Big Data Analytics with Hadoop 3

Build highly effective analytics solutions to gain valuable insight into your big data

Sridhar Alla

Packt

BIRMINGHAM - MUMBAI

Big Data Analytics with Hadoop 3

Commissioning Editor: Amey Varangaonkar
Acquisition Editor: Varsha Shetty
Content Development Editor: Cheryl Dsa
Technical Editor: Sagar Sawant
Copy Editors: Vikrant Phadke, Safis Editing
Project Coordinator: Nidhi Joshi
Proofreader: Safis Editing
Indexer: Rekha Nair
Graphics: Tania Dutta
Production Coordinator: Arvindkumar Gupta

First published: May 2018

Production reference: 1280518

Published by Packt Publishing Ltd.
Livery Place
35 Livery Street
Birmingham
B3 2PB, UK.

ISBN 978-1-78862-884-6

`www.packtpub.com`

Contributors

About the author

Sridhar Alla is a big data expert helping companies solve complex problems in distributed computing, large scale data science and analytics practice. He presents regularly at several prestigious conferences and provides training and consulting to companies. He holds a bachelor's in computer science from JNTU, India.

He loves writing code in Python, Scala, and Java. He also has extensive hands-on knowledge of several Hadoop-based technologies, TensorFlow, NoSQL, IoT, and deep learning.

I thank my loving wife, Rosie Sarkaria for all the love and patience during the many months I spent writing this book. I thank my parents Ravi and Lakshmi Alla for all the support and encouragement. I am very grateful to my wonderful niece Niharika and nephew Suman Kalyan who helped me with screenshots, proof reading and testing the code snippets.

About the reviewers

V. Naresh Kumar has more than a decade of professional experience in designing, implementing, and running very large-scale internet applications in Fortune 500 Companies. He is a full-stack architect with hands-on experience in e-commerce, web hosting, healthcare, big data, analytics, data streaming, advertising, and databases. He admires open source and contributes to it actively. He keeps himself updated with emerging technologies, from Linux system internals to frontend technologies. He studied in BITS- Pilani, Rajasthan, with a joint degree in computer science and economics.

Manoj R. Patil is a big data architect at TatvaSoft—an IT services and consulting firm. He has a bachelor's degree in engineering from COEP, Pune. He is a proven and highly skilled business intelligence professional with 18 years, experience in IT. He is a seasoned BI and big data consultant with exposure to all the leading platforms.

Previously, he worked for numerous organizations, including Tech Mahindra and Persistent Systems. Apart from authoring a book on Pentaho and big data, he has been an avid reviewer of various titles in the respective fields from Packt and other leading publishers.

Manoj would like to thank his entire family, especially his two beautiful angels, Ayushee and Ananyaa for understanding during the review process. He would also like to thank Packt for giving this opportunity, the project co-ordinator and the author.

Table of Contents

Preface

Apache Hadoop is the most popular platform for big data processing, and can be combined with a host of other big data tools to build powerful analytics solutions. *Big Data Analytics with Hadoop 3* shows you how to do just that, by providing insights into the software as well as its benefits with the help of practical examples.

Once you have taken a tour of Hadoop 3's latest features, you will get an overview of HDFS, MapReduce, and YARN, and how they enable faster, more efficient big data processing. You will then move on to learning how to integrate Hadoop with open source tools, such as Python and R, to analyze and visualize data and perform statistical computing on big data. As you become acquainted with all of this, you will explore how to use Hadoop 3 with Apache Spark and Apache Flink for real-time data analytics and stream processing. In addition to this, you will understand how to use Hadoop to build analytics solutions in the cloud and an end-to-end pipeline to perform big data analysis using practical use cases.

By the end of this book, you will be well-versed with the analytical capabilities of the Hadoop ecosystem. You will be able to build powerful solutions to perform big data analytics and get insights effortlessly.

Who this book is for

Big Data Analytics with Hadoop 3 is for you if you are looking to build high-performance analytics solutions for your enterprise or business using Hadoop 3's powerful features, or if you're new to big data analytics. A basic understanding of the Java programming language is required.

What this book covers

`Chapter 1`, *Introduction to Hadoop*, introduces you to the world of Hadoop and its core components, namely, HDFS and MapReduce.

`Chapter 2`, *Overview of Big Data Analytics*, introduces the process of examining large datasets to uncover patterns in data, generating reports, and gathering valuable insights.

`Chapter 3`, *Big Data Processing with MapReduce,* introduces the concept of MapReduce, which is the fundamental concept behind most of the big data computing/processing systems.

`Chapter 4`, *Scientific Computing and Big Data Analysis with Python and Hadoop,* provides an introduction to Python and an analysis of big data using Hadoop with the aid of Python packages.

`Chapter 5`, *Statistical Big Data Computing with R and Hadoop,* provides an introduction to R and demonstrates how to use R to perform statistical computing on big data using Hadoop.

`Chapter 6`, *Batch Analytics with Apache Spark,* introduces you to Apache Spark and demonstrates how to use Spark for big data analytics based on a batch processing model.

`Chapter 7`, *Real-Time Analytics with Apache Spark,* introduces the stream processing model of Apache Spark and demonstrates how to build streaming-based, real-time analytical applications.

`Chapter 8`, *Batch Analytics with Apache Flink,* covers Apache Flink and how to use it for big data analytics based on a batch processing model.

`Chapter 9`, *Stream Processing with Apache Flink,* introduces you to DataStream APIs and stream processing using Flink. Flink will be used to receive and process real-time event streams and store the aggregates and results in a Hadoop cluster.

`Chapter 10`, *Visualizing Big Data,* introduces you to the world of data visualization using various tools and technologies such as Tableau.

`Chapter 11`, *Introduction to Cloud Computing,* introduces Cloud computing and various concepts such as IaaS, PaaS, and SaaS. You will also get a glimpse into the top Cloud providers.

`Chapter 12`, *Using Amazon Web Services,* introduces you to AWS and various services in AWS useful for performing big data analytics using **Elastic Map Reduce** (**EMR**) to set up a Hadoop cluster in AWS Cloud.

To get the most out of this book

The examples have been implemented using Scala, Java, R, and Python on a Linux 64-bit. You will also need, or be prepared to install, the following on your machine (preferably the latest version):

- Spark 2.3.0 (or higher)
- Hadoop 3.1 (or higher)
- Flink 1.4
- Java (JDK and JRE) 1.8+
- Scala 2.11.x (or higher)
- Python 2.7+/3.4+
- R 3.1+ and RStudio 1.0.143 (or higher)
- Eclipse Mars or Idea IntelliJ (latest)

Regarding the operating system: Linux distributions are preferable (including Debian, Ubuntu, Fedora, RHEL, and CentOS) and, to be more specific, for example, as regards Ubuntu, it is recommended having a complete 14.04 (LTS) 64-bit (or later) installation, VMWare player 12, or Virtual box. You can also run code on Windows (XP/7/8/10) or macOS X (10.4.7+).

Regarding hardware configuration: Processor Core i3, Core i5 (recommended) ~ Core i7 (to get the best result). However, multicore processing would provide faster data processing and scalability. At least 8 GB RAM (recommended) for a standalone mode. At least 32 GB RAM for a single VM and higher for cluster. Enough storage for running heavy jobs (depending on the dataset size you will be handling) preferably at least 50 GB of free disk storage (for stand alone and SQL warehouse).

Download the example code files

You can download the example code files for this book from your account at `www.packtpub.com`. If you purchased this book elsewhere, you can visit `www.packtpub.com/support` and register to have the files emailed directly to you.

You can download the code files by following these steps:

1. Log in or register at `www.packtpub.com`.
2. Select the **SUPPORT** tab.
3. Click on **Code Downloads & Errata**.
4. Enter the name of the book in the **Search** box and follow the onscreen instructions.

Once the file is downloaded, please make sure that you unzip or extract the folder using the latest version of:

- WinRAR/7-Zip for Windows
- Zipeg/iZip/UnRarX for Mac
- 7-Zip/PeaZip for Linux

The code bundle for the book is also hosted on GitHub at `https://github.com/PacktPublishing/Big-Data-Analytics-with-Hadoop-3`. In case there's an update to the code, it will be updated on the existing GitHub repository.

We also have other code bundles from our rich catalog of books and videos available at `https://github.com/PacktPublishing/`. Check them out!

Download the color images

We also provide a PDF file that has color images of the screenshots/diagrams used in this book. You can download it here: `http://www.packtpub.com/sites/default/files/downloads/BigDataAnalyticswithHadoop3_ColorImages.pdf`.

Conventions used

There are a number of text conventions used throughout this book.

`CodeInText`: Indicates code words in text, database table names, folder names, filenames, file extensions, pathnames, dummy URLs, user input, and Twitter handles. Here is an example: "This file, `temperatures.csv`, is available as a download and once downloaded, you can move it into `hdfs` by running the command, as shown in the following code."

A block of code is set as follows:

```
hdfs dfs -copyFromLocal temperatures.csv /user/normal
```

When we wish to draw your attention to a particular part of a code block, the relevant lines or items are set in bold:

```
Map-Reduce Framework -- output average temperature per city name
    Map input records=35
    Map output records=33
    Map output bytes=208
    Map output materialized bytes=286
```

Any command-line input or output is written as follows:

```
$ ssh-keygen -t rsa -P '' -f ~/.ssh/id_rsa
$ cat ~/.ssh/id_rsa.pub >> ~/.ssh/authorized_keys
$ chmod 0600 ~/.ssh/authorized_keys
```

Bold: Indicates a new term, an important word, or words that you see on screen. For example, words in menus or dialog boxes appear in the text like this. Here is an example: "Clicking on the **Datanodes** tab shows all the nodes."

Warnings or important notes appear like this.

Tips and tricks appear like this.

Get in touch

Feedback from our readers is always welcome.

General feedback: Email `feedback@packtpub.com` and mention the book title in the subject of your message. If you have questions about any aspect of this book, please email us at `questions@packtpub.com`.

Errata: Although we have taken every care to ensure the accuracy of our content, mistakes do happen. If you have found a mistake in this book, we would be grateful if you would report this to us. Please visit `www.packtpub.com/submit-errata`, selecting your book, clicking on the Errata Submission Form link, and entering the details.

Piracy: If you come across any illegal copies of our works in any form on the Internet, we would be grateful if you would provide us with the location address or website name. Please contact us at `copyright@packtpub.com` with a link to the material.

If you are interested in becoming an author: If there is a topic that you have expertise in and you are interested in either writing or contributing to a book, please visit `authors.packtpub.com`.

Reviews

Please leave a review. Once you have read and used this book, why not leave a review on the site that you purchased it from? Potential readers can then see and use your unbiased opinion to make purchase decisions, we at Packt can understand what you think about our products, and our authors can see your feedback on their book. Thank you!

For more information about Packt, please visit `packtpub.com`.

1
Introduction to Hadoop

This chapter introduces the reader to the world of Hadoop and the core components of Hadoop, namely the **Hadoop Distributed File System** (**HDFS**) and MapReduce. We will start by introducing the changes and new features in the Hadoop 3 release. Particularly, we will talk about the new features of HDFS and **Yet Another Resource Negotiator** (**YARN**), and changes to client applications. Furthermore, we will also install a Hadoop cluster locally and demonstrate the new features such as **erasure coding** (**EC**) and the timeline service. As as quick note, `Chapter 10`, *Visualizing Big Data* shows you how to create a Hadoop cluster in AWS.

In a nutshell, the following topics will be covered throughout this chapter:

- HDFS
    - High availability
    - Intra-DataNode balancer
    - EC
    - Port mapping
- MapReduce
    - Task-level optimization
- YARN
    - Opportunistic containers
    - Timeline service v.2
    - Docker containerization
- Other changes
- Installation of Hadoop 3.1
    - HDFS
    - YARN
    - EC
    - Timeline service v.2

Hadoop Distributed File System

HDFS is a software-based filesystem implemented in Java and it sits on top of the native filesystem. The main concept behind HDFS is that it divides a file into blocks (typically 128 MB) instead of dealing with a file as a whole. This allows many features such as distribution, replication, failure recovery, and more importantly distributed processing of the blocks using multiple machines. Block sizes can be 64 MB, 128 MB, 256 MB, or 512 MB, whatever suits the purpose. For a 1 GB file with 128 MB blocks, there will be 1024 MB/128 MB equal to eight blocks. If you consider a replication factor of three, this makes it 24 blocks. HDFS provides a distributed storage system with fault tolerance and failure recovery. HDFS has two main components: the **NameNode** and the **DataNode**. The NameNode contains all the metadata of all content of the filesystem: filenames, file permissions, and the location of each block of each file, and hence it is the most important machine in HDFS. DataNodes connect to the NameNode and store the blocks within HDFS. They rely on the NameNode for all metadata information regarding the content in the filesystem. If the NameNode does not have any information, the DataNode will not be able to serve information to any client who wants to read/write to the HDFS.

It is possible for NameNode and DataNode processes to be run on a single machine; however, generally HDFS clusters are made up of a dedicated server running the NameNode process and thousands of machines running the DataNode process. In order to be able to access the content information stored in the NameNode, it stores the entire metadata structure in memory. It ensures that there is no data loss as a result of machine failures by keeping a track of the replication factor of blocks. Since it is a single point of failure, to reduce the risk of data loss on account of the failure of a NameNode, a secondary NameNode can be used to generate snapshots of the primary NameNode's memory structures.

DataNodes have large storage capacities and, unlike the NameNode, HDFS will continue to operate normally if a DataNode fails. When a DataNode fails, the NameNode automatically takes care of the now diminished replication of all the data blocks in the failed DataNode and makes sure the replication is built back up. Since the NameNode knows all locations of the replicated blocks, any clients connected to the cluster are able to proceed with little to no hiccups.

In order to make sure that each block meets the minimum required replication factor, the NameNode replicates the lost blocks.

The following diagram depicts the mapping of files to blocks in the NameNode, and the storage of blocks and their replicas within the DataNodes:

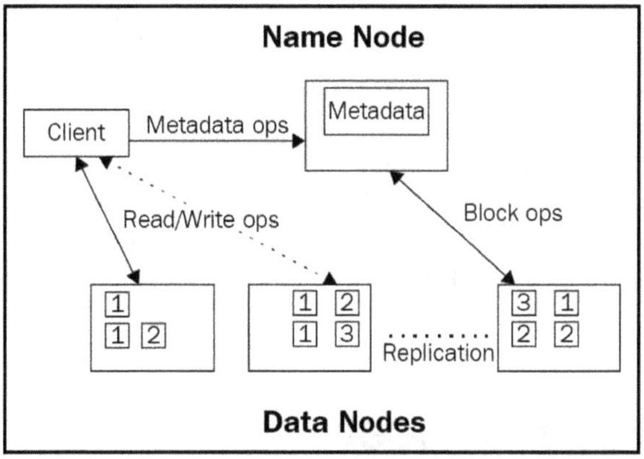

The NameNode, as shown in the preceding diagram, has been the single point of failure since the beginning of Hadoop.

High availability

The loss of NameNodes can crash the cluster in both Hadoop 1.x as well as Hadoop 2.x. In Hadoop 1.x, there was no easy way to recover, whereas Hadoop 2.x introduced high availability (active-passive setup) to help recover from NameNode failures.

The following diagram shows how high availability works:

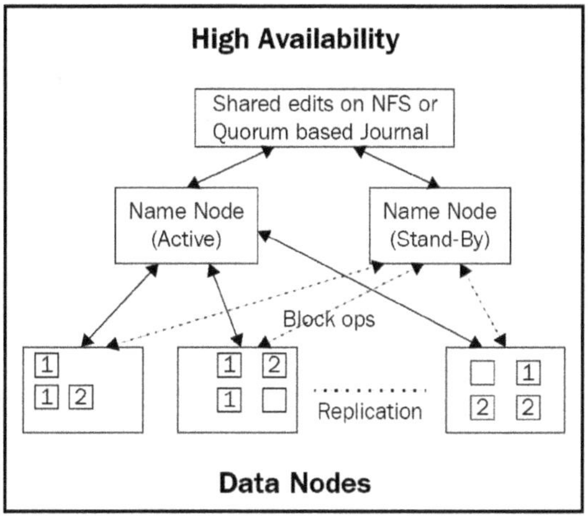

In Hadoop 3.x you can have two passive NameNodes along with the active node, as well as five **JournalNodes** to assist with recovery from catastrophic failures:

- **NameNode machines**: The machines on which you run the active and standby NameNodes. They should have equivalent hardware to each other and to what would be used in a non-HA cluster.
- **JournalNode machines**: The machines on which you run the JournalNodes. The JournalNode daemon is relatively lightweight, so these daemons may reasonably be collocated on machines with other Hadoop daemons, for example NameNodes, the **JobTracker**, or the YARN **ResourceManager**.

Intra-DataNode balancer

HDFS has a way to balance the data blocks across the data nodes, but there is no such balancing inside the same data node with multiple hard disks. Hence, a 12-spindle DataNode can have out of balance physical disks. But why does this matter to performance? Well, by having out of balance disks, the blocks at DataNode level might be the same as other DataNodes but the reads/writes will be skewed because of imbalanced disks. Hence, Hadoop 3.x introduces the intra-node balancer to balance the physical disks inside each data node to reduce the skew of the data.

This increases the reads and writes performed by any process running on the cluster, such as a **mapper** or **reducer**.

Erasure coding

HDFS has been the fundamental component since the inception of Hadoop. In Hadoop 1.x as well as Hadoop 2.x, a typical HDFS installation uses a replication factor of three.

Compared to the default replication factor of three, EC is probably the biggest change in HDFS in years and fundamentally doubles the capacity for many datasets by bringing down the replication factor from 3 to about 1.4. Let's now understand what EC is all about.

EC is a method of data protection in which data is broken into fragments, expanded, encoded with redundant data pieces, and stored across a set of different locations or storage. If at some point during this process data is lost due to corruption, then it can be reconstructed using the information stored elsewhere. Although EC is more CPU intensive, this greatly reduces the storage needed for the reliable storing of large amounts of data (HDFS). HDFS uses replication to provide reliable storage and this is expensive, typically requiring three copies of data to be stored, thus causing a 200% overhead in storage space.

Port numbers

In Hadoop 3.x, many of the ports for various services have been changed.

Previously, the default ports of multiple Hadoop services were in the Linux ephemeral port range (32768–61000). This indicated that at startup, services would sometimes fail to bind to the port with another application due to a conflict.

These conflicting ports have been moved out of the ephemeral range, affecting the NameNode, Secondary NameNode, DataNode, and KMS.

The changes are listed as follows:

- **NameNode ports**: 50470 → 9871, 50070 → 9870, and 8020 → 9820
- **Secondary NameNode ports**: 50091 → 9869 and 50090 → 9868
- **DataNode ports:** 50020 → 9867, 50010 → 9866, 50475 → 9865, and 50075 → 9864

MapReduce framework

An easy way to understand this concept is to imagine that you and your friends want to sort out piles of fruit into boxes. For that, you want to assign each person the task of going through one raw basket of fruit (all mixed up) and separating out the fruit into various boxes. Each person then does the same task of separating the fruit into the various types with this basket of fruit. In the end, you end up with a lot of boxes of fruit from all your friends. Then, you can assign a group to put the same kind of fruit together in a box, weigh the box, and seal the box for shipping. A classic example of showing the MapReduce framework at work is the word count example. The following are the various stages of processing the input data, first splitting the input across multiple worker nodes and then finally generating the output, the word counts:

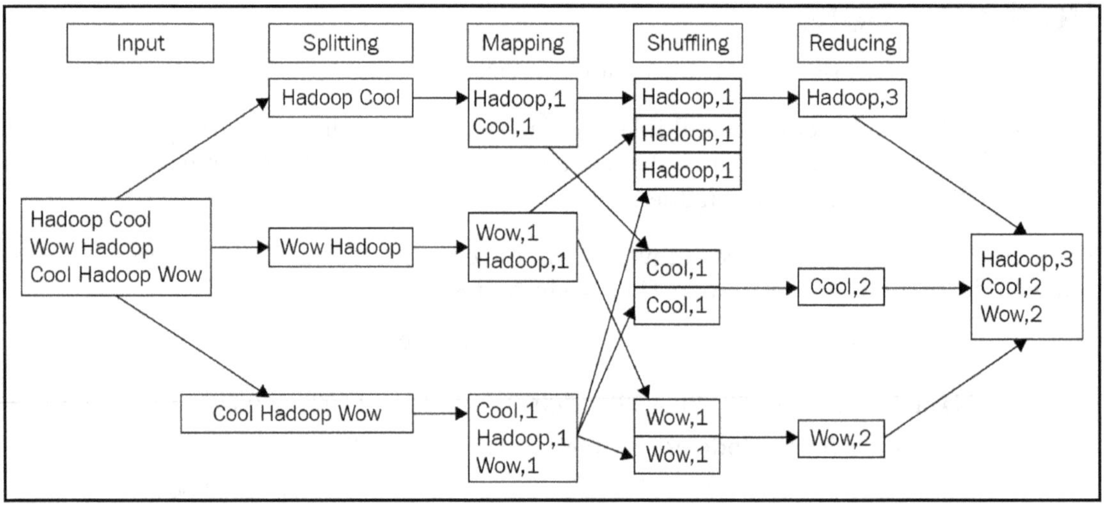

The MapReduce framework consists of a single ResourceManager and multiple NodeManagers (usually, NodeManagers coexist with the DataNodes of HDFS).

Task-level native optimization

MapReduce has added support for a native implementation of the map output collector. This new support can result in a performance improvement of about 30% or more, particularly for shuffle-intensive jobs.

The native library will build automatically with `Pnative`. Users may choose the new collector on a job-by-job basis by setting `mapreduce.job.map.output.collector.class=org.apache.hadoop.mapred.nativetask.NativeMapOutputCollectorDelegator` in their job configuration.

The basic idea is to be able to add a `NativeMapOutputCollector` in order to handle key/value pairs emitted by mapper. As a result of this `sort`, `spill`, and `IFile` serialization can all be done in native code. A preliminary test (on Xeon E5410, jdk6u24) showed promising results as follows:

- `sort` is about 3-10 times faster than Java (only binary string compare is supported)
- `IFile` serialization speed is about three times faster than Java: about 500 MB per second. If CRC32C hardware is used, things can get much faster in the range of 1 GB or higher per second
- Merge code is not completed yet, so the test uses enough `io.sort.mb` to prevent mid-spill

YARN

When an application wants to run, the client launches the ApplicationMaster, which then negotiates with the ResourceManager to get resources in the cluster in the form of containers. A container represents CPUs (cores) and memory allocated on a single node to be used to run tasks and processes. Containers are supervised by the NodeManager and scheduled by the ResourceManager.

Examples of containers:

- One core and 4 GB RAM
- Two cores and 6 GB RAM
- Four cores and 20 GB RAM

Some containers are assigned to be mappers and others to be reducers; all this is coordinated by the ApplicationMaster in conjunction with the ResourceManager. This framework is called **YARN**:

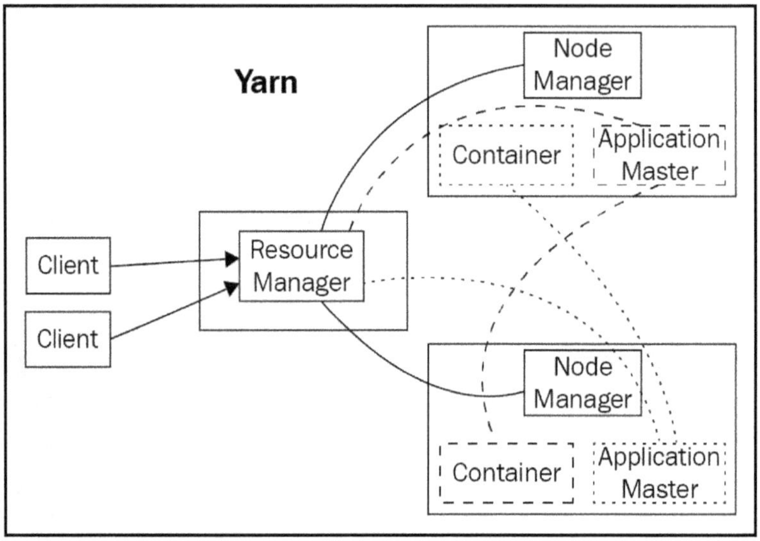

Using YARN, several different applications can request for and execute tasks on containers, sharing the cluster resources pretty well. However, as the size of the clusters grows and the variety of applications and requirements change, the efficiency of the resource utilization is not as good over time.

Opportunistic containers

Opportunistic containers can be transmitted to a NodeManager even if their execution at that particular time cannot begin immediately, unlike YARN containers, which are scheduled in a node if and only if there are unallocated resources.

In these types of scenarios, opportunistic containers will be queued at the NodeManager till the required resources are available for use. The ultimate goal of these containers is to enhance the cluster resource utilization and in turn improve task throughput.

Types of container execution

There are two types of container, as follows:

- **Guaranteed containers**: These containers correspond to the existing YARN containers. They are assigned by the capacity scheduler. They are transmitted to a node if and only if there are resources available to begin their execution immediately.
- **Opportunistic containers**: Unlike guaranteed containers, in this case we cannot guarantee that there will be resources available to begin their execution once they are dispatched to a node. On the contrary, they will be queued at the NodeManager itself until resources become available.

YARN timeline service v.2

The YARN timeline service v.2 addresses the following two major challenges:

- Enhancing the scalability and reliability of the timeline service
- Improving usability by introducing flows and aggregation

Enhancing scalability and reliability

Version 2 adopts a more scalable distributed writer architecture and backend storage, as opposed to v.1 which does not scale well beyond small clusters as it used a single instance of writer/reader architecture and backend storage.

Since Apache HBase scales well even to larger clusters and continues to maintain a good read and write response time, v.2 prefers to select it as the primary backend storage.

Usability improvements

Many a time, users are more interested in the information obtained at the level of flows or in logical groups of YARN applications. For this reason, it is more convenient to launch a series of YARN applications to complete a logical workflow.

In order to achieve this, v.2 supports the notion of flows and aggregates metrics at the flow level.

Architecture

YARN Timeline Service v.2 uses a set of collectors (writers) to write data to the back-end storage. The collectors are distributed and co-located with the application masters to which they are dedicated. All data that belong to that application are sent to the application level timeline collectors with the exception of the resource manager timeline collector.

For a given application, the application master can write data for the application to the co-located timeline collectors (which is an NM auxiliary service in this release). In addition, node managers of other nodes that are running the containers for the application also write data to the timeline collector on the node that is running the application master.

The resource manager also maintains its own timeline collector. It emits only YARN-generic
life-cycle events to keep its volume of writes reasonable.

The timeline readers are separate daemons separate from the timeline collectors, and they are dedicated to serving queries via REST API:

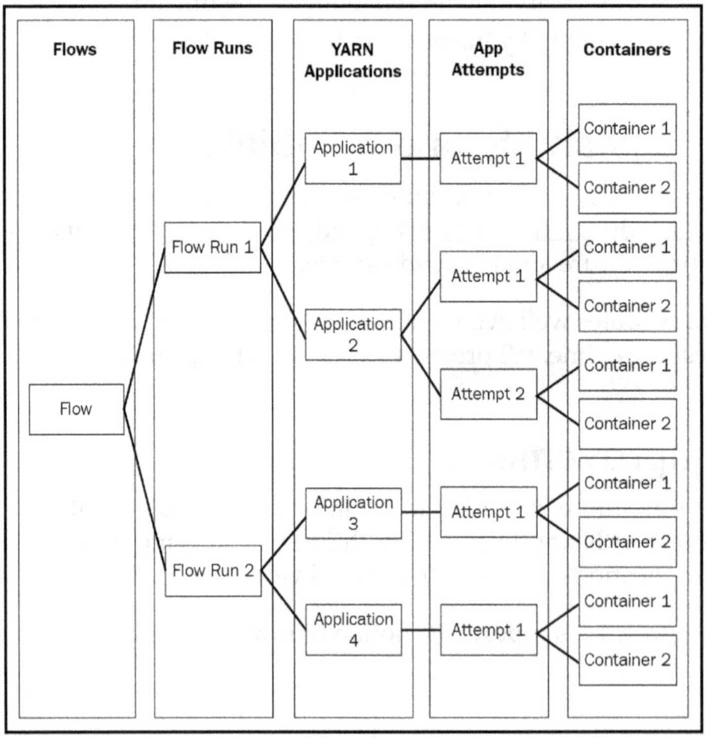

The following diagram illustrates the design at a high level:

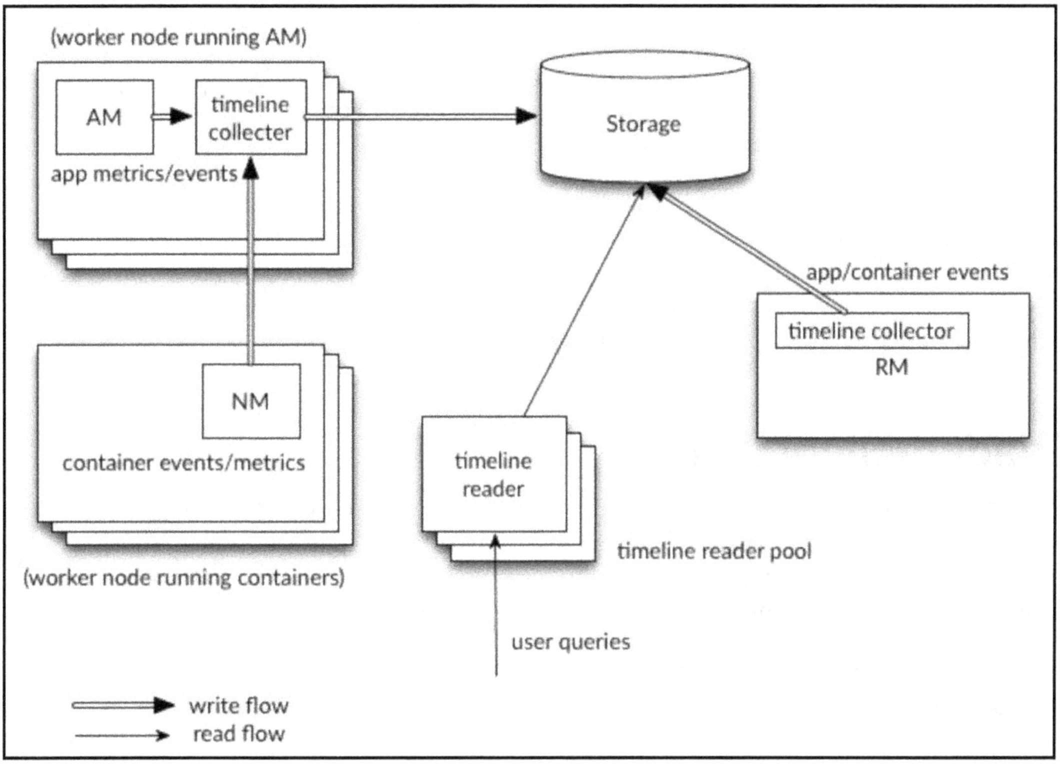

Other changes

There are other changes coming up in Hadoop 3, which are mainly to make it easier to maintain and operate. Particularly, the command-line tools have been revamped to better suit the needs of operational teams.

Minimum required Java version

All Hadoop JARs are now compiled to target a runtime version of Java 8. Hence, users that are still using Java 7 or lower must upgrade to Java 8.

Shell script rewrite

The Hadoop shell scripts have been rewritten to fix many long-standing bugs and include some new features.

Incompatible changes are documented in the release notes. You can find them at `https://issues.apache.org/jira/browse/HADOOP-9902`.

There are more details available in the documentation at `https://hadoop.apache.org/docs/r3.0.0/hadoop-project-dist/hadoop-common/UnixShellGuide.html`. The documentation present at `https://hadoop.apache.org/docs/r3.0.0/hadoop-project-dist/hadoop-common/UnixShellAPI.html` will appeal to power users, as it describes most of the new functionalities, particularly those related to extensibility.

Shaded-client JARs

The new `hadoop-client-api` and `hadoop-client-runtime` artifacts have been added, as referred to by `https://issues.apache.org/jira/browse/HADOOP-11804`. These artifacts shade Hadoop's dependencies into a single JAR. As a result, it avoids leaking Hadoop's dependencies onto the application's classpath.

Hadoop now also supports integration with Microsoft Azure Data Lake and Aliyun Object Storage System as an alternative for Hadoop-compatible filesystems.

Installing Hadoop 3

In this section, we shall see how to install a single-node Hadoop 3 cluster on your local machine. In order to do this, we will be following the documentation given at `https://hadoop.apache.org/docs/current/hadoop-project-dist/hadoop-common/SingleCluster.html`.

This document gives us a detailed description of how to install and configure a single-node Hadoop setup in order to carry out simple operations using Hadoop MapReduce and the HDFS quickly.

Prerequisites

Java 8 must be installed for Hadoop to be run. If Java 8 does not exist on your machine, then you can download and install Java 8: `https://www.java.com/en/download/`.

The following will appear on your screen when you open the download link in the browser:

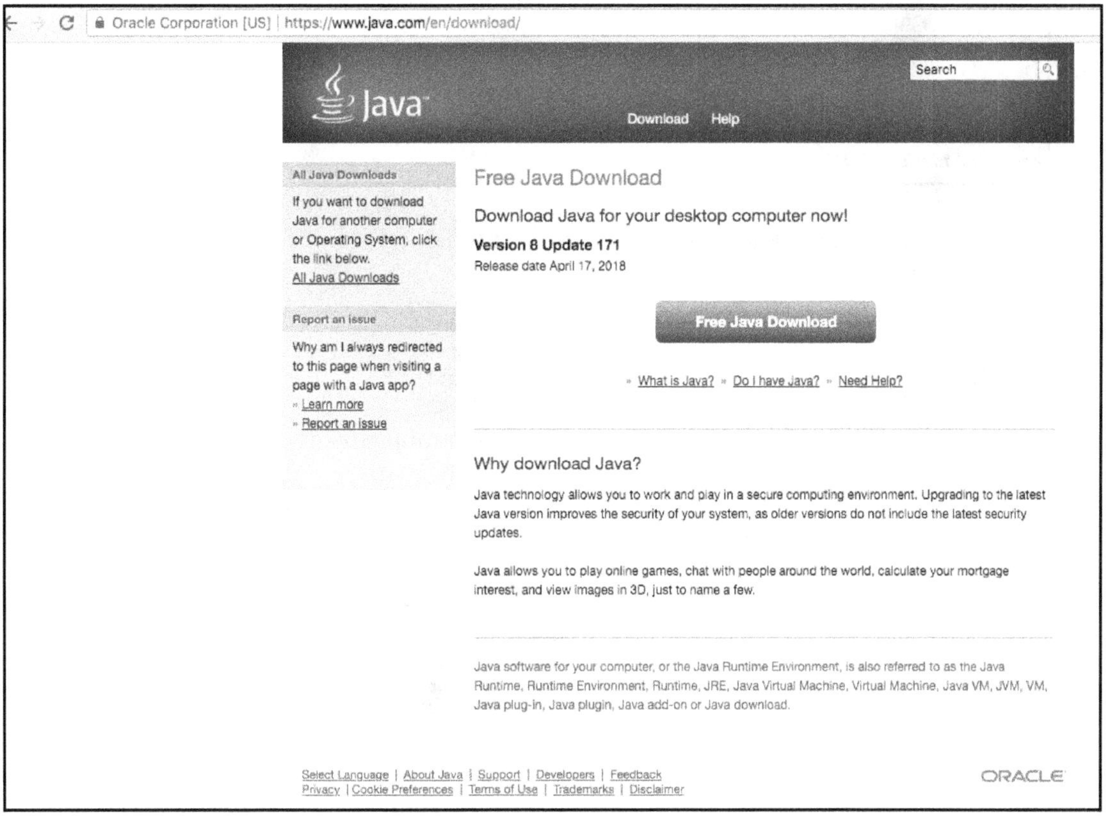

Downloading

Download the Hadoop 3.1 version using the following link: `http://apache.spinellicreations.com/hadoop/common/hadoop-3.1.0/`.

The following screenshot is the page shown when the download link is opened in the browser:

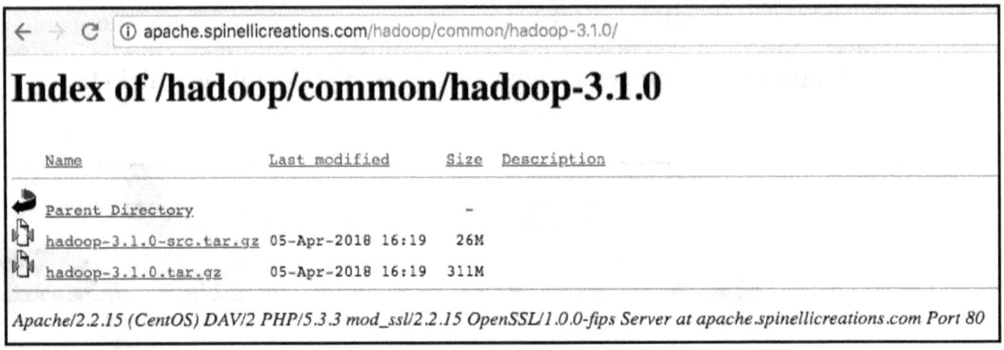

When you get this page in your browser, simply download the `hadoop-3.1.0.tar.gz` file to your local machine.

Installation

Perform the following steps to install a single-node Hadoop cluster on your machine:

1. Extract the downloaded file using the following command:

```
tar -xvzf hadoop-3.1.0.tar.gz
```

2. Once you have extracted the Hadoop binaries, just run the following commands to test the Hadoop binaries and make sure the binaries works on our local machine:

```
cd hadoop-3.1.0

mkdir input

cp etc/hadoop/*.xml input

bin/hadoop jar share/hadoop/mapreduce/hadoop-mapreduce-
examples-3.1.0.jar grep input output 'dfs[a-z.]+'

cat output/*
```

If everything runs as expected, you will see an output directory showing some output, which shows that the sample command worked.

A typical error at this point will be missing Java. You might want to check and see if you have Java installed on your machine and the `JAVA_HOME` environment variable set correctly.

Setup password-less ssh

Now check if you can `ssh` to the `localhost` without a passphrase by running a simple command, shown as follows:

```
$ ssh localhost
```

If you cannot `ssh` to `localhost` without a passphrase, execute the following commands:

```
$ ssh-keygen -t rsa -P '' -f ~/.ssh/id_rsa
$ cat ~/.ssh/id_rsa.pub >> ~/.ssh/authorized_keys
$ chmod 0600 ~/.ssh/authorized_keys
```

Setting up the NameNode

Make the following changes to the configuration file `etc/hadoop/core-site.xml`:

```
<configuration>
    <property>
        <name>fs.defaultFS</name>
        <value>hdfs://localhost:9000</value>
    </property>
</configuration>
```

Make the following changes to the configuration file `etc/hadoop/hdfs-site.xml`:

```
<configuration>
    <property>
        <name>dfs.replication</name>
        <value>1</value>
    </property>
        <name>dfs.name.dir</name>
        <value><YOURDIRECTORY>/hadoop-3.1.0/dfs/name</value>
    </property>
</configuration>
```

Starting HDFS

Follow these steps as shown to start HDFS (NameNode and DataNode):

1. Format the filesystem:

```
$ ./bin/hdfs namenode -format
```

2. Start the NameNode daemon and the DataNode daemon:

```
$ ./sbin/start-dfs.sh
```

   The Hadoop daemon log output is written to the `$HADOOP_LOG_DIR` directory (defaults to `$HADOOP_HOME/logs`).

3. Browse the web interface for the NameNode; by default it is available at `http://localhost:9870/`.
4. Make the HDFS directories required to execute MapReduce jobs:

```
$ ./bin/hdfs dfs -mkdir /user
$ ./bin/hdfs dfs -mkdir /user/<username>
```

5. When you're done, stop the daemons with the following:

```
$ ./sbin/stop-dfs.sh
```

6. Open a browser to check your local Hadoop, which can be launched in the browser as `http://localhost:9870/`. The following is what the HDFS installation looks like:

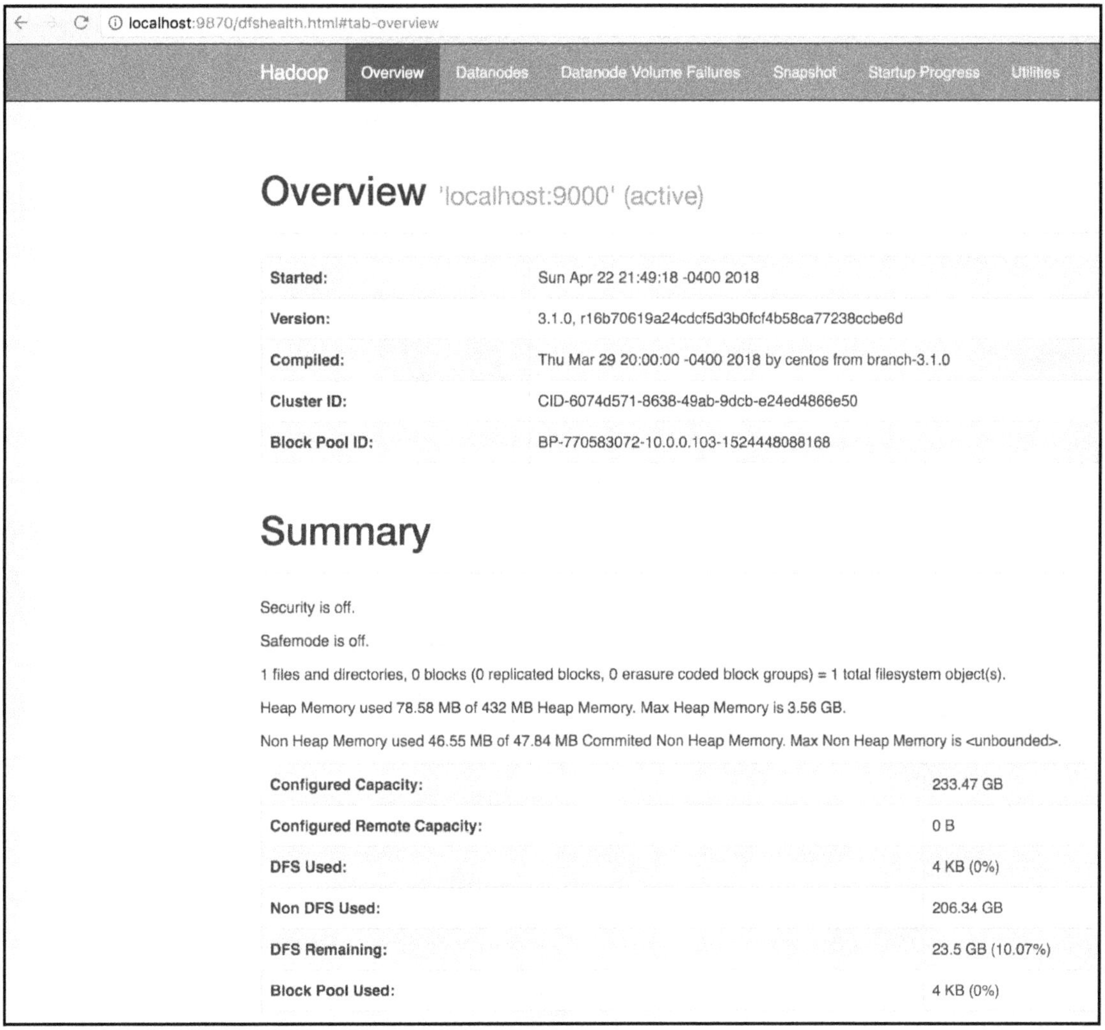

7. Clicking on the **Datanodes** tab shows the nodes as shown in the following screenshot:

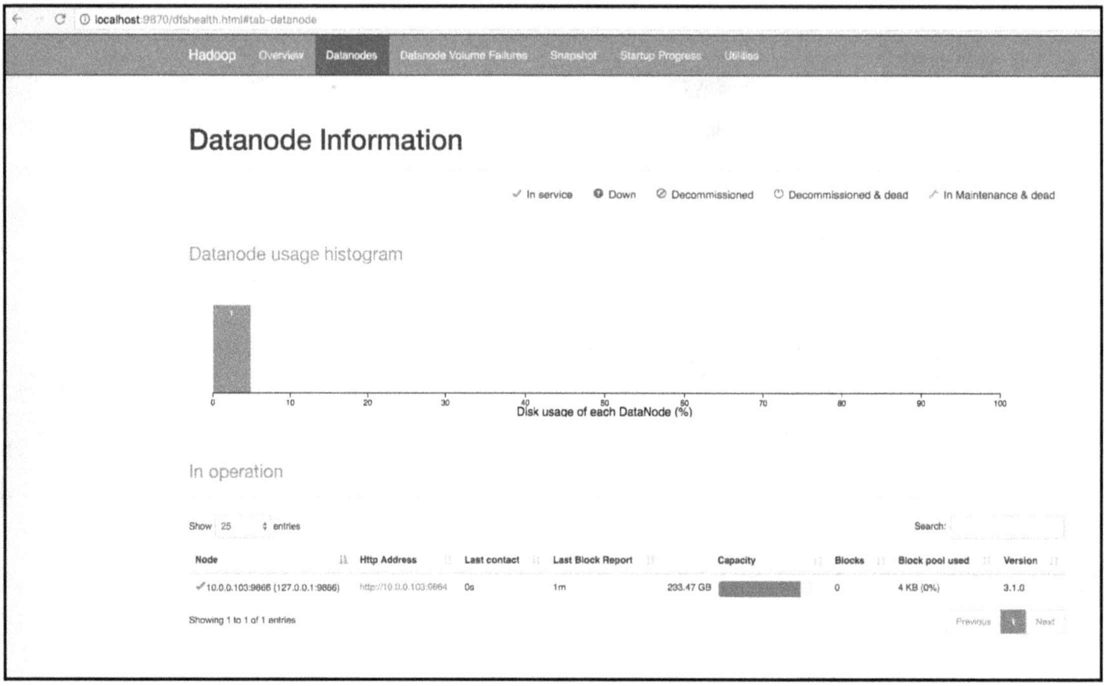

Figure: Screenshot showing the nodes in the Datanodes tab

8. Clicking on the **logs** will show the various logs in your cluster, as shown in the following screenshot:

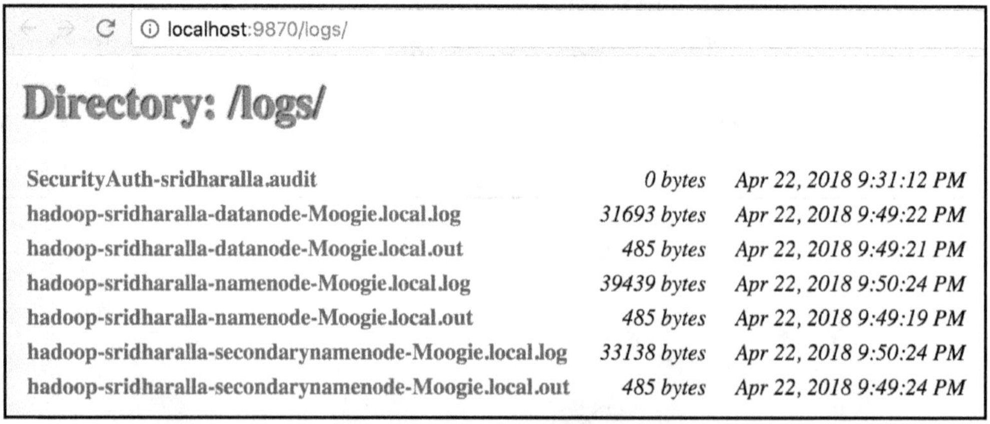

9. As shown in the following screenshot, you can also look at the various JVM metrics of your cluster components:

localhost:9870/jmx


```
{
  "beans" : [ {
    "name" : "Hadoop:service=NameNode,name=JvmMetrics",
    "modelerType" : "JvmMetrics",
    "tag.Context" : "jvm",
    "tag.ProcessName" : "NameNode",
    "tag.SessionId" : null,
    "tag.Hostname" : "Moogie.local",
    "MemNonHeapUsedM" : 47.575027,
    "MemNonHeapCommittedM" : 49.148438,
    "MemNonHeapMaxM" : -1.0,
    "MemHeapUsedM" : 103.684074,
    "MemHeapCommittedM" : 432.0,
    "MemHeapMaxM" : 3641.0,
    "MemMaxM" : 3641.0,
    "GcCount" : 8,
    "GcTimeMillis" : 247,
    "GcNumWarnThresholdExceeded" : 0,
    "GcNumInfoThresholdExceeded" : 0,
    "GcTotalExtraSleepTime" : 435,
    "ThreadsNew" : 0,
    "ThreadsRunnable" : 10,
    "ThreadsBlocked" : 0,
    "ThreadsWaiting" : 6,
    "ThreadsTimedWaiting" : 36,
    "ThreadsTerminated" : 0,
    "LogFatal" : 0,
    "LogError" : 0,
    "LogWarn" : 8,
    "LogInfo" : 130
  }, {
    "name" : "JMImplementation:type=MBeanServerDelegate",
    "modelerType" : "javax.management.MBeanServerDelegate",
    "MBeanServerId" : "Moogie.local_1524448157872",
    "SpecificationName" : "Java Management Extensions",
    "SpecificationVersion" : "1.4",
```


10. As shown in the following screenshot, you can also check the configuration. This is a good place to look at the entire configuration and all the default settings:

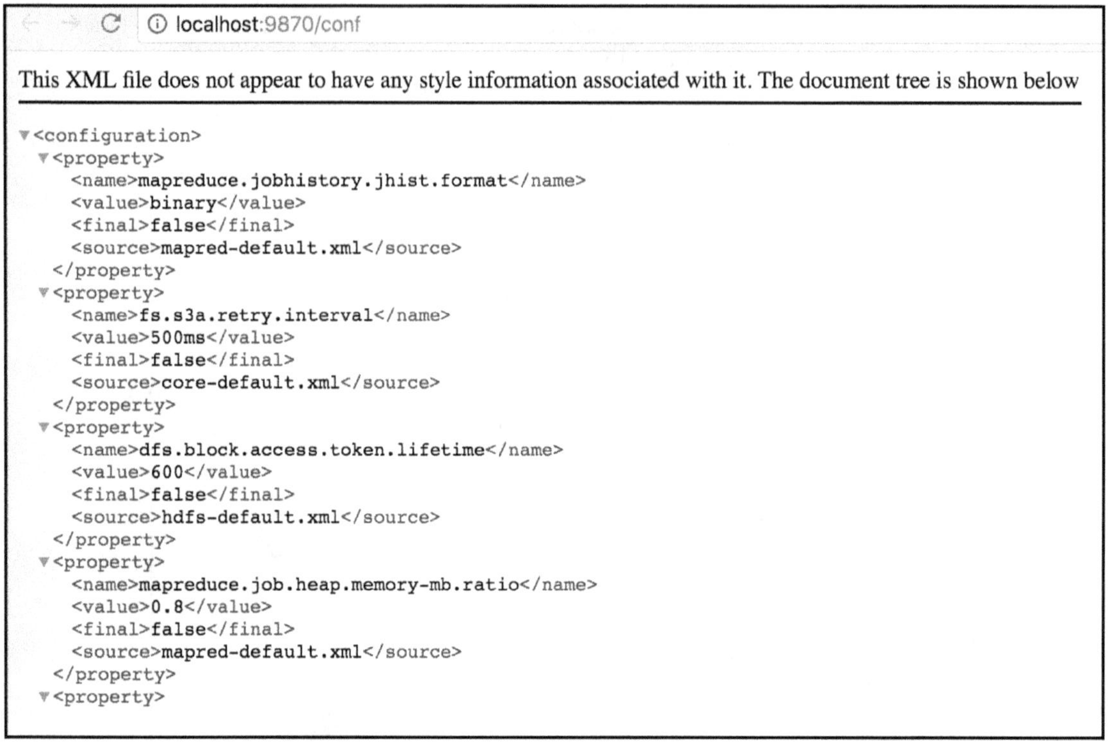

11. You can also browse the filesystem of your newly installed cluster, as shown in the following screenshot:

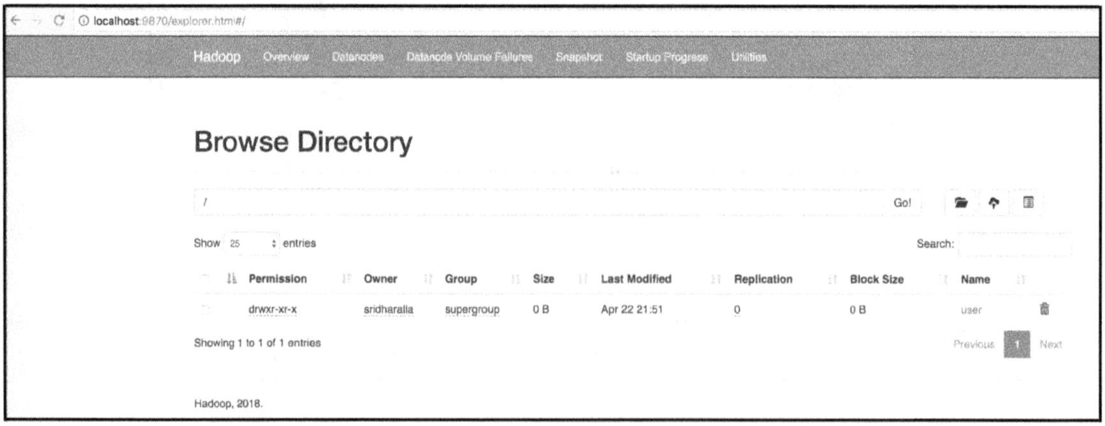

Figure: Screenshot showing the Browse Directory and how you can browse the filesystem in you newly installed cluster

At this point, we should all be able to see and use a basic HDFS cluster. But this is just a HDFS filesystem with some directories and files. We also need a job/task scheduling service to actually use the cluster for computational needs rather than just storage.

Setting up the YARN service

In this section, we will set up a YARN service and start the components needed to run and operate a YARN cluster:

1. Start the ResourceManager daemon and the NodeManager daemon:

```
$ sbin/start-yarn.sh
```

2. Browse the web interface for the ResourceManager; by default it is available at: `http://localhost:8088/`
3. Run a MapReduce job
4. When you're done, stop the daemons with the following:

```
$ sbin/stop-yarn.sh
```

The following is the YARN ResourceManager, which you can view by putting the URL `http://localhost:8088/` into the browser:

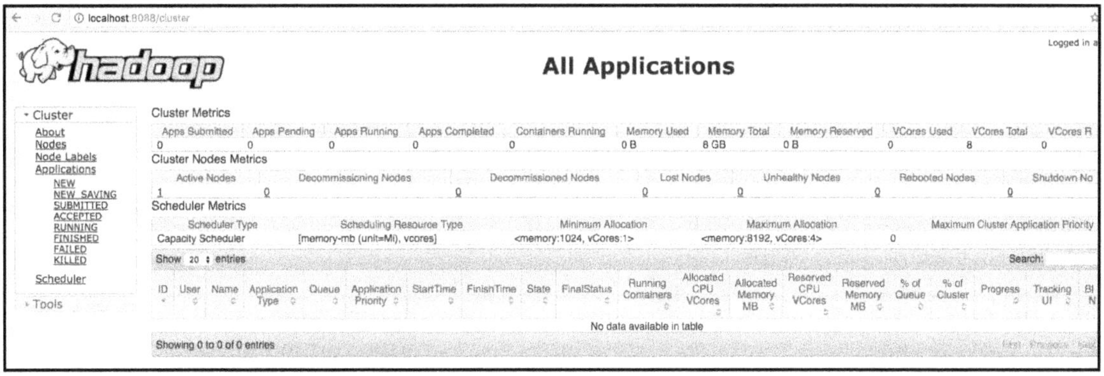

Figure: Screenshot of YARN ResouceManager

The following is a view showing the queues of resources in the cluster, along with any applications running. This is also the place where you can see and monitor the running jobs:

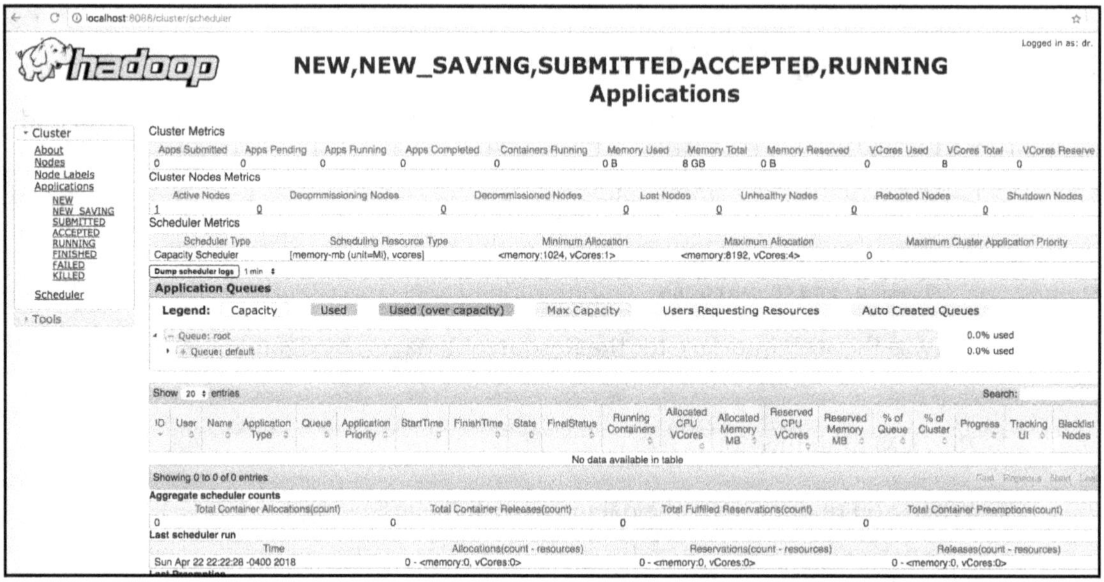

Figure: Screenshot of queues of resources in the cluster

At this time, we should be able to see the running YARN service in our local cluster running Hadoop 3.1.0. Next, we will look at some new features in Hadoop 3.x.

Erasure Coding

EC is a key change in Hadoop 3.x promising a significant improvement in HDFS utilization efficiencies as compared to earlier versions where replication factor of 3 for instance caused immense wastage of precious cluster file system for all kinds of data no matter what the relative importance was to the tasks at hand.

EC can be setup using policies and assigning the policies to directories in HDFS. For this, HDFS provides an ec subcommand to perform administrative commands related to EC:

```
hdfs ec [generic options]
     [-setPolicy -path <path> [-policy <policyName>] [-replicate]]
     [-getPolicy -path <path>]
     [-unsetPolicy -path <path>]
```

```
[-listPolicies]
[-addPolicies -policyFile <file>]
[-listCodecs]
[-enablePolicy -policy <policyName>]
[-disablePolicy -policy <policyName>]
[-help [cmd ...]]
```

The following are the details of each command:

- `[-setPolicy -path <path> [-policy <policyName>] [-replicate]]`: Sets an EC policy on a directory at the specified path.
    - `path`: An directory in HDFS. This is a mandatory parameter. Setting a policy only affects newly created files, and does not affect existing files.
    - `policyName`: The EC policy to be used for files under this directory. This parameter can be omitted if a `dfs.namenode.ec.system.default.policy` configuration is set. The EC policy of the path will be set with the default value in configuration.
    - `-replicate`: Apply the special REPLICATION policy on the directory, force the directory to adopt 3x replication scheme.
    - `-replicate and -policy <policyName>`: These are optional arguments. They cannot be specified at the same time.
- `[-getPolicy -path <path>]`: Get details of the EC policy of a file or directory at the specified path.
- `[-unsetPolicy -path <path>]`: Unset an EC policy set by a previous call to `setPolicy` on a directory. If the directory inherits the EC policy from an ancestor directory, `unsetPolicy` is a no-op. Unsetting the policy on a directory which doesn't have an explicit policy set will not return an error.
- `[-listPolicies]`: Lists all (enabled, disabled and removed) EC policies registered in HDFS. Only the enabled policies are suitable for use with the `setPolicy` command.
- `[-addPolicies -policyFile <file>]`: Add a list of EC policies. Please refer `etc/hadoop/user_ec_policies.xml.template` for the example policy file. The maximum cell size is defined in property `dfs.namenode.ec.policies.max.cellsize` with the default value 4 MB. Currently HDFS allows the user to add 64 policies in total, and the added policy ID is in range of 64 to 127. Adding policy will fail if there are already 64 policies added.

- `[-listCodecs]`: Get the list of supported EC codecs and coders in system. A coder is an implementation of a codec. A codec can have different implementations, thus different coders. The coders for a codec are listed in a fall back order.
- `[-removePolicy -policy <policyName>]`: It removes an EC policy
- `[-enablePolicy -policy <policyName>]`: It enables an EC policy
- `[-disablePolicy -policy <policyName>]`: It disables an EC policy

By using `-listPolicies`, you can list all the EC policies currently setup in your cluster along with the state of such policies whether they are `ENABLED` or `DISABLED`:

```
Moogie:hadoop-3.1.0 sridharalla$ ./bin/hdfs ec -listPolicies
2018-04-22 22:55:59,587 WARN util.NativeCodeLoader: Unable to load native-hadoop library for your platform... using builtin-java classes
where applicable
Erasure Coding Policies:
ErasureCodingPolicy=[Name=RS-10-4-1024k, Schema=[ECSchema=[Codec=rs, numDataUnits=10, numParityUnits=4]], CellSize=1048576, Id=5], State=
DISABLED
ErasureCodingPolicy=[Name=RS-3-2-1024k, Schema=[ECSchema=[Codec=rs, numDataUnits=3, numParityUnits=2]], CellSize=1048576, Id=2], State=DI
SABLED
ErasureCodingPolicy=[Name=RS-6-3-1024k, Schema=[ECSchema=[Codec=rs, numDataUnits=6, numParityUnits=3]], CellSize=1048576, Id=1], State=EN
ABLED
ErasureCodingPolicy=[Name=RS-LEGACY-6-3-1024k, Schema=[ECSchema=[Codec=rs-legacy, numDataUnits=6, numParityUnits=3]], CellSize=1048576, I
d=3], State=DISABLED
ErasureCodingPolicy=[Name=XOR-2-1-1024k, Schema=[ECSchema=[Codec=xor, numDataUnits=2, numParityUnits=1]], CellSize=1048576, Id=4], State=
DISABLED
```

Lets test out EC in our cluster. First we will create directories in the HDFS shown as follows:

```
./bin/hdfs dfs -mkdir /user/normal
./bin/hdfs dfs -mkdir /user/ec
```

Once the two directories are created then you can set the policy on any path:

```
./bin/hdfs ec -setPolicy -path /user/ec -policy RS-6-3-1024k
Set RS-6-3-1024k erasure coding policy on /user/ec
```

Now copying any content into the `/user/ec` folder falls into the newly set `policy`.

Type the command shown as follows to test this:

```
./bin/hdfs dfs -copyFromLocal ~/Documents/OnlineRetail.csv /user/ec
```

The following screenshot shows the result of the copying, as expected the system complains as we don't really have a cluster on our local system enough to implement EC. But this should give us an idea of what is needed and how it would look:

```
Moogie:hadoop-3.1.0 sridharalla$ ./bin/hdfs dfs -copyFromLocal ~/Documents/OnlineRetail.csv /user/ec
2018-04-22 23:48:25,379 WARN util.NativeCodeLoader: Unable to load native-hadoop library for your platform... using builtin-java classes
where applicable
2018-04-22 23:48:26,284 WARN erasurecode.ErasureCodeNative: ISA-L support is not available in your platform... using builtin-java codec
here applicable
copyFromLocal: File /user/ec/OnlineRetail.csv._COPYING_ could only be written to 1 of the 6 required nodes for RS-6-3-1024k. There are 1
datanode(s) running and no node(s) are excluded in this operation.
```

Intra-DataNode balancer

While HDFS always had a great feature of balancing the data between the data nodes in the cluster, often this resulted in skewed disks within data nodes. For instance, if you have four disks, two disks might take the bulk of the data and the other two might be under-utilized. Given that physical disks (say 7,200 or 10,000 rpm) are slow to read/write, this kind of skewing of data results in poor performance. Using an intra-node balancer, we can rebalance the data amongst the disks.

Run the command shown in the following example to invoke disk balancing on a DataNode:

```
./bin/hdfs diskbalancer -plan 10.0.0.103
```

The following is the output of the disk balancer command:

```
Moogie:hadoop-3.1.0 sridharalla$ ./bin/hdfs diskbalancer -plan 10.0.0.103
2018-04-23 00:00:14,789 WARN util.NativeCodeLoader: Unable to load native-hadoop library for your platform... using builtin-java classes
where applicable
2018-04-23 00:00:15,691 INFO planner.GreedyPlanner: Starting plan for Node : 10.0.0.103:9867
2018-04-23 00:00:15,691 INFO planner.GreedyPlanner: Compute Plan for Node : 10.0.0.103:9867 took 16 ms
2018-04-23 00:00:15,692 INFO command.Command: No plan generated. DiskBalancing not needed for node: 10.0.0.103 threshold used: 10.0
No plan generated. DiskBalancing not needed for node: 10.0.0.103 threshold used: 10.0
```

Installing YARN timeline service v.2

As stated in the *YARN timeline service v.2* section, v.2 always selects Apache HBase as the primary backing storage, since Apache HBase scales well even to larger clusters and continues to maintain a good read and write response time.

There are a few steps that need to be performed to prepare the storage for timeline service v.2:

1. Set up the HBase cluster
2. Enable the co-processor
3. Create the schema for timeline service v.2

Each step is explained in more detail in the following sections.

Setting up the HBase cluster

The first step involves picking an Apache HBase cluster to use as the storage cluster. The version of Apache HBase that is supported with the timeline service v.2 is 1.2.6. The 1.0.x versions no longer work with timeline service v.2. Later versions of HBase have not been tested yet with the timeline service.

Simple deployment for HBase

If you are intent on a simple deploy profile for the Apache HBase cluster where the data loading is light but the data needs to persist across node comings and goings, you could consider the *Standalone HBase* over *HDFS* deploy mode.

`http://mirror.cogentco.com/pub/apache/hbase/1.2.6/`

The following screenshot is the download link to HBase 1.2.6:

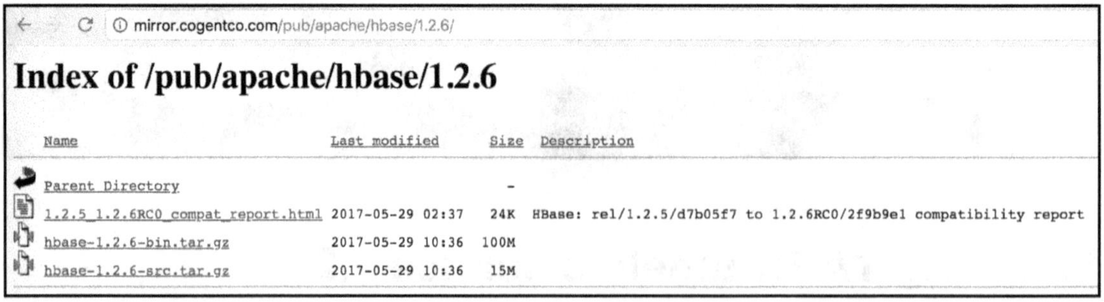

Download `hbase-1.2.6-bin.tar.gz` to your local machine. Then extract the HBase binaries:

```
tar -xvzf hbase-1.2.6-bin.tar.gz
```

The following is the content of the extracted HBase:

Moogie:~ sridharalla$ cd hbase-1.2.6
Moogie:hbase-1.2.6 sridharalla$ ls
CHANGES.txt LICENSE.txt README.txt conf hbase-webapps
LEGAL NOTICE.txt bin docs lib

This is a useful variation on the standalone HBase setup and has all HBase daemons running inside one JVM but rather than persisting to the local filesystem, it persists to an HDFS instance. Writing to HDFS where data is replicated ensures that data is persisted across node comings and goings. To configure this standalone variant, edit your `hbasesite.xml` setting the `hbase.rootdir` to point at a directory in your HDFS instance but then set `hbase.cluster.distributed` to `false`.

The following is the `hbase-site.xml` with the `hdfs` port `9000` for the local cluster we have installed mentioned as a property. If you leave this out there wont be a HBase cluster installed.

```
<configuration>
    <property>
        <name>hbase.rootdir</name>
        <value>hdfs://localhost:9000/hbase</value>
    </property>
    <property>
        <name>hbase.cluster.distributed</name>
        <value>false</value>
    </property>
</configuration>
```

Next step is to start HBase. We will do this by using `start-hbase.sh` script:

```
./bin/start-hbase.sh
```

The following screenshot shows the HBase cluster we just installed:

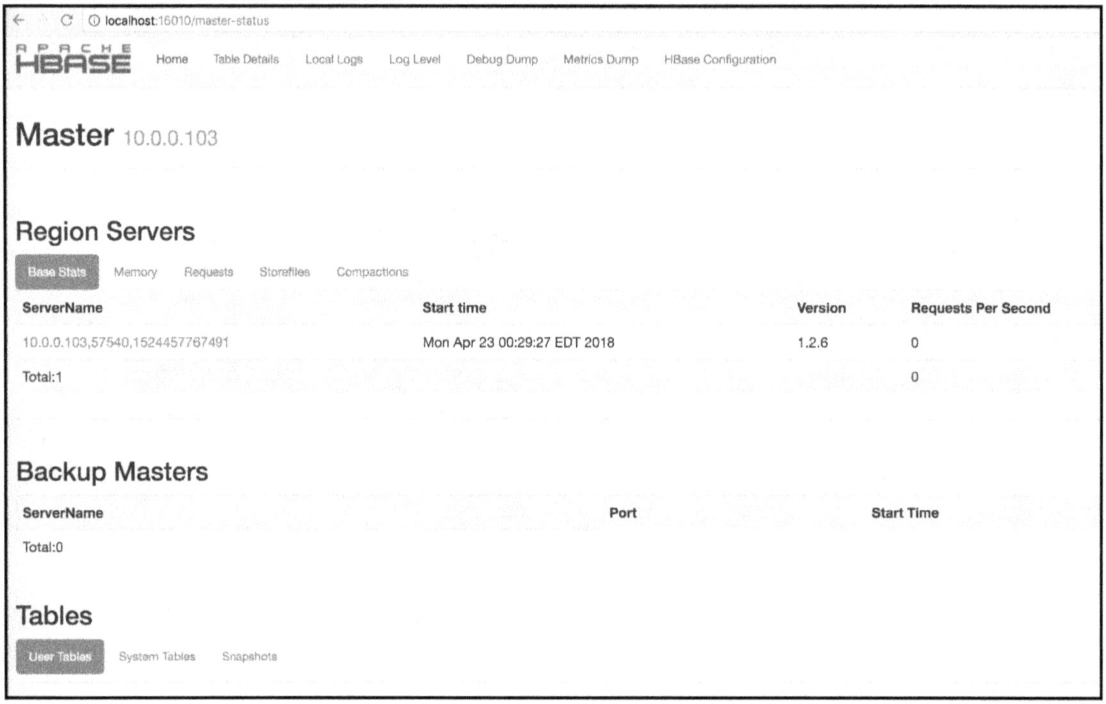

The following screenshot shows are more attributes of the HBase cluster setup showing versions, of various components:

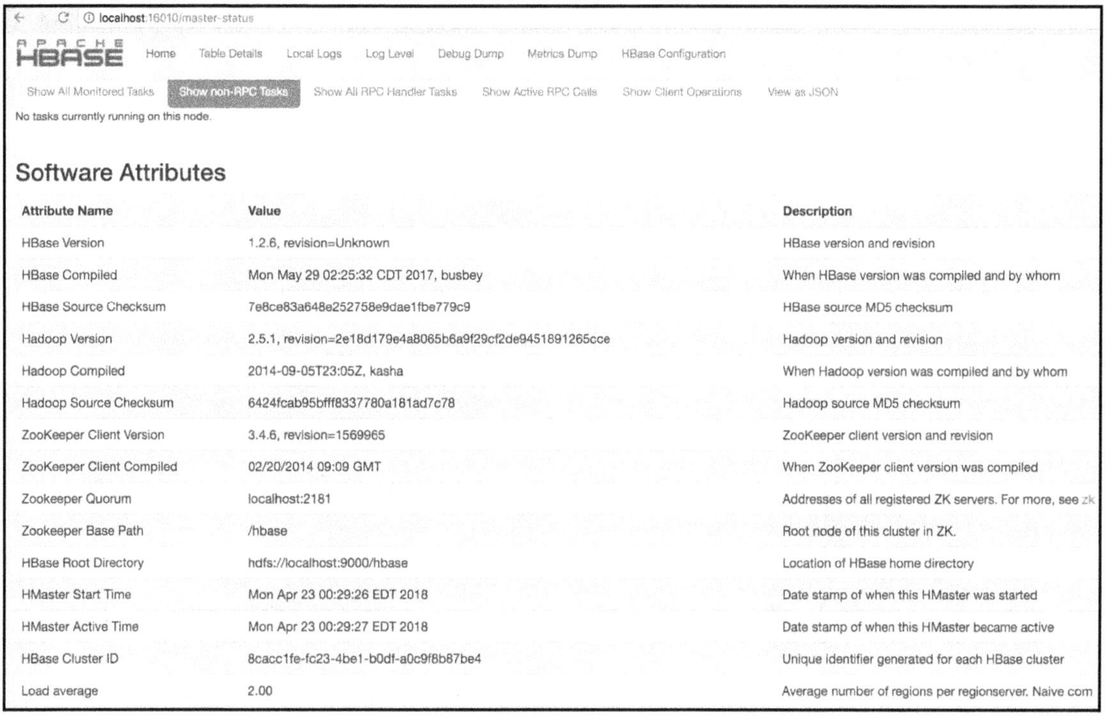

Attribute Name	Value	Description
HBase Version	1.2.6, revision=Unknown	HBase version and revision
HBase Compiled	Mon May 29 02:25:32 CDT 2017, busbey	When HBase version was compiled and by whom
HBase Source Checksum	7e8ce83a648e252758e9dae1fbe779c9	HBase source MD5 checksum
Hadoop Version	2.5.1, revision=2e18d179e4a8065b6a9f29cf2de9451891265cce	Hadoop version and revision
Hadoop Compiled	2014-09-05T23:05Z, kasha	When Hadoop version was compiled and by whom
Hadoop Source Checksum	6424fcab95bfff8337780a181ad7c78	Hadoop source MD5 checksum
ZooKeeper Client Version	3.4.6, revision=1569965	ZooKeeper client version and revision
ZooKeeper Client Compiled	02/20/2014 09:09 GMT	When ZooKeeper client version was compiled
Zookeeper Quorum	localhost:2181	Addresses of all registered ZK servers. For more, see zk
Zookeeper Base Path	/hbase	Root node of this cluster in ZK.
HBase Root Directory	hdfs://localhost:9000/hbase	Location of HBase home directory
HMaster Start Time	Mon Apr 23 00:29:26 EDT 2018	Date stamp of when this HMaster was started
HMaster Active Time	Mon Apr 23 00:29:27 EDT 2018	Date stamp of when this HMaster became active
HBase Cluster ID	8cacc1fe-fc23-4be1-b0df-a0c9f8b87be4	Unique identifier generated for each HBase cluster
Load average	2.00	Average number of regions per regionserver. Naive com

Figure: Screenshot of attributes of the HBase cluster setup and the versions of different components

Once you have an Apache HBase cluster ready to use, perform the steps in the following section.

Enabling the co-processor

In this version, the co-processor is loaded dynamically.

Copy the timeline service `.jar` to HDFS from where HBase can load it. It is needed for the flowrun table creation in the schema creator. The default HDFS location is `/hbase/coprocessor`.

For example:

```
hadoop fs -mkdir /hbase/coprocessor hadoop fs -put hadoop-yarn-server-
timelineservice-hbase-3.0.0-alpha1-SNAPSHOT.jar /hbase/coprocessor/hadoop-
yarn-server-timelineservice.jar
```

To place the JAR at a different location on HDFS, there also exists a YARN configuration setting called `yarn.timeline-service.hbase.coprocessor.jar.hdfs.location`, shown as follows:

```
<property>
  <name>yarn.timeline-service.hbase.coprocessor.jar.hdfs.location</name>
  <value>/custom/hdfs/path/jarName</value>
</property>
```

Create the timeline service schema using the schema creator tool. For this to happen, we also need to make sure the JARs are all found correctly:

```
export
HADOOP_CLASSPATH=$HADOOP_CLASSPATH:/Users/sridharalla/hbase-1.2.6/lib/:/Use
rs/sridharalla/hadoop-3.1.0/share/hadoop/yarn/timelineservice/
```

Once we have the classpath corrected, we can create the HBase schema/tables using a simple command, shown as follows:

```
./bin/hadoop
org.apache.hadoop.yarn.server.timelineservice.storage.TimelineSchemaCreator
-create -skipExistingTable
```

The following is the HBase schema created as a result of the preceding command:

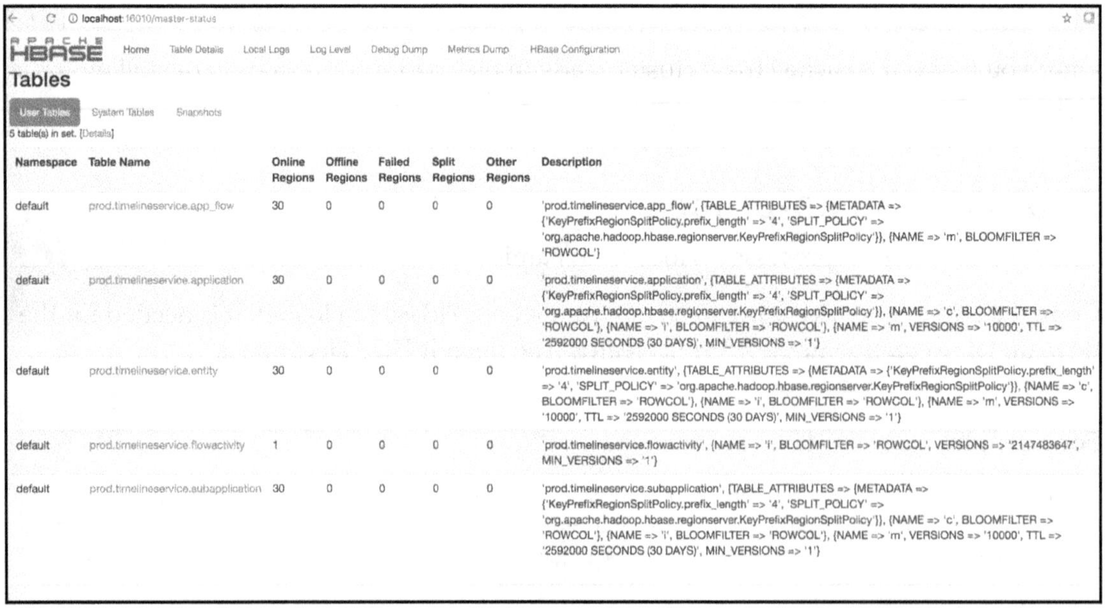

Namespace	Table Name	Online Regions	Offline Regions	Failed Regions	Split Regions	Other Regions	Description
default	prod.timelineservice.app_flow	30	0	0	0	0	'prod.timelineservice.app_flow', {TABLE_ATTRIBUTES => {METADATA => {'KeyPrefixRegionSplitPolicy.prefix_length' => '4', 'SPLIT_POLICY' => 'org.apache.hadoop.hbase.regionserver.KeyPrefixRegionSplitPolicy'}}, {NAME => 'm', BLOOMFILTER => 'ROWCOL'}
default	prod.timelineservice.application	30	0	0	0	0	'prod.timelineservice.application', {TABLE_ATTRIBUTES => {METADATA => {'KeyPrefixRegionSplitPolicy.prefix_length' => '4', 'SPLIT_POLICY' => 'org.apache.hadoop.hbase.regionserver.KeyPrefixRegionSplitPolicy'}}, {NAME => 'c', BLOOMFILTER => 'ROWCOL'}, {NAME => 'i', BLOOMFILTER => 'ROWCOL'}, {NAME => 'm', VERSIONS => '10000', TTL => '2592000 SECONDS (30 DAYS)', MIN_VERSIONS => '1'}
default	prod.timelineservice.entity	30	0	0	0	0	'prod.timelineservice.entity', {TABLE_ATTRIBUTES => {METADATA => {'KeyPrefixRegionSplitPolicy.prefix_length' => '4', 'SPLIT_POLICY' => 'org.apache.hadoop.hbase.regionserver.KeyPrefixRegionSplitPolicy'}}, {NAME => 'c', BLOOMFILTER => 'ROWCOL'}, {NAME => 'i', BLOOMFILTER => 'ROWCOL'}, {NAME => 'm', VERSIONS => '10000', TTL => '2592000 SECONDS (30 DAYS)', MIN_VERSIONS => '1'}
default	prod.timelineservice.flowactivity	1	0	0	0	0	'prod.timelineservice.flowactivity', {NAME => 'i', BLOOMFILTER => 'ROWCOL', VERSIONS => '2147483647', MIN_VERSIONS => '1'}
default	prod.timelineservice.subapplication	30	0	0	0	0	'prod.timelineservice.subapplication', {TABLE_ATTRIBUTES => {METADATA => {'KeyPrefixRegionSplitPolicy.prefix_length' => '4', 'SPLIT_POLICY' => 'org.apache.hadoop.hbase.regionserver.KeyPrefixRegionSplitPolicy'}}, {NAME => 'c', BLOOMFILTER => 'ROWCOL'}, {NAME => 'i', BLOOMFILTER => 'ROWCOL'}, {NAME => 'm', VERSIONS => '10000', TTL => '2592000 SECONDS (30 DAYS)', MIN_VERSIONS => '1'}

Enabling timeline service v.2

The following are the basic configurations to start timeline service v.2:

```
<property>
  <name>yarn.timeline-service.version</name>
  <value>2.0f</value>
</property>

<property>
  <name>yarn.timeline-service.enabled</name>
  <value>true</value>
</property>

<property>
  <name>yarn.nodemanager.aux-services</name>
  <value>mapreduce_shuffle,timeline_collector</value>
</property>

<property>
  <name>yarn.nodemanager.aux-services.timeline_collector.class</name>
<value>org.apache.hadoop.yarn.server.timelineservice.collector.PerNodeTimel
ineCollectorsAuxService</value>
</property>

<property>
  <description> This setting indicates if the yarn system metrics is
published by RM and NM by on the timeline service. </description>
  <name>yarn.system-metrics-publisher.enabled</name>
  <value>true</value>
</property>

<property>
  <description>This setting is to indicate if the yarn container events are
published by RM to the timeline service or not. This configuration is for
ATS V2. </description>
  <name>yarn.rm.system-metrics-publisher.emit-container-events</name>
  <value>true</value>
</property>
```

Also, add the `hbase-site.xml` configuration file to the client Hadoop cluster configuration so that it can write data to the Apache HBase cluster you are using, or set `yarn.timeline-service.hbase.configuration.file` to the file URL pointing to `hbase-site.xml` for the same purpose of writing the data to HBase, for example:

```
<property>
  <description>This is an Optional URL to an hbase-site.xml configuration
file. It is to be used to connect to the timeline-service hbase cluster. If
it is empty or not specified, the HBase configuration will be loaded from
the classpath. Else, they will override those from the ones present on the
classpath. </description>
  <name>yarn.timeline-service.hbase.configuration.file</name>
  <value>file:/etc/hbase/hbase-site.xml</value>
</property>
```

Running timeline service v.2

Restart the ResourceManager as well as the node managers to pick up the new configuration. The collectors start within the resource manager and the node managers in an embedded manner.

The timeline service reader is a separate YARN daemon, and it can be started using the following syntax:

```
$ yarn-daemon.sh start timelinereader
```

Enabling MapReduce to write to timeline service v.2

To write MapReduce framework data to timeline service v.2, enable the following configuration in `mapred-site.xml`:

```
<property>
  <name>mapreduce.job.emit-timeline-data</name>
  <value>true</value>
</property>
```

The timeline service is still evolving so you should try it out only to test out the features and not in production, and wait for the more widely adopted version, which should be available sometime soon.

Summary

In this chapter, we have discussed the new features in Hadoop 3.x and how it improves the reliability and performance of Hadoop 2.x. We also walked through the installation of a standalone Hadoop cluster on the local machine.

In the next chapter, we will take a peek into the world of big data analytics.

2
Overview of Big Data Analytics

In this chapter, we will talk about big data analytics, starting with a general point of view and then taking a deep dive into some common technologies used to gain insights into data. This chapter introduces the reader to the process of examining large data sets to uncover patterns in data, generating reports, and gathering valuable insights. We will particularly focus on the seven Vs of big data. We will also learn about data analysis and big data; we will see the challenges that big data provides and how they are dealt with in distributed computing, and look at approaches using Hive and Tableau to showcase the most commonly used technologies.

In a nutshell, the following topics will be covered throughout this chapter:

- Introduction to data analytics
- Introduction to big data
- Distributed computing using Apache Hadoop
- MapReduce framework
- Hive
- Apache Spark

Introduction to data analytics

Data analytics is the process of applying qualitative and quantitative techniques when examining data, with the goal of providing valuable insights. Using various techniques and concepts, data analytics can provide the means to explore the data **exploratory data analysis** (**EDA**) as well as draw conclusions about the data **confirmatory data analysis** (**CDA**). The EDA and CDA are fundamental concepts of data analytics, and it is important to understand the differences between the two.

EDA involves the methodologies, tools, and techniques used to explore data with the intention of finding patterns in the data and relationships between various elements of the data. CDA involves the methodologies, tools, and techniques used to provide an insight or conclusion for a specific question, based on hypothesis and statistical techniques, or simple observation of the data.

Inside the data analytics process

Once data is deemed ready, it can be analyzed and explored by data scientists using statistical methods such as SAS. Data governance also becomes a factor to ensure the proper collection and protection of the data. Another less well known role is that of a **data steward** who specializes in understanding the data to the byte; exactly where it is coming from, all transformations that occur, and what the business really needs from the column or field of data.

Various entities in the business might be dealing with addresses differently, such as the following:

```
123 N Main St vs 123 North Main Street.
```

But, our analytics depend on getting the correct address field, else both the addresses mentioned will be considered different and our analytics will not have the same accuracy.

The analytics process starts with data collection based on what the analysts might need from the data warehouse, collecting all sorts of data in the organization (sales, marketing, employee, payroll, HR, and so on). Data stewards and governance teams are important here to make sure the right data is collected and that any information deemed confidential or private is not accidentally exported out, even if the end users are all employees. **Social Security Numbers** (**SSNs**) or full addresses might not be a good idea to include in analytics as this can cause a lot of problems to the organization.

Data quality processes must be established to make sure that the data being collected and engineered is correct and will match the needs of the data scientists. At this stage, the main goal is to find and fix data quality problems that could affect the accuracy of analytical needs. Common techniques are profiling the data, cleansing the data to make sure that the information in a dataset is consistent, and also that any errors and duplicate records are removed.

Analytical applications can thus be realized using several disciplines, teams, and skillsets. Analytical applications can be used to generate reports all the way to automatically triggering business actions. For example, you can simply a create daily sales report to be emailed out to all managers every day at 8 AM in the morning. But, you can also integrate with business process management applications or some custom stock trading applications to take action, such as buying, selling, or alerting on activities in the stock market. You can also think of taking in news articles or social media information to further influence what decisions to be made.

Data visualization is an important piece of data analytics and it's hard to understand numbers when you are looking at a lot of metrics and calculation. Rather, there is an increasing dependence on **business intelligence** (**BI**) tools, such as Tableau, QlikView, and so on, to explore and analyze the data. Of course, large-scale visualization, such as showing all Uber cars in the country or heat maps showing water supply in New York City, requires more custom applications or specialized tools to be built.

Managing and analyzing data has always been a challenge across many organizations of different sizes across all industries. Businesses have always struggled to find a pragmatic approach to capturing information about their customers, products, and services. When the company only had a handful of customers who bought a few of their items, it was not that difficult. It was not as big of a challenge. But over time, companies in the markets started growing. Things have become more complicated. Now, we have branding information and social media. We have things that are sold and bought over the internet. We need to come up with different solutions. With web development, organizations, pricing, social networks, and segmentations, there's a lot of different data that we're dealing with that brings a lot more complexity when it comes to dealing, managing, organizing, and trying to gain some insight from the data.

Introduction to big data

Twitter, Facebook, Amazon, Verizon, Macy's, and Whole Foods are all companies that run their business using data analytics and base many of the decisions on the analytics. Think about what kind of data they are collecting, how much data they might be collecting, and then how they might be using the data.

Let's look at the grocery store example seen earlier; what if the store starts expanding its business to set up hundreds of stores? Naturally, the sales transactions will have to be collected and stored at a scale hundreds of times more than the single store. But then, no business works independently any more. There is a lot of information out there, starting from local news, tweets, Yelp reviews, customer complaints, survey activities, competition from other stores, the changing demographics or economy of the local area, and so on. All such additional data can help in better understanding the customer behavior and the revenue models.

For example, if we see increasing negative sentiment regarding the store's parking facility, then we could analyze this and take corrective action such as validated parking or negotiating with the city's public transportation department to provide more frequent trains or buses for better reach. Such an increasing quantity and variety of data, while it provides better analytics also poses challenges to the business IT organization trying to store and process and analyze all the data. It is, in fact, not uncommon to see TBs of data.

Every day, we create more than two quintillion bytes of data (2 EB), and it is estimated that more than 90% of the data has been generated in last few years alone:

```
1 KB = 1024 Bytes
1 MB = 1024 KB
1 GB = 1024 MB
1 TB = 1024 GB ~ 1,000,000 MB
1 PB = 1024 TB ~ 1,000,000 GB ~ 1,000,000,000 MB
1 EB = 1024 PB ~ 1,000,000 TB ~ 1,000,000,000 GB ~ 1,000,000,000,000 MB
```

Such large amounts of data since the 1990s and the need to understand and make sense of the data, gave rise to the term big data.

In 2001, *Doug Laney*, then an analyst at consultancy Meta Group Inc (which got acquired by Gartner), introduced the idea of three Vs (that is, Variety, Velocity, and Volume). Now, we refer to four Vs instead of three Vs with the addition of Veracity of data to the three Vs.

The following are the four Vs of big data, used to describe the properties of big data.

Variety of data

Data can be obtained from a number of sources, such as weather sensors, car sensors, census data, Facebook updates, tweets, transactions, sales, and marketing. The data format is both structured and unstructured as well. Data types can also be different, binary, text, JSON, and XML. Variety really begins to scratch the surface of the depth of the data.

Velocity of data

Data can be from a data warehouse, batch mode file archives, near real-time updates, or instantaneous real-time updates from the Uber ride you just booked. Velocity refers to the increasing speed at which this data is created, and the increasing speed at which the data can be processed, stored, and analyzed by relational databases.

Volume of data

Data can be collected and stored for an hour, a day, a month, a year, or 10 years. The size of data is growing to 100s of TBs for many companies. Volume refers to the scale of the data, which is part of what makes big data big.

Veracity of data

Data can be analyzed for actionable insights, but with so much data of all types being analyzed from across data sources, it is very difficult to ensure correctness and proof of accuracy.

The following are the four Vs of big data:

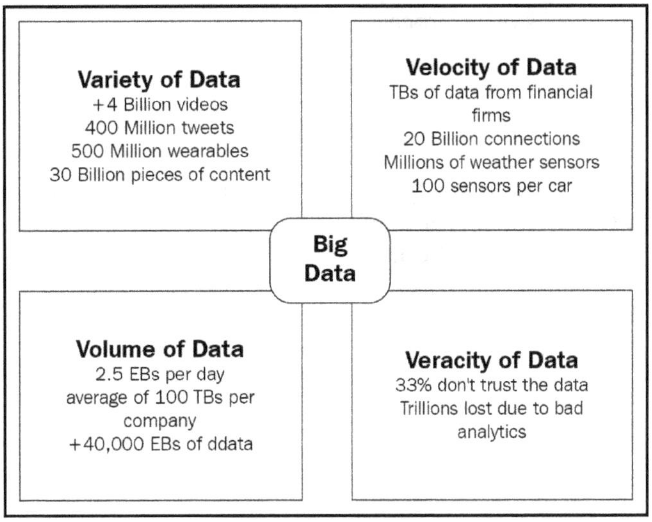

To make sense of all the data and apply data analytics to big data, we need to expand the concept of data analytics to operate at a much larger scale that deals with the four Vs of big data. This changes not only the tools and technologies and methodologies used in analyzing the data, but also changes the way we even approach the problem. If a SQL database was used for data in a business in 1999, to handle the data now for the same business, we will need a distributed SQL database that is scalable and adaptable to the nuances of the big data space.

The four Vs described earlier are no longer sufficient to cover the capabilities and needs of big data analytics, hence nowadays it's common to hear about the seven Vs instead of the four Vs.

Variability of data

Variability refers to data whose meaning is constantly changing. Many a time, organizations need to develop sophisticated programs in order to be able to understand context in them and decode their exact meaning.

Visualization

Visualization comes in the picture when you need to present the data in a readable and accessible manner after it has been processed.

Value

Big data is large and is increasing everyday, however the data is also messy, noisy, and constantly changing. It is available for all in a variety of formats and is in no position to be used without analysis and visualization.

Distributed computing using Apache Hadoop

We are surrounded by devices such as the smart refrigerator, smart watch, phone, tablet, laptops, kiosks at the airport, ATMs dispensing cash to you, and many many more, with the help of which we are now able to do things that were unimaginable just a few years ago. We are so used to applications such as Instagram, Snapchat, Gmail, Facebook, Twitter, and Pinterest that it is next to impossible to go a day without access to such applications. Today, cloud computing has introduced us to the following concepts:

- Infrastructure as a Service
- Platform as a Service
- Software as a Service

Behind the scenes is the world of highly scalable distributed computing, which makes it possible to store and process **Petabytes** (**PB**) of data:

- 1 EB = 1024 PB (50 million Blu-ray movies)
- 1 PB = 1024 TB (50,000 Blu-ray movies)
- 1 TB = 1024 GB (50 Blu-ray movies)

The average size of one Blu-ray disc for a movie is ~ 20 GB.

Now, the paradigm of distributed computing is not really a genuinely new topic and has been pursued in some shape or form over decades, primarily at research facilities as well as by a few commercial product companies. **Massively parallel processing** (**MPP**) is a paradigm that was in use decades ago in several areas such as oceanography, earthquake monitoring, and space exploration. Several companies, such as Teradata, also implemented MPP platforms and provided commercial products and applications.

Eventually, tech companies such as Google and Amazon, among others, pushed the niche area of scalable distributed computing to a new stage of evolution, which eventually led to the creation of Apache Spark by Berkeley University. Google published a paper on MapReduce as well as **Google File System** (**GFS**), which brought the principles of distributed computing to be used by everyone. Of course, due credit needs to be given to *Doug Cutting*, who made it possible by implementing the concepts given in the Google white papers and introducing the world to Hadoop. The Apache Hadoop framework is an open source software framework written in Java. The two main areas provided by the framework are storage and processing. For storage, the Apache Hadoop framework uses **Hadoop Distributed File System** (**HDFS**), which is based on the GFS paper released on October 2003. For processing or computing, the framework depends on MapReduce, which is based on a Google paper on MapReduce released in December 2004 MapReduce framework evolved from V1 (based on JobTracker and TaskTracker) to V2 (based on YARN).

The MapReduce framework

MapReduce is a framework used to compute a large amount of data in a Hadoop cluster. MapReduce uses YARN to schedule the mappers and reducers as tasks, using the containers.

An example of a MapReduce job to count frequencies of words is shown in the following diagram:

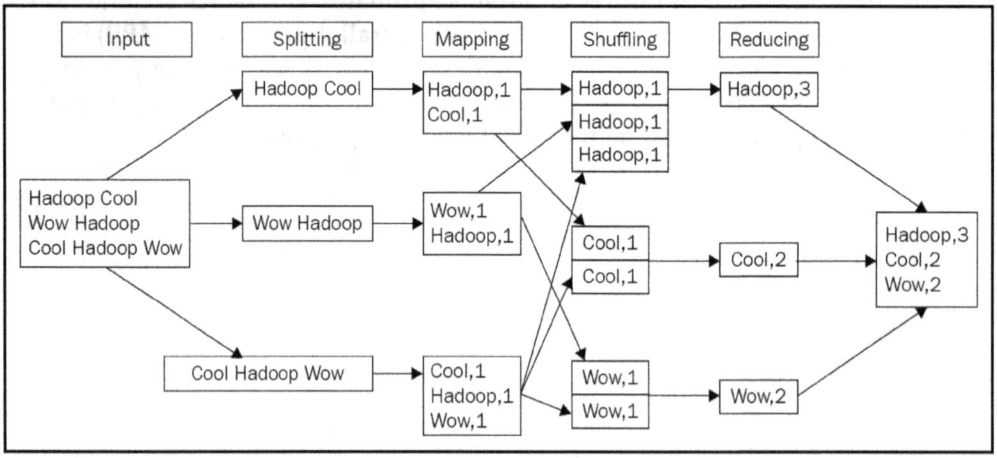

MapReduce works closely with YARN to plan the job and the various tasks in the job, requests computing resources from the cluster manager (resource manager), schedules the execution of the tasks on the compute resources of the cluster, and then executes the plan of execution. Using MapReduce, you can read write many different types of files of varying formats and perform very complex computations in a distributed manner. We will see more of this in the next chapter on MapReduce frameworks.

Hive

Hive provides a SQL layer abstraction over the MapReduce framework with several optimizations. This is needed because of the complexity of writing code using the MapReduce framework. For example, a simple count of the records in a specific file takes at least a few dozen lines of code, which is not productive to anyone. Hive abstracts the MapReduce code by encapsulating the logic from the SQL statement into a MapReduce framework code, which is automatically generated and executed on the backend. This saves incredible amounts of time for anyone who needs to spend more time on doing something useful with the data, rather than going through the boiler plate coding for every single task that needs to be executed and every single computation that's desired as part of your job:

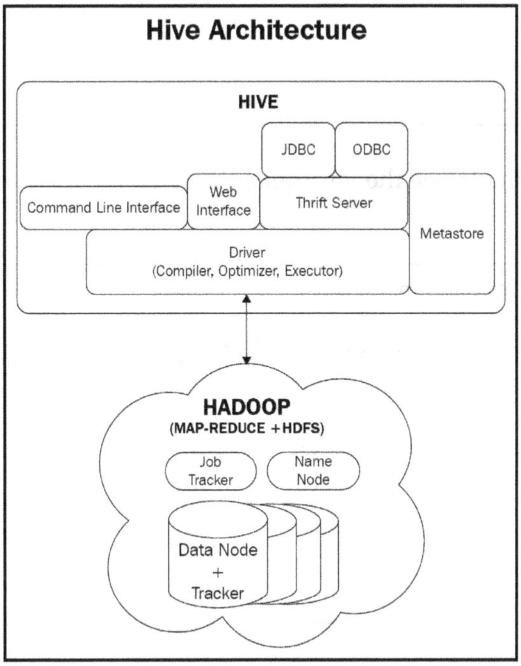

Hive is not designed for online transaction processing and does not offer real-time queries and row-level updates.

In this section, we will look at Hive and how to use it to perform analytics, `https://hive.apache.org/downloads.html`:

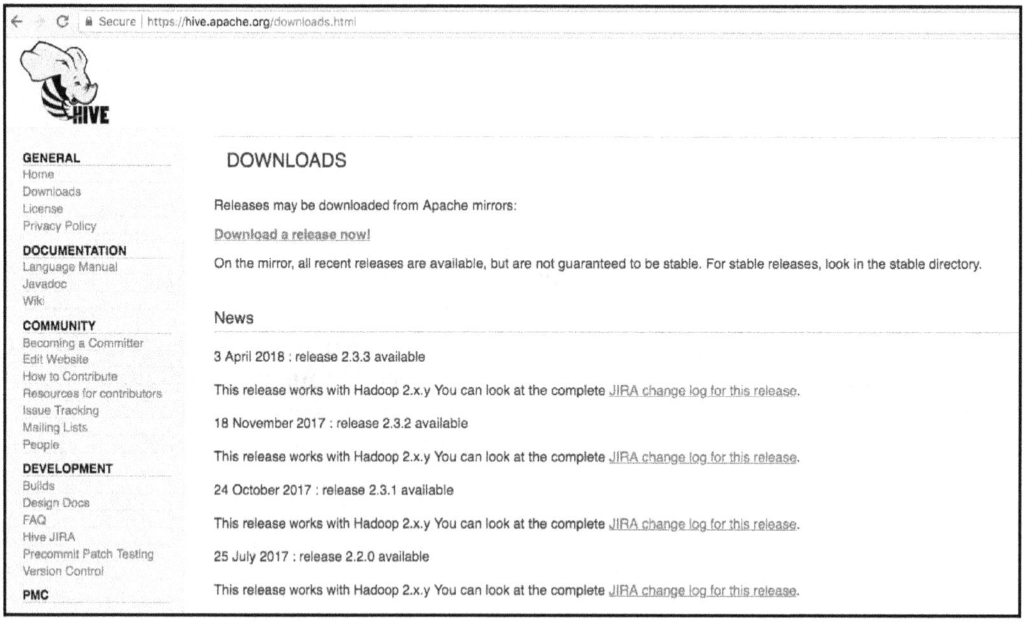

Click on the download link to see the various downloadable files as shown in the following screenshot:

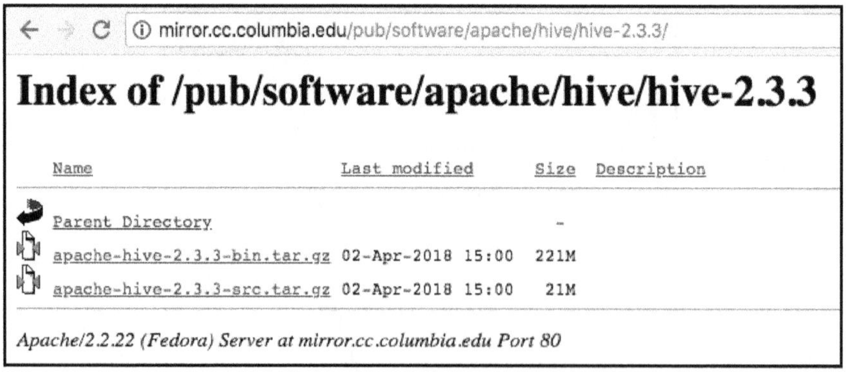

Downloading and extracting the Hive binaries

In this section, we will extract the downloaded binaries and then configure the Hive binaries to get everything started:

```
tar -xvzf apache-hive-2.3.3-bin.tar.gz
```

Once the Hive bundle is extracted, do the following to create a `hive-site.xml`:

```
cd apache-hive-2.3.3-bin
vi conf/hive-site.xml
```

At the top of the properties list, paste the following:

```
<property>
 <name>system:java.io.tmpdir</name>
 <value>/tmp/hive/java</value>
</property>
```

At the bottom of the `hive-site.xml` add the following properties:

```
<property>
 <name>hive.metastore.local</name>
 <value>TRUE</value>

</property>
<property>
 <name>hive.metastore.warehouse.dir</name>
 <value>/usr/hive/warehouse</value>
 </property>
```

After this, using the Hadoop commands, create the HDFS paths needed for `hive`:

```
cd hadoop-3.1.0
./bin/hadoop fs -mkdir -p /usr/hive/warehouse
./bin/hadoop fs -chmod g+w /usr/hive/warehouse
```

Installing Derby

Hive works by leveraging the MapReduce framework and uses the tables and schemas to create the mappers and reducers for the MapReduce jobs that are run behind the scenes. In order to maintain the metadata about the data, Hive uses Derby which is an easy to use database. In this section, we will look at installing Derby to be used in our Hive installation, `https://db.apache.org/derby/derby_downloads.html`:

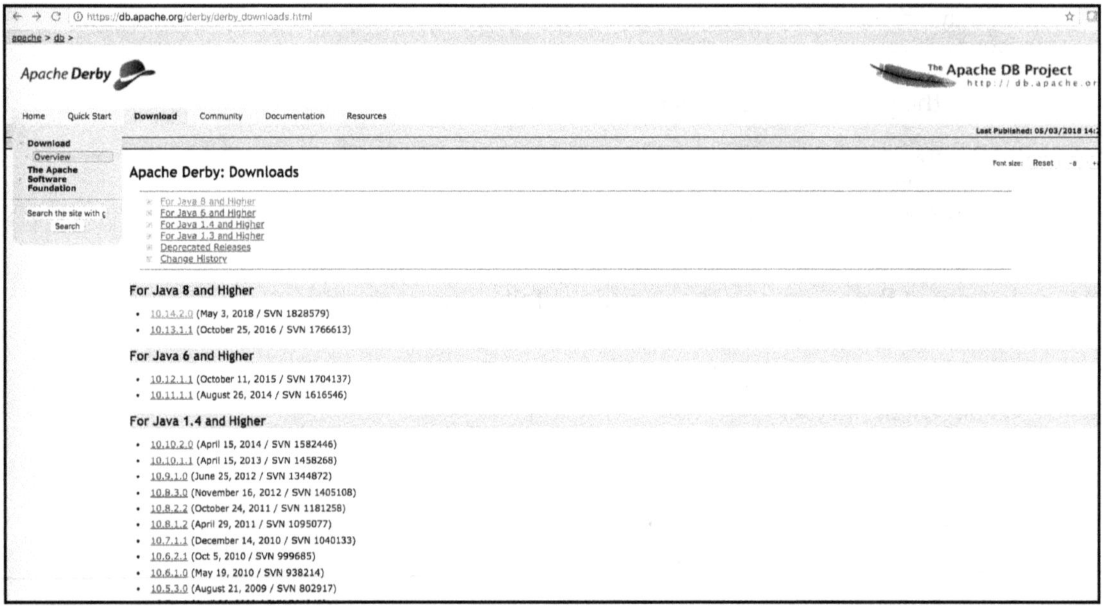

1. Extract Derby using a command, as shown in the following code:

```
tar -xvzf db-derby-10.14.1.0-bin.tar.gz
```

2. Then, change directory into `derby` and create a directory named `data`. In fact, there are several commands to be run so we are going to list all of them in the following code:

```
export HIVE_HOME=<YOURDIRECTORY>/apache-hive-2.3.3-bin
export HADOOP_HOME=<YOURDIRECTORY>/hadoop-3.1.0
export DERBY_HOME=<YOURDIRECTORY>/db-derby-10.14.1.0-bin
export PATH=$PATH:$HADOOP_HOME/bin:$HIVE_HOME/bin:$DERBY_HOME/bin
mkdir $DERBY_HOME/data
cp $DERBY_HOME/lib/derbyclient.jar $HIVE_HOME/lib
cp $DERBY_HOME/lib/derbytools.jar $HIVE_HOME/lib
```

3. Now, start up the Derby server using a simple command, as shown in the following code:

```
nohup startNetworkServer -h 0.0.0.0
```

4. Once this is done, you have to create and initialize the `derby` instance:

```
schematool -dbType derby -initSchema --verbose
```

5. Now, you are ready to open the `hive` console:

```
hive
```

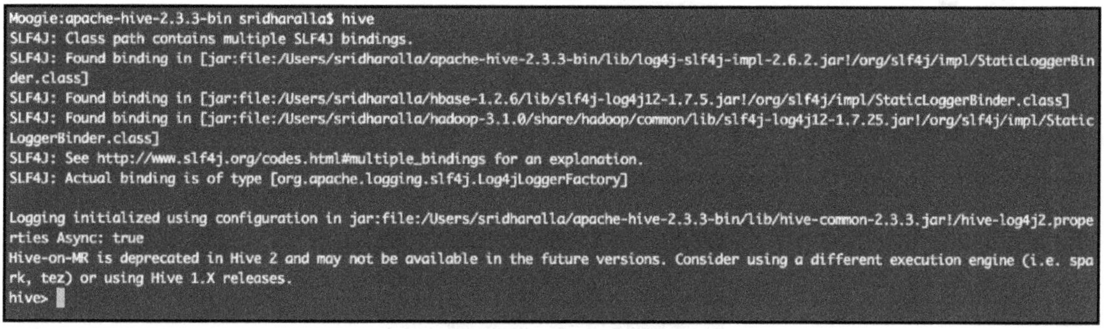
Moogie:apache-hive-2.3.3-bin sridharalla$ hive
SLF4J: Class path contains multiple SLF4J bindings.
SLF4J: Found binding in [jar:file:/Users/sridharalla/apache-hive-2.3.3-bin/lib/log4j-slf4j-impl-2.6.2.jar!/org/slf4j/impl/StaticLoggerBinder.class]
SLF4J: Found binding in [jar:file:/Users/sridharalla/hbase-1.2.6/lib/slf4j-log4j12-1.7.5.jar!/org/slf4j/impl/StaticLoggerBinder.class]
SLF4J: Found binding in [jar:file:/Users/sridharalla/hadoop-3.1.0/share/hadoop/common/lib/slf4j-log4j12-1.7.25.jar!/org/slf4j/impl/StaticLoggerBinder.class]
SLF4J: See http://www.slf4j.org/codes.html#multiple_bindings for an explanation.
SLF4J: Actual binding is of type [org.apache.logging.slf4j.Log4jLoggerFactory]
Logging initialized using configuration in jar:file:/Users/sridharalla/apache-hive-2.3.3-bin/lib/hive-common-2.3.3.jar!/hive-log4j2.properties Async: true
Hive-on-MR is deprecated in Hive 2 and may not be available in the future versions. Consider using a different execution engine (i.e. spark, tez) or using Hive 1.X releases.
hive>

Using Hive

As opposed to relational data warehouses, nested data models have complex types such as array, map, and struct. We can partition tables based on the values of one or more columns with the `PARTITIONED BY` clause. Moreover, tables or partitions can be bucketed using `CLUSTERED BY` columns, and data can be sorted within that bucket via `SORT BY` columns:

- **Tables**: They are very similar to RDBMS tables and contain rows and tables.
- **Partitions**: Hive tables can have more than one partition. They are mapped to subdirectories and filesystems as well.
- **Buckets**: Data can also be divided into buckets in Hive. They can be stored as files in partitions in the underlying filesystem.

The Hive query language provides the basic SQL-like operations. Here are few of the tasks that HQL can do easily:

- Create and manage tables and partitions
- Support various relational, arithmetic, and logical operators
- Evaluate functions
- Download the contents of a table to a local directory or the results of queries to the HDFS directory

Creating a database

We first have to create a database to hold all the tables created in Hive. This step is easy and similar to most other databases:

```
create database mydb;
```

The following is the `hive` console showing the query execution:

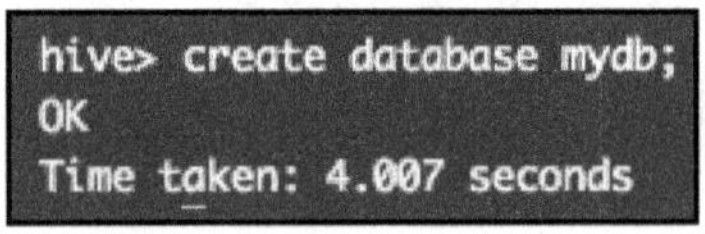
hive> create database mydb;
OK
Time taken: 4.007 seconds

We then begin using the database we just created to create the tables required by our database as follows:

```
use mydb;
```

The following is the `hive` console showing the query execution:

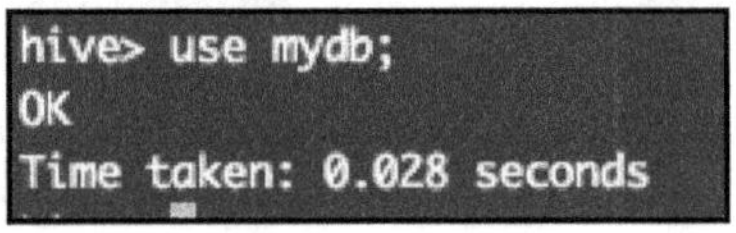
hive> use mydb;
OK
Time taken: 0.028 seconds

Creating a table

Once we have created a database, we are ready to create a table in the database. The table creation is syntactically similar to most RDBMS (database systems such as Oracle, MySQL):

```
create external table OnlineRetail (
 InvoiceNo string,
 StockCode string,
 Description string,
 Quantity integer,
 InvoiceDate string,
 UnitPrice float,
 CustomerID string,
 Country string
 ) ROW FORMAT DELIMITED
 FIELDS TERMINATED BY ','
 LOCATION '/user/normal';
```

The following is the `hive` console and what it looks like:

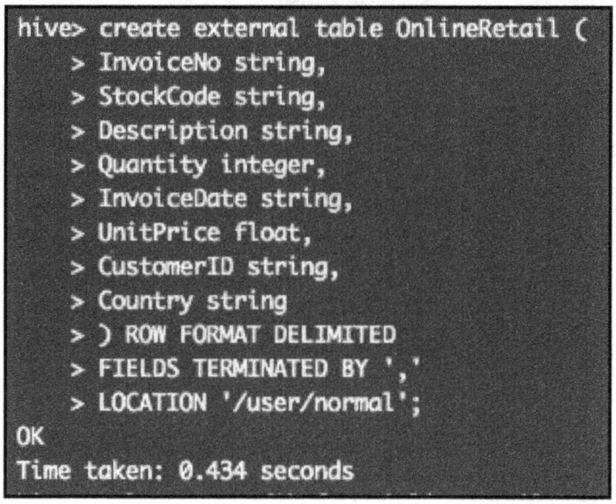
hive> create external table OnlineRetail (
> InvoiceNo string,
> StockCode string,
> Description string,
> Quantity integer,
> InvoiceDate string,
> UnitPrice float,
> CustomerID string,
> Country string
>) ROW FORMAT DELIMITED
> FIELDS TERMINATED BY ','
> LOCATION '/user/normal';
OK
Time taken: 0.434 seconds

We will not get into the syntax of query statements, rather, we will discuss how to improve the query performance significantly using the stinger initiative as follows:

```
select count(*) from OnlineRetail;
```

The following is the `hive` console showing the query execution:

```
hive> select count(*) from OnlineRetail;
WARNING: Hive-on-MR is deprecated in Hive 2 and may not be available in the future
(i.e. spark, tez) or using Hive 1.X releases.
Query ID = sridharalla_20180423173731_d68999d5-5618-4170-a3a8-42be21851d51
Total jobs = 1
Launching Job 1 out of 1
Number of reduce tasks determined at compile time: 1
In order to change the average load for a reducer (in bytes):
  set hive.exec.reducers.bytes.per.reducer=<number>
In order to limit the maximum number of reducers:
  set hive.exec.reducers.max=<number>
In order to set a constant number of reducers:
  set mapreduce.job.reduces=<number>
Job running in-process (local Hadoop)
2018-04-23 17:37:35,267 Stage-1 map = 100%,  reduce = 100%
Ended Job = job_local961179496_0001
MapReduce Jobs Launched:
Stage-Stage-1:  HDFS Read: 10714480 HDFS Write: 0 SUCCESS
Total MapReduce CPU Time Spent: 0 msec
OK
65500
Time taken: 3.518 seconds, Fetched: 1 row(s)
```

SELECT statement syntax

Here's the syntax of Hive's `SELECT` statement:

```
SELECT [ALL | DISTINCT] select_expr, select_expr, ...
FROM table_reference
[WHERE where_condition]
[GROUP BY col_list]
[HAVING having_condition]
[CLUSTER BY col_list | [DISTRIBUTE BY col_list] [SORT BY col_list]]
[LIMIT number]
;
```

`SELECT` is the projection operator in HiveQL. The points are:

- `SELECT` scans the table specified by the `FROM` clause
- `WHERE` gives the condition of what to filter

- `GROUP BY` gives a list of columns that specifies how to aggregate the records
- `CLUSTER BY`, `DISTRIBUTE BY`, and `SORT BY` specify the sort order and algorithm
- `LIMIT` specifies how many records to retrieve:

```
Select Description, count(*) as c from OnlineRetail group By Description
order by c DESC limit 5;
```

The following is the `hive` console showing the query execution:

```
WHITE HANGING HEART T-LIGHT HOLDER      358
REGENCY CAKESTAND 3 TIER        278
HEART OF WICKER SMALL   224
HAND WARMER BABUSHKA DESIGN     213
SCOTTIE DOG HOT WATER BOTTLE    207
Time taken: 3.206 seconds, Fetched: 5 row(s)
```

```
select * from OnlineRetail limit 5;
```

The following is the `hive` console showing the query execution:

```
hive> select * from OnlineRetail limit 5;
OK
InvoiceNo       StockCode       Description     NULL    InvoiceDate     NULL    CustomerID      Country
536365  85123A  WHITE HANGING HEART T-LIGHT HOLDER      6       12/1/10 8:26    2.55    17850   United Kingdom
536365  71053   WHITE METAL LANTERN     6       12/1/10 8:26    3.39    17850   United Kingdom
536365  84406B  CREAM CUPID HEARTS COAT HANGER  8       12/1/10 8:26    2.75    17850   United Kingdom
536365  84029G  KNITTED UNION FLAG HOT WATER BOTTLE     6       12/1/10 8:26    3.39    17850   United Kingdom
Time taken: 5.25 seconds, Fetched: 5 row(s)
```

```
select lower(description), quantity from OnlineRetail limit 5;
```

The following is the `hive` console showing the query execution:

```
hive> select lower(description), quantity from OnlineRetail limit 5;
OK
description     NULL
white hanging heart t-light holder      6
white metal lantern     6
cream cupid hearts coat hanger  8
knitted union flag hot water bottle     6
Time taken: 0.154 seconds, Fetched: 5 row(s)
```

WHERE clauses

A `WHERE` clause is used to filter the result set by using predicate operators and logical operators with the help of the following:

- List of predicate operators
- List of logical operators
- List of functions

Here is an example of using the `WHERE` clause:

```
select * from OnlineRetail where Description='WHITE METAL LANTERN' limit 5;
```

The following is the `hive` console showing the query execution:

```
hive> select * from OnlineRetail where Description='WHITE METAL LANTERN' limit 5;
OK
536365  71053   WHITE METAL LANTERN     6       12/1/10 8:26    3.39    17850   United Kingdom
536373  71053   WHITE METAL LANTERN     6       12/1/10 9:02    3.39    17850   United Kingdom
536375  71053   WHITE METAL LANTERN     6       12/1/10 9:32    3.39    17850   United Kingdom
536396  71053   WHITE METAL LANTERN     6       12/1/10 10:51   3.39    17850   United Kingdom
536406  71053   WHITE METAL LANTERN     8       12/1/10 11:33   3.39    17850   United Kingdom
Time taken: 0.144 seconds, Fetched: 5 row(s)
```

The following query shows us how to use the `group by` clause:

```
select Description, count(*) from OnlineRetail group by Description limit
5;
```

The following is the `hive` console showing the query execution:

```
        166
 4 PURPLE FLOCK DINNER CANDLES  4
 OVAL WALL MIRROR DIAMANTE      22
 SET 2 TEA TOWELS I LOVE LONDON         102
"ACRYLIC HANGING JEWEL  1
Time taken: 1.6 seconds, Fetched: 5 row(s)
```

The following query is an example of using the `group by` clause and specify conditions to filter the results obtained with the help of the `having` clause:

```
select Description, count(*) as cnt from OnlineRetail group by Description
having cnt> 100 limit 5;
```

The following is the `hive` console showing the query execution:

The following query is another example of using the group by clause, filtering the result with the having clause and sorting our result using the `order by` clause, here using `DESC`:

```
select Description, count(*) as cnt from OnlineRetail group by Description
having cnt> 100 order by cnt DESC limit 5;
```

The following is the `hive` console showing the query execution:

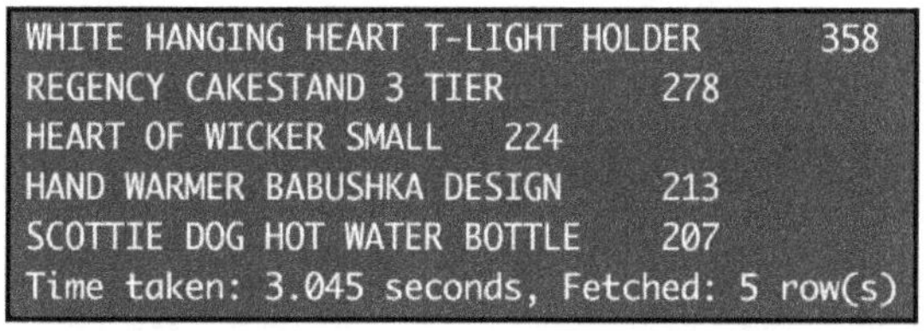

INSERT statement syntax

The syntax of Hive's `INSERT` statement is as follows:

```
-- append new rows to tablename1
INSERT INTO TABLE tablename1 select_statement1 FROM from_statement;

-- replace contents of tablename1
INSERT OVERWRITE TABLE tablename1 select_statement1 FROM from_statement;

-- more complex example using WITH clause
WITH tablename1 AS (select_statement1 FROM from_statement) INSERT
[OVERWRITE/INTO] TABLE tablename2 select_statement2 FROM tablename1;
```

Primitive types

Types are associated with the columns in the tables. Let's take a look at the types supported and their description in the following table:

Types	Description
Integers	• TINYINT: 1 byte integer • SMALLINT: 2 byte integer • INT: 4 byte integer • BIGINT: 8 byte integer
Boolean type	• BOOLEAN: TRUE/FALSE
Floating point numbers	• FLOAT: Single precision • DOUBLE: Double precision
Fixed point numbers	• DECIMAL: A fixed point value of user defined scale and precision
String types	• STRING: Sequence of characters in a specified character set • VARCHAR: Sequence of characters in a specified character set with a maximum length • CHAR: Sequence of characters in a specified character set with a defined length
Date and time types	• TIMESTAMP: A specific point in time, up to nanosecond precision • DATE: A date
Binary types	• BINARY: A sequence of bytes

Complex types

We can build complex types from primitive and other composite types with the help of the following:

- **Structs**: The elements within the type can be accessed using the DOT (.) notation.
- **Maps (key-value tuples)**: The elements are accessed using the ['element name'] notation.
- **Arrays (indexable lists)**: The elements in the array have to be in the same type. You can access the elements using the [n] notation where n is an index (zero-based) into the array.

Built-in operators and functions

The following operators and functions listed are not necessarily up to date. (Hive operators and UDFs have more current information). In Beeline or the Hive CLI, use these commands to show the latest documentation:

```
SHOW FUNCTIONS;
DESCRIBE FUNCTION <function_name>;
DESCRIBE FUNCTION EXTENDED <function_name>;
```

All Hive keywords are case insensitive, including the names of Hive operators and functions.

Built-in operators

Relational operators: Depending on whether the comparison between the operands holds or not, the following operators compare the passed operands and generate a `TRUE` or `FALSE` value:

Operataors	Type	Description
`A = B`	all primitive types	`TRUE` if expression `A` is equivalent to expression `B`; otherwise `FALSE`
`A != B`	all primitive types	`TRUE` if expression `A` is *not* equivalent to expression `B`; otherwise `FALSE`
`A < B`	all primitive types	`TRUE` if expression `A` is less than expression `B`; otherwise `FALSE`
`A <= B`	all primitive types	`TRUE` if expression `A` is less than or equal to expression `B`; otherwise `FALSE`
`A > B`	all primitive types	`TRUE` if expression `A` is greater than expression `B`; otherwise `FALSE`
`A >= B`	all primitive types	`TRUE` if expression `A` is greater than or equal to expression `B` otherwise `FALSE`
`A IS NULL`	all types	`TRUE` if expression `A` evaluates to `NULL` otherwise `FALSE`
`A IS NOT NULL`	all types	`FALSE` if expression `A` evaluates to `NULL` otherwise `TRUE`

A LIKE B	strings	TRUE if string A matches the SQL simple regular expression B, otherwise FALSE. The comparison is done character by character. The _ character in B matches any character in A (similar to . in posix regular expressions), and the % character in B matches an arbitrary number of characters in A (similar to .* in posix regular expressions). For example, foobar LIKE foo evaluates to FALSE where as foobar LIKE foo___ evaluates to TRUE and so does 'foobar' LIKEfoo%. To escape % use \ (% matches one % character). If the data contains a semicolon, and you want to search for it, it needs to be escaped; columnValue LIKE a\;b
A RLIKE B	strings	NULL if A or B is NULL, TRUE if any (possibly empty) substring of A matches the Java regular expression B (see Java regular expressions syntax), otherwise FALSE. For example, 'foobar' rlike 'foo' evaluates to TRUE and so does 'foobar' rlike '^f.*r$'.
A REGEXP B	strings	Same as RLIKE

Arithmetic operators: The following operators support various common arithmetic operations on the operands. All of them return number types:

Operators	Type	Description
A + B	all number types	Gives the result of adding A and B. The type of the result is the same as the common parent (in the type hierarchy) of the types of the operands, for example, since every integer is a float. Therefore, float is a containing type of integer so the + operator on a float and an int will result in a float.
A - B	all number types	Gives the result of subtracting B from A. The type of the result is the same as the common parent (in the type hierarchy) of the types of the operands.
A * B	all number types	Gives the result of multiplying A and B. The type of the result is the same as the common parent (in the type hierarchy) of the types of the operands. Note that if the multiplication is causing overflow, you will have to cast one of the operators to a type higher in the type hierarchy.

A / B	all number types	Gives the result of dividing B from A. The type of the result is the same as the common parent (in the type hierarchy) of the types of the operands. If the operands are integer types, then the result is the quotient of the division.
A % B	all number types	Gives the reminder resulting from dividing A by B. The type of the result is the same as the common parent (in the type hierarchy) of the types of the operands.
A & B	all number types	Gives the result of bitwise AND of A and B. The type of the result is the same as the common parent (in the type hierarchy) of the types of the operands.
A | B	all number types	Gives the result of bitwise OR of A and B. The type of the result is the same as the common parent (in the type hierarchy) of the types of the operands.
A ^ B	all number types	Gives the result of bitwise XOR of A and B. The type of the result is the same as the common parent (in the type hierarchy) of the types of the operands.
~A	all number types	Gives the result of bitwise NOT of A. The type of the result is the same as the type of A.

Logical operators: The following operators provide support for creating logical expressions. All of them return Boolean TRUE or FALSE depending upon the Boolean values of the operands:

Operators	**Type**	**Description**
A AND B	Boolean	TRUE if both A and B are TRUE, otherwise FALSE
A && B	Boolean	Same as A AND B
A OR B	Boolean	TRUE if either A or B or both are TRUE, otherwise FALSE
A || B	Boolean	Same as A OR B
NOT A	Boolean	TRUE if A is FALSE, otherwise FALSE
!A	Boolean	Same as NOT A

Operators on complex types: The following operators provide mechanisms to access elements in complex types:

Operators	**Type**	**Description**
A[n]	A is an array and n is an int	Returns the nth element in the array A. The first element has index 0, for example, if A is an array comprising of ['foo', 'bar'] then A[0] returns 'foo' and A[1] returns 'bar'

M[key]	M is a Map<K, V> and key has type K	Returns the value corresponding to the key in the map for example, if M is a map comprising of ('f' -> 'foo', 'b' -> 'bar', 'all' -> 'foobar') then M['all'] returns 'foobar'.
S.x	S is a struct	Returns the x field of S, for example, for struct foobar (int foo, int bar) foobar. foo returns the integer stored in the foo field of the struct.

Built-in functions

Hive supports the following built-in functions:

Data type	Function	Description
BIGINT	round(double a)	Returns the rounded BIGINT value of the double.
BIGINT	floor(double a)	Returns the maximum BIGINT value that is equal or less than the double.
BIGINT	ceil(double a)	Returns the minimum BIGINT value that is equal or greater than the double.
double	rand(), rand(int seed)	Returns a random number (that changes from row to row). Specifying the seed will make sure the generated random number sequence is deterministic.
string	concat(string A, string B,...)	Returns the string resulting from concatenating B after A. For example, concat('foo', 'bar') results in 'foobar'. This function accepts an arbitrary number of arguments and returns the concatenation of all of them.
string	substr(string A, int start)	Returns the substring of A starting from start position till the end of string A. For example, substr('foobar', 4) results in 'bar'.
string	substr(string A, int start, int length)	Returns the substring of A starting from start position with the given length, for example, substr('foobar', 4, 2) results in 'ba'.
string	upper(string A)	Returns the string resulting from converting all characters of A to uppercase, for example, upper('fOoBaR') results in 'FOOBAR'.

<table>
<tr><td>string</td><td>ucase(string A)</td><td>Same as upper.</td></tr>
<tr><td>string</td><td>lower(string A)</td><td>Returns the string resulting from converting all characters of B to lowercase, for example, lower('fOoBaR') results in 'foobar'.</td></tr>
<tr><td>string</td><td>lcase(string A)</td><td>Same as lower.</td></tr>
<tr><td>string</td><td>trim(string A)</td><td>Returns the string resulting from trimming spaces from both ends of A, for example, trim('foobar ') results in 'foobar'.</td></tr>
<tr><td>string</td><td>ltrim(string A)</td><td>Returns the string resulting from trimming spaces from the beginning (left hand side) of A. For example, ltrim(' foobar ') results in 'foobar '.</td></tr>
<tr><td>string</td><td>rtrim(string A)</td><td>Returns the string resulting from trimming spaces from the end (right hand side) of A. For example, rtrim(' foobar') results in 'foobar'.</td></tr>
<tr><td>string</td><td>regexp_replace(string A, string B, string C)</td><td>Returns the string resulting from replacing all substrings in B that match the Java regular expression syntax (See Java regular expressions syntax) with C. For example, regexp_replace('foobar', 'oo|ar',) returns 'fb'.</td></tr>
<tr><td>int</td><td>size(Map<K.V>)</td><td>Returns the number of elements in the map type.</td></tr>
<tr><td>int</td><td>size(Array<T>)</td><td>Returns the number of elements in the array type.</td></tr>
<tr><td>value of <type></td><td>cast(<expr> as <type>)</td><td>Converts the results of the expression expr to <type>, for example, cast('1' as BIGINT) will convert the string '1' to its integral representation. A null is returned if the conversion does not succeed.</td></tr>
<tr><td>string</td><td>from_unixtime(int unixtime)</td><td>Convert the number of seconds from the UNIX epoch (1970-01-01 00:00:00 UTC) to a string representing the timestamp of that moment in the current system time zone in the format of 1970-01-01 00:00:00.</td></tr>
</table>

string	to_date(string timestamp)	Return the date part of a timestamp string: to_date("1970-01-01 00:00:00") = "1970-01-01".
int	year(string date)	Return the year part of a date or a timestamp string: year("1970-01-01 00:00:00") = 1970, year("1970-01-01") = 1970.
int	month(string date)	Return the month part of a date or a timestamp string: month("1970-11-01 00:00:00") = 11, month("1970-11-01") = 11.
int	day(string date)	Return the day part of a date or a timestamp string: day("1970-11-01 00:00:00") = 1, day("1970-11-01") = 1.
string	get_json_object(string json_string, string path)	Extract a json object from a json string based on the json path specified, and return json string of the extracted a .json object. It will return null if the input json string is invalid.

The following built-in aggregate functions are supported in Hive:

Data type	**Functions**	**Description**
BIGINT	count(*), count(expr), count(DISTINCT expr[, expr_.])	count(*) – Returns the total number of retrieved rows, including rows containing NULL values; count(expr) – Returns the number of rows for which the supplied expression is non-NULL; count(DISTINCT expr[, expr]) – Returns the number of rows for which the supplied expressions are unique and non-NULL.
DOUBLE	sum(col), sum(DISTINCT col)	Returns the sum of the elements in the group or the sum of the distinct values of the column in the group.
DOUBLE	avg(col), avg(DISTINCT col)	Returns the average of the elements in the group or the average of the distinct values of the column in the group.
DOUBLE	min(col)	Returns the minimum value of the column in the group.
DOUBLE	max(col)	Returns the maximum value of the column in the group.

Language capabilities

Hive's SQL provides the following basic SQL operations that can work on tables or partitions:

- Filter rows from a table with the help of a `WHERE` clause
- Select certain columns from the table using a `SELECT` clause
- Perform equijoins between two tables
- Evaluate aggregations on multiple `group by` columns for the data stored in a table
- Store the results of a query into another table
- Download the contents of a table to a local (for example, `nfs`) directory
- Store the results of a query in a `hadoop dfs` directory
- Manage tables and partitions (create, drop, and alter)
- Plug in custom scripts in the language of choice for custom map/reduce jobs

A cheat sheet on retrieving information

The following table shows us how to retrieve information for some commonly used functions:

Function	Hive
Retrieving Information (General)	`SELECT from_columns FROM table WHERE conditions;`
Retrieving All Values	`SELECT * FROM table;`
Retrieving Some Values	`SELECT * FROM table WHERE rec_name = "value";`
Retrieving With Multiple Criteria	`SELECT * FROM TABLE WHERE rec1 = "value1" AND rec2 = "value2";`
Retrieving Specific Columns	`SELECT column_name FROM table;`
Retrieving Unique Output	`SELECT DISTINCT column_name FROM table;`
Sorting	`SELECT col1, col2 FROM table ORDER BY col2;`
Sorting Reverse	`SELECT col1, col2 FROM table ORDER BY col2 DESC;`
Counting Rows	`SELECT COUNT(*) FROM table;`
Grouping With Counting	`SELECT owner, COUNT(*) FROM table GROUP BY owner;`
Maximum Value	`SELECT MAX(col_name) AS label FROM table;`

Selecting from multiple tables (Join same table using alias w/"AS")	`SELECT pet.name, comment FROM pet JOIN event ON (pet.name = event.name)`

Apache Spark

Apache Spark is a unified distributed computing engine across different workloads and platforms. Spark can connect to different platforms and process different data workloads using a variety of paradigms such as Spark Streaming, Spark ML, Spark SQL, and Spark Graphx.

Apache Spark is a fast in-memory data processing engine with elegant and expressive development APIs, which allow data workers to efficiently execute streaming machine learning or SQL workloads that require fast interactive access to data sets.

Additional libraries built on top of the core allow the workloads for streaming, SQL, graph processing, and machine learning. SparkML, for instance, is designed for data science and its abstraction makes data science easier.

Spark provides real-time streaming, queries, machine learning, and graph processing. Before Apache Spark, we had to use different technologies for different types of workloads. One for batch analytics, one for interactive queries, one for real-time streaming processing, and another for machine learning algorithms. However, Apache Spark can do all of these just using Apache Spark instead of using multiple technologies that are not always integrated.

Using Apache Spark, all types of workloads could be processed and Spark also supports Scala, Java, R, and Python as a means of writing the client programs.

Apache Spark is an open source distributed computing engine which has key advantages over the MapReduce paradigm:

- Uses in-memory processing as much as possible
- General purpose engine to be used for batch, real-time workloads
- Compatible with YARN and also Mesos
- Integrates well with HBase, Cassandra, MongoDB, HDFS, Amazon S3, and other filesystems and data sources

Spark was created in Berkeley back in 2009 and was a result of the project to build Mesos, a cluster management framework to support different kinds of cluster computing systems.

Hadoop and Apache Spark are both popular big data frameworks, but they don't really serve the same purposes. While Hadoop provides the distributed storage and MapReduce distributed computing framework, Spark on the other hand is a data processing framework that operates on the distributed data storage provided by other technologies.

> Spark is generally a lot faster than MapReduce because of the way it processes data. MapReduce operates on splits using disk operations, Spark operates on the dataset much more efficiently than MapReduce with the main reason behind the performance improvement of Apache Spark being the efficient off-heap in-memory processing rather than solely relying on disk-based computations.

MapReduce's processing style can be sufficient if your data operations and reporting requirements are mostly static, and it is okay to use batch processing for your purposes, but if you need to do analytics on streaming data or the processing requirements needed in multistage processing logic, you probably want to want to go with Spark.

The following is the Apache Spark stack:

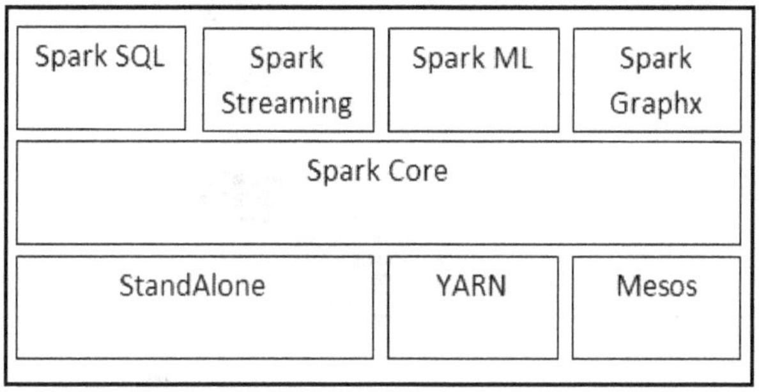

Visualization using Tableau

Whichever method we use to perform distributed computing on big data, its very hard to comprehend the meaning of the data without the aid of tools such as Tableau, which can provide an easy to understand visualization of data.

We can do visualization using many tools such as Cognos, Tableau, Zoom data, KineticaDB, Python Matplotlib, R + Shiny, JavaScript, and so on. We will cover visualization in more detail in `Chapter 10`, *Visualizing Big Data.*

The following is a simple horizontal bar chart in Tableau:

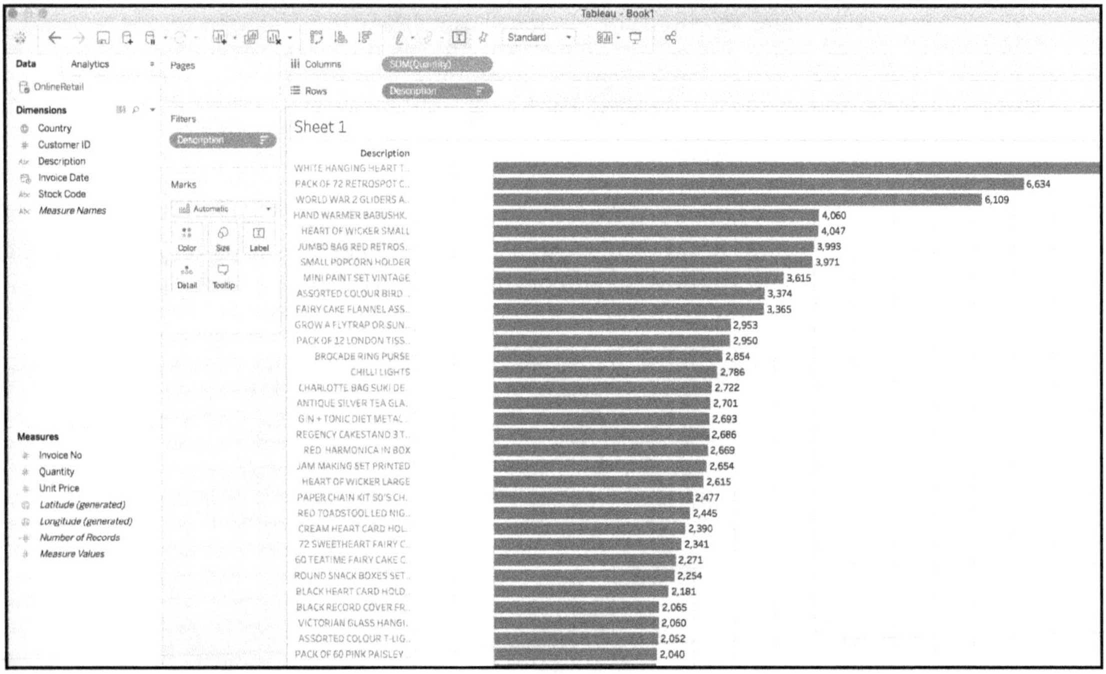

Figure: Screenshot showing a simple horizontal bar chart in Tableau

The following is a geospatial view of data in Tableau:

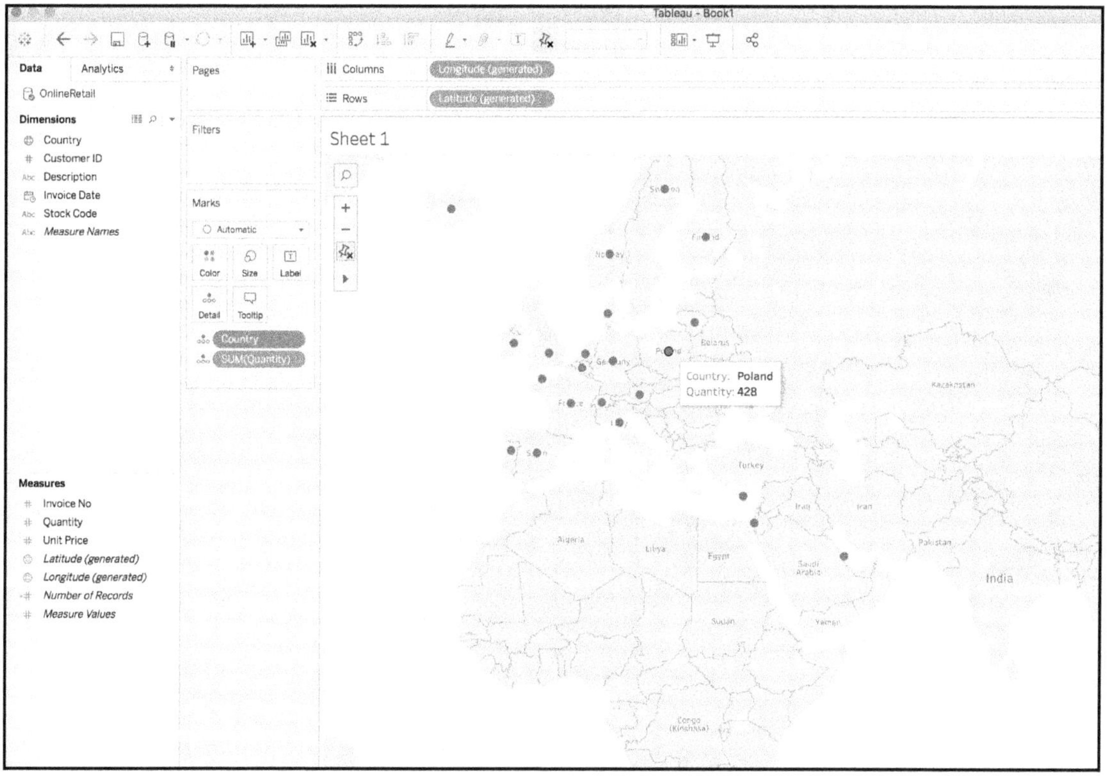

Figure: Screenshot of a geospatial view of data in Tableau

Summary

In this chapter, we have discussed big data analytics, various concepts of big data analytics, and the seven Vs of big data—Volume, Velocity, Veracity, Variety, Value, Vision, and Visualization. We also looked at some of the technologies that aid in performing analytics, such as Hive and Tableau.

In the next chapter, we will explore the world of MapReduce and the most used patterns in performing distributed computing.

3
Big Data Processing with MapReduce

This chapter will puts everything we have learned in the book into a practical use case of building an end-to-end pipeline to perform big data analytics.

In a nutshell, the following topics will be covered throughout this chapter:

- The MapReduce framework
- MapReduce job types:
    - Single mapper jobs
    - Single mapper reducer jobs
    - Multiple mappers reducer jobs
- MapReduce patterns:
    - Aggregation patterns
    - Filtering patterns
    - Join patterns

The MapReduce framework

MapReduce is a framework used to compute a large amount of data in a Hadoop cluster. MapReduce uses YARN to schedule the mappers and reducers as tasks, using the containers. The MapReduce framework enables you to write distributed applications to process large amounts of data from a filesystem, such as a **Hadoop Distributed File System** (**HDFS**), in a reliable and fault-tolerant manner. When you want to use the MapReduce framework to process data, it works through the creation of a job, which then runs on the framework to perform the tasks needed. A MapReduce job usually works by splitting the input data across worker nodes, running the mapper tasks in a parallel manner.

At this time, any failures that happen, either at the HDFS level or the failure of a mapper task, are handled automatically, to be fault-tolerant. Once the mappers have completed, in the results are copied over the network to other machines running the reducer tasks.

An example of using a MapReduce job to count frequencies of words is shown in the following diagram:

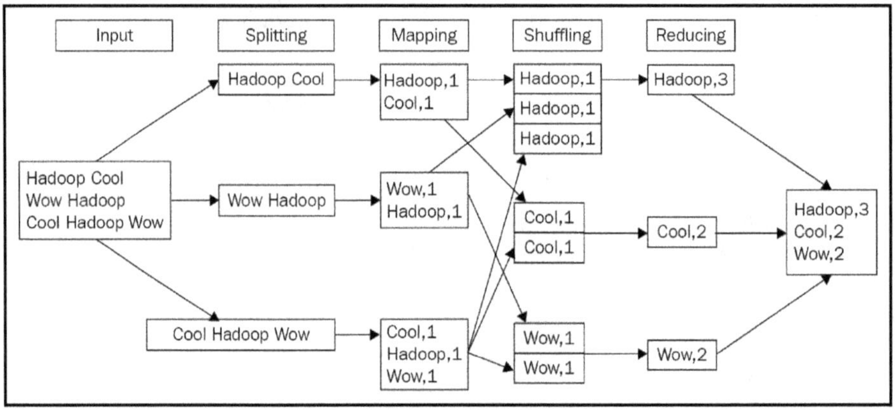

MapReduce uses YARN as a resource manager, which is shown in the following diagram:

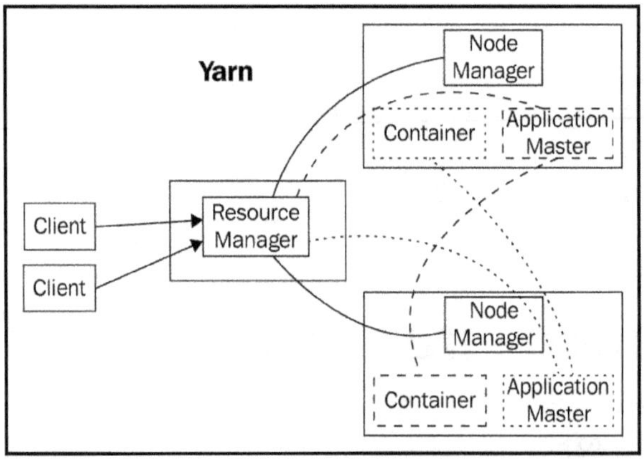

The term MapReduce actually refers to two separate and distinct tasks that Hadoop programs perform. The first is the map job, which takes a set of data and converts it into another set of data, where individual elements are broken down into tuples (key/value pairs).

The reduce job takes the output from a map as input and combines those data tuples into a smaller set of tuples. As the sequence of the name MapReduce implies, the reduce job is always performed after the map job.

The input to a MapReduce job is a set of files in the data store that is spread out over the HDFS. In Hadoop, these files are split with an input format, which defines how to separate a file into input splits. An input split is a byte-oriented view of a chunk of the file, to be loaded by a map task. Each map task in Hadoop is broken into the following phases: record reader, mapper, combiner, and partitioner. The output of the map tasks, called the **intermediate keys and values**, is sent to the reducers. The reduce tasks are broken into the following phases: shuffle, sort, reducer, and output format. The nodes in which the map tasks run are optimally on the nodes in which the data rests. This way, the data typically does not have to move over the network, and can be computed on the local machine.

Throughout this chapter, we will look at different use cases, and how to use a MapReduce job to produce the output desired; for this purpose, we will use a simple dataset.

Dataset

The first dataset is a table of cities containing the city `ID` and the name of the `City`:

```
Id,City
1,Boston
2,New York
3,Chicago
4,Philadelphia
5,San Francisco
7,Las Vegas
```

This file, `cities.csv`, is available as a download, and, once downloaded, you can move it into `hdfs` by running the command, as shown in the following code:

```
hdfs dfs -copyFromLocal cities.csv /user/normal
```

The second dataset is that of daily temperature measurements for a city, and this contains the `Date` of measurement, the city `ID`, and the `Temperature` on the particular date for the specific city:

```
Date,Id,Temperature
2018-01-01,1,21
2018-01-01,2,22
2018-01-01,3,23
2018-01-01,4,24
2018-01-01,5,25
```

```
2018-01-01,6,22
2018-01-02,1,23
2018-01-02,2,24
2018-01-02,3,25
```

This file, `temperatures.csv`, is available as a download, and, once downloaded, you can move it into `hdfs` by running the command, as shown in the following code:

```
hdfs dfs -copyFromLocal temperatures.csv /user/normal
```

The following are the programming components of a MapReduce program:

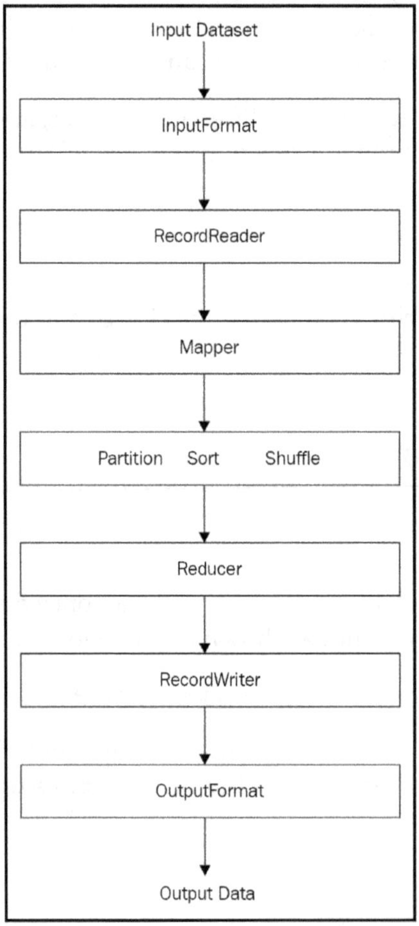

Record reader

The input reader divides the input into appropriately sized splits (in practice, typically, 64 MB to 128 MB), and the framework assigns one split to each map function. The input reader reads data from stable storage (typically, a distributed filesystem) and generates key/value pairs.

> A common example will read a directory full of text files and return each line as a record.

The record reader translates an input split generated by input format into records. The purpose of the record reader is to parse the data into records, but not to parse the record itself. It passes the data to the mapper in the form of a key/value pair. Usually, the key in this context is positional information, and the value is the chunk of data that composes a record. Customized record readers are outside of the scope of this book. We generally assume you have an appropriate record reader for your data. LineRecordReader is the default RecordReader that `TextInputFormat` provides and it treats each line of the input file as the new value; the associated key is byte offset. LineRecordReader always skips the first line in the split (or part of it), if it is not the first split. It reads one line after the boundary of the split at the end (if data is available, so it is not the last split).

Map

The `map` function takes a series of key/value pairs, processes each, and generates zero or more output key/value pairs. The input and output types of the map can be (and often are) different from each other.

If the application is doing a word count, the `map` function will break the line into words and output a key/value pair for each word. Each output pair will contain the word as the key and the number of instances of that word in the line as the value.

In the mapper, code is executed on each key/value pair from the record reader to produce zero or more new key/value pairs, called the **intermediate output of the mapper** (which also consists of key/value pairs). The decision of what the key and value from each record is directly related to what the MapReduce job is accomplishing. The key is what the data will be grouped on and the value is the part of the data to be used in the reducer to generate the necessary output. One of the key items discussed in the patterns is how the different types of use cases also determine the particular key/value logic. In fact, the semantics of this logic is a key differentiator between MapReduce design patterns.

Combiner

If every output of every mapper is directly sent over to every reducer, this will consume a significant amount of resources and time. The combiner, an optional localized reducer, can group data in the map phase. It takes the intermediate keys from the mapper and applies a user-provided method to aggregate values in the small scope of that one mapper. For example, because the count of an aggregation is the sum of the counts of each part, you can produce an intermediate count, and then sum those intermediate counts for the final result. In many situations, this significantly reduces the amount of data that has to move over the network. For instance, if we look at the datasets of cities and temperatures, sending (Boston, 66) requires fewer bytes than sending (Boston, 20), (Boston, 25), (Boston, 21), three times over the network. Combiners often provide significant performance gains with no downsides.

We will point out which patterns benefit from using a combiner, and which ones cannot use a combiner. A combiner is not guaranteed to execute, so it cannot be a part of the overall algorithm.

Partitioner

The partitioner takes the intermediate key/value pairs from the mapper (or combiner if it is being used) and splits them up into shards, one shard per reducer.

Each `map` function output is allocated to a particular reducer by the application's `partition` function for sharding purposes. The `partition` function, is given the key and the number of reducers and returns the index of the desired reducer.

A typical default is to hash the key and use the `hash` value to module the number of reducers:

```
partitionId = hash(key) % R, where R is number of Reducers
```

It is important to pick a `partition` function that gives an approximately uniform distribution of data per shard for load-balancing purposes; otherwise the MapReduce operation can be held up waiting for slow reducers to finish (that is, the reducers assigned the larger shares of the skewed data).

Between the map and reduce stages, the data is shuffled (parallel sorted and then exchanged between nodes) in order to move the data from the map node that produced them to the shard in which they will be reduced. The shuffle can sometimes take longer than the computation time, depending on network bandwidth, CPU speeds, data produced, and time taken by map and reduce computations.

By default, the partitioner computes the hash code of each object, which is typically an md5 checksum. Then, it randomly distributes the keyspace evenly over the reducers, but still ensures that keys with the same values in different mappers end up at the same reducer. The default behavior of the partitioner can be customized with operations such as sorting. The partitioned data is written to the local filesystem for each map task and waits to be pulled by its corresponding reducer.

Shuffle and sort

Once the mappers are done with the input data processing (essentially, splitting the data and generating key/value pairs), the output has to be distributed across the cluster to start the reduce tasks. Hence, a reduce task starts with the shuffle and sort step, by taking the output files written by all of the mappers and subsequent partitioners and downloads them to the local machine in which the reducer task is running. These individual data pieces are then sorted by key into one larger list of key/value pairs. The purpose of this sort is to group equivalent keys together, so that their values can be iterated over easily in the reduce task. The framework handles everything automatically, with the ability for the custom code to control how the keys are sorted and grouped.

Reduce

The reducer takes the grouped data as input and runs a `reduce` function once per key grouping. The function is passed the key and an iterator over all of the values associated with that key. A wide range of processing can happen in this function, as we'll see in many of our patterns. The data can be aggregated, filtered, and combined in a number of ways. Once the `reduce` function is done, it sends zero or more key/value pairs to the final step, the output format. Like the `map` function, the `reduce` function will change from job to job since it is a core piece of logic in the solution. The reducer can have a lot of customization including writing output to HDFS, output to Elasticsearch index, and output to RDBMS or a NoSQL such as Cassandra, HBase, and so on.

Output format

The output format translates the final key/value pair from the `reduce` function and writes it out to a file by a record writer. By default, it will separate the key and value with a tab and separate records with a newline character. This can typically be customized to provide richer output formats, but in the end, the data is written out to HDFS, regardless of format. Not only is writing to HDFS supported by default but also output to Elasticsearch index, output to RDBMS, or a NoSQL such as Cassandra, HBase, and so on.

MapReduce job types

MapReduce jobs can be written in multiple ways, depending on what the desired outcome is. The fundamental structure of a MapReduce job is as follows:

```
import java.io.IOException;
import java.util.StringTokenizer;
import java.util.Map;
import java.util.HashMap;
import org.apache.hadoop.conf.Configuration;
import org.apache.hadoop.fs.Path;
import org.apache.hadoop.io.IntWritable;
import org.apache.hadoop.io.Text;
import org.apache.hadoop.mapreduce.Job;
import org.apache.hadoop.mapreduce.Mapper;
import org.apache.hadoop.mapreduce.Reducer;
import org.apache.hadoop.mapreduce.lib.input.FileInputFormat;
import org.apache.hadoop.mapreduce.lib.output.FileOutputFormat;
import org.apache.hadoop.util.GenericOptionsParser;
import org.apache.commons.lang.StringEscapeUtils;

public class EnglishWordCounter {
public static class WordMapper
extends Mapper<Object, Text, Text, IntWritable> {
...
}
public static class CountReducer
extends Reducer<Text, IntWritable, Text, IntWritable> {
...
}

public static void main(String[] args) throws Exception {
Configuration conf = new Configuration();
Job job = new Job(conf, "English Word Counter");
job.setJarByClass(EnglishWordCounter.class);
```

```
job.setMapperClass(WordMapper.class);
job.setCombinerClass(CountReducer.class);
job.setReducerClass(CountReducer.class);
job.setOutputKeyClass(Text.class);
job.setOutputValueClass(IntWritable.class);
FileInputFormat.addInputPath(job, new Path(args[0]));
FileOutputFormat.setOutputPath(job, new Path(args[1]));
System.exit(job.waitForCompletion(true) ? 0 : 1);
}
}
```

The purpose of the driver is to orchestrate the jobs. The first few lines of `main` are all about parsing command-line arguments. Then, we start setting up the job object by telling it what classes to use for computations and what input paths and output paths to use.

Let's look at the `Mapper` code, which simply tokenizes the input string and writes each word as an output of the mapper:

```
public static class WordMapper
extends Mapper<Object, Text, Text, IntWritable> {
private final static IntWritable one = new IntWritable(1);
private Text word = new Text();
public void map(Object key, Text value, Context context)
throws IOException, InterruptedException {
// Grab the "Text" field, since that is what we are counting over
String txt = value.toString()
StringTokenizer itr = new StringTokenizer(txt);
while (itr.hasMoreTokens()) {
word.set(itr.nextToken());
context.write(word, one);
}
}
}
```

Finally, there is comes the reducer code, which is relatively simple. The `reduce` function gets called once per key grouping; in this case, each word. We'll iterate through the values, which will be numbers, and take a running sum. The final value of this running sum will be the sum of the ones:

```
public static class CountReducer
extends Reducer<Text, IntWritable, Text, IntWritable> {
private IntWritable result = new IntWritable();
public void reduce(Text key, Iterable<IntWritable> values,
Context context) throws IOException, InterruptedException {
int sum = 0;
for (IntWritable val : values) {
sum += val.get();
```

```
}
result.set(sum);
context.write(key, result);
}
}
```

There are basic types of MapReduce jobs, as shown in the following points.

Single mapper job

Single mapper jobs are used in transformation use cases. If we want to change only the format of data, such as some kind of transformation, then this pattern is used:

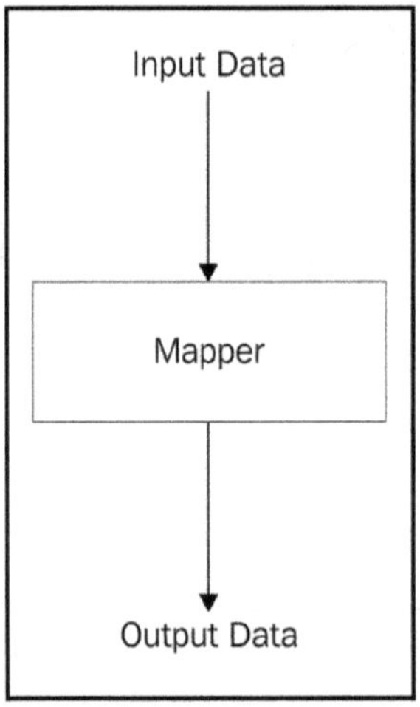

Scenario	Some cities have short names as BOS, NYC, and so on
Map (Key, Value)	Key: city Name Value: ShortName → if city is Boston/boston then converted to BOS else if city is New York/new york then convert to NYC

Now, let's look at a complete example of a Single mapper only job. For this, we will simply try to output the cityID and temperature from the `temperature.csv` file seen earlier.

The following is the code:

```
package io.somethinglikethis;

import org.apache.hadoop.conf.Configuration;
import org.apache.hadoop.fs.Path;
```

```
import org.apache.hadoop.io.IntWritable;
import org.apache.hadoop.io.Text;
import org.apache.hadoop.mapreduce.Job;
import org.apache.hadoop.mapreduce.Mapper;
import org.apache.hadoop.mapreduce.Reducer;
import org.apache.hadoop.mapreduce.lib.input.FileInputFormat;
import org.apache.hadoop.mapreduce.lib.output.FileOutputFormat;
import java.io.IOException;

public class SingleMapper
{
    public static void main(String[] args) throws Exception {
        Configuration conf = new Configuration();
        Job job = new Job(conf, "City Temperature Job");
        job.setMapperClass(TemperatureMapper.class);
        job.setOutputKeyClass(Text.class);
        job.setOutputValueClass(IntWritable.class);

        FileInputFormat.addInputPath(job, new Path(args[0]));
        FileOutputFormat.setOutputPath(job, new Path(args[1]));

        System.exit(job.waitForCompletion(true) ? 0 : 1);
    }

    /*
    Date,Id,Temperature
    2018-01-01,1,21
    2018-01-01,2,22
    */
    private static class TemperatureMapper
            extends Mapper<Object, Text, Text, IntWritable> {

        public void map(Object key, Text value, Context context)
                throws IOException, InterruptedException {
            String txt = value.toString();
            String[] tokens = txt.split(",");
            String date = tokens[0];
            String id = tokens[1].trim();
            String temperature = tokens[2].trim();
            if (temperature.compareTo("Temperature") != 0)
                context.write(new Text(id), new
IntWritable(Integer.parseInt(temperature)));
        }
    }


}
```

To execute this job, you have to create a Maven project using your favorite editor and edit `pom.xml` to look like the following code:

```
<?xml version="1.0" encoding="UTF-8"?>

<project xmlns="http://maven.apache.org/POM/4.0.0"
xmlns:xsi="http://www.w3.org/2001/XMLSchema-instance"
  xsi:schemaLocation="http://maven.apache.org/POM/4.0.0
http://maven.apache.org/xsd/maven-4.0.0.xsd">
  <modelVersion>4.0.0</modelVersion>
  <packaging>jar</packaging>
  <groupId>io.somethinglikethis</groupId>
  <artifactId>mapreduce</artifactId>
  <version>1.0-SNAPSHOT</version>

  <name>mapreduce</name>
  <!-- FIXME change it to the project's website -->
  <url>http://somethinglikethis.io</url>

  <properties>
    <project.build.sourceEncoding>UTF-8</project.build.sourceEncoding>
    <maven.compiler.source>1.7</maven.compiler.source>
    <maven.compiler.target>1.7</maven.compiler.target>
  </properties>

  <dependencies>
    <dependency>
      <groupId>junit</groupId>
      <artifactId>junit</artifactId>
      <version>4.11</version>
      <scope>test</scope>
    </dependency>
    <dependency>
      <groupId>org.apache.hadoop</groupId>
      <artifactId>hadoop-mapreduce-client-core</artifactId>
      <version>3.1.0</version>
    </dependency>
    <dependency>
      <groupId>org.apache.hadoop</groupId>
      <artifactId>hadoop-client</artifactId>
      <version>3.1.0</version>
    </dependency>
  </dependencies>
  <build>
      <plugins>
        <plugin>
          <groupId>org.apache.maven.plugins</groupId>
```

```
            <artifactId>maven-shade-plugin</artifactId>
            <version>3.1.1</version>
            <executions>
                <execution>
                    <phase>package</phase>
                    <goals>
                        <goal>shade</goal>
                    </goals>
                </execution>
            </executions>
              <configuration>
                  <finalName>uber-${project.artifactId}-
${project.version}</finalName>
                  <transformers>
                      <transformer
implementation="org.apache.maven.plugins.shade.resource.ServicesResourceTra
nsformer"/>
                  </transformers>
                  <filters>
                      <filter>
                          <artifact>*:*</artifact>
                          <excludes>
                              <exclude>META-INF/*.SF</exclude>
                              <exclude>META-INF/*.DSA</exclude>
                              <exclude>META-INF/*.RSA</exclude>
                              <exclude>META-INF/LICENSE*</exclude>
                              <exclude>license/*</exclude>
                          </excludes>
                      </filter>
                  </filters>
              </configuration>
          </plugin>
      </plugins>
  </build>
</project>
```

Once you have the code, you can use Maven to build the shaded/fat `.jar` as the following:

```
Moogie:mapreduce sridharalla$ mvn clean compile package
[INFO] Scanning for projects...
[INFO]
[INFO] --------------------------------------------------------------------
----
[INFO] Building mapreduce 1.0-SNAPSHOT
[INFO] --------------------------------------------------------------------
----
[INFO]
[INFO] --- maven-clean-plugin:2.5:clean (default-clean) @ mapreduce ---
```

```
[INFO] Deleting /Users/sridharalla/git/mapreduce/target
.......
............
```

You should see a `uber-mapreduce-1.0-SNAPSHOT.jar` in the target directory; now we are ready to execute the job.

TIP: Make sure that the local Hadoop cluster, as seen in `Chapter 1`, *Introduction to Hadoop*, is started, and that you are able to browse to `http://localhost:9870`.

To execute the job, we will use the Hadoop binaries and the fat `.jar` we just built earlier as shown in the following code:

```
export PATH=$PATH:/Users/sridharalla/hadoop-3.1.0/bin
hdfs dfs -chmod -R 777 /user/normal
```

Now, run the command, as shown in the following code:

```
hadoop jar target/uber-mapreduce-1.0-SNAPSHOT.jar
io.somethinglikethis.SingleMapper /user/normal/temperatures.csv
/user/normal/output/SingleMapper
```

The job will run, and you should be able to see output as shown in the following code:

```
Moogie:target sridharalla$ hadoop jar uber-mapreduce-1.0-SNAPSHOT.jar
io.somethinglikethis.SingleMapper /user/normal/temperatures.csv
/user/normal/output/SingleMapper
2018-05-20 18:38:01,399 WARN util.NativeCodeLoader: Unable to load native-
hadoop library for your platform... using builtin-java classes where
applicable
2018-05-20 18:38:02,248 INFO impl.MetricsConfig: loaded properties from
hadoop-metrics2.properties
......
```

Pay particular attention to the output counters:

```
Map-Reduce Framework
 Map input records=28
 Map output records=27
 Map output bytes=162
 Map output materialized bytes=222
 Input split bytes=115
 Combine input records=0
 Combine output records=0
 Reduce input groups=6
```

```
Reduce shuffle bytes=222
Reduce input records=27
Reduce output records=27
Spilled Records=54
Shuffled Maps =1
Failed Shuffles=0
Merged Map outputs=1
GC time elapsed (ms)=13
Total committed heap usage (bytes)=1084227584
```

This shows that 27 records were output from the mapper, and there is no reducer action and all input records are output on a 1:1 basis. You will be able to check this using the HDFS browser by simply using `http://localhost:9870` and jumping into the output directory shown under `/user/normal/output` as shown in the following screenshot:

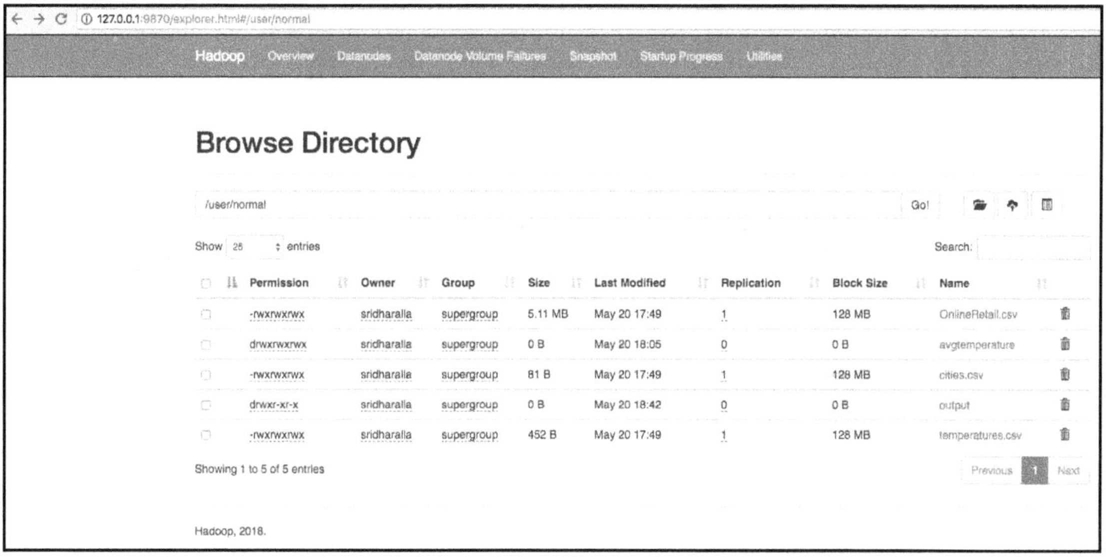

Figure: Screenshot showing how to check output from output directory

Now find the `SingleMapper` folder and go into this directory as shown in the following screenshot:

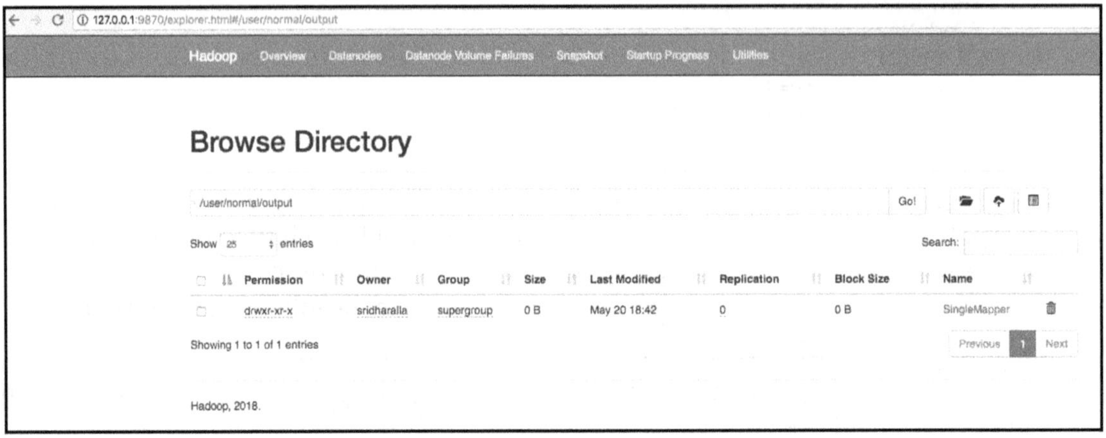

Figure: Screenshot showing SingleMapper folder

Going further down into this `SingleMapper` folder:

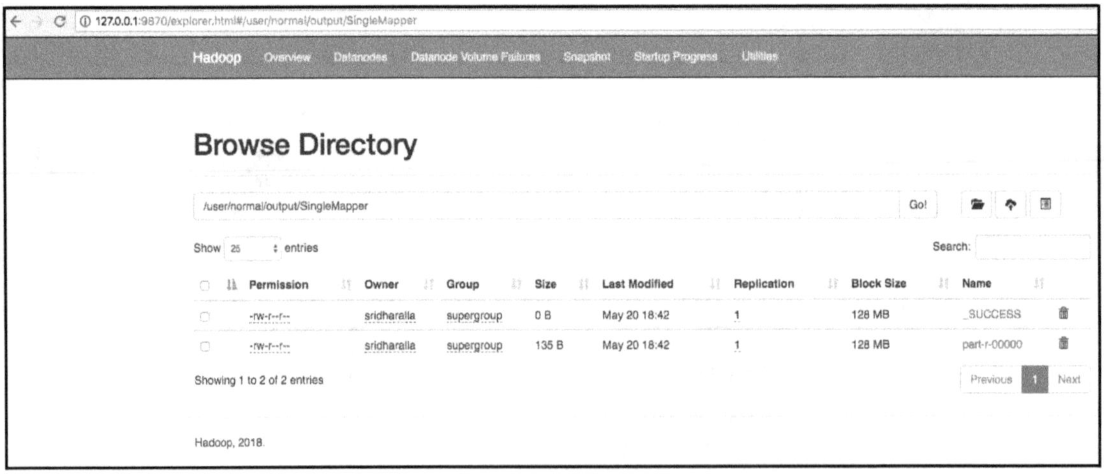

Figure: Screenshot showing further down in the SingleMapper folder

Finally, click on the `part-r-00000` file seen in the following screenshot:

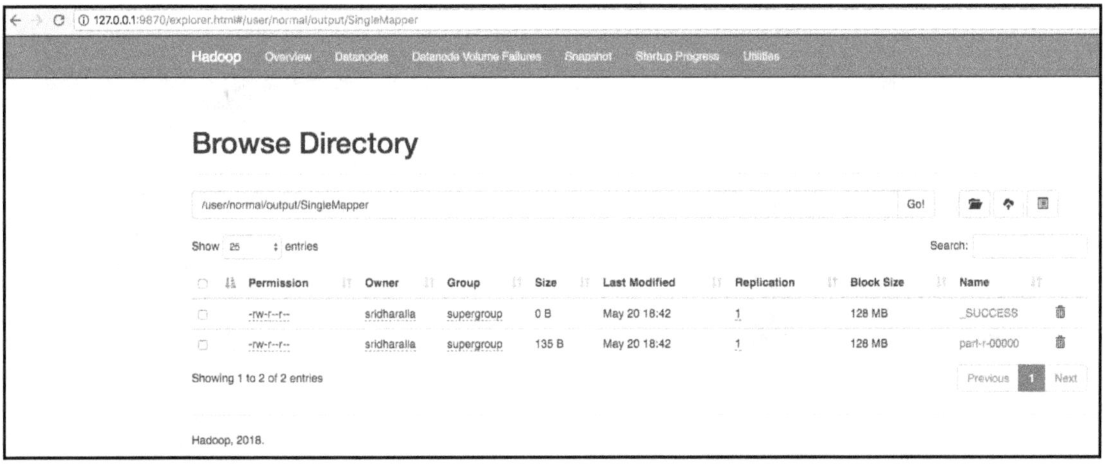

Figure: Screenshot showing the file to be selected

You will see a screen showing the file properties as seen in the following screenshot:

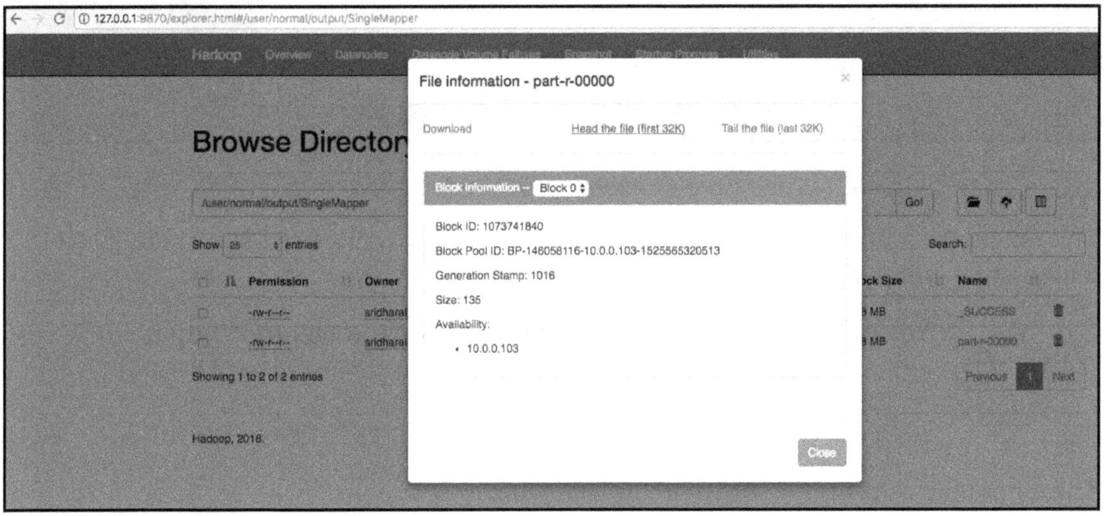

Figure: screenshot showing the file properties

Using head/tail option in the preceding screenshot you can view the content of the file as shown in the following screenshot:

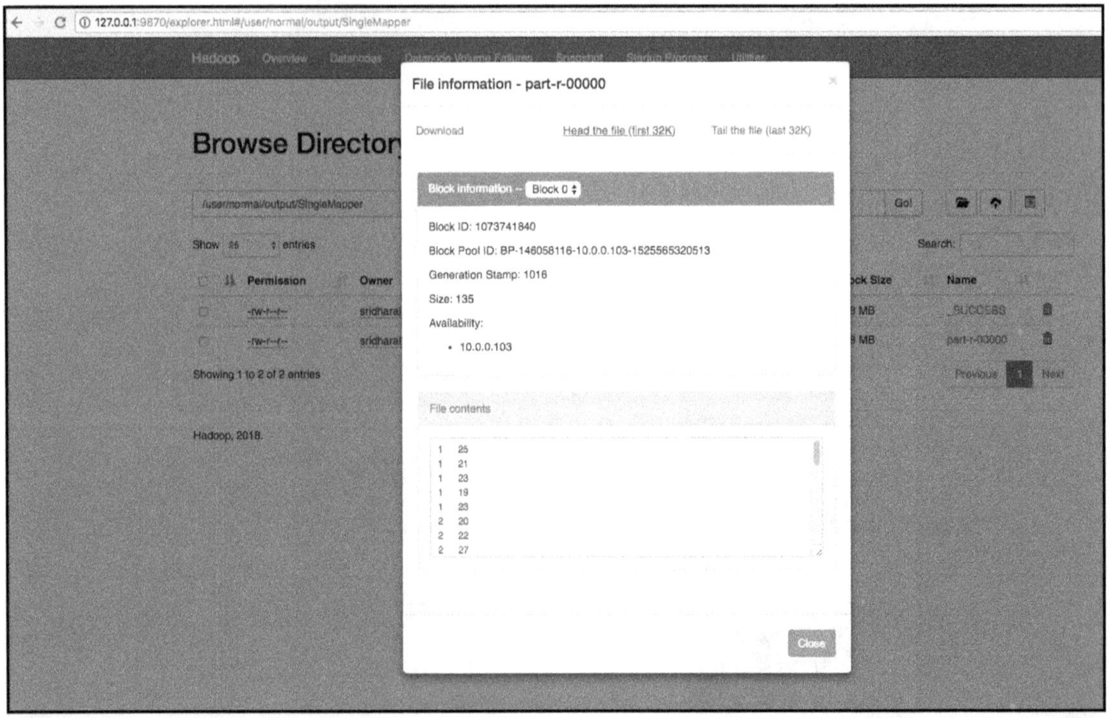

Figure: Screenshot showing content of the file

This shows the output of the `SingleMapper` job as simply writing each row's cityID and temperature without any calculations.

> **TIP:** You can also use the command line to view the contents of output `hdfs dfs -cat /user/normal/output/SingleMapper/part-r-00000`.

The output file contents are shown in the following code:

```
1 25
1 21
1 23
1 19
1 23
2 20
```

```
2 22
2 27
2 24
2 26
3 21
3 25
3 22
3 25
3 23
4 21
4 26
4 23
4 24
4 22
5 18
5 24
5 22
5 25
5 24
6 22
6 22
```

This concludes the `SingleMapper` job execution and the output is as expected.

Single mapper reducer job

Single mapper reducer jobs are used in aggregation use cases. If we want to do some aggregation the such as count, by key, then this pattern is used:

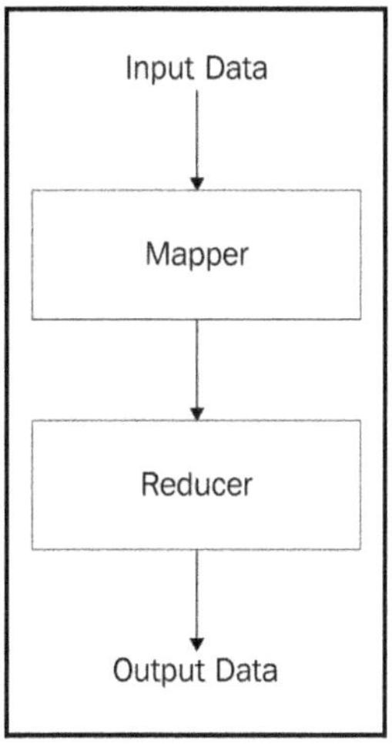

Scenario	Counting the total/average temperature of cities
Map (Key, Value)	Key: city Value: Their temperatures
Reduce	Group by city, and take average temperature for each city

Now let's look at a complete example of a single mapper reducer only job. For this, we will simply try to output the cityID and average temperature from the `temperature.csv` file seen earlier.

The following is the code:

```
package io.somethinglikethis;

import org.apache.hadoop.conf.Configuration;
import org.apache.hadoop.fs.Path;
import org.apache.hadoop.io.IntWritable;
import org.apache.hadoop.io.Text;
import org.apache.hadoop.mapreduce.Job;
import org.apache.hadoop.mapreduce.Mapper;
import org.apache.hadoop.mapreduce.Reducer;
import org.apache.hadoop.mapreduce.lib.input.FileInputFormat;
import org.apache.hadoop.mapreduce.lib.output.FileOutputFormat;

import java.io.IOException;


public class SingleMapperReducer
{
    public static void main(String[] args) throws Exception {
        Configuration conf = new Configuration();
        Job job = new Job(conf, "City Temperature Job");
        job.setMapperClass(TemperatureMapper.class);
        job.setReducerClass(TemperatureReducer.class);
        job.setOutputKeyClass(Text.class);
        job.setOutputValueClass(IntWritable.class);

        FileInputFormat.addInputPath(job, new Path(args[0]));
        FileOutputFormat.setOutputPath(job, new Path(args[1]));

        System.exit(job.waitForCompletion(true) ? 0 : 1);
    }

    /*
    Date,Id,Temperature
    2018-01-01,1,21
    2018-01-01,2,22
```

```
    */
    private static class TemperatureMapper
            extends Mapper<Object, Text, Text, IntWritable> {

        public void map(Object key, Text value, Context context)
                throws IOException, InterruptedException {
            String txt = value.toString();
            String[] tokens = txt.split(",");
            String date = tokens[0];
            String id = tokens[1].trim();
            String temperature = tokens[2].trim();
            if (temperature.compareTo("Temperature") != 0)
                context.write(new Text(id), new
IntWritable(Integer.parseInt(temperature)));
        }
    }

    private static class TemperatureReducer
            extends Reducer<Text, IntWritable, Text, IntWritable> {
        private IntWritable result = new IntWritable();
        public void reduce(Text key, Iterable<IntWritable> values,
                           Context context) throws IOException,
InterruptedException {
            int sum = 0;
            int n = 0;
            for (IntWritable val : values) {
                sum += val.get();
                n +=1;
            }
            result.set(sum/n);
            context.write(key, result);
        }
    }
}
```

Now, run this command:

```
hadoop jar target/uber-mapreduce-1.0-SNAPSHOT.jar
io.somethinglikethis.SingleMapperReducer /user/normal/temperatures.csv
/user/normal/output/SingleMapperReducer
```

The job will run and you should be able to see output as shown in the following code showing the output counters:

```
Map-Reduce Framework
    Map input records=28
    Map output records=27
    Map output bytes=162
```

```
Map output materialized bytes=222
Input split bytes=115
Combine input records=0
Combine output records=0
Reduce input groups=6
Reduce shuffle bytes=222
Reduce input records=27
Reduce output records=6
Spilled Records=54
Shuffled Maps =1
Failed Shuffles=0
Merged Map outputs=1
GC time elapsed (ms)=12
Total committed heap usage (bytes)=1080557568
```

This shows that 27 records were output from mapper, and there are six output records from reducer. You will be able to check this using the HDFS browser, simply by using `http://localhost:9870` and jumping into the output directory shown under `/user/normal/output`, as shown in the following screenshot:

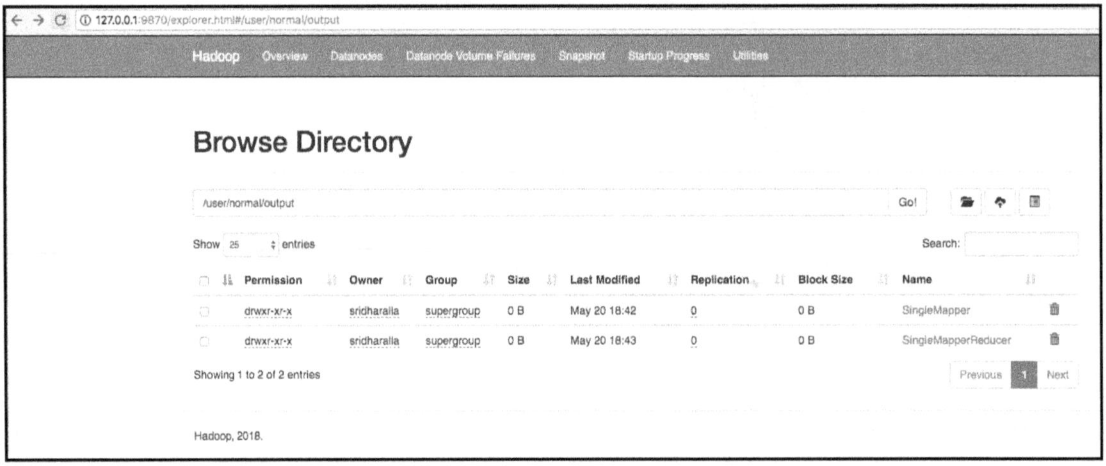

Figure: screenshot showing how to check output in the output directory

Now, find the `SingleMapperReducer` folder, go into this directory and then drilldown as in *SingleMapper* section; then using the head/tail option in the preceding screenshot, you can view the contents of the file, as shown in the following screenshot:

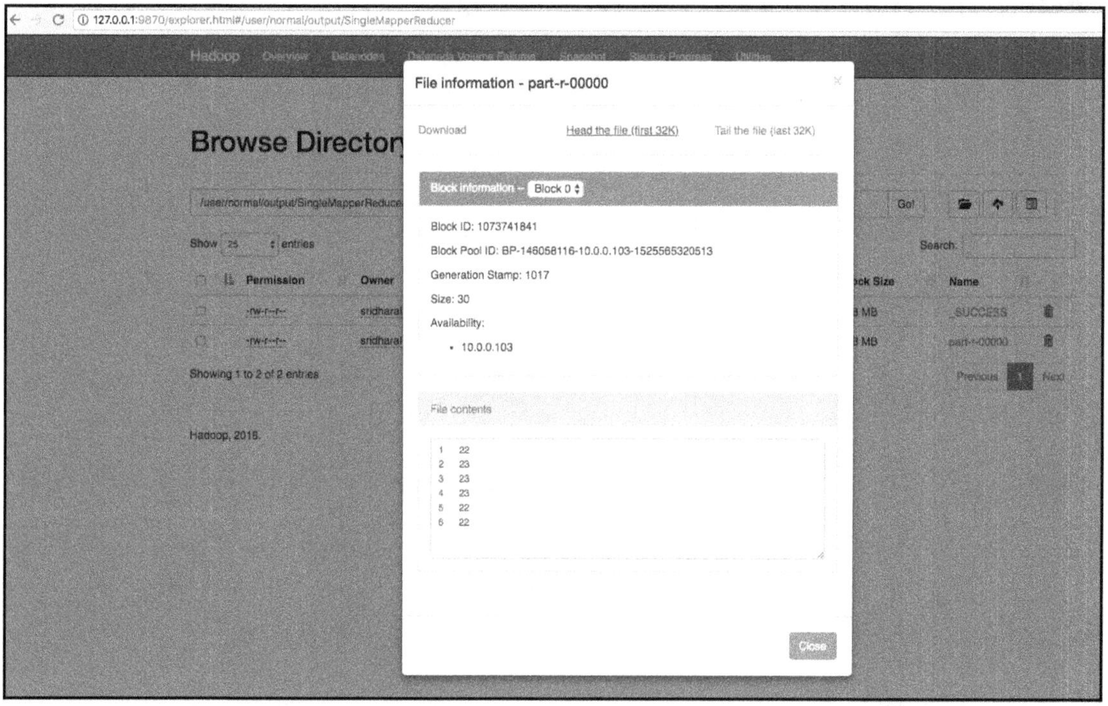

This shows the output of the `SingleMapperReducer` job, writing each row's cityID and average temperature for each cityID.

TIP

You can also use command line to view the contents of output `hdfs dfs -cat /user/normal/output/SingleMapperReducer/part-r-00000`.

The output file contents are as shown in the following code:

```
1 22
2 23
3 23
4 23
5 22
6 22
```

This concludes the `SingleMapperReducer` job execution and the output is as expected.

Multiple mappers reducer job

Multiple mappers reducer jobs are used in join use cases. In this design pattern, our input is taken from multiple input files to yield joined/aggregated output:

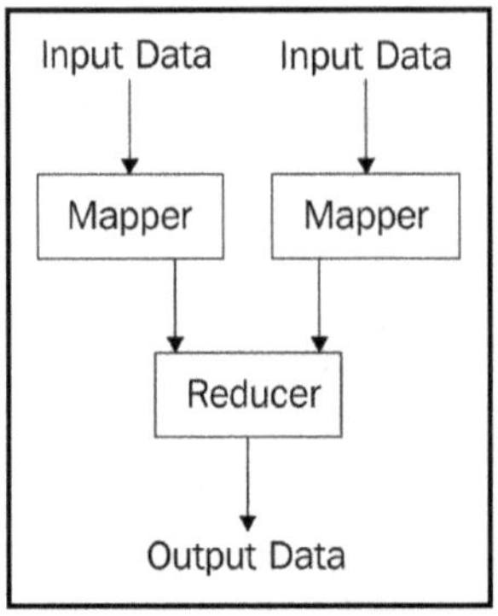

Scenario	We have to find the average of city-wide temperature, but we have two files with different schema, one for cities and the other for temperature. Input File 1 City ID to Name Input File 2 Temperature for each city per day
Map (Key, Value)	Map 1 (For input 1) We need to write a program to split cityID, Name and according to the cityID, write the Name Then prepare the key/value pair (cityID, Name) Map 2 (For input 2) We need to write a program to split date, cityID, temperature and according to the cityID, write the temperature Then prepare the key/value pair (cityID, temperature)
Reduce	Group by cityID And take average temperature for each city Name.

Now let's look at a complete example of a single mapper reducer job. For this, we will simply try to output the cityID and average temperature from the `temperature.csv` file seen earlier.

The following is the code:

```
package io.somethinglikethis;

import org.apache.hadoop.conf.Configuration;
import org.apache.hadoop.fs.Path;
import org.apache.hadoop.io.IntWritable;
import org.apache.hadoop.io.Text;
import org.apache.hadoop.mapreduce.Job;
import org.apache.hadoop.mapreduce.Mapper;
import org.apache.hadoop.mapreduce.Reducer;
import org.apache.hadoop.mapreduce.lib.input.FileInputFormat;
import org.apache.hadoop.mapreduce.lib.input.MultipleInputs;
import org.apache.hadoop.mapreduce.lib.input.TextInputFormat;
import org.apache.hadoop.mapreduce.lib.output.FileOutputFormat;

import java.io.IOException;


public class MultipleMappersReducer
{
    public static void main(String[] args) throws Exception {
        Configuration conf = new Configuration();
        Job job = new Job(conf, "City Temperature Job");
        job.setMapperClass(TemperatureMapper.class);
        MultipleInputs.addInputPath(job, new Path(args[0]),
TextInputFormat.class, CityMapper.class);
        MultipleInputs.addInputPath(job, new Path(args[1]),
TextInputFormat.class, TemperatureMapper.class);

        job.setMapOutputKeyClass(Text.class);
        job.setMapOutputValueClass(Text.class);
        job.setReducerClass(TemperatureReducer.class);
        job.setOutputKeyClass(Text.class);
        job.setOutputValueClass(IntWritable.class);

        FileOutputFormat.setOutputPath(job, new Path(args[2]));

        System.exit(job.waitForCompletion(true) ? 0 : 1);
    }


    /*
```

```
Id,City
1,Boston
2,New York
*/
private static class CityMapper

        extends Mapper<Object, Text, Text, Text> {

    public void map(Object key, Text value, Context context)
            throws IOException, InterruptedException {
        String txt = value.toString();
        String[] tokens = txt.split(",");
        String id = tokens[0].trim();
        String name = tokens[1].trim();
        if (name.compareTo("City") != 0)
            context.write(new Text(id), new Text(name));
    }
}


/*
Date,Id,Temperature
2018-01-01,1,21
2018-01-01,2,22
*/
private static class TemperatureMapper
        extends Mapper<Object, Text, Text, Text> {

    public void map(Object key, Text value, Context context)
            throws IOException, InterruptedException {
        String txt = value.toString();
        String[] tokens = txt.split(",");
        String date = tokens[0];
        String id = tokens[1].trim();
        String temperature = tokens[2].trim();
        if (temperature.compareTo("Temperature") != 0)
            context.write(new Text(id), new Text(temperature));
    }
}



private static class TemperatureReducer
        extends Reducer<Text, Text, Text, IntWritable> {
    private IntWritable result = new IntWritable();
    private Text cityName = new Text("Unknown");
    public void reduce(Text key, Iterable<Text> values,
                       Context context) throws IOException,
```

```
InterruptedException {
            int sum = 0;
            int n = 0;

            cityName = new Text("city-"+key.toString());

            for (Text val : values) {
                String strVal = val.toString();
                if (strVal.length() <=3)
                {
                    sum += Integer.parseInt(strVal);
                    n +=1;
                } else {
                    cityName = new Text(strVal);
                }
            }
            if (n==0) n = 1;
            result.set(sum/n);
            context.write(cityName, result);
        }
    }
}
```

Now, run the command, as shown in the following code:

```
hadoop jar target/uber-mapreduce-1.0-SNAPSHOT.jar
io.somethinglikethis.MultipleMappersReducer /user/normal/cities.csv
/user/normal/temperatures.csv /user/normal/output/MultipleMappersReducer
```

The job will run and you should be able to see output as shown in the following output counters:

```
Map-Reduce Framework -- mapper for temperature.csv
    Map input records=28
    Map output records=27
    Map output bytes=135
    Map output materialized bytes=195
    Input split bytes=286
    Combine input records=0
    Spilled Records=27
    Failed Shuffles=0
    Merged Map outputs=0
    GC time elapsed (ms)=0
    Total committed heap usage (bytes)=430964736

Map-Reduce Framework.  -- mapper for cities.csv
    Map input records=7
    Map output records=6
```

```
        Map output bytes=73
        Map output materialized bytes=91
        Input split bytes=273
        Combine input records=0
        Spilled Records=6
        Failed Shuffles=0
        Merged Map outputs=0
        GC time elapsed (ms)=10
        Total committed heap usage (bytes)=657457152

    Map-Reduce Framework -- output average temperature per city name
        Map input records=35
        Map output records=33
        Map output bytes=208
        Map output materialized bytes=286
        Input split bytes=559
        Combine input records=0
        Combine output records=0
        Reduce input groups=7
        Reduce shuffle bytes=286
        Reduce input records=33
        Reduce output records=7
        Spilled Records=66
        Shuffled Maps =2
        Failed Shuffles=0
        Merged Map outputs=2
        GC time elapsed (ms)=10
        Total committed heap usage (bytes)=1745879040
```

This shows that 27 records were output from one Mapper, six records were output from Mapper2 and seven records were output by the reducer. You will be able to check this using the HDFS browser, simply by using `http://localhost:9870` and jumping into the output directory shown under `/user/normal/output`, as shown in the following screenshot:

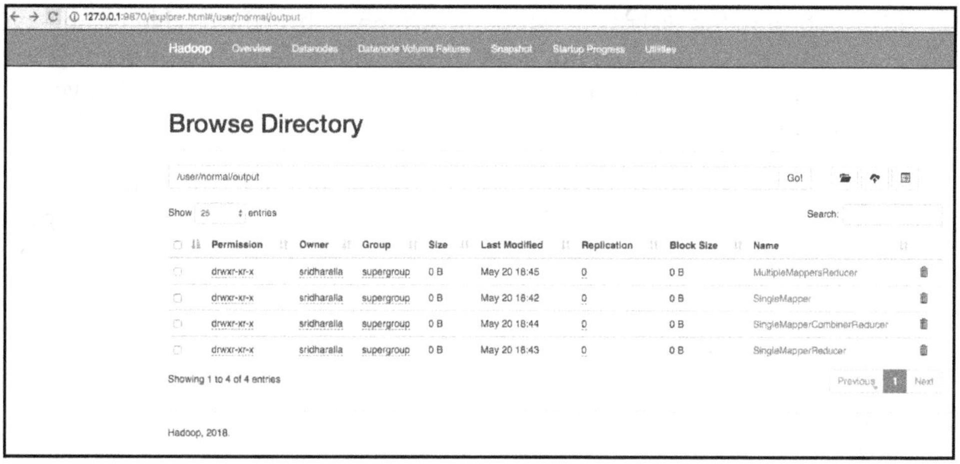

Figure: Check output in output directory

Now find the `MultipleMappersReducer` folder go into the directory, and then drill down as in the *SingleMapper* section; then, using the head/tail option in the preceding screenshot, you can view the content of the file, as shown in the following screenshot:

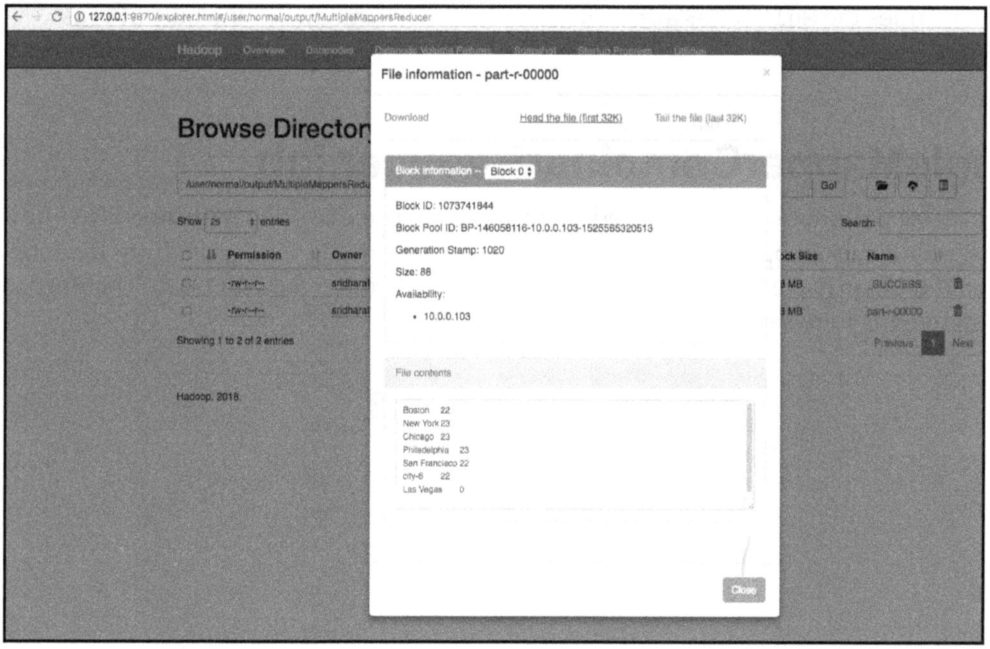

Figure: Content of the file

This shows the output of the `MultipleMappersReducer` job as the cityName and average temperature per city. If a cityID does not have corresponding temperature records in `temperature.csv`, the average is shown as 0. Similarly, if a cityID does not have a name in `cities.csv`, then the city name is shown as city-N.

> TIP
> You can also use the command line to view the contents of output `hdfs dfs -cat /user/normal/output/MultipleMappersReducer/part-r-00000`.

The output file contents are shown in the following code:

```
Boston 22
New York 23
Chicago 23
Philadelphia 23
San Francisco 22
city-6 22  //city ID 6 has no name in cities.csv only temperature
measurements
Las Vegas 0 // city of Las vegas has no temperature measurements in
temperature.csv
```

This concludes the `MultipleMappersReducer` job execution, and the output is as expected.

SingleMapperCombinerReducer job

`SingleMapperReducer` jobs are used in aggregation use cases. A **combiner**, also known as a **semi-reducer**, is an optional class that operates by accepting the inputs from the map class and thereafter passing the output key/value pairs to the **reducer** class. The purpose of the combiner is to reduce the workload of the **reducer**:

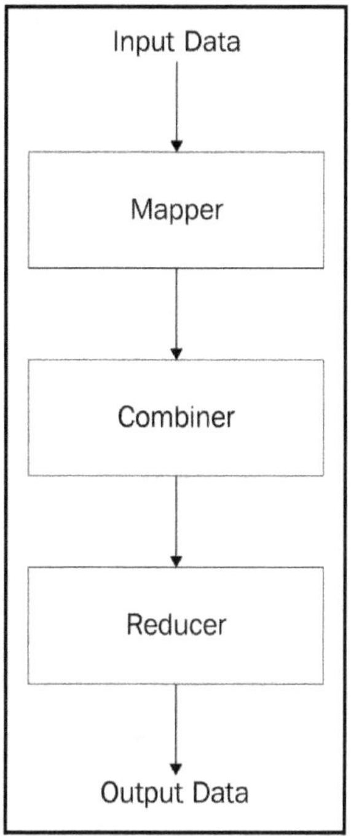

In the MapReduce program, 25% of the work is done in the map stage, which is also known as the **data preparation stage**, which works in parallel. At the same time, 75% of the work is done in the **reduce** stage, which is known as the **calculation stage**, and is not parallel. Therefore, it is slower than the map phase. To reduce time, some work in the reduce phase can be done in the combiner phase.

For example, if we have a combiner, then we will send (Boston, 66) from a mapper, which sees (Boston, 22), (Boston, 24), (Boston, 20) as input records, instead of sending three individual key/pair records across the network.

Scenario

There are several cities, with a daily temperature provided for each city, and we have to calculate the city's average salary. However, there are certain rules to calculate the average. After calculating the city-wise total for each city, we can compute the average of temperature for each city:

Input Files (several files)	**Map (Parallel) (, Value = Name)**	**Combiner (Parallel)**	**Reducer (Not Parallel)**	**Output**
City 1	1<10,20,25,45,15,45,25,20> 2 <10,30,20,25,35>	1 <250,20> 2 <120,10>	1 Boston, < 250,20,155, 10,90,90,30> 2 New York, <120,10,175,10,135, 10,110,10,130,10>	Boston <645> New York <720>
City 2	1<Boston> 2 <New York>	1 <Boston> 2 <New York>		

Now, let's look at the complete example of a `SingleMapperCombinerReducer` job. For this, we will simply try to output the cityID and the average temperature from the `temperature.csv` file seen earlier.

The following is the code:

```
package io.somethinglikethis;

import org.apache.hadoop.conf.Configuration;
import org.apache.hadoop.fs.Path;
import org.apache.hadoop.io.IntWritable;
import org.apache.hadoop.io.Text;
import org.apache.hadoop.mapreduce.Job;
import org.apache.hadoop.mapreduce.Mapper;
import org.apache.hadoop.mapreduce.Reducer;
import org.apache.hadoop.mapreduce.lib.input.FileInputFormat;
import org.apache.hadoop.mapreduce.lib.output.FileOutputFormat;

import java.io.IOException;


public class SingleMapperCombinerReducer
{
    public static void main(String[] args) throws Exception {
```

```
        Configuration conf = new Configuration();
        Job job = new Job(conf, "City Temperature Job");
        job.setMapperClass(TemperatureMapper.class);
        job.setCombinerClass(TemperatureReducer.class);
        job.setReducerClass(TemperatureReducer.class);
        job.setOutputKeyClass(Text.class);
        job.setOutputValueClass(IntWritable.class);

        FileInputFormat.addInputPath(job, new Path(args[0]));
        FileOutputFormat.setOutputPath(job, new Path(args[1]));

        System.exit(job.waitForCompletion(true) ? 0 : 1);
    }


    /*
    Date,Id,Temperature
    2018-01-01,1,21
    2018-01-01,2,22
    */
    private static class TemperatureMapper
            extends Mapper<Object, Text, Text, IntWritable> {

        public void map(Object key, Text value, Context context)
                throws IOException, InterruptedException {
            String txt = value.toString();
            String[] tokens = txt.split(",");
            String date = tokens[0];
            String id = tokens[1].trim();
            String temperature = tokens[2].trim();
            if (temperature.compareTo("Temperature") != 0)
                context.write(new Text(id), new
IntWritable(Integer.parseInt(temperature)));
        }
    }



    private static class TemperatureReducer
            extends Reducer<Text, IntWritable, Text, IntWritable> {
        private IntWritable result = new IntWritable();
        public void reduce(Text key, Iterable<IntWritable> values,
                           Context context) throws IOException,
InterruptedException {
            int sum = 0;
            int n = 0;
            for (IntWritable val : values) {
                sum += val.get();
```

```
                n +=1;
            }
            result.set(sum/n);
            context.write(key, result);
        }
    }
}
```

Now, run the command, as shown in the following code:

```
hadoop jar target/uber-mapreduce-1.0-SNAPSHOT.jar
io.somethinglikethis.SingleMapperCombinerReducer
/user/normal/temperatures.csv
/user/normal/output/SingleMapperCombinerReducer
```

The job will run, and you should be able to see output as shown in the following output counters:

```
Map-Reduce Framework
    Map input records=28
    Map output records=27
    Map output bytes=162
    Map output materialized bytes=54
    Input split bytes=115
    Combine input records=27
    Combine output records=6
    Reduce input groups=6
    Reduce shuffle bytes=54
    Reduce input records=6
    Reduce output records=6
    Spilled Records=12
    Shuffled Maps =1
    Failed Shuffles=0
    Merged Map outputs=1
    GC time elapsed (ms)=11
    Total committed heap usage (bytes)=1077936128
```

This shows that 27 records were output from mapper and there are 6 output records from reducer. However, note that there is now a combiner which takes 27 input records and outputs 6 records clearly demonstrating the performance gain by reducing the records shuffled from mappers to reducers. You will be able to check this using the HDFS browser by simply using `http://localhost:9870` and jumping into the output directory shown under `/user/normal/output`, as shown in the following screenshot:

Now find the `SingleMapperCombinerReducer` folder and go into this directory and then drilldown as in *SingleMapper* section earlier and then using head/tail option in the preceding screen you can view the content of the file as shown in the following screenshot:

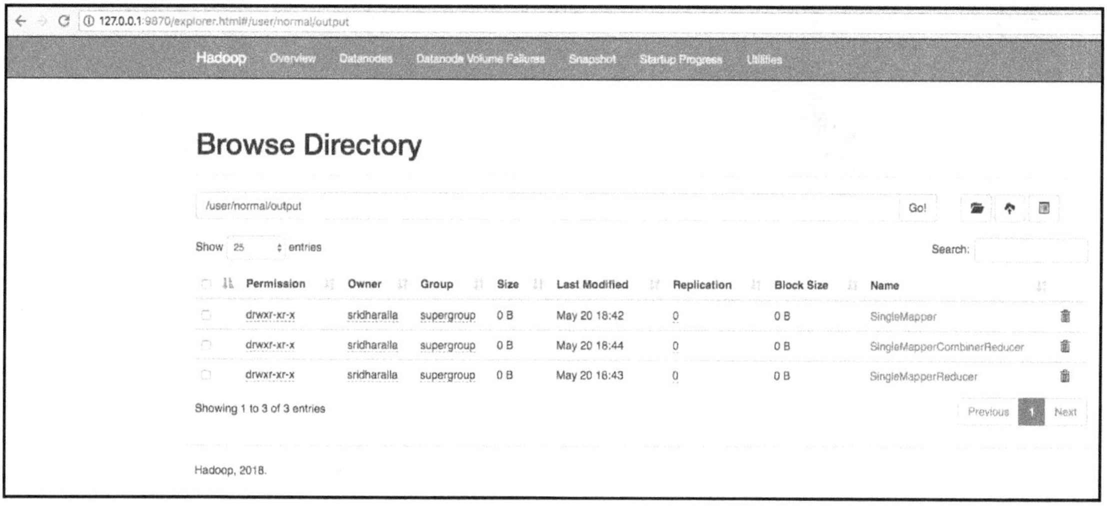

Figure: Check output in output directory

This shows the output of the `SingleMapperCombinerReducer` job as writing each row's cityID and the average temperature per cityID:

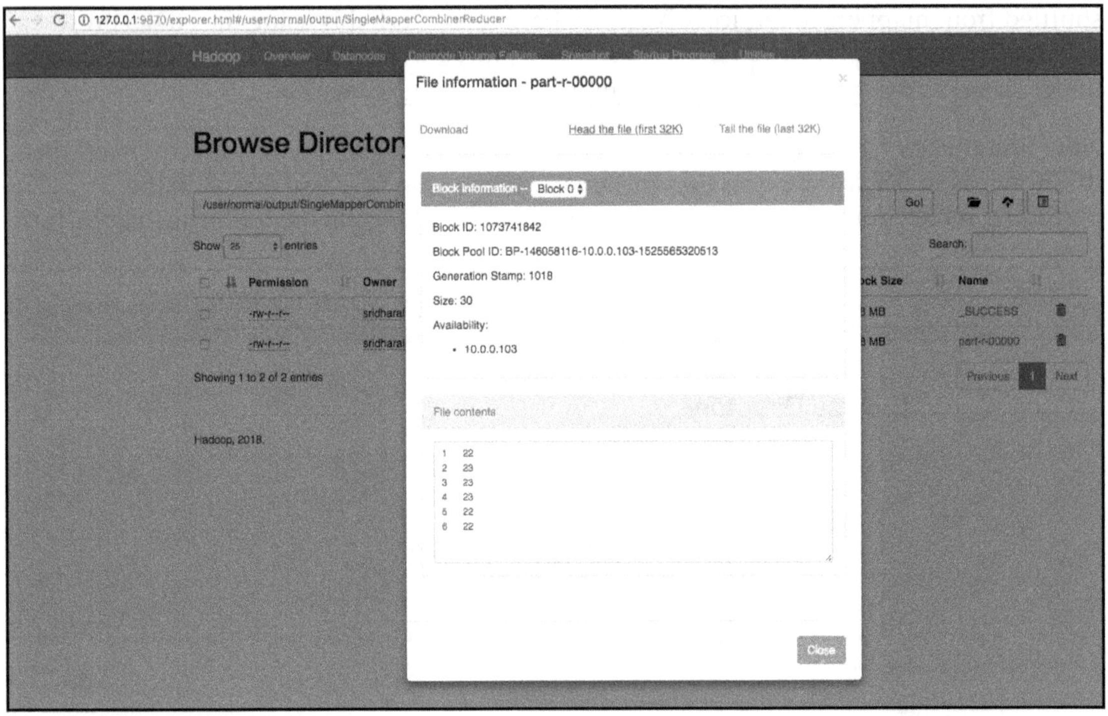

Figure: Screenshot showing output of the SingleMapperCombinerReducer

TIP

You can also use command line to view contents of output `hdfs dfs -cat /user/normal/output/SingleMapperCombinerReducer/part-r-00000`.

The output file contents are shown in the following code:

```
1 22
2 23
3 23
4 23
5 22
6 22
```

This concludes the `SingleMapperCombinerReducer` job execution and the output is as expected.

Next, we will look into more details on the patterns used in writing MapReduce jobs.

MapReduce patterns

A MapReduce pattern is a template for solving a common and general data manipulation problem with MapReduce. A pattern is not specific to a domain, such as text processing or graph analysis, but it is a general approach to solving a problem. Using design patterns is all about using tried and true design principles to build better software.

Design patterns have been making developers, lives easier for years. They are tools for solving problems in a reusable and general way, so that the developer can spend less time figuring out how they're going to overcome a hurdle and move on to the next one.

Aggregation patterns

This chapter focuses on design patterns that produce a top-level, summarized view of your data, so you can glean insights not available from looking at a localized set of records alone. Aggregation, or summarization, analytics are all about grouping similar data together and then performing an operation, such as calculating a statistic, building an index, or simply counting.

The patterns in this chapter are numerical summarizations, inverted index, and counting with counters:

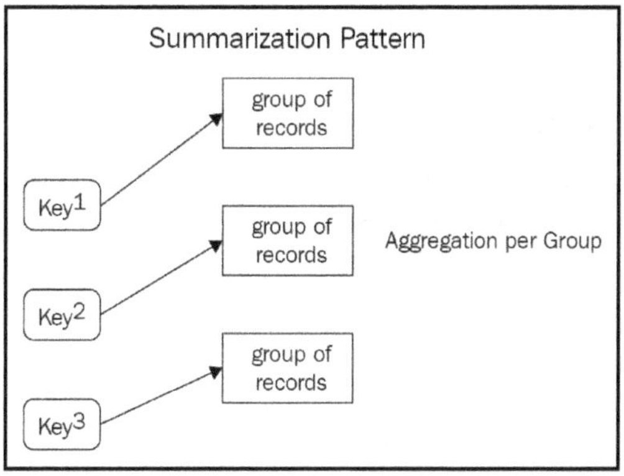

The aggregation pattern is a general pattern for calculating aggregate statistical values over your data, and is discussed in detail. It is important to use the combiner properly, and to understand the calculation you are performing before writing the code. Basically, the logic is to group records together by a key field and calculate a numerical aggregate per group.

Aggregations, or numerical summarizations, can be used when both of the following are true:

- You are dealing with numerical data or counting
- The data can be grouped by specific fields

Average temperature by city

The application outputs each city of a record as the key and each temperature as the value, thus grouping by cities. The reduce phase then adds up the integers and outputs each unique city with the average temperature.

Record count

A very common summarization is to get a count of records grouped by key, and maybe have a breakdown into daily, weekly, and monthly counts.

Min/max/count

This is an analytic to determine the minimum, maximum, and count of a particular event, such as the first time a city was sampled, the last time a city was sampled, and the number of times the temperature was measured in between that time period. You don't have to collect all three of these aggregates at the same time, or any of the other use cases listed here, if you are only interested in one of them.

Average/median/standard deviation

This is similar to min/max/count, but not as straightforward an implementation because these operations are not associative. A combiner can be used for all three, but requires a more complex approach than just reusing the reducer implementation.

A minimum, maximum, and count example, calculating the minimum, maximum, and count of a given field, are all excellent applications of the numerical summarization pattern.

> **TIP:** `SingleMapperReducer` job seen earlier is a good example for aggregation pattern.

Depending on the use case, an aggregation pattern can be customized to generate the intended output.

Filtering patterns

Also known as **transformation patterns**, filtering patterns find a subset of data, whether it be small, like a top 10 listing, or large, like the results of a deduplication:

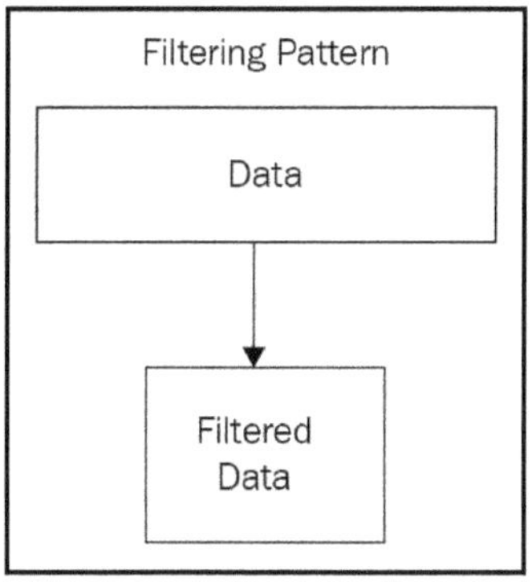

Four patterns are presented in this chapter: filtering, bloom filtering, top ten, and distinct.

As the most basic pattern, filtering serves as an abstract pattern for some of the other patterns. Filtering simply evaluates each record separately and decides, based on some condition, whether it should stay or go. Filter out records that are not of interest and keep ones that are. Consider an evaluation function `f` that takes a record and returns a Boolean value of `true` or `false`. If this function returns `true`, keep the record; otherwise, toss it out.

> **TIP:** The `SingleMapper` job seen earlier is a good example of a filtering patterns.

Depending on the use case, a transformation pattern can be customized to generate the intended output.

Join patterns

Data is all over the place, and while it's very valuable on its own, we can discover interesting relationships when we start analyzing these sets together. This is where join patterns come in to play. Joins can be used to enrich data with a smaller reference set or they can be used to filter out or select records that are in some type of special list.

To understand these patterns and their implementations, you should refer to the `MultipleMappersReducer` job earlier in this chapter.

The abbreviated code is shown as follows, showing the two mappers and one reducer classes:

```
public class MultipleMappersReducer
{
    public static void main(String[] args) throws Exception {
        Configuration conf = new Configuration();
        Job job = new Job(conf, "City Temperature Job");
        job.setMapperClass(TemperatureMapper.class);
        MultipleInputs.addInputPath(job, new Path(args[0]),
TextInputFormat.class, CityMapper.class);
        MultipleInputs.addInputPath(job, new Path(args[1]),
TextInputFormat.class, TemperatureMapper.class);

        job.setMapOutputKeyClass(Text.class);
        job.setMapOutputValueClass(Text.class);
        job.setReducerClass(TemperatureReducer.class);
        job.setOutputKeyClass(Text.class);
        job.setOutputValueClass(IntWritable.class);

        FileOutputFormat.setOutputPath(job, new Path(args[2]));

        System.exit(job.waitForCompletion(true) ? 0 : 1);
    }

    /*
    Id,City
    1,Boston
    2,New York
    */
    private static class CityMapper
```

```
            extends Mapper<Object, Text, Text, Text> {

        public void map(Object key, Text value, Context context)
                throws IOException, InterruptedException {
            String txt = value.toString();
            String[] tokens = txt.split(",");
            String id = tokens[0].trim();
            String name = tokens[1].trim();
            if (name.compareTo("City") != 0)
                context.write(new Text(id), new Text(name));
        }
    }

    /*
    Date,Id,Temperature
    2018-01-01,1,21
    2018-01-01,2,22
    */
    private static class TemperatureMapper
            extends Mapper<Object, Text, Text, Text> {

        public void map(Object key, Text value, Context context)
                throws IOException, InterruptedException {
            String txt = value.toString();
            String[] tokens = txt.split(",");
            String date = tokens[0];
            String id = tokens[1].trim();
            String temperature = tokens[2].trim();
            if (temperature.compareTo("Temperature") != 0)
                context.write(new Text(id), new Text(temperature));
        }
    }

    private static class TemperatureReducer
            extends Reducer<Text, Text, Text, IntWritable> {
        private IntWritable result = new IntWritable();
        private Text cityName = new Text("Unknown");
        public void reduce(Text key, Iterable<Text> values,
                           Context context) throws IOException,
InterruptedException {
            int sum = 0;
            int n = 0;

            cityName = new Text("city-"+key.toString());

            for (Text val : values) {
                String strVal = val.toString();
                if (strVal.length() <=3)
```

```
                {
                    sum += Integer.parseInt(strVal);
                    n +=1;
                } else {
                    cityName = new Text(strVal);
                }
            }
            if (n==0) n = 1;
            result.set(sum/n);
            context.write(cityName, result);
        }
    }
}
```

The output of this job is shown in the following code:

```
Boston 22
New York 23
Chicago 23
Philadelphia 23
San Francisco 22
city-6 22 //city ID 6 has no name in cities.csv only temperature
measurements
Las Vegas 0 // city of Las vegas has no temperature measurements in
temperature.csv
```

Inner join

Inner join requires the left and right tables to have the same column. If you have duplicate or multiple copies of the keys on either the left or right side, the join will quickly blow up into a sort of cartesian join, taking a lot longer to complete than if designed correctly, to minimize the multiple keys:

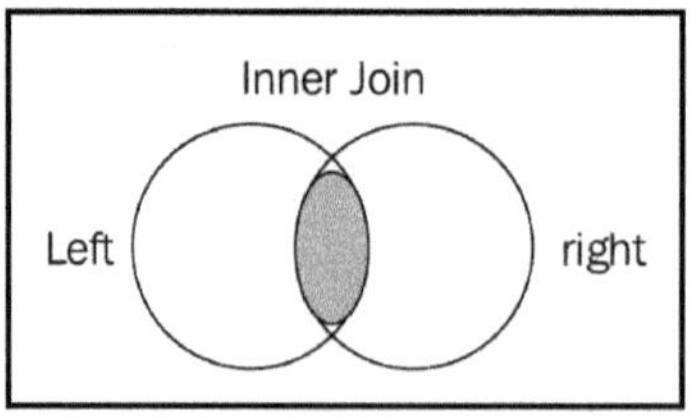

We will consider the cities and temperatures only if the cityID has both records as shown in the following code:

```
private static class InnerJoinReducer
        extends Reducer<Text, Text, Text, IntWritable> {
    private IntWritable result = new IntWritable();
    private Text cityName = new Text("Unknown");
    public void reduce(Text key, Iterable<Text> values,
                        Context context) throws IOException,
InterruptedException {
        int sum = 0;
        int n = 0;
        for (Text val : values) {
            String strVal = val.toString();
            if (strVal.length() <=3)
            {
                sum += Integer.parseInt(strVal);
                n +=1;
            } else {
                cityName = new Text(strVal);
            }
        }
        if (n!=0 && cityName.toString().compareTo("Unknown") !=0) {
            result.set(sum / n);
            context.write(cityName, result);
        }
    }
}
```

The output will be as shown in the following code (without city-6 or Las Vegas, as shown earlier in original output):

```
Boston 22
New York 23
Chicago 23
Philadelphia 23
San Francisco 22
```

Left anti join

Left anti join gives only those rows from the left hand side table based that are not present in the right hand side table. Use this when you want to keep rows from the left table only when not present in right table. This provides very good performance, as only one table is fully considered and the other is only checked for the join condition:

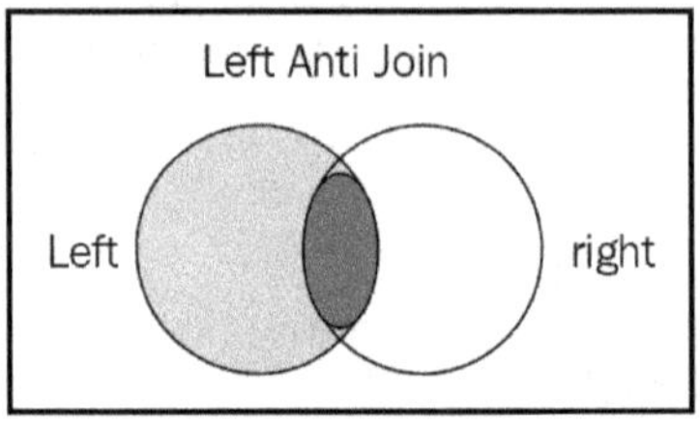

We will consider the cities and temperatures if the cityID has only, name and no temperature records, as shown in the following code:

```
private static class LeftAntiJoinReducer
        extends Reducer<Text, Text, Text, IntWritable> {
    private IntWritable result = new IntWritable();
    private Text cityName = new Text("Unknown");
    public void reduce(Text key, Iterable<Text> values,
                         Context context) throws IOException,
InterruptedException {
        int sum = 0;
        int n = 0;

        for (Text val : values) {
            String strVal = val.toString();
            if (strVal.length() <=3)
            {
                sum += Integer.parseInt(strVal);
                n +=1;
            } else {
                cityName = new Text(strVal);
            }
        }
        if (n==0 ) {
            if (n==0) n=1;
            result.set(sum / n);
            context.write(cityName, result);
        }
    }
}
```

The output will be as shown in the following code:

```
Las Vegas 0 // city of Las vegas has no temperature measurements in
temperature.csv
```

Left outer join

Left outer join gives all rows present in the left-hand side table, in addition to the rows that are common to both of the tables (inner join). If used on tables with little in common, can result in very large results, and thus, slow performance:

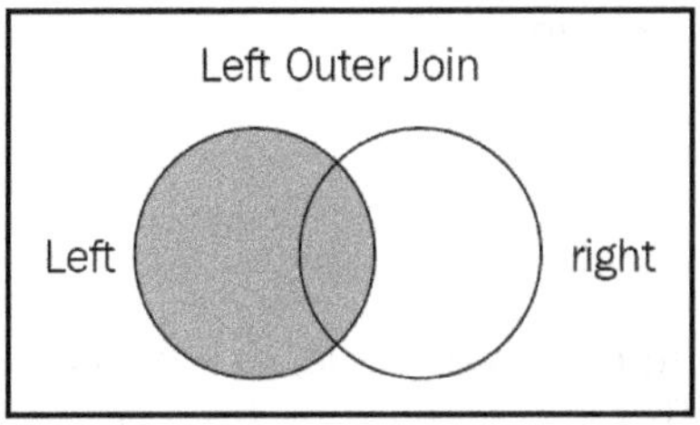

We will consider the cities and temperatures only if the cityID has both records or cityID is in `cities.csv` only, as shown in the following code:

```
private static class LeftOuterJoinReducer
        extends Reducer<Text, Text, Text, IntWritable> {
    private IntWritable result = new IntWritable();
    private Text cityName = new Text("Unknown");
    public void reduce(Text key, Iterable<Text> values,
                       Context context) throws IOException,
InterruptedException {
        int sum = 0;
        int n = 0;

        for (Text val : values) {
            String strVal = val.toString();
            if (strVal.length() <=3)
            {
                sum += Integer.parseInt(strVal);
                n +=1;
            } else {
                cityName = new Text(strVal);
            }
        }
        if (cityName.toString().compareTo("Unknown") !=0)) {
            if (n==0) n = 1;
```

```
                result.set(sum / n);
                context.write(cityName, result);
            }
        }
    }
```

The output is shown in the following code:

```
Boston 22
New York 23
Chicago 23
Philadelphia 23
San Francisco 22
Las Vegas 0 // city of Las vegas has no temperature measurements in
temperature.csv
```

Right outer join

Right outer join gives all rows in right side table, as well as the common rows on both the left and right (inner join). Use this to get all of the rows in the right table, along with the rows found in both left and right tables. Fills in `NULL` if not in left. The performance here is similar to the left outer join previously mentioned in this table:

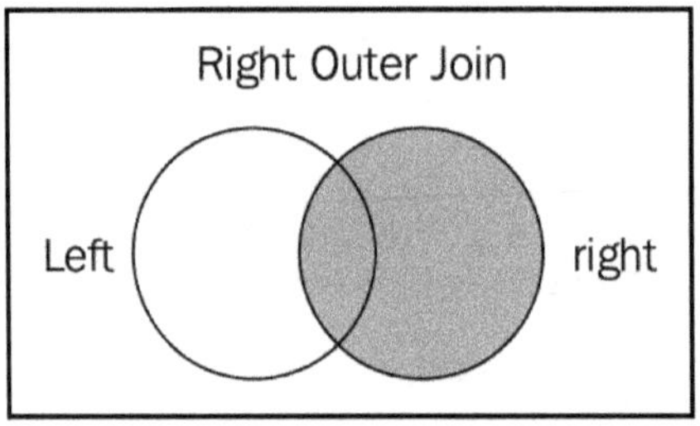

We will consider the cities and temperatures only if the cityID has both records or only temperature measurements are included, as shown in the following code:

```
private static class RightOuterJoinReducer
        extends Reducer<Text, Text, Text, IntWritable> {
    private IntWritable result = new IntWritable();
    private Text cityName = new Text("Unknown");
    public void reduce(Text key, Iterable<Text> values,
                       Context context) throws IOException,
InterruptedException {
        int sum = 0;
        int n = 0;
```

```
            for (Text val : values) {
                String strVal = val.toString();
                if (strVal.length() <=3)
                {
                    sum += Integer.parseInt(strVal);
                    n +=1;
                } else {
                    cityName = new Text(strVal);
                }
            }
           if (n !=0) {
             result.set(sum / n);
             context.write(cityName, result);
            }
        }
    }
```

The output will be as follows:

```
Boston 22
New York 23
Chicago 23
Philadelphia 23
San Francisco 22
city-6 22 //city ID 6 has no name in cities.csv only temperature
measurements
```

Full outer join

Full outer join gives all (matched and unmatched) rows from the tables at the left and right side of the join clause. We use this when we want to keep all of the rows from both tables. A full outer join returns all rows when there is a match in ONE of the tables. If used on tables with little in common, it can result in very large results, and thus, slow performance:

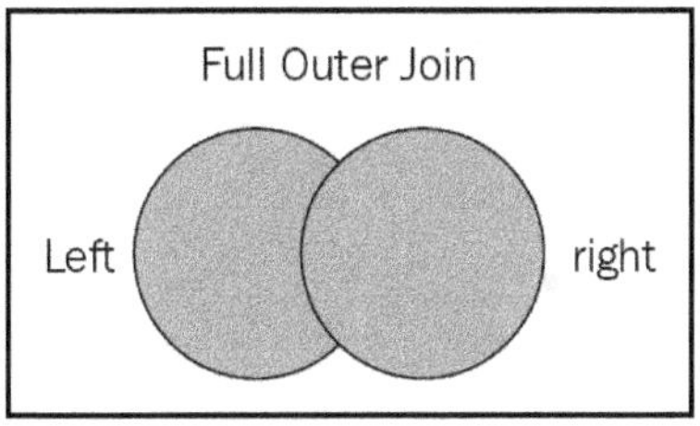

We will consider the cities and temperatures only if the cityID has both records, or if it exists in one of the tables, as shown in the following code:

```
private static class FullOuterJoinReducer
        extends Reducer<Text, Text, Text, IntWritable> {
    private IntWritable result = new IntWritable();
    private Text cityName = new Text("Unknown");
    public void reduce(Text key, Iterable<Text> values,
                        Context context) throws IOException,
InterruptedException {
        int sum = 0;
        int n = 0;

        for (Text val : values) {
            String strVal = val.toString();
            if (strVal.length() <=3)
            {
                sum += Integer.parseInt(strVal);
                n +=1;
            } else {
                cityName = new Text(strVal);
            }
        }
        if (n==0) n = 1;
        result.set(sum/n);
        context.write(cityName, result);
    }
}
```

The output will be as follows:

```
Boston 22
New York 23
Chicago 23
Philadelphia 23
San Francisco 22
city-6 22 //city ID 6 has no name in cities.csv only temperature
measurements
Las Vegas 0 // city of Las vegas has no temperature measurements in
temperature.csv
```

Left semi join

Left semi join gives only rows from the left side table, if, and only if, they exist in the right side table. Use this to get rows from left table, if, and only if, the rows are found in the right table. This is the opposite of the left anti join seen in the previous section. It does not include right side values. It provides very good performance, as only one table is fully considered, and the other is only checked for the join condition:

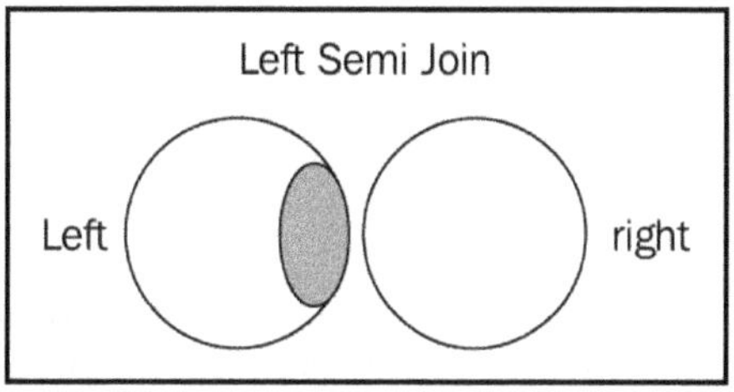

This is similar to left outer join, except that we will only output left table records from `cities.csv`.

Cross join

Cross join matches every row from the left with every row from the right, generating a Cartesian cross product. This is to be used with caution, as it is the worst performing join, to be used in specific use cases only:

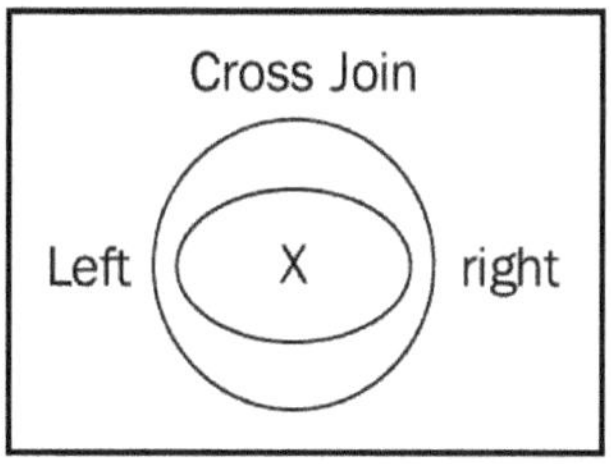

This will output all temperatures for all cities, generating 6 x 6 records (36 output records). This join is usually not used, as the output can be very large, and it is not that useful in most cases.

Thus, we can implement different joins using the multiple mapper approach.

> **TIP:** The multiple mappers reducer job seen earlier is a good example of a join pattern.

Depending on the use case, a join pattern can be customized to generate the intended output.

Summary

In this chapter, we discussed the MapReduce framework, various components of the MapReduce framework, and the various patterns in the MapReduce paradigm, which can be used to design and develop MapReduce code to meet specific objectives.

In the next chapter, we will look at the Python language, and how it can be used to perform analytics on big data.

4
Scientific Computing and Big Data Analysis with Python and Hadoop

In this chapter, we provide an introduction to Python and analyzing big data using Hadoop and Python packages. We will be looking at a basic Python installation, opening a Jupyter Notebook, and working through some examples.

In a nutshell, the following topics will be covered in this chapter:

- Installation:
    - Downloading and installing Python
    - Downloading and installing Anaconda
    - Installing Jupyter Notebook
- Data analysis

Installation

In this section, we will look at the steps involved in installing and setting up Jupyter Notebook with the Python interpreter to perform data analysis.

Installing standard Python

Go to the Python download page at `http://www.python.org/download/` with your web browser. Python is supported on Windows, macOS, and Linux, and you will find the different installations:

- Python releases for Windows at `https://www.python.org/downloads/windows/`
- Python releases for macOS X at `https://www.python.org/downloads/mac-osx/`
- Python source releases (Linux and Unix) at `https://www.python.org/downloads/source/`

When you click on the download page, you will see the following screen:

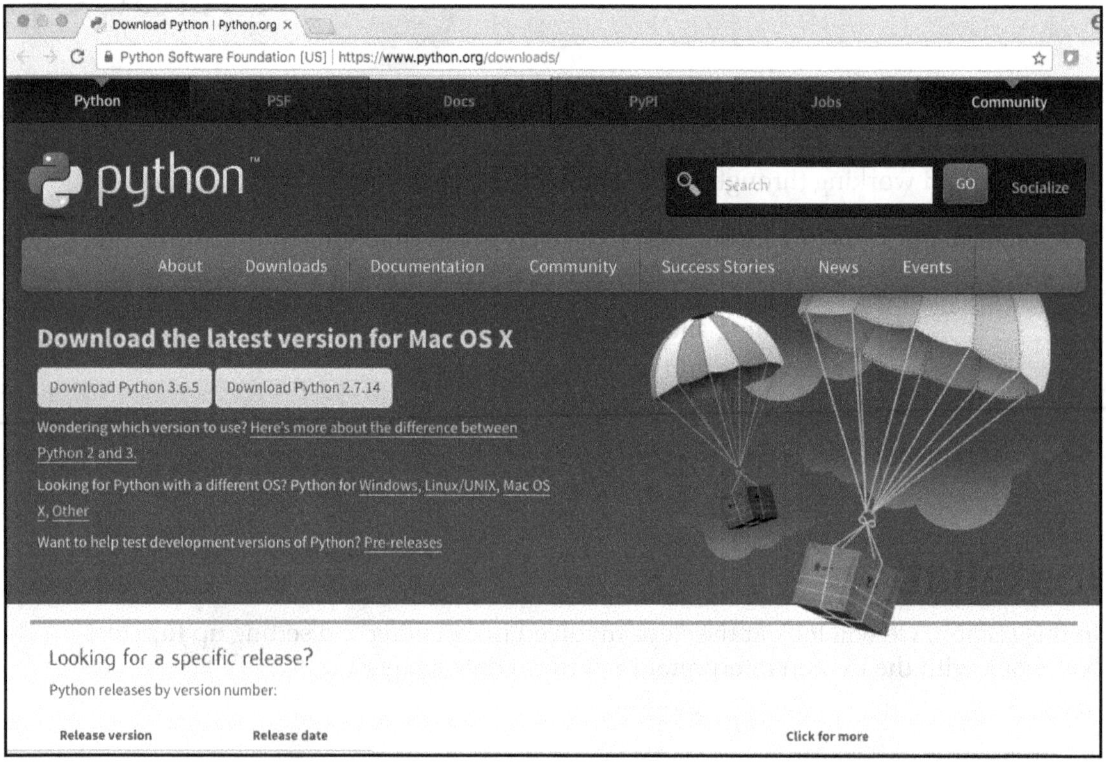

If you click on a specific version, such as 3.6.5, then you will be taken to a different page, as shown in the following screenshot:

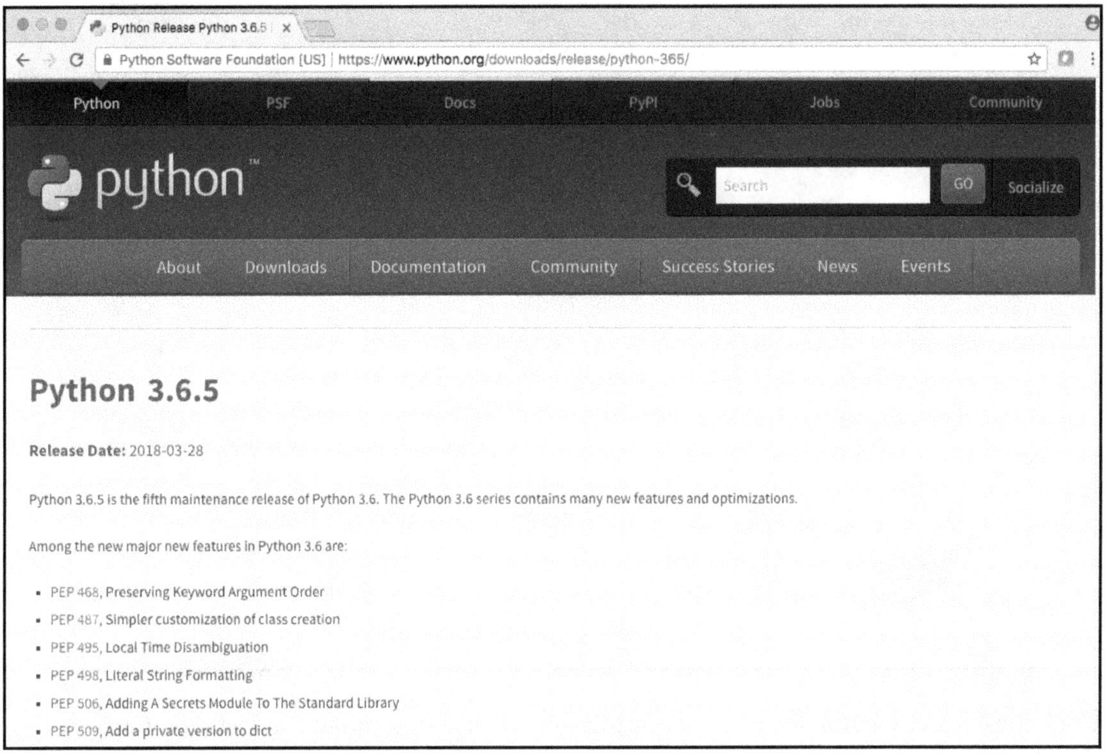

You can read the release notes and then proceed to download the Python version by simply scrolling down the page, as shown in the following screenshot:

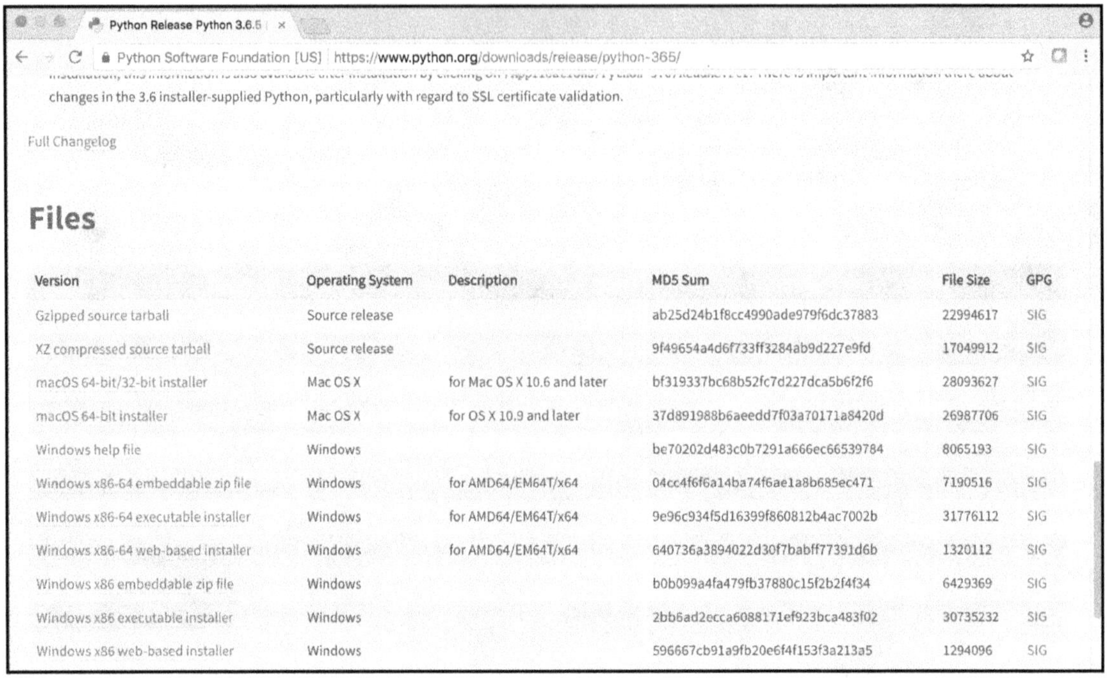

Version	Operating System	Description	MD5 Sum	File Size	GPG
Gzipped source tarball	Source release		ab25d24b1f8cc4990ade979f6dc37883	22994617	SIG
XZ compressed source tarball	Source release		9f49654a4d6f733ff3284ab9d227e9fd	17049912	SIG
macOS 64-bit/32-bit installer	Mac OS X	for Mac OS X 10.6 and later	bf319337bc68b52fc7d227dca5b6f2f6	28093627	SIG
macOS 64-bit installer	Mac OS X	for OS X 10.9 and later	37d891988b6aeedd7f03a70171a8420d	26987706	SIG
Windows help file	Windows		be70202d483c0b7291a666ec66539784	8065193	SIG
Windows x86-64 embeddable zip file	Windows	for AMD64/EM64T/x64	04cc4f6f6a14ba74f6ae1a8b685ec471	7190516	SIG
Windows x86-64 executable installer	Windows	for AMD64/EM64T/x64	9e96c934f5d16399f860812b4ac7002b	31776112	SIG
Windows x86-64 web-based installer	Windows	for AMD64/EM64T/x64	640736a3894022d30f7babff77391d6b	1320112	SIG
Windows x86 embeddable zip file	Windows		b0b099a4fa479fb37880c15f2b2f4f34	6429369	SIG
Windows x86 executable installer	Windows		2bb6ad2ecca6088171ef923bca483f02	30735232	SIG
Windows x86 web-based installer	Windows		596667cb91a9fb20e6f4f153f3a213a5	1294096	SIG

Click the correct version for your operating system and download the installer. Once the download is complete, install Python on your computer.

Installing Anaconda

The standard Python install has limitations, so you have to install Jupyter, other packages, `pip`, and so on, to make the installation production ready for you. Anaconda is an all-in-one installer with an emphasis on science: it includes Python, the standard library, and many useful third-party libraries.

Using a browser, type the URL `https://www.anaconda.com/download/` – this will take you to the Anaconda download page, as shown in the following screenshot:

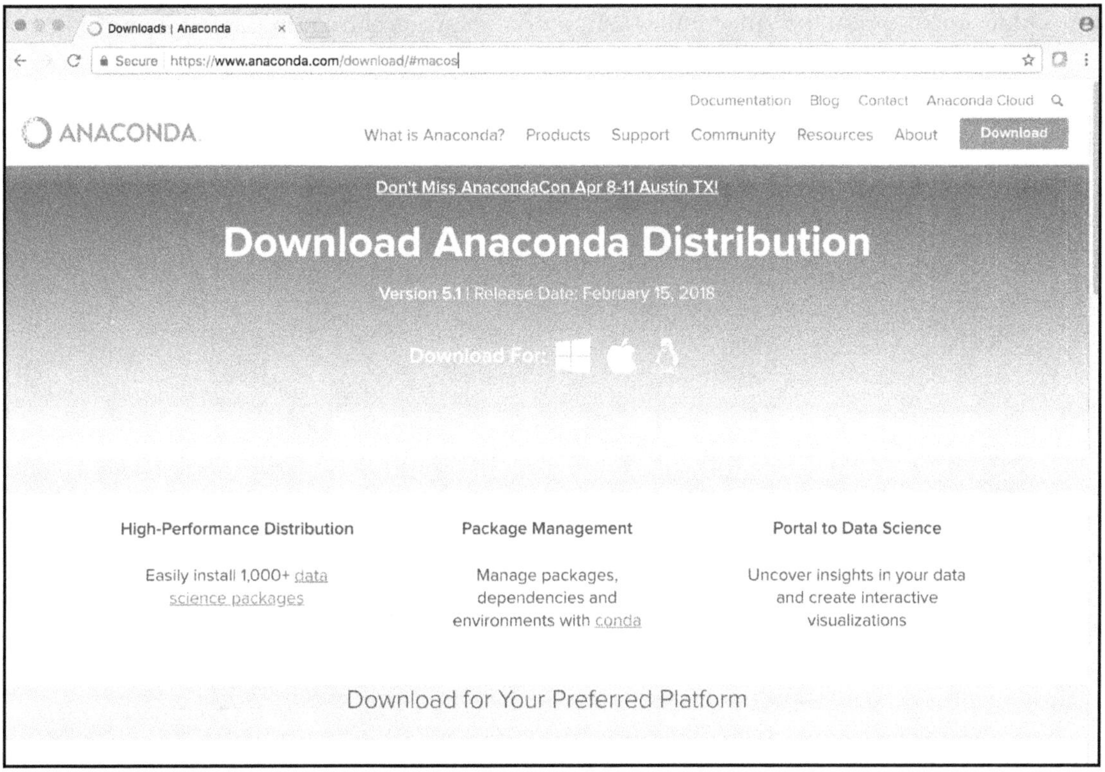

Download the appropriate version of Anaconda for your platform and then install it using the instructions on the web page `https://docs.anaconda.com/anaconda/install/`.

Once installation is complete, you should be able to just open Anaconda Navigator (on Windows, this is in the **Start** menu and on the Mac, you can simply search).

TIP: On Linux, typically you have to use the command line to launch Jupyter Notebook.

On a Mac, for instance, the Anaconda Navigator appears as shown in the following screenshot:

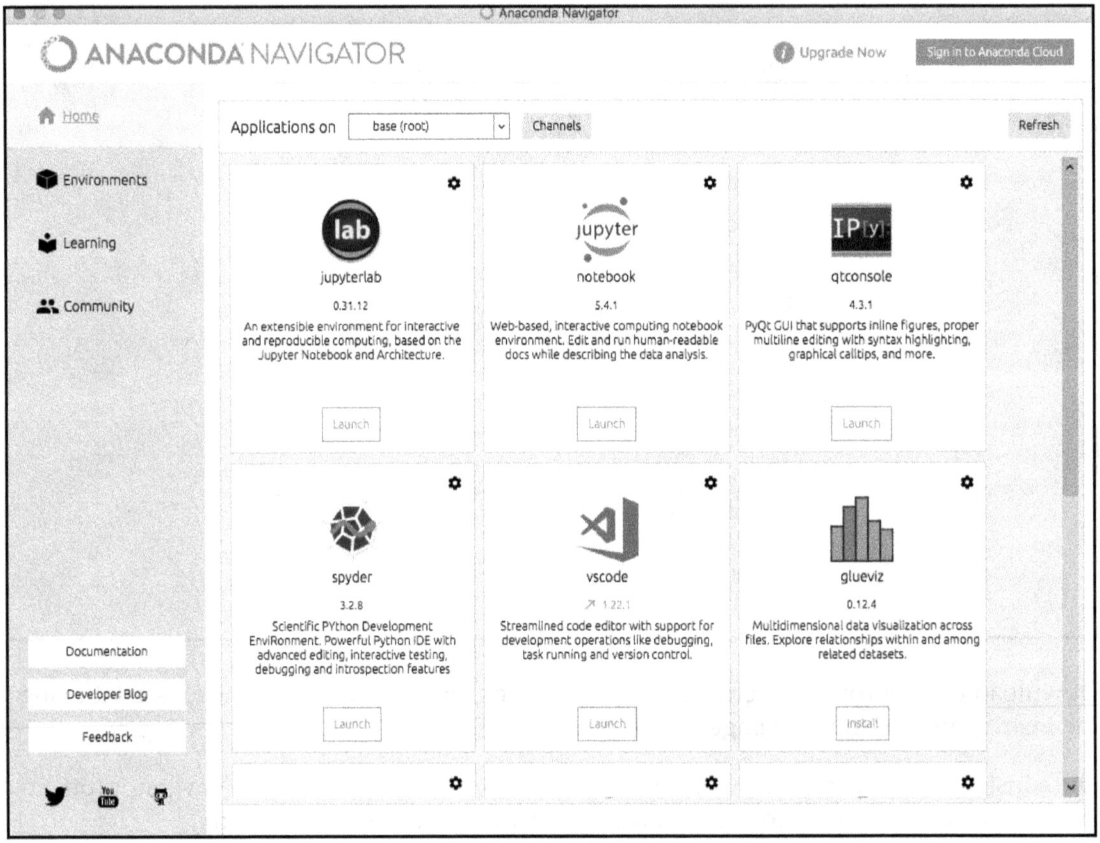

If you are using Anaconda Navigator, simply clicking on the Jupyter Notebook **Launch** button will launch Jupyter, as shown in the following screenshot:

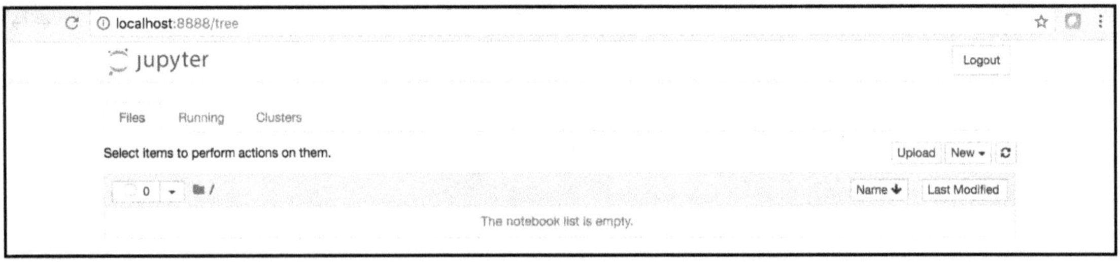

Using Conda

The Conda command line is by far the most useful and easy-to-use tool to set up your Python installation successfully. Conda supports multiple environments that can coexist so you can set up a Python 2.7 environment as well as a Python 3.6 environment. If you are into deep learning, you can set up TensorFlow as a separate environment and so on.

TIP

You can download and install `conda` by browsing to the URL `https://conda.io/docs/user-guide/install/index.html`.

The following screenshot is the Conda installation page:

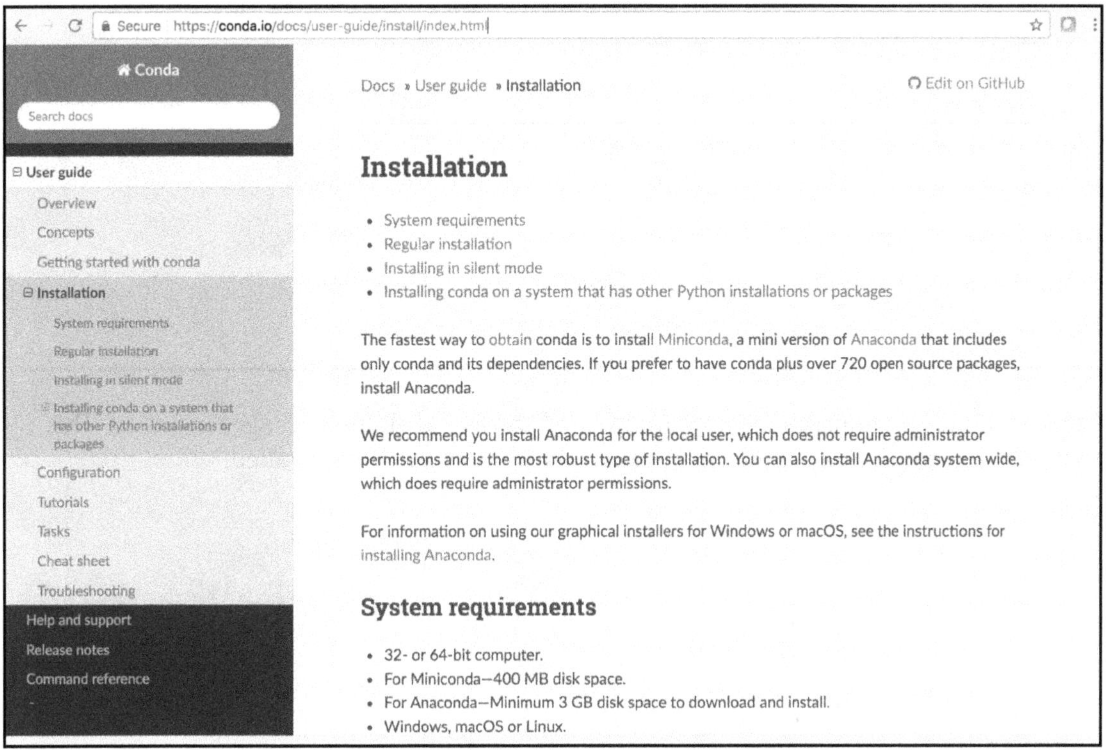

Follow the instructions to install Conda on your machine after downloading Conda from the links, as shown in the following screenshot:

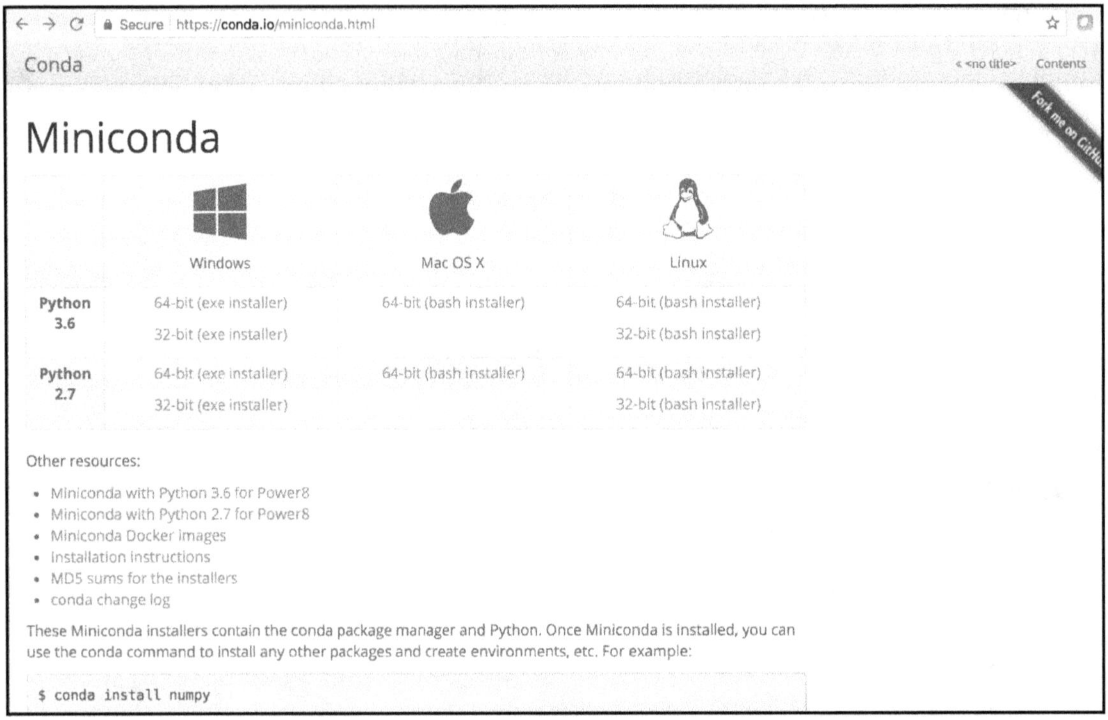

Typing `conda list` on the command line will show you all the packages installed. This will help you understand which versions of which packages are installed:

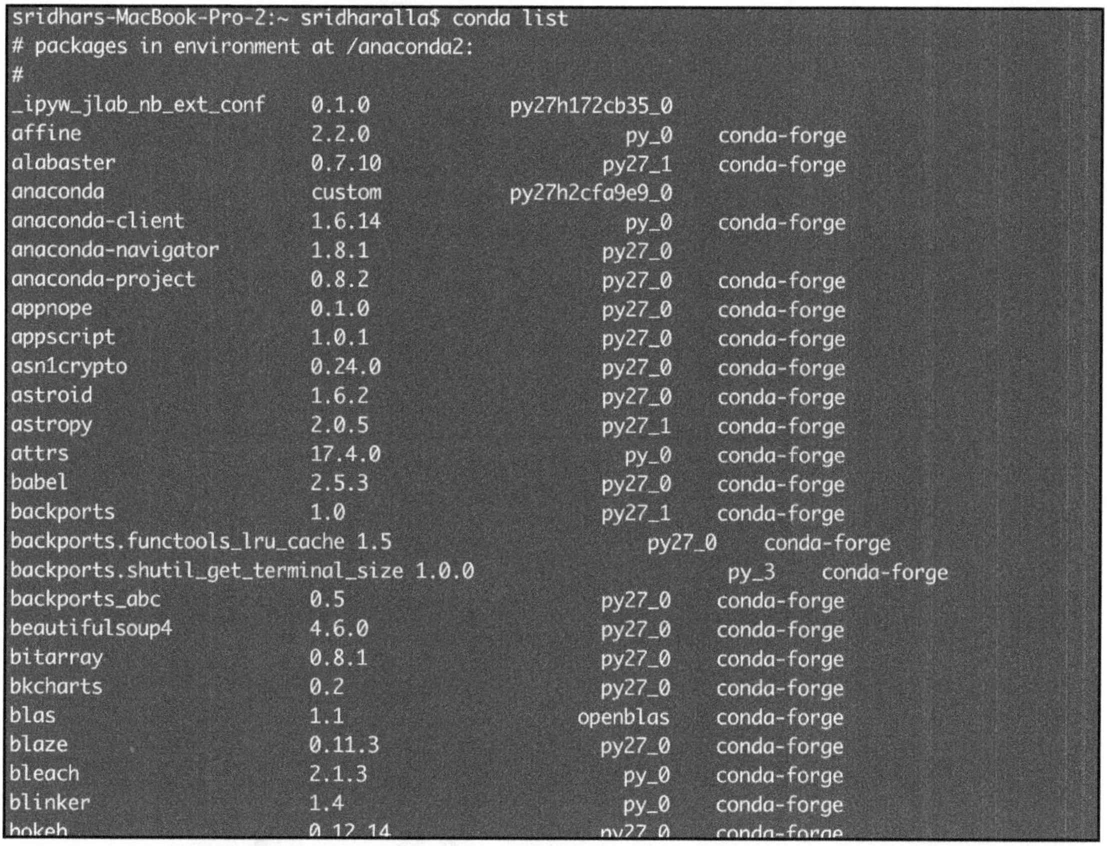

```
sridhars-MacBook-Pro-2:~ sridharalla$ conda list
# packages in environment at /anaconda2:
#
_ipyw_jlab_nb_ext_conf    0.1.0          py27h172cb35_0
affine                    2.2.0                    py_0    conda-forge
alabaster                 0.7.10                 py27_1    conda-forge
anaconda                  custom         py27h2cfa9e9_0
anaconda-client           1.6.14                   py_0    conda-forge
anaconda-navigator        1.8.1                  py27_0
anaconda-project          0.8.2                  py27_0    conda-forge
appnope                   0.1.0                  py27_0    conda-forge
appscript                 1.0.1                  py27_0    conda-forge
asn1crypto                0.24.0                 py27_0    conda-forge
astroid                   1.6.2                  py27_0    conda-forge
astropy                   2.0.5                  py27_1    conda-forge
attrs                     17.4.0                   py_0    conda-forge
babel                     2.5.3                  py27_0    conda-forge
backports                 1.0                    py27_1    conda-forge
backports.functools_lru_cache 1.5                   py27_0    conda-forge
backports.shutil_get_terminal_size 1.0.0                   py_3    conda-forge
backports_abc             0.5                    py27_0    conda-forge
beautifulsoup4            4.6.0                  py27_0    conda-forge
bitarray                  0.8.1                  py27_0    conda-forge
bkcharts                  0.2                    py27_0    conda-forge
blas                      1.1                  openblas    conda-forge
blaze                     0.11.3                 py27_0    conda-forge
bleach                    2.1.3                    py_0    conda-forge
blinker                   1.4                      py_0    conda-forge
bokeh                     0.12.14                py27_0    conda-forge
```

Installing a package is easy using `conda`. It's as simple as `conda install <package name>`.

For instance, type in:

```
conda install scikit-learn
```

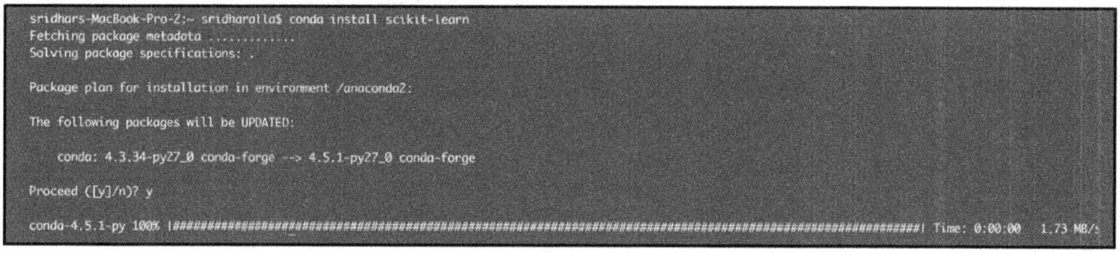

```
sridhars-MacBook-Pro-2:~ sridharalla$ conda install scikit-learn
Fetching package metadata ............
Solving package specifications: .

Package plan for installation in environment /anaconda2:

The following packages will be UPDATED:

    conda: 4.3.34-py27_0 conda-forge --> 4.5.1-py27_0 conda-forge

Proceed ([y]/n)? y

conda-4.5.1-py 100% |################################################################################| Time: 0:00:00   1.73 MB/s
```

More importantly, `conda install Jupyter` installs the Jupyter Notebook ,which requires a lot of other packages:

```
    - jupyter


The following packages will be downloaded:

    package                    |            build
    ---------------------------|-----------------
    libxml2-2.9.8              |       hf84eae3_0         2.0 MB
    backports_abc-0.5          |  py27h7b3c97b_0          12 KB
    jsonschema-2.6.0           |  py27h7ed5aa4_0          61 KB
    markupsafe-1.0             |  py27h97b2822_1          24 KB
    notebook-5.4.1             |           py27_0         6.6 MB
    libpng-1.6.34              |       hb9fc6fc_0         334 KB
    bleach-2.1.3               |           py27_0          32 KB
    ca-certificates-2018.03.07 |                0         124 KB
    decorator-4.3.0            |           py27_0          15 KB
    xz-5.2.3                   |       h55aa19d_2         357 KB
    gstreamer-1.14.0           |       hb453b48_1         3.8 MB
    pyzmq-17.0.0               |  py27h14c3975_1          440 KB
    jupyter_console-5.2.0      |  py27hc6bee7e_1           34 KB
    icu-58.2                   |       h9c2bf20_1        22.5 MB
    ipython-5.6.0              |           py27_0        1020 KB
    pandocfilters-1.4.2        |  py27h428e1e5_1           12 KB
    tornado-5.0.1              |           py27_1         617 KB
    prompt_toolkit-1.0.15      |  py27h1b593e1_0          333 KB
    sip-4.19.8                 |  py27hf484d3e_0          291 KB
    ptyprocess-0.5.2           |  py27h4ccb14c_0           22 KB
    widgetsnbextension-3.2.0   |           py27_0         1.7 MB
    openssl-1.0.2o             |       h20670df_0         3.4 MB
    simplegeneric-0.8.1        |           py27_2           9 KB
    freetype-2.8               |       hab7d2ae_1         804 KB
    pickleshare-0.7.4          |  py27h09770e1_0           11 KB
    pygments-2.2.0             |  py27h4a8b6f5_0          1.3 MB
    libsodium-1.0.16           |       h1bed415_0         302 KB
    gst-plugins-base-1.14.0    |       hbbd80ab_1         6.3 MB
    zeromq-4.2.5               |       h439df22_0         567 KB
```

Let's try another important package:

```
conda install pandas
```

```
[root@4b726275a804 /]# conda install pandas
Solving environment: done

## Package Plan ##

  environment location: /root/miniconda2

  added / updated specs:
    - pandas


The following packages will be downloaded:

    package                    |            build
    ---------------------------|-----------------
    intel-openmp-2018.0.0      |                8         620 KB
    mkl_fft-1.0.1              |  py27h3010b51_0         137 KB
    pytz-2018.4                |          py27_0         211 KB
    mkl-2018.0.2               |                1       205.2 MB
    pandas-0.22.0              |  py27hf484d3e_0        10.5 MB
    mkl_random-1.0.1           |  py27h629b387_0         361 KB
    libgfortran-ng-7.2.0       |      hdf63c60_3         1.2 MB
    numpy-1.14.2               |  py27hdbf6ddf_1         4.1 MB
    ------------------------------------------------------------
                                           Total:       222.3 MB

The following NEW packages will be INSTALLED:

    intel-openmp:   2018.0.0-8
    libgfortran-ng: 7.2.0-hdf63c60_3
    mkl:            2018.0.2-1
    mkl_fft:        1.0.1-py27h3010b51_0
    mkl_random:     1.0.1-py27h629b387_0
    numpy:          1.14.2-py27hdbf6ddf_1
    pandas:         0.22.0-py27hf484d3e_0
    pytz:           2018.4-py27_0
```

Other important packages are:

```
conda install scikit-learn
conda install matplotlib
conda install seaborn
```

In addition to the `conda` installs, we would need to install packages to access HDFS (Hadoop) and open files (parquet format):

```
pip install hdfs
pip install pyarrow
```

Jupyter Notebook configuration can be generated by running a command as follows:

```
[root@4b726275a804 /]# jupyter notebook --generate-config
 Writing default config to: /root/.jupyter/jupyter_notebook_config.py
```

Jupyter needs authentication, which is a token by default. However, if you want to create a password-based authentication, then just run the command shown in the following code to set up a password:

```
[root@4b726275a804 /]# jupyter notebook password
 Enter password:
 Verify password:
 [NotebookPasswordApp] Wrote hashed password to
/root/.jupyter/jupyter_notebook_config.json
```

Now, we are ready to launch the Notebook, so type the following command:

```
jupyter notebook --allow-root --no-browser --ip=* --port=8888
```

The following is the console when the preceding command is being run:

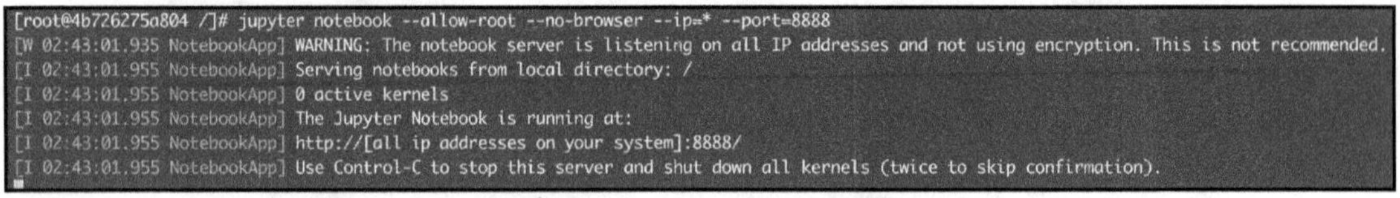

When you open the browser and put in `localhost:8888`, the browser will open the login screen and then you have to put in the password set in the preceding steps:

Once the password is supplied, the Jupyter Notebook portal opens up which shows any existing Notebooks. In this case, we have no prior Notebooks so the next step is to create one. Click **New** and then select **Python 2** for your new Notebook:

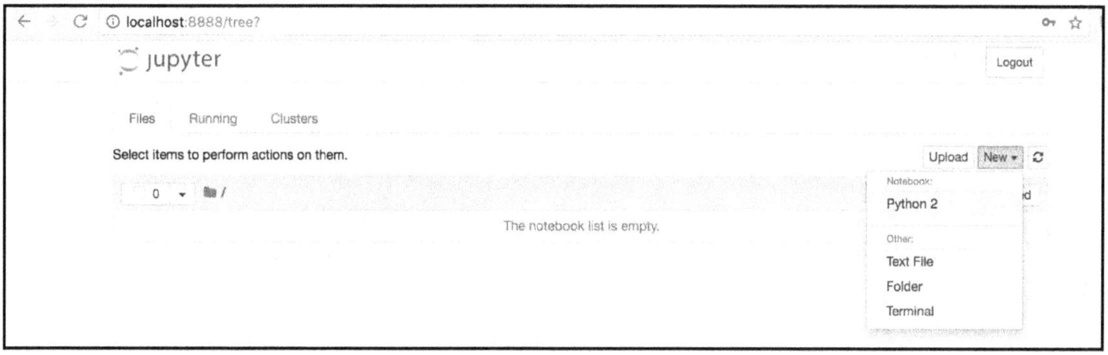

The following is a new Notebook where you can now type in some test code, as shown in the following screenshot:

Now that we have installed Python and Jupyter Notebook, we are ready to do data analysis using the Notebooks and the Python language. In the next section, we will look deep into the different types of data analysis that can be done.

Data analysis

Download `OnlineRetail.csv` from the link provided with the book. Then, you can load the file using Pandas.

The following is a simple way of reading a local file using Pandas:

```
import pandas as pd
path = '/Users/sridharalla/Documents/OnlineRetail.csv'
df = pd.read_csv(path)
```

However, since we are analyzing data in a Hadoop cluster, we should be using `hdfs` not a local system. The following is an example of how the `hdfs` file can be loaded into a `pandas` DataFrame:

```
import pandas as pd
from hdfs import InsecureClient
client_hdfs = InsecureClient('http://localhost:9870')
with client_hdfs.read('/user/normal/OnlineRetail.csv', encoding = 'utf-8')
as reader:
 df = pd.read_csv(reader,index_col=0)
```

The following is what the following line of code does:

```
df.head(3)
```

You will get the following result:

```
In [11]: df.head(3)
Out[11]:
```

	InvoiceNo	StockCode	Description	Quantity	InvoiceDate	UnitPrice	CustomerID	Country
0	536365	85123A	WHITE HANGING HEART T-LIGHT HOLDER	6	12/1/10 8:26	2.55	17850.0	United Kingdom
1	536365	71053	WHITE METAL LANTERN	6	12/1/10 8:26	3.39	17850.0	United Kingdom
2	536365	84406B	CREAM CUPID HEARTS COAT HANGER	8	12/1/10 8:26	2.75	17850.0	United Kingdom

Basically, it displays the top three entries in the DataFrame.

We can now experiment with the data. Enter the following:

```
len(df)
```

That should output this:

```
65499
```

That just means the length, or size, of the DataFrame. It's telling us that there are `65,499` entries in the whole file.

Now do this:

```
df2 = df.loc[df.UnitPrice > 3.0]
df2.head(3)
```

We defined a new DataFrame called `df2`, and we set it as all the entries in the original DataFrame with unit prices greater than three.

Then, we tell it to display the top three entries, as seen in the following screenshot:

	InvoiceNo	StockCode	Description	Quantity	InvoiceDate	UnitPrice	CustomerID	Country
1	536365	71053	WHITE METAL LANTERN	6	12/1/10 8:26	3.39	17850.0	United Kingdom
3	536365	84029G	KNITTED UNION FLAG HOT WATER BOTTLE	6	12/1/10 8:26	3.39	17850.0	United Kingdom
4	536365	84029E	RED WOOLLY HOTTIE WHITE HEART.	6	12/1/10 8:26	3.39	17850.0	United Kingdom

The following lines of code select the indices with data that has a unit price above `3.0` and set their description to `Miscellaneous`. Then it displays the first three items:

```
df.loc[df.UnitPrice > 3.0, ['Description']] = 'Miscellaneous'
df.head(3)
```

And this is the result:

```
In [45]: df.loc[df.UnitPrice > 3.0, ['Description']] = 'Miscellaneous'
         df.head(3)
Out[45]:
```

	InvoiceNo	StockCode	Description	Quantity	InvoiceDate	UnitPrice	CustomerID	Country
0	536365	85123A	WHITE HANGING HEART T-LIGHT HOLDER	1	12/1/10 8:26	2.55	17850.0	United Kingdom
1	536365	71053	Miscellaneous	1	12/1/10 8:26	3.39	17850.0	United Kingdom
2	536365	84406B	CREAM CUPID HEARTS COAT HANGER	1	12/1/10 8:26	2.75	17850.0	United Kingdom

As you can see, entry number 2 (with the index of 1) has its description changed to `Miscellaneous` because its unit price is $3.39 (which is over 3 as we specified earlier).

The line of code outputs the data with index 2:

```
df.loc[2]
```

The output is as follows:

```
In [55]: df.loc[2]

Out[55]: InvoiceNo                                 536365
         StockCode                                 84406B
         Description    CREAM CUPID HEARTS COAT HANGER
         Quantity                                       8
         InvoiceDate                         12/1/10 8:26
         UnitPrice                                   2.75
         CustomerID                                 17850
         Country                           United Kingdom
         Name: 2, dtype: object
```

And finally, we can create a plot of the **Quantity** column as shown in the following code:

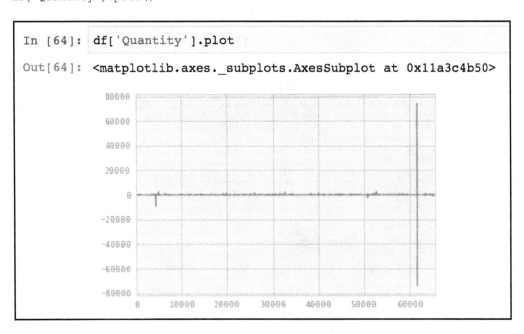

```
df['Quantity'].plot()
```

```
In [64]: df['Quantity'].plot()

Out[64]: <matplotlib.axes._subplots.AxesSubplot at 0x11a3c4b50>
```

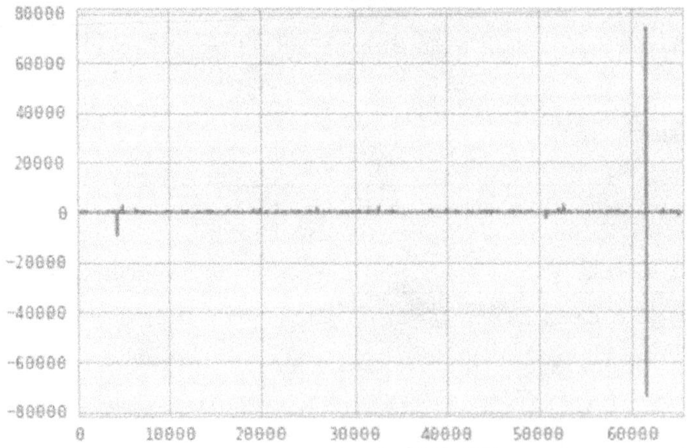

There are plenty more functions to explore.

Here's an example of the usage of the `.append()` function.

We define a new `df` object, `df3`, and we set it equal to the first 10 rows of `df` combined with the rows 200–209 of `df`. In other words, we append rows 200–209 to rows 0–9 of `df`:

```
df3 = df[0:10].append(df[200:210])
df3
```

And this is the resulting output:

```
In [35]: df3 = df[0:10].append(df[200:210])
         df3
Out[35]:
```

	InvoiceNo	StockCode	Description	Quantity	InvoiceDate	UnitPrice	CustomerID	Country
0	536365	85123A	WHITE HANGING HEART T-LIGHT HOLDER	6	12/1/10 8:26	2.55	17850.0	United Kingdom
1	536365	71053	Miscellaneous	6	12/1/10 8:26	3.39	17850.0	United States
2	536365	84406B	CREAM CUPID HEARTS COAT HANGER	8	12/1/10 8:26	2.75	17850.0	United Kingdom
3	536365	84029G	Miscellaneous	6	12/1/10 8:26	3.39	17850.0	United States
4	536365	84029E	Miscellaneous	6	12/1/10 8:26	3.39	17850.0	United States
5	536365	22752	Miscellaneous	2	12/1/10 8:26	7.65	17850.0	United States
6	536365	21730	Miscellaneous	6	12/1/10 8:26	4.25	17850.0	United States
7	536366	22633	HAND WARMER UNION JACK	6	12/1/10 8:28	1.85	17850.0	United Kingdom
8	536366	22632	HAND WARMER RED POLKA DOT	6	12/1/10 8:28	1.85	17850.0	United Kingdom
9	536367	84879	ASSORTED COLOUR BIRD ORNAMENT	32	12/1/10 8:34	1.69	13047.0	United Kingdom
200	536389	35004C	Miscellaneous	6	12/1/10 10:03	5.45	12431.0	United States
201	536389	35004G	Miscellaneous	4	12/1/10 10:03	6.35	12431.0	United States
202	536389	85014B	Miscellaneous	6	12/1/10 10:03	5.95	12431.0	United States
203	536389	85014A	Miscellaneous	3	12/1/10 10:03	5.95	12431.0	United States
204	536389	22193	Miscellaneous	2	12/1/10 10:03	8.50	12431.0	United States
205	536389	22726	Miscellaneous	4	12/1/10 10:03	3.75	12431.0	United States
206	536389	22727	Miscellaneous	4	12/1/10 10:03	3.75	12431.0	United States
207	536389	22192	Miscellaneous	2	12/1/10 10:03	8.50	12431.0	United States
208	536389	22191	Miscellaneous	2	12/1/10 10:03	8.50	12431.0	United States
209	536389	22195	LARGE HEART MEASURING SPOONS	24	12/1/10 10:03	1.65	12431.0	Australia

Now, imagine that you're only concerned with a few columns, namely **StockCode**, **Quantity**, **InvoiceDate**, and **UnitPrice**. We can define a new `DataFrame` object to contain only those columns in the data:

```
df4 = pd.DataFrame(df, columns=['StockCode', 'Quantity', 'InvoiceDate',
'UnitPrice']
df4.head(3)
```

And this is the following result:

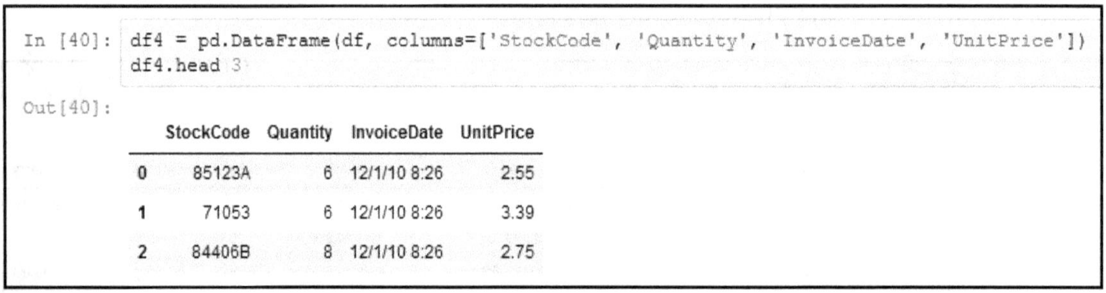
In [40]: df4 = pd.DataFrame(df, columns=['StockCode', 'Quantity', 'InvoiceDate', 'UnitPrice'])
df4.head(3)
Out[40]:

	StockCode	Quantity	InvoiceDate	UnitPrice
0	85123A	6	12/1/10 8:26	2.55
1	71053	6	12/1/10 8:26	3.39
2	84406B	8	12/1/10 8:26	2.75

Pandas offers different ways to combine data. More specifically, we can **merge**, **concatenate**, **join**, and **append**. We have already covered append, so now we will take a look at concatenating data.

Take a look at this code block:

```
d1 = df[0:10]
d2 = df[10:20]

d3 = pd.concat([d1, d2])
d3
```

Basically, we set `d1` to be a `DataFrame` object containing the first 10 indices in `df`. Then, we set `d2` to be the next ten indices in `df`. Finally, we set `d3` to be the concatenation of `d1` and `d2`. This is the result once they are concatenated:

```
In [166]: d1 = df[0:10]
          d2 = df[10:20]

          d3 = pd.concat([d1, d2])
          d3
```

Out[166]:

	InvoiceNo	StockCode	Description	Quantity	InvoiceDate	UnitPrice	CustomerID	Country
0	536365	85123A	WHITE HANGING HEART T-LIGHT HOLDER	6	12/1/10 8:26	2.55	17850.0	United Kingdom
1	536365	71053	WHITE METAL LANTERN	6	12/1/10 8:26	3.39	17850.0	United Kingdom
2	536365	84406B	CREAM CUPID HEARTS COAT HANGER	8	12/1/10 8:26	2.75	17850.0	United Kingdom
3	536365	84029G	KNITTED UNION FLAG HOT WATER BOTTLE	6	12/1/10 8:26	3.39	17850.0	United Kingdom
4	536365	84029E	RED WOOLLY HOTTIE WHITE HEART.	6	12/1/10 8:26	3.39	17850.0	United Kingdom
5	536365	22752	SET 7 BABUSHKA NESTING BOXES	2	12/1/10 8:26	7.65	17850.0	United Kingdom
6	536365	21730	GLASS STAR FROSTED T-LIGHT HOLDER	6	12/1/10 8:26	4.25	17850.0	United Kingdom
7	536366	22633	HAND WARMER UNION JACK	6	12/1/10 8:28	1.85	17850.0	United Kingdom
8	536366	22632	HAND WARMER RED POLKA DOT	6	12/1/10 8:28	1.85	17850.0	United Kingdom
9	536367	84879	ASSORTED COLOUR BIRD ORNAMENT	32	12/1/10 8:34	1.69	13047.0	United Kingdom
10	536367	22745	POPPY'S PLAYHOUSE BEDROOM	6	12/1/10 8:34	2.10	13047.0	United Kingdom
11	536367	22748	POPPY'S PLAYHOUSE KITCHEN	6	12/1/10 8:34	2.10	13047.0	United Kingdom
12	536367	22749	FELTCRAFT PRINCESS CHARLOTTE DOLL	8	12/1/10 8:34	3.75	13047.0	United Kingdom
13	536367	22310	IVORY KNITTED MUG COSY	6	12/1/10 8:34	1.65	13047.0	United Kingdom
14	536367	84969	BOX OF 6 ASSORTED COLOUR TEASPOONS	6	12/1/10 8:34	4.25	13047.0	United Kingdom
15	536367	22623	BOX OF VINTAGE JIGSAW BLOCKS	3	12/1/10 8:34	4.95	13047.0	United Kingdom
16	536367	22622	BOX OF VINTAGE ALPHABET BLOCKS	2	12/1/10 8:34	9.95	13047.0	United Kingdom
17	536367	21754	HOME BUILDING BLOCK WORD	3	12/1/10 8:34	5.95	13047.0	United Kingdom
18	536367	21755	LOVE BUILDING BLOCK WORD	3	12/1/10 8:34	5.95	13047.0	United Kingdom
19	536367	21777	RECIPE BOX WITH METAL HEART	4	12/1/10 8:34	7.95	13047.0	United Kingdom

We can do more with this. We can specify keys that will make it easier to distinguish between `d1` and `d2`. Take a look at the following line of code:

```
d3 = pd.concat([d1, d2], keys=['d1', 'd2'])
```

```
In [179]: d1 = df[0:10]
          d2 = df[10:20]

          d3 = pd.concat([d1, d2], keys=['d1', 'd2'])
          d3
```

Out[179]:

		InvoiceNo	StockCode	Description	Quantity	InvoiceDate	UnitPrice	CustomerID	Country
d1	0	536365	85123A	WHITE HANGING HEART T-LIGHT HOLDER	6	12/1/10 8:26	2.55	17850.0	United Kingdom
	1	536365	71053	WHITE METAL LANTERN	6	12/1/10 8:26	3.39	17850.0	United Kingdom
	2	536365	84406B	CREAM CUPID HEARTS COAT HANGER	8	12/1/10 8:26	2.75	17850.0	United Kingdom
	3	536365	84029G	KNITTED UNION FLAG HOT WATER BOTTLE	6	12/1/10 8:26	3.39	17850.0	United Kingdom
	4	536365	84029E	RED WOOLLY HOTTIE WHITE HEART.	6	12/1/10 8:26	3.39	17850.0	United Kingdom
	5	536365	22752	SET 7 BABUSHKA NESTING BOXES	2	12/1/10 8:26	7.65	17850.0	United Kingdom
	6	536365	21730	GLASS STAR FROSTED T-LIGHT HOLDER	6	12/1/10 8:26	4.25	17850.0	United Kingdom
	7	536366	22633	HAND WARMER UNION JACK	6	12/1/10 8:28	1.85	17850.0	United Kingdom
	8	536366	22632	HAND WARMER RED POLKA DOT	6	12/1/10 8:28	1.85	17850.0	United Kingdom
	9	536367	84879	ASSORTED COLOUR BIRD ORNAMENT	32	12/1/10 8:34	1.69	13047.0	United Kingdom
d2	10	536367	22745	POPPY'S PLAYHOUSE BEDROOM	6	12/1/10 8:34	2.10	13047.0	United Kingdom
	11	536367	22748	POPPY'S PLAYHOUSE KITCHEN	6	12/1/10 8:34	2.10	13047.0	United Kingdom
	12	536367	22749	FELTCRAFT PRINCESS CHARLOTTE DOLL	8	12/1/10 8:34	3.75	13047.0	United Kingdom
	13	536367	22310	IVORY KNITTED MUG COSY	6	12/1/10 8:34	1.65	13047.0	United Kingdom
	14	536367	84969	BOX OF 6 ASSORTED COLOUR TEASPOONS	6	12/1/10 8:34	4.25	13047.0	United Kingdom
	15	536367	22623	BOX OF VINTAGE JIGSAW BLOCKS	3	12/1/10 8:34	4.95	13047.0	United Kingdom
	16	536367	22622	BOX OF VINTAGE ALPHABET BLOCKS	2	12/1/10 8:34	9.95	13047.0	United Kingdom
	17	536367	21754	HOME BUILDING BLOCK WORD	3	12/1/10 8:34	5.95	13047.0	United Kingdom
	18	536367	21755	LOVE BUILDING BLOCK WORD	3	12/1/10 8:34	5.95	13047.0	United Kingdom
	19	536367	21777	RECIPE BOX WITH METAL HEART	4	12/1/10 8:34	7.95	13047.0	United Kingdom

As you can see, it is much easier to differentiate the two datasets. We can call the keys anything we want, even simple keys like x and y will work. If we had three datasets `d1`, `d2`, and some `d3`, we can say the keys are (x, y, z) so that we can distinguish between all three datasets.

Now, we move on to concatenation with different columns. By default, the `concat()` function uses **outer** join. This means that it combines all the columns. Think of two sets, A and B, where set A contains all the column names belonging to `d1` and set B contains all the column names belonging to `d2`. If we concatenate `d1` and `d2` using the line of code we used earlier, the columns we will see are represented by the union of A and B.

We can also specify that we want to use **inner** join, which is represented by the intersection of A and B. Take a look at the following lines of code:

```
d4 = pd.DataFrame(df, columns=['InvoiceNo', 'StockCode',
'Description'])[0:10]
d5 = pd.DataFrame(df, columns=['StockCode', 'Description',
'Quantity'])[0:10]

pd.concat([d4, d5])
```

```
In [183]: d4 = pd.DataFrame(df, columns=['InvoiceNo', 'StockCode', 'Description'])[0:10]
          d5 = pd.DataFrame(df, columns=['StockCode', 'Description', 'Quantity'])[0:10]

          pd.concat( d4, d5 )
Out[183]:
```

	Description	InvoiceNo	Quantity	StockCode
0	WHITE HANGING HEART T-LIGHT HOLDER	536365	NaN	85123A
1	WHITE METAL LANTERN	536365	NaN	71053
2	CREAM CUPID HEARTS COAT HANGER	536365	NaN	84406B
3	KNITTED UNION FLAG HOT WATER BOTTLE	536365	NaN	84029G
4	RED WOOLLY HOTTIE WHITE HEART.	536365	NaN	84029E
5	SET 7 BABUSHKA NESTING BOXES	536365	NaN	22752
6	GLASS STAR FROSTED T-LIGHT HOLDER	536365	NaN	21730
7	HAND WARMER UNION JACK	536366	NaN	22633
8	HAND WARMER RED POLKA DOT	536366	NaN	22632
9	ASSORTED COLOUR BIRD ORNAMENT	536367	NaN	84879
0	WHITE HANGING HEART T-LIGHT HOLDER	NaN	6.0	85123A
1	WHITE METAL LANTERN	NaN	6.0	71053
2	CREAM CUPID HEARTS COAT HANGER	NaN	8.0	84406B
3	KNITTED UNION FLAG HOT WATER BOTTLE	NaN	6.0	84029G
4	RED WOOLLY HOTTIE WHITE HEART.	NaN	6.0	84029E
5	SET 7 BABUSHKA NESTING BOXES	NaN	2.0	22752
6	GLASS STAR FROSTED T-LIGHT HOLDER	NaN	6.0	21730
7	HAND WARMER UNION JACK	NaN	6.0	22633
8	HAND WARMER RED POLKA DOT	NaN	6.0	22632
9	ASSORTED COLOUR BIRD ORNAMENT	NaN	32.0	84879

As you can see, it used all the column labels.

Remember that by default, `concat()` uses outer join. So, saying `pd.concat([d4, d5])` is the same as saying:

```
pd.concat([d4, d5], join='outer')
```

Now, we use inner join. Keep everything else the same, but change the call to the `concat()` function. Look at the following line of code:

```
pd.concat([d4, d5], join='inner')
```

That should now output:

```
In [184]: d4 = pd.DataFrame(df, columns=['InvoiceNo', 'StockCode', 'Description'])[0:10]
          d5 = pd.DataFrame(df, columns=['StockCode', 'Description', 'Quantity'])[0:10]

          pd.concat([d4, d5], join = 'inner')

Out[184]:
```

	StockCode	Description
0	85123A	WHITE HANGING HEART T-LIGHT HOLDER
1	71053	WHITE METAL LANTERN
2	84406B	CREAM CUPID HEARTS COAT HANGER
3	84029G	KNITTED UNION FLAG HOT WATER BOTTLE
4	84029E	RED WOOLLY HOTTIE WHITE HEART.
5	22752	SET 7 BABUSHKA NESTING BOXES
6	21730	GLASS STAR FROSTED T-LIGHT HOLDER
7	22633	HAND WARMER UNION JACK
8	22632	HAND WARMER RED POLKA DOT
9	84879	ASSORTED COLOUR BIRD ORNAMENT
0	85123A	WHITE HANGING HEART T-LIGHT HOLDER
1	71053	WHITE METAL LANTERN
2	84406B	CREAM CUPID HEARTS COAT HANGER
3	84029G	KNITTED UNION FLAG HOT WATER BOTTLE
4	84029E	RED WOOLLY HOTTIE WHITE HEART.
5	22752	SET 7 BABUSHKA NESTING BOXES
6	21730	GLASS STAR FROSTED T-LIGHT HOLDER
7	22633	HAND WARMER UNION JACK
8	22632	HAND WARMER RED POLKA DOT
9	84879	ASSORTED COLOUR BIRD ORNAMENT

As you can see, this time we only have the column labels that both d4 and d5 had in common. And once again, we can add keys to make it easier to distinguish between the two datasets in the table.

Merge is slightly more complicated. This time, you can choose between outer join, inner join, left join, and right join, and you can also choose the column to merge on.

Let's keep modifying our original definitions of d4 and of d5:

```
d4 = pd.DataFrame(df, columns=['InvoiceNo', 'StockCode',
'Description'])[0:11]
d5 = pd.DataFrame(df, columns=['StockCode', 'Description',
'Quantity'])[10:20]
```

The brackets you see at the end of the d4 definition mean we're taking the first 11 elements of that particular DataFrame, as defined. The brackets at the end of the d5 definition mean we're taking the elements 10 through 20 to put into d5, as opposed to the whole thing.

It is noticeable to see that they will have an overlapping element, and this will come into play soon.

First, let's start with the merge function. Let's do a left join merge of d4 and d5:

```
pd.merge(d4, d5, how='left')
```

```
In [222]: pd.merge(d4, d5, how='left')
```

Out[222]:

	InvoiceNo	StockCode	Description	Quantity
0	536365	85123A	WHITE HANGING HEART T-LIGHT HOLDER	NaN
1	536365	71053	WHITE METAL LANTERN	NaN
2	536365	84406B	CREAM CUPID HEARTS COAT HANGER	NaN
3	536365	84029G	KNITTED UNION FLAG HOT WATER BOTTLE	NaN
4	536365	84029E	RED WOOLLY HOTTIE WHITE HEART.	NaN
5	536365	22752	SET 7 BABUSHKA NESTING BOXES	NaN
6	536365	21730	GLASS STAR FROSTED T-LIGHT HOLDER	NaN
7	536366	22633	HAND WARMER UNION JACK	NaN
8	536366	22632	HAND WARMER RED POLKA DOT	NaN
9	536367	84879	ASSORTED COLOUR BIRD ORNAMENT	NaN
10	536367	22745	POPPY'S PLAYHOUSE BEDROOM	6.0

What this did was use all the columns of the left DataFrame in the pair d4 and d5 and added the columns of d5 to that. As you can see, since we defined d5 to contain elements 10 through 20, there are no values of quantity from indices 0 through 10. However, since element 11 is in both d5 and d4, we see a data value for that under **Quantity**.

Similarly, we can do the same thing for right join:

```
pd.merge(d4, d5, how='right')
```

```
In [223]: pd.merge(d4, d5, how='right')

Out[223]:
```

	InvoiceNo	StockCode	Description	Quantity
0	536367	22745	POPPY'S PLAYHOUSE BEDROOM	6
1	NaN	22748	POPPY'S PLAYHOUSE KITCHEN	6
2	NaN	22749	FELTCRAFT PRINCESS CHARLOTTE DOLL	8
3	NaN	22310	IVORY KNITTED MUG COSY	6
4	NaN	84969	BOX OF 6 ASSORTED COLOUR TEASPOONS	6
5	NaN	22623	BOX OF VINTAGE JIGSAW BLOCKS	3
6	NaN	22622	BOX OF VINTAGE ALPHABET BLOCKS	2
7	NaN	21754	HOME BUILDING BLOCK WORD	3
8	NaN	21755	LOVE BUILDING BLOCK WORD	3
9	NaN	21777	RECIPE BOX WITH METAL HEART	4

Now, it uses the column labels of d5 as well as the data of d5 (which spans from elements 10 through 20). As you can see, the data at index 0 is shared with d4, hence why it's completed in this particular table. This is because element number 11 (with index 10) overlaps with the first element of d5 (index 10).

Now we do inner join:

```
pd.merge(d4, d5, how='inner')
```

```
In [224]: pd.merge(d4, d5, how='inner')
Out[224]:
```

	InvoiceNo	StockCode	Description	Quantity
0	536367	22745	POPPY'S PLAYHOUSE BEDROOM	6

Inner join means it only includes elements that both DataFrames have in common. In this case, the element shown there is element number 11, with index 10 in `df`. Because it exists in both `d4` and in `d5`, it has data for both **InvoiceNo** and for **Quantity** (since the data for **InvoiceNo** exists in `d4` and the data for **Quantity** exists in `d5`).

Now, we will do outer join:

```
pd.merge(d4, d5, how='outer')
```

```
In [225]: pd.merge(d4, d5, how='outer')
Out[225]:
```

	InvoiceNo	StockCode	Description	Quantity
0	536365	85123A	WHITE HANGING HEART T-LIGHT HOLDER	NaN
1	536365	71053	WHITE METAL LANTERN	NaN
2	536365	84406B	CREAM CUPID HEARTS COAT HANGER	NaN
3	536365	84029G	KNITTED UNION FLAG HOT WATER BOTTLE	NaN
4	536365	84029E	RED WOOLLY HOTTIE WHITE HEART.	NaN
5	536365	22752	SET 7 BABUSHKA NESTING BOXES	NaN
6	536365	21730	GLASS STAR FROSTED T-LIGHT HOLDER	NaN
7	536366	22633	HAND WARMER UNION JACK	NaN
8	536366	22632	HAND WARMER RED POLKA DOT	NaN
9	536367	84879	ASSORTED COLOUR BIRD ORNAMENT	NaN
10	536367	22745	POPPY'S PLAYHOUSE BEDROOM	6.0
11	NaN	22748	POPPY'S PLAYHOUSE KITCHEN	6.0
12	NaN	22749	FELTCRAFT PRINCESS CHARLOTTE DOLL	8.0
13	NaN	22310	IVORY KNITTED MUG COSY	6.0
14	NaN	84969	BOX OF 6 ASSORTED COLOUR TEASPOONS	6.0
15	NaN	22623	BOX OF VINTAGE JIGSAW BLOCKS	3.0
16	NaN	22622	BOX OF VINTAGE ALPHABET BLOCKS	2.0
17	NaN	21754	HOME BUILDING BLOCK WORD	3.0
18	NaN	21755	LOVE BUILDING BLOCK WORD	3.0
19	NaN	21777	RECIPE BOX WITH METAL HEART	4.0

As you can see, outer join means it includes all columns (the union of the columns in `d4` and in `d5`).

Any data values that don't exist are labeled NaN. For example, there is no column labeled **InvoiceNo** in `d5`, so all the data values there are shown as NaN.

Now, let's talk about joining on a column. We can introduce a new parameter, `on=`, in our function call. Here is an example of merging on the **StockCode** column:

```
pd.merge(d4, d5, on='StockCode', how='left')
```

```
In [227]: pd.merge(d4, d5, on='StockCode', how='left')
```

Out[227]:

	InvoiceNo	StockCode	Description_x	Description_y	Quantity
0	536365	85123A	WHITE HANGING HEART T-LIGHT HOLDER	NaN	NaN
1	536365	71053	WHITE METAL LANTERN	NaN	NaN
2	536365	84406B	CREAM CUPID HEARTS COAT HANGER	NaN	NaN
3	536365	84029G	KNITTED UNION FLAG HOT WATER BOTTLE	NaN	NaN
4	536365	84029E	RED WOOLLY HOTTIE WHITE HEART.	NaN	NaN
5	536365	22752	SET 7 BABUSHKA NESTING BOXES	NaN	NaN
6	536365	21730	GLASS STAR FROSTED T-LIGHT HOLDER	NaN	NaN
7	536366	22633	HAND WARMER UNION JACK	NaN	NaN
8	536366	22632	HAND WARMER RED POLKA DOT	NaN	NaN
9	536367	84879	ASSORTED COLOUR BIRD ORNAMENT	NaN	NaN
10	536367	22745	POPPY'S PLAYHOUSE BEDROOM	POPPY'S PLAYHOUSE BEDROOM	6.0

The graph is similar to the table generated when we merge `d4` and `d5` using left join. However, the exception is that since **Description** is a column shared by both `d4` and `d5`, it adds both of them but distinguishes between them with **_x** and **_y** respectively.

As you can see in the last entry, it is shared by both `d4` and `d5`, so both **Description_x** and **Description_y** are the same.

Remember, we can only enter column names that both DataFrames share in common. So, we can do either **StockCode** or **Description** to merge on.

This is what it looks like if we merge on **Description** instead:

```
pd.merge(d4, d5, on='Description', how='left')
```

```
In [228]: pd.merge(d4, d5, on='Description', how='left')

Out[228]:
```

	InvoiceNo	StockCode_x	Description	StockCode_y	Quantity
0	536365	85123A	WHITE HANGING HEART T-LIGHT HOLDER	NaN	NaN
1	536365	71053	WHITE METAL LANTERN	NaN	NaN
2	536365	84406B	CREAM CUPID HEARTS COAT HANGER	NaN	NaN
3	536365	84029G	KNITTED UNION FLAG HOT WATER BOTTLE	NaN	NaN
4	536365	84029E	RED WOOLLY HOTTIE WHITE HEART.	NaN	NaN
5	536365	22752	SET 7 BABUSHKA NESTING BOXES	NaN	NaN
6	536365	21730	GLASS STAR FROSTED T-LIGHT HOLDER	NaN	NaN
7	536366	22633	HAND WARMER UNION JACK	NaN	NaN
8	536366	22632	HAND WARMER RED POLKA DOT	NaN	NaN
9	536367	84879	ASSORTED COLOUR BIRD ORNAMENT	NaN	NaN
10	536367	22745	POPPY'S PLAYHOUSE BEDROOM	22745	6.0

Again, it distinguishes between the column that they both share by adding **_x** and **_y** respectively to represent `d4` and `d5`.

We can actually pass in a list of column names instead of a single column name. So, now we have:

```
pd.merge(d4, d5, on=['StockCode', 'Description'], how='left')
```

```
In [229]: pd.merge d4, d5, on=['StockCode', 'Description'], how='left'
```

Out[229]:

	InvoiceNo	StockCode	Description	Quantity
0	536365	85123A	WHITE HANGING HEART T-LIGHT HOLDER	NaN
1	536365	71053	WHITE METAL LANTERN	NaN
2	536365	84406B	CREAM CUPID HEARTS COAT HANGER	NaN
3	536365	84029G	KNITTED UNION FLAG HOT WATER BOTTLE	NaN
4	536365	84029E	RED WOOLLY HOTTIE WHITE HEART.	NaN
5	536365	22752	SET 7 BABUSHKA NESTING BOXES	NaN
6	536365	21730	GLASS STAR FROSTED T-LIGHT HOLDER	NaN
7	536366	22633	HAND WARMER UNION JACK	NaN
8	536366	22632	HAND WARMER RED POLKA DOT	NaN
9	536367	84879	ASSORTED COLOUR BIRD ORNAMENT	NaN
10	536367	22745	POPPY'S PLAYHOUSE BEDROOM	6.0

However, in this case, we can see that this is the same table as:

```
pd.merge(d4, d5, how='left')
```

That's because in this particular case, the list we passed in contained all the column names both of them shared. This would not be the case if they shared three columns and we only passed in two.

To illustrate that, suppose this:

```
d4 = pd.DataFrame(df, columns=['InvoiceNo', 'StockCode', 'Description',
'UnitPrice'])[0:11]
d5 = pd.DataFrame(df, columns=['StockCode', 'Description', 'Quantity',
'UnitPrice'])[10:20]
```

Now, let's try this again:

```
pd.merge(d4, d5, on=['StockCode', 'Description'], how='left')
```

So, now our table will look like:

```
In [232]: pd.merge d4, d5, on=['StockCode', 'Description'], how='left'
```

Out[232]:

	InvoiceNo	StockCode	Description	UnitPrice_x	Quantity	UnitPrice_y
0	536365	85123A	WHITE HANGING HEART T-LIGHT HOLDER	2.55	NaN	NaN
1	536365	71053	WHITE METAL LANTERN	3.39	NaN	NaN
2	536365	84406B	CREAM CUPID HEARTS COAT HANGER	2.75	NaN	NaN
3	536365	84029G	KNITTED UNION FLAG HOT WATER BOTTLE	3.39	NaN	NaN
4	536365	84029E	RED WOOLLY HOTTIE WHITE HEART.	3.39	NaN	NaN
5	536365	22752	SET 7 BABUSHKA NESTING BOXES	7.65	NaN	NaN
6	536365	21730	GLASS STAR FROSTED T-LIGHT HOLDER	4.25	NaN	NaN
7	536366	22633	HAND WARMER UNION JACK	1.85	NaN	NaN
8	536366	22632	HAND WARMER RED POLKA DOT	1.85	NaN	NaN
9	536367	84879	ASSORTED COLOUR BIRD ORNAMENT	1.69	NaN	NaN
10	536367	22745	POPPY'S PLAYHOUSE BEDROOM	2.10	6.0	2.1

We can also specify that we want all columns to be present, even the shared ones.

Consider this:

```
pd.merge(d4, d5, left_index = True, right_index=True, how='outer')
```

You can specify any type of joining that you want, and it will still display all the columns. However, in this example, it will be using an outer join:

```
In [237]: pd.merge d4, d5, left_index = True, right_index=True, how='outer'
```

Out[237]:

	InvoiceNo	StockCode_x	Description_x	UnitPrice_x	StockCode_y	Description_y	Quantity	UnitPrice_y
0	536365	85123A	WHITE HANGING HEART T-LIGHT HOLDER	2.55	NaN	NaN	NaN	NaN
1	536365	71053	WHITE METAL LANTERN	3.39	NaN	NaN	NaN	NaN
2	536365	84406B	CREAM CUPID HEARTS COAT HANGER	2.75	NaN	NaN	NaN	NaN
3	536365	84029G	KNITTED UNION FLAG HOT WATER BOTTLE	3.39	NaN	NaN	NaN	NaN
4	536365	84029E	RED WOOLLY HOTTIE WHITE HEART.	3.39	NaN	NaN	NaN	NaN
5	536365	22752	SET 7 BABUSHKA NESTING BOXES	7.65	NaN	NaN	NaN	NaN
6	536365	21730	GLASS STAR FROSTED T-LIGHT HOLDER	4.25	NaN	NaN	NaN	NaN
7	536366	22633	HAND WARMER UNION JACK	1.85	NaN	NaN	NaN	NaN
8	536366	22632	HAND WARMER RED POLKA DOT	1.85	NaN	NaN	NaN	NaN
9	536367	84879	ASSORTED COLOUR BIRD ORNAMENT	1.69	NaN	NaN	NaN	NaN
10	536367	22745	POPPY'S PLAYHOUSE BEDROOM	2.10	22745	POPPY'S PLAYHOUSE BEDROOM	6.0	2.10
11	NaN	NaN	NaN	NaN	22748	POPPY'S PLAYHOUSE KITCHEN	6.0	2.10
12	NaN	NaN	NaN	NaN	22749	FELTCRAFT PRINCESS CHARLOTTE DOLL	8.0	3.75
13	NaN	NaN	NaN	NaN	22310	IVORY KNITTED MUG COSY	6.0	1.65
14	NaN	NaN	NaN	NaN	84969	BOX OF 6 ASSORTED COLOUR TEASPOONS	6.0	4.25
15	NaN	NaN	NaN	NaN	22623	BOX OF VINTAGE JIGSAW BLOCKS	3.0	4.95
16	NaN	NaN	NaN	NaN	22622	BOX OF VINTAGE ALPHABET BLOCKS	2.0	9.95
17	NaN	NaN	NaN	NaN	21754	HOME BUILDING BLOCK WORD	3.0	5.95
18	NaN	NaN	NaN	NaN	21755	LOVE BUILDING BLOCK WORD	3.0	5.95
19	NaN	NaN	NaN	NaN	21777	RECIPE BOX WITH METAL HEART	4.0	7.95

Now, we can move on to the `join()` function. One thing to note is that it will not allow us to join two DataFrames if they share a column name. So, the following is not allowed:

```
d4 = pd.DataFrame(df, columns=['StockCode', 'Description',
'UnitPrice'])[0:11]
d5 = pd.DataFrame(df, columns=[ 'Description', 'Quantity',
'InvoiceNo'])[10:20]
d4.join(d5)
```

Otherwise, it would result in an error.

Now, look at the following lines of code:

```
d4 = pd.DataFrame(df, columns=['StockCode', 'UnitPrice'])[0:11]
d5 = pd.DataFrame(df, columns=[ 'Description', 'Quantity'])[10:20]
d4.join(d5)
```

That would result in this table:

```
In [242]: d4 = pd.DataFrame(df, columns=['StockCode', 'UnitPrice'])[0:11]
          d5 = pd.DataFrame(df, columns=[ 'Description', 'Quantity'])[10:20]
          d4.join d5
```

Out[242]:

	StockCode	UnitPrice	Description	Quantity
0	85123A	2.55	NaN	NaN
1	71053	3.39	NaN	NaN
2	84406B	2.75	NaN	NaN
3	84029G	3.39	NaN	NaN
4	84029E	3.39	NaN	NaN
5	22752	7.65	NaN	NaN
6	21730	4.25	NaN	NaN
7	22633	1.85	NaN	NaN
8	22632	1.85	NaN	NaN
9	84879	1.69	NaN	NaN
10	22745	2.10	POPPY'S PLAYHOUSE BEDROOM	6.0

So it takes the `d4` table and adds the columns and corresponding data from `d5`. Since `d5` has no data for description or quantity from indices 0 through 9, they are all displayed as NaN. Since `d5` and `d4` both share data for index 10, that element has all its data displayed in the corresponding columns.

We can also join them the other way around:

```
d4 = pd.DataFrame(df, columns=['StockCode', 'UnitPrice'])[0:11]
d5 = pd.DataFrame(df, columns=[ 'Description', 'Quantity'])[10:20]
d5.join(d4)
```

```
In [243]: d4 = pd.DataFrame(df, columns=['StockCode', 'UnitPrice'])[0:11]
          d5 = pd.DataFrame(df, columns=[ 'Description', 'Quantity'])[10:20]
          d5.join d4
Out[243]:
```

	Description	Quantity	StockCode	UnitPrice
10	POPPY'S PLAYHOUSE BEDROOM	6	22745	2.1
11	POPPY'S PLAYHOUSE KITCHEN	6	NaN	NaN
12	FELTCRAFT PRINCESS CHARLOTTE DOLL	8	NaN	NaN
13	IVORY KNITTED MUG COSY	6	NaN	NaN
14	BOX OF 6 ASSORTED COLOUR TEASPOONS	6	NaN	NaN
15	BOX OF VINTAGE JIGSAW BLOCKS	3	NaN	NaN
16	BOX OF VINTAGE ALPHABET BLOCKS	2	NaN	NaN
17	HOME BUILDING BLOCK WORD	3	NaN	NaN
18	LOVE BUILDING BLOCK WORD	3	NaN	NaN
19	RECIPE BOX WITH METAL HEART	4	NaN	NaN

It's the same logic, except the columns of `d4` and corresponding data are added onto the table for `d5`.

Next, we can combine the data using `combine_first()`.

Look at the following code:

```
d6 = pd.DataFrame.copy(df)[0:5]
d7 = pd.DataFrame.copy(df)[2:8]


d6.loc[3, ['Quantity']] = 110
d6.loc[4, ['Quantity']] = 110

d7.loc[3, ['Quantity']] = 210
d7.loc[4, ['Quantity']] = 210
pd.concat([d6, d7], keys=['d6', 'd7'])
```

The `.copy` added after `pd.DataFrame` ensures that we make a copy of the original `df` as opposed to editing the original `df` itself. That way, `d6` changing the quantity to `110` for indices `3` and `4` shouldn't affect `d7`, and vice versa. Keep in mind, this won't work if you pass in a list of columns to select, so you can't have something like:

```
pd.DataFrame(df, columns=['Quantity', 'UnitPrice'])
```

After running the preceding code, this is the resulting table:

```
In [59]: d6 = pd.DataFrame.copy(df)[0:5]
         d7 = pd.DataFrame.copy(df)[2:8]

         d6.loc[3, ['Quantity']] = 110
         d6.loc[4, ['Quantity']] = 110

         d7.loc[3, ['Quantity']] = 210
         d7.loc[4, ['Quantity']] = 210
         pd.concat([d6, d7], keys=['d6', 'd7'])
```

Out[59]:

		InvoiceNo	StockCode	Description	Quantity	InvoiceDate	UnitPrice	CustomerID	Country
d6	0	536365	85123A	WHITE HANGING HEART T-LIGHT HOLDER	6	12/1/10 8:26	2.55	17850.0	United Kingdom
	1	536365	71053	WHITE METAL LANTERN	6	12/1/10 8:26	3.39	17850.0	United Kingdom
	2	536365	84406B	CREAM CUPID HEARTS COAT HANGER	8	12/1/10 8:26	2.75	17850.0	United Kingdom
	3	536365	84029G	KNITTED UNION FLAG HOT WATER BOTTLE	110	12/1/10 8:26	3.39	17850.0	United Kingdom
	4	536365	84029E	RED WOOLLY HOTTIE WHITE HEART.	110	12/1/10 8:26	3.39	17850.0	United Kingdom
d7	2	536365	84406B	CREAM CUPID HEARTS COAT HANGER	8	12/1/10 8:26	2.75	17850.0	United Kingdom
	3	536365	84029G	KNITTED UNION FLAG HOT WATER BOTTLE	210	12/1/10 8:26	3.39	17850.0	United Kingdom
	4	536365	84029E	RED WOOLLY HOTTIE WHITE HEART.	210	12/1/10 8:26	3.39	17850.0	United Kingdom
	5	536365	22752	SET 7 BABUSHKA NESTING BOXES	2	12/1/10 8:26	7.65	17850.0	United Kingdom
	6	536365	21730	GLASS STAR FROSTED T-LIGHT HOLDER	6	12/1/10 8:26	4.25	17850.0	United Kingdom
	7	536366	22633	HAND WARMER UNION JACK	6	12/1/10 8:28	1.85	17850.0	United Kingdom

Notice that both `d6` and `d7` have elements in common, namely the elements with indices 2 through 4.

Now, take a look at this code:

```
d6.combine_first(d7)
```

```
In [61]: d6.combine_first d7
```

Out[61]:

	InvoiceNo	StockCode	Description	Quantity	InvoiceDate	UnitPrice	CustomerID	Country
0	536365	85123A	WHITE HANGING HEART T-LIGHT HOLDER	6.0	12/1/10 8:26	2.55	17850.0	United Kingdom
1	536365	71053	WHITE METAL LANTERN	6.0	12/1/10 8:26	3.39	17850.0	United Kingdom
2	536365	84406B	CREAM CUPID HEARTS COAT HANGER	8.0	12/1/10 8:26	2.75	17850.0	United Kingdom
3	536365	84029G	KNITTED UNION FLAG HOT WATER BOTTLE	110.0	12/1/10 8:26	3.39	17850.0	United Kingdom
4	536365	84029E	RED WOOLLY HOTTIE WHITE HEART.	110.0	12/1/10 8:26	3.39	17850.0	United Kingdom
5	536365	22752	SET 7 BABUSHKA NESTING BOXES	2.0	12/1/10 8:26	7.65	17850.0	United Kingdom
6	536365	21730	GLASS STAR FROSTED T-LIGHT HOLDER	6.0	12/1/10 8:26	4.25	17850.0	United Kingdom
7	536366	22633	HAND WARMER UNION JACK	6.0	12/1/10 8:28	1.85	17850.0	United Kingdom

What this did was combine the data of `d7` data with that of `d6`, but with preference given to `d6`. Remember that we set the quantity of indices 3 and 4 to `110` in `d6`. As you can see, the data of `d6` was kept where both datasets had indices in common. Now look at this line of code:

```
d7.combine_first(d6)
```

```
In [63]: d7.combine_first d6
```

Out[63]:

	InvoiceNo	StockCode	Description	Quantity	InvoiceDate	UnitPrice	CustomerID	Country
0	536365	85123A	WHITE HANGING HEART T-LIGHT HOLDER	6.0	12/1/10 8:26	2.55	17850.0	United Kingdom
1	536365	71053	WHITE METAL LANTERN	6.0	12/1/10 8:26	3.39	17850.0	United Kingdom
2	536365	84406B	CREAM CUPID HEARTS COAT HANGER	8.0	12/1/10 8:26	2.75	17850.0	United Kingdom
3	536365	84029G	KNITTED UNION FLAG HOT WATER BOTTLE	210.0	12/1/10 8:26	3.39	17850.0	United Kingdom
4	536365	84029E	RED WOOLLY HOTTIE WHITE HEART.	210.0	12/1/10 8:26	3.39	17850.0	United Kingdom
5	536365	22752	SET 7 BABUSHKA NESTING BOXES	2.0	12/1/10 8:26	7.65	17850.0	United Kingdom
6	536365	21730	GLASS STAR FROSTED T-LIGHT HOLDER	6.0	12/1/10 8:26	4.25	17850.0	United Kingdom
7	536366	22633	HAND WARMER UNION JACK	6.0	12/1/10 8:28	1.85	17850.0	United Kingdom

Now you'll see that where both elements had indices in common (at indices 3 and 4), the data of `d7` was kept.

You can also get the occurrence counts of every value in a category of choice using `value_counts()`. Take a look at this code:

```
pd.value_counts(df['Country'])
```

```
In [8]: pd.value_counts(df['Country'])

Out[8]: United Kingdom     61186
        Germany              982
        France               967
        EIRE                 504
        Spain                355
        Portugal             212
        Netherlands          186
        Switzerland          175
        Norway               147
        Australia            142
        Belgium              142
        Italy                112
        Cyprus                99
        Japan                 69
        Sweden                41
        Lithuania             35
        Poland                33
        Iceland               31
        Denmark               20
        Channel Islands       17
        Finland               17
        Israel                16
        Austria                9
        Bahrain                2
        Name: Country, dtype: int64
```

One thing to consider during your merges is the fact that you might come across duplicate data values. To resolve these, use `.drop_duplicates()`.

Consider this:

```
d1 = pd.DataFrame(df, columns = ['InvoiceNo', 'StockCode',
'Description'])[0:100]
d2 = pd.DataFrame(df, columns = ['Description', 'InvoiceDate',
'Quantity'])[0:100]

pd.merge(d1, d2)
```

```
In [48]: d1 = pd.DataFrame(df, columns = ['InvoiceNo', 'StockCode', 'Description'])[0:100]
         d2 = pd.DataFrame(df, columns = ['Description', 'InvoiceDate', 'Quantity'])[0:100]

         pd.merge(d1, d2)

Out[48]:
```

	InvoiceNo	StockCode	Description	InvoiceDate	Quantity
0	536365	85123A	WHITE HANGING HEART T-LIGHT HOLDER	12/1/10 8:26	6
1	536365	85123A	WHITE HANGING HEART T-LIGHT HOLDER	12/1/10 9:02	6
2	536365	85123A	WHITE HANGING HEART T-LIGHT HOLDER	12/1/10 9:32	6
3	536373	85123A	WHITE HANGING HEART T-LIGHT HOLDER	12/1/10 8:26	6
4	536373	85123A	WHITE HANGING HEART T-LIGHT HOLDER	12/1/10 9:02	6
5	536373	85123A	WHITE HANGING HEART T-LIGHT HOLDER	12/1/10 9:32	6
6	536375	85123A	WHITE HANGING HEART T-LIGHT HOLDER	12/1/10 8:26	6
7	536375	85123A	WHITE HANGING HEART T-LIGHT HOLDER	12/1/10 9:02	6
8	536375	85123A	WHITE HANGING HEART T-LIGHT HOLDER	12/1/10 9:32	6
9	536365	71053	WHITE METAL LANTERN	12/1/10 8:26	6
10	536365	71053	WHITE METAL LANTERN	12/1/10 9:02	6
11	536365	71053	WHITE METAL LANTERN	12/1/10 9:32	6
12	536373	71053	WHITE METAL LANTERN	12/1/10 8:26	6
13	536373	71053	WHITE METAL LANTERN	12/1/10 9:02	6
14	536373	71053	WHITE METAL LANTERN	12/1/10 9:32	6
15	536375	71053	WHITE METAL LANTERN	12/1/10 8:26	6
16	536375	71053	WHITE METAL LANTERN	12/1/10 9:02	6
17	536375	71053	WHITE METAL LANTERN	12/1/10 9:32	6
18	536365	84406B	CREAM CUPID HEARTS COAT HANGER	12/1/10 8:26	8
19	536365	84406B	CREAM CUPID HEARTS COAT HANGER	12/1/10 9:02	8
20	536365	84406B	CREAM CUPID HEARTS COAT HANGER	12/1/10 9:32	8
21	536373	84406B	CREAM CUPID HEARTS COAT HANGER	12/1/10 8:26	8

And if we scroll all the way to the bottom:

158	536378	22386	JUMBO BAG PINK POLKADOT	12/1/10 9:37	10
159	536378	85099C	JUMBO BAG BAROQUE BLACK WHITE	12/1/10 9:37	10
160	536378	21033	JUMBO BAG CHARLIE AND LOLA TOYS	12/1/10 9:37	10
161	536378	20723	STRAWBERRY CHARLOTTE BAG	12/1/10 9:37	10
162	536378	84997B	RED 3 PIECE RETROSPOT CUTLERY SET	12/1/10 9:37	12
163	536378	84997C	BLUE 3 PIECE POLKADOT CUTLERY SET	12/1/10 9:37	6
164	536378	21094	SET/6 RED SPOTTY PAPER PLATES	12/1/10 9:37	12
165	536378	20725	LUNCH BAG RED RETROSPOT	12/1/10 9:37	10
166	536378	21559	STRAWBERRY LUNCH BOX WITH CUTLERY	12/1/10 9:37	6
167	536378	22352	LUNCH BOX WITH CUTLERY RETROSPOT	12/1/10 9:37	6
168	536378	21212	PACK OF 72 RETROSPOT CAKE CASES	12/1/10 9:37	120
169	536378	21975	PACK OF 60 DINOSAUR CAKE CASES	12/1/10 9:37	24
170	536378	21977	PACK OF 60 PINK PAISLEY CAKE CASES	12/1/10 9:37	24
171	536378	84991	60 TEATIME FAIRY CAKE CASES	12/1/10 9:37	24

172 rows × 5 columns

As you can see, there are many duplicate data entries. To remove them all, we can use `drop_duplicates()`. In addition, we can specify what column data we can use to determine which entries are duplicates to be removed. For example, we can use `StockCode` to remove all duplicate entries, assuming that each item has a unique stock code. We could also assume a unique description for each item and remove items that way. So, now look at this code:

```
d1 = pd.DataFrame(df, columns = ['InvoiceNo', 'StockCode',
'Description'])[0:100]
d2 = pd.DataFrame(df, columns = ['Description', 'InvoiceDate',
'Quantity'])[0:100]

pd.merge(d1, d2).drop_duplicates(['StockCode'])
```

```
In [62]: d1 = pd.DataFrame(df, columns = ['InvoiceNo', 'StockCode', 'Description'])[0:100]
         d2 = pd.DataFrame(df, columns = ['Description', 'InvoiceDate', 'Quantity'])[0:100]

         pd.merge(d1, d2).drop_duplicates(['StockCode'])
```

Out[62]:

	InvoiceNo	StockCode	Description	InvoiceDate	Quantity
0	536365	85123A	WHITE HANGING HEART T-LIGHT HOLDER	12/1/10 8:26	6
9	536365	71053	WHITE METAL LANTERN	12/1/10 8:26	6
18	536365	84406B	CREAM CUPID HEARTS COAT HANGER	12/1/10 8:26	8
27	536365	84029G	KNITTED UNION FLAG HOT WATER BOTTLE	12/1/10 8:26	6
36	536365	84029E	RED WOOLLY HOTTIE WHITE HEART.	12/1/10 8:26	6
45	536365	22752	SET 7 BABUSHKA NESTING BOXES	12/1/10 8:26	2
54	536365	21730	GLASS STAR FROSTED T-LIGHT HOLDER	12/1/10 8:26	6
63	536366	22633	HAND WARMER UNION JACK	12/1/10 8:28	6
72	536366	22632	HAND WARMER RED POLKA DOT	12/1/10 8:28	6
81	536367	84879	ASSORTED COLOUR BIRD ORNAMENT	12/1/10 8:34	32
82	536367	22745	POPPY'S PLAYHOUSE BEDROOM	12/1/10 8:34	6
83	536367	22748	POPPY'S PLAYHOUSE KITCHEN	12/1/10 8:34	6
84	536367	22749	FELTCRAFT PRINCESS CHARLOTTE DOLL	12/1/10 8:34	8
85	536367	22310	IVORY KNITTED MUG COSY	12/1/10 8:34	6
86	536367	84969	BOX OF 6 ASSORTED COLOUR TEASPOONS	12/1/10 8:34	6
87	536367	22623	BOX OF VINTAGE JIGSAW BLOCKS	12/1/10 8:34	3
88	536367	22622	BOX OF VINTAGE ALPHABET BLOCKS	12/1/10 8:34	2

And if we scroll to the bottom:

165	536378	20725	LUNCH BAG RED RETROSPOT	12/1/10 9:37	10
166	536378	21559	STRAWBERRY LUNCH BOX WITH CUTLERY	12/1/10 9:37	6
167	536378	22352	LUNCH BOX WITH CUTLERY RETROSPOT	12/1/10 9:37	6
168	536378	21212	PACK OF 72 RETROSPOT CAKE CASES	12/1/10 9:37	120
169	536378	21975	PACK OF 60 DINOSAUR CAKE CASES	12/1/10 9:37	24
170	536378	21977	PACK OF 60 PINK PAISLEY CAKE CASES	12/1/10 9:37	24
171	536378	84991	60 TEATIME FAIRY CAKE CASES	12/1/10 9:37	24

73 rows × 5 columns

You will see that many duplicate entries are removed. We could have also passed in either `Description`, `StockCode`, or `Description` and it would have yielded the same results.

You'll notice then that the indices are all over the place. We can use `reset_index()` to fix it. Look at the following code:

```
d1 = pd.DataFrame(df, columns = ['InvoiceNo', 'StockCode',
'Description'])[0:100]
d2 = pd.DataFrame(df, columns = ['Description', 'InvoiceDate',
'Quantity'])[0:100]

d3 = pd.merge(d1, d2).drop_duplicates(['StockCode'])
d3.reset_index()
```

This is what that will look like:

```
In [66]: d3.reset_index()
Out[66]:
```

	index	InvoiceNo	StockCode	Description	InvoiceDate	Quantity
0	0	536365	85123A	WHITE HANGING HEART T-LIGHT HOLDER	12/1/10 8:26	6
1	9	536365	71053	WHITE METAL LANTERN	12/1/10 8:26	6
2	18	536365	84406B	CREAM CUPID HEARTS COAT HANGER	12/1/10 8:26	8
3	27	536365	84029G	KNITTED UNION FLAG HOT WATER BOTTLE	12/1/10 8:26	6
4	36	536365	84029E	RED WOOLLY HOTTIE WHITE HEART.	12/1/10 8:26	6
5	45	536365	22752	SET 7 BABUSHKA NESTING BOXES	12/1/10 8:26	2
6	54	536365	21730	GLASS STAR FROSTED T-LIGHT HOLDER	12/1/10 8:26	6
7	63	536366	22633	HAND WARMER UNION JACK	12/1/10 8:28	6
8	72	536366	22632	HAND WARMER RED POLKA DOT	12/1/10 8:28	6
9	81	536367	84879	ASSORTED COLOUR BIRD ORNAMENT	12/1/10 8:34	32
10	82	536367	22745	POPPY'S PLAYHOUSE BEDROOM	12/1/10 8:34	6
11	83	536367	22748	POPPY'S PLAYHOUSE KITCHEN	12/1/10 8:34	6
12	84	536367	22749	FELTCRAFT PRINCESS CHARLOTTE DOLL	12/1/10 8:34	8
13	85	536367	22310	IVORY KNITTED MUG COSY	12/1/10 8:34	6
14	86	536367	84969	BOX OF 6 ASSORTED COLOUR TEASPOONS	12/1/10 8:34	6

Now clearly, that is not what you probably had in mind. It reset the index, yes, but it added the old index as a column. There is a simple fix, and that is to introduce a new parameter. Now, look at this code:

```
d3.reset_index(drop=True)
```

```
In [67]: d3.reset_index drop=True
Out[67]:
```

	InvoiceNo	StockCode	Description	InvoiceDate	Quantity
0	536365	85123A	WHITE HANGING HEART T-LIGHT HOLDER	12/1/10 8:26	6
1	536365	71053	WHITE METAL LANTERN	12/1/10 8:26	6
2	536365	84406B	CREAM CUPID HEARTS COAT HANGER	12/1/10 8:26	8
3	536365	84029G	KNITTED UNION FLAG HOT WATER BOTTLE	12/1/10 8:26	6
4	536365	84029E	RED WOOLLY HOTTIE WHITE HEART.	12/1/10 8:26	6
5	536365	22752	SET 7 BABUSHKA NESTING BOXES	12/1/10 8:26	2
6	536365	21730	GLASS STAR FROSTED T-LIGHT HOLDER	12/1/10 8:26	6
7	536366	22633	HAND WARMER UNION JACK	12/1/10 8:28	6
8	536366	22632	HAND WARMER RED POLKA DOT	12/1/10 8:28	6
9	536367	84879	ASSORTED COLOUR BIRD ORNAMENT	12/1/10 8:34	32
10	536367	22745	POPPY'S PLAYHOUSE BEDROOM	12/1/10 8:34	6
11	536367	22748	POPPY'S PLAYHOUSE KITCHEN	12/1/10 8:34	6
12	536367	22749	FELTCRAFT PRINCESS CHARLOTTE DOLL	12/1/10 8:34	8
13	536367	22310	IVORY KNITTED MUG COSY	12/1/10 8:34	6
14	536367	84969	BOX OF 6 ASSORTED COLOUR TEASPOONS	12/1/10 8:34	6
15	536367	22623	BOX OF VINTAGE JIGSAW BLOCKS	12/1/10 8:34	3
16	536367	22622	BOX OF VINTAGE ALPHABET BLOCKS	12/1/10 8:34	2
17	536367	21754	HOME BUILDING BLOCK WORD	12/1/10 8:34	3
18	536367	21755	LOVE BUILDING BLOCK WORD	12/1/10 8:34	3

Much better. By default, `drop=False`, so if you don't want the old index to be added to the data as a new column, then remember to set `drop=True`.

You may remember the `.plot()` function from earlier. You can use this to help visualize DataFrames, especially if they are large.

Here is one such example involving a single column:

```
d8 = pd.DataFrame(df, columns=['Quantity'])[0:100]
d8.plot()
```

Here, only the first 100 elements are selected to make the graph less crowded and illustrate the example better.

Now, you'll have:

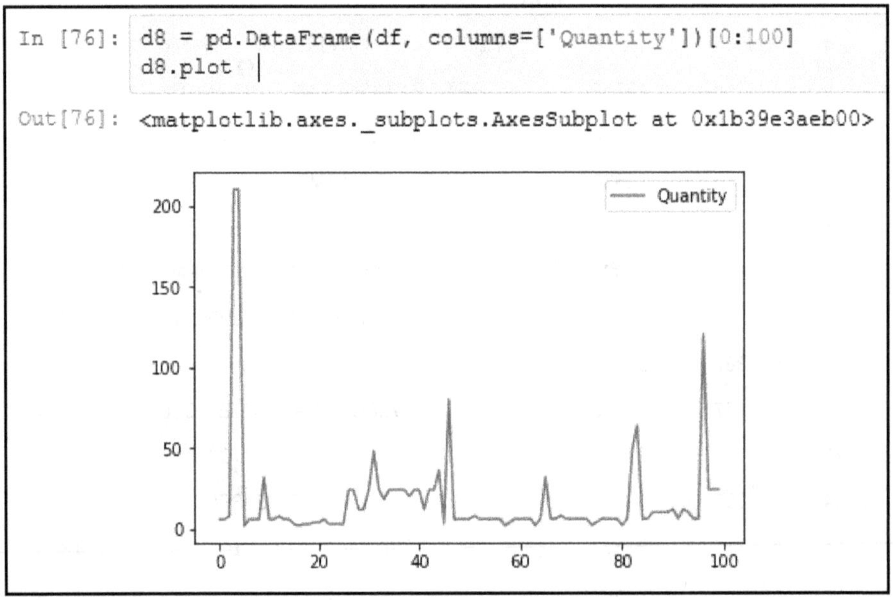

Now, suppose that you want multiple columns to show up. Look at the following:

```
d8 = pd.DataFrame(df, columns=['Quantity', 'UnitPrice'])[0:100]
d8.plot()
```

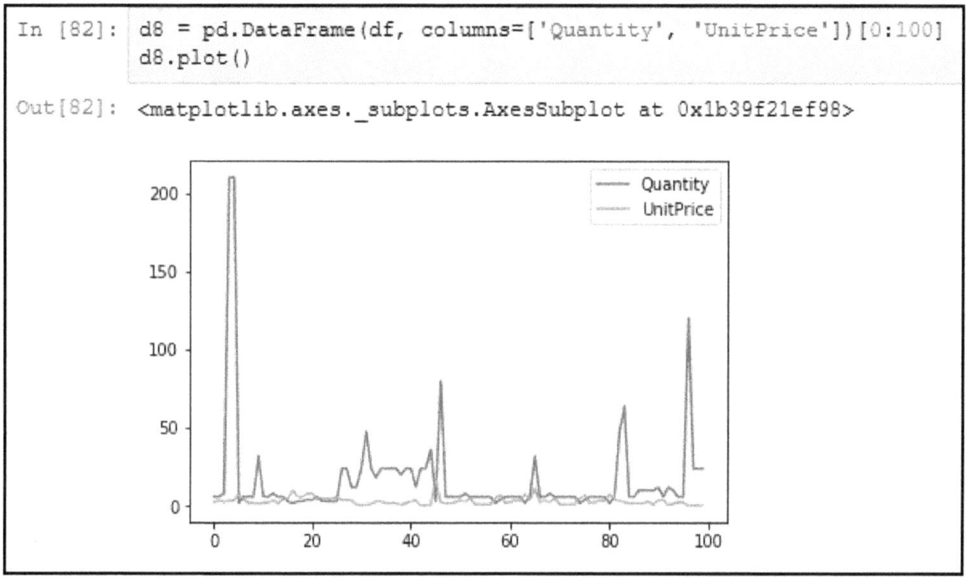

Just remember that it will not plot qualitative data columns such as **Description**, but only things that can be graphed such as **Quantity** and **UnitPrice**.

Summary

In this chapter, we have discussed Python and how to use Python to perform data analysis with Jupyter Notebook. We also looked at several different operations that can be done using Python.

In the next chapter, we will look at another popular analytical language, R, and how R can be used to perform data analysis.

5 Statistical Big Data Computing with R and Hadoop

This chapter provides an introduction to R and how to use R to perform statistical computing on big data using Hadoop. We will see alternatives ranging from open source R on workstations to parallelized commercial products such as Revolution R Enterprise, and many other options in between will present themselves. Between these extremes lie a range of options with unique abilities: scaling data, performance, capability, and ease of use. And so, the right choice or choices depend on your data size, budget, skill, patience, and governance limitations.

In this chapter, we will summarize the alternatives and some of their advantages using pure open source R. Also, we will describe the options for achieving even greater scale, speed, stability, and ease of development by combining open source and commercial technologies.

In a nutshell, the following topics will be covered in this chapter:

- Introduction to integrating R with Hadoop
- Methods of integrating R and Hadoop
- Data analytics with R

Introduction

This chapter is written to help current R users who are novices in Hadoop understand and select solutions to evaluate. As with most things open source, the first consideration is of course monetary. Isn't it always? The good news is that there are multiple alternatives that are free, and additional capabilities are under development in various open source projects.

We generally see four options for building R and Hadoop integration using entirely open source stacks:

- Install R on workstations and connect to the data in Hadoop
- Install R on a shared server and connect to Hadoop
- Utilize Revolution R Open
- Execute R inside of MapReduce using RMR2

Let's walk through each option in detail in the following sections.

Install R on workstations and connect to the data in Hadoop

This baseline approach's greatest advantage is simplicity and cost. It's free. End to end free. What else in life is? Through the packages Revolution contributed as open source, including `rhdfs` and `rhbase`, R users can directly ingest data from both the `hdfs` filesystem and the `hbase` database subsystems in Hadoop. Both connectors are part of the RHadoop package created and maintained by Revolution and are the go-to choice.

Additional options exist as well. The RHive package executes Hive's HQL (SQL-like query language) directly from R, and provides functions for retrieving metadata from Hive, such as database names, table names, column names, and so on. The `rhive` package, in particular, has the advantage that its data operations some work to be pushed down into Hadoop, avoiding data movement and parallelizing operations for big speed increases. A similar push-down can be achieved with `rhbase` as well. However, neither are particularly rich environments, and complex analytical problems will invariably reveal some gaps in capability.

Beyond the somewhat limited push-down capabilities, R's best at working on modest data sampled from `hdfs`, `hbase`, or `hive`; in this way, current R users can get going with Hadoop quickly.

Install R on a shared server and connect to Hadoop

Once you're tired of R's memory barriers on your laptop, the obvious next path is a shared server. With today's technologies, you can equip a powerful server for only a few thousand dollars and easily share it between a few users. When using Windows or Linux with 256 GB or 512 GB of RAM, R can be used to analyze files up to the hundreds of gigabytes, albeit not as fast as perhaps you'd like.

Like option one, R on a shared server can also leverage the push-down capabilities of the `rhbase` and `rhive` packages to achieve parallelism and avoid data movement. However, as with workstations, the push-down capabilities of `rhive` and `rhbase` are limited.

And of course, while lots of RAM keeps the dreaded out-of-memory exhaustion at bay, it does little for compute performance and depends on sharing the skills learned (or perhaps not learned) in kindergarten. For these reasons, consider a shared server to be a great add-on to R on workstations but not a complete substitute.

Utilize Revolution R Open

Replacing the CRAN download of R with the R distribution **Revolution R Open** (**RRO**) enhances performance further. RRO is, like R itself, open source and 100% R. It is free to download. It accelerates math computations using the Intel Math Kernel Libraries and is 100% compatible with the algorithms in CRAN and other repositories such as BioConductor. No changes are required to R scripts, and the acceleration the MKL libraries offer varies from negligible to an order of magnitude for scripts making intensive use of certain math and linear algebra primitives. You can anticipate that RRO can double your average performance if you're doing math operations in the language. As with options one and two, RRO can be used with connectors such as `rhdfs`, and it can connect and push work down into Hadoop through `rhbase` and `rhive`.

Execute R inside of MapReduce using RMR2

Once you find that your problem set is too big, or your patience is being taxed on a workstation or server and the limitations of `rhbase` and `rhive` push-down are impeding progress, you're ready to run R inside of Hadoop.

The open source RHadoop project includes `rhdfs`, `rhbase`, and `plyrmr`, and also a package called `rmr2` that enables R users to build Hadoop MapReduce operations using R functions. Using mappers, R functions are applied to all the data blocks that compose an `hdfs` file, an `hbase` table, or other datasets; the results can be sent to a reducer, also an R function, for aggregation or analysis. All the work is conducted inside of Hadoop but is built in R. Let's be clear: applying R functions to each `hdfs` file segment is a great way to accelerate computation. But for the most part, it is the avoidance of moving data that really accentuates performance. To do this, `rmr2` applies R functions to the data residing on Hadoop nodes rather than moving the data to where R resides.

While `rmr2` gives essentially unlimited capabilities, as a data scientist or statistician, your thoughts will soon turn to computing entire algorithms in R on large datasets. Using `rmr2` in this way complicates development for the R programmer because he or she must write the entire logic of the desired algorithm or adapt existing CRAN algorithms. He/she must then validate that the algorithm is accurate and reflects the expected mathematical result, and write code for the myriad corner cases such as missing data.

`rmr2` requires coding on your part to manage parallelization. This may be trivial for data transformation operations, aggregates, and so on, or quite tedious if you're trying to train predictive models or build classifiers on large datasets. While `rmr2` can be more tedious than other approaches, it is not untenable, and most R programmers will find `rmr2` much easier than resorting to Java-based development of Hadoop mappers and reducers. While somewhat tedious, it:

- Is fully open source
- Helps to parallelize computation to address larger datasets
- Skips painful data movement
- Is widely used, so you'll find help available
- Is free

`rmr2` is not the only option in this category; a similar package called `rhipe` is also there and provides similar capabilities. `rhipe` is described at `https://www.rhipe.com/download-confirmation/` and is downloadable from GitHub.

Summary and outlook for pure open source options

The range of open source-based options for using R with Hadoop is expanding. The Apache Spark community, for example, is rapidly improving R integration via the predictably named SparkR. Today, SparkR provides access to Spark from R, much as `rmr2` and `rhipe` do for Hadoop MapReduce today.

We expect that in future, the SparkR team will add support for Spark's MLlib machine learning algorithm library, providing execution directly from R. Availability dates haven't been widely published.

Perhaps the most exciting observation is that R has become **table stakes** for platform vendors. Our partners at Cloudera, Hortonworks, MapR, and others, along with database vendors and others, are all keenly aware of the dominance of R in the large and growing data science community, and of R's importance as a means to extract insights and value from the burgeoning data repositories built atop Hadoop.

In a subsequent post, I'll review the options for creating even greater performance, simplicity, portability, and scale available to R users by expanding the scope from open source-only solutions to those like Revolution R Enterprise for Hadoop.

R is an amazing data science programming tool to run statistical data analysis on models and translate the results of analysis into colorful graphics. There is no doubt that R is the most preferred programming tool for statisticians, data scientists, data analysts, and data architects, but it falls short when working with large datasets. One major drawback with the R programming language is that all objects are loaded into the main memory of a single-machine. Large datasets of sizes in petabytes cannot be loaded into the RAM memory; this is when Hadoop integrated with R is an ideal solution. To adapt to the in-memory, single machine limitation of the R programming language, data scientists have to limit their data analysis to a sample of data from the large data set. This limitation of the R programming language comes as a major hindrance when dealing with big data. Since R is not very scalable, the core R engine can process only a limited amount of data.

On the contrary, distributed processing frameworks such as Hadoop are scalable for complex operations and tasks on large datasets (petabyte range) but do not have strong statistical analysis capabilities. As Hadoop is a popular framework for big data processing, integrating R with Hadoop is the next logical step. Using R on Hadoop will provide a highly scalable data analytics platform that can be scaled depending on the size of the dataset. Integrating Hadoop with R lets data scientists run R in parallel on large datasets as none of the data science libraries in the R language will work on a dataset that is larger than its memory. Big data analytics with R and Hadoop competes with the cost-value return offered by commodity hardware clusters for vertical scaling.

Methods of integrating R and Hadoop

Data analysts or data scientists working with Hadoop might have R packages or R scripts that they use for data processing. To use these R scripts or R packages with Hadoop, they need to rewrite these R scripts in the Java programming language or any other language that implements Hadoop MapReduce. This is a burdensome process and could lead to unwanted errors. To integrate Hadoop with the R programming language, we need to use a software that is already written for R, with the data being stored in the distributed of storage Hadoop. There are many solutions for using the R language to perform large computations, but all these solutions require that the data be loaded into the memory before it is distributed to the computing nodes. This is not an ideal solution for large datasets. Here are some commonly used methods to integrate Hadoop with R to make the best use of the analytical capabilities of R for large datasets.

RHADOOP – install R on workstations and connect to data in Hadoop

The most commonly used open source analytics solution to integrate the R programming language with Hadoop is **RHadoop**. RHadoop, developed by Revolution analytics, lets users directly ingest data from HBase database subsystems and HDFS filesystems. The RHadoop package is the go-to solution for using R on Hadoop because of its simplicity and cost advantage. RHadoop is a collection of five different packages which allows Hadoop users to manage and analyze data using the R programming language. The RHadoop package is compatible with open source Hadoop and also with the popular Hadoop distributions Cloudera, Hortonworks and MapR:

- `rhbase`: The `rhbase` package provides database management functions for HBase within R using a Thrift server. This package needs to be installed on the node that will run the R client. Using `rhbase`, data engineers and data scientists can read, write, and modify data stored in HBase tables from within R.
- `rhdfs`: The `rhdfs` package provides R programmers with connectivity to the Hadoop distributed filesystem so that they read, write, or modify the data stored in Hadoop HDFS.
- `plyrmr`: This package supports data manipulation operations on large datasets managed by Hadoop. `plyrmr` (`plyr` for MapReduce) provides data manipulation operations present in popular packages such as `reshape2` and `plyr`. This package depends on Hadoop MapReduce to perform operations but abstracts most of the MapReduce details.

- `ravro`: This package lets users read and write Avro files from local and HDFS filesystems.
- `rmr2` (execute R inside Hadoop MapReduce): Using this package, R programmers can perform statistical analysis on the data stored in a Hadoop cluster. Using `rmr2` might be a cumbersome process to integrate R with Hadoop, but many R programmers find using `rmr2` much easier than depending on Java-based Hadoop mappers and reducers. `rmr2` might be a little tedious but it eliminates data movement and helps parallelize computation to handle large datasets.

RHIPE – execute R inside Hadoop MapReduce

R and Hadoop Integrated Programming Environment (RHIPE) is an R library that allows users to run Hadoop MapReduce jobs within the R programming language. R programmers just have to write R Map and R Reduce functions, and the RHIPE library will transfer them and invoke the corresponding Hadoop Map and Hadoop Reduce tasks. RHIPE uses a protocol buffer encoding scheme to transfer the Map and Reduce inputs. The advantage of using RHIPE over other parallel R packages is that it integrates well with Hadoop and provides a data distribution scheme using HDFS across a cluster of machines, which provides fault tolerance and optimizes processor usage.

R and Hadoop Streaming

The Hadoop Streaming API allows users to run Hadoop MapReduce jobs with any executable script that reads data from standard input and writes data to standard output as a mapper or reducer. Thus, the Hadoop Streaming API can be used along with R programming scripts in the Map or Reduce phases. This method to integrate R and Hadoop does not require any client-side integration because streaming jobs are launched through the Hadoop command line. MapReduce jobs submitted undergo data transformation through UNIX standard streams and serialization to ensure Java complaint input to Hadoop, irrespective of the language of the input script provided by the programmer.

What do you think is the best way to integrate R with Hadoop?

RHIVE – install R on workstations and connect to data in Hadoop

If you want your Hive queries to be launched from the R interface, then RHIVE is the go-to package with functions for retrieving metadata such as database names, column names, and table names from Apache Hive. RHIVE provides rich statistical libraries and algorithms available in the R programming language for the data stored in Hadoop by extending HiveQL with R language functions. RHIVE functions allow users to apply R statistical learning models to the data stored in Hadoop cluster that has been cataloged using Apache Hive. The advantage of using RHIVE for Hadoop R integration is that it parallelizes operations and avoids data movement because data operations are pushed down into Hadoop.

ORCH – Oracle connector for Hadoop

ORCH can be used on non-Oracle Hadoop clusters or on any other Oracle big data appliance. Mappers and reducers are written in R and MapReduce jobs are executed from R environments through a high-level interface. With ORCH for R Hadoop integration, R programmers do not have to learn a new programming language such as Java to get into the details of a Hadoop environment, such as Hadoop cluster hardware or software. The ORCH connector also allows users to test the ability of MapReduce programs locally through the same function call, long before they are deployed on the Hadoop cluster.

The number of open source options for performing big data analytics with R and Hadoop is continuously expanding, but for simple Hadoop MapReduce jobs, R and Hadoop Streaming still prove to be the best solution. The combination of R and Hadoop together is a must-have toolkit for professionals working with big data to create fast predictive analytics combined with the performance, scalability, and flexibility you need.

Most Hadoop users claim that the advantage of using R is its exhaustive list of data science libraries for statistics and data visualization. However, the data science libraries in R are non-distributed in nature, which makes data retrieval a time-consuming affair. This is an inbuilt limitation of the R programming language, but if we just ignore it, then R and Hadoop together can make big data analytics an ecstasy!

Data analytics

R allows us to conduct a wide variety of data analytics. Everything we have done with `pandas` in Python, we are able to do in R as well.

Take a look at the following code:

```
df = read.csv(file=file.choose(), header=T, fill=T, sep=",",
stringsAsFactors=F)
```

`file.choose()` means there will be a new window that will allow you to select the data file to be opened. `header=T` means it will read the header. `fill=T` means it will fill in NaN for any undefined or missing data values. Finally, `sep=","` means that it knows how to distinguish between the different data values in the `.csv` file. In this case, they are all separated by commas. `stringsAsFactors` tells it to treat all the string values as strings, not as factors. This allows us to replace values in the data later on.

Now, you should see this:

Figure: Screenshot of output you will obtain

Press *Enter*. You should see something like this if you are on Windows:

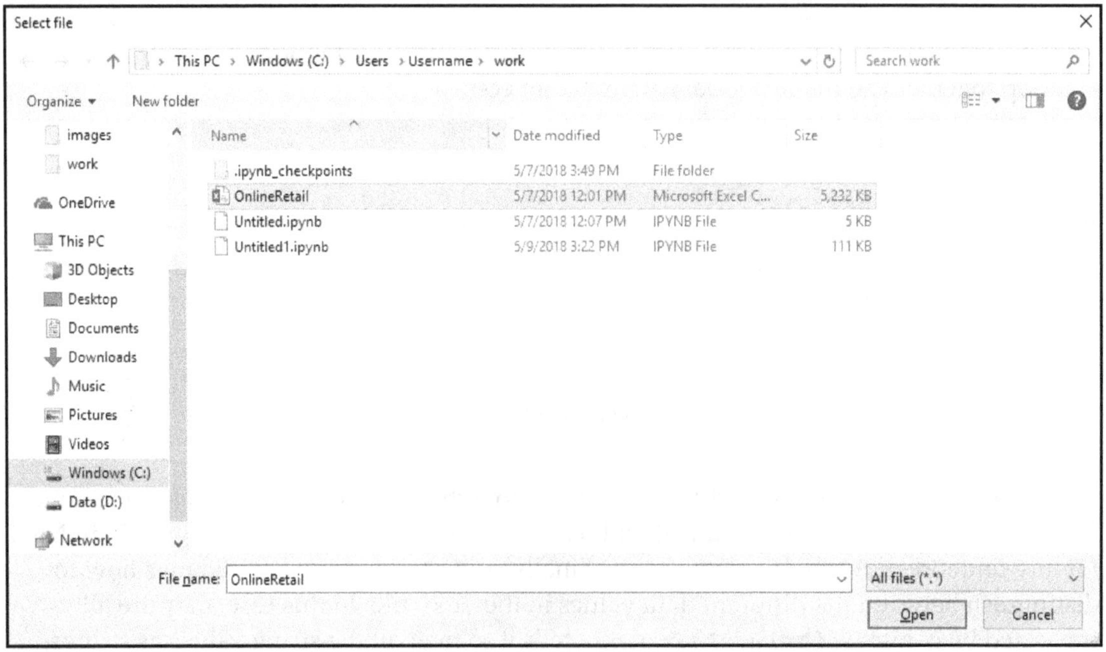

Regardless of the OS, you should see a window that opens up to allow you to choose a file. Next, you should see this:

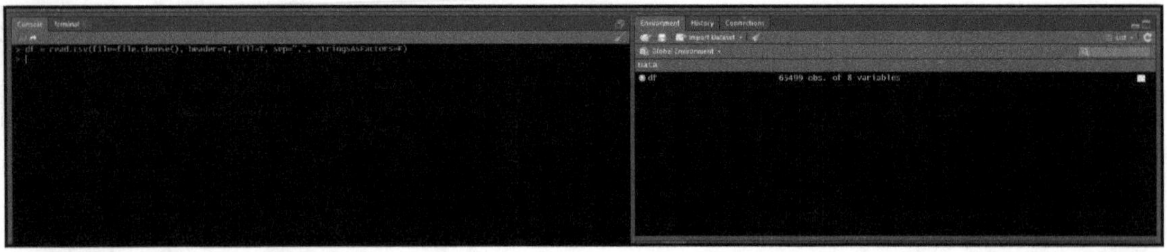

If you look to the right, you'll see a new field called `df`. If you click on it, you can see its contents:

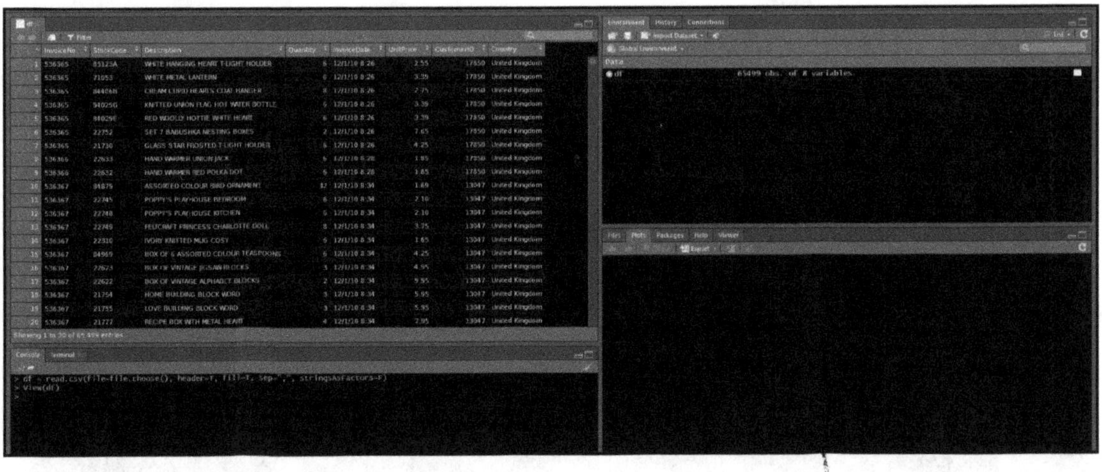

Now, that we have a data frame created, we can begin some analytics.

We can get some information about the number of rows and columns, as well as the length of the data frame and the column names. Look at the following lines of code and their respective outputs:

```
> is.data.frame(df)
[1] TRUE

> ncol(df)
[1] 8

> length(df)
[1] 8

> nrow(df)
[1] 27080

> names(df)
[1] "InvoiceNo" "StockCode" "Description" "Quantity" "InvoiceDate"
    "UnitPrice" "CustomerID" "Country"

> colnames(df)
[1] "InvoiceNo" "StockCode" "Description" "Quantity" "InvoiceDate"
    "UnitPrice" "CustomerID" "Country"
```

Now, we can move on to creating data subsets. Take a look at this code:

```
d1 = df[1:3]
```

This is what it results in:

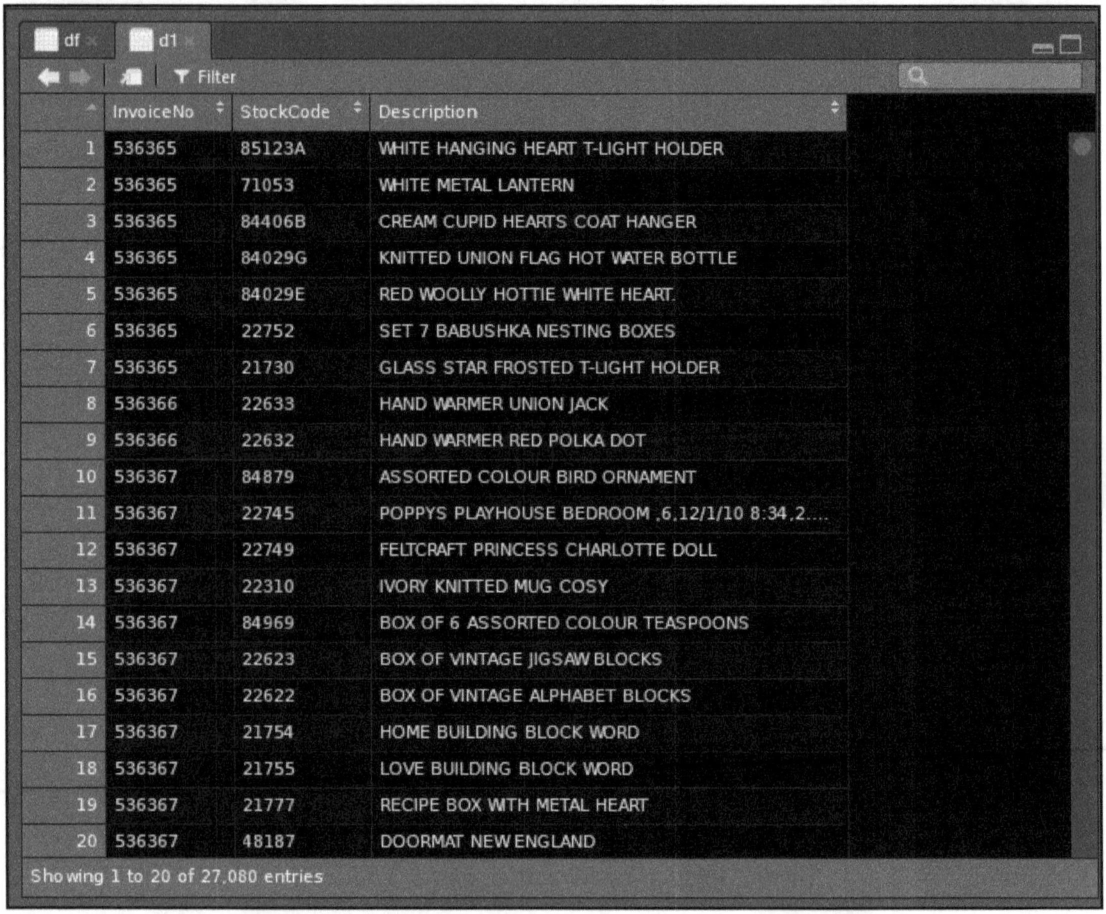

	InvoiceNo	StockCode	Description
1	536365	85123A	WHITE HANGING HEART T-LIGHT HOLDER
2	536365	71053	WHITE METAL LANTERN
3	536365	84406B	CREAM CUPID HEARTS COAT HANGER
4	536365	84029G	KNITTED UNION FLAG HOT WATER BOTTLE
5	536365	84029E	RED WOOLLY HOTTIE WHITE HEART.
6	536365	22752	SET 7 BABUSHKA NESTING BOXES
7	536365	21730	GLASS STAR FROSTED T-LIGHT HOLDER
8	536366	22633	HAND WARMER UNION JACK
9	536366	22632	HAND WARMER RED POLKA DOT
10	536367	84879	ASSORTED COLOUR BIRD ORNAMENT
11	536367	22745	POPPYS PLAYHOUSE BEDROOM ,6,12/1/10 8:34,2....
12	536367	22749	FELTCRAFT PRINCESS CHARLOTTE DOLL
13	536367	22310	IVORY KNITTED MUG COSY
14	536367	84969	BOX OF 6 ASSORTED COLOUR TEASPOONS
15	536367	22623	BOX OF VINTAGE JIGSAW BLOCKS
16	536367	22622	BOX OF VINTAGE ALPHABET BLOCKS
17	536367	21754	HOME BUILDING BLOCK WORD
18	536367	21755	LOVE BUILDING BLOCK WORD
19	536367	21777	RECIPE BOX WITH METAL HEART
20	536367	48187	DOORMAT NEW ENGLAND

Showing 1 to 20 of 27,080 entries

So basically, we selected columns 1, 2, and 3 as the set of data for `d1`. We can also select what rows we want in addition to what columns we want. Let's redefine `d1`:

```
d1 = df[1:10, c(1:3)]
```

	InvoiceNo	StockCode	Description
1	536365	85123A	WHITE HANGING HEART T-LIGHT HOLDER
2	536365	71053	WHITE METAL LANTERN
3	536365	84406B	CREAM CUPID HEARTS COAT HANGER
4	536365	84029G	KNITTED UNION FLAG HOT WATER BOTTLE
5	536365	84029E	RED WOOLLY HOTTIE WHITE HEART.
6	536365	22752	SET 7 BABUSHKA NESTING BOXES
7	536365	21730	GLASS STAR FROSTED T-LIGHT HOLDER
8	536366	22633	HAND WARMER UNION JACK
9	536366	22632	HAND WARMER RED POLKA DOT
10	536367	84879	ASSORTED COLOUR BIRD ORNAMENT

Showing 1 to 10 of 10 entries

We can also access an individual column of the data frame. Take a look at this:

```
v1 = df[[3]]
```

This assigns the whole column of data to `v1`. Now, let's access the first five elements of `v1`:

```
v1[1:5]
```

```
> v1[1:5]
[1] "WHITE HANGING HEART T-LIGHT HOLDER"  "WHITE METAL LANTERN"                "CREAM CUPID HEARTS COAT HANGER"
[4] "KNITTED UNION FLAG HOT WATER BOTTLE" "RED WOOLLY HOTTIE WHITE HEART."
```

We can also do this:

```
v2 = df$Description
v2[1:5]
```

```
> v2 = df$Description
> v2[1:5]
[1] "WHITE HANGING HEART T-LIGHT HOLDER"  "WHITE METAL LANTERN"                "CREAM CUPID HEARTS COAT HANGER"
[4] "KNITTED UNION FLAG HOT WATER BOTTLE" "RED WOOLLY HOTTIE WHITE HEART."
> |
```

We can even access each individual row, assuming we know a specific data value. Here, we use the stock code:

```
d1[d1$StockCode == "85123A", ]
```

```
> d1[d1$StockCode == "85123A", ]
  InvoiceNo StockCode                        Description
1    536365    85123A WHITE HANGING HEART T-LIGHT HOLDER
```

We can access a specific row we want:

```
d1 = df[1:10, c(1:8)]
d1[2, c(1:8)]
```

```
> d1 = df[1:10, c(1:8)]
> d1[2, c(1:8)]
  InvoiceNo StockCode          Description Quantity  InvoiceDate UnitPrice CustomerID        Country
2    536365     71053 WHITE METAL LANTERN         6 12/1/10 8:26      3.39      17850 United Kingdom
```

Similar to the `.head()` function in Python, there is a `head()` function in R. Look at this code:

```
head(df)
```

```
> head(df)
  InvoiceNo StockCode                         Description Quantity  InvoiceDate UnitPrice CustomerID        Country
1    536365    85123A  WHITE HANGING HEART T-LIGHT HOLDER        6 12/1/10 8:26      2.55      17850 United Kingdom
2    536365     71053                 WHITE METAL LANTERN        6 12/1/10 8:26      3.39      17850 United Kingdom
3    536365    84406B      CREAM CUPID HEARTS COAT HANGER        8 12/1/10 8:26      2.75      17850 United Kingdom
4    536365    84029G KNITTED UNION FLAG HOT WATER BOTTLE        6 12/1/10 8:26      3.39      17850 United Kingdom
5    536365    84029E      RED WOOLLY HOTTIE WHITE HEART.        6 12/1/10 8:26      3.39      17850 United Kingdom
6    536365     22752        SET 7 BABUSHKA NESTING BOXES        2 12/1/10 8:26      7.65      17850 United Kingdom
> |
```

We can add another parameter to choose the number of rows that we want to display. Let's say that we want to display the first `10` rows. Here is the code:

```
head(df, 10)
```

```
> head(df, 10)
   InvoiceNo StockCode                         Description Quantity  InvoiceDate UnitPrice CustomerID        Country
1     536365    85123A  WHITE HANGING HEART T-LIGHT HOLDER        6 12/1/10 8:26      2.55      17850 United Kingdom
2     536365     71053                 WHITE METAL LANTERN        6 12/1/10 8:26      3.39      17850 United Kingdom
3     536365    84406B      CREAM CUPID HEARTS COAT HANGER        8 12/1/10 8:26      2.75      17850 United Kingdom
4     536365    84029G KNITTED UNION FLAG HOT WATER BOTTLE        6 12/1/10 8:26      3.39      17850 United Kingdom
5     536365    84029E      RED WOOLLY HOTTIE WHITE HEART.        6 12/1/10 8:26      3.39      17850 United Kingdom
6     536365     22752        SET 7 BABUSHKA NESTING BOXES        2 12/1/10 8:26      7.65      17850 United Kingdom
7     536365     21730   GLASS STAR FROSTED T-LIGHT HOLDER        6 12/1/10 8:26      4.25      17850 United Kingdom
8     536366     22633              HAND WARMER UNION JACK        6 12/1/10 8:28      1.85      17850 United Kingdom
9     536366     22632           HAND WARMER RED POLKA DOT        6 12/1/10 8:28      1.85      17850 United Kingdom
10    536367     84879       ASSORTED COLOUR BIRD ORNAMENT       32 12/1/10 8:34      1.69      13047 United Kingdom
>
```

We can have a negative number as the second parameter. Look at the following:

```
head(d1, -2)
```

```
> head(d1, -2)
  InvoiceNo StockCode                         Description Quantity  InvoiceDate UnitPrice CustomerID        Country
1    536365    85123A  WHITE HANGING HEART T-LIGHT HOLDER        6 12/1/10 8:26      2.55      17850 United Kingdom
2    536365     71053                 WHITE METAL LANTERN        6 12/1/10 8:26      3.39      17850 United Kingdom
3    536365    84406B      CREAM CUPID HEARTS COAT HANGER        8 12/1/10 8:26      2.75      17850 United Kingdom
4    536365    84029G KNITTED UNION FLAG HOT WATER BOTTLE        6 12/1/10 8:26      3.39      17850 United Kingdom
5    536365    84029E      RED WOOLLY HOTTIE WHITE HEART.        6 12/1/10 8:26      3.39      17850 United Kingdom
6    536365     22752        SET 7 BABUSHKA NESTING BOXES        2 12/1/10 8:26      7.65      17850 United Kingdom
7    536365     21730   GLASS STAR FROSTED T-LIGHT HOLDER        6 12/1/10 8:26      4.25      17850 United Kingdom
8    536366     22633              HAND WARMER UNION JACK        6 12/1/10 8:28      1.85      17850 United Kingdom
```

Similarly, we can display the last *n* rows using `tail()`. Look at the following:

```
tail(d1, 4)
```

```
> d1 = df[0:10, c(1:8)]
> tail(d1, 4)
   InvoiceNo StockCode                       Description Quantity  InvoiceDate UnitPrice CustomerID        Country
7     536365     21730 GLASS STAR FROSTED T-LIGHT HOLDER        6 12/1/10 8:26      4.25      17850 United Kingdom
8     536366     22633            HAND WARMER UNION JACK        6 12/1/10 8:28      1.85      17850 United Kingdom
9     536366     22632         HAND WARMER RED POLKA DOT        6 12/1/10 8:28      1.85      17850 United Kingdom
10    536367     84879     ASSORTED COLOUR BIRD ORNAMENT       32 12/1/10 8:34      1.69      13047 United Kingdom
> |
```

We can also have a negative number as the second parameter, like with `head()`. Look at this line of code:

```
tail(d1, -2)
```

This displays *nrow(d1) + n* rows, where *n* is the parameter passed into the `tail()` function:

```
> tail(d1, -2)
   InvoiceNo StockCode                         Description Quantity  InvoiceDate UnitPrice CustomerID        Country
3     536365    84406B      CREAM CUPID HEARTS COAT HANGER        8 12/1/10 8:26      2.75      17850 United Kingdom
4     536365    84029G KNITTED UNION FLAG HOT WATER BOTTLE        6 12/1/10 8:26      3.39      17850 United Kingdom
5     536365    84029E      RED WOOLLY HOTTIE WHITE HEART.        6 12/1/10 8:26      3.39      17850 United Kingdom
6     536365     22752        SET 7 BABUSHKA NESTING BOXES        2 12/1/10 8:26      7.65      17850 United Kingdom
7     536365     21730   GLASS STAR FROSTED T-LIGHT HOLDER        6 12/1/10 8:26      4.25      17850 United Kingdom
8     536366     22633              HAND WARMER UNION JACK        6 12/1/10 8:28      1.85      17850 United Kingdom
9     536366     22632           HAND WARMER RED POLKA DOT        6 12/1/10 8:28      1.85      17850 United Kingdom
10    536367     84879       ASSORTED COLOUR BIRD ORNAMENT       32 12/1/10 8:34      1.69      13047 United Kingdom
>
```

We can do some basic statistical analysis of a column. However, we will have to convert the data first. We can do `min()`, `max()`, `mean()`, and more. Take a look at this:

```
min(as.numeric(df$UnitPrice))
[1] 0
min(df$UnitPrice)
[1] 0
```

`as.numeric()` means that any data values that are strings will be converted to a number. In this case, none of them are a string value, otherwise you'd see `min(df$UnitPrice)` result in `0`:

```
max(df$UnitPrice)
[1] 16888.02

mean(df$UnitPrice)
[1] 5.857586

median(df$UnitPrice)
[1] 2.51

quantile(df$UnitPrice)
```

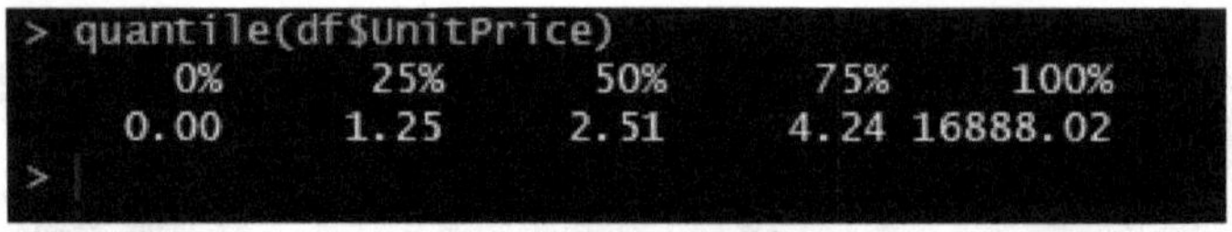
```
> quantile(df$UnitPrice)
      0%      25%      50%      75%     100%
    0.00     1.25     2.51     4.24 16888.02
>
```

We can add another parameter here to customize the percentage values we want:

```
quantile(df$UnitPrice, c(0, .1, .5, .9)
```

```
> quantile(df$UnitPrice, c(0, .1, .5, .9))
  0%  10%  50%  90%
0.00 0.83 2.51 7.95
>
```

```
sd(df$UnitPrice)
```

```
> sd(df$UnitPrice)
[1] 145.796
>
```

That tells us the standard deviation of `df$UnitPrice`. We can also find the variance:

```
var(df$UnitPrice)
```

```
> var(df$UnitPrice)
[1] 21256.46
>
```

```
range(df$UnitPrice)
```

```
> range(df$UnitPrice)
[1]     0.00 16888.02
>
```

We can also get a five-number summary, which tells us the minimum, the first quantile, the median (which is also the 50% mark), the third quantile (the 75% mark), and the maximum:

```
fivenum(df$UnitPrice)
```

```
> fivenum(df$UnitPrice)
[1]     0.00     1.25     2.51     4.24 16888.02
>
```

We can also plot a column of choice. Look at this:

```
plot(df$UnitPrice)
```

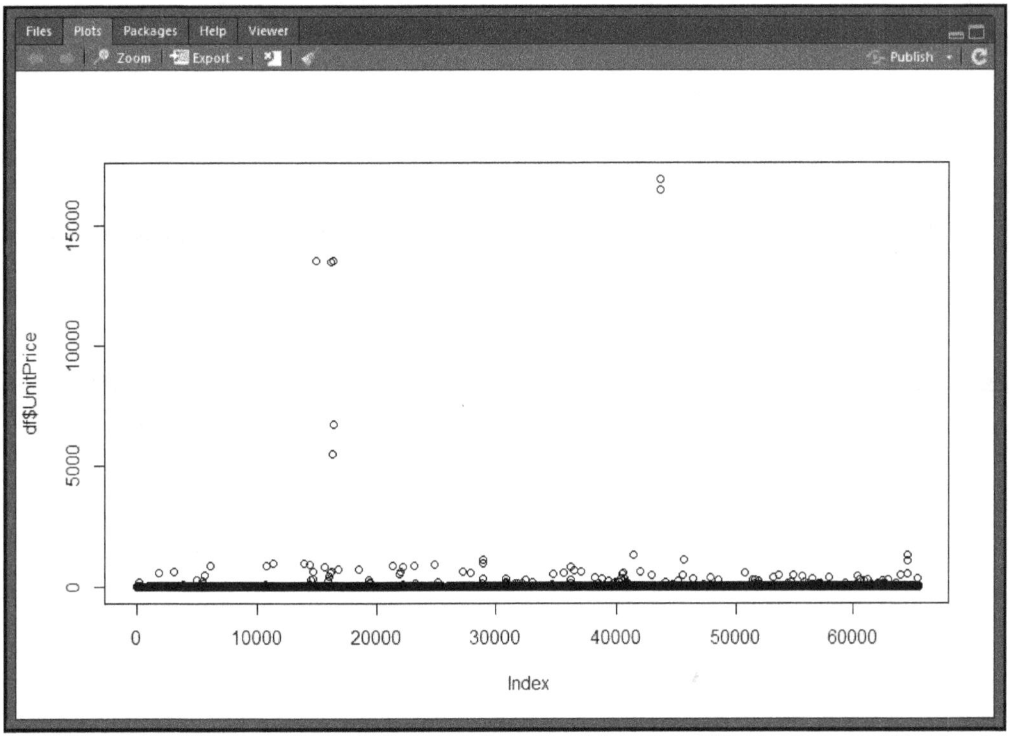

There are different types of plot we can have. We can introduce another parameter to specify the type of plot we want. Look at the following lines of code and their resulting graphs:

```
plot(df$UnitPrice, type="p")
```

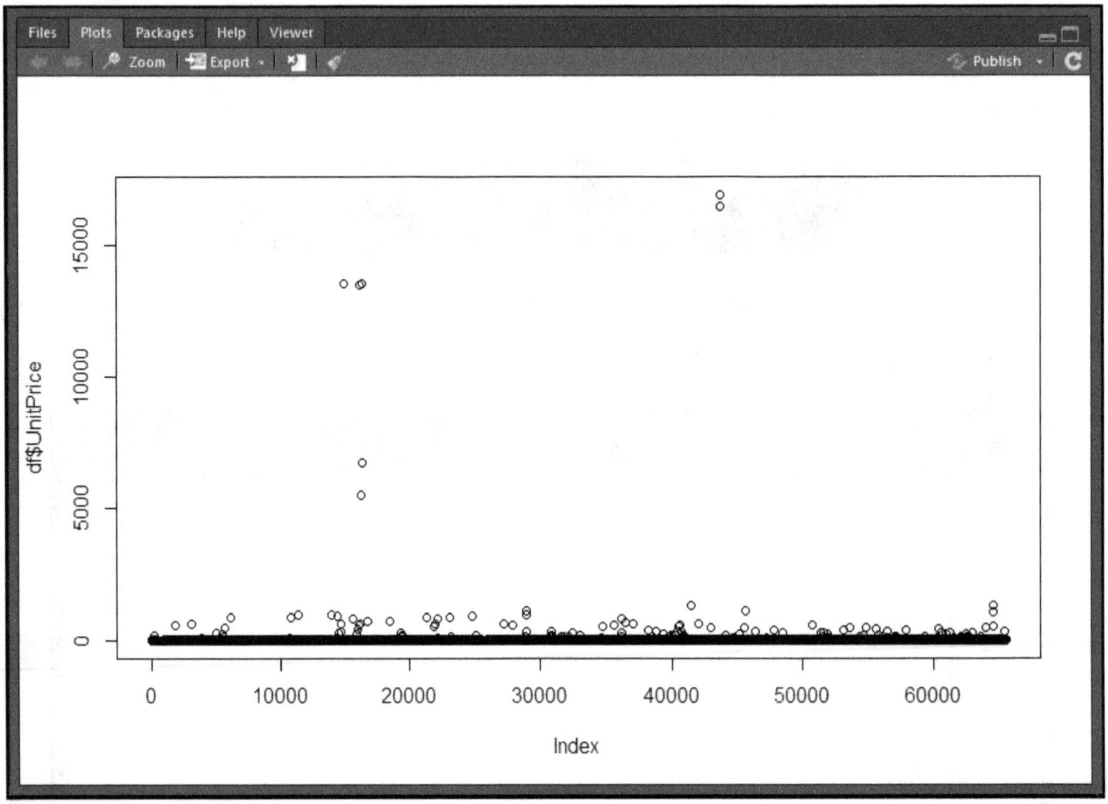

As you can see, it is the same graph as the one we saw earlier. However, the graph is a little crowded, so let's use a smaller range:

```
d1 = df[0:30, c(1:8)]
plot(d1$UnitPrice)
```

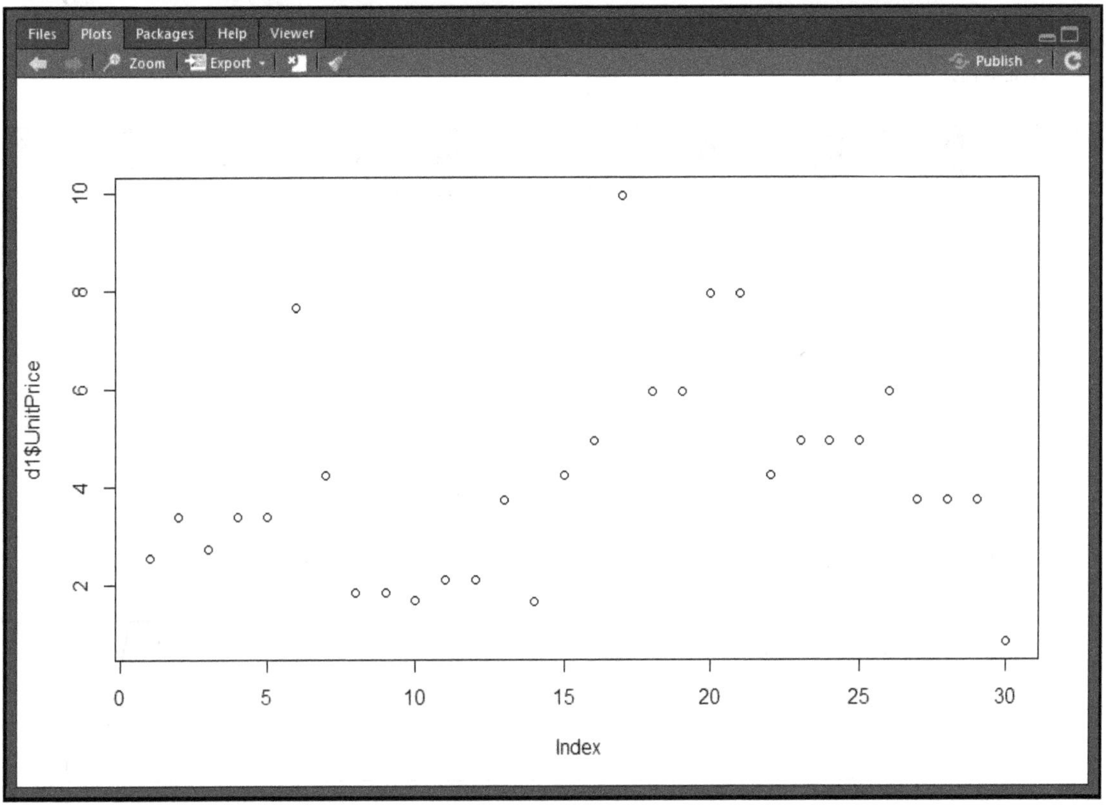

Let's make it easier and redefine `d1` to just have the `UnitPrice` column:

```
d1 = d1$UnitPrice
plot(d1, type="p")
```

The graph should be the same as the one preceding one.

Now, let's move on:

```
plot(d1, type="l")
```

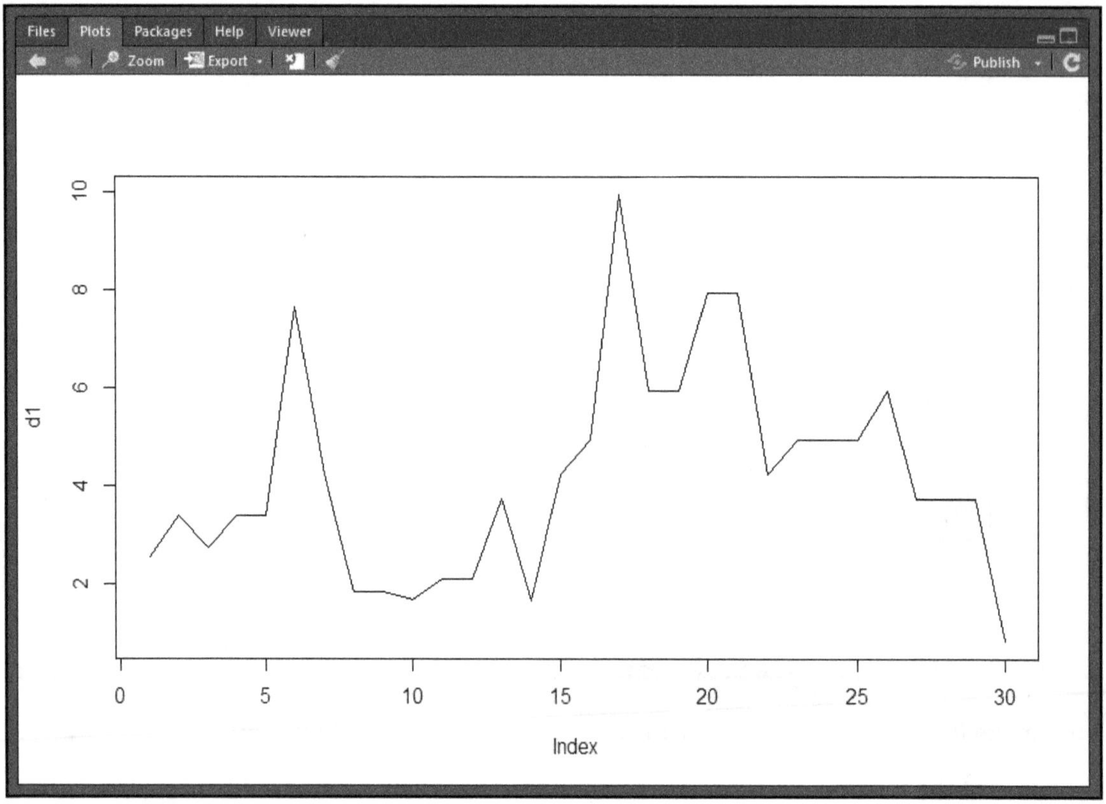

This is a line graph of `d1`:

```
plot(d1, type="b")
```

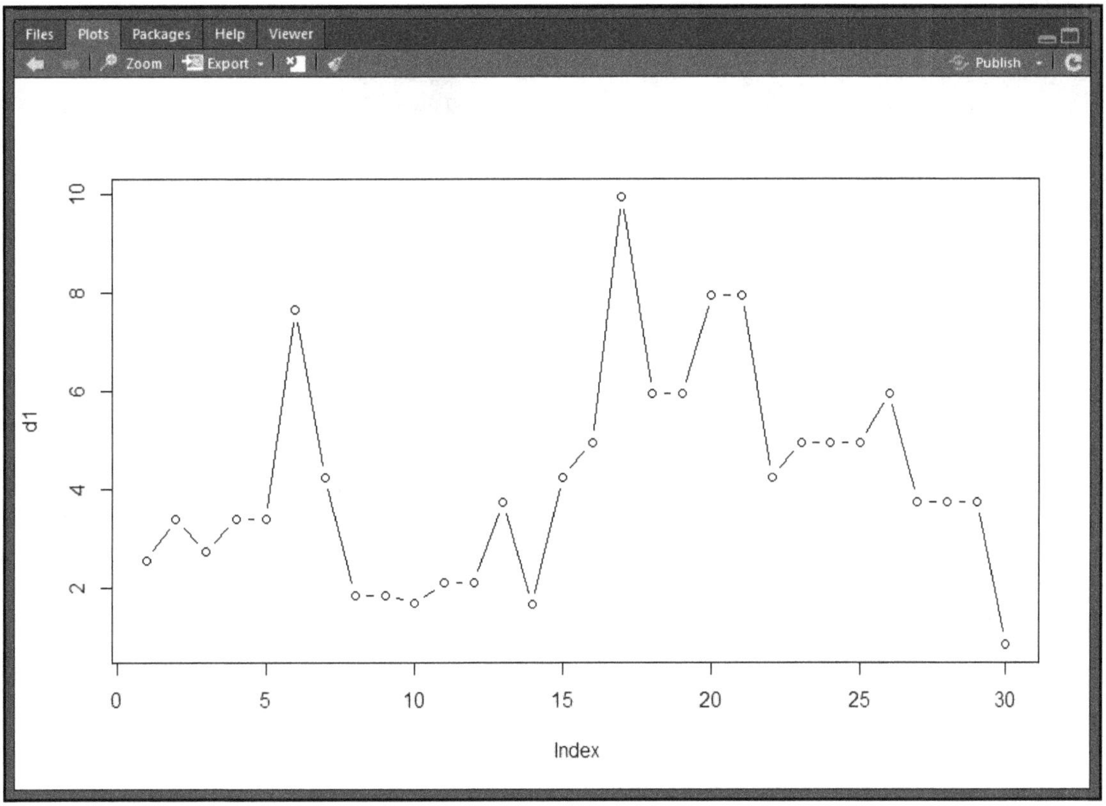

This is a combined line and point graph of `d1`. However, they are not overlaid on top of each other:

```
plot(d1, type="c")
```

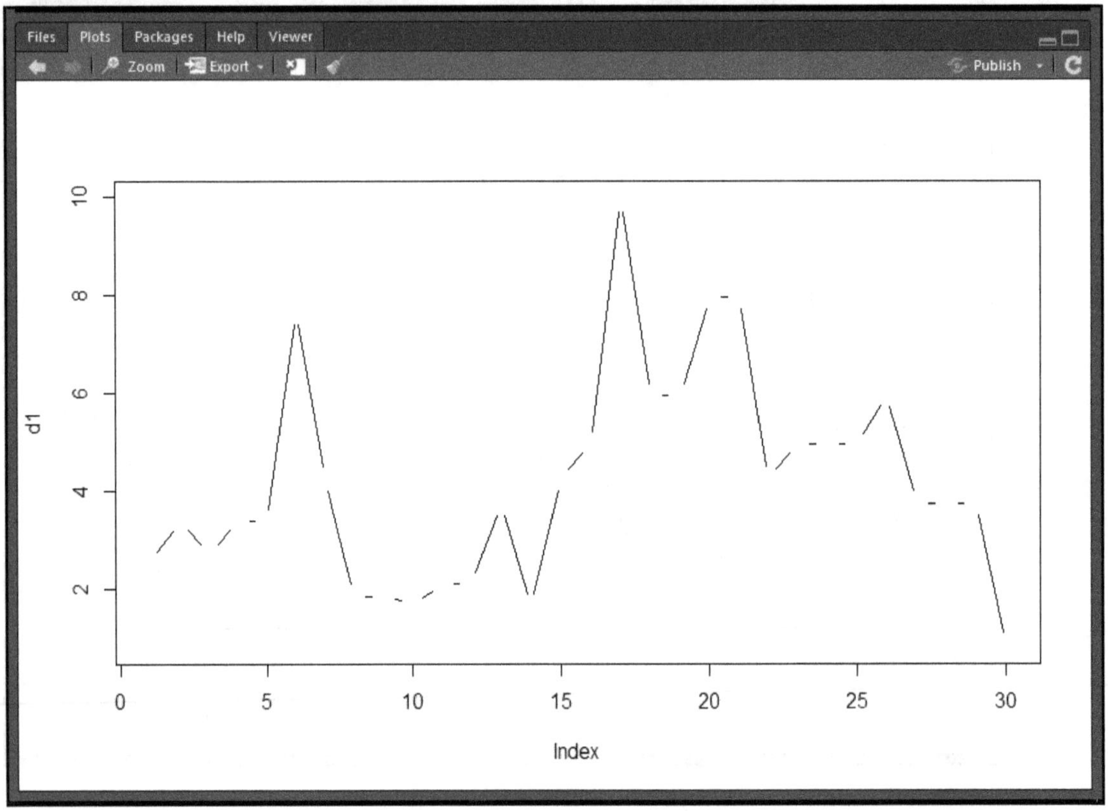

This graph is the graph of only the lines from the combined graph we saw earlier with `type="b"`:

```
plot(d1, type="o")
```

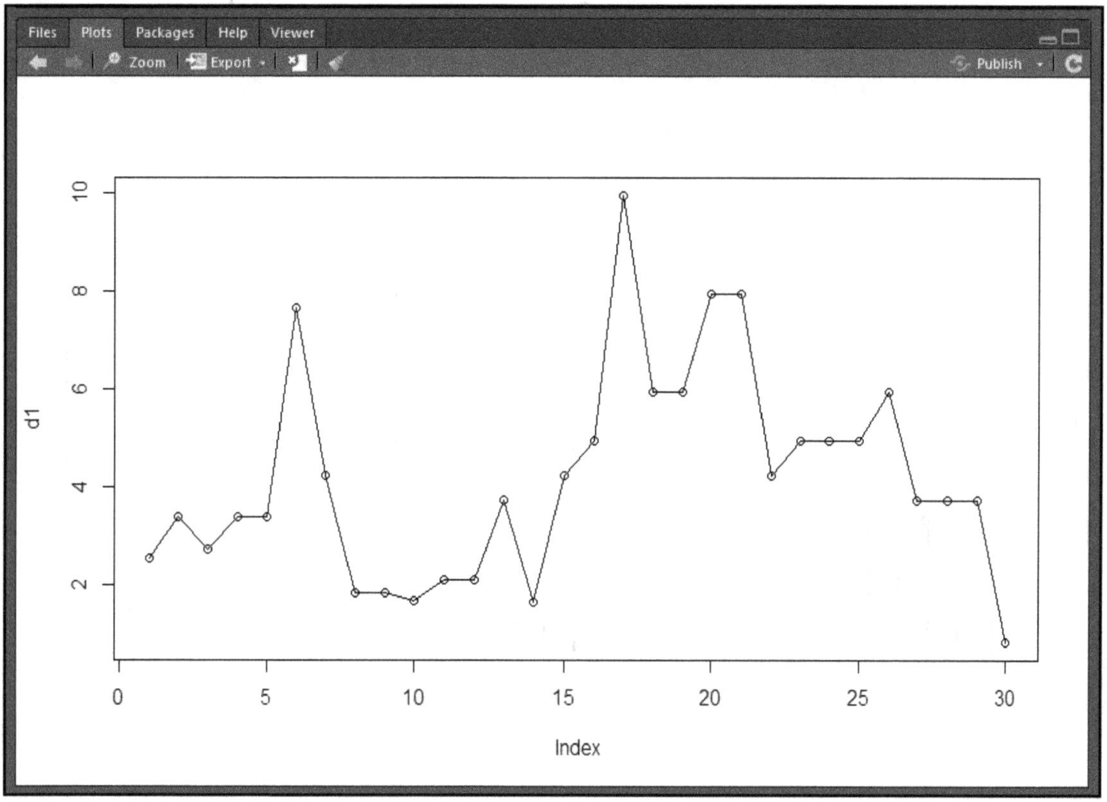

This is an overplotted graph of `d1`. This means that the line and point graphs are overlaid on top of each other:

```
plot(d1, type="h")
```

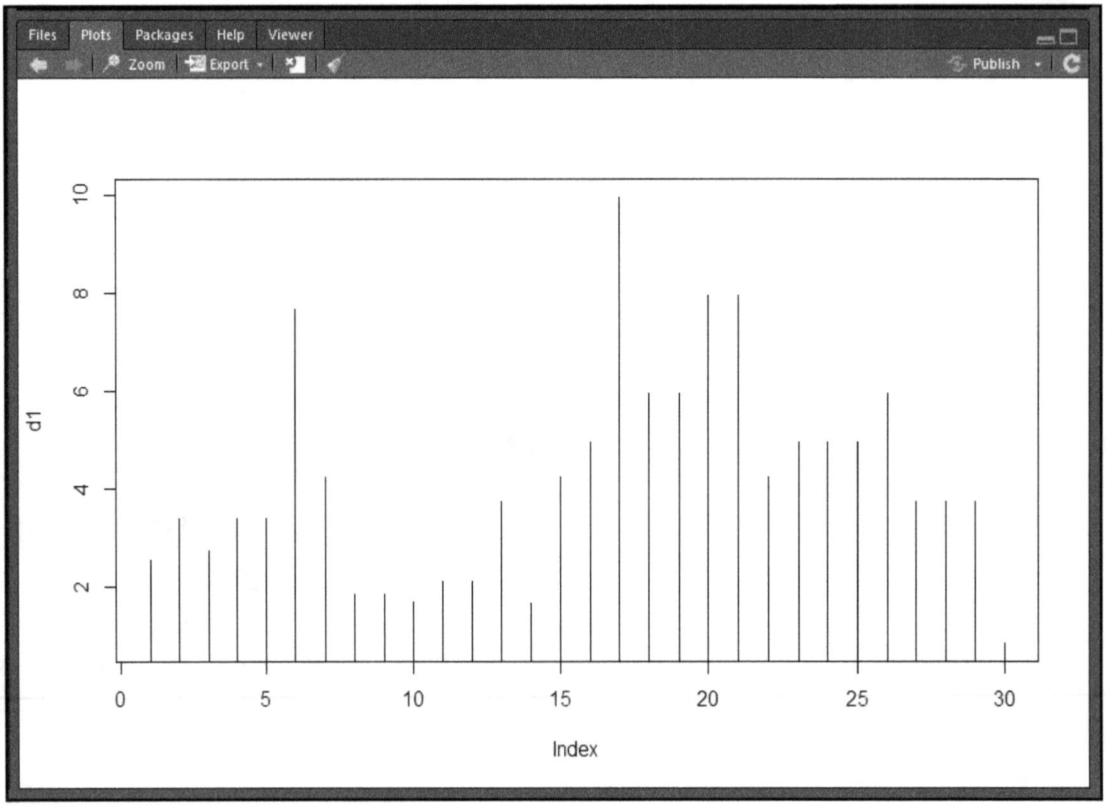

This is a histogram of `d1`:

```
plot(d1, type="s")
```

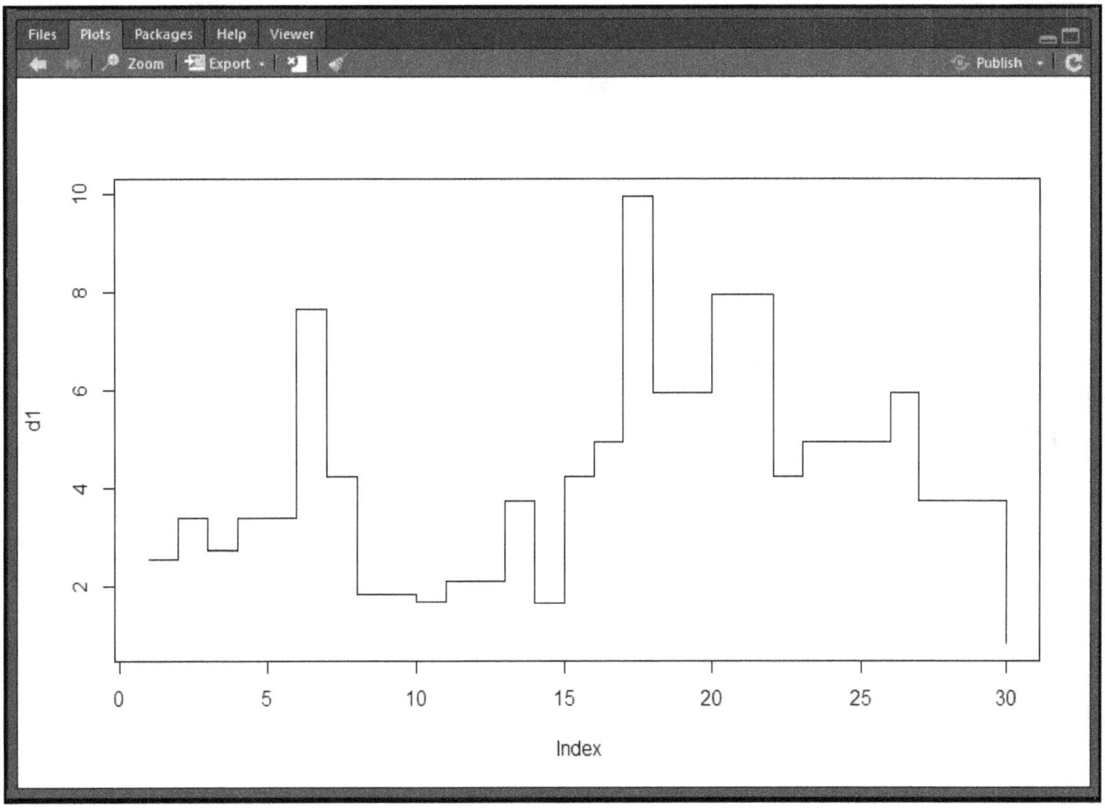

This is a step graph:

```
plot(d1, type="S")
```

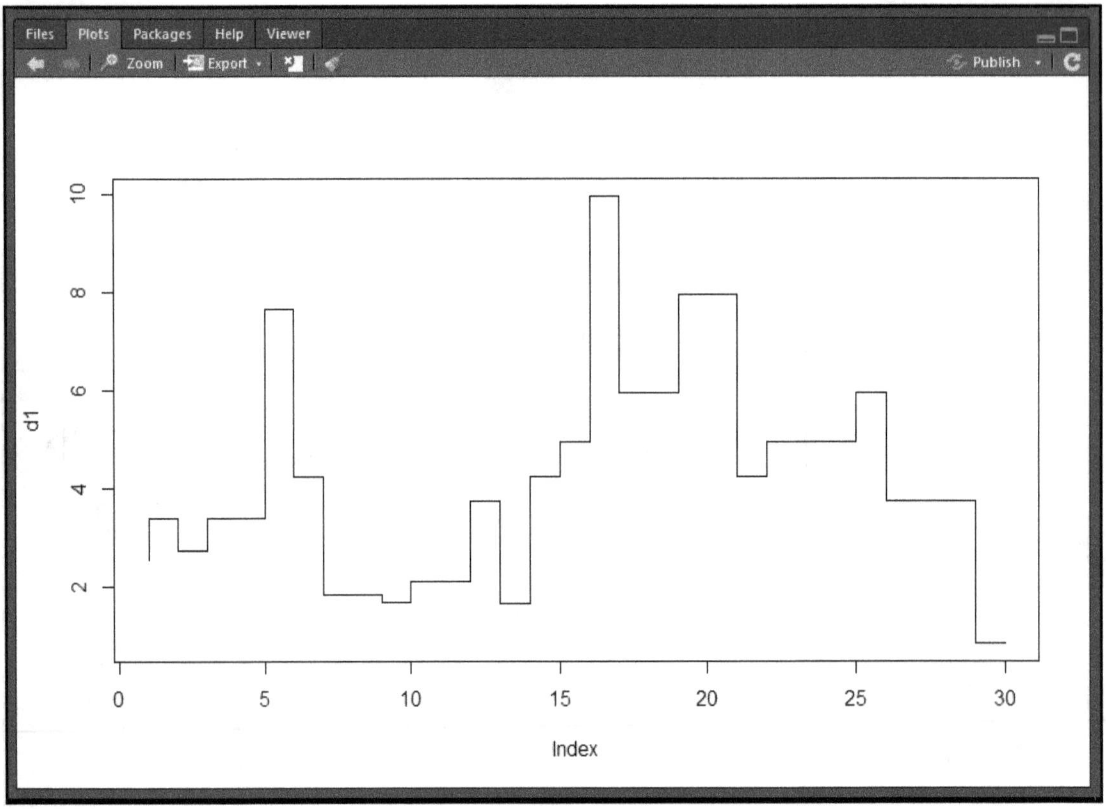

The difference between the two graphs is that the first step graph, where `type="s"`, is where the graph goes horizontally first then vertical. The second step graph has `type="S"`, and moves vertically first before moving horizontally. It is possible to see this difference by looking at the graphs.

There are also other parameters that we can use, such as:

```
#Note: these are parameters, not individual lines of code.

#The title of the graph
main="Title"

#Subtitle for the graph
sub="title"
```

```
#Label for the x-axis
xlab="X Axis"

#Label for the y-axis
ylab="Y Axis"

#The aspect ratio between y and x.
asp=1
```

Now for an example:

```
plot(d1, type="h", main="Graph of Unit Prices vs Index", sub ="First 30
Rows", xlab = "Row Index", ylab="Prices", asp=1.4)
```

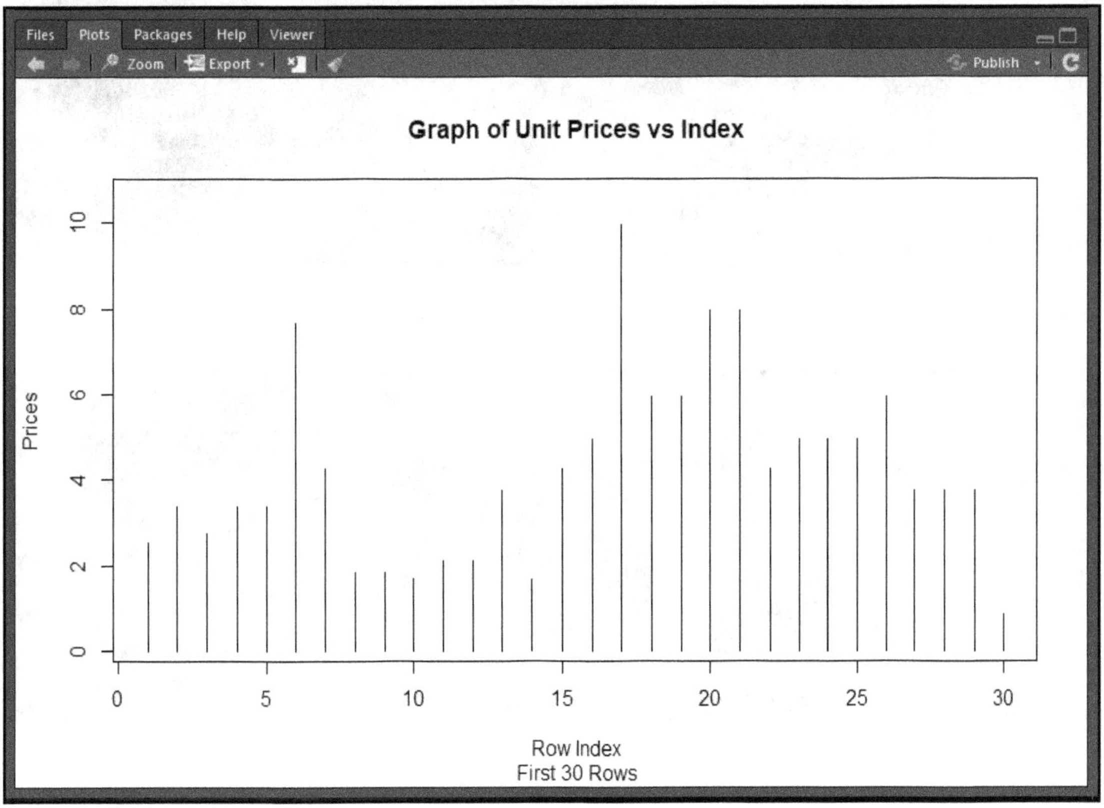

To add two different data frames together, we use `rbind()`.

Look at the following code:

```
d2 = df[0:10, c(1:8)]
d3 = df[21:30, c(1:8)]
d4 = rbind(d2, d3)
```

This is `d2`:

	InvoiceNo	StockCode	Description	Quantity	InvoiceDate	UnitPrice	CustomerID	Country
1	536365	85123A	WHITE HANGING HEART T-LIGHT HOLDER	6	12/1/10 8:26	2.55	17850	United Kingdom
2	536365	71053	WHITE METAL LANTERN	6	12/1/10 8:26	3.39	17850	United Kingdom
3	536365	84406B	CREAM CUPID HEARTS COAT HANGER	8	12/1/10 8:26	2.75	17850	United Kingdom
4	536365	84029G	KNITTED UNION FLAG HOT WATER BOTTLE	6	12/1/10 8:26	3.39	17850	United Kingdom
5	536365	84029E	RED WOOLLY HOTTIE WHITE HEART.	6	12/1/10 8:26	3.39	17850	United Kingdom
6	536365	22752	SET 7 BABUSHKA NESTING BOXES	2	12/1/10 8:26	7.65	17850	United Kingdom
7	536365	21730	GLASS STAR FROSTED T-LIGHT HOLDER	6	12/1/10 8:26	4.25	17850	United Kingdom
8	536366	22633	HAND WARMER UNION JACK	6	12/1/10 8:28	1.85	17850	United Kingdom
9	536366	22632	HAND WARMER RED POLKA DOT	6	12/1/10 8:28	1.85	17850	United Kingdom
10	536367	84879	ASSORTED COLOUR BIRD ORNAMENT	32	12/1/10 8:34	1.69	13047	United Kingdom

This is `d3`:

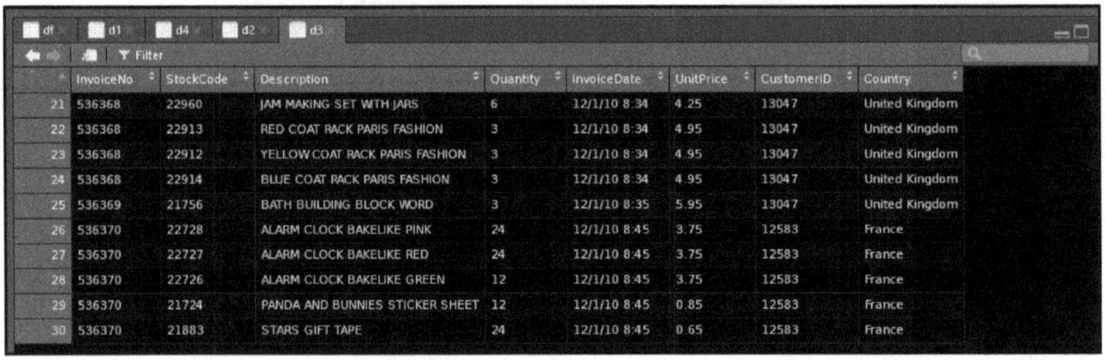

	InvoiceNo	StockCode	Description	Quantity	InvoiceDate	UnitPrice	CustomerID	Country
21	536368	22960	JAM MAKING SET WITH JARS	6	12/1/10 8:34	4.25	13047	United Kingdom
22	536368	22913	RED COAT RACK PARIS FASHION	3	12/1/10 8:34	4.95	13047	United Kingdom
23	536368	22912	YELLOW COAT RACK PARIS FASHION	3	12/1/10 8:34	4.95	13047	United Kingdom
24	536368	22914	BLUE COAT RACK PARIS FASHION	3	12/1/10 8:34	4.95	13047	United Kingdom
25	536369	21756	BATH BUILDING BLOCK WORD	3	12/1/10 8:35	5.95	13047	United Kingdom
26	536370	22728	ALARM CLOCK BAKELIKE PINK	24	12/1/10 8:45	3.75	12583	France
27	536370	22727	ALARM CLOCK BAKELIKE RED	24	12/1/10 8:45	3.75	12583	France
28	536370	22726	ALARM CLOCK BAKELIKE GREEN	12	12/1/10 8:45	3.75	12583	France
29	536370	21724	PANDA AND BUNNIES STICKER SHEET	12	12/1/10 8:45	0.85	12583	France
30	536370	21883	STARS GIFT TAPE	24	12/1/10 8:45	0.65	12583	France

And now, this is d4:

	InvoiceNo	StockCode	Description	Quantity	InvoiceDate	UnitPrice	CustomerID	Country
1	536365	85123A	WHITE HANGING HEART T-LIGHT HOLDER	6	12/1/10 8:26	2.55	17850	United Kingdom
2	536365	71053	WHITE METAL LANTERN	6	12/1/10 8:26	3.39	17850	United Kingdom
3	536365	84406B	CREAM CUPID HEARTS COAT HANGER	8	12/1/10 8:26	2.75	17850	United Kingdom
4	536365	84029G	KNITTED UNION FLAG HOT WATER BOTTLE	6	12/1/10 8:26	3.39	17850	United Kingdom
5	536365	84029E	RED WOOLLY HOTTIE WHITE HEART.	6	12/1/10 8:26	3.39	17850	United Kingdom
6	536365	22752	SET 7 BABUSHKA NESTING BOXES	2	12/1/10 8:26	7.65	17850	United Kingdom
7	536365	21730	GLASS STAR FROSTED T-LIGHT HOLDER	6	12/1/10 8:26	4.25	17850	United Kingdom
8	536366	22633	HAND WARMER UNION JACK	6	12/1/10 8:28	1.85	17850	United Kingdom
9	536366	22632	HAND WARMER RED POLKA DOT	6	12/1/10 8:28	1.85	17850	United Kingdom
10	536367	84879	ASSORTED COLOUR BIRD ORNAMENT	32	12/1/10 8:34	1.69	13047	United Kingdom
21	536368	22960	JAM MAKING SET WITH JARS	6	12/1/10 8:34	4.25	13047	United Kingdom
22	536368	22913	RED COAT RACK PARIS FASHION	3	12/1/10 8:34	4.95	13047	United Kingdom
23	536368	22912	YELLOW COAT RACK PARIS FASHION	3	12/1/10 8:34	4.95	13047	United Kingdom
24	536368	22914	BLUE COAT RACK PARIS FASHION	3	12/1/10 8:34	4.95	13047	United Kingdom
25	536369	21756	BATH BUILDING BLOCK WORD	3	12/1/10 8:35	5.95	13047	United Kingdom
26	536370	22728	ALARM CLOCK BAKELIKE PINK	24	12/1/10 8:45	3.75	12583	France
27	536370	22727	ALARM CLOCK BAKELIKE RED	24	12/1/10 8:45	3.75	12583	France
28	536370	22726	ALARM CLOCK BAKELIKE GREEN	12	12/1/10 8:45	3.75	12583	France
29	536370	21724	PANDA AND BUNNIES STICKER SHEET	12	12/1/10 8:45	0.85	12583	France
30	536370	21883	STARS GIFT TAPE	24	12/1/10 8:45	0.65	12583	France

One thing to note is that all data frames passed into `rbind()` must have the same columns. The order does not matter.

We can also merge two data frames.

Look at this code:

```
d2 = df[0:11, c("InvoiceNo", "StockCode", "Description")]
d3 = df[11:20, c("StockCode", "Description", "Quantity")]
d4 = merge(d2, d3)
```

This is d2:

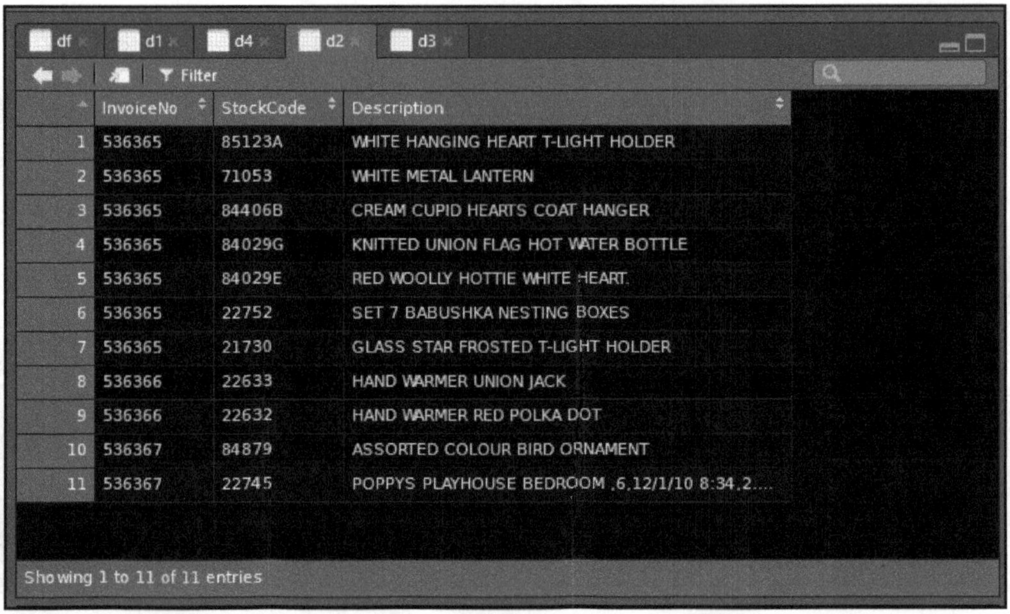

	InvoiceNo	StockCode	Description
1	536365	85123A	WHITE HANGING HEART T-LIGHT HOLDER
2	536365	71053	WHITE METAL LANTERN
3	536365	84406B	CREAM CUPID HEARTS COAT HANGER
4	536365	84029G	KNITTED UNION FLAG HOT WATER BOTTLE
5	536365	84029E	RED WOOLLY HOTTIE WHITE HEART.
6	536365	22752	SET 7 BABUSHKA NESTING BOXES
7	536365	21730	GLASS STAR FROSTED T-LIGHT HOLDER
8	536366	22633	HAND WARMER UNION JACK
9	536366	22632	HAND WARMER RED POLKA DOT
10	536367	84879	ASSORTED COLOUR BIRD ORNAMENT
11	536367	22745	POPPYS PLAYHOUSE BEDROOM ,6,12/1/10 8:34,2....

Showing 1 to 11 of 11 entries

This is d3:

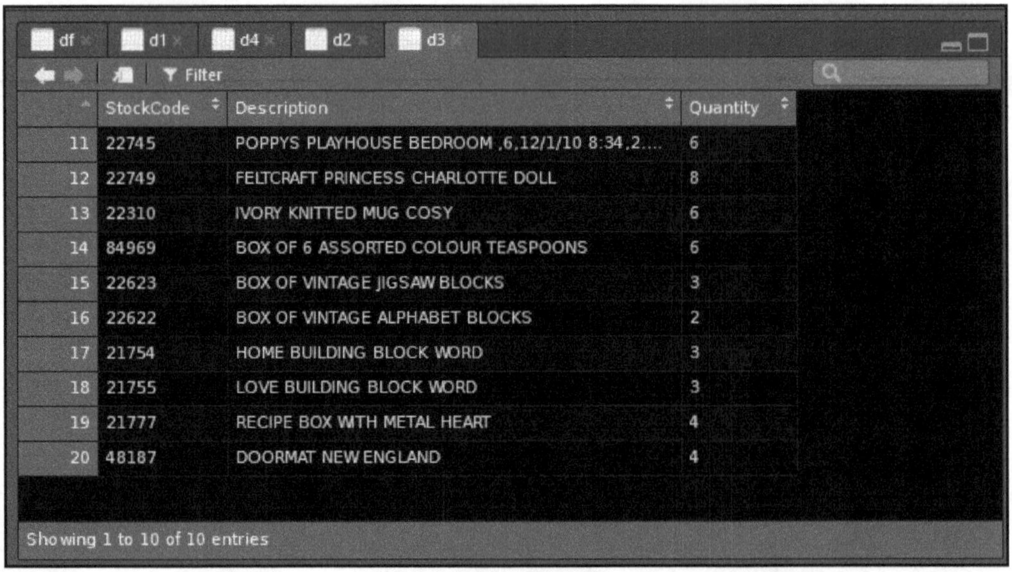

	StockCode	Description	Quantity
11	22745	POPPYS PLAYHOUSE BEDROOM ,6,12/1/10 8:34,2....	6
12	22749	FELTCRAFT PRINCESS CHARLOTTE DOLL	8
13	22310	IVORY KNITTED MUG COSY	6
14	84969	BOX OF 6 ASSORTED COLOUR TEASPOONS	6
15	22623	BOX OF VINTAGE JIGSAW BLOCKS	3
16	22622	BOX OF VINTAGE ALPHABET BLOCKS	2
17	21754	HOME BUILDING BLOCK WORD	3
18	21755	LOVE BUILDING BLOCK WORD	3
19	21777	RECIPE BOX WITH METAL HEART	4
20	48187	DOORMAT NEW ENGLAND	4

Showing 1 to 10 of 10 entries

This is `d4`:

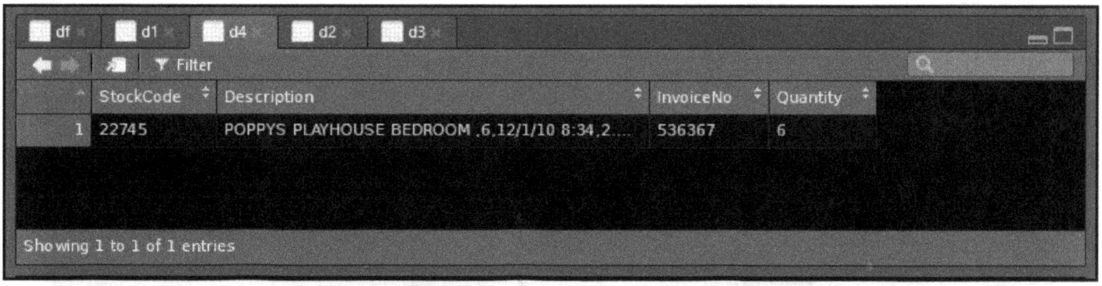

	StockCode	Description	InvoiceNo	Quantity
1	22745	POPPYS PLAYHOUSE BEDROOM ,6,12/1/10 8:34,2....	536367	6

Showing 1 to 1 of 1 entries

So by default, `merge()` uses inner join.

Now, let's look at outer join:

```
d4 = merge(d2, d3, all=T)
```

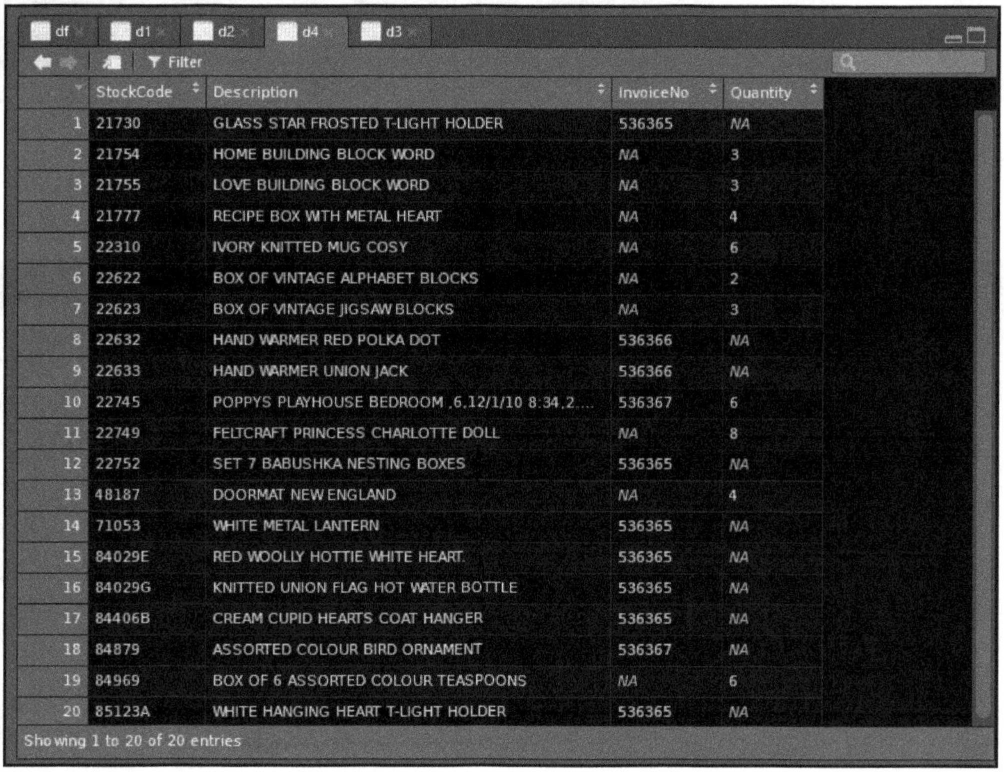

	StockCode	Description	InvoiceNo	Quantity
1	21730	GLASS STAR FROSTED T-LIGHT HOLDER	536365	NA
2	21754	HOME BUILDING BLOCK WORD	NA	3
3	21755	LOVE BUILDING BLOCK WORD	NA	3
4	21777	RECIPE BOX WITH METAL HEART	NA	4
5	22310	IVORY KNITTED MUG COSY	NA	6
6	22622	BOX OF VINTAGE ALPHABET BLOCKS	NA	2
7	22623	BOX OF VINTAGE JIGSAW BLOCKS	NA	3
8	22632	HAND WARMER RED POLKA DOT	536366	NA
9	22633	HAND WARMER UNION JACK	536366	NA
10	22745	POPPYS PLAYHOUSE BEDROOM ,6,12/1/10 8:34,2....	536367	6
11	22749	FELTCRAFT PRINCESS CHARLOTTE DOLL	NA	8
12	22752	SET 7 BABUSHKA NESTING BOXES	536365	NA
13	48187	DOORMAT NEW ENGLAND	NA	4
14	71053	WHITE METAL LANTERN	536365	NA
15	84029E	RED WOOLLY HOTTIE WHITE HEART.	536365	NA
16	84029G	KNITTED UNION FLAG HOT WATER BOTTLE	536365	NA
17	84406B	CREAM CUPID HEARTS COAT HANGER	536365	NA
18	84879	ASSORTED COLOUR BIRD ORNAMENT	536367	NA
19	84969	BOX OF 6 ASSORTED COLOUR TEASPOONS	NA	6
20	85123A	WHITE HANGING HEART T-LIGHT HOLDER	536365	NA

Showing 1 to 20 of 20 entries

This is left outer join:

```
d4 = merge(d2, d3, all.x=T)
```

	StockCode	Description	InvoiceNo	Quantity
1	21730	GLASS STAR FROSTED T-LIGHT HOLDER	536365	NA
2	22632	HAND WARMER RED POLKA DOT	536366	NA
3	22633	HAND WARMER UNION JACK	536366	NA
4	22745	POPPYS PLAYHOUSE BEDROOM ,6,12/1/10 8:34,2....	536367	6
5	22752	SET 7 BABUSHKA NESTING BOXES	536365	NA
6	71053	WHITE METAL LANTERN	536365	NA
7	84029E	RED WOOLLY HOTTIE WHITE HEART.	536365	NA
8	84029G	KNITTED UNION FLAG HOT WATER BOTTLE	536365	NA
9	84406B	CREAM CUPID HEARTS COAT HANGER	536365	NA
10	84879	ASSORTED COLOUR BIRD ORNAMENT	536367	NA
11	85123A	WHITE HANGING HEART T-LIGHT HOLDER	536365	NA

Showing 1 to 11 of 11 entries

This is right outer join:

```
d4 = merge(d2, d3, all.y=T)
```

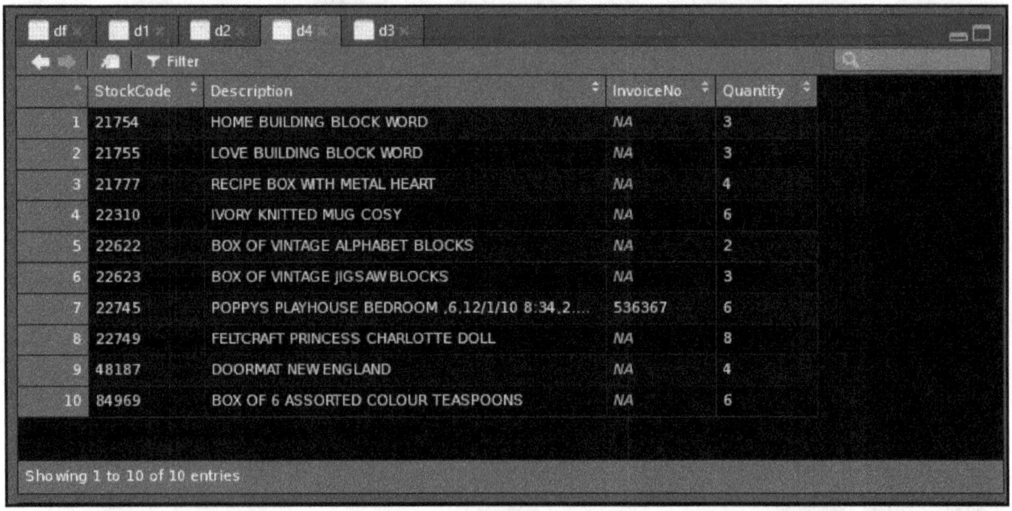

	StockCode	Description	InvoiceNo	Quantity
1	21754	HOME BUILDING BLOCK WORD	NA	3
2	21755	LOVE BUILDING BLOCK WORD	NA	3
3	21777	RECIPE BOX WITH METAL HEART	NA	4
4	22310	IVORY KNITTED MUG COSY	NA	6
5	22622	BOX OF VINTAGE ALPHABET BLOCKS	NA	2
6	22623	BOX OF VINTAGE JIGSAW BLOCKS	NA	3
7	22745	POPPYS PLAYHOUSE BEDROOM ,6,12/1/10 8:34,2....	536367	6
8	22749	FELTCRAFT PRINCESS CHARLOTTE DOLL	NA	8
9	48187	DOORMAT NEW ENGLAND	NA	4
10	84969	BOX OF 6 ASSORTED COLOUR TEASPOONS	NA	6

Showing 1 to 10 of 10 entries

And finally, cross join:

```
d4 = merge(d2, d3, by=NULL)
```

	InvoiceNo	StockCode.x	Description.x	StockCode.y	Description.y	Quantity
1	536365	85123A	WHITE HANGING HEART T-LIGHT HOLDER	22745	POPPYS PLAYHOUSE BEDROOM ,6,12/1/10 8:34,2...	6
2	536365	71053	WHITE METAL LANTERN	22745	POPPYS PLAYHOUSE BEDROOM ,6,12/1/10 8:34,2...	6
3	536365	84406B	CREAM CUPID HEARTS COAT HANGER	22745	POPPYS PLAYHOUSE BEDROOM ,6,12/1/10 8:34,2...	6
4	536365	84029G	KNITTED UNION FLAG HOT WATER BOTTLE	22745	POPPYS PLAYHOUSE BEDROOM ,6,12/1/10 8:34,2...	6
5	536365	84029E	RED WOOLLY HOTTIE WHITE HEART.	22745	POPPYS PLAYHOUSE BEDROOM ,6,12/1/10 8:34,2...	6
6	536365	22752	SET 7 BABUSHKA NESTING BOXES	22745	POPPYS PLAYHOUSE BEDROOM ,6,12/1/10 8:34,2...	6
7	536365	21730	GLASS STAR FROSTED T-LIGHT HOLDER	22745	POPPYS PLAYHOUSE BEDROOM ,6,12/1/10 8:34,2...	6
8	536366	22633	HAND WARMER UNION JACK	22745	POPPYS PLAYHOUSE BEDROOM ,6,12/1/10 8:34,2...	6
9	536366	22632	HAND WARMER RED POLKA DOT	22745	POPPYS PLAYHOUSE BEDROOM ,6,12/1/10 8:34,2...	6
10	536367	84879	ASSORTED COLOUR BIRD ORNAMENT	22745	POPPYS PLAYHOUSE BEDROOM ,6,12/1/10 8:34,2...	6
11	536367	22745	POPPYS PLAYHOUSE BEDROOM ,6,12/1/10 8:34,2...	22745	POPPYS PLAYHOUSE BEDROOM ,6,12/1/10 8:34,2...	6
12	536365	85123A	WHITE HANGING HEART T-LIGHT HOLDER	22749	FELTCRAFT PRINCESS CHARLOTTE DOLL	8
13	536365	71053	WHITE METAL LANTERN	22749	FELTCRAFT PRINCESS CHARLOTTE DOLL	8
14	536365	84406B	CREAM CUPID HEARTS COAT HANGER	22749	FELTCRAFT PRINCESS CHARLOTTE DOLL	8
15	536365	84029G	KNITTED UNION FLAG HOT WATER BOTTLE	22749	FELTCRAFT PRINCESS CHARLOTTE DOLL	8
16	536365	84029E	RED WOOLLY HOTTIE WHITE HEART.	22749	FELTCRAFT PRINCESS CHARLOTTE DOLL	8
17	536365	22752	SET 7 BABUSHKA NESTING BOXES	22749	FELTCRAFT PRINCESS CHARLOTTE DOLL	8
18	536365	21730	GLASS STAR FROSTED T-LIGHT HOLDER	22749	FELTCRAFT PRINCESS CHARLOTTE DOLL	8
19	536366	22633	HAND WARMER UNION JACK	22749	FELTCRAFT PRINCESS CHARLOTTE DOLL	8

Showing 1 to 20 of 110 entries

Just as in pandas, we can use `by=` to specify between the two data items with a `.x` and `.y` instead of `_x` and `_y`. Look at the following:

```
d4 = merge(d2, d3, by="StockCode", all=T)
```

This is an outer join on the `StockCode` column.

This is the result:

	StockCode	InvoiceNo	Description.x	Description.y	Quantity
1	21730	536365	GLASS STAR FROSTED T-LIGHT HOLDER	NA	NA
2	21754	NA	NA	HOME BUILDING BLOCK WORD	3
3	21755	NA	NA	LOVE BUILDING BLOCK WORD	3
4	21777	NA	NA	RECIPE BOX WITH METAL HEART	4
5	22310	NA	NA	IVORY KNITTED MUG COSY	6
6	22622	NA	NA	BOX OF VINTAGE ALPHABET BLOCKS	2
7	22623	NA	NA	BOX OF VINTAGE JIGSAW BLOCKS	3
8	22632	536366	HAND WARMER RED POLKA DOT	NA	NA
9	22633	536366	HAND WARMER UNION JACK	NA	NA
10	22745	536367	POPPYS PLAYHOUSE BEDROOM ,6,12/1/10 8:34,2...	POPPYS PLAYHOUSE BEDROOM ,6,12/1/10 8:34,2...	6
11	22749	NA	NA	FELTCRAFT PRINCESS CHARLOTTE DOLL	8
12	22752	536365	SET 7 BABUSHKA NESTING BOXES	NA	NA
13	48187	NA	NA	DOORMAT NEW ENGLAND	4
14	71053	536365	WHITE METAL LANTERN	NA	NA
15	84029E	536365	RED WOOLLY HOTTIE WHITE HEART.	NA	NA
16	84029G	536365	KNITTED UNION FLAG HOT WATER BOTTLE	NA	NA
17	84406B	536365	CREAM CUPID HEARTS COAT HANGER	NA	NA
18	84879	536367	ASSORTED COLOUR BIRD ORNAMENT	NA	NA
19	84969	NA	NA	BOX OF 6 ASSORTED COLOUR TEASPOONS	6
20	85123A	536365	WHITE HANGING HEART T-LIGHT HOLDER	NA	NA

Showing 1 to 20 of 20 entries

We can always keep a log of all our commands in case something happens. Execute this code to save the command log:

```
savehistory(file="logname.Rhistory")
```

And to load history:

```
loadhistory(file="logname.Rhistory")
```

If you want to check your history, simply do this:

```
history()
```

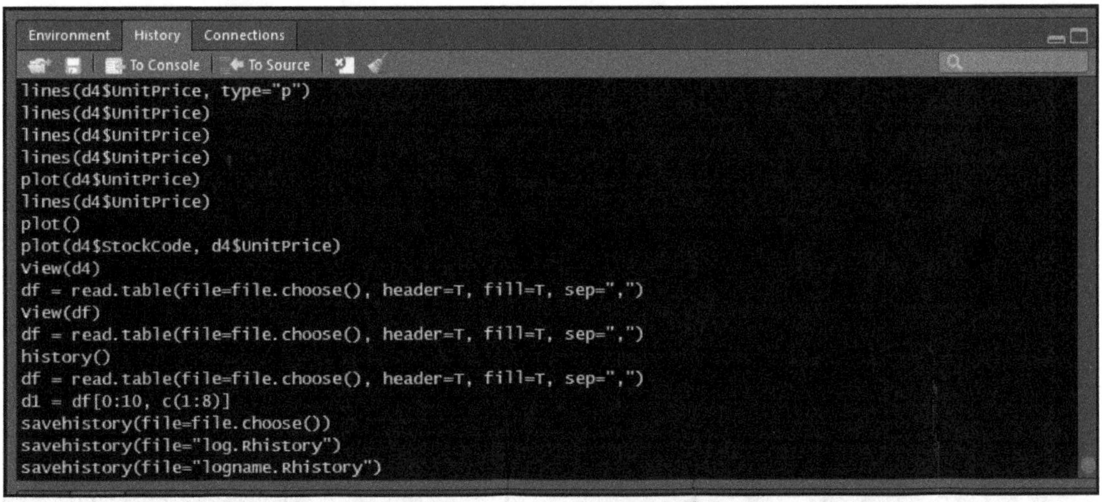

Environment
History
Connections
To Console
To Source
lines(d4$UnitPrice, type="p")
lines(d4$UnitPrice)
lines(d4$UnitPrice)
lines(d4$UnitPrice)
plot(d4$UnitPrice)
lines(d4$UnitPrice)
plot()
plot(d4$StockCode, d4$UnitPrice)
View(d4)
df = read.table(file=file.choose(), header=T, fill=T, sep=",")
View(df)
df = read.table(file=file.choose(), header=T, fill=T, sep=",")
history()
df = read.table(file=file.choose(), header=T, fill=T, sep=",")
d1 = df[0:10, c(1:8)]
savehistory(file=file.choose())
savehistory(file="log.Rhistory")
savehistory(file="logname.Rhistory")

We can check the data to see whether there's any blank data. Look at the code:

```
colSums(is.na(df))
```

Now, let's repeat this again. Recall how earlier when we merged two data frames, we had NaN for some data values:

```
d2 = df[0:11, c("InvoiceNo", "StockCode", "Description")]
d3 = df[11:20, c("StockCode", "Description", "Quantity")]
```

Now, let's do an outer merge on them:

```
d4 = merge(d2, d3, all=T)
```

Now, let's try this line of code:

```
colSums(is.na(d4))
```

> colSums(is.na(d4))
StockCode Description InvoiceNo Quantity
0 0 9 10

We can also replace values in the data.

Now, suppose that you want to change the description of every item with a price greater than three to `"Miscellaneous"`. Take a look at this example code:

```
d1 = df[0:30, c(1:8)]
```

	InvoiceNo	StockCode	Description	Quantity	InvoiceDate	UnitPrice	CustomerID	Country
1	536365	85123A	WHITE HANGING HEART T-LIGHT HOLDER	6	12/1/10 8:26	2.55	17850	United Kingdom
2	536365	71053	WHITE METAL LANTERN	6	12/1/10 8:26	3.39	17850	United Kingdom
3	536365	84406B	CREAM CUPID HEARTS COAT HANGER	8	12/1/10 8:26	2.75	17850	United Kingdom
4	536365	84029G	KNITTED UNION FLAG HOT WATER BOTTLE	6	12/1/10 8:26	3.39	17850	United Kingdom
5	536365	84029E	RED WOOLLY HOTTIE WHITE HEART.	6	12/1/10 8:26	3.39	17850	United Kingdom
6	536365	22752	SET 7 BABUSHKA NESTING BOXES	2	12/1/10 8:26	7.65	17850	United Kingdom
7	536365	21730	GLASS STAR FROSTED T-LIGHT HOLDER	6	12/1/10 8:26	4.25	17850	United Kingdom
8	536366	22633	HAND WARMER UNION JACK	6	12/1/10 8:28	1.85	17850	United Kingdom
9	536366	22632	HAND WARMER RED POLKA DOT	6	12/1/10 8:28	1.85	17850	United Kingdom
10	536367	84879	ASSORTED COLOUR BIRD ORNAMENT	32	12/1/10 8:34	1.69	13047	United Kingdom
11	536367	22745	POPPY'S PLAYHOUSE BEDROOM	6	12/1/10 8:34	2.10	13047	United Kingdom
12	536367	22748	POPPY'S PLAYHOUSE KITCHEN	6	12/1/10 8:34	2.10	13047	United Kingdom
13	536367	22749	FELTCRAFT PRINCESS CHARLOTTE DOLL	8	12/1/10 8:34	3.75	13047	United Kingdom
14	536367	22310	IVORY KNITTED MUG COSY	6	12/1/10 8:34	1.65	13047	United Kingdom
15	536367	84969	BOX OF 6 ASSORTED COLOUR TEASPOONS	6	12/1/10 8:34	4.25	13047	United Kingdom
16	536367	22623	BOX OF VINTAGE JIGSAW BLOCKS	3	12/1/10 8:34	4.95	13047	United Kingdom
17	536367	22622	BOX OF VINTAGE ALPHABET BLOCKS	2	12/1/10 8:34	9.95	13047	United Kingdom
18	536367	21754	HOME BUILDING BLOCK WORD	3	12/1/10 8:34	5.95	13047	United Kingdom
19	536367	21755	LOVE BUILDING BLOCK WORD	3	12/1/10 8:34	5.95	13047	United Kingdom
20	536367	21777	RECIPE BOX WITH METAL HEART	4	12/1/10 8:34	7.95	13047	United Kingdom

Now, look at this:

```
d1[d1$UnitPrice > 3, "Description"] <- "Miscellaneous"
```

	InvoiceNo	StockCode	Description	Quantity	InvoiceDate	UnitPrice	CustomerID	Country
1	536365	85123A	WHITE HANGING HEART T-LIGHT HOLDER	6	12/1/10 8:26	2.55	17850	United Kingdom
2	536365	71053	Miscellaneous	6	12/1/10 8:26	3.39	17850	United Kingdom
3	536365	84406B	CREAM CUPID HEARTS COAT HANGER	8	12/1/10 8:26	2.75	17850	United Kingdom
4	536365	84029G	Miscellaneous	6	12/1/10 8:26	3.39	17850	United Kingdom
5	536365	84029E	Miscellaneous	6	12/1/10 8:26	3.39	17850	United Kingdom
6	536365	22752	Miscellaneous	2	12/1/10 8:26	7.65	17850	United Kingdom
7	536365	21730	Miscellaneous	6	12/1/10 8:26	4.25	17850	United Kingdom
8	536366	22633	HAND WARMER UNION JACK	6	12/1/10 8:28	1.85	17850	United Kingdom
9	536366	22632	HAND WARMER RED POLKA DOT	6	12/1/10 8:28	1.85	17850	United Kingdom
10	536367	84879	ASSORTED COLOUR BIRD ORNAMENT	32	12/1/10 8:34	1.69	13047	United Kingdom
11	536367	22745	POPPY'S PLAYHOUSE BEDROOM	6	12/1/10 8:34	2.10	13047	United Kingdom
12	536367	22748	POPPY'S PLAYHOUSE KITCHEN	6	12/1/10 8:34	2.10	13047	United Kingdom
13	536367	22749	Miscellaneous	8	12/1/10 8:34	3.75	13047	United Kingdom
14	536367	22310	IVORY KNITTED MUG COSY	6	12/1/10 8:34	1.65	13047	United Kingdom
15	536367	84969	Miscellaneous	6	12/1/10 8:34	4.25	13047	United Kingdom
16	536367	22623	Miscellaneous	3	12/1/10 8:34	4.95	13047	United Kingdom
17	536367	22622	Miscellaneous	2	12/1/10 8:34	9.95	13047	United Kingdom
18	536367	21754	Miscellaneous	3	12/1/10 8:34	5.95	13047	United Kingdom
19	536367	21755	Miscellaneous	3	12/1/10 8:34	5.95	13047	United Kingdom
20	536367	21777	Miscellaneous	4	12/1/10 8:34	7.95	13047	United Kingdom

Showing 1 to 20 of 30 entries

```
> d1 = df[0:30, c(1:8)]
> d1[d1$UnitPrice > 3, "Description"] <- "Miscellaneous"
>
```

Now we see that everything with a unit price greater that three has a description of "`Miscellaneous`".

We can use other operators besides >, and we can replace values in other columns too.

Here is another example.

Let's say that every item with the invoice number `536365` actually came from the `United States`.

Now, since they all share the same invoice number and invoice date, we can use either one to select the desired rows:

```
d1[d1$InvoiceNo == 536365, "Country"] = "United States"
```

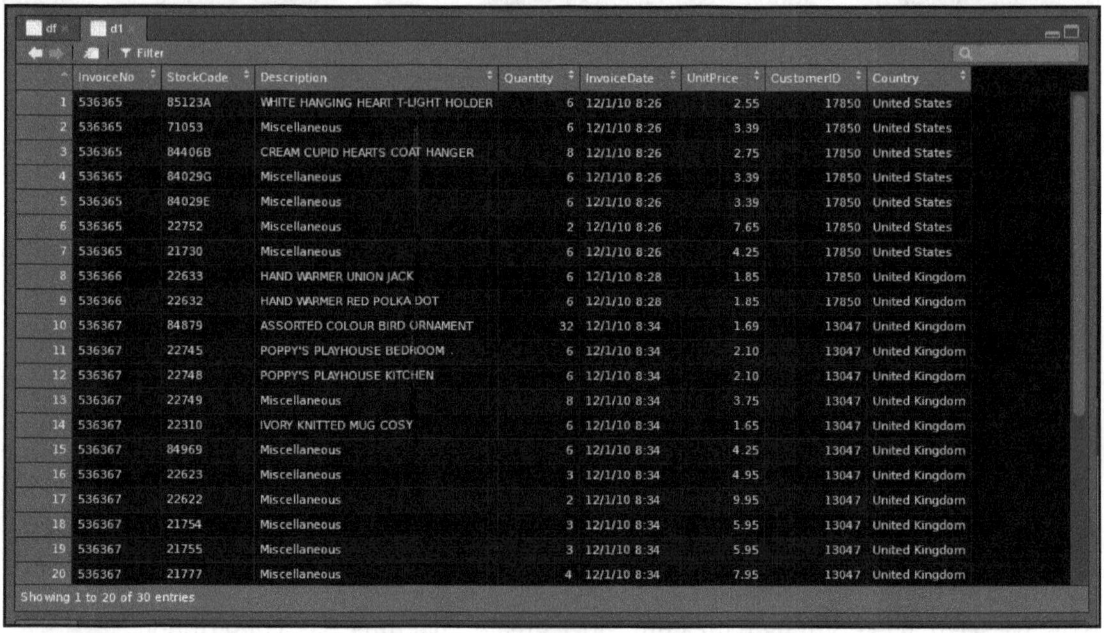

	InvoiceNo	StockCode	Description	Quantity	InvoiceDate	UnitPrice	CustomerID	Country
1	536365	85123A	WHITE HANGING HEART T-LIGHT HOLDER	6	12/1/10 8:26	2.55	17850	United States
2	536365	71053	Miscellaneous	6	12/1/10 8:26	3.39	17850	United States
3	536365	84406B	CREAM CUPID HEARTS COAT HANGER	8	12/1/10 8:26	2.75	17850	United States
4	536365	84029G	Miscellaneous	6	12/1/10 8:26	3.39	17850	United States
5	536365	84029E	Miscellaneous	6	12/1/10 8:26	3.39	17850	United States
6	536365	22752	Miscellaneous	2	12/1/10 8:26	7.65	17850	United States
7	536365	21730	Miscellaneous	6	12/1/10 8:26	4.25	17850	United States
8	536366	22633	HAND WARMER UNION JACK	6	12/1/10 8:28	1.85	17850	United Kingdom
9	536366	22632	HAND WARMER RED POLKA DOT	6	12/1/10 8:28	1.85	17850	United Kingdom
10	536367	84879	ASSORTED COLOUR BIRD ORNAMENT	32	12/1/10 8:34	1.69	13047	United Kingdom
11	536367	22745	POPPY'S PLAYHOUSE BEDROOM	6	12/1/10 8:34	2.10	13047	United Kingdom
12	536367	22748	POPPY'S PLAYHOUSE KITCHEN	6	12/1/10 8:34	2.10	13047	United Kingdom
13	536367	22749	Miscellaneous	8	12/1/10 8:34	3.75	13047	United Kingdom
14	536367	22310	IVORY KNITTED MUG COSY	6	12/1/10 8:34	1.65	13047	United Kingdom
15	536367	84969	Miscellaneous	6	12/1/10 8:34	4.25	13047	United Kingdom
16	536367	22623	Miscellaneous	3	12/1/10 8:34	4.95	13047	United Kingdom
17	536367	22622	Miscellaneous	2	12/1/10 8:34	9.95	13047	United Kingdom
18	536367	21754	Miscellaneous	3	12/1/10 8:34	5.95	13047	United Kingdom
19	536367	21755	Miscellaneous	3	12/1/10 8:34	5.95	13047	United Kingdom
20	536367	21777	Miscellaneous	4	12/1/10 8:34	7.95	13047	United Kingdom

Showing 1 to 20 of 30 entries

Notice that this time we used = instead of <-. In this context, they both are assigning something, so either one can be used.

Summary

In this chapter, we discussed how R can be used to perform data analysis. We also described different options for integrating R and Hadoop.

In the next chapter, we will learn about Apache Spark and how to use it for big data analytics based on a batch processing model.

6
Batch Analytics with Apache Spark

In this chapter, you will learn about Apache Spark and how to use it for big data analytics based on a batch processing model. Spark SQL is a component on top of Spark Core that can be used to query structured data. It is becoming the de facto tool, replacing Hive as the choice for batch analytics on Hadoop.

Moreover, you will learn how to use Spark for the analysis of structured data (unstructured data such as a document containing arbitrary text, or some other format that has to be transformed into a structured form). We will see how DataFrames/datasets are the cornerstone here, and how SparkSQL's APIs make querying structured data simple yet robust.

We will also introduce datasets and see the difference between datasets, DataFrames, and RDDs. In a nutshell, the following topics will be covered in this chapter:

- SparkSQL and DataFrames
- DataFrames and the SQL API
- DataFrame schema
- Datasets and encoders
- Loading and saving data
- Aggregations
- Joins

SparkSQL and DataFrames

Before Apache Spark, Apache Hive was the go-to technology whenever anyone wanted to run an SQL-like query on large amount of data. Apache Hive essentially translated an SQL query into MapReduce, like logic automatically making it very easy to perform many kinds of analytics on big data without actually learning to write complex code in Java and Scala.

With the advent of Apache Spark, there was a paradigm shift in how we could perform analysis at a big data scale. Spark SQL provides an SQL-like layer on top of Apache Spark's distributed computation abilities that is rather simple to use. In fact, Spark SQL can be used as an online analytical processing database. Spark SQL works by parsing the SQL-like statement into an **abstract syntax tree** (**AST**), subsequently converting that plan to a logical plan and then optimizing the logical plan into a physical plan that can be executed, as shown in the following diagram:

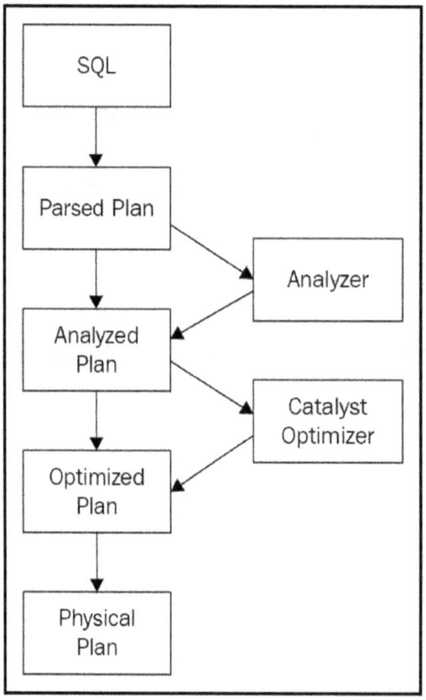

The final execution uses the underlying DataFrame API, making it very easy for anyone to use DataFrame APIs by simply using an SQL-like interface rather than learning all the internals. Since this book dives into the technical details of various APIs, we will primarily cover the DataFrame APIs, showing Spark SQL API at some places to contrast the different ways of using the APIs. Thus, the DataFrame API is the underlying layer beneath Spark SQL. In this chapter, we will show you how to create DataFrames using various techniques, including SQL queries and performing operations on the DataFrames.

A DataFrame is an abstraction over the **resilient distributed dataset** (**RDD**) dealing with higher-level functions optimized using a catalyst optimizer, and is also highly performant via the Tungsten initiative.

Since its inception, Project Tungsten has been the largest change to Spark's execution engine. Its main focus lies in enhancing efficiency of CPU and memory for Spark applications. This project comprises three initiatives:

- Memory management and binary processing
- Cache-aware computation
- Code generation

TIP: For more information, you can check out `https://databricks.com/blog/2015/04/28/project-tungsten-bringing-spark-closer-to-bare-metal.html`.

You can think of a dataset as an efficient table over an RDD with a heavily optimized binary representation of the data. The binary representation is achieved using encoders that serialize the various objects into a binary structure for much better performance than RDD representation. Since DataFrame uses the RDD internally anyway, a DataFrame/dataset is also distributed exactly like an RDD and thus is also a distributed dataset. Obviously, this also means datasets are immutable.

The following is an illustration of the binary representation of data:

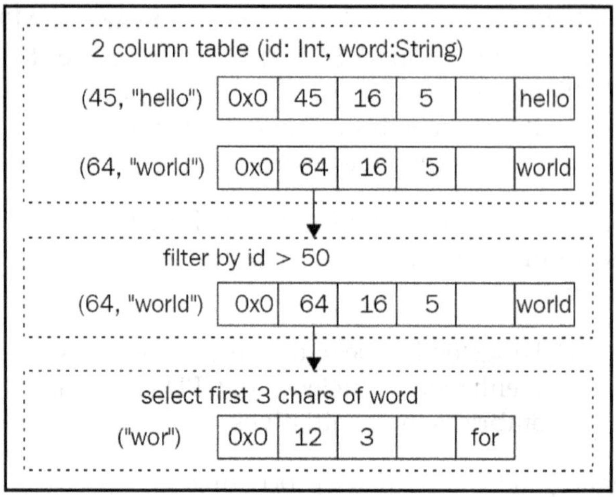

Datasets were added in Spark 1.6 and provide the benefit of strong typing on top of DataFrames. In fact, since Spark 2.0 the DataFrame is simply an alias of a Dataset.

> `http://spark.apache.org/sql/` defines the DataFrame type as a *Dataset[Row]*, which means that most of the APIs will work well with both dataset and *DataFrame.type DataFrame = Dataset[Row]*.

A DataFrame is conceptually similar to a table in a relational database. Hence, a DataFrame contains rows of data with each row consisting of several columns. One of the first things we need to keep in mind is that just like RDDs, DataFrames are also immutable. This property of DataFrames being immutable means every transformation or action creates a new DataFrame.

Let's start by looking more into DataFrames and how they are different from RDDs. RDDs, as seen before, represent a low-level API for data manipulation in Apache Spark. The DataFrames were created on top of RDDs to abstract the low-level inner workings of RDDs and expose high-level APIs which are easier to use and provide lot of functionality out of the box. DataFrame was created following similar concepts found in the Python pandas package, R language, Julia language, and so on.

As we mentioned before, the DataFrame translates the SQL code and domain-specific language expressions into optimized execution plans to be run on top of Spark Core APIs in order for the SQL statements to perform a wide variety of operations. DataFrames support many different types of input data sources and many types of operations. This includes all types of SQL operations such as joins, group by, aggregations, and window functions as most of the databases.

Spark SQL is also quite similar to the Hive query language and since Spark provides a natural adapter to Apache Hive, users who have been working in Apache Hive can easily transfer their knowledge and apply to Spark SQL, thus minimizing the transition time. The DataFrame essentially depends on the concept of table as seen previously.

The table can be operated very similarly to how Apache Hive works. In fact, many of the operations on the tables in Apache Spark are similar to how Apache Hive handles tables and operates on the tables. Once you have a table that is the DataFrame, the DataFrame can be registered as a table and you can operate on the data using Spark SQL statements in lieu of the DataFrame APIs.

The DataFrame depends on the catalyst optimizer and the Tungsten performance improvement, so let's briefly examine how the catalyst optimizer works. The catalyst optimizer creates a parsed logical plan from the input SQL and then analyzes the logical plan by looking at all the various attributes and columns used in the SQL statement. Once the analyzed logical plan is created, the catalyst optimizer further tries to optimize the plan by combining several operations and also rearranging the logic to get better performance.

> In order to understand the catalyst optimizer, think about it as a common sense logic optimizer which can reorder operations such as filters and transformations, sometimes grouping several operations into one so as to minimize the amount of data that is shuffled across the worker nodes. For example, the catalyst optimizer may decide to broadcast the smaller datasets when performing joint operations between different datasets. Use explain to look at the execution plan of any DataFrame. The catalyst optimizer also computes statistics of the DataFrames columns and partitions improving the speed of execution.

For example, if there are transformations and filters on the data partitions then the order in which we filter data and apply transformations matters a lot to the overall performance of the operations. As a result of all the optimizations, the optimized logical plan is generated which is then converted to a physical plan.

Obviously, several physical plans are possible to execute the same SQL statement and generate the same result. The cost optimization logic determines and picks a good physical plan based on the cost optimizations and estimations. Tungsten performance improvements are another key ingredient in the secret sauce behind the phenomenal performance improvements offered by Spark 2.x compared to previous releases such as Spark 1.6 or older.

Tungsten implements a complete overhaul of memory management and other performance improvements. Most important memory management improvements use binary encoding of objects and reference them in both off-heap and on-heap memory. Thus, Tungsten allows usage of office heap memory by using the binary encoding mechanism to encode all the objects. Binary encoded objects take up much less memory.

Project Tungsten also improve shuffle performance. The data is typically loaded into DataFrames through the `DataFrameReader` and data is saved from DataFrames through `DataFrameWriter`.

DataFrame APIs and the SQL API

A DataFrame can be created in several ways; some of them are as follows:

- Execute SQL queries, load external data such as Parquet, JSON, CSV, Text, Hive, JDBC, and so on
- Convert RDDs to DataFrames
- Load a CSV file

We will take a look at `statesPopulation.csv` here, which we will then load as a DataFrame.

The CSV has the following format of the population of US states from the years 2010 to 2016:

State	**Year**	**Population**
Alabama	2010	47,85,492
Alaska	2010	714,031
Arizona	2010	64,08,312
Arkansas	2010	2,921,995
California	2010	37,332,685

Since this CSV has a header, we can use it to quickly load into a DataFrame with an implicit schema detection:

```
scala> val statesDF = spark.read.option("header",
"true").option("inferschema", "true").option("sep",
",").csv("statesPopulation.csv")
statesDF: org.apache.spark.sql.DataFrame = [State: string, Year: int ... 1
more field]
```

Once we load the DataFrame, it can be examined for the schema:

```
scala> statesDF.printSchema
root
|-- State: string (nullable = true)
|-- Year: integer (nullable = true)
|-- Population: integer (nullable = true)
```

```
option("header",
"true").option("inferschema", "true").option("sep", ",")
```

tells Spark that the CSV has a header; a comma separator is used to separate the fields/columns and also that schema can be inferred implicitly.

The DataFrame works by parsing the logical plan, analyzing the logical plan, optimizing the plan and then finally executing the physical plan of execution.

Using explain on DataFrame shows the plan of execution:

```
scala> statesDF.explain(true)
== Parsed Logical Plan ==
Relation[State#0,Year#1,Population#2] csv
== Analyzed Logical Plan ==
State: string, Year: int, Population: int
Relation[State#0,Year#1,Population#2] csv
== Optimized Logical Plan ==
Relation[State#0,Year#1,Population#2] csv
== Physical Plan ==
*FileScan csv [State#0,Year#1,Population#2] Batched: false, Format: CSV,
Location: InMemoryFileIndex[file:/Users/salla/states.csv],
PartitionFilters: [], PushedFilters: [], ReadSchema:
struct<State:string,Year:int,Population:int>
```

A DataFrame can also be registered as a table name (shown as follows) which will then allow you to type SQL statements like a relational database:

```
scala> statesDF.createOrReplaceTempView("states")
```

Once we have the DataFrame as a structured DataFrame or a table, we can run commands to operate on the data:

```
scala> statesDF.show(5)
scala> spark.sql("select * from states limit 5").show
+----------+----+----------+
| State|Year|Population|
+----------+----+----------+
| Alabama|2010| 4785492|
| Alaska|2010| 714031|
| Arizona|2010| 6408312|
| Arkansas|2010| 2921995|
|California|2010| 37332685|
+----------+----+----------+
```

If you see in the preceding piece of code, we have written an SQL-like statement and executed it using the `spark.sql` API.

TIP: Note that the Spark SQL is simply converted to the DataFrame API for execution and the SQL is only a DSL for ease of use.

Using the `sort` operation on the DataFrame, you can order the rows in the DataFrame by any column. We see the effects of descending sort using the `Population` column as follows. The rows are ordered by the `Population` in a descending order:

```
scala> statesDF.sort(col("Population").desc).show(5)
scala> spark.sql("select * from states order by Population desc limit
5").show
+----------+----+----------+
| State|Year|Population|
 +----------+----+----------+
|California|2016| 39250017|
|California|2015| 38993940|
|California|2014| 38680810|
|California|2013| 38335203|
|California|2012| 38011074|
+----------+----+----------+
```

Using `groupBy` we can group the DataFrame by any column. Following is the code to group the rows by `State` and then add up the `Population` counts for each `State`:

```
scala> statesDF.groupBy("State").sum("Population").show(5)
scala> spark.sql("select State, sum(Population)
from states group by State
limit 5").show
+---------+---------------+
| State|sum(Population)|
+---------+---------------+
| Utah| 20333580|
| Hawaii| 9810173|
|Minnesota| 37914011|
| Ohio| 81020539|
| Arkansas| 20703849|
+---------+---------------+
```

Using the `agg` operation, you can perform many different operations on columns of the DataFrame such as finding the `min`, `max`, and `avg` of a column. You can also perform the operation and rename the column at the same time to suit your use case:

```
scala>
statesDF.groupBy("State").agg(sum("Population").alias("Total")).show(5)
scala> spark.sql("select State, sum(Population) as Total from states group
by State limit 5").show
+---------+--------+
| State| Total|
+---------+--------+
| Utah|20333580|
| Hawaii| 9810173|
|Minnesota|37914011|
| Ohio|81020539|
| Arkansas|20703849|
+---------+--------+
```

Naturally, the more complicated the logic gets, the more the execution plan also gets complicated. Let's look at the plan for the preceding operation of `groupBy` and `agg` API invocations to better understand what is really going on under the hood. The following is the code showing the execution plan of the `group by` clause and a summation of population per `State`:

```
scala>
statesDF.groupBy("State").agg(sum("Population").alias("Total")).explain(tru
e)
== Parsed Logical Plan ==
'Aggregate [State#0], [State#0, sum('Population) AS Total#31886]
```

```
+- Relation[State#0,Year#1,Population#2] csv
== Analyzed Logical Plan ==
State: string, Total: bigint
Aggregate [State#0], [State#0, sum(cast(Population#2 as bigint)) AS
Total#31886L]
+- Relation[State#0,Year#1,Population#2] csv
== Optimized Logical Plan ==
Aggregate [State#0], [State#0, sum(cast(Population#2 as bigint)) AS
Total#31886L]
+- Project [State#0, Population#2]
+- Relation[State#0,Year#1,Population#2] csv
== Physical Plan ==
*HashAggregate(keys=[State#0], functions=[sum(cast(Population#2 as
bigint))], output=[State#0, Total#31886L])
+- Exchange hashpartitioning(State#0, 200)
+- *HashAggregate(keys=[State#0], functions=[partial_sum(cast(Population#2
as bigint))], output=[State#0, sum#31892L])
+- *FileScan csv [State#0,Population#2] Batched: false, Format: CSV,
Location: InMemoryFileIndex[file:/Users/salla/states.csv],
PartitionFilters: [], PushedFilters: [], ReadSchema:
struct<State:string,Population:int>
```

DataFrame operations can be chained together very well so that the execution takes advantage of the cost optimization (the Tungsten performance improvements and catalyst optimizer working together). We can also chain the operations together in a single statement as follows, where we not only group the data by the `State` column and then sum the `Population` value but also sort the DataFrame by the summation column:

```
scala>
statesDF.groupBy("State").agg(sum("Population").alias("Total")).sort(col("T
otal").desc).show(5)
scala> spark.sql("select State, sum(Population) as Total from states group
by State order by Total desc limit 5").show
+----------+---------+
| State| Total|
+----------+---------+
|California|268280590
| Texas|185672865|
| Florida|137618322|
| New York|137409471|
| Illinois| 89960023|
+----------+---------+
```

The preceding chained operation consists of multiple transformations and actions which can be visualized using the following diagram:

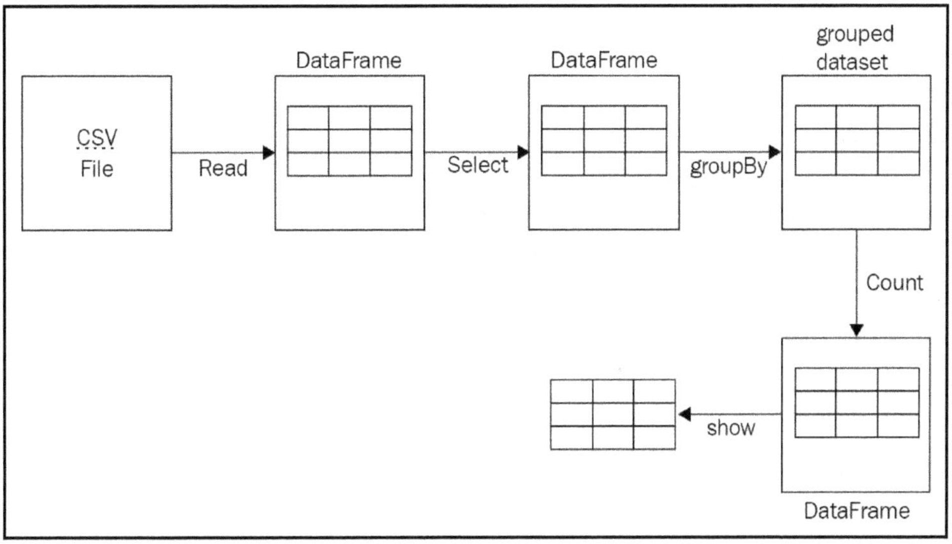

It's also possible to create multiple aggregations at the same time as follows:

```
scala> statesDF.groupBy("State").agg(
min("Population").alias("minTotal"),
max("Population").alias("maxTotal"),
avg("Population").alias("avgTotal"))
.sort(col("minTotal").desc).show(5)
scala> spark.sql("select State, min(Population) as minTotal,
max(Population) as maxTotal, avg(Population) as avgTotal from states group
by State order by minTotal desc limit 5").show
+----------+--------+--------+--------------------+
| State|minTotal|maxTotal| avgTotal|
+----------+--------+--------+--------------------+
|California|37332685|39250017|3.8325798571428575E7|
| Texas|25244310|27862596| 2.6524695E7|
| New York|19402640|19747183| 1.962992442857143E7|
| Florida|18849098|20612439|1.9659760285714287E7|
| Illinois|12801539|12879505|1.2851431857142856E7|
+----------+--------+--------+--------------------+
```

Pivots

One of the best ways to transform a table in order to create a different view that will be more suitable to perform multiple summarizations and aggregations is **pivoting**. We can achieve this by taking the values of a column and making each of the values an actual column.

Let us understand this better with the help of an example. We will pivot the rows of the DataFrame by `Year` and examine the result. The result we obtain now depicts the values from the `Year` column and each has formed a new column. The end result of this is that rather than just looking at the year column we can use the per year columns created to summarize and aggregate by `Year`:

```
scala> statesDF.groupBy("State").pivot("Year").sum("Population").show(5)
+---------+--------+--------+--------+--------+--------+--------+--------+
| State| 2010| 2011| 2012| 2013| 2014| 2015| 2016|
+---------+--------+--------+--------+--------+--------+--------+--------+
| Utah| 2775326| 2816124| 2855782| 2902663| 2941836| 2990632| 3051217|
| Hawaii| 1363945| 1377864| 1391820| 1406481| 1416349| 1425157| 1428557|
|Minnesota| 5311147| 5348562| 5380285| 5418521| 5453109| 5482435| 5519952|
| Ohio|11540983|11544824|11550839|11570022|11594408|11605090|11614373|
| Arkansas| 2921995| 2939493| 2950685| 2958663| 2966912| 2977853| 2988248|
+---------+--------+--------+--------+--------+--------+--------+--------+
```

Filters

Filter is also supported by DataFrames and can be used to generate a new DataFrame by filtering the DataFrame rows. The `Filter` enables a very important transformation of the data to narrow down the DataFrame to our use case. Let's look at the execution plan for the filtering of the DataFrame to only consider state of `California`:

```
scala> statesDF.filter("State == 'California'").explain(true)
== Parsed Logical Plan ==
'Filter ('State = California)
+- Relation[State#0,Year#1,Population#2] csv
== Analyzed Logical Plan ==
State: string, Year: int, Population: int
Filter (State#0 = California)
+- Relation[State#0,Year#1,Population#2] csv
== Optimized Logical Plan ==
Filter (isnotnull(State#0) && (State#0 = California))
+- Relation[State#0,Year#1,Population#2] csv
== Physical Plan ==
*Project [State#0, Year#1, Population#2]
```

```
+- *Filter (isnotnull(State#0) && (State#0 = California))
+- *FileScan csv [State#0,Year#1,Population#2] Batched: false, Format:
CSV, Location: InMemoryFileIndex[file:/Users/salla/states.csv],
PartitionFilters: [], PushedFilters: [IsNotNull(State),
EqualTo(State,California)], ReadSchema:
struct<State:string,Year:int,Population:int>
```

Now that we can seen the execution plan, let's now execute the `filter` command as follows:

```
scala> statesDF.filter("State == 'California'").show
+----------+----+----------+
| State|Year|Population|
+----------+----+----------+
|California|2010| 37332685|
|California|2011| 37676861|
|California|2012| 38011074|
|California|2013| 38335203|
|California|2014| 38680810|
|California|2015| 38993940|
|California|2016| 39250017|
+----------+----+----------+
```

User-defined functions

User-defined functions (**UDFs**) define new column-based functions that extend the functionality of Spark SQL. The creation of UDFs can be of help in cases where the built-in functions in Spark cannot handle our requirements.

> `udf()` internally calls a case class `UserDefinedFunction` which in turn calls `ScalaUDF` internally.

Let's go through an example of a UDF which simply converts `State` column values to uppercase. First, we create the function we need in Scala as shown in the following code snippets:

```
import org.apache.spark.sql.functions._
scala> val toUpper: String => String = _.toUpperCase
toUpper: String => String = <function1>
```

Then we have to encapsulate the created function inside the `udf` to create the UDF:

```
scala> val toUpperUDF = udf(toUpper)
toUpperUDF: org.apache.spark.sql.expressions.UserDefinedFunction =
UserDefinedFunction(<function1>,StringType,Some(List(StringType)))
```

Now that we have created the `udf`, we can use it to convert the `State` column to uppercase:

```
scala> statesDF.withColumn("StateUpperCase",
toUpperUDF(col("State"))).show(5)
+----------+----+----------+--------------+
| State|Year|Population|StateUpperCase|
+----------+----+----------+--------------+
| Alabama|2010| 4785492| ALABAMA|
| Alaska|2010| 714031| ALASKA|
| Arizona|2010| 6408312| ARIZONA|
| Arkansas|2010| 2921995| ARKANSAS|
|California|2010| 37332685| CALIFORNIA|
+----------+----+----------+--------------+
```

Schema – structure of data

A schema is the description of the structure of your data and can be either implicit or explicit. There are two main ways to convert existing RDDs into datasets as the DataFrames are internally based on the RDD; they are as follows:

- Using reflection to infer the schema of the RDD
- Through a programmatic interface with the help of which you can take an existing RDD and render a schema to convert the RDD into a dataset with schema

Implicit schema

Let's look at an example of loading a **comma-separated values** (**CSV**) file into a DataFrame. Whenever a text file contains a header, the read API can infer the schema by reading the header line. We also have the option to specify the separator to be used to split the text file lines.

We read the `csv` inferring the schema from the header line and use the comma (`,`) as the separator. We also show the use of the `schema` command and the `printSchema` command to verify the schema of the input file:

```
scala> val statesDF = spark.read.option("header", "true")
 .option("inferschema", "true")
 .option("sep", ",")
 .csv("statesPopulation.csv")
statesDF: org.apache.spark.sql.DataFrame = [State: string, Year: int ... 1
more field]
scala> statesDF.schema
res92: org.apache.spark.sql.types.StructType = StructType(
StructField(State,StringType,true),
StructField(Year,IntegerType,true),
StructField(Population,IntegerType,true))
scala> statesDF.printSchema
root
|-- State: string (nullable = true)
|-- Year: integer (nullable = true)
|-- Population: integer (nullable = true)
```

Explicit schema

A schema is described using `StructType` which is a collection of `StructField` objects.

> `StructType` and `StructField` belong to the `org.apache.spark.sql.types` package. `DataTypes` such as `IntegerType` and `StringType` also belong to the `org.apache.spark.sql.types` package.

Using these imports, we can define a custom explicit schema.

First, import the necessary classes:

```
scala> import org.apache.spark.sql.types.{StructType, IntegerType,
StringType}
import org.apache.spark.sql.types.{StructType, IntegerType, StringType}
```

Define a schema with two columns/fields and an integer followed by a string:

```
scala> val schema = new StructType().add("i", IntegerType).add("s",
StringType)
schema: org.apache.spark.sql.types.StructType =
StructType(StructField(i,IntegerType,true), StructField(s,StringType,true))
```

It's easy to print the just created `schema`:

```
scala> schema.printTreeString
root
|-- i: integer (nullable = true)
|-- s: string (nullable = true)
```

There is also an option to print JSON, which is as follows, using the `prettyJson` function:

```
scala> schema.prettyJson
res85: String =
{
"type" : "struct",
"fields" : [ {
"name" : "i",
"type" : "integer",
"nullable" : true,
"metadata" : { }
}, {
"name" : "s",
"type" : "string",
"nullable" : true,
"metadata" : { }
} ]
}
```

All data types of Spark SQL are located in the package `org.apache.spark.sql.types`.

You can access them by using:

```
import org.apache.spark.sql.types._
```

Encoders

Spark 2.x supports a different way of defining schema for complex datatypes. First, let's look at a simple example. `Encoders` must be imported using the import statement in order for you to use `Encoders`:

```
import org.apache.spark.sql.Encoders
```

Let's look at a simple example of a defined tuple as a datatype to be used in the dataset APIs:

```
scala> Encoders.product[(Integer, String)].schema.printTreeString
root
|-- _1: integer (nullable = true)
|-- _2: string (nullable = true)
```

The preceding code looks complicated to use all the time, so we can also define a `case class` for our needs and then use it.

We can define a case `class Record` with two fields, an `Integer` and a `String`:

```
scala> case class Record(i: Integer, s: String)
defined class Record
```

Using `Encoders` we can easily create a schema on top of the `case class`, thus allowing us to use the various APIs with ease:

```
scala> Encoders.product[Record].schema.printTreeString
root
|-- i: integer (nullable = true)
|-- s: string (nullable = true)
```

All datatypes of Spark SQL are located in the package `org.apache.spark.sql.types`.

You can access them by using:

```
import org.apache.spark.sql.types._
```

You should use the `DataTypes` object in your code in order to create complex `Spark SQL` types such as arrays or maps as shown in the following:

```
scala> import org.apache.spark.sql.types.DataTypes
import org.apache.spark.sql.types.DataTypes
scala> val arrayType = DataTypes.createArrayType(IntegerType)
arrayType: org.apache.spark.sql.types.ArrayType =
ArrayType(IntegerType,true)
```

Following are the data types supported in SparkSQL APIs:

Data type	**Value type in Scala**	**API to access or create a data type**
ByteType	Byte	ByteType
ShortType	Short	ShortType
IntegerType	Int	IntegerType
LongType	Long	LongType
FloatType	Float	FloatType
DoubleType	Double	DoubleType
DecimalType	java.math.BigDecimal	DecimalType
StringType	String	StringType
BinaryType	Array[Byte]	BinaryType
BooleanType	Boolean	BooleanType
TimestampType	java.sql.Timestamp	TimestampType
DateType	java.sql.Date	DateType
ArrayType	scala.collection.Seq	ArrayType(elementType, [containsNull])
MapType	scala.collection.Map	MapType(keyType, valueType, [valueContainsNull])Note: The default value of valueContainsNull is true.
StructType	org.apache.spark.sql.Row	StructType(fields).Note: Fields is a Seq of StructFields. Also, two fields with the same name are not allowed.

Loading datasets

Spark SQL can read data from external storage systems such as files, Hive tables, and JDBC databases through the `DataFrameReader` interface.

The format of the API call is `spark.read.inputtype`:

- Parquet
- CSV
- Hive table
- JDBC

- ORC
- Text
- JSON

Let's look at a couple of simple examples of reading CSV files into DataFrames:

```
scala> val statesPopulationDF = spark.read.option("header",
"true").option("inferschema", "true").option("sep",
",").csv("statesPopulation.csv")
statesPopulationDF: org.apache.spark.sql.DataFrame = [State: string, Year:
int ... 1 more field]
scala> val statesTaxRatesDF = spark.read.option("header",
"true").option("inferschema", "true").option("sep",
",").csv("statesTaxRates.csv")
statesTaxRatesDF: org.apache.spark.sql.DataFrame = [State: string, TaxRate:
double]
```

Saving datasets

Spark SQL can save data to external storage systems like files, Hive tables and JDBC databases through the `DataFrameWriter` interface.

Format of the API call is `dataframe.write.outputtype`:

- Parquet
- ORC
- Text
- Hive table
- JSON
- CSV
- JDBC

Let's look at couple of examples of writing or saving a DataFrame to a CSV file:

```
scala> statesPopulationDF.write.option("header",
"true").csv("statesPopulation_dup.csv")
scala> statesTaxRatesDF.write.option("header",
"true").csv("statesTaxRates_dup.csv")
```

Aggregations

Aggregation is the method of collecting data together based on a condition and performing analytics on the data. Aggregation is very important to make sense of data of all sizes as just having raw records of data is not that useful for most use cases.

> Imagine a table containing one temperature measurement per day for every city in the world for five years.

For example, if you see the following table and then the aggregated view of the same data then it is obvious that just raw records do not help you understand the data. Shown below is the raw data in the form of a table:

City	**Date**	**Temperature**
Boston	12/23/2016	32
New York	12/24/2016	36
Boston	12/24/2016	30
Philadelphia	12/25/2016	34
Boston	12/25/2016	28

Shown below is the average temperature per city:

City	**Average Temperature**
Boston	30 - (32 + 30 + 28)/3
New York	36
Philadelphia	34

Aggregate functions

Aggregations can be performed with the help of functions that can be found in the `org.apache.spark.sql.functions` package. In addition to this, custom aggregation functions can also be created, also known as **user-defined aggregation functions** (**UDAF**).

> Each grouping operation returns a `RelationalGroupedDataset` on which aggregations can be specified.

We will load the sample data to illustrate all the different types of aggregate functions in this section:

```
val statesPopulationDF = spark.read.option("header", "true").
 option("inferschema", "true").
 option("sep", ",").csv("statesPopulation.csv")
```

count

Count is the most basic aggregate function which simply counts the number of rows for the column specified. `countDistinct` is an extension of `count`; it also eliminates duplicates.

The `count` API has several implementations as follows. The exact API used depends on the specific use case:

```
def count(columnName: String): TypedColumn[Any, Long]
 Aggregate function: returns the number of items in a group.
def count(e: Column): Column
 Aggregate function: returns the number of items in a group.
def countDistinct(columnName: String, columnNames: String*): Column
 Aggregate function: returns the number of distinct items in a group.
def countDistinct(expr: Column, exprs: Column*): Column
 Aggregate function: returns the number of distinct items in a group.
```

Let's take a look at some examples of invoking `count` and `countDistinct` on the DataFrame to print the row counts:

```
import org.apache.spark.sql.functions._
scala> statesPopulationDF.select(col("*")).agg(count("State")).show
scala> statesPopulationDF.select(count("State")).show
+------------+
|count(State)|
+------------+
| 350|
+------------+
scala> statesPopulationDF.select(col("*")).agg(countDistinct("State")).show
scala> statesPopulationDF.select(countDistinct("State")).show
+---------------------+
|count(DISTINCT State)|
+---------------------+
| 50|
```

first

Gets the first record in the `RelationalGroupedDataset`.

The `first` API has several implementations as follows. The exact API used depends on the specific use case:

```
def first(columnName: String): Column
 Aggregate function: returns the first value of a column in a group.
def first(e: Column): Column
 Aggregate function: returns the first value in a group.
def first(columnName: String, ignoreNulls: Boolean): Column
 Aggregate function: returns the first value of a column in a group.
def first(e: Column, ignoreNulls: Boolean): Column
 Aggregate function: returns the first value in a group.
```

Let's look at example of invoking first on the DataFrame to output the first row:

```
import org.apache.spark.sql.functions._
 scala> statesPopulationDF.select(first("State")).show
+-------------------+
|first(State, false)|
+-------------------+
| Alabama|
+-------------------+
```

last

Gets the last record in the `RelationalGroupedDataset`.

The `last` API has several implementations as follows. The exact API used depends on the specific use case:

```
def last(columnName: String): Column
 Aggregate function: returns the last value of the column in a group.
def last(e: Column): Column
 Aggregate function: returns the last value in a group.
def last(columnName: String, ignoreNulls: Boolean): Column
 Aggregate function: returns the last value of the column in a group.
def last(e: Column, ignoreNulls: Boolean): Column
 Aggregate function: returns the last value in a group.
```

Let's look at example of invoking last on the DataFrame to output the last row:

```
import org.apache.spark.sql.functions._
 scala> statesPopulationDF.select(last("State")).show
```

```
+-----------------+
|last(State, false)|
+-----------------+
| Wyoming|
+-----------------+
```

approx_count_distinct

If you need an approximate count of the distinct records, approximate distinct count is a much faster way to do so instead of performing an exact count which usually needs lot of shuffles and other operations.

The `approx_count_distinct` API has several implementations as follows. The exact API used depends on the specific use case:

```
def approx_count_distinct(columnName: String, rsd: Double): Column
 Aggregate function: returns the approximate number of distinct items in a
 group.
def approx_count_distinct(e: Column, rsd: Double): Column
 Aggregate function: returns the approximate number of distinct items in a
group.
def approx_count_distinct(columnName: String): Column
 Aggregate function: returns the approximate number of distinct items in a
group.
def approx_count_distinct(e: Column): Column
 Aggregate function: returns the approximate number of distinct items in a
group.
```

Let's look at example of invoking `approx_count_distinct` on the DataFrame to print the approximate count of the DataFrame:

```
import org.apache.spark.sql.functions._
 scala>
statesPopulationDF.select(col("*")).agg(approx_count_distinct("State")).sho
w
 +---------------------------+
 |approx_count_distinct(State)|
 +---------------------------+
 | 48|
 +---------------------------+
 scala> statesPopulationDF.select(approx_count_distinct("State", 0.2)).show
 +---------------------------+
 |approx_count_distinct(State)|
 +---------------------------+
 | 49|
 +---------------------------+
```

min

`min` is the minimum column value of one of the columns in the DataFrame. An example of `min` is if you want to check the minimum temperature of a city.

The `min` API has several implementations as follows. The exact API used depends on the specific use case:

```
def min(columnName: String): Column
 Aggregate function: returns the minimum value of the column in a group.
def min(e: Column): Column
 Aggregate function: returns the minimum value of the expression in a
group.
```

Let's look at example of invoking `min` on the DataFrame to print the minimum `Population`:

```
import org.apache.spark.sql.functions._
 scala> statesPopulationDF.select(min("Population")).show
 +---------------+
 |min(Population)|
 +---------------+
 |  564513|
+---------------+
```

max

`max` is the maximum column value of one of the columns in the DataFrame. An example of this is if you want to check the maximum temperature of a city.

The `max` API has several implementations as follows. The exact API used depends on the specific use case:

```
def max(columnName: String): Column
 Aggregate function: returns the maximum value of the column in a group.
def max(e: Column): Column
 Aggregate function: returns the maximum value of the expression in a
group.
```

Let's look at example of invoking `max` on the DataFrame to print the maximum `Population`:

```
import org.apache.spark.sql.functions._
 scala> statesPopulationDF.select(max("Population")).show
+---------------+
 |max(Population)|
 +---------------+
 | 39250017|
 +---------------+
```

avg

The average of the values is calculated by adding the values and dividing them by the number of values.

The average of *1, 2, 3* is *(1 + 2 + 3) / 3 = 6/3 = z*.

The `avg` API has several implementations as follows. The exact API used depends on the specific use case:

```
def avg(columnName: String): Column
 Aggregate function: returns the average of the values in a group.
def avg(e: Column): Column
 Aggregate function: returns the average of the values in a group.
```

Let's look at example of invoking `avg` on the DataFrame to print the average population:

```
import org.apache.spark.sql.functions._
 scala> statesPopulationDF.select(avg("Population")).show
 +-----------------+
 | avg(Population)|
 +-----------------+
 |6253399.371428572|
 +----------------+
```

sum

Computes the sum of the values of the column. Optionally, `sumDistinct` can be used to only add up distinct values.

The `sum` API has several implementations as follows. The exact API used depends on the specific use case:

```
def sum(columnName: String): Column
 Aggregate function: returns the sum of all values in the given column.
def sum(e: Column): Column
 Aggregate function: returns the sum of all values in the expression.
def sumDistinct(columnName: String): Column
 Aggregate function: returns the sum of distinct values in the expression
def sumDistinct(e: Column): Column
 Aggregate function: returns the sum of distinct values in the expression.
```

Let's look at example of invoking sum on the DataFrame to print summation (total) `Population`:

```
import org.apache.spark.sql.functions._
scala> statesPopulationDF.select(sum("Population")).show
 +---------------+
 |sum(Population)|
 +---------------+
 | 2188689780|
 +---------------+
```

kurtosis

`kurtosis` is a way of quantifying differences in shapes of distributions, which may look very similar in terms of means and variances yet is actually different.

The `kurtosis` API has several implementations as follows. The exact API used depends on the specific use case:

```
def kurtosis(columnName: String): Column
 Aggregate function: returns the kurtosis of the values in a group.
def kurtosis(e: Column): Column
 Aggregate function: returns the kurtosis of the values in a group.
```

Let's look at an example of invoking `kurtosis` on the DataFrame on the `Population` column:

```
import org.apache.spark.sql.functions._
scala> statesPopulationDF.select(kurtosis("Population")).show
 +--------------------+
 |kurtosis(Population)|
 +--------------------+
 | 7.727421920829375|
 +--------------------+
```

skewness

`skewness` measures the asymmetry the values in your data around the average or mean.

The `skewness` API has several implementations as follows. The exact API used depends on the specific use case:

```
def skewness(columnName: String): Column
 Aggregate function: returns the skewness of the values in a group.
def skewness(e: Column): Column
 Aggregate function: returns the skewness of the values in a group.
```

Let's look at example of invoking `skewness` on the DataFrame on the `Population` column:

```
import org.apache.spark.sql.functions._
 scala> statesPopulationDF.select(skewness("Population")).show
 +--------------------+
 |skewness(Population)|
 +--------------------+
 | 2.5675329049100024|
 +--------------------+
```

Variance

The variance is the average of the squared differences of each of the values from the mean.

The `var` API has several implementations as follows. The exact API used depends on the specific use case:

```
def var_pop(columnName: String): Column
 Aggregate function: returns the population variance of the values in a
group.
def var_pop(e: Column): Column
 Aggregate function: returns the population variance of the values in a
```

```
group.
def var_samp(columnName: String): Column
 Aggregate function: returns the unbiased variance of the values in a
group.
def var_samp(e: Column): Column
 Aggregate function: returns the unbiased variance of the values in a
group.
```

Now, let's look at example of invoking `var_pop` on the DataFrame measuring variance of `Population`:

```
import org.apache.spark.sql.functions._
scala> statesPopulationDF.select(var_pop("Population")).show
 +--------------------+
 | var_pop(Population)|
 +--------------------+
 |4.948359064356177E13|
 +--------------------+
```

Standard deviation

The standard deviation is the square root of the variance (see previous section).

The `stddev` API has several implementations as follows. The exact API used depends on the specific use case:

```
def stddev(columnName: String): Column
 Aggregate function: alias for stddev_samp.
def stddev(e: Column): Column
 Aggregate function: alias for stddev_samp.
def stddev_pop(columnName: String): Column
 Aggregate function: returns the population standard deviation of the
 expression in a group.
def stddev_pop(e: Column): Column
 Aggregate function: returns the population standard deviation of the
 expression in a group.
def stddev_samp(columnName: String): Column
 Aggregate function: returns the sample standard deviation of the
expression in a group.
def stddev_samp(e: Column): Column
Aggregate function: returns the sample standard deviation of the expression
in a group.
```

Let's look at an example of invoking `stddev` on the DataFrame, printing the standard deviation of `Population`:

```
import org.apache.spark.sql.functions._
scala> statesPopulationDF.select(stddev("Population")).show
 +----------------------+
 |stddev_samp(Population)|
 +----------------------+
 | 7044528.191173398|
 +----------------------+
```

Covariance

Covariance is a measure of the joint variability of two random variables.

The `covar` API has several implementations as follows. The exact API used depends on the specific use case:

```
def covar_pop(columnName1: String, columnName2: String): Column
 Aggregate function: returns the population covariance for two columns.
def covar_pop(column1: Column, column2: Column): Column
 Aggregate function: returns the population covariance for two columns.
def covar_samp(columnName1: String, columnName2: String): Column
 Aggregate function: returns the sample covariance for two columns.
def covar_samp(column1: Column, column2: Column): Column
 Aggregate function: returns the sample covariance for two columns.
```

Let's look at an example of invoking `covar_pop` on the DataFrame to calculate the covariance between the `Year` and `Population` columns:

```
import org.apache.spark.sql.functions._
scala> statesPopulationDF.select(covar_pop("Year", "Population")).show
 +---------------------------+
 |covar_pop(Year, Population)|
 +---------------------------+
 | 183977.56000006935|
 +---------------------------+
```

groupBy

A common task seen in data analysis is to group the data into different categories and then perform calculations on the resultant groups of data.

Let's run the groupBy function on the DataFrame to print aggregate counts of each State:

```
scala> statesPopulationDF.groupBy("State").count.show(5)
+---------+-----+
| State|count|
+---------+-----+
| Utah| 7|
| Hawaii| 7|
|Minnesota| 7|
| Ohio| 7|
| Arkansas| 7|
+---------+-----+
```

You can also groupBy and then apply any of the aggregate functions seen previously such as min, max, avg, stddev, and so on:

```
import org.apache.spark.sql.functions._
scala> statesPopulationDF.groupBy("State").agg(min("Population"),
avg("Population")).show(5)
+---------+---------------+--------------------+
| State|min(Population)| avg(Population)|
+---------+---------------+--------------------+
| Utah| 2775326| 2904797.1428571427|
| Hawaii| 1363945| 1401453.2857142857|
|Minnesota| 5311147| 5416287.285714285|
| Ohio| 11540983|1.1574362714285715E7|
| Arkansas| 2921995| 2957692.714285714|
+---------+---------------+--------------------+
```

Rollup

Rollup is a multi-dimensional aggregation used to perform hierarchical or nested calculations. For example, if we want to show the number of records for each State and Year group as well as for each State (aggregating over all years to give a grand total for each State irrespective of the Year), we can use rollup as follows:

```
scala> statesPopulationDF.rollup("State", "Year").count.show(5)
+------------+----+-----+
| State|Year|count|
+------------+----+-----+
|South Dakota|2010| 1|
| New York|2012| 1|
| California|2014| 1|
| Wyoming|2014| 1|
| Hawaii|null| 7|
+------------+----+-----+
```

Cube

`Cube` is a multi-dimensional aggregation used to perform hierarchical or nested calculations just like `rollup` but with the difference that `cube` does the same operation for all dimensions. For example, if we want to show the number of records for each `State` and `Year` group as well as for each `State` (aggregating over all year's to give a grand total for each `State` irrespective of the `Year`), we can use `cube`as follows:

```
scala> statesPopulationDF.cube("State", "Year").count.show(5)
+------------+----+-----+
| State|Year|count|
+------------+----+-----+
|South Dakota|2010| 1|
| New York|2012| 1|
| null|2014| 50|
| Wyoming|2014| 1|
| Hawaii|null| 7|
+------------+----+-----+
```

Window functions

Window functions allow you to perform aggregations over a window of data rather than entire data or some filtered data. The use cases of such window functions are:

- Cumulative sum
- Delta from previous value for same key
- Weighted moving average

You can specify a window looking at three rows *T-1*, *T*, and *T+1*, and by performing a simple calculation. You can also specify a window over the latest/most recent 10 values:

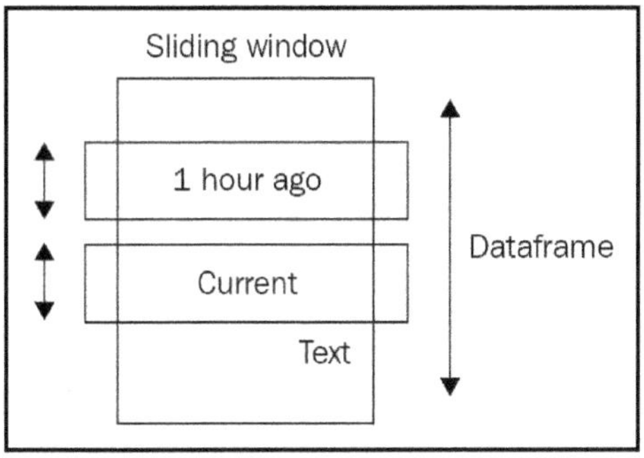

The API for the `Window` specification requires three properties, the `partitionBy()`, `orderBy()`, and the `rowsBetween()`. The `partitionBy` chunks the data into the partitions/groups as specified by `partitionBy()`. `orderBy()` is used to order the data within each partition of data.

The `rowsBetween()` specifies the window frame or the span of the sliding window to perform the calculations.

To try out the Windows function, there are certain packages that are needed. You can import the necessary packages using the import directive as follows:

```
import org.apache.spark.sql.expressions.Window
import org.apache.spark.sql.functions.col
import org.apache.spark.sql.functions.max
```

Now we are ready to write some code to learn about the `Window` functions. Let's create a window specification for the partitions sorted by `Population` and partitioned by `State`. Also, specify that we want to consider all rows until current row as part of the `Window`:

```
val windowSpec = Window
 .partitionBy("State")
 .orderBy(col("Population").desc)
 .rowsBetween(Window.unboundedPreceding, Window.currentRow)
```

Compute the rank over the `Window` specification. The result will be a rank (row number) added to each row as long as it falls within the `Window` specified. In this example, we chose to partition by `State` and then order the rows of each `State` further in descending order. Hence, each `State` row has its own rank number assigned:

```
import org.apache.spark.sql.functions._
 scala> statesPopulationDF.select(col("State"), col("Year"),
 max("Population").over(windowSpec), rank().over(windowSpec)).sort("State",
 "Year").show(10)
 +-------+----+------------------------------------------------------------
-
 ------------------------------------------------------------------+-------
-
 --------------------------------------------------------------------------
-
 --------------------------------+
| State|Year|max(Population) OVER (PARTITION BY State ORDER BY Population
 DESC NULLS LAST ROWS BETWEEN UNBOUNDED PRECEDING AND CURRENT ROW)|RANK()
 OVER (PARTITION BY State ORDER BY Population DESC NULLS LAST ROWS BETWEEN
 UNBOUNDED PRECEDING AND CURRENT ROW)|
 +-------+----+------------------------------------------------------------
```

```
-
 ---------------------------------------------------------------------+--------
-
 ------------------------------------------------------------------------------
-
 -----------------------------------+
|Alabama|2010| 4863300| 6|
 |Alabama|2011| 4863300| 7|
 |Alabama|2012| 4863300| 5|
 |Alabama|2013| 4863300| 4|
 |Alabama|2014| 4863300| 3|
```

ntiles

`ntiles` is a popular aggregation over a window and is commonly used to divide an input dataset into *n* parts.

For example, if we want to partition the `statesPopulationDF` by `State` (window specification is shown previously), order by population, and then divide into two portions, we can use `ntile` over the `windowspec`:

```
import org.apache.spark.sql.functions._
scala> statesPopulationDF.select(col("State"), col("Year"),
 ntile(2).over(windowSpec), rank().over(windowSpec)).sort("State",
 "Year").show(10)
+-------+----+-----------------------------------------------------------------
 --------------------------------------------------------------+---------------
-
 ------------------------------------------------------------------------------
-
 ---------------------------+
| State|Year|ntile(2) OVER (PARTITION BY State ORDER BY Population DESC
 NULLS LAST ROWS BETWEEN UNBOUNDED PRECEDING AND CURRENT ROW)|RANK() OVER
 (PARTITION BY State ORDER BY Population DESC NULLS LAST ROWS BETWEEN
 UNBOUNDED PRECEDING AND CURRENT ROW)|
 +-------+----+----------------------------------------------------------------
-
 --------------------------------------------------------------+---------------
-
 ------------------------------------------------------------------------------
-
 ---------------------------+
 |Alabama|2010| 2| 6|
 |Alabama|2011| 2| 7|
 |Alabama|2012| 2| 5|
```

```
|Alabama|2013|  1|  4|
|Alabama|2014|  1|  3|
|Alabama|2015|  1|  2|
|Alabama|2016|  1|  1|
| Alaska|2010|  2|  7|
| Alaska|2011|  2|  6|
| Alaska|2012|  2|  5|
+-------+----+-----------------------------------------------------------
-
 ---------------------------------------------------------+--------------
-
 -----------------------------------------------------------
```

As shown previously, we have used the `Window` function and `ntile()` together to divide the rows of each `State` into two equal portions.

A popular use of this function is to compute decile used in data science models.

Joins

In traditional databases, joins are used to join one transaction table with another lookup table to generate a more complete view. For example, if you have a table of online transactions sorted by customer ID and another table containing the customer city and customer ID, you can use join to generate reports on the transactions sorted by city.

Transactions table: This table has three columns, the **CustomerID**, the **Purchased item**, and how much the customer paid for the item:

CustomerID	Purchased Item	Price Paid
1	Headphones	25.00
2	Watch	20.00
3	Keyboard	20.00
1	Mouse	10.00
4	Cable	10.00
3	Headphones	30.00

Customer Info table: This table has two columns the **CustomerID** and the **City** the customer lives in:

Customer ID	**City**
1	Boston
2	New York
3	Philadelphia
4	Boston

Joining the transaction table with the customer info table will generate a view as follows:

Customer ID	**Purchased Item**	**Price Paid**	**City**
1	Headphone	25.00	Boston
2	Watch	100.00	New York
3	Keyboard	20.00	Philadelphia
1	Mouse	10.00	Boston
4	Cable	10.00	Boston
3	Headphones	30.00	Philadelphia

Now, we can use this joined view to generate a report of `Total` sale price sorted sorted by `City`:

City	**#Items**	**Total Sale Price**
Boston	3	45.00
Philadelphia	2	50.00
New York	1	100.00

Joins are an important function of Spark SQL as they enable you to bring two datasets together as seen previously. Spark, of course, is not only meant to generate some report but is used to process data at Peta byte scale to handle real-time streaming use cases, machine learning algorithms, or plain analytics. In order to accomplish these goals, Spark provides the API functions needed.

A typical join between two datasets takes place using one or more keys of the left and right datasets and then evaluates a conditional expression on the sets of keys as a Boolean expression. If the result of the Boolean expression returns `true`, then the join is successful, or else the joined DataFrame will not contain the corresponding join. The `join` API has six different implementations:

```
join(right: Dataset[_]): DataFrame
 Condition-less inner join
 join(right: Dataset[_], usingColumn: String): DataFrame
```

```
Inner join with a single column
join(right: Dataset[_], usingColumns: Seq[String]): DataFrame
Inner join with multiple columns
join(right: Dataset[_], usingColumns: Seq[String], joinType: String):
DataFrame
Join with multiple columns and a join type (inner, outer,....)
join(right: Dataset[_], joinExprs: Column): DataFrame
Inner Join using a join expression
join(right: Dataset[_], joinExprs: Column, joinType: String): DataFrame
Join using a Join expression and a join type (inner, outer, ...)
```

We will use one of the APIs to understand how to use the `join` API; however, you can choose to use other APIs depending on the use case:

```
def join(right: Dataset[_], joinExprs: Column, joinType: String):
DataFrame
Join with another DataFrame using the given join expression
right: Right side of the join.
joinExprs: Join expression.
joinType : Type of join to perform. Default is inner join
// Scala:
import org.apache.spark.sql.functions._
import spark.implicits._
df1.join(df2, $"df1Key" === $"df2Key", "outer")
```

Note that joins will be covered in detail in the next few sections.

Inner workings of join

Join works by operating on the partitions of a DataFrame using multiple executors. However, the actual operations and the subsequent performance depends on the type of join and the nature of the datasets being joined. In the next section, we will look at the different types of joins.

Shuffle join

A join between two big datasets involves shuffle join where partitions of both left and right datasets are spread across the executors. Shuffles are expensive and it's important to analyze the logic to make sure the distribution of partitions and shuffles are done optimally.

The following is an illustration of how shuffle join works internally:

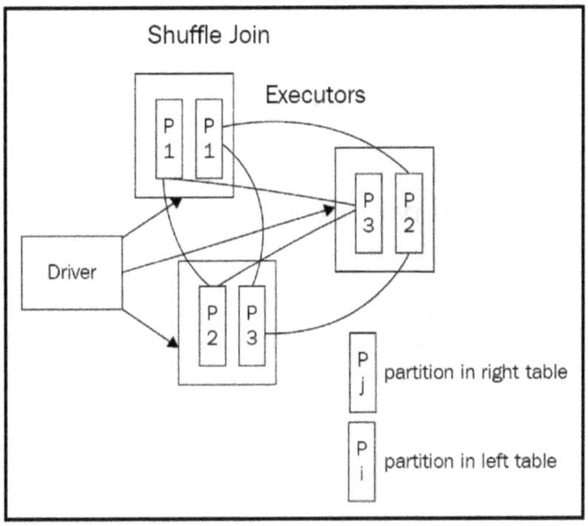

Broadcast join

A join that is carried out between one large dataset and a smaller dataset by broadcasting the smaller dataset to all executors where a partition from left dataset exists is called a **broadcast join**.

The following is an illustration of how a broadcast join works internally:

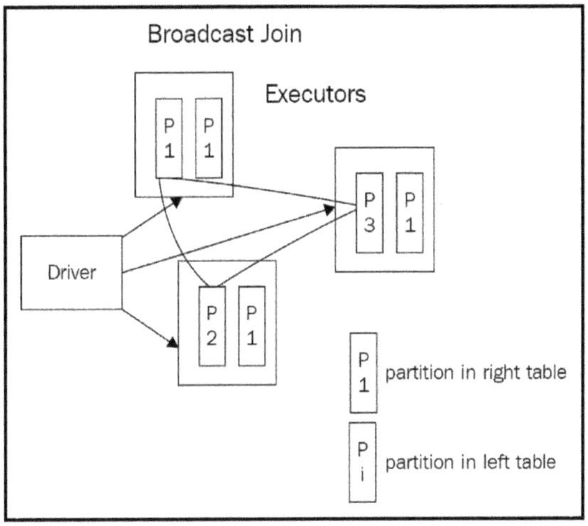

Join types

The following is the table of different types of joins. This is important as the choice made when joining two datasets makes all the difference in the output and also the performance:

JoinType	Description
inner	The inner join compares each row from left to rows from right and combines matched pairs of rows from left and right datasets only when both have non-`NULL` values.
outer, full, fullouter	The full outer join gives all rows from the left and right hand side tables. If we want to keep all the rows from both tables, we use full outer join. Full outer join returns all rows when there is a match in ONE of the tables
leftanti	Left anti join gives only those rows from the left hand side table based that are not present in the right hand side table.
left, leftouter	The left outer join gives all rows in left plus common rows of left and right (inner join). Fills in `NULL` if not in right.
leftsemi	The left semi join gives only rows in left based on existence on right-side. The does not include right-side values.
right, rightouter	The right outer join gives all rows in right plus common rows of left and right (inner join). Fills in `NULL` if not in left.

We will examine how the different join types work by using the sample datasets:

```
scala> val statesPopulationDF = spark.read.option("header",
 "true").option("inferschema", "true").option("sep",
 ",").csv("statesPopulation.csv")
 statesPopulationDF: org.apache.spark.sql.DataFrame = [State: string, Year:
 int ... 1 more field]
scala> val statesTaxRatesDF = spark.read.option("header",
 "true").option("inferschema", "true").option("sep",
 ",").csv("statesTaxRates.csv")
 statesTaxRatesDF: org.apache.spark.sql.DataFrame = [State: string,
TaxRate:
 double]
scala> statesPopulationDF.count
 res21: Long = 357
scala> statesTaxRatesDF.count
 res32: Long = 47
%sql
 statesPopulationDF.createOrReplaceTempView("statesPopulationDF")
 statesTaxRatesDF.createOrReplaceTempView("statesTaxRatesDF")
```

Inner join

Inner join results in rows from both `statesPopulationDF` and `statesTaxRatesDF` when `State` is non-`NULL` in both datasets:

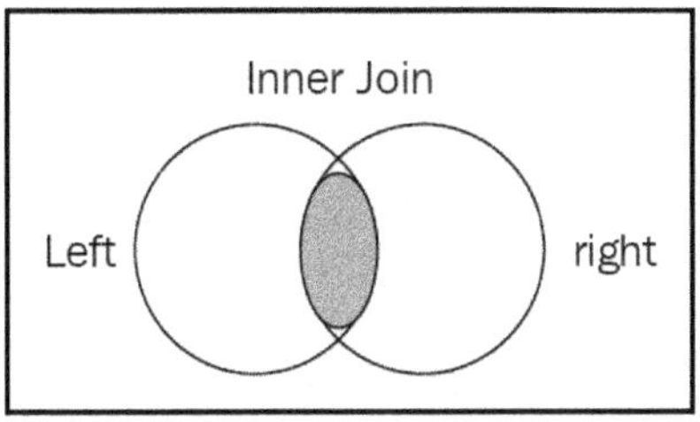

Join the two datasets by the `State` column as follows:

```
val joinDF = statesPopulationDF.join(statesTaxRatesDF,
 statesPopulationDF("State") === statesTaxRatesDF("State"), "inner")
%sql
 val joinDF = spark.sql("SELECT * FROM statesPopulationDF INNER JOIN
 statesTaxRatesDF ON statesPopulationDF.State = statesTaxRatesDF.State")
scala> joinDF.count
 res22: Long = 329
scala> joinDF.show
 +--------------------+----+----------+--------------------+-------+
 | State|Year|Population| State|TaxRate|
+--------------------+----+----------+--------------------+-------+
 | Alabama|2010| 4785492| Alabama| 4.0|
 | Arizona|2010| 6408312| Arizona| 5.6|
 | Arkansas|2010| 2921995| Arkansas| 6.5|
 | California|2010| 37332685| California| 7.5|
 | Colorado|2010| 5048644| Colorado| 2.9|
 | Connecticut|2010| 3579899| Connecticut| 6.35|
```

You can run the `explain()` on the `joinDF` to look at the execution plan:

```
scala> joinDF.explain
 == Physical Plan ==
*BroadcastHashJoin [State#570], [State#577], Inner, BuildRight
 :- *Project [State#570, Year#571, Population#572]
 : +- *Filter isnotnull(State#570)
 : +- *FileScan csv [State#570,Year#571,Population#572] Batched: false,
Format: CSV, Location: InMemoryFileIndex[file:/Users/salla/spark-2.1.0-
binhadoop2.7/
 statesPopulation.csv], PartitionFilters: [], PushedFilters:
 [IsNotNull(State)], ReadSchema:
```

```
 struct<State:string,Year:int,Population:int>
 +- BroadcastExchange HashedRelationBroadcastMode(List(input[0, string,
 true]))
 +- *Project [State#577, TaxRate#578]
 +- *Filter isnotnull(State#577)
 +- *FileScan csv [State#577,TaxRate#578] Batched: false, Format: CSV,
Location: InMemoryFileIndex[file:/Users/salla/spark-2.1.0-binhadoop2.7/
 statesTaxRates.csv], PartitionFilters: [],
PushedFilters:[IsNotNull(State)], ReadSchema:
struct<State:string,TaxRate:double>
```

Left outer join

Left outer join results in all rows from `statesPopulationDF`, including any common in `statesPopulationDF` and `statesTaxRatesDF`:

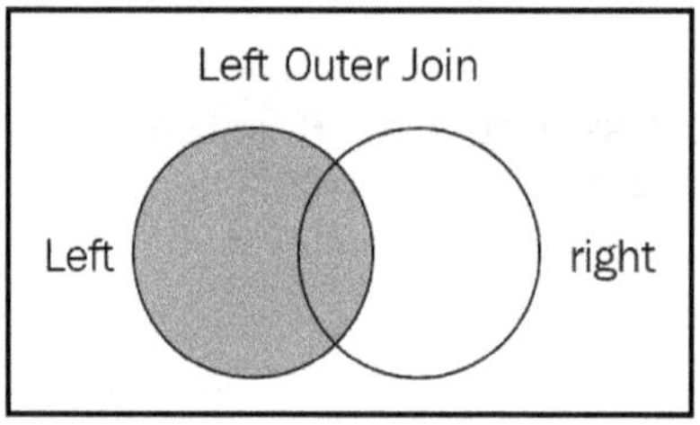

Join the two datasets via the `State` column as shown as follows:

```
val joinDF = statesPopulationDF.join(statesTaxRatesDF,
 statesPopulationDF("State") === statesTaxRatesDF("State"), "leftouter")
%sql
 val joinDF = spark.sql("SELECT * FROM statesPopulationDF LEFT OUTER JOIN
statesTaxRatesDF ON statesPopulationDF.State = statesTaxRatesDF.State")
 scala> joinDF.count
 res22: Long = 357
 scala> joinDF.show(5)
 +----------+----+----------+----------+-------+
 | State|Year|Population| State|TaxRate|
 +----------+----+----------+----------+-------+
 | Alabama|2010| 4785492| Alabama| 4.0|
 | Alaska|2010| 714031| null| null|
 | Arizona|2010| 6408312| Arizona| 5.6|
 | Arkansas|2010| 2921995| Arkansas| 6.5|
 |California|2010| 37332685|California| 7.5|
 +----------+----+----------+----------+-------+
```

Right outer join

Right outer join results in all rows from `statesTaxRatesDF`, including any common in `statesPopulationDF` and `statesTaxRatesDF`:

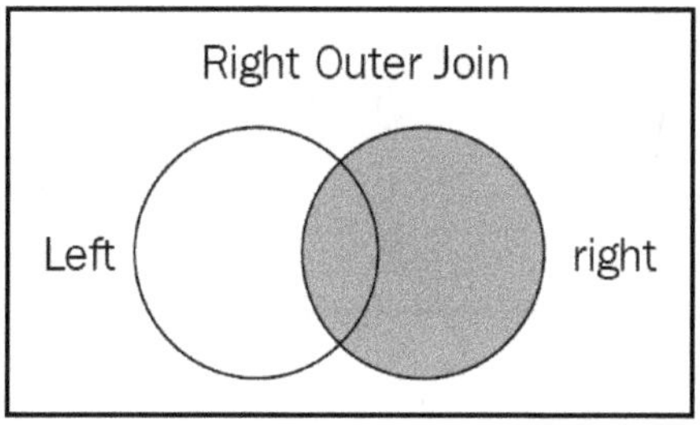

Join the two datasets via the `State` column as follows:

```
val joinDF = statesPopulationDF.join(statesTaxRatesDF,
 statesPopulationDF("State") === statesTaxRatesDF("State"), "rightouter")
%sql
 val joinDF = spark.sql("SELECT * FROM statesPopulationDF RIGHT OUTER JOIN
 statesTaxRatesDF ON statesPopulationDF.State = statesTaxRatesDF.State")
scala> joinDF.count
 res22: Long = 323
scala> joinDF.show
 +--------------------+----+----------+--------------------+-------+
 | State|Year|Population| State|TaxRate|
 +--------------------+----+----------+--------------------+-------+
 | Colorado|2011| 5118360| Colorado| 2.9|
 | Colorado|2010| 5048644| Colorado| 2.9|
 | null|null| null|Connecticut| 6.35|
 | Florida|2016| 20612439| Florida| 6.0|
 | Florida|2015| 20244914| Florida| 6.0|
 | Florida|2014| 19888741| Florida| 6.0|
```

Outer join

Outer join results in all rows from `statesPopulationDF` and `statesTaxRatesDF`:

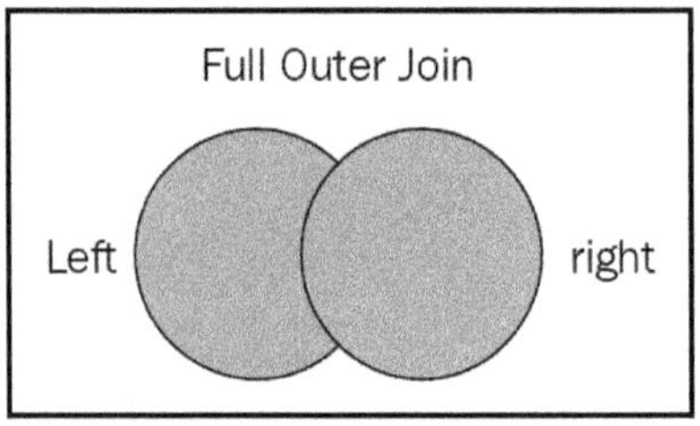

Join the two datasets via the `State` column as follows:

```
val joinDF = statesPopulationDF.join(statesTaxRatesDF,
 statesPopulationDF("State") === statesTaxRatesDF("State"), "fullouter")
%sql
 val joinDF = spark.sql("SELECT * FROM statesPopulationDF FULL OUTER JOIN
 statesTaxRatesDF ON statesPopulationDF.State = statesTaxRatesDF.State")
scala> joinDF.count
 res22: Long = 351
scala> joinDF.show
 +--------------------+----+----------+--------------------+-------+
 | State|Year|Population| State|TaxRate|
 +--------------------+----+----------+--------------------+-------+
 | Delaware|2010| 899816| null| null|
 | Delaware|2011| 907924| null| null|
 | West Virginia|2010| 1854230| West Virginia| 6.0|
 | West Virginia|2011| 1854972| West Virginia| 6.0|
 | Missouri|2010| 5996118| Missouri| 4.225|
 | null|null| null| Connecticut| 6.35|
```

Left anti join

Left anti join results in rows from only `statesPopulationDF` if and only if there is no corresponding row in `statesTaxRatesDF`:

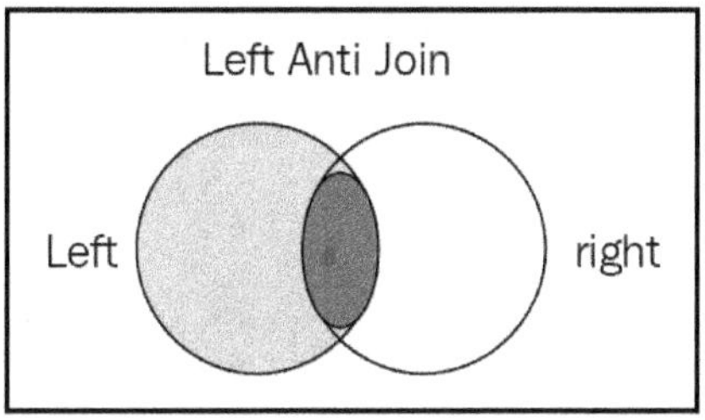

Join the two datasets via the `State` column as follows:

```
val joinDF = statesPopulationDF.join(statesTaxRatesDF,
 statesPopulationDF("State") === statesTaxRatesDF("State"), "leftanti")
 %sql
 val joinDF = spark.sql("SELECT * FROM statesPopulationDF LEFT ANTI JOIN
 statesTaxRatesDF ON statesPopulationDF.State = statesTaxRatesDF.State")
scala> joinDF.count
res22: Long = 28
 scala> joinDF.show(5)
 +--------+----+----------+
 | State|Year|Population|
 +--------+----+----------+
 | Alaska|2010| 714031|
 |Delaware|2010| 899816|
 | Montana|2010| 990641|
 | Oregon|2010| 3838048|
 | Alaska|2011| 722713|
 +--------+----+----------+
```

Left semi join

Left semi join results in rows from only `statesPopulationDF` if and only if there is a corresponding row in `statesTaxRatesDF`:

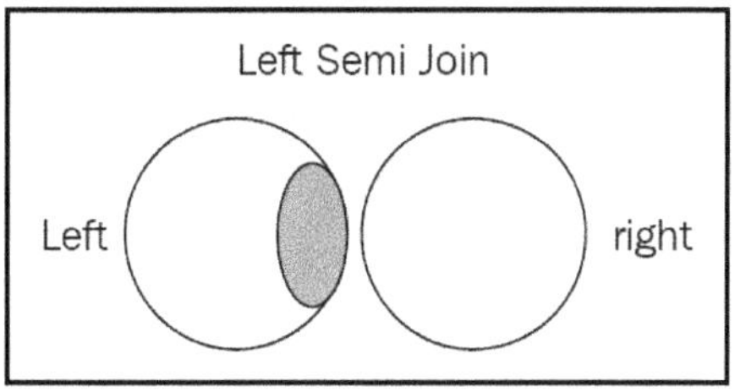

Join the two datasets by the `State` column as follows:

```
val joinDF = statesPopulationDF.join(statesTaxRatesDF,
 statesPopulationDF("State") === statesTaxRatesDF("State"), "leftsemi")
 %sql

val joinDF = spark.sql("SELECT * FROM statesPopulationDF LEFT SEMI JOIN
 statesTaxRatesDF ON statesPopulationDF.State = statesTaxRatesDF.State")

scala> joinDF.count

res22: Long = 322
 scala> joinDF.show(5)
 +----------+----+----------+
 | State|Year|Population|
 +----------+----+----------+
 | Alabama|2010| 4785492|
 | Arizona|2010| 6408312|
 | Arkansas|2010| 2921995|
 |California|2010| 37332685|
 | Colorado|2010| 5048644|
 +----------+----+----------+
```

Cross join

Cross join matches every row from the left with every row from the right, generating a cartesian cross product:

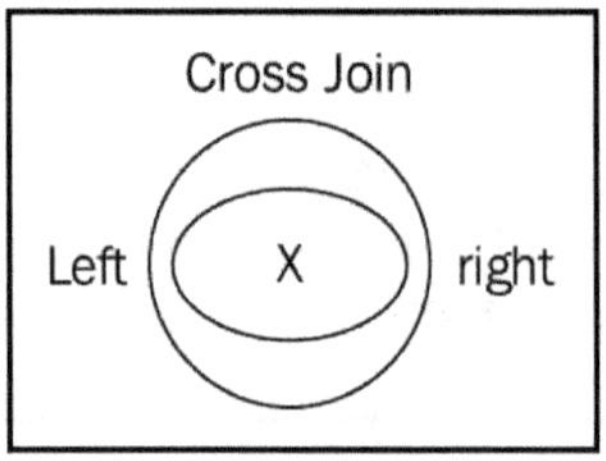

Join the two datasets via the `State` column as follows:

```
scala> val joinDF=statesPopulationDF.crossJoin(statesTaxRatesDF)
 joinDF: org.apache.spark.sql.DataFrame = [State: string, Year: int ... 3
 more fields]
%sql
val joinDF = spark.sql("SELECT * FROM statesPopulationDF CROSS JOIN
 statesTaxRatesDF")
 scala> joinDF.count
```

```
res46: Long = 16450
scala> joinDF.show(10)
+-------+----+----------+-----------+-------+
| State|Year|Population| State|TaxRate|
+-------+----+----------+-----------+-------+
|Alabama|2010| 4785492| Alabama| 4.0|
|Alabama|2010| 4785492| Arizona| 5.6|
|Alabama|2010| 4785492| Arkansas| 6.5|
|Alabama|2010| 4785492| California| 7.5|
|Alabama|2010| 4785492| Colorado| 2.9|
|Alabama|2010| 4785492|Connecticut| 6.35|
|Alabama|2010| 4785492| Florida| 6.0|
|Alabama|2010| 4785492| Georgia| 4.0|
|Alabama|2010| 4785492| Hawaii| 4.0|
|Alabama|2010| 4785492| Idaho| 6.0|
+-------+----+----------+-----------+-------+
```

TIP

You can also use join with cross `joinType` instead of calling the cross join API: `statesPopulationDF.join(statesTaxRatesDF, statesPopulationDF("State").isNotNull, "cross").count`.

Performance implications of join

The join type chosen directly impacts the performance of the join. This is because joins require shuffling data between executors to execute the tasks, hence different joins and even the order of the joins needs to be considered while using join. The following is a table you could use as a reference when writing join code:

JoinType	Performance considerations and tips
inner	Inner join requires the left and right tables to have the same column. If you have duplicate or multiple copies of the keys on either left or right side, the join will quickly blow up into sort of a cartesian join, taking lot longer to complete than if designed correctly to minimize the multiple keys.
cross	Cross Join matches every row from the left with every row from the right, generating a cartesian cross product. This is to be used with caution as this is the worst performance join, to be used in specific use cases only.

outer, full, fullouter	Full outer join gives all (matched and unmatched) rows from the tables at the left and right side of the join clause. Use this when we want to keep all the rows from both tables, we use full outer join. Full outer join returns all rows when there is a match in ONE of the tables. If used on tables with little in common, it can result in very large results and thus slow performance.
leftanti	Left anti join gives only those rows from the left hand side table based that are not present in the right hand side table. Use this when we want to keep rows from left table only when not present in right table. Very good performance as only one table is fully considered and the other is only checked for the join condition.
left, leftouter	Left outer join gives all rows present in the left hand side table in addition to the rows that are common to both the tables (inner join). If used on tables with little in common, can result in very large results and thus slow performance.
leftsemi	Left semi join gives only rows from the left side table if and only if they exist in the right side table. Use this to get rows from left table if and only if the rows are found in the right table. This is the opposite of leftanti join seen above. Does not include right side values. Very good performance as only one table is fully considered and the other is only checked for the join condition.
right, rightouter	Right outer join gives all rows in right side table as well as the common rows of left and right (inner join). Use this to get all rows in right table along with the rows found in both left and right tables. Fills in `NULL` if not in left. Performance is similar to the left outer join mentioned previously in this table.

Summary

In this chapter, we have discussed the origin of DataFrames and how Spark SQL provides the SQL interface on top of DataFrame. The power of DataFrames is such that the execution times have decreased over the original RDD-based computations. Having such a powerful layer with a simple SQL-like interface makes it all the more powerful. We also looked at various APIs to create and manipulate DataFrames and dug deeper into the sophisticated features of aggregations, including `groupBy`, `Window`, `rollup`, and `cubes`. Finally, we also looked at the concept of joining datasets and the various types of joins possible such as inner, outer, cross, and so on.

We will explore the exciting world of real-time data processing and analytics in `Chapter 7`, *Real-Time Analytics with Apache Spark.*

7
Real-Time Analytics with Apache Spark

In this chapter, we will introduce the stream-processing model of Apache Spark, and show you how to build streaming-based, real-time analytical applications. This chapter will focus on Spark Streaming, and will show you how to process data streams using the Spark API.

More specifically, the reader will learn how to process Twitter's tweets, as well as how to process real-time data streams in several ways. Basically, the chapter will focus on the following:

- A short introduction to streaming
- Spark Streaming
- Discretized Streams
- Stateful and stateless transformations
- Checkpointing
- Operating with other streaming platforms (such as Apache Kafka)
- Structured Streaming

Streaming

In the modern world, an increasing number of people are becoming interconnected to one another via the internet. With the advent of the smartphone, this trend has skyrocketed. Nowadays, the smartphone can be used to do many things, such as check social media, order food online, and call a cab online. We are finding ourselves more reliant on the internet than ever before, and we will only become more reliant in the future. With this development comes a massive increase in data generation. As the internet began to boom, the very nature of data processing changed. Any time one of the apps or service is accessed on the phone, real-time data processing is taking place. Because there is a lot at stake in terms of the quality of their applications, companies are forced to improve data processing, and with improvements come paradigm shifts. One paradigm that is currently being researched and used is the idea of a highly scalable, real-time (or as close to real-time as possible) processing engine on a high-end infrastructure. It must function quickly and be receptive to changes and failures. Basically, the data processing must be as close to real-time as possible, without interruptions.

Most of the systems being monitored generate lots of data as indefinite but continuous streams of events. The same challenge of collecting, storing, and processing data remains, as it would with any other data-processing system. Additional complications result from real-time needs. A highly scalable architecture is required in order to collect and process these indefinite streams, and so many iterations of these systems exist, such as Flink, AMQ, Storm, and Spark. Newer, more modern systems are very efficient and flexible, meaning that companies can reach their goals even more easily and efficiently than ever before. These new technological developments allow for data consumption from a variety of sources, as well as for data processing and usage. And all of this with minimal delays.

When you use your smartphone to order a pizza, you are able to make a credit card payment and have the pizza delivered straight to your address. Some bus systems allow you to track individual buses on a map in real time, and if you need to wait for the bus, you can use your smartphone to find a nearby Starbucks and grab a coffee.

By looking at the expected time of arrival, you can make an informed decision about a trip to the airport. If the car will arrive in an amount of time that might be detrimental to your flight plans, you can cancel your ride and get in a nearby taxi. In the event that traffic would prevent an on-time arrival at the airport, you can reschedule or cancel your flight.

To understand how all of that data is processed in real time, we must first understand the basics of streaming architectures. It is essential for a real-time streaming architecture to collect large amounts of data at high rates, but to also ensure that it becomes processed.

The following is a generic stream-processing system, with a producer putting events into a messaging system while a consumer is reading from the messaging system:

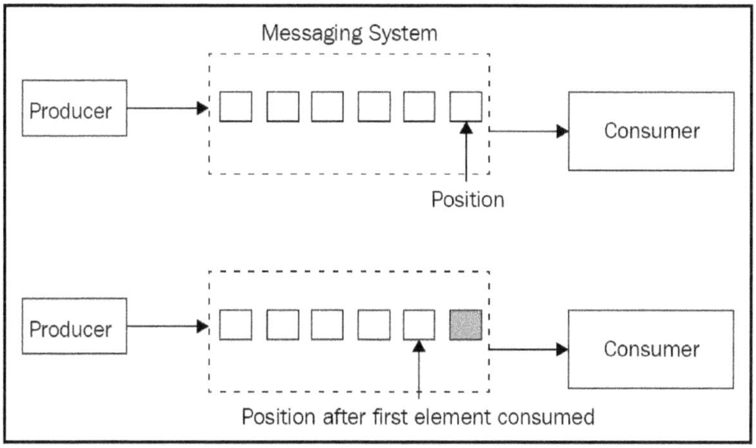

Real-time streaming data can be processed according to the following three paradigms:

- At-least-once processing
- At-most-once processing
- Exactly-once processing

Exactly-once processing is the most ideal situation, but it is hard to achieve it in various scenarios. We must compromise on the properties of exactly-once processing in situations where it would be very complex to implement such criteria.

At-least-once processing

In the at-least-once processing paradigm, the position of the last received event is saved only after it is processed, and the results are stored somewhere. In the event of a failure, the consumer will still be able to read and reprocess the old events. However, it cannot be assumed that the received events were either never processed or partially processed, so there could be a duplication of results after the previous event is called again. This is what it means when the name says the data has been processed at least once.

This paradigm is ideal for any application that updates a ticker or gauge to show a current value. However, sums, counters, or any things that depend on the accuracy of those types of aggregations are not ideal for at-least-once processing, mainly because duplicate events lead to incorrect results.

The sequence proceeds as follows:

- Save results
- Save offsets

The following diagram represents the at-least-once processing paradigm:

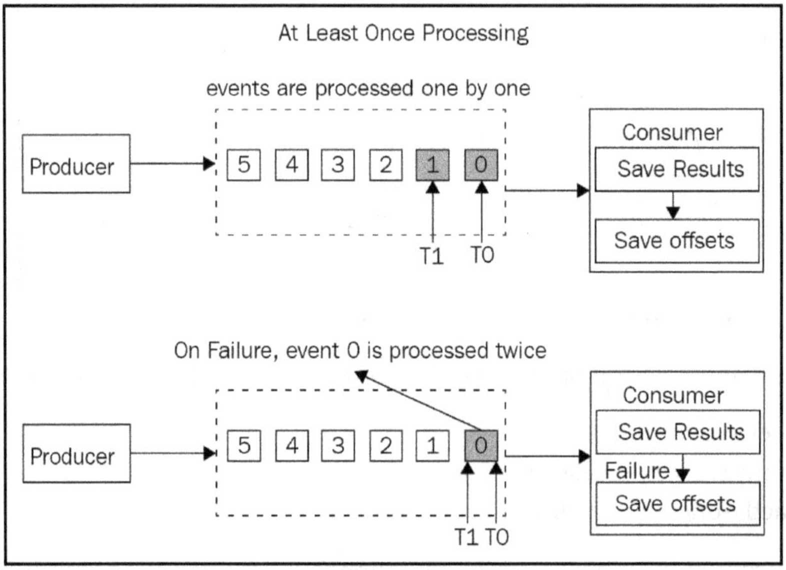

At-most-once processing

In this paradigm, the position of the last event is saved before it is actually processed, and the results are stored somewhere. In case of a failure and consumer restart, the old events won't be read again. However, there could be the potential for a loss of events, since they can never be retrieved again because of the fact that we cannot assume all received events were processed. This is what the paradigm means when it states that events are either not processed, or processed once, at the most. It is ideal for situations that require a ticker or gauge to be updated to display a current value. Additionally, any aggregations, such as cumulative sums or counters, may work as well, if accuracy is not mandatory, or if all events are needed. Any lost events will cause missing or incorrect results.

The sequence proceeds as follows:

- Save results
- Save offsets

If there is a failure and the consumer ends up restarting, there will be offsets for every event (provided that they all process before failure occurs), but an event might end up going missing as shown in the following diagram:

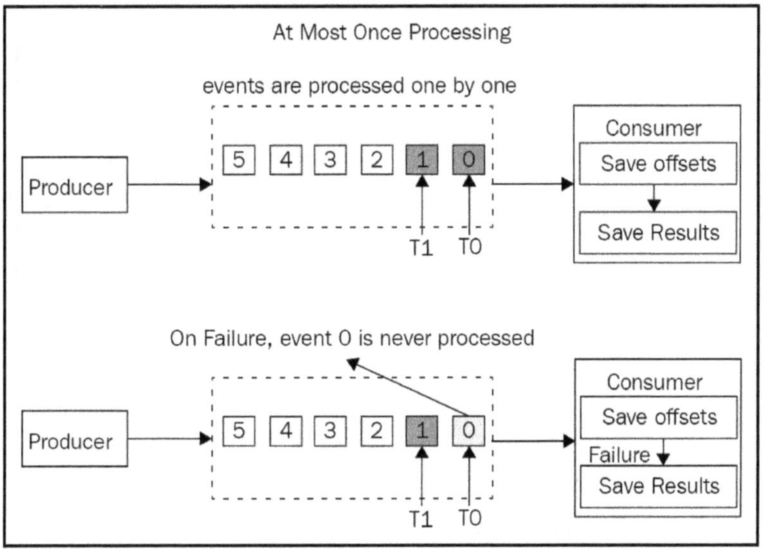

Exactly-once processing

This paradigm is similar to at-least-once processing. It saves the last event received only after it is actually processed, and the results are stored somewhere, so that in the case of failure and consumer restart, the old events can be reread and reprocessed. However, there is cause for potential duplication, since it cannot be assumed that all the events were either not processed or were only partially processed. Unlike at-least-once processing, any duplicate events are dropped and not processed, resulting in exactly-once processing.

This is ideal for any application in which accuracy is important, such as applications involving aggregations such as accurate counters, or anything else that needs an event processed only once and without loss.

The sequence proceeds as follows:

- Save results
- Save offsets

The following is what occurs when the consumer restarts after a failure. The events have been processed already, but the offsets have not been saved as shown in the following diagram:

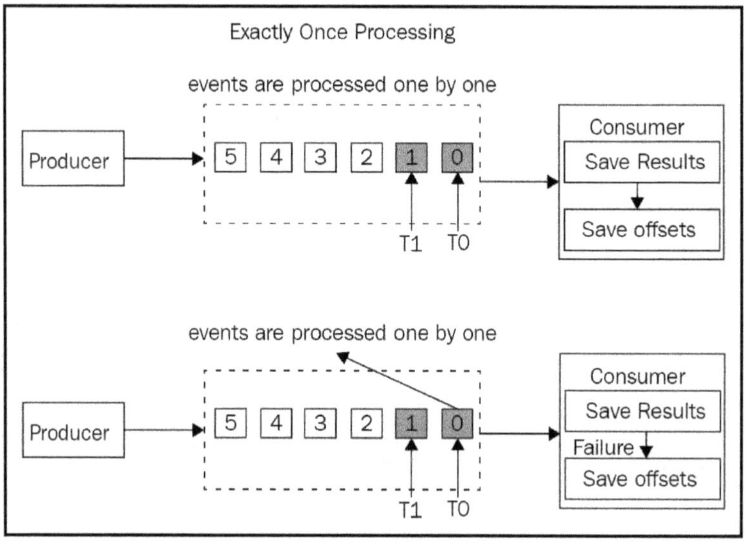

How does exactly-once processing duplicate? Two processes are involved:

- Idempotent updates
- Transactional updates

Spark Streaming implements structure streaming in Spark 2.0 and higher, which supports exactly-once processing. Structure streaming will be covered later on in this chapter.

In idempotent updates, results are saved based on a unique key or ID that is generated. In the case of a duplication, the generated key or ID will already be in the results (a database, for example), so the consumer can remove the duplicate without updating the results. However, this can become complicated, since generating a unique keys for every event is not a simple task, as additional processing is required on the consumer's end. Additionally, the database could be separate for results and offsets.

In transactional updates, results are saved in batches that require a transaction to begin and a transaction to commit, so in the event of a commit, the events will be successfully processed. In the event of a duplication, they can be dropped without updating results. However, these are more complicated than idempotent updates, since now, transaction data needs to be stored. Another disadvantage is that the database could be required to stay the same for results and offsets.

> Decisions on using at-least-once processing or at-most-once processing should be made after looking into the use case that you are trying to build, to keep a reasonable level of accuracy and performance.

Spark Streaming

Spark Streaming wasn't the first streaming architecture. Over time, multiple technologies have been developed in order to address various real-time processing needs. One of the first popular stream processor technologies was Twitter Storm, and it was used in many businesses. Spark includes the streaming library, which has grown to become the most widely used technology today. This is mainly because Spark Streaming holds some significant advantages over all of the other technologies, the most important being its integration of Spark Streaming APIs within its core API. Not only that, but Spark Streaming is also integrated with Spark ML and Spark SQL, along with GraphX. Because of all of these integrations, Spark is a powerful and versatile streaming technology.

Note that `https://spark.apache.org/docs/2.1.0/streaming-programming-guide.html` has more information on Spark Streaming Flink, Heron (Twitter Storm's successor), and Samza and their various features; for example, their ability to handle events while minimizing latency. However, Spark Streaming consumes data and processes it in microbatches. The size of these microbatches is of a minimum of 500 milliseconds.

> Apache Apex, Flink, Samza, Heron, Gearpump, and other new technologies are all competitors of Spark Streaming in some cases. Spark Streaming, will not be the right fit if you need true, event-by-event processing.

Spark Streaming works by creating batches of events at certain time intervals, as configured by the user, and delivering them for processing at another specified time interval.

Spark Streaming supports several input sources and can write results to several sinks:

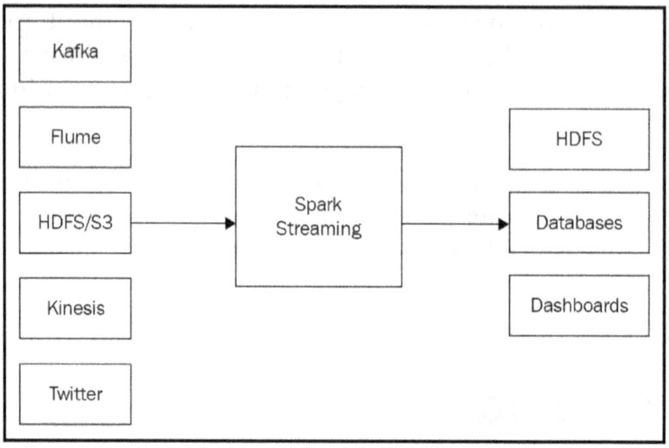

Similar to `SparkContext`, Spark Streaming contains a `StreamingContext`, the primary point of entry for the streaming to take place. The `StreamingConext` depends on the `SparkContext`, and the `SparkContext` can actually be used directly in the streaming task. The `StreamingContext` is similar to the `SparkContext`, the difference being that `StreamingContext` requires a specification, by the program, of a time interval/duration of batching interval, ranging from minutes to milliseconds:

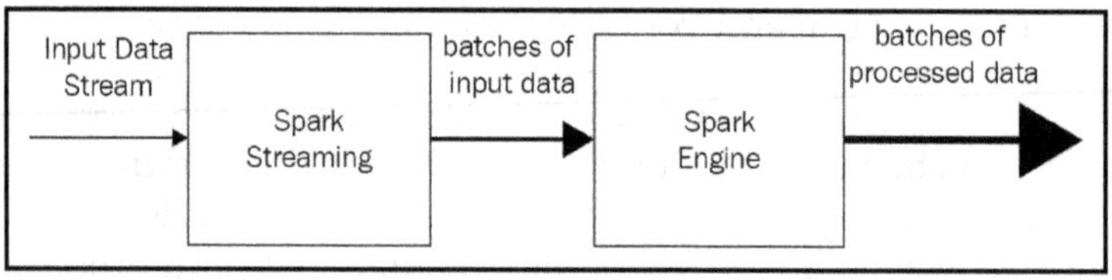

The `SparkContext` is the main point of entry. The `StreamingContext` reuses the logic that is part of `SparkContext` (task scheduling and resource management).

StreamingContext

As the main point of entry for streaming, `StreamingContext` handles the streaming application's actions, including checkpointing and transformations of the RDD.

Creating StreamingContext

A new `StreamingContext` may be created in one of several ways:

- Create a `StreamingContext` by using an existing `SparkContext`:

```
StreamingContext(sparkContext: SparkContext, batchDuration:
Duration)
scala> val ssc = new StreamingContext(sc, Seconds(10))
```

- Create a `StreamingContext` by providing the configuration necessary for a new one:

```
StreamingContext(conf: SparkConf, batchDuration: Duration)
scala> val conf =
newSparkConf().setMaster("local[1]").setAppName("TextStreams")
scala> val ssc = new StreamingContext(conf, Seconds(10))
```

- The `getOrCreate` function is used to recreate a `StreamingContext` from a previous checkpoint data piece, or to create a new `StreamingContext`. If the data does not exist, then the `StreamingContext` will be created by calling the provided `creatingFunc` as follows:

```
def getOrCreate(
checkpointPath: String,
creatingFunc: () => StreamingContext,
hadoopConf: Configuration = SparkHadoopUtil.get.conf,
createOnError: Boolean = false
): StreamingContext
```

Starting StreamingContext

The streaming application is started by starting the execution of the streams defined using the `StreamingContext`:

```
def start(): Unit
scala> ssc.start()
```

Stopping StreamingContext

All processing stops when the `StreamingContext` is stopped. You will need to create a new `StreamingContext`, and you must invoke `start()` to restart the application. There are two useful APIs to stop stream processing:

- Stop stream execution immediately (this does not wait for received data to be processed) by using the following:

```
def stop(stopSparkContext: Boolean)
scala> ssc.stop(false)
```

- Stop the execution of the streams, with an option for allowing the received data to be processed, by using the following:

```
def stop(stopSparkContext: Boolean, stopGracefully: Boolean)
scala> ssc.stop(true, true)
```

Input streams

Several types of input streams exists, all of which need `StreamingContext` to be created, as shown in the following sections.

receiverStream

An input stream is created with any user-implemented receiver. It is customizable:

More details can be found at `http://spark.apache.org/docs/latest/streaming-custom-receivers.html`:

```
API declaration for receiverStream:
def receiverStream[T]: ClassTag](receiver: Receiver[T]):
ReceiverInputDStream[T]
```

socketTextStream

The `socketTextStream` uses the TCP source `hostname:port` to create an input stream. Data is received through the TCP socket, and the received bytes are interpreted as UTF8, encoded in `\n` delimiter lines:

```
def socketTextStream(hostname: String, port: Int,
storageLevel: StorageLevel = StorageLevel.MEMORY_AND_DISK_SER_2):
ReceiverInputDStream[String]
```

rawSocketStream

The `rawSocketStream` uses the network source `hostname:port` to create an input stream. It is the most efficient method with which to receive data:

```
def rawSocketStream[T: ClassTag](hostname: String, port: Int,
storageLevel: StorageLevel = StorageLevel.MEMORY_AND_DISK_SER_2):
ReceiverInputDStream[T]
```

fileStream

The `fileStream` creates an input stream that monitors a Hadoop-compatible filesystem. It reads new files using a given key-value type and input format. Any filenames starting with `.` are ignored. Invoking an atomic file rename function, a filename starting with `.` is renamed to a usable filename that can be picked up by the `fileStream` and have its contents processed:

```
def fileStream[K: ClassTag, V: ClassTag, F <: NewInputFormat[K, V]:
ClassTag] (directory: String): InputDStream[(K, V)]
```

textFileStream

The `textFileStream` command creates an input stream that monitors a Hadoop-compatible filesystem. It reads new files, as text files with the key as `Longwritable`, the value as `text`, and the input format as `TextInputFormat`. Any files that have names starting with `.` are ignored:

```
def textFileStream(directory: String): Dstream[String]
```

binaryRecordsStream

Using `binaryRecordsStream`, an input stream that monitors a Hadoop-compatible filesystem is created. Any filenames starting with `.` are ignored:

```
def binaryRecordsStream(directory: String, recordLength: Int):
Dstream[Array[Byte]]
```

queueStream

Using `queueStream`, an input stream is created from a queue of RDDs. Within each batch, either one or all of the RDDs returned by the queue are processed:

```
def queueStream[T: ClassTag](queue: Queue[RDD[T]], oneAtATime: Boolean =
true): InputDStream[T]
```

textFileStream example

The following is an example of Spark Streaming using the `textFileStream` method. A `StreamingContext` is created from the Spark shell `SparkContext` (`sc`) with an interval of `10` seconds. The `textFileStream` will start, which will then monitor the directory named `streamfiles` and process any new files that are found in the directory. In the example, the number of elements in the RDD will be printed:

```
scala> import org.apache.spark._
scala> import org.apache.spark.streaming._
scala> val ssc = new StreamingContext(sc, Seconds(10))
scala> val filestream = ssc.textFileStream("streamfiles")
scala> filestream.foreachRDD(rdd => {println(rdd.count())})
scala> ssc.start
```

twitterStream example

The following is another example of how Twitter tweets can be processed using Spark Streaming:

1. Open a terminal and change the directory to `spark-2.1.1-bin-hadoop2.7`.
2. Create a folder named `streamouts` under the `spark-2.1.1-bin-hadoop2.7` folder, in which you have Spark installed. The `Streamouts` object will collect the tweet and convert it to text files when the application is running.
3. Download these JARs into the directory: `http://central.maven.org/maven2/org/apache/bahir/spark-streaming-twitter_2.11/2.1.0/spark-streaming-twitter_2.11-2.1.0.jar`, `http://central.maven.org/maven2/org/twitter4j/twitter4j-core/4.0.6/twitter4j-core-4.0.6.jar`, and `http://central.maven.org/maven2/org/twitter4j/twitter4j-stream/4.0.6/twitter4j-stream-4.0.6.jar`.

4. Launch the `spark-shell` with all the JARs needed for the Twitter integration, specified here as `./bin/spakr-shell -jars twitter4j-stream-4.0.6.jar`, `twitter4j-core-4.0.6.jar`, and `spark-streaming-twitter_2.11-2.1.0.jar`.

5. Sample code can now be written. The following is the code to test the Twitter event processing:

```
import org.apache.spark._
import org.apache.spark.streaming._
import org.apache.spark.streaming.twitter._
import twitter4j.auth.OAuthAuthorization
import twitter4j.conf.ConfigurationBuilder
//you can replace the next 4 settings with your own twitter account
settings.
System.setProperty("twitter4j.oauth.consumerKey",
"8wVysSpBc0LGzbwKMRh8hldSm")
System.setProperty("twitter4j.oauth.consumerSecret",
"FpV5MUDWliR6sInqIYIdkKMQEKaAUHdGJkEb4MVhDkh7dXtXPZ")
System.setProperty("twitter4j.oauth.accessToken",
"817207925756358656-
yR0JR92VBdA2rBbgJaF7PYREbiV8VZq")
System.setProperty("twitter4j.oauth.accessTokenSecret",
"JsiVkUItwWCGyOLQEtnRpEhbXyZS9jNSzcMtycn68aBaS")
val ssc = new StreamingContext(sc, Seconds(10))
val twitterStream = TwitterUtils.createStream(ssc, None)
twitterStream.saveAsTextFiles("streamouts/tweets", "txt")
ssc.start()
```

The `streamouts` folder will now contain several tweet output text files. These can be opened and checked to ensure they contain tweets.

Discretized Streams

Discretized Streams (**DStreams**) are an abstraction that Spark Streaming is built on. Each DStream is represented as a sequence of RDDs, each being created at a specific time interval. The DStream can then be processed similar to a regular RDD using concepts such as a directed cyclic graph-based execution plan (DAG). Just like a regular RDD processing, any transformations and actions that are part of the execution plan are handled in the case of a DStream as shown in the following diagram:

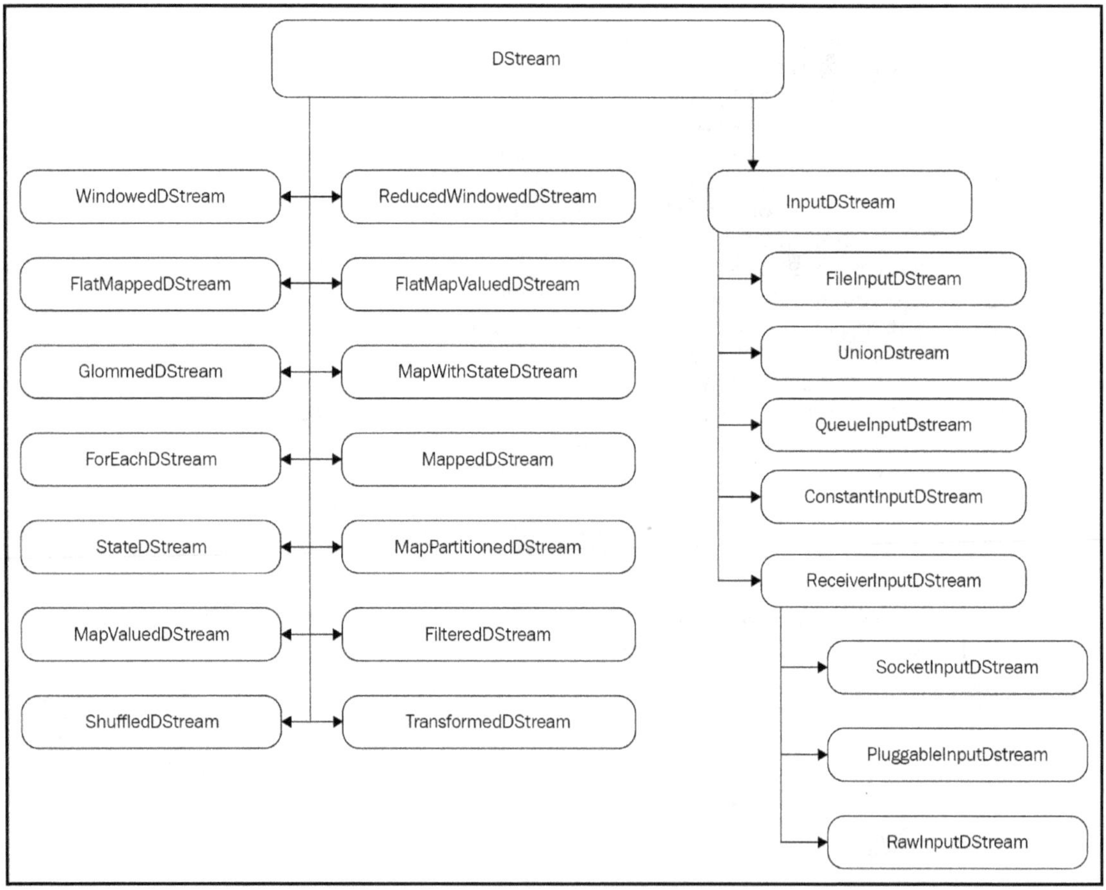

A DStream divides a very long stream of data into smaller chunks based on time intervals and processes each of those chunks as an RDD. These micro-batches are processed independently, with each microbatch being stateless. Assume that the batch interval is five seconds, with the events being consumed in real time, and that a microbatch goes off for further processing as an RDD. One thing to note about Spark Streaming is that the API calls that are used to process microbatch events are integrated into the Spark APIs to be integrated with the rest of the architecture. Whenever a microbatch is created, it becomes an RDD, allowing for seamless processing using Spark APIs as shown in the following diagram:

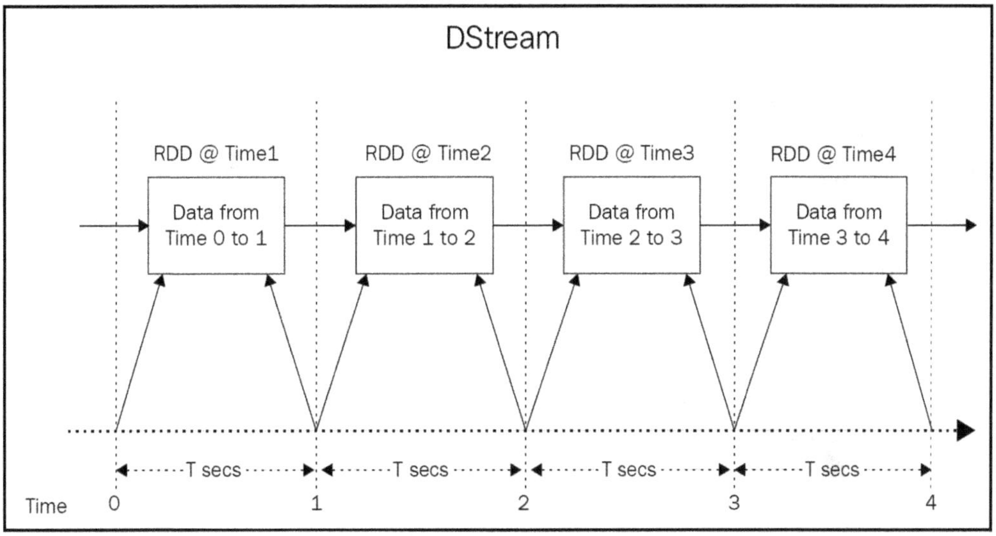

The `DStream` class appears similar to the following example:

```
class DStream[T: ClassTag] (var ssc: StreamingContext)
//hashmap of RDDs in the DStream
var generatedRDDs = new HashMap[Time, RDD[T]]()
```

In this example, a `StreamingContext` is created, and it spawns a microbatch every five seconds, to create an RDD that is similar to a Spark Core API RDD. These RDDs in the data stream can be processed like any other RDDs. The steps to build a streaming application are as follows:

1. Create a `StreamingContext` from a `SparkContext`.
2. Create a `DStream` from a streaming.
3. Contexts provide transformations and actions that can be applied to the RDDs.
4. Start the streaming application by calling `start` on the `StreamingContext`. The Spark Streaming application handles the process of consuming and processing in real time.

> No further operations may be added once the Spark Streaming application is started. A stopped `StreamingContext` cannot be restarted ,either, and a new `StreamingContext` will have to be made.

The following is an example of how to create a streaming job that accesses Twitter:

1. Create a `StreamingContext` from a `SparkContext`:

```
scala> val ssc = new StreamingContext(sc, Seconds(5))
ssc: org.apache.spark.streaming.StreamingContext =
org.apache.spark.streaming.StreamingContext@8ea5756
```

2. Create a `DStream` from the `StreamingContext`:

```
scala> val twitterStream = TwitterUtils.createStream(ssc, None)
twitterStream:
org.apache.spark.streaming.dstream.ReceiverInputDStream[twitter4j.S
tatus] =
org.apache.spark.streaming.twitter.TwitterInputDStream@46219d14
```

3. Provide transformations and actions that can be applied to each individual RDD:

```
val aggStream = twitterStream
.flatMap(x => x.getText.split(" ")).filter(_.startsWith("#"))
.map(x => (x, 1))
.reduceByKey(_ + _)
```

4. Start the streaming application by calling `start` on the `StreamingContext`:

```
ssc.start()
//to stop just call stop on the StreamingContext
ssc.stop(false)
```

In *step 2*, we created a `DSTream` of the `ReceiverInputDStream` type. This is an abstract class that defines any `InputDStream` that must start a receiver on worker nodes as being be able to receive external data.

This example shows what we see when we are receiving from Twitter Stream:

```
class InputDStream[T: ClassTag](_ssc: StreamingContext) extends
DStream[T](_ssc)
class ReceiverInputDStream[T: ClassTag](_ssc: StreamingContext) extends
InputDStream[T](_ssc)
```

Running a transformation, `flatMap()`, on the `twitterStream` will result in a `FlatMappedDStream`, as shown in the following code:

```
scala> val wordStream = twitterStream.flatMap(x => x.getText().split(" "))
wordStream: org.apache.spark.streaming.dstream.DStream[String] =
org.apache.spark.streaming.dstream.FlatMappedDStream@1ed2dbd5
```

Transformations

Transformations on DStreams are similar to those that are applicable to a Spark Core RDD. DStreams consist of RDDs, so a transformation applies to each RDD to generate a transformed RDD for each RDD, creating a transformed DStream. Each transformation creates a specified DStream derived class.

There are many DStream classes that are built for a functionalities; map transformations, window functions, reduce actions, and different `InputStream` types are implemented using different DStream-derived classes.

The following table showcases the possible types of transformations:

Transformation	Meaning
`map(func)`	Applies the `transformation` function to each element of the DStream and returns a new DStream.
`filter(func)`	Filters out the records of the `DStream` to return a new DStream.
`repartition(numPartitions)`	Creates more or fewer partitions to redistribute the data to change the parallelism.
`union(otherStream)`	Combines the elements in two source DStreams and returns a new DStream.
`count()`	Returns a new DStream by counting the number of elements in each RDD of the source DStream.
`reduce(func)`	Returns a new DStream by applying the `reduce` function on each element of the source DStream.

`countByValue()`	Computes the frequency of each `Key` and returns a new DStream of `(Key, Long)` pairs.
`reduceByKey(func, [numTasks])`	Aggregates the data by `Key` in the source DStream's RDDs and returns a new DStream of `(Key, Value)` pairs.
`join(otherStream, [numTasks])`	Joins two DStreams of `(K, V)` and `(K, W)` pairs and returns a new DStream of `(K, (V, W))` pairs, combining the values from both DStreams.
`cogroup(otherStream, [numTasks])`	The `cogroup` transformation, when called on a DStream of `(K, V)` and `(K, W)` pairs, will return a new DStream of `(K, Seq(V), Seq(W))` tuples.
`transform(func)`	Applies a transformation function on each RDD of the source DStream and returns a new DStream.
`updateStateByKey(func)`	Updates the state for each key by applying the given function on the previous state of the key and the new values for the key. Typically used to maintain the state machine.

Windows operations

Spark Streaming allows for windowed processing, which enables you to apply transformations over a sliding window of events. This sliding window is created over a specified interval.

Every time a window slides over a DStream, the source RDDs that fall into the window specification are combined to create a windowed DStream as shown in the following diagram. The window must have two specified parameters:

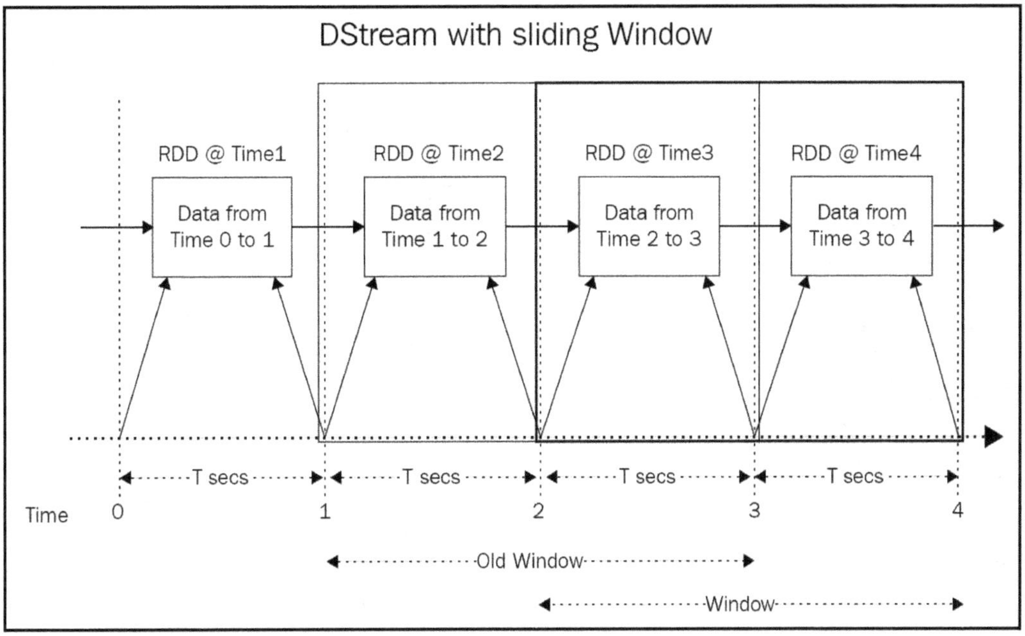

- Window length – specifies the interval length considered
- Sliding interval – the interval at which a window is created

The window length and the sliding interval are required to be a multiple of the block interval.

The following is a table of some common transformations:

Transformation	**Meaning**
`window(windowLength, slideInterval)`	Creates a window on the source DStream and returns it as a new DStream.
`countByWindow(windowLength, slideInterval)`	Returns a count of elements in the DStream by applying a sliding window.

`reduceByWindow(func, windowLength,slideInterval)`	Returns a new DStream by applying the `reduce` function to each element of the source DStream after creating a sliding window of `windowLength` length.
`reduceByKeyAndWindow(func, windowLength, slideInterval, [numTasks])`	Aggregates the data by `Key` in the window applied to the source DStream's RDDs and returns a new DStream of `(Key, Value)` pairs. The computation is provided by the `func` function.
`reduceByKeyAndWindow(func, invFunc, windowLength, slideInterval, [numTasks])`	Aggrega – the interval at which a window w applied to the source DStream's RDDs and returns a new DStream of `(Key, Value)` pairs. The key difference between the preceding function and this one is the `invFunc`, which provides the computation to be done at the beginning of the sliding window.
`countByValueAndWindow(windowLength, slideInterval, [numTasks])`	Computes the frequency of each `Key` and returns a new DStream of `(Key, Long)` pairs within the sliding window, as specified.

Let's revisit the Twitter Stream example. The goal now is to print the five most-used words in tweets streamed every 5 seconds, with a 15-second-length window that slides every 10 seconds. To run that code, go through the following steps:

1. Open a terminal and change the directory to `spark-2.1.1-bin-hadoop2.7`.
2. Create a folder named `streamouts` under the `spark-2.1.1-bin-hadoop2.7` folder, where Spark is installed. Upon running the application, the `streamouts` folder will contain all of the tweet-to-text files.

3. Download the following JARs, and place them in the directory: `http://central.maven.org/maven2/org/apache/bahir/spark-streaming-twitter_2.11/2.1.0/spark-streaming-twitter_2.11-2.1.0.jar`, `http://central.maven.org/maven2/org/twitter4j/twitter4j-core/4.0.6/twitter4j-core-4.0.6.jar`, and `http://central.maven.org/maven2/org/twitter4j/twitter4j-stream/4.0.6/twitter4j-stream-4.0.6.jar`.
4. Launch the Spark shell with the JARs required for integrating the specified tweets; `./bin/spark-shell --jars twitter4j-stream-4.0.6.jar,twitter4j-core-4.0.6.jar,spark-streaming-twitter_2.11-2.1.0.jar`.
5. The following is some sample code to test the tweet processing:

```
import org.apache.log4j.Logger
import org.apache.log4j.Level
Logger.getLogger("org").setLevel(Level.OFF)
import java.util.Date
import org.apache.spark._
import org.apache.spark.streaming._
import org.apache.spark.streaming.twitter._
import twitter4j.auth.OAuthAuthorization
import twitter4j.conf.ConfigurationBuilder
System.setProperty("twitter4j.oauth.consumerKey","8wVysSpBc0LGzbwKM
Rh8hldSm")
System.setProperty("twitter4j.oauth.consumerSecret",
"FpV5MUDWliR6sInqIYIdkKMQEKaAUHdGJkEb4MVhDkh7dXtXPZ")
System.setProperty("twitter4j.oauth.accessToken",
"817207925756358656-yR0JR92VBdA2rBbgJaF7PYREbiV8VZq")
System.setProperty("twitter4j.oauth.accessTokenSecret",
"JsiVkUItwWCGyOLQEtnRpEhbXyZS9jNSzcMtycn68aBaS")

val ssc = new StreamingContext(sc, Seconds(5))
val twitterStream = TwitterUtils.createStream(ssc, None)
val aggStream = twitterStream
.flatMap(x => x.getText.split(" "))
.filter(_.startsWith("#"))
.map(x => (x, 1))
.reduceByKeyAndWindow(_ + _, _ - _, Seconds(15), Seconds(10), 5)

ssc.checkpoint("checkpoints")
aggStream.checkpoint(Seconds(10))
aggStream.foreachRDD((rdd, time) => {
val count = rdd.count()
if (count > 0) {
val dt = new Date(time.milliseconds)
println(s"\n\n$dt rddCount = $count\nTop 5 words\n")
```

```
val top5 = rdd.sortBy(_._2, ascending = false).take(5)
top5.foreach {
case (word, count) =>
println(s"[$word] - $count")
}}})
ssc.start
//wait 60 seconds
ss.stop(false)
The output is shown on the console every 15 seconds, looking like
the following:
Mon May 29 02:44:50 EDT 2017 rddCount = 1453
Top 5 words
[#RT] - 64
[#de] - 24
[#a] - 15
[#to] - 15
[#the] - 13
Mon May 29 02:45:00 EDT 2017 rddCount = 3312
Top 5 words
[#RT] - 161
[#df] - 47
[#a] - 35
[#the] - 29
[#to] - 29
```

Stateful/stateless transformations

Spark Streaming uses the concept of DStreams, which are basically microbatches of data that are RDDs. We also saw some transformations that can be applied to DStreams. DStream transformations can be grouped into two types: stateless and stateful transformations.

In a stateless transformation, whether or not each microbatch of data is processed does not depend on the previous data batches, so each batch is fully independent of whatever batches of data preceded it.

In stateful transformations, whether or not each microbatch of data is processed depends partially or wholly on the previous batches of data, so each batch considers what happened prior to it and uses that information while being processed.

Stateless transformations

One DStream is transformed into another by applying transformations to each RDD in the DStream as shown in the following diagram. Some examples include `map()`, `flatMap()`, `union()`, `join()`, and `reduceBykey()`.

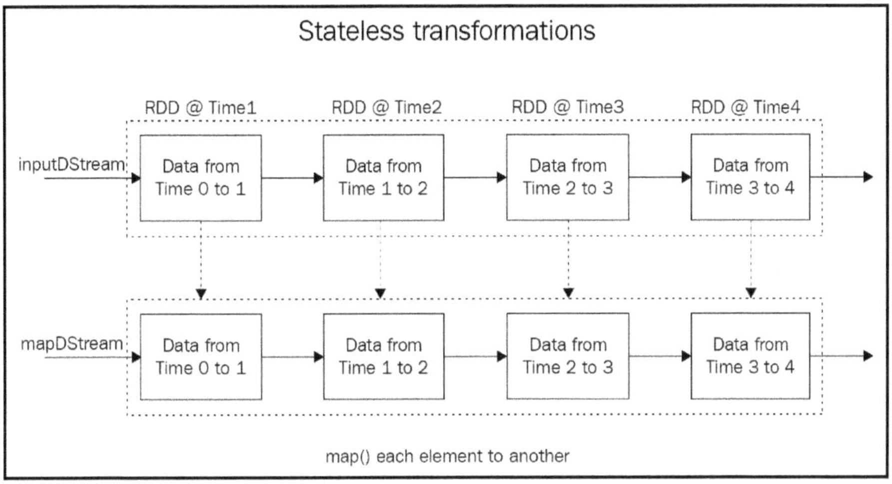

Stateful transformations

Stateful transformations are applied to a DStream, but they depend on the previous state of processing. Examples include `countByValueAndWindow()`, `reduceByKeyAndWindow()`, `mapWithState()`, and `updateStateByKey()`. All window-based transformations are stateful by definition; we must keep track of the window length and the sliding interval of the DStream.

Checkpointing

As it is expected that real-time streaming applications will run for extended periods of time while remaining resilient to failure, Spark Streaming implements a mechanism called **checkpointing**. This mechanism tracks enough information to be able to recover from any failures. There are two types of data checkpointing:

- Metadata checkpointing
- Data checkpointing

Checkpointing is enabled by calling `checkpoint()` on the `StreamingContext`:

```
def checkpoint(directory: String)
```

This specifies the directory where the checkpoint data is to be stored. Note that this must be a filesystem that is fault tolerant, such as HDFS.

Once the directory for the checkpoint is set, any DStream can be checkpointed into it, based on an interval. Revisiting the Twitter example, each DStream can be checkpointed every 10 seconds:

```
val ssc = new StreamingContext(sc, Seconds(5))
val twitterStream = TwitterUtils.createStream(ssc, None)
val wordStream = twitterStream.flatMap(x => x.getText().split(" "))
val aggStream = twitterStream
.flatMap(x => x.getText.split(" ")).filter(_.startsWith("#"))
.map(x => (x, 1))
.reduceByKeyAndWindow(_ + _, _ - _, Seconds(15), Seconds(10), 5)
ssc.checkpoint("checkpoints")
aggStream.checkpoint(Seconds(10))
wordStream.checkpoint(Seconds(10))
```

Metadata checkpointing

Metadata checkpointing saves information that defines streaming operations that are represented by a DAG to the HDFS. This can be utilized to recover the DAG in the event of a failure, allowing for the application to be restarted. The driver then restarts and reads all of the metadata from the HDFS, and rebuilds the DAG while recovering the operational state before the crash.

Data checkpointing

Data checkpointing saves the RDDs to the HDFS. In the case of a failure in the streaming application, the RDDs can be recovered, and the processing can continue where it left off. Not only is recovery good in the case of data checkpointing, but it also helps when RDDs are lost because of cache cleanup or the loss of an executor. Now, any generated RDDs do not need to wait for parent RDDs in the DAG lineage to be reprocessed.

It is necessary for checkpointing to be enabled for any applications that have the following requirements:

- Stateful transformations are applied. If `updateStateBykey()` or `reduceByKeyAndWindow()` (along with their inverse functions) are used, then the checkpoint directory has to be given in order for RDD checkpointing to take place.
- Recovering from driver failures while running the application. Metadata checkpoints help to recover information on progress.

If there are no stateful transformations, then the application can be run without having checkpointing enabled.

> There could be a loss of received, but not yet processed, data.

Something to take note of is that RDD checkpointing means saving each RDD to storage. This would have the effect of increasing the processing time of the batches that have RDDs checkpointed. So, the checkpointing interval must be set and adjusted so as to not hinder performance, which is important when dealing with the expectations of real-time processing.

Tiny batch sizes (1 second, for example) mean that checkpointing occurs too frequently, and this might reduce the operation throughput. Conversely, checkpointing infrequently will cause the task size to grow, causing processing delays because of the large amount of queued data.

Stateful transformations that need RDD checkpointing have a default checkpointing interval of 10 seconds, at the very least. A good setting to start with is a checkpointing interval of 5 to 10 DStream sliding intervals.

Driver failure recovery

We can achieve driver failure recovery with the help of `StreamingContext.getOrCreate()`. As previously mentioned, this will either initialize a `StreamingContext` from a checkpoint that already exists, or create a new one.

We will not implement a function called `createStreamContext0`, which creates a `StreamingContext` and sets up DStreams to interpret tweets and generate the top five most-used hashtags, using a window every 15 seconds. Instead of invoking `createStreamContext()` and then calling `ssc.start()`, we will invoke `getOrCreate()`, so that if a checkpoint exists, then the `StreamingContext` will be recreated from the data in the `checkpoint Directory`. If there is no such directory, or if the application is on its first run, then `createStreamContext()` will be invoked:

```
val ssc = StreamingContext.getOrCreate(checkpointDirectory,
createStreamContext _)
```

The following code shows how the function is defined, and how `getOrCreate()` can be invoked:

```
val checkpointDirectory = "checkpoints"
//Creating and setting up a new StreamingContext
def createStreamContext(): StreamingContext = {
val ssc = new StreamingContext(sc, Seconds(5))
val twitterStream = TwitterUtils.createStream(ssc, None)
val wordStream = twitterStream.flatMap(x => x.getText().split(" "))
val aggStream = twitterStream
.flatMap(x => x.getText.split(" ")).filter(_.startsWith("#"))
.map(x => (x, 1))
.reduceByKeyAndWindow(_ + _, _ - _, Seconds(15), Seconds(10), 5)
ssc.checkpoint(checkpointDirectory)
aggStream.checkpoint(Seconds(10))
wordStream.checkpoint(Seconds(10))
aggStream.foreachRDD((rdd, time) => {
val count = rdd.count()
if (count > 0) {
val dt = new Date(time.milliseconds)
println(s"\n\n$dt rddCount = $count\nTop 5 words\n")
val top10 = rdd.sortBy(_._2, ascending = false).take(5)
top10.foreach {
case (word, count) =>
println(s"[$word] - $count")
}
}
})
ssc
}
//Retrieve StreamingContext from checkpoint data or create a new one
val ssc = StreamingContext.getOrCreate(checkpointDirectory,
createStreamContext _)
```

Interoperability with streaming platforms (Apache Kafka)

Spark Streaming integrates well with Apache Kafka, currently the most popular messaging platform. This integration has several approaches, and the mechanism has improved over time with regards to performance and reliability.

There are three main approaches:

- Receiver-based approach
- Direct Stream approach
- Structured Streaming

Receiver-based

The first integration between Spark and Kafka is the receiver-based integration. In the receiver-based approach, the driver starts the receivers on the executors, which then pull data using a high-level API from the Kafka brokers. Since the events are being pulled from the Kafka brokers, the receivers update the offsets into Zookeeper, which is also used by the Kafka cluster. The important aspect here is the use of the **write ahead log** (**WAL**), which is what the receiver writes to as it collects data from Kafka. If there is a problem and the executors and receivers have to restart or are lost, the WAL can be utilized to recover the events and process them. As a result, this design, based on logging, helps to provide durability, as well as consistency.

An input DStream of events is created by each receiver from a Kafka topic while it queries Zookeeper for Kafka topics, brokers, and offsets. Parallelism is made complicated by logged-in, running receivers, since the workload will not be properly distributed as the application is scaled. Another problem is the dependence upon HDFS, along with write operation duplication. There is also a need for reliability with regards to the exactly-once paradigm of processing, since only an idempotent approach will work. Transactional approaches will not work in the receiver-based approach, because there is not a way to access offset ranges from Zookeeper or the HDFS location. The receiver-based approach is also more general purpose, since it works with any messaging system as shown in the following diagram:

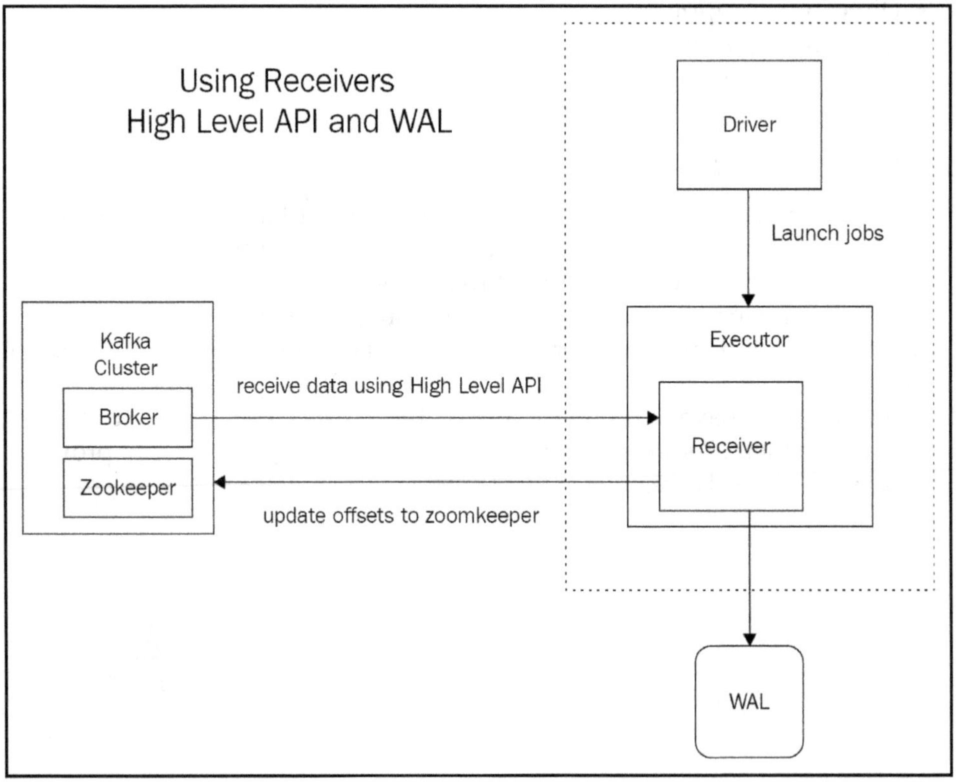

A receiver-based stream can be created by invoking the `createStream()` API:

```
def createStream(
ssc: StreamingContext,
// StreamingContext object
zkQuorum: String,
//Zookeeper quorum (hostname:port,hostname:port,..)
```

```
groupId: String,
//Group id for the consumer
topics: Map[String, Int],
//Map of (topic_name to numPartitions) to consume
storageLevel: StorageLevel = StorageLevel.MEMORY_AND_DISK_SER_2
//Storage level to use for storing the received objects
(default: StorageLevel.MEMORY_AND_DISK_SER_2)
): ReceiverInputDStream[(String, String)]
//DStream of (Kafka message key,
Kafka message value)
```

An example of the creation of a receiver-based stream that pulls messages from Kafka brokers is as follows:

```
val topicMap = topics.split(",").map((_, numThreads.toInt)).toMap
val lines = KafkaUtils.createStream(ssc, zkQuorum, group,
topicMap).map(_._2)
```

Direct Stream

An input stream that directly pulls messages from Kafka brokers without using a receiver can be created, and this ensures that each Kafka message is included in the transformations only once as shown in the following diagram:

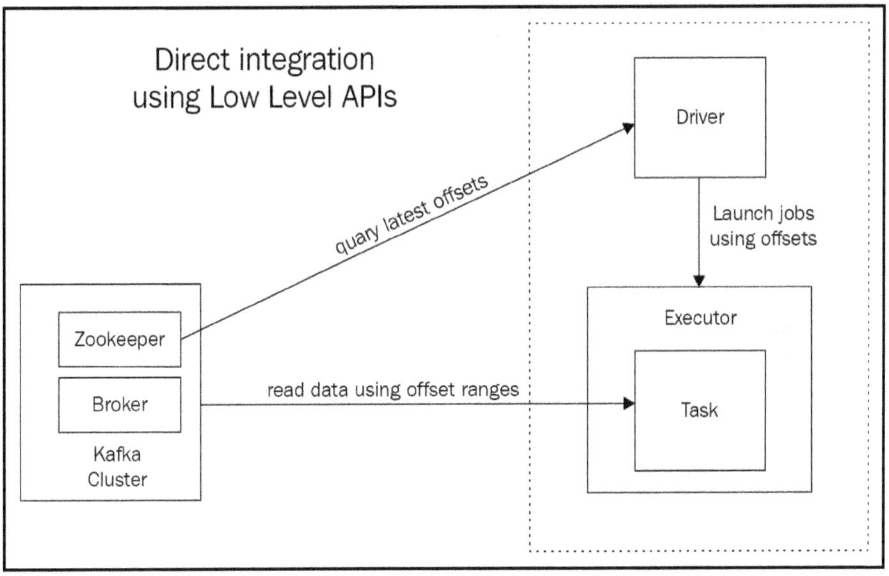

The properties of a Direct Stream are as follows:

- **No receivers**: It does not use a receiver, but directly queries Kafka.
- **Offsets**: It does not use Zookeeper to store offsets, and any consumed offsets are tracked by the stream itself. The offsets used in each batch can be accessed from the RDDs that are generated.
- **Failure recovery**: Checkpointing in the streaming context must be enabled to recover from driver failures.
- **End-to-end schematics**: The stream guarantees that all of the records are received and transformed exactly once, but it does not ensure that the transformed data is outputted exactly once.

A Direct Stream can be created as follows, using the Kafka Utils `createDirectStream()` API:

```
def createDirectStream[
K: ClassTag,
//K type of Kafka message key
V: ClassTag,
//V type of Kafka message value
KD <: Decoder[K]: ClassTag,
//KD type of Kafka message key decoder
VD <: Decoder[V]: ClassTag,
//VD type of Kafka message value decoder
R: ClassTag
//R type returned by messageHandler
](
ssc: StreamingContext,
//StreamingContext object
kafkaParams: Map[String, String],
/*
kafkaParams Kafka <a
href="http://kafka.apache.org/documentation.html#configuration">
configuration parameters</a>. Requires "metadata.broker.list" or
"bootstrap.servers"
to be set with Kafka broker(s) (NOT Zookeeper servers) specified in
host1:port1,host2:port2 form.
*/
fromOffsets: Map[TopicAndPartition, Long],
//fromOffsets Per-
topic/partition Kafka offsets defining the (inclusive) starting point of
the stream
messageHandler: MessageAndMetadata[K, V] => R
//messageHandler Function
```

```
for translating each message and metadata into the desired type
): InputDStream[R]
//DStream of R
```

The following is an example of a Direct Stream that pulls data from Kafka topics to create a DStream:

```
val topicsSet = topics.split(",").toSet
val kafkaParams : Map[String, String] =
Map("metadata.broker.list" -> brokers,
"group.id" -> groupid )
val rawDstream = KafkaUtils.createDirectStream[String, String,
StringDecoder, StringDecoder](ssc, kafkaParams, topicsSet)
```

The Direct Stream API can be used only with Kafka, so it is not for general purpose use.

Structured Streaming

Structured Streaming is new as of Apache Spark 2.0+, and it is still in the alpha phase of development. In the next section, there are details on and examples of how to use Structured Streaming. You can also refer to `https://spark.apache.org/docs/latest/structured-streaming-kafka-integration.html` for more information on Kafka integration in Structured Streaming.

An example of how you can use a Kafka source stream in Structured Streaming is shown in the following code snippet:

```
val ds1 = spark
.readStream
.format("kafka")
.option("kafka.bootstrap.servers", "host1:port1,host2:port2")
.option("subscribe", "topic1")
.load()
ds1.selectExpr("CAST(key AS STRING)", "CAST(value AS STRING)")
.as[(String, String)]
```

The following is an example of how you can use a Kafka source instead of source stream (if you want to take a batch analytics approach):

```
val ds1 = spark
.read
.format("kafka")
.option("kafka.bootstrap.servers", "host1:port1,host2:port2")
.option("subscribe", "topic1")
.load()
ds1.selectExpr("CAST(key AS STRING)", "CAST(value AS STRING)")
.as[(String, String)]
```

Getting deeper into Structured Streaming

Structured Streaming is a fault-tolerant, scalable stream-processing engine, built on top of the Spark SQL engine. Structured Streaming, however, allows you to specify an event time in the data being received, so that any late data will be taken care of automatically. One thing to note is that Structured Streaming is still in its alpha stages in Spark 2.1, and the APIs are labelled as experimental. You can refer to `https://spark.apache.org/docs/latest/structured-streaming-programming-guide.html` for more information.

The driving idea behind Structured Streaming is to treat a data stream as an unbounded table that is constantly being added to. Computations and SQL queries can then be applied to this table, as can normally be done with batch data. For instance, a Spark SQL query will process the unbounded table. As the DStream changes with time, an increasing amount of data will be processed to generate a table of results. This table can be written to an external sink, known as the **output**.

We will now look at an example of the creation of a Structured Streaming query by listening to the input of the localhost port `9999`. On a Linux or macOS, it is easy to start a server on port `9999`:

```
nc -lk 9999
```

The following is an example of the creation of an `inputStream` by calling on SparkSession's `readStream` API, and then extracting those words from the lines. Then, the words are grouped and the occurrences are counted before the results are finally written to the output stream:

```
//Creating stream reading from localhost 999
val inputLines = spark.readStream
.format("socket")
```

```
.option("host", "localhost")
.option("port", 9999)
.load()
inputLines: org.apache.spark.sql.DataFrame = [value: string]
// Splitting the inputLines into words
val words = inputLines.as[String].flatMap(_.split(" "))
words: org.apache.spark.sql.Dataset[String] = [value: string]
// Generating running word count
val wordCounts = words.groupBy("value").count()
wordCounts: org.apache.spark.sql.DataFrame = [value: string, count: bigint]
val query = wordCounts.writeStream
.outputMode("complete")
.format("console")

query:
org.apache.spark.sql.streaming.DataStreamWriter[org.apache.spark.sql.Row] =
org.apache.spark.sql.streaming.DataStreamWriter@4823f4d0
query.start()
```

As long as words are typed into the Terminal, the query will be updated, and will keep generating results by printing them on the console:

```
scala> -------------------------------------------
Batch: 0
-------------------------------------------
+-----+-----+
|value|count|
+-----+-----+
| dog| 1|
+-----+-----+
-------------------------------------------
Batch: 1
-------------------------------------------
+-----+-----+
|value|count|
+-----+-----+
| dog| 1|
| cat| 1|
+-----+-----+
scala> -------------------------------------------
Batch: 2
-------------------------------------------
+-----+-----+
|value|count|
+-----+-----+
| dog| 2|
| cat| 1|
+-----+-----+
```

Handling event time and late date

Event time is the time inside the data. Spark Streaming used to define the time as the received time for DStream purposes, but for many applications that need the event time, this is not enough. For example, if you require the number of times that a hashtag appears in a tweet every minute, then you will need the time when the data was generated, not the time when Spark received the event.

The following is an extension of the previous example of Structured Streaming, listening on server port `9999`. The `Timestamp` is now enabled as a part of the input data, so now, we can perform window operations on the unbounded table:

```
import java.sql.Timestamp
import org.apache.spark.sql.SparkSession
import org.apache.spark.sql.functions._
// Creating DataFrame that represent the stream of input lines from
connection
to host:port
val inputLines = spark.readStream
.format("socket")
.option("host", "localhost")
.option("port", 9999)
.option("includeTimestamp", true)
.load()
// Splitting the lines into words, retaining timestamps
val words = inputLines.as[(String, Timestamp)].flatMap(line =>
line._1.split(" ").map(word => (word, line._2))
).toDF("word", "timestamp")
// Grouping the data by window and word and computing the count of each
val windowedCounts = words.withWatermark("timestamp", "10 seconds")
.groupBy(
window($"timestamp", "10 seconds", "10 seconds"), $"word"
).count().orderBy("window")
// Begin executing the query which will print the windowed word counts to
the
console
val query = windowedCounts.writeStream.outputMode("complete")
.format("console")
.option("truncate", "false")

query.start()
query.awaitTermination()
```

Fault-tolerance semantics

The exactly-once paradigm is complicated in traditional streaming that uses an external database/storage to maintain offsets. Structured Streaming is still changing, and has several challenges to conquer before it sees widespread use.

Summary

Over the course of this chapter, the concepts of the stream-processing system, Spark Streaming, DStreams in Apache Spark, DStreams, DAG and DStream lineages, and transformations and actions were covered. Additionally, window-stream processing and a practical example of processing Twitter tweets using Spark Streaming were covered. Then, the receiver-based and direct-stream approaches of data consumption were covered with regards to Kafka, and finally, the newly developing technology of Structured Streaming was covered. Currently, it aims to solve many current challenges, such as fault tolerance, the use of exactly-once semantics in the stream, and the simplification of the integration with messaging systems, such as Kafka, while maintaining flexibility and extensibility to integrate with other input stream types.

In the next chapter, we will explore Apache Flink, which is a key challenger to Spark as a computing platform.

8
Batch Analytics with Apache Flink

This chapter will introduce the reader to Apache Flink, illustrating how to use Flink for big data analysis, based on the batch processing model. We will look at DataSet APIs, which provide easy-to-use methods for performing batch analysis on big data.

In this chapter, we will cover the following topics:

- Introduction to Apache Flink
- Installing Flink
- Using the Scala shell
- Using the Flink cluster UI
- Batch Analytics using Flink

Introduction to Apache Flink

Flink is an open source framework for distributed stream processing, and has the following features:

- It provides results that are accurate, even in the case of out-of-order or late-arriving data
- It is stateful and fault tolerant, and can seamlessly recover from failures while maintaining an exactly-once application state
- It performs at a large scale, running on thousands of nodes with very good throughput and latency characteristics

The following is a screenshot from the official documentation that shows how Apache Flink can be used:

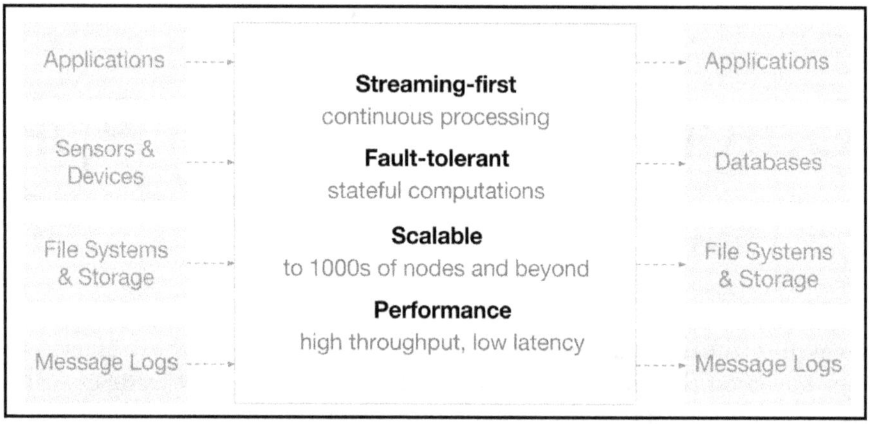

Another way of viewing the Apache Flink framework is shown in the following screenshot:

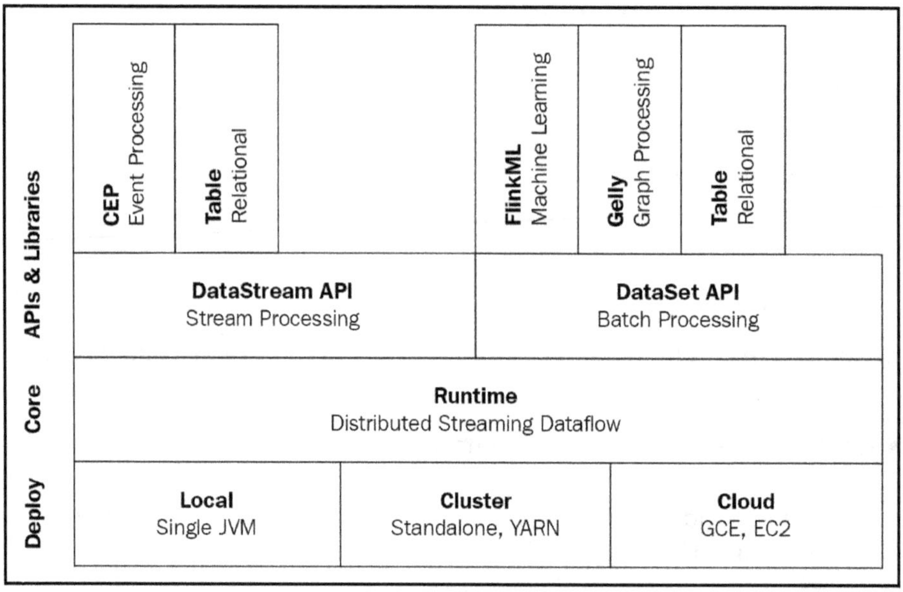

All Flink programs are executed lazily, when the program's main method is executed, the data loading and transformations do not happen directly. Rather, each operation is created and added to the program's plan. The operations are actually executed when the execution is explicitly triggered by an `execute()` call on the execution environment. Whether the program is executed locally or on a cluster depends on the type of execution environment The lazy evaluation lets you construct sophisticated programs that Flink executes as one holistically planned unit.

Flink programs look like regular programs that transform collections of data. Each program consists of the same basic parts:

1. Obtain an execution environment
2. Load the initial data
3. Specify transformations, aggregations, joins on this data
4. Specify where to put the results of your computations
5. Trigger the program execution

Continuous processing for unbounded datasets

Before we go into detail about Apache Flink, let's review, at a higher level, the types of datasets that you're likely to encounter when processing data, as well as the types of execution models you can choose for processing. These two ideas are often conflated; it will be useful to know what makes them different.

Firstly, there are two types of datasets:

- **Unbounded**: Infinite datasets that are added to continuously
- **Bounded**: Finite, unchanging datasets

Many real-world datasets that are traditionally thought of as bounded or batch are, in reality, unbounded datasets. This is true whether the data is stored in a sequence of directories on HDFS, or in a log-based system, such as **Apache Kafka**.

Some examples of unbounded datasets include, but are not limited to, the following:

- End users interacting with mobile or web applications
- Physical sensors providing measurements
- Financial markets
- Machine log data

Secondly, just like the two types of datasets, there are also two types of execution models:

- **Streaming**: Processing that executes continuously, as long as data is being produced
- **Batch**: Processing that is executed and runs to completeness in a finite amount of time, releasing computing resources when finished

It's possible, though not necessarily optimal, to process either type of dataset with either type of execution model. For instance, batch execution has long been applied to unbounded datasets, despite potential problems with windowing, state management, and out-of-order data.

Flink relies on a streaming execution model, which is an intuitive fit for processing unbounded datasets: streaming execution is continuously processing data that is continuously produced. An alignment between the type of dataset and the type of execution model offers many advantages with regard to accuracy and performance.

Flink, the streaming model, and bounded datasets

In Apache Flink, you can use both a DataStream API for working with unbounded data and a DataSet API for working with bounded data. Flink makes the relationship between bounded and unbounded datasets quite natural. A bounded dataset can be treated as simply a special case of an unbounded one, so it's possible to apply all of the same concepts to both types of datasets.

A bounded dataset is handled inside of Flink as a **finite stream**, with only a few minor differences in how Flink manages bounded versus unbounded datasets. As a result, it's possible to use Flink to process both bounded and unbounded data, with both APIs running on the same distributed streaming execution engine: a simple yet powerful architecture.

Installing Flink

In this section, we will download and install Apache Flink.

Flink runs on Linux, OS X, and Windows. To be able to run Flink, the only requirement is having a working Java 7.x (or higher) installation. If you are using Windows, please take a look at the Flink on Windows guide at `https://ci.apache.org/projects/flink/flink-docs-release-1.4/start/flink_on_windows.html`, which describes how to run Flink on Windows for local setups.

You can check your version of Java by issuing the following command:

```
java -version
```

If you have Java 8, the output will look something like this:

```
java version "1.8.0_111"
Java(TM) SE Runtime Environment (build 1.8.0_111-b14)
Java HotSpot(TM) 64-Bit Server VM (build 25.111-b14, mixed mode)
```

Downloading Flink

Download the Apache Flink binaries relevant to your platform at `https://flink.apache.org/downloads.html`:

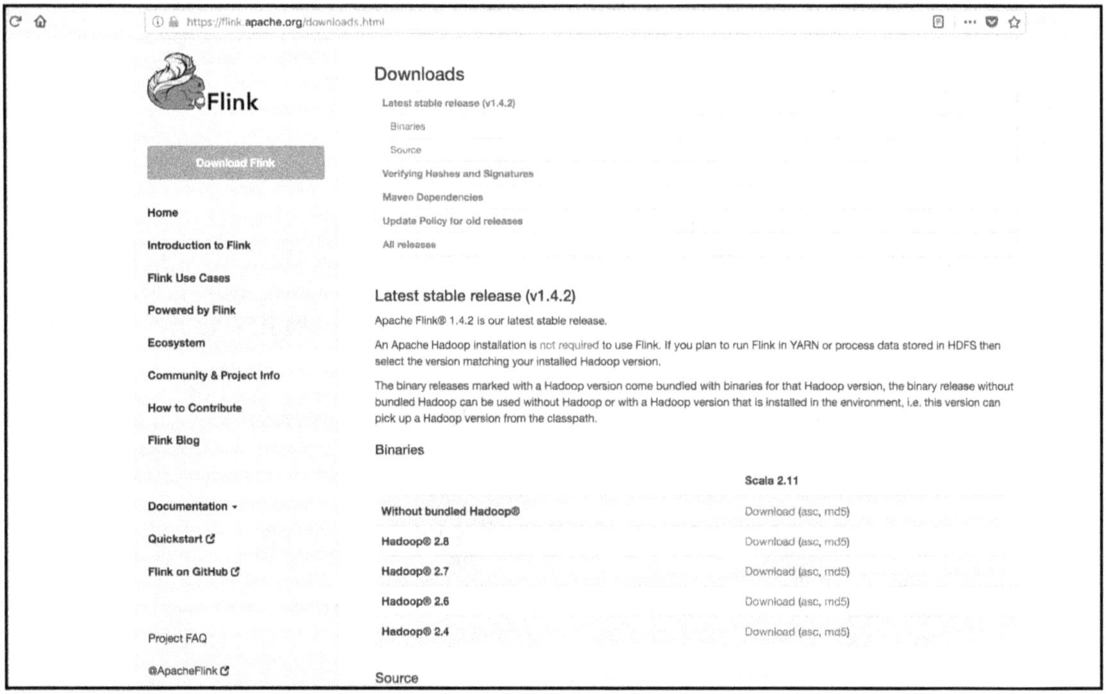

Figure: Screenshot showing Apache Flink libraries

Download Hadoop version 2.8 by clicking on **Download**. You will see the download page in your browser, as shown in the following screenshot:

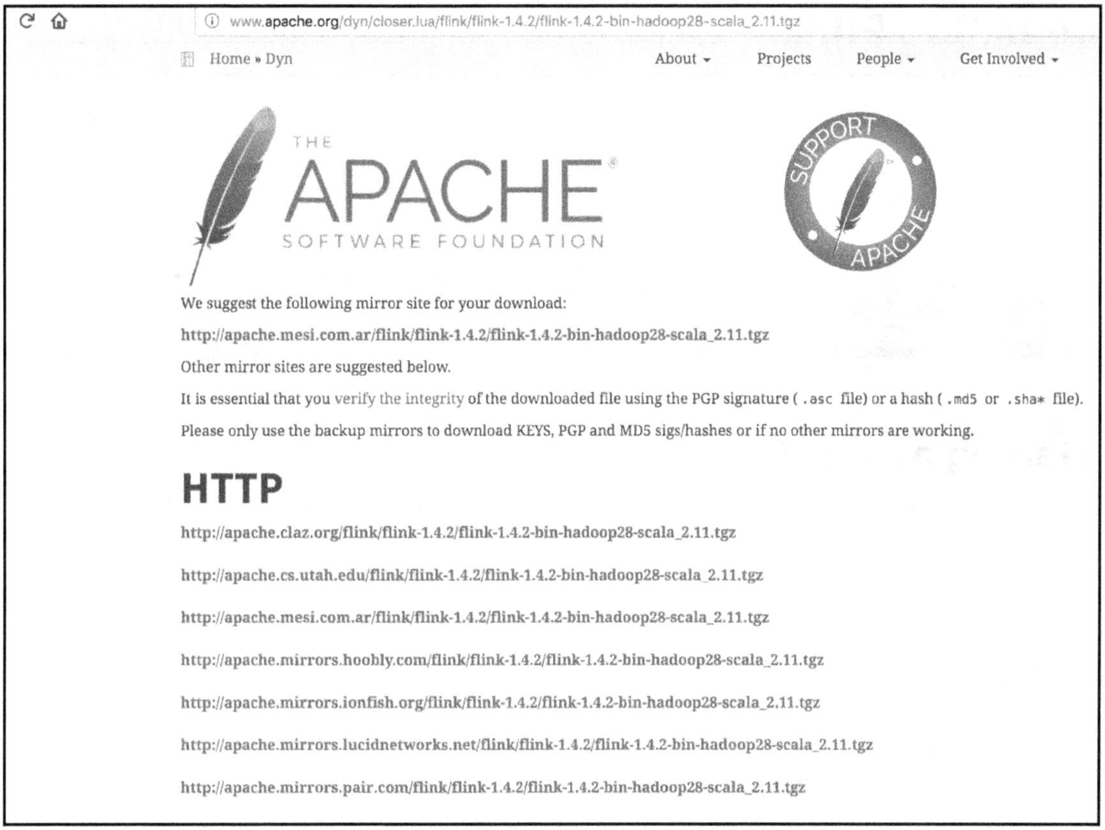

Figure: Screenshot showing Hadoop version to be downloaded

In this instance, I downloaded `flink-1.4.2-bin-hadoop28-scala_2.11.tgz`, which is the most recent version available.

Once downloaded, extract the binaries. On a Mac or a Linux machine, you can use the `tar` command:

```
Moogie:~ sridharalla$ tar -xvzf flink-1.4.2-bin-hadoop28-scala_2.11.tgz
x flink-1.4.2/
x flink-1.4.2/lib/
x flink-1.4.2/lib/flink-dist_2.11-1.4.2.jar
```

Installing Flink

First, change the directory to the location from which you extracted Apache Flink:

```
cd flink-1.4.2
```

You will see the following contents:

```
Moogie:flink-1.4.2 sridharalla$ ls
LICENSE         README.txt      conf            lib             opt             tools
NOTICE          bin             examples        log             resources
```

Starting a local Flink cluster

You can start a local cluster by simply using the following script in the `bin` folder:

```
./bin/start-local.sh
```

Once you run the script, you should see the cluster started.

Check the JobManager's web frontend at `http://localhost:8081` and make sure that everything is up and running. The web frontend should report a single available **Task Managers** instance:

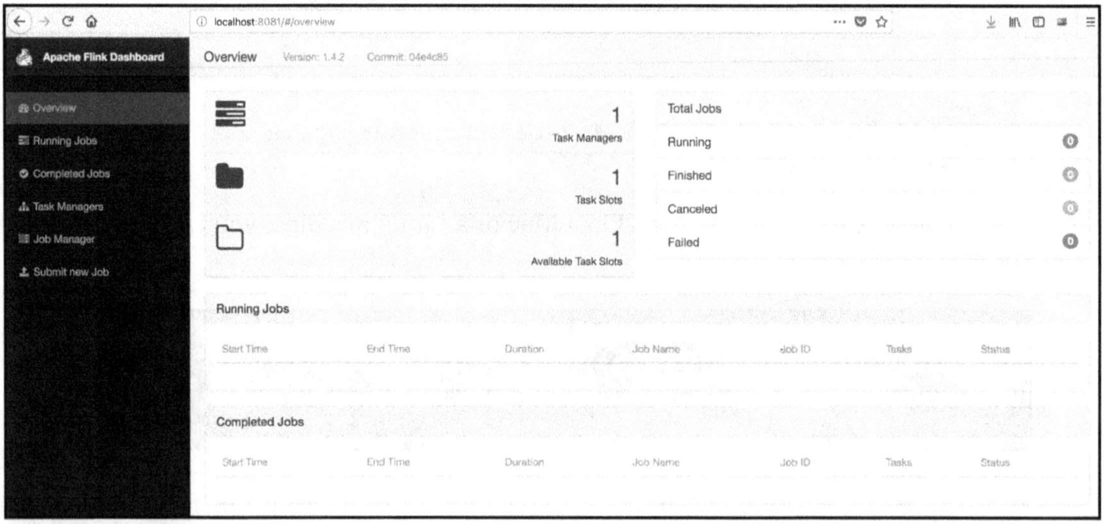

You can also verify that the system is running by checking the log files in the `logs` directory:

```
tail log/flink-*-jobmanager-*.log
```

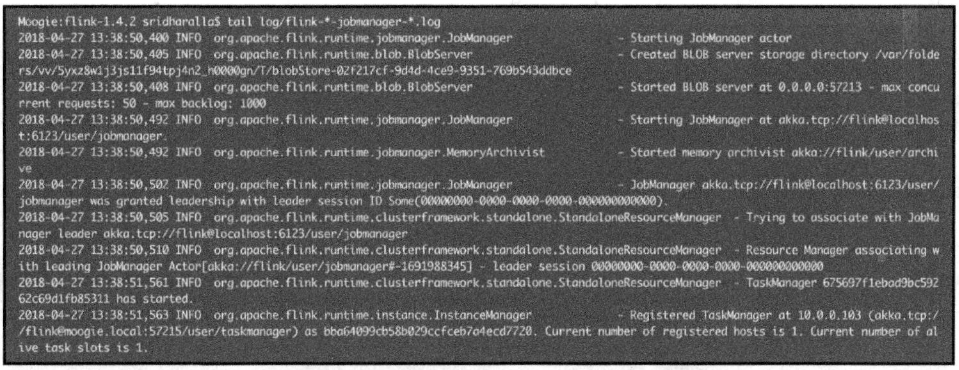
Moogie:flink-1.4.2 sridharalla$ tail log/flink-*-jobmanager-*.log
2018-04-27 13:38:50,400 INFO org.apache.flink.runtime.jobmanager.JobManager - Starting JobManager actor
2018-04-27 13:38:50,405 INFO org.apache.flink.runtime.blob.BlobServer - Created BLOB server storage directory /var/folde
rs/vv/5yxz8w1j3js11f94tpj4n2_h0000gn/T/blobStore-02f217cf-9d4d-4ce9-9351-769b543ddbce
2018-04-27 13:38:50,408 INFO org.apache.flink.runtime.blob.BlobServer - Started BLOB server at 0.0.0.0:57213 - max concu
rrent requests: 50 - max backlog: 1000
2018-04-27 13:38:50,492 INFO org.apache.flink.runtime.jobmanager.JobManager - Starting JobManager at akka.tcp://flink@localhos
t:6123/user/jobmanager.
2018-04-27 13:38:50,492 INFO org.apache.flink.runtime.jobmanager.MemoryArchivist - Started memory archivist akka://flink/user/archi
ve
2018-04-27 13:38:50,502 INFO org.apache.flink.runtime.jobmanager.JobManager - JobManager akka.tcp://flink@localhost:6123/user/
jobmanager was granted leadership with leader session ID Some(00000000-0000-0000-0000-000000000000).
2018-04-27 13:38:50,505 INFO org.apache.flink.runtime.clusterframework.standalone.StandaloneResourceManager - Trying to associate with JobMa
nager leader akka.tcp://flink@localhost:6123/user/jobmanager
2018-04-27 13:38:50,510 INFO org.apache.flink.runtime.clusterframework.standalone.StandaloneResourceManager - Resource Manager associating w
ith leading JobManager Actor[akka://flink/user/jobmanager#-1691988345] - leader session 00000000-0000-0000-0000-000000000000
2018-04-27 13:38:51,561 INFO org.apache.flink.runtime.clusterframework.standalone.StandaloneResourceManager - TaskManager 675697f1ebad9bc592
62c69d1fb85311 has started.
2018-04-27 13:38:51,563 INFO org.apache.flink.runtime.instance.InstanceManager - Registered TaskManager at 10.0.0.103 (akka.tcp:/
/flink@moogie.local:57215/user/taskmanager) as bba64099cb58b029ccfceb7a4ecd7720. Current number of registered hosts is 1. Current number of al
ive task slots is 1.

To use a Scala shell, enter the following code:

```
./bin/start-scala-shell.sh remote localhost 6123
```

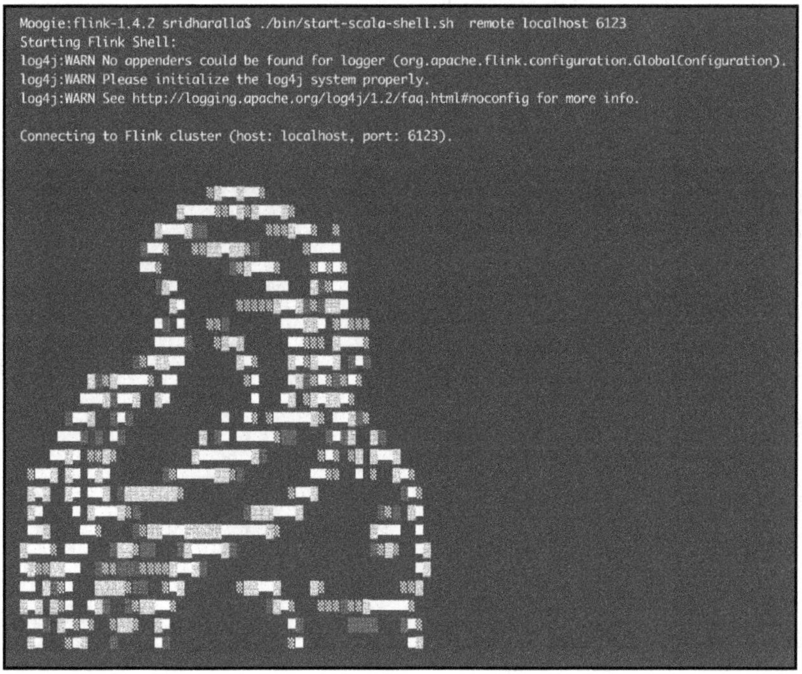
Moogie:flink-1.4.2 sridharalla$ ./bin/start-scala-shell.sh remote localhost 6123
Starting Flink Shell:
log4j:WARN No appenders could be found for logger (org.apache.flink.configuration.GlobalConfiguration).
log4j:WARN Please initialize the log4j system properly.
log4j:WARN See http://logging.apache.org/log4j/1.2/faq.html#noconfig for more info.
Connecting to Flink cluster (host: localhost, port: 6123).

To load data, enter the following code:

```
val dataSet = benv
.readTextFile("OnlineRetail.csv")
dataSet.count()
```

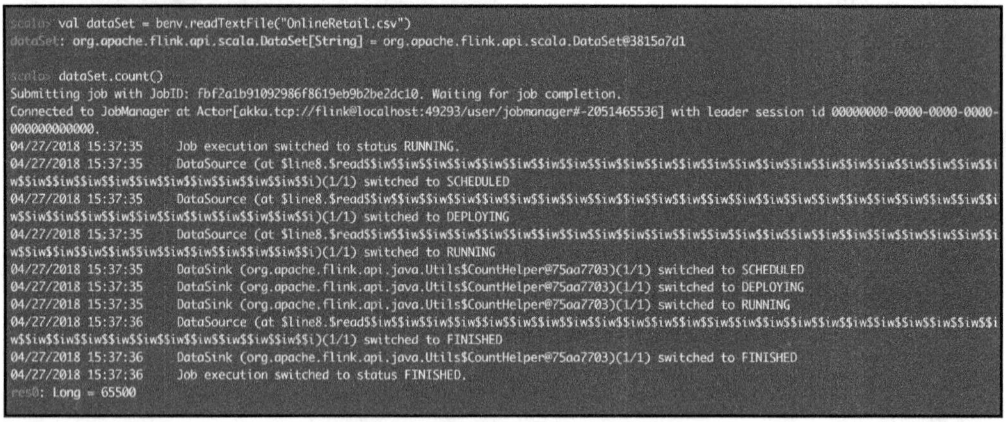

```
scala> val dataSet = benv.readTextFile("OnlineRetail.csv")
dataSet: org.apache.flink.api.scala.DataSet[String] = org.apache.flink.api.scala.DataSet@3815a7d1

scala> dataSet.count()
Submitting job with JobID: fbf2a1b91092986f8619eb9b2be2dc10. Waiting for job completion.
Connected to JobManager at Actor[akka.tcp://flink@localhost:49293/user/jobmanager#-2051465536] with leader session id 00000000-0000-0000-0000-000000000000.
04/27/2018 15:37:35     Job execution switched to status RUNNING.
04/27/2018 15:37:35     DataSource (at $line8.$read$$iw$$iw$$iw$$iw$$iw$$iw$$iw$$iw$$iw$$iw$$iw$$iw$$iw$$iw$$iw$$iw$$iw$$iw$$iw$$iw$$iw$$iw$$iw$$iw$$iw$$iw$$iw$$iw$$iw$$iw$$i)(1/1) switched to SCHEDULED
04/27/2018 15:37:35     DataSource (at $line8.$read$$iw$$iw$$iw$$iw$$iw$$iw$$iw$$iw$$iw$$iw$$iw$$iw$$iw$$iw$$iw$$iw$$iw$$iw$$iw$$iw$$iw$$iw$$iw$$iw$$iw$$iw$$iw$$iw$$iw$$iw$$i)(1/1) switched to DEPLOYING
04/27/2018 15:37:35     DataSource (at $line8.$read$$iw$$iw$$iw$$iw$$iw$$iw$$iw$$iw$$iw$$iw$$iw$$iw$$iw$$iw$$iw$$iw$$iw$$iw$$iw$$iw$$iw$$iw$$iw$$iw$$iw$$iw$$iw$$iw$$iw$$iw$$i)(1/1) switched to RUNNING
04/27/2018 15:37:35     DataSink (org.apache.flink.api.java.Utils$CountHelper@75aa7703)(1/1) switched to SCHEDULED
04/27/2018 15:37:35     DataSink (org.apache.flink.api.java.Utils$CountHelper@75aa7703)(1/1) switched to DEPLOYING
04/27/2018 15:37:35     DataSink (org.apache.flink.api.java.Utils$CountHelper@75aa7703)(1/1) switched to RUNNING
04/27/2018 15:37:36     DataSource (at $line8.$read$$iw$$iw$$iw$$iw$$iw$$iw$$iw$$iw$$iw$$iw$$iw$$iw$$iw$$iw$$iw$$iw$$iw$$iw$$iw$$iw$$iw$$iw$$iw$$iw$$iw$$iw$$iw$$iw$$iw$$iw$$i)(1/1) switched to FINISHED
04/27/2018 15:37:36     DataSink (org.apache.flink.api.java.Utils$CountHelper@75aa7703)(1/1) switched to FINISHED
04/27/2018 15:37:36     Job execution switched to status FINISHED.
res0: Long = 65500
```

You can print the first five rows of the dataset by using the following code. The results are shown in the screenshot following the code:

```
dataSet
.first(5)
.print()
```

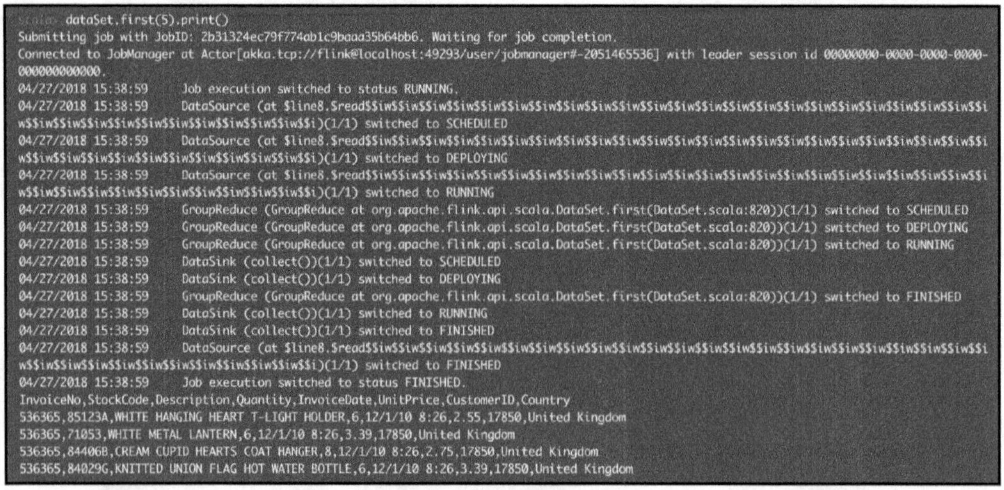

```
scala> dataSet.first(5).print()
Submitting job with JobID: 2b31324ec79f774ab1c9baaa35b64bb6. Waiting for job completion.
Connected to JobManager at Actor[akka.tcp://flink@localhost:49293/user/jobmanager#-2051465536] with leader session id 00000000-0000-0000-0000-000000000000.
04/27/2018 15:38:59     Job execution switched to status RUNNING.
04/27/2018 15:38:59     DataSource (at $line8.$read$$iw$$iw$$iw$$iw$$iw$$iw$$iw$$iw$$iw$$iw$$iw$$iw$$iw$$iw$$iw$$iw$$iw$$iw$$iw$$iw$$iw$$iw$$iw$$iw$$iw$$iw$$iw$$iw$$iw$$iw$$i)(1/1) switched to SCHEDULED
04/27/2018 15:38:59     DataSource (at $line8.$read$$iw$$iw$$iw$$iw$$iw$$iw$$iw$$iw$$iw$$iw$$iw$$iw$$iw$$iw$$iw$$iw$$iw$$iw$$iw$$iw$$iw$$iw$$iw$$iw$$iw$$iw$$iw$$iw$$iw$$iw$$i)(1/1) switched to DEPLOYING
04/27/2018 15:38:59     DataSource (at $line8.$read$$iw$$iw$$iw$$iw$$iw$$iw$$iw$$iw$$iw$$iw$$iw$$iw$$iw$$iw$$iw$$iw$$iw$$iw$$iw$$iw$$iw$$iw$$iw$$iw$$iw$$iw$$iw$$iw$$iw$$iw$$i)(1/1) switched to RUNNING
04/27/2018 15:38:59     GroupReduce (GroupReduce at org.apache.flink.api.scala.DataSet.first(DataSet.scala:820))(1/1) switched to SCHEDULED
04/27/2018 15:38:59     GroupReduce (GroupReduce at org.apache.flink.api.scala.DataSet.first(DataSet.scala:820))(1/1) switched to DEPLOYING
04/27/2018 15:38:59     GroupReduce (GroupReduce at org.apache.flink.api.scala.DataSet.first(DataSet.scala:820))(1/1) switched to RUNNING
04/27/2018 15:38:59     DataSink (collect())(1/1) switched to SCHEDULED
04/27/2018 15:38:59     DataSink (collect())(1/1) switched to DEPLOYING
04/27/2018 15:38:59     GroupReduce (GroupReduce at org.apache.flink.api.scala.DataSet.first(DataSet.scala:820))(1/1) switched to FINISHED
04/27/2018 15:38:59     DataSink (collect())(1/1) switched to RUNNING
04/27/2018 15:38:59     DataSink (collect())(1/1) switched to FINISHED
04/27/2018 15:38:59     DataSource (at $line8.$read$$iw$$iw$$iw$$iw$$iw$$iw$$iw$$iw$$iw$$iw$$iw$$iw$$iw$$iw$$iw$$iw$$iw$$iw$$iw$$iw$$iw$$iw$$iw$$iw$$iw$$iw$$iw$$iw$$iw$$iw$$i)(1/1) switched to FINISHED
04/27/2018 15:38:59     Job execution switched to status FINISHED.
InvoiceNo,StockCode,Description,Quantity,InvoiceDate,UnitPrice,CustomerID,Country
536365,85123A,WHITE HANGING HEART T-LIGHT HOLDER,6,12/1/10 8:26,2.55,17850,United Kingdom
536365,71053,WHITE METAL LANTERN,6,12/1/10 8:26,3.39,17850,United Kingdom
536365,84406B,CREAM CUPID HEARTS COAT HANGER,8,12/1/10 8:26,2.75,17850,United Kingdom
536365,84029G,KNITTED UNION FLAG HOT WATER BOTTLE,6,12/1/10 8:26,3.39,17850,United Kingdom
```

You can perform a simple transformation by using `map()`:

```
dataSet
.map(x => x.split(",")(2))
.first(5)
.print()
```

```
scala> dataSet.map(x => x.split(",")(2)).first(5).print()
Submitting job with JobID: 6513e762d3a224dfa3ba3a611d5a8136. Waiting for job completion.
Connected to JobManager at Actor[akka.tcp://flink@localhost:49293/user/jobmanager#-2051465536] with leader session id 00000000-0000-0000-0000-
000000000000.
04/27/2018 15:39:51     Job execution switched to status RUNNING.
04/27/2018 15:39:51     CHAIN DataSource (at $line8.$read$$iw$$iw$$iw$$iw$$iw$$iw$$iw$$iw$$iw$$iw$$iw$$iw$$iw$$iw$$iw$$iw$$iw$$iw$$iw$
$iw$$iw$$iw$$iw$$iw$$iw$$iw$$iw$$iw$$iw$$iw$$i) -> Map (Map at $line13.$read$$iw$$iw$$iw$$iw$$iw$$iw$$iw$$iw$$iw$$iw$$iw$$iw$$iw$$
iw$$iw$$iw$$iw$$iw$$iw$$iw$$iw$$iw$$iw$$iw$$iw$$iw$$iw$$iw$$iw$$iw$$iw$$iw$$iw$.<init>(<console>:65))(1/1) switched to SCHEDULED
04/27/2018 15:39:51     CHAIN DataSource (at $line8.$read$$iw$$iw$$iw$$iw$$iw$$iw$$iw$$iw$$iw$$iw$$iw$$iw$$iw$$iw$$iw$$iw$$iw$$iw$$iw$
$iw$$iw$$iw$$iw$$iw$$iw$$iw$$iw$$iw$$iw$$iw$$i) -> Map (Map at $line13.$read$$iw$$iw$$iw$$iw$$iw$$iw$$iw$$iw$$iw$$iw$$iw$$iw$$iw$$
iw$$iw$$iw$$iw$$iw$$iw$$iw$$iw$$iw$$iw$$iw$$iw$$iw$$iw$$iw$$iw$$iw$$iw$$iw$$iw$.<init>(<console>:65))(1/1) switched to DEPLOYING
04/27/2018 15:39:51     CHAIN DataSource (at $line8.$read$$iw$$iw$$iw$$iw$$iw$$iw$$iw$$iw$$iw$$iw$$iw$$iw$$iw$$iw$$iw$$iw$$iw$$iw$$iw$
$iw$$iw$$iw$$iw$$iw$$iw$$iw$$iw$$iw$$iw$$iw$$i) -> Map (Map at $line13.$read$$iw$$iw$$iw$$iw$$iw$$iw$$iw$$iw$$iw$$iw$$iw$$iw$$iw$$
iw$$iw$$iw$$iw$$iw$$iw$$iw$$iw$$iw$$iw$$iw$$iw$$iw$$iw$$iw$$iw$$iw$$iw$$iw$$iw$.<init>(<console>:65))(1/1) switched to RUNNING
04/27/2018 15:39:51     GroupReduce (GroupReduce at org.apache.flink.api.scala.DataSet.first(DataSet.scala:820))(1/1) switched to SCHEDULED
04/27/2018 15:39:51     GroupReduce (GroupReduce at org.apache.flink.api.scala.DataSet.first(DataSet.scala:820))(1/1) switched to DEPLOYING
04/27/2018 15:39:51     GroupReduce (GroupReduce at org.apache.flink.api.scala.DataSet.first(DataSet.scala:820))(1/1) switched to RUNNING
04/27/2018 15:39:51     DataSink (collect())(1/1) switched to SCHEDULED
04/27/2018 15:39:51     DataSink (collect())(1/1) switched to DEPLOYING
04/27/2018 15:39:51     GroupReduce (GroupReduce at org.apache.flink.api.scala.DataSet.first(DataSet.scala:820))(1/1) switched to FINISHED
04/27/2018 15:39:51     DataSink (collect())(1/1) switched to RUNNING
04/27/2018 15:39:51     DataSink (collect())(1/1) switched to FINISHED
04/27/2018 15:39:51     CHAIN DataSource (at $line8.$read$$iw$$iw$$iw$$iw$$iw$$iw$$iw$$iw$$iw$$iw$$iw$$iw$$iw$$iw$$iw$$iw$$iw$$iw$$iw$
$iw$$iw$$iw$$iw$$iw$$iw$$iw$$iw$$iw$$iw$$iw$$i) -> Map (Map at $line13.$read$$iw$$iw$$iw$$iw$$iw$$iw$$iw$$iw$$iw$$iw$$iw$$iw$$iw$$
iw$$iw$$iw$$iw$$iw$$iw$$iw$$iw$$iw$$iw$$iw$$iw$$iw$$iw$$iw$$iw$$iw$$iw$$iw$$iw$.<init>(<console>:65))(1/1) switched to FINISHED
04/27/2018 15:39:51     Job execution switched to status FINISHED.
Description
WHITE HANGING HEART T-LIGHT HOLDER
WHITE METAL LANTERN
CREAM CUPID HEARTS COAT HANGER
KNITTED UNION FLAG HOT WATER BOTTLE
```

```
dataSet
.flatMap(x => x.split(","))
.map(x=> (x,1))
.groupBy(0)
.sum(1)
.first(10)
.print()
```

```
(,25447)
( ",95)
( 1 HANGER ,30)
( 3 TIER,1)
( 4 PURPLE FLOCK DINNER CANDLES,4)
( BACK DOOR ",31)
( BAROQUE",3)
( BILLBOARD FONTS DESIGN",12)
( BIRTHDAY CARD,28)
( BLUE",1)
```

Using the Flink cluster UI

Using the Flink cluster UI, you can understand and monitor what's running in your cluster and dig deeply into various jobs and tasks. You can monitor the job statuses, cancel jobs, or debug any problems with the jobs. By looking at logs, you can also diagnose problems with your code, and fix them.

The following is a list of **Completed Jobs**:

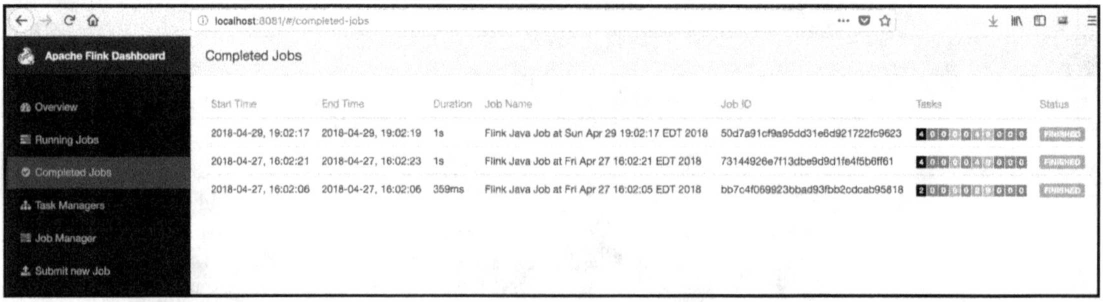

You can drill down into any particular job to see more details about the job's execution:

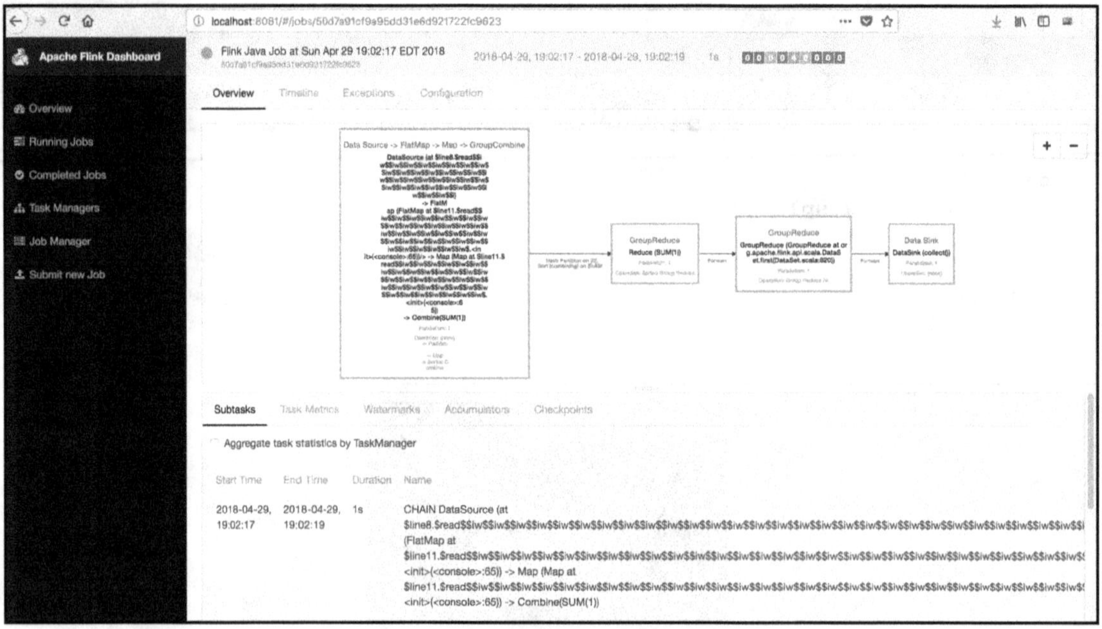

Figure: Drilling down a particular job to see job's execution

You can look at the **Timeline** of the job to get more details:

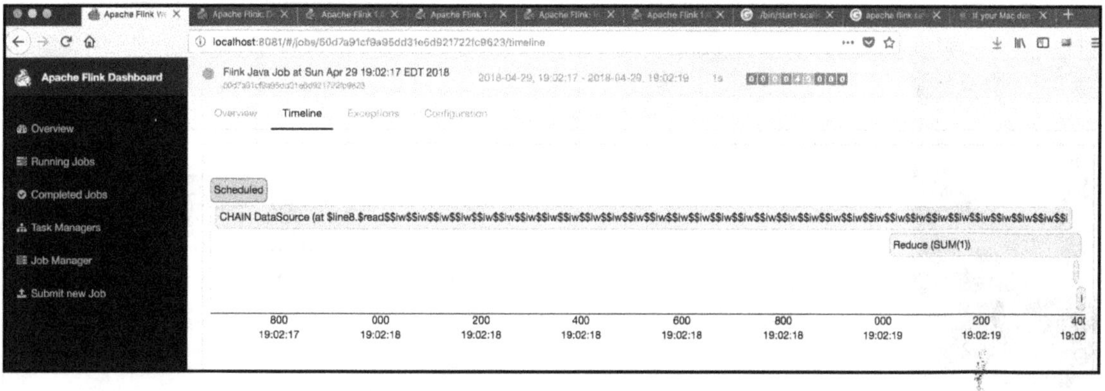

Figure: Screenshot to see Timeline of a job

The following screenshot shows the **Task Managers** tab, showing all of the task managers. This helps you understand the number and status of the task managers:

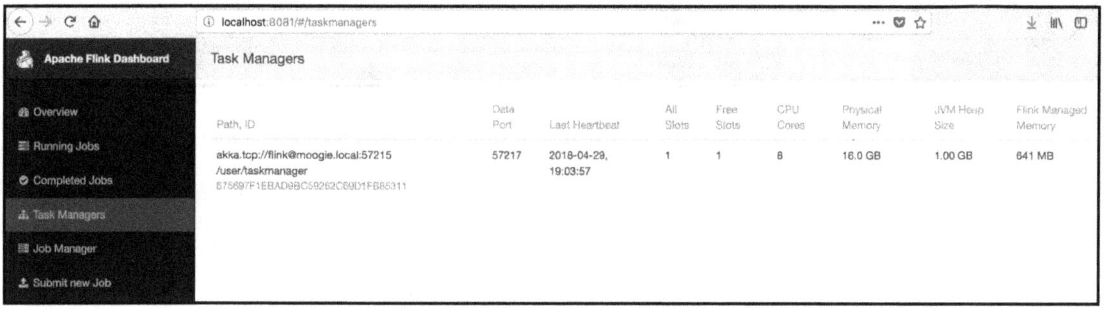

You can also check the **Logs**, as shown in the following screenshot:

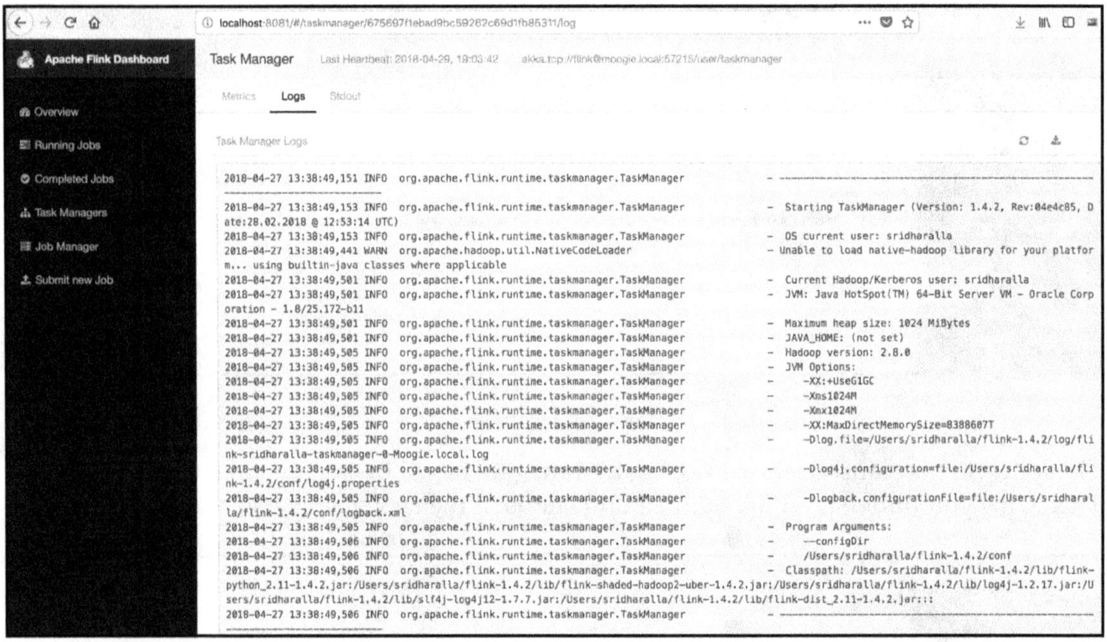

The **Metrics** tab gives you details of the memory and CPU resources:

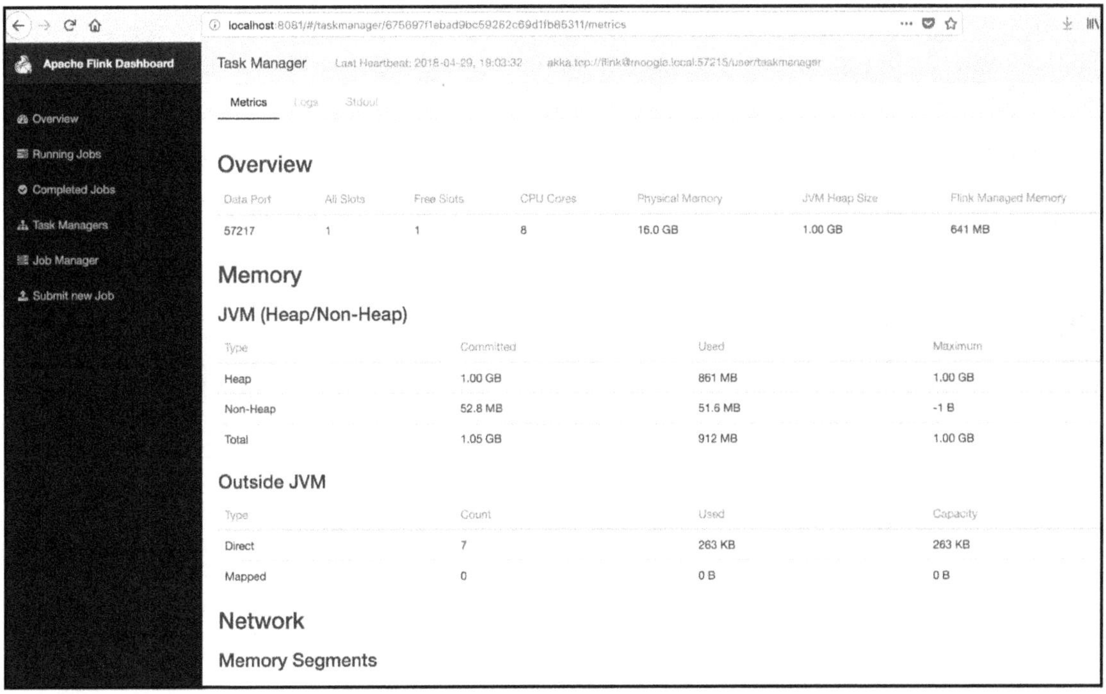

Figure: Screenshot showing details of the memory and CPU resources in Metrics tab

You can also submit JARs as jobs, in lieu of writing everything in the Scala shell, as seen previously:

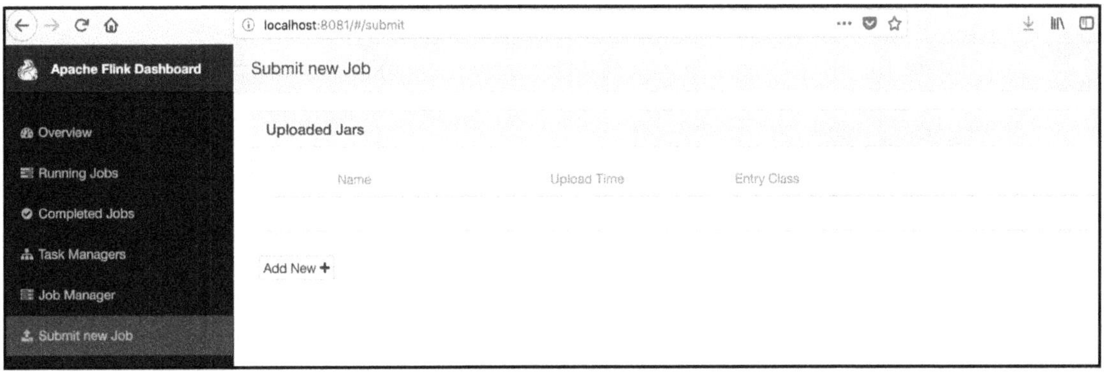

Batch analytics

Batch Analytics in Apache Flink are quite similar to the streaming analytics in the way Flink handles both types of analytics using same APIs. This gives a lot of flexibility and allows code reuse across both the different types of analytics.

In this section, we will look at some analytical jobs on the sample data we are using `OnlineRetail.csv`. We will also be loading `cities.csv` and `temperature.csv` to do some more join operations.

Reading file

Flink comes with several built-in formats to create data sets from common file formats. Many of them have shortcut methods on the execution environment.

File-based

File based sources can be read using APIs which are listed as follows:

- `readTextFile(path)/TextInputFormat`: Reads files line wise and returns them as strings.
- `readTextFileWithValue(path)/TextValueInputFormat`: Reads files line wise and returns them as `StringValues`. `StringValues` are mutable strings.
- `readCsvFile(path)/CsvInputFormat`: Parses files of comma (or another char) delimited fields. Returns a DataSet of tuples, case class objects, or POJOs. Supports the basic Java types and their `Value` counterparts as field types.
- `readFileOfPrimitives(path, delimiter)/PrimitiveInputFormat`: Parses files of new-line (or another char sequence) delimited primitive data types such as `String` or `Integer` using the given delimiter.
- `readHadoopFile(FileInputFormat, Key, Value, path)/FileInputFormat`: Creates a `JobConf` and reads file from the specified path with the specified `FileInputFormat`, `Key` class and `Value` class and returns them as `Tuple2<Key, Value>`.
- `readSequenceFile(Key, Value, path)/SequenceFileInputFormat`: Creates a `JobConf` and reads file from the specified path with type `SequenceFileInputFormat`, `Key` class and `Value` class and returns them as `Tuple2<Key, Value>`.

Collection-based

Collection (data structures such as lists, arrays, and so on) based sources can be read using APIs which are listed as follows:

- `fromCollection(Seq)`: Creates a DataSet from a `Seq`. All elements in the collection must be of the same type.
- `fromCollection(Iterator)`: Creates a DataSet from an `Iterator`. The class specifies the data type of the elements returned by the iterator.
- `fromElements(elements: _*)`: Creates a DataSet from the given sequence of objects. All objects must be of the same type.
- `fromParallelCollection(SplittableIterator)`: Creates a DataSet from an iterator, in parallel. The class specifies the data type of the elements returned by the iterator.
- `generateSequence(from, to)`: Generates the sequence of numbers in the given interval, in parallel.

Generic

Generic (Custom) sources can be read using APIs which are listed as follows:

- `readFile(inputFormat, path)/FileInputFormat`: Accepts a file input format
- `createInput(inputFormat)/InputFormat`: Accepts a generic input format

We will look at one of the APIs which is `readTextFile()`. Reading a file using this API results in loading a file (local text file, hdfs file, Amazon s3 file, and so on) into a DataSet. This DataSet contains the locations of the partitions of the data being loaded thus being able to support TBs of data.

Let's load the example `OnlineRetail.csv` as shown in the following code:

```
val dataSet = benv.readTextFile("OnlineRetail.csv")
dataSet.first(10).print()
```

This will print the contents of the DataSet once loaded as shown in the following code:

```
InvoiceNo,StockCode,Description,Quantity,InvoiceDate,UnitPrice,CustomerID,C
ountry
 536365,85123A,WHITE HANGING HEART T-LIGHT HOLDER,6,12/1/10
8:26,2.55,17850,United Kingdom
 536365,71053,WHITE METAL LANTERN,6,12/1/10 8:26,3.39,17850,United Kingdom
```

```
 536365,84406B,CREAM CUPID HEARTS COAT HANGER,8,12/1/10
8:26,2.75,17850,United Kingdom
 536365,84029G,KNITTED UNION FLAG HOT WATER BOTTLE,6,12/1/10
8:26,3.39,17850,United Kingdom
 536365,84029E,RED WOOLLY HOTTIE WHITE HEART.,6,12/1/10
8:26,3.39,17850,United Kingdom
 536365,22752,SET 7 BABUSHKA NESTING BOXES,2,12/1/10 8:26,7.65,17850,United
Kingdom
 536365,21730,GLASS STAR FROSTED T-LIGHT HOLDER,6,12/1/10
8:26,4.25,17850,United Kingdom
 536366,22633,HAND WARMER UNION JACK,6,12/1/10 8:28,1.85,17850,United
Kingdom
 536366,22632,HAND WARMER RED POLKA DOT,6,12/1/10 8:28,1.85,17850,United
Kingdom
```

If you notice the preceding example, you see that the first line/row is actually a header row hence is not useful in any analysis. You can filter out one or more rows using the `filter()` function.

Following is the loading of the file and removal of the first line and return a DataSet:

```
val dataSet =benv
    .readTextFile("OnlineRetail.csv")
    .filter(!_.startsWith("InvoiceNo"))
dataSet.first(10).print()
```

This will print the contents of the DataSet once loaded as shown in the following code:

```
 536365,85123A,WHITE HANGING HEART T-LIGHT HOLDER,6,12/1/10
8:26,2.55,17850,United Kingdom
 536365,71053,WHITE METAL LANTERN,6,12/1/10 8:26,3.39,17850,United Kingdom
 536365,84406B,CREAM CUPID HEARTS COAT HANGER,8,12/1/10
8:26,2.75,17850,United Kingdom
 536365,84029G,KNITTED UNION FLAG HOT WATER BOTTLE,6,12/1/10
8:26,3.39,17850,United Kingdom
 536365,84029E,RED WOOLLY HOTTIE WHITE HEART.,6,12/1/10
8:26,3.39,17850,United Kingdom
 536365,22752,SET 7 BABUSHKA NESTING BOXES,2,12/1/10 8:26,7.65,17850,United
Kingdom
 536365,21730,GLASS STAR FROSTED T-LIGHT HOLDER,6,12/1/10
8:26,4.25,17850,United Kingdom
 536366,22633,HAND WARMER UNION JACK,6,12/1/10 8:28,1.85,17850,United
Kingdom
 536366,22632,HAND WARMER RED POLKA DOT,6,12/1/10 8:28,1.85,17850,United
Kingdom
 536367,84879,ASSORTED COLOUR BIRD ORNAMENT,32,12/1/10
8:34,1.69,13047,United Kingdom
```

Clearly this time we do not see the header row:

```
InvoiceNo,StockCode,Description,Quantity,InvoiceDate,UnitPrice,CustomerID,C
ountry
```

We will now look into more operations that can be performed on the DataSet loaded.

Transformations

Transformations change a DataSet into a new DataSet by applying the transformation logic to each row of the original DataSet. As an example, if we want to eliminate the first header row from the input then we can use a `filter()` operation to do this.

Following is application of two `filter()` operations to first remove the header and then making sure we have the correct number of columns in each row which happens to be 8 in this case:

```
val dataSet = benv.readTextFile("OnlineRetail.csv")
    .filter(!_.startsWith("InvoiceNo"))
    .filter(_.split(",").length == 8)

dataSet.map(x => x.split(",")(2))
    .first(10).print()
```

This will print the contents of the DataSet once loaded as shown in the following code:

```
WHITE HANGING HEART T-LIGHT HOLDER
WHITE METAL LANTERN
CREAM CUPID HEARTS COAT HANGER
KNITTED UNION FLAG HOT WATER BOTTLE
RED WOOLLY HOTTIE WHITE HEART.
SET 7 BABUSHKA NESTING BOXES
GLASS STAR FROSTED T-LIGHT HOLDER
HAND WARMER UNION JACK
HAND WARMER RED POLKA DOT
```

Similarly you can print the quantity column from the DataSet:

```
dataSet.map(x => x.split(",")(3))
    .first(10).print()
```

This will print the contents of the DataSet once loaded as shown in the following code:

```
6
6
8
6
6
2
6
6
6
```

Similarly you can print the tuple of description and quantity columns from the DataSet:

```
dataSet.map(x => (x.split(",")(2), x.split(",")(3).toInt))
    .first(10).print()
```

This will print the contents of the DataSet once loaded as shown in the following code:

```
(WHITE HANGING HEART T-LIGHT HOLDER,6)
(WHITE METAL LANTERN,6)
(CREAM CUPID HEARTS COAT HANGER,8)
(KNITTED UNION FLAG HOT WATER BOTTLE,6)
(RED WOOLLY HOTTIE WHITE HEART.,6)
(SET 7 BABUSHKA NESTING BOXES,2)
(GLASS STAR FROSTED T-LIGHT HOLDER,6)
(HAND WARMER UNION JACK,6)
(HAND WARMER RED POLKA DOT,6)
```

This section gives a brief overview of the available transformations and can be found at `https://ci.apache.org/projects/flink/flink-docs-release-1.4/dev/batch/dataset_transformations.html`:

Transformation	Description
Map	Takes one element and produces one element. `data.map { x => x.toInt }`
FlatMap	Takes one element and produces zero, one, or more elements. `data.flatMap { str => str.split(" ") }`
MapPartition	Transforms a parallel partition in a single function call. The function get the partition as an Iterator and can produce an arbitrary number of result values. The number of elements in each partition depends on the degree-of-parallelism and previous operations. `data.mapPartition { in => in map { (_, 1) } }`

Transformation	Description
Filter	Evaluates a boolean function for each element and retains those for which the function returns true. **IMPORTANT**: The system assumes that the function does not modify the element on which the predicate is applied. Violating this assumption can lead to incorrect results. `data.filter { _ > 1000 }`
Reduce	Combines a group of elements into a single element by repeatedly combining two elements into one. Reduce may be applied on a full data set, or on a grouped data set. `data.reduce { _ + _ }`
ReduceGroup	Combines a group of elements into one or more elements. `reduceGroup` may be applied on a full data set, or on a grouped data set. `data.reduceGroup { elements => elements.sum }`

Aggregate	Aggregates a group of values into a single value. Aggregation functions can be thought of as built-in reduce functions. Aggregate may be applied on a full data set, or on a grouped data set.
	`val input: DataSet[(Int, String, Double)] = // [...]`
	`val output: DataSet[(Int, String, Double)] =`
	`input.aggregate(SUM, 0).aggregate(MIN, 2)`
	You can also use short-hand syntax for minimum, maximum, and sum aggregations.
	`val input: DataSet[(Int, String, Double)] = // [...]`
	`val output: DataSet[(Int, String, Double)] = input.sum(0).min(2)`

Distinct	Returns the distinct elements of a data set. It removes the duplicate entries from the input DataSet, with respect to all fields of the elements, or a subset of fields. `data.distinct()`

Transformation	Description

Join	Joins two data sets by creating all pairs of elements that are equal on their keys. Optionally uses a `JoinFunction` to turn the pair of elements into a single element, or a `FlatJoinFunction` to turn the pair of elements into arbitrarily many (including none) elements.
	`// In this case tuple fields are used as keys. "0" is the join field on the first tuple`
	`// "1" is the join field on the second tuple.`
	`val result = input1.join(input2).where(0).equalTo(1)`
	You can specify the way that the runtime executes the join via Join Hints. The hints describe whether the join happens through partitioning or broadcasting, and whether it uses a sort-based or a hash-based algorithm. Please refer to the Transformations Guide at `https://ci.apache.org/projects/flink/flink-docs-release-1.4/dev/batch/dataset_transformations.html#join-algorithm-hints` for a list of possible hints and an example. If no hint is specified, the system will try to make an estimate of the input sizes and pick the best strategy according to those estimates.
	`// This executes a join by broadcasting the first data set`
	`// using a hash table for the broadcast data`
	`val result = input1.join(input2, JoinHint.BROADCAST_HASH_FIRST)`
	`                   .where(0).equalTo(1)`
	Note that the join transformation works only for equi-joins. Other join types need to be expressed using OuterJoin or CoGroup.

OuterJoin	Performs a left, right, or full outer join on two data sets. Outer joins are similar to regular (inner) joins and create all pairs of elements that are equal on their keys. In addition, records of the outer side (left, right, or both in case of full) are preserved if no matching key is found in the other side. Matching pairs of elements (or one element and a null value for the other input) are given to a `JoinFunction` to turn the pair of elements into a single element, or to a `FlatJoinFunction` to turn the pair of elements into arbitrarily many (including none) elements.
	`val joined = left.leftOuterJoin(right).where(0).equalTo(1) {`
	`   (left, right) =>`
	`     val a = if (left == null) "none" else left._1`
	`     (a, right)`
	`  }`

CoGroup	The two-dimensional variant of the reduce operation. Groups each input on one or more fields and then joins the groups. The transformation function is called per pair of groups. See the keys section at `https://ci.apache.org/projects/flink/flink-docs-release-1.4/dev/api_concepts.html#specifying-keys` to learn how to define coGroup keys. `data1.coGroup(data2).where(0).equalTo(1)`

Transformation	Description

Cross	Builds the Cartesian product (cross product) of two inputs, creating all pairs of elements. Optionally uses a `CrossFunction` to turn the pair of elements into a single element
	`val data1: DataSet[Int] = // [...]`
	`val data2: DataSet[String] = // [...]`
	`val result: DataSet[(Int, String)] = data1.cross(data2)`
	Note: Cross is potentially a very compute-intensive operation which can challenge even large compute clusters! It is advised to hint the system with the DataSet sizes by using `crossWithTiny()` and `crossWithHuge()`.

Union	Produces the union of two data sets. `data.union(data2)`

Rebalance	Evenly rebalances the parallel partitions of a data set to eliminate data skew. Only Map-like transformations may follow a rebalance transformation.
	`val data1: DataSet[Int] = // [...]`
	`val result: DataSet[(Int, String)] = data1.rebalance().map(...)`

Hash-Partition	Hash-partitions a data set on a given key. Keys can be specified as position keys, expression keys, and key selector functions.
	`val in: DataSet[(Int, String)] = // [...]`
	`val result = in.partitionByHash(0).mapPartition { ... }`

Range-Partition	Range-partitions a data set on a given key. Keys can be specified as position keys, expression keys, and key selector functions.
	`val in: DataSet[(Int, String)] = // [...]`
	`val result = in.partitionByRange(0).mapPartition { ... }`

Custom Partitioning	Manually specify a partitioning over the data.
	Note: This method works only on single field keys.
	`val in: DataSet[(Int, String)] = // [...]`
	`val result = in`
	`  .partitionCustom(partitioner: Partitioner[K], key)`

Sort Partition	Locally sorts all partitions of a data set on a specified field in a specified order. Fields can be specified as tuple positions or field expressions. Sorting on multiple fields is done by chaining `sortPartition()` calls.
	`val in: DataSet[(Int, String)] = // [...]`
	`val result = in.sortPartition(1, Order.ASCENDING).mapPartition {`
	`... }`

Transformation	Description

First-n	Returns the first n (arbitrary) elements of a data set. First-n can be applied on a regular data set, a grouped data set, or a grouped-sorted data set. Grouping keys can be specified as key-selector functions, tuple positions or case class fields.
	`val in: DataSet[(Int, String)] = // [...]`
	`// regular data set`
	`val result1 = in.first(3)`
	`// grouped data set`
	`val result2 = in.groupBy(0).first(3)`
	`// grouped-sorted data set`
	`val result3 = in.groupBy(0).sortGroup(1, Order.ASCENDING).first(3)`

GroupBy

`groupBy` operation helps to aggregate the rows of the DataSet by some columns. `groupBy()` takes index of column which is used to aggregate the rows by.

Following command groups by `Description` and prints first 10 records.

```
dataSet.map(x => (x.split(",")(2), x.split(",")(3).toInt))
    .groupBy(0)
    .first(10).print()
```

This will print the contents of the DataSet once loaded which are shown as follows:

```
(WOODLAND DESIGN COTTON TOTE BAG,1)
(WOODLAND DESIGN COTTON TOTE BAG,1)
(WOODLAND DESIGN COTTON TOTE BAG,6)
(WOODLAND DESIGN COTTON TOTE BAG,1)
(WOODLAND DESIGN COTTON TOTE BAG,2)
(WOODLAND DESIGN COTTON TOTE BAG,1)
(WOODLAND DESIGN COTTON TOTE BAG,6)
(WOODLAND DESIGN COTTON TOTE BAG,1)
(WOODLAND DESIGN COTTON TOTE BAG,1)
(WOODLAND DESIGN COTTON TOTE BAG,12)
(WOODLAND PARTY BAG + STICKER SET,2)
(WOODLAND PARTY BAG + STICKER SET,16)
(WOODLAND PARTY BAG + STICKER SET,1)
(WOODLAND PARTY BAG + STICKER SET,8)
(WOODLAND PARTY BAG + STICKER SET,4)
```

The `groupBy()` API is defined as follows:

```
/**
 * Groups a {@link Tuple} {@link DataSet} using field position keys.
 *
 * <p><b>Note: Field position keys only be specified for Tuple
DataSets.</b>
 *
 * <p>The field position keys specify the fields of Tuples on which the
DataSet is grouped.
 * This method returns an {@link UnsortedGrouping} on which one of the
following grouping transformation
 * can be applied.
 * <ul>
 * <li>{@link UnsortedGrouping#sortGroup(int,
org.apache.flink.api.common.operators.Order)} to get a {@link
SortedGrouping}.
 * <li>{@link UnsortedGrouping#aggregate(Aggregations, int)} to apply an
Aggregate transformation.
 * <li>{@link
UnsortedGrouping#reduce(org.apache.flink.api.common.functions.ReduceFunctio
n)} to apply a Reduce transformation.
 * <li>{@link
UnsortedGrouping#reduceGroup(org.apache.flink.api.common.functions.GroupRed
uceFunction)} to apply a GroupReduce transformation.
 * </ul>
 *
 * @param fields One or more field positions on which the DataSet will be
grouped.
 * @return A Grouping on which a transformation needs to be applied to
obtain a transformed DataSet.
 *
 * @see Tuple
 * @see UnsortedGrouping
 * @see AggregateOperator
 * @see ReduceOperator
 * @see org.apache.flink.api.java.operators.GroupReduceOperator
 * @see DataSet
 */
 public UnsortedGrouping<T> groupBy(int... fields) {
 return new UnsortedGrouping<>(this, new Keys.ExpressionKeys<>(fields,
getType()));
 }
```

Aggregation

Aggregation operation applies logic to the grouped rows of the DataSet after applying `groupBy()` by some columns. `groupBy()` takes index of column which is used to aggregate the rows by and the aggregation operation takes index of the column to aggregate on.

Following command groups by `Description` and adds the `Quantities` for each Description and then prints first 10 records.

```
dataSet.map(x => (x.split(",")(2), x.split(",")(3).toInt))
    .groupBy(0)
    .sum(1)
    .first(10).print()
```

This will print the contents of the DataSet once loaded as shown in the following code:

```
(,-2117)
(*Boombox Ipod Classic,1)
(*USB Office Mirror Ball,2)
(10 COLOUR SPACEBOY PEN,823)
(12 COLOURED PARTY BALLOONS,102)
(12 DAISY PEGS IN WOOD BOX,62)
(12 EGG HOUSE PAINTED WOOD,16)
(12 IVORY ROSE PEG PLACE SETTINGS,80)
(12 MESSAGE CARDS WITH ENVELOPES,238)
(12 PENCIL SMALL TUBE WOODLAND,444)
```

Following command groups by `Description` and adds the `Quantities` for each `Description` and then prints the top `Description` with maximum `Quantity`:

```
dataSet.map(x => (x.split(",")(2), x.split(",")(3).toInt))
    .groupBy(0)
    .sum(1)
    .max(1)
    .first(10).print()
```

This will print the contents of the DataSet once loaded as shown in the following code:

```
(reverse 21/5/10 adjustment,8189)
```

Following command groups by `Description` and adds the `Quantities` for each `Description` and then prints the top `Description` with minimum `Quantity`:

```
dataSet.map(x => (x.split(",")(2), x.split(",")(3).toInt))
     .groupBy(0)
     .sum(1)
     .min(1)
     .first(10).print()
```

This will print the contents of the DataSet once loaded as shown in the following code:

```
(reverse 21/5/10 adjustment,-7005)
```

The `sum()` API is defined as follows:

```
// private helper that allows to set a different call location name
 private AggregateOperator<T> aggregate(Aggregations agg, int field, String
callLocationName) {
 return new AggregateOperator<T>(this, agg, field, callLocationName);
 }
/**
 * Syntactic sugar for aggregate (SUM, field).
 * @param field The index of the Tuple field on which the aggregation
function is applied.
 * @return An AggregateOperator that represents the summed DataSet.
 *
 * @see org.apache.flink.api.java.operators.AggregateOperator
 */
 public AggregateOperator<T> sum (int field) {
 return this.aggregate (Aggregations.SUM, field,
Utils.getCallLocationName());
 }
```

Joins

```
val cities = benv.readTextFile("cities.csv")
```

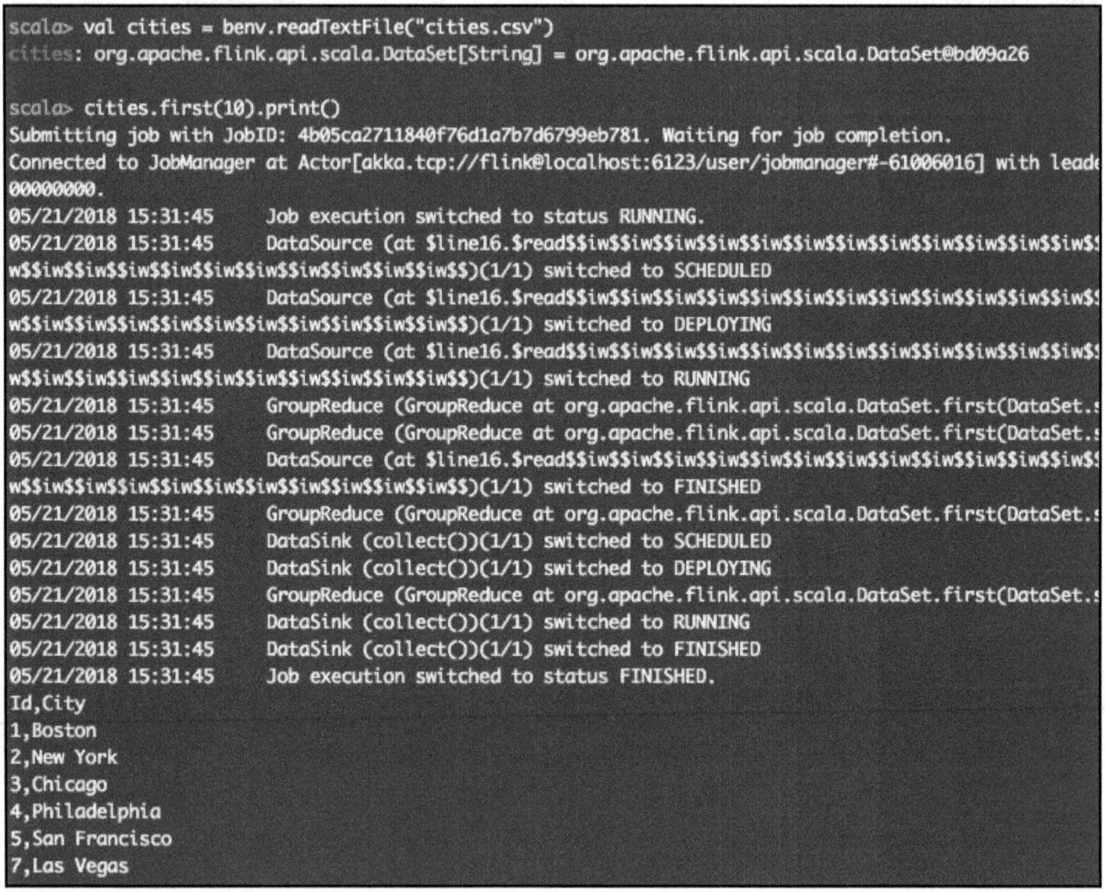
scala> val cities = benv.readTextFile("cities.csv")
cities: org.apache.flink.api.scala.DataSet[String] = org.apache.flink.api.scala.DataSet@bd09a26
scala> cities.first(10).print()
Submitting job with JobID: 4b05ca2711840f76d1a7b7d6799eb781. Waiting for job completion.
Connected to JobManager at Actor[akka.tcp://flink@localhost:6123/user/jobmanager#-61006016] with lead
00000000.
05/21/2018 15:31:45 Job execution switched to status RUNNING.
05/21/2018 15:31:45 DataSource (at $line16.$read$$iw$$iw$$iw$$iw$$iw$$iw$$iw$$iw$$iw$$iw$$iw$
w$$iw$$iw$$iw$$iw$$iw$$iw$$iw$$iw$$iw$$iw$$)(1/1) switched to SCHEDULED
05/21/2018 15:31:45 DataSource (at $line16.$read$$iw$$iw$$iw$$iw$$iw$$iw$$iw$$iw$$iw$$iw$$iw$
w$$iw$$iw$$iw$$iw$$iw$$iw$$iw$$iw$$iw$$iw$$)(1/1) switched to DEPLOYING
05/21/2018 15:31:45 DataSource (at $line16.$read$$iw$$iw$$iw$$iw$$iw$$iw$$iw$$iw$$iw$$iw$$iw$
w$$iw$$iw$$iw$$iw$$iw$$iw$$iw$$iw$$iw$$iw$$)(1/1) switched to RUNNING
05/21/2018 15:31:45 GroupReduce (GroupReduce at org.apache.flink.api.scala.DataSet.first(DataSet.
05/21/2018 15:31:45 GroupReduce (GroupReduce at org.apache.flink.api.scala.DataSet.first(DataSet.
05/21/2018 15:31:45 DataSource (at $line16.$read$$iw$$iw$$iw$$iw$$iw$$iw$$iw$$iw$$iw$$iw$$iw$
w$$iw$$iw$$iw$$iw$$iw$$iw$$iw$$iw$$iw$$iw$$)(1/1) switched to FINISHED
05/21/2018 15:31:45 GroupReduce (GroupReduce at org.apache.flink.api.scala.DataSet.first(DataSet.
05/21/2018 15:31:45 DataSink (collect())(1/1) switched to SCHEDULED
05/21/2018 15:31:45 DataSink (collect())(1/1) switched to DEPLOYING
05/21/2018 15:31:45 GroupReduce (GroupReduce at org.apache.flink.api.scala.DataSet.first(DataSet.
05/21/2018 15:31:45 DataSink (collect())(1/1) switched to RUNNING
05/21/2018 15:31:45 DataSink (collect())(1/1) switched to FINISHED
05/21/2018 15:31:45 Job execution switched to status FINISHED.
Id,City
1,Boston
2,New York
3,Chicago
4,Philadelphia
5,San Francisco
7,Las Vegas

```
Id,City
1,Boston
2,New York
3,Chicago
4,Philadelphia
5,San Francisco
7,Las Vegas
```

```
val temp = benv.readTextFile("temperatures.csv")
```

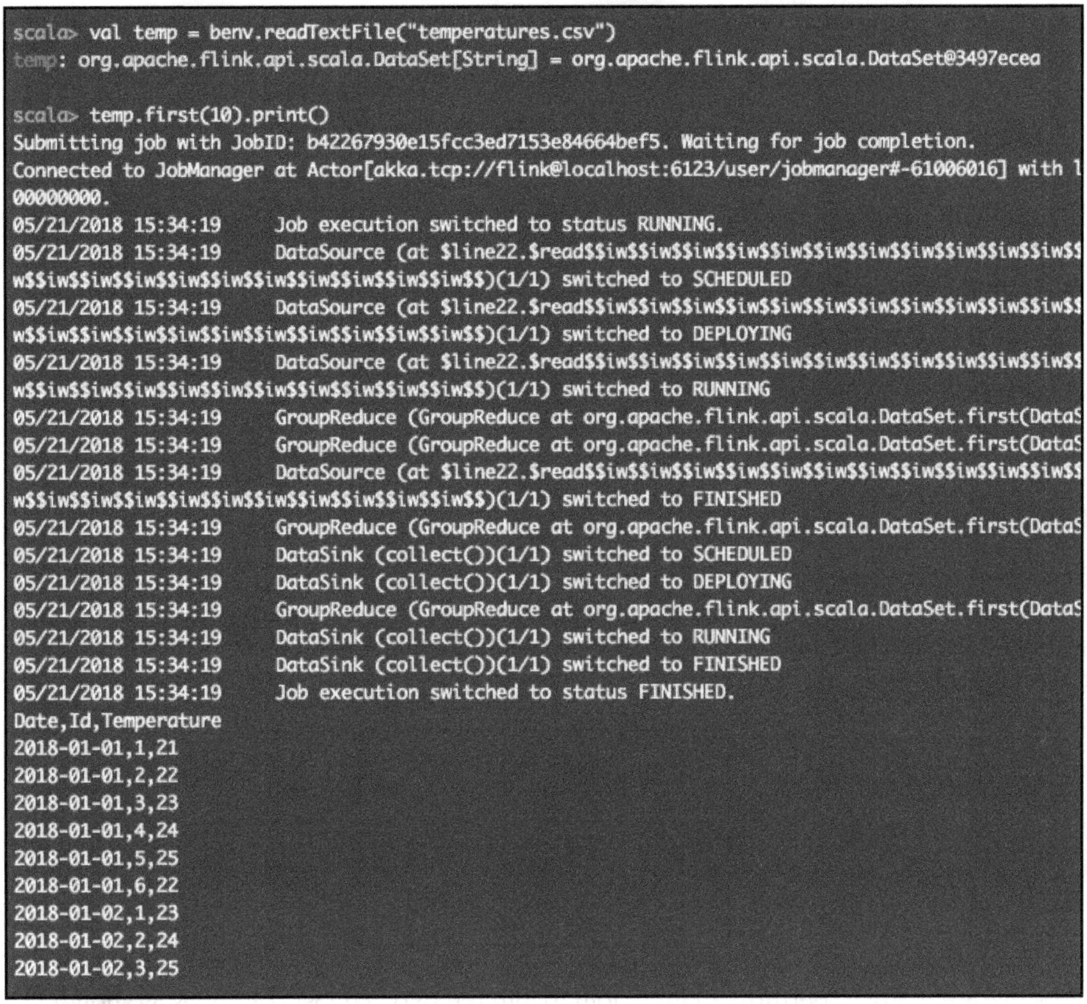
scala> val temp = benv.readTextFile("temperatures.csv")
temp: org.apache.flink.api.scala.DataSet[String] = org.apache.flink.api.scala.DataSet@3497ecea
scala> temp.first(10).print()
Submitting job with JobID: b42267930e15fcc3ed7153e84664bef5. Waiting for job completion.
Connected to JobManager at Actor[akka.tcp://flink@localhost:6123/user/jobmanager#-61006016] with 1
00000000.
05/21/2018 15:34:19 Job execution switched to status RUNNING.
05/21/2018 15:34:19 DataSource (at $line22.$read$$iw$$iw$$iw$$iw$$iw$$iw$$iw$$iw$$iw$$iw$$iw$$
w$$iw$$iw$$iw$$iw$$iw$$iw$$iw$$iw$$iw$$iw$$)(1/1) switched to SCHEDULED
05/21/2018 15:34:19 DataSource (at $line22.$read$$iw$$iw$$iw$$iw$$iw$$iw$$iw$$iw$$iw$$iw$$iw$$
w$$iw$$iw$$iw$$iw$$iw$$iw$$iw$$iw$$iw$$iw$$)(1/1) switched to DEPLOYING
05/21/2018 15:34:19 DataSource (at $line22.$read$$iw$$iw$$iw$$iw$$iw$$iw$$iw$$iw$$iw$$iw$$iw$$
w$$iw$$iw$$iw$$iw$$iw$$iw$$iw$$iw$$iw$$iw$$)(1/1) switched to RUNNING
05/21/2018 15:34:19 GroupReduce (GroupReduce at org.apache.flink.api.scala.DataSet.first(DataS
05/21/2018 15:34:19 GroupReduce (GroupReduce at org.apache.flink.api.scala.DataSet.first(DataS
05/21/2018 15:34:19 DataSource (at $line22.$read$$iw$$iw$$iw$$iw$$iw$$iw$$iw$$iw$$iw$$iw$$iw$$
w$$iw$$iw$$iw$$iw$$iw$$iw$$iw$$iw$$iw$$iw$$)(1/1) switched to FINISHED
05/21/2018 15:34:19 GroupReduce (GroupReduce at org.apache.flink.api.scala.DataSet.first(DataS
05/21/2018 15:34:19 DataSink (collect())(1/1) switched to SCHEDULED
05/21/2018 15:34:19 DataSink (collect())(1/1) switched to DEPLOYING
05/21/2018 15:34:19 GroupReduce (GroupReduce at org.apache.flink.api.scala.DataSet.first(DataS
05/21/2018 15:34:19 DataSink (collect())(1/1) switched to RUNNING
05/21/2018 15:34:19 DataSink (collect())(1/1) switched to FINISHED
05/21/2018 15:34:19 Job execution switched to status FINISHED.
Date,Id,Temperature
2018-01-01,1,21
2018-01-01,2,22
2018-01-01,3,23
2018-01-01,4,24
2018-01-01,5,25
2018-01-01,6,22
2018-01-02,1,23
2018-01-02,2,24
2018-01-02,3,25

```
Date,Id,Temperature
2018-01-01,1,21
2018-01-01,2,22
2018-01-01,3,23
2018-01-01,4,24
2018-01-01,5,25
2018-01-01,6,22
2018-01-02,1,23
2018-01-02,2,24
2018-01-02,3,25
```

Let us now load the cities.csv and temperatures.csv into DataSets and remove the header.

```
 val cities = benv.readTextFile("cities.csv")
    .filter(!_.contains("Id,"))
val temp = benv.readTextFile("temperatures.csv")
    .filter(!_.contains("Id,"))
```

Then we will transform the DataSets to a DataSet of tuples. The first DataSet which is the cities DataSet will yield <cityId, cityName> tuples. The second DataSet which is the temperatures DataSet will yield <cityId, temperature> tuples.

```
val cities2 = cities.map(x => (x.split(",")(0), x.split(",")(1)))
cities2.first(10).print()
val temp2 = temp.map(x => (x.split(",")(1), x.split(",")(2)))
temp2.first(10).print()
```

Inner join

Inner join requires the left and right tables to have the same column. If you have duplicate or multiple copies of the keys on either left or right side, the join will quickly blow up into sort of a cartesian join, taking lot longer to complete than if designed correctly to minimize the multiple keys:

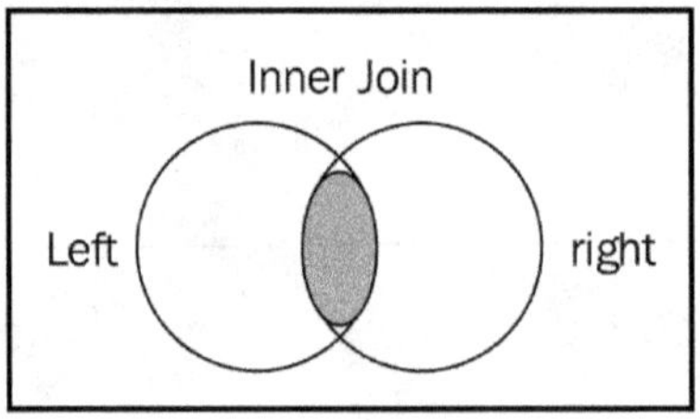

Now, we are ready to perform an inner join to join the two DataSets of tuples as shown in the following code:

```
cities2.join(temp2)
 .where(0)
 .equalTo(0)
 .first(10).print()
```

The output of this job is as follows showing the tuples from the two DataSets where cityID exists in both DataSets:

```
((1,Boston),(1,21))
((2,New York),(2,22))
((3,Chicago),(3,23))
((4,Philadelphia),(4,24))
((5,San Francisco),(5,25))
((1,Boston),(1,23))
((2,New York),(2,24))
((3,Chicago),(3,25))
((4,Philadelphia),(4,26))
((5,San Francisco),(5,18))
```

Now, if we apply aggregation and add the temperatures for each city, we will get the total temperature per city. You can do this by writing the code as shown in the following code:

```
cities2
    .join(temp2)
    .where(0)
    .equalTo(0)
    .map(x=> (x._1._2, x._2._2.toInt))
    .groupBy(0)
    .sum(1)
    .first(10).print()
```

This shows the following result:

```
(Boston,111)
(Chicago,116)
(New York,119)
(Philadelphia,116)
(San Francisco,113)
```

The job can be seen in flink UI:

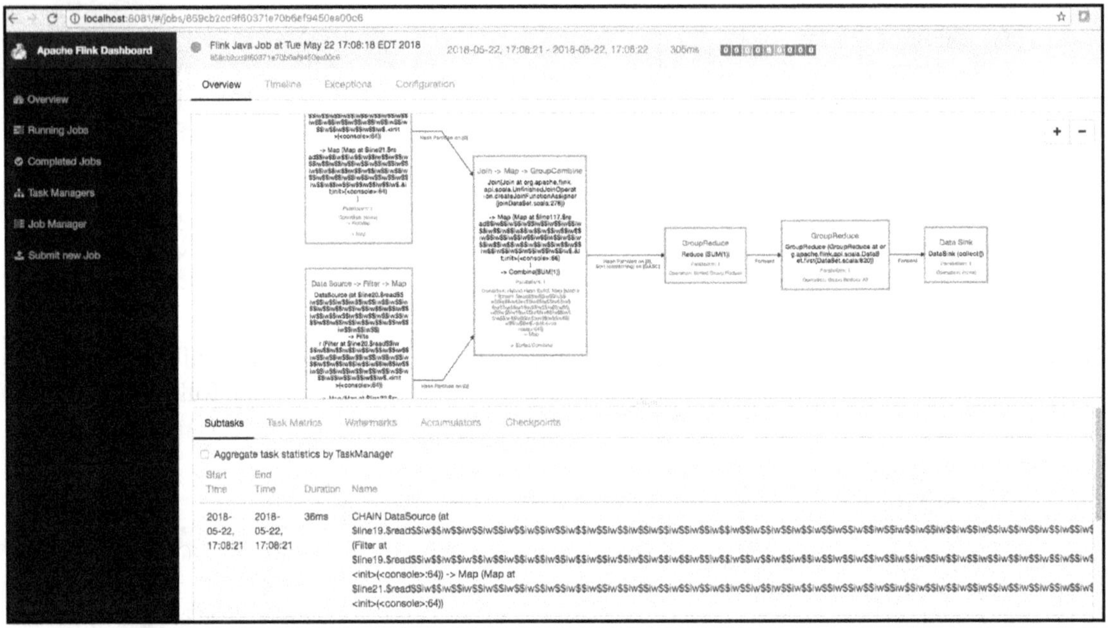

The `join()` API is defined as follows:

```
/**
 * Initiates a Join transformation.
 *
 * <p>A Join transformation joins the elements of two
 * {@link DataSet DataSets} on key equality and provides multiple ways to
combine
 * joining elements into one DataSet.
 *
 * <p>This method returns a {@link JoinOperatorSets} on which one of the
{@code where} methods
 * can be called to define the join key of the first joining (i.e., this)
DataSet.
 *
 * @param other The other DataSet with which this DataSet is joined.
 * @return A JoinOperatorSets to continue the definition of the Join
transformation.
 *
 * @see JoinOperatorSets
 * @see DataSet
 */
```

```
public <R> JoinOperatorSets<T, R> join(DataSet<R> other) {
return new JoinOperatorSets<>(this, other);
}
```

Left outer join

Left outer join gives all rows present in the left hand side table in addition to the rows that are common to both the tables (inner join). If used on tables with little in common, can result in very large results and thus slow performance:

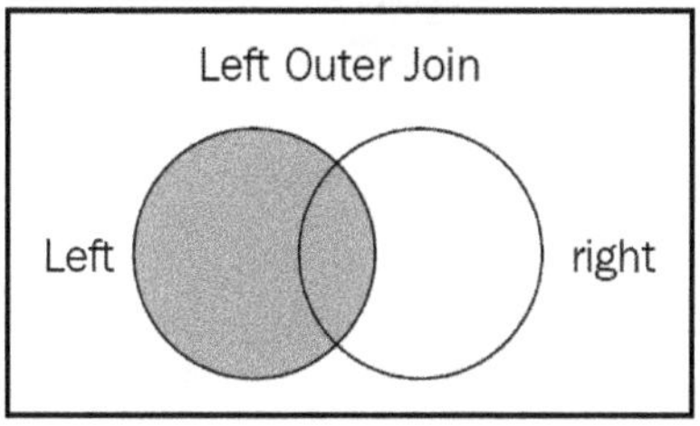

Now, we are ready to perform a left outer join to join the two DataSets of tuples as shown in the following code:

```
cities2
    .leftOuterJoin(temp2)
    .where(0)
    .equalTo(0) {
        (x,y) => (x, if (y==null) (x._1,0) else (x._1, y._2.toInt))
    }
    .map(x=> (x._1._2, x._2._2.toInt))
    .groupBy(0)
    .sum(1)
    .first(10).print()
```

The output of this job is as follows showing the tuples from the two DataSets where cityID exists in left or both DataSets:

```
(Boston,111)
(Chicago,116)
(Las Vegas,0)    // Las vegas has no records in temperatures DataSet so is
assigned 0
(New York,119)
(Philadelphia,116)
(San Francisco,113)
```

The job can be seen in flink UI:

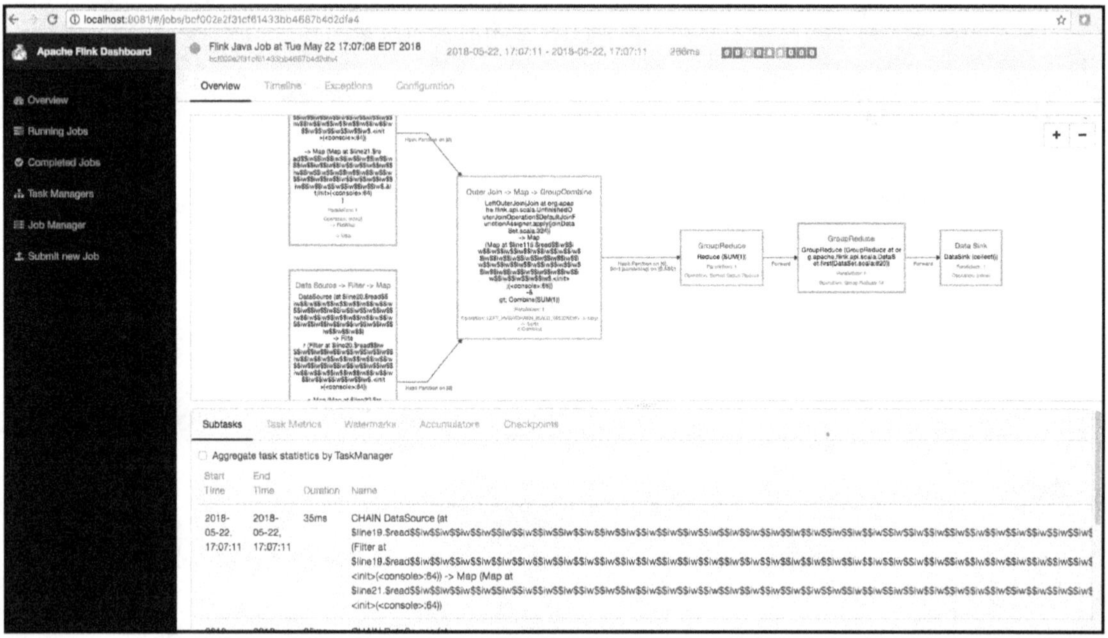

The `leftOuterJoin()` API is defined as follows:

```
/**
 * Initiates a Left Outer Join transformation.
 *
 * <p>An Outer Join transformation joins two elements of two
 * {@link DataSet DataSets} on key equality and provides multiple ways to
combine
 * joining elements into one DataSet.
 *
 * <p>Elements of the <b>left</b> DataSet (i.e. {@code this}) that do not
have a matching
 * element on the other side are joined with {@code null} and emitted to
the
 * resulting DataSet.
 *
 * @param other The other DataSet with which this DataSet is joined.
 * @return A JoinOperatorSet to continue the definition of the Join
transformation.
 *
 * @see org.apache.flink.api.java.operators.join.JoinOperatorSetsBase
 * @see DataSet
```

```
*/
public <R> JoinOperatorSetsBase<T, R> leftOuterJoin(DataSet<R> other) {
return new JoinOperatorSetsBase<>(this, other, JoinHint.OPTIMIZER_CHOOSES,
JoinType.LEFT_OUTER);
}
```

Right outer join

Right outer join gives all rows in right side table as well as the common rows of left and right (inner join). Use this to get all rows in right table along with the rows found in both left and right tables. Fills in `NULL` if not in left. Performance is similar to the left outer join mentioned previously in this table:

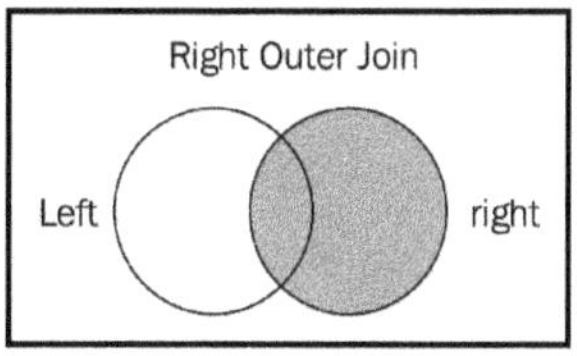

Now, we are ready to perform a right outer join to join the two DataSets of tuples as shown in the following code:

```
cities2
    .rightOuterJoin(temp2)
    .where(0)
    .equalTo(0) {
        (x,y) => (if (x==null) (y._1,"unknown") else (y._1, x._2), y)
    }
    .map(x=> (x._1._2, x._2._2.toInt))
    .groupBy(0)
    .sum(1)
    .first(10).print()
```

The output of this job is as follows showing the tuples from the two DataSets where cityID exists in right or both DataSets:

```
(Boston,111)
(Chicago,116)
(New York,119)
(Philadelphia,116)
(San Francisco,113)
(unknown,44) . // note that only right hand side temperatures DataSet has
id 6 which is not in cities DataSet
```

The job can be seen in flink UI:

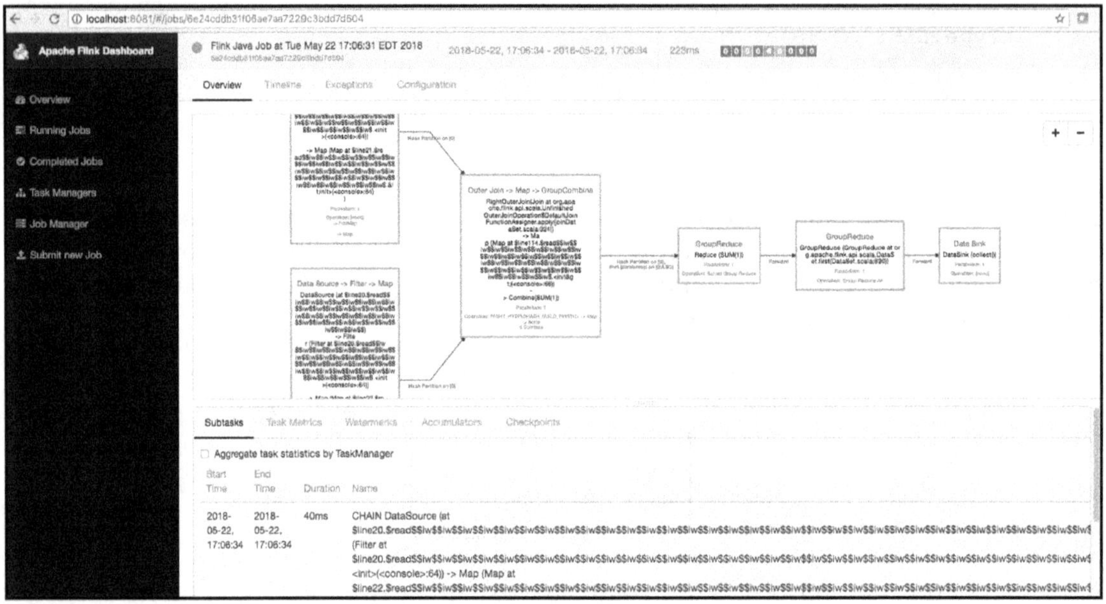

The `rightOuterJoin()` API is defined as follows:

```
/**
 * Initiates a Right Outer Join transformation.
 *
 * <p>An Outer Join transformation joins two elements of two
 * {@link DataSet DataSets} on key equality and provides multiple ways to
combine
 * joining elements into one DataSet.
 *
 * <p>Elements of the <b>right</b> DataSet (i.e. {@code other}) that do not
have a matching
 * element on {@code this} side are joined with {@code null} and emitted to
the
 * resulting DataSet.
 *
 * @param other The other DataSet with which this DataSet is joined.
 * @return A JoinOperatorSet to continue the definition of the Join
transformation.
 *
 * @see org.apache.flink.api.java.operators.join.JoinOperatorSetsBase
 * @see DataSet
 */
```

```
public <R> JoinOperatorSetsBase<T, R> rightOuterJoin(DataSet<R> other) {
 return new JoinOperatorSetsBase<>(this, other, JoinHint.OPTIMIZER_CHOOSES,
JoinType.RIGHT_OUTER);
 }
```

Full outer join

Full outer join gives all (matched and unmatched) rows from the tables at the left and right side of the join clause. Use this when we want to keep all the rows from both tables, we use full outer join. Full outer join returns all rows when there is a match in ONE of the tables. If used on tables with little in common, it can result in very large results and thus slow performance:

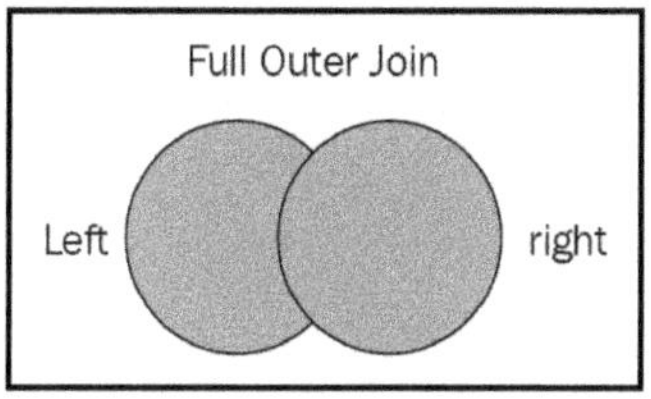

Now, we are ready to perform a full outer join to join the two DataSets of tuples as shown in the following code:

```
cities2
    .fullOuterJoin(temp2)
    .where(0)
    .equalTo(0) {
        (x,y) => (if (x==null) (y._1,"unknown") else (x._1, x._2),
                if (y==null) (x._1,0) else (y._1, y._2.toInt))
    }
    .map(x=> (x._1._2, x._2._2.toInt))
    .groupBy(0)
    .sum(1)
    .first(10).print()
```

The output of this job is as follows showing the tuples from the two DataSets where cityID exists in either or both DataSets:

```
(Boston,111)
(Chicago,116)
(Las Vegas,0) // Las vegas has no records in temperatures DataSet so is
assigned 0
(New York,119)
(Philadelphia,116)
```

```
(San Francisco,113)
(unknown,44) // note that only right hand side temperatures DataSet has id
6 which is not in cities DataSet
```

The job can be seen in flink UI:

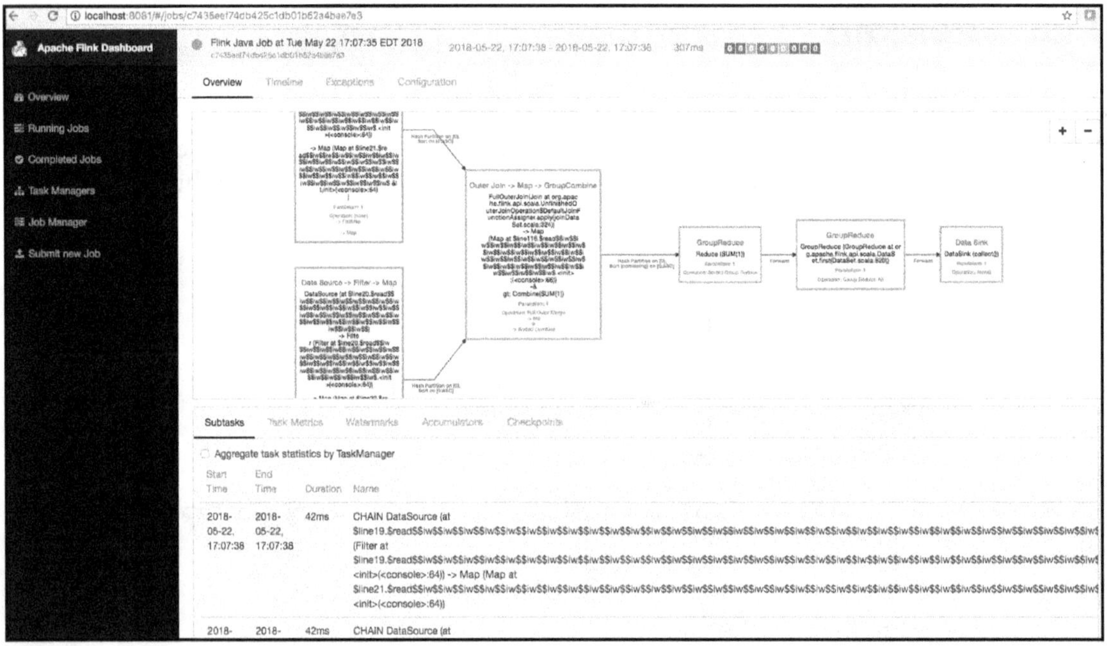

The `fullOuterJoin()` API is defined as follows:

```
/**
 * Initiates a Full Outer Join transformation.
 *
 * <p>An Outer Join transformation joins two elements of two
 * {@link DataSet DataSets} on key equality and provides multiple ways to
combine
 * joining elements into one DataSet.
 *
 * <p>Elements of <b>both</b> DataSets that do not have a matching
 * element on the opposing side are joined with {@code null} and emitted to
the
 * resulting DataSet.
 *
 * @param other The other DataSet with which this DataSet is joined.
 * @return A JoinOperatorSet to continue the definition of the Join
transformation.
```

```
 *
 * @see org.apache.flink.api.java.operators.join.JoinOperatorSetsBase
 * @see DataSet
 */
 public <R> JoinOperatorSetsBase<T, R> fullOuterJoin(DataSet<R> other) {
 return new JoinOperatorSetsBase<>(this, other, JoinHint.OPTIMIZER_CHOOSES,
JoinType.FULL_OUTER);
 }
```

Writing to a file

Data sinks consume DataSets and are used to store or return them. Data sink operations are described using an OutputFormat. Flink comes with a variety of built-in output formats that are encapsulated behind operations on the DataSet:

- `writeAsText()/TextOutputFormat`: Writes elements line-wise as Strings. The strings are obtained by calling the `toString()` method of each element.
- `writeAsCsv(...)/CsvOutputFormat`: Writes tuples as comma-separated value files. Row and field delimiters are configurable. The value for each field comes from the `toString()` method of the objects.
- `print()/printToErr()`: Prints the `toString()` value of each element on the standard out/standard error stream.
- `write()/FileOutputFormat`: Method and base class for custom file outputs. Supports custom object-to-bytes conversion.
- `output()/OutputFormat`: Most generic output method, for data sinks that are not file based (such as storing the result in a database).

Let us write the results of inner join of cities and temperatures to a file using `writeAsText()`.

TIP

No output will be seen until you call `benv.execute()`.

First, create a DataSet for the inner join of cities and temperatures:

```
val results = cities2
    .join(temp2)
    .where(0)
    .equalTo(0)
    .map(x=> (x._1._2, x._2._2.toInt))
    .groupBy(0)
    .sum(1)
```

Then call the `writeAsText()` on the results DataSet and call `execute()` on the DataSink as shown in the following code:

```
results.writeAsText("file:///Users/sridharalla/flink-1.4.2/results.txt").se
tParallelism(1)
benv.execute()
```

If you open the file you just created, you will see the results of the join operation as seen in the following code:

```
(Boston,111)
(Chicago,116)
(New York,119)
(Philadelphia,116)
(San Francisco,113)
```

The job can be seen in flink UI:

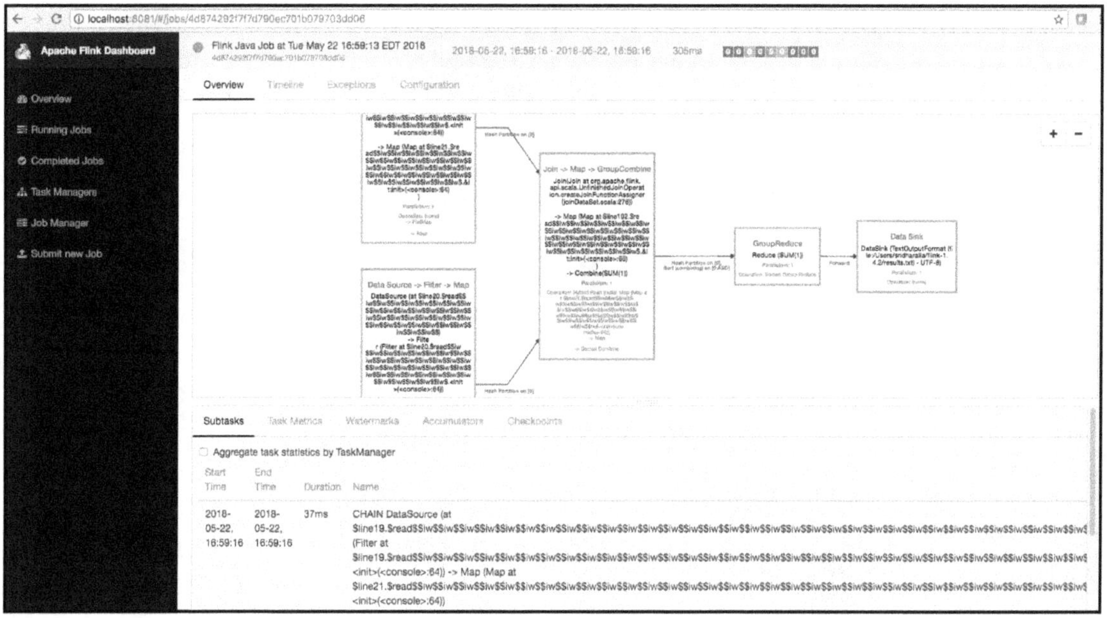

Summary

In this chapter, we have discussed Apache Flink and how Flink can be used to perform batch analysis on a large amount of data. We explored Flink and inner workings of Flink. Then we loaded and analyzed data performing transformations and aggregation operations. Then we explored how to perform Join operations on big data.

In the next chapter, we will discuss real-time analytics using Apache Flink.

9
Stream Processing with Apache Flink

In this chapter, we will look at stream processing using Apache Flink and how the framework can be used to process data as soon as it arrives to build exciting real-time applications. We will start with the DataStream API and look at various operations that can be performed.

We will be looking at the following:

- Data processing using the DataStream API
- Transformations
- Aggregations
- Window
- Physical partitioning
- Rescaling
- Data sinks
- Event time and watermarks
- Kafka connector
- Twitter connector
- Elasticsearch connector
- Cassandra connector

Introduction to streaming execution model

Flink is an open source framework for distributed stream processing that:

- Provides results that are accurate, even in the case of out-of-order or late-arriving data
- Is stateful and fault tolerant, and can seamlessly recover from failures while maintaining an exactly-once application state
- Performs on a large scale, running on thousands of nodes with very good throughput and latency characteristics

The following diagram is a generalized view of stream processing:

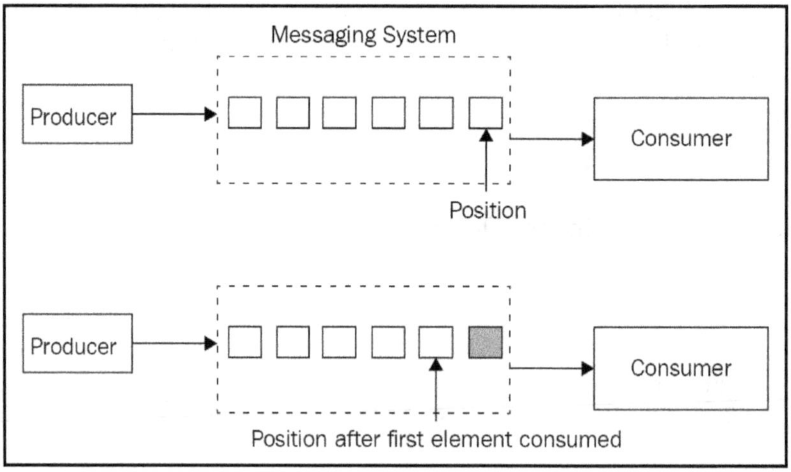

Many of Flink's features - state management, handling out-of-order data, flexible windowing – are essential for computing accurate results on unbounded datasets and are enabled by Flink's streaming execution model:

- Flink guarantees exactly-once semantics for stateful computations. Stateful means that applications can maintain an aggregation or summary of data that has been processed over time, and Flink's checkpointing mechanism ensures exactly-once semantics for an application's state in the event of a failure:

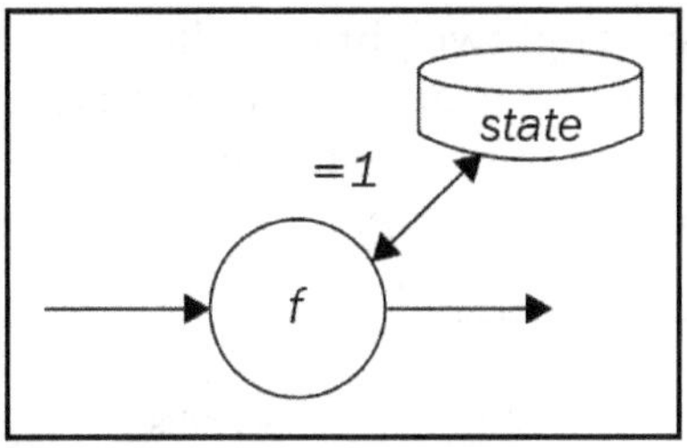

- Flink supports stream processing and windowing with event-time semantics. Event time makes it easy to compute accurate results over streams where events arrive out of order and where events may arrive delayed:

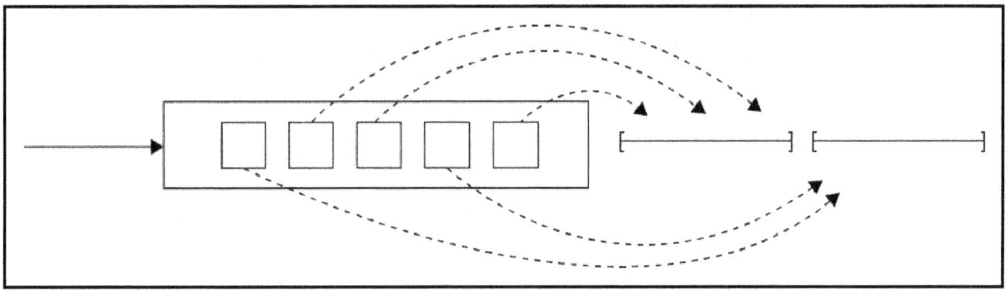

- Flink supports flexible windowing based on time, count, or sessions, in addition to data-driven windows. Windows can be customized with flexible triggering conditions to support sophisticated streaming patterns. Flink's windowing makes it possible to model the reality of the environment in which data is created:

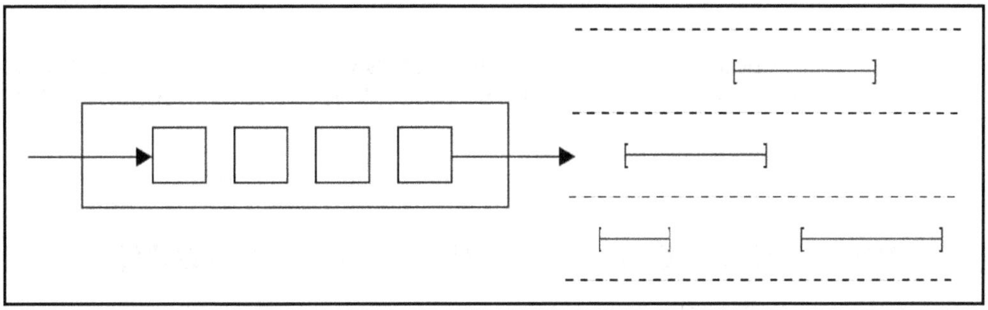

- Flink's fault tolerance is lightweight and allows the system to maintain high throughput rates and provide exactly-once consistency guarantees at the same time. Flink recovers from failures with zero data loss while the trade-off between reliability and latency is negligible:

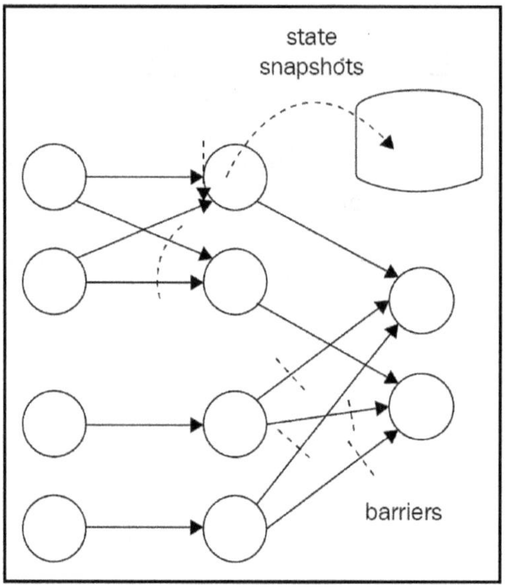

- Flink is capable of high throughput and low latency (processing lots of data quickly).
- Flink's savepoints provide a state versioning mechanism, making it possible to update applications or reprocess historic data with no lost state and minimal downtime.
- Flink is designed to run on large-scale clusters with many thousands of nodes, and in addition to a standalone cluster mode, Flink provides support for YARN and Mesos.

Data processing using the DataStream API

It is crucial to have robust analytics in place to process real-time data. This is more important for domains that are data-driven. Flink enables you to do real-time analytics using its DataStream API. This streaming data processing API helps you cater to **Internet of Things** (**IoT**) applications and store, process, and analyze data in real time or near real time.

In the following sections, let's examine each of the elements related to the DataStream API:

- Execution environment
- Data sources
- Transformations
- Data sinks
- Connectors

Execution environment

To write a Flink program, you need an execution environment. You can use an existing environment or create a new environment.

Based on your requirements, Flink allows you to use an existing Flink environment, create a local environment, or create a remote environment.

Use the `getExecutionEnvironment()` command to accomplish different tasks based on your requirement:

- To execute on a local environment in an IDE, it starts a local execution environment
- To execute a JAR, the Flink cluster manager executes the program in a distributed manner
- To create your own local or remote environment, you can use methods such as `createLocalEnvironment()` and `createRemoteEnvironment` (string host, int port, string, and `.jar` files)

Data sources

Flink gets data from different sources. It has many inbuilt source functions to fetch data seamlessly. Several pre-implemented data source functions in Flink simplify data sourcing. Flink also allows you to write custom data source functions when the existing functions are not enough for data sourcing.

The DataStream API is documented here: `https://ci.apache.org/projects/flink/flink-docs-release-1.4/dev/datastream_api.html`.

Here are some existing data source functions in Flink:

- Socket-based data sourcing
- File-based data sourcing

Socket-based

The DataStream API enables you to read from a socket. Look at the following piece of code for a simple illustration of the streaming API:

```
// Data type for words with count
case class WordWithCount(word: String, count: Long)
// get input data by connecting to the socket
val text = senv.socketTextStream("127.0.0.1", 9000, '\n')
// parse the data, group it, window it, and aggregate the counts
val windowCounts = text
 .flatMap { w => w.split("\\s") }
 .map { w => WordWithCount(w, 1) }
 .keyBy("word")
 .timeWindow(Time.seconds(5), Time.seconds(1))
 .sum("count")
// print the results with a single thread, rather than in parallel
windowCounts.print().setParallelism(1)
senv.execute("Socket Window WordCount")
```

The preceding code connects to port `9000` on the localhost, receives and processes text, splitting the strings into individual words (space separated). Then, the code counts the frequencies of the words in a window of `5` seconds and prints them.

To run this example, we will use the Scala shell for Flink:

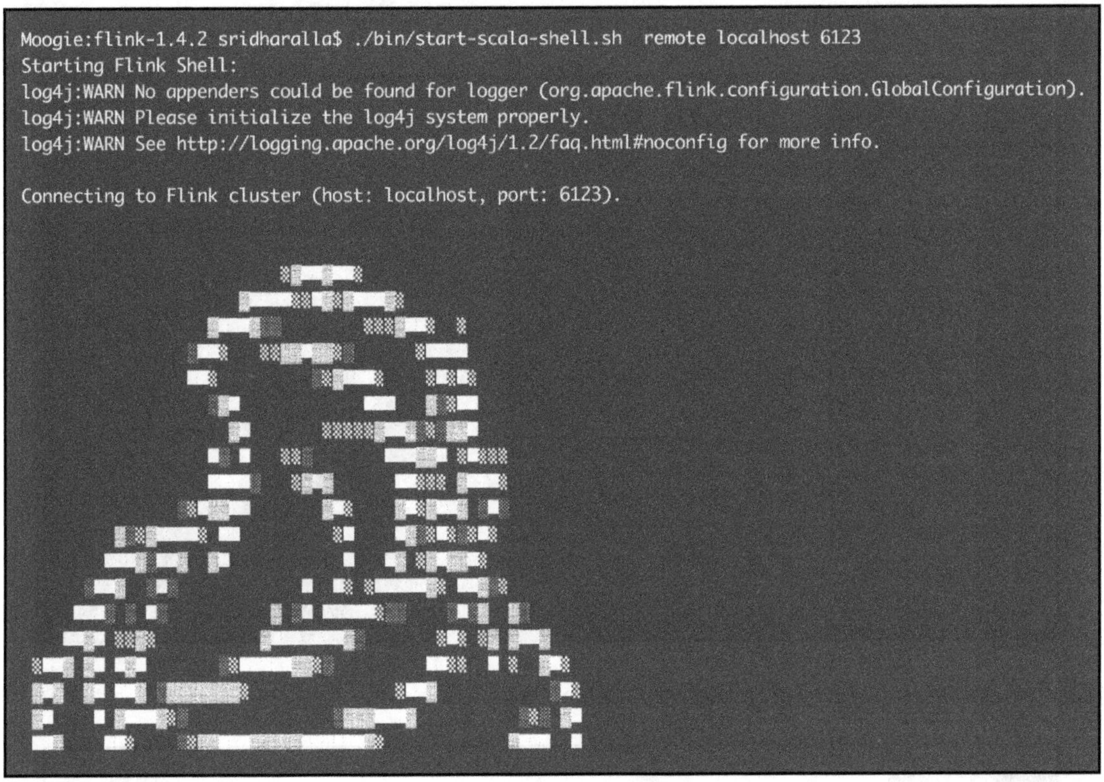
Moogie:flink-1.4.2 sridharalla$ ./bin/start-scala-shell.sh remote localhost 6123
Starting Flink Shell:
log4j:WARN No appenders could be found for logger (org.apache.flink.configuration.GlobalConfiguration).
log4j:WARN Please initialize the log4j system properly.
log4j:WARN See http://logging.apache.org/log4j/1.2/faq.html#noconfig for more info.
Connecting to Flink cluster (host: localhost, port: 6123).

Now, start a local server running `nc` as follows on any Linux system:

Moogie:~ sridharalla$ nc -l 9000

Now, run the code in the shell to connect to port `9000` and listen for data:

```
// Data type for words with count
case class WordWithCount(word: String, count: Long)

// get input data by connecting to the socket
val text = senv.socketTextStream("127.0.0.1", 9000, '\n')

// parse the data, group it, window it, and aggregate the counts
val windowCounts = text
    .flatMap { w => w.split("\\s") }
    .map { w => WordWithCount(w, 1) }
    .keyBy("word")
    .timeWindow(Time.seconds(5), Time.seconds(1))
    .sum("count")

// print the results with a single thread, rather than in parallel
windowCounts.print().setParallelism(1)

senv.execute("Socket Window WordCount")

// Exiting paste mode, now interpreting.

Submitting job with JobID: 557deeac32d01c1061ff4b558b97b7c8. Waiting for job completion.
Connected to JobManager at Actor[akka.tcp://flink@localhost:6123/user/jobmanager#-598835017] with leader session id 00000000-0000-0000-0000
0000000000.
04/29/2018 21:19:57     Job execution switched to status RUNNING.
04/29/2018 21:19:57     Source: Socket Stream(1/1) switched to SCHEDULED
04/29/2018 21:19:57     Flat Map -> Map(1/1) switched to SCHEDULED
04/29/2018 21:19:57     TriggerWindow(SlidingProcessingTimeWindows(5000, 1000), ReducingStateDescriptor{serializer=$line19.$read$$iw$$iw$$iw$
iw$$iw$$iw$$iw$$iw$$iw$$iw$$iw$$iw$$iw$$iw$$iw$$iw$$iw$$iw$$iw$$iw$$iw$$iw$$iw$$iw$$iw$$iw$$iw$$iw$$iw$$iw$$iw$$iw$$iw$$iw$$anon$2$$a
on$1@895bda3c, reduceFunction=org.apache.flink.streaming.api.functions.aggregation.SumAggregator@375febef}, ProcessingTimeTrigger(), Windowed
tream.reduce(WindowedStream.java:241))(1/1) switched to SCHEDULED
```

You can see the job running in the web console now:

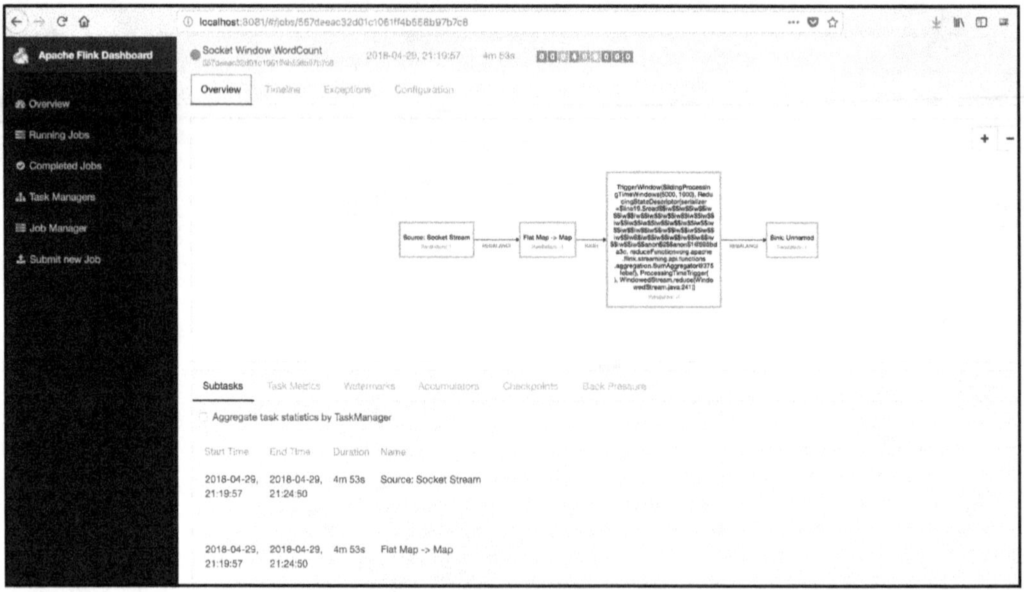

You can look into the tasks for a deeper understanding:

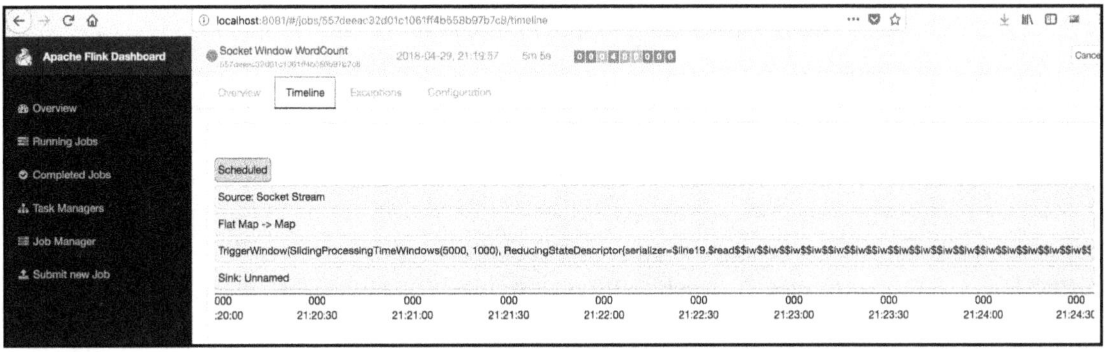

Figure: Screenshot showing a view of the tasks

If you start typing text into the `nc` server console, you will start seeing output in the `log` folder.

In my case, I see a `log` file for `taskmanager`:

```
tail -f log/flink-sridharalla-taskmanager-1-Moogie.local.out
```

The following is what you will see when you tail the `log` file:

```
WordWithCount(hellow,1)
WordWithCount(hellow,1)
WordWithCount(world,1)
```

Now that we have seen running sample code, let's look at the API for the socket stream.

Specify the host and port in the API to read data from a socket:

```
socketTextStream(hostName, port);
```

You can also specify the delimiter:

```
socketTextStream(hostName,port,delimiter)
```

You can also specify the maximum number of times the API must fetch the data from a socket:

```
socketTextStream(hostName,port,delimiter, maxRetry)
```

File-based

Use the file-based source functions in Flink to stream data from a file source. Use `readTextFile(String path)` to stream data from a specified file. By default, the string path has the default value `TextInputFormat`. This implies that it reads text and strings line by line.

If the file format is different from text, specify the format using these functions:

```
readFile(FileInputFormat<Out> inputFormat, String path)
```

Using the `readFileStream()` function, Flink can read file streams as they are produced:

```
readFileStream(String filePath, long intervalMillis,
FileMonitoringFunction.WatchType watchType)
```

Specify the file path, the polling interval in which the file path should be polled, and the watch type. Watch types are of three types:

- `FileMonitoringFunction.WatchType.ONLY_NEW_FILES`: Use to process only new files
- `FileMonitoringFunction.WatchType.PROCESS_ONLY_APPENDED`: Use to process only appended contents of files
- `FileMonitoringFunction.WatchType.REPROCESS_WITH_APPENDED`: Use to reprocess not only the appended contents of files, but also the previous content in the file

If the file is not a text file, then you can use this function to define the file input format:

```
readFile(fileInputFormat, path, watchType, interval, pathFilter, typeInfo)
```

This command divides the reading file task into two sub-tasks:

- One sub-task only monitors the file path based on the specified `WatchType`
- The second sub-task does the actual file reading in parallel

The sub-task that monitors the file path is a non-parallel sub-task. It continuously scans the file path based on the polling interval and reports files to be processed, splits the files, and assigns the splits to the respective downstream threads.

Transformations

Data transformations transform the data stream from one form to another. Input can be one or more data streams, and the output can be zero, or one or more data streams. In the following sections, let's examine different transformations.

map

This is one of the simplest transformations, where the input is one data stream and the output is also one data stream:

In Java:

```
inputStream.map(new MapFunction<Integer, Integer>() {
@Override
public Integer map(Integer value) throws Exception {
return 5 * value;
}
});
```

In Scala:

```
inputStream.map { x => x * 5 }
```

flatMap

`flatMap` takes one record as input and gives an output of zero, one, or more than one record:

In Java:

```
inputStream.flatMap(new FlatMapFunction<String, String>() {
@Override
public void flatMap(String value, Collector<String> out)
throws Exception {
    for(String word: value.split(" ")){
        out.collect(word);
    }
});
```

In Scala:

```
inputStream.flatMap { str => str.split(" ") }
```

filter

The `filter` function evaluates the conditions and based on the conditions being met, gives records as output:

The `filter` function can output zero records also.

In Java:

```
inputStream.filter(new FilterFunction<Integer>() {
@Override
    public boolean filter(Integer value) throws Exception {
        return value != 1;
    }
});
```

In Scala:

```
inputStream.filter { _ != 1 }
```

keyBy

`keyBy` logically partitions the stream based on the key. It uses `hash` functions to partition the stream. It returns `KeyedDataStream`:

In Java:

```
inputStream.keyBy("someKey");
```

In Scala:

```
inputStream.keyBy("someKey")
```

reduce

`reduce` rolls out the `KeyedDataStream` by reducing the last reduced value by the current value. The following code does the sum reduce of a `KeyedDataStream`:

In Java:

```
keyedInputStream. reduce(new ReduceFunction<Integer>() {
@Override
    public Integer reduce(Integer value1, Integer value2)
        throws Exception {
            return value1 + value2;
        }
});
```

In Scala:

```
keyedInputStream. reduce { _ + _ }
```

fold

`fold` rolls out `KeyedDataStream` by combining the last folder's stream with the current record. It emits back the data stream:

In Java:

```
keyedInputStream keyedStream.fold("Start", new FoldFunction<Integer,
String>() {
@Override
    public String fold(String current, Integer value) {
        return current + "=" + value;
    }
});
```

In Scala:

```
keyedInputStream.fold("Start")((str, i) => { str + "=" + i })
```

The preceding function, when applied on a stream of (1,2,3,4,5), would emit a stream like this: `Start=1=2=3=4=5`.

Aggregations

The DataStream API supports various aggregations such as `min`, `max`, `sum`, and so on. These functions can be applied on `KeyedDataStream` to get rolling aggregations:

In Java:

```
keyedInputStream.sum(0)
keyedInputStream.sum("key")
keyedInputStream.min(0)
keyedInputStream.min("key")
keyedInputStream.max(0)
keyedInputStream.max("key")
keyedInputStream.minBy(0)
keyedInputStream.minBy("key")
keyedInputStream.maxBy(0)
keyedInputStream.maxBy("key")
```

In Scala:

```
keyedInputStream.sum(0)
keyedInputStream.sum("key")
keyedInputStream.min(0)
keyedInputStream.min("key")
keyedInputStream.max(0)
keyedInputStream.max("key")
keyedInputStream.minBy(0)
keyedInputStream.minBy("key")
keyedInputStream.maxBy(0)
keyedInputStream.maxBy("key")
```

The difference between `max` and `maxBy` is that `max` returns the maximum value in a stream, but `maxBy` returns a key that has a maximum value. The same applies to `min` and `minBy`.

window

The `window` function allows the grouping of existing `KeyedDataStreams` by time or other conditions. The following transformation emits groups of records by a time window of `10` seconds:

In Java:

```
inputStream.keyBy(0).window(TumblingEventTimeWindows.of(Time.seconds(10)));
```

In Scala:

```
inputStream.keyBy(0).window(TumblingEventTimeWindows.of(Time.seconds(10)))
```

Flink defines slices of data called windows to process potentially infinite data streams.

This helps the processing of data in chunks using transformations. To do windowing on a stream, assign a key on which the distribution can be made and a function that describes what transformations to perform on a windowed stream.

To slice streams into windows, you can use pre-implemented Flink window assigners. Use options such as tumbling windows, sliding windows, and global and session windows.

Flink also allows you to write custom window assigners by extending the `WindowAssigner` class.

Let's examine how these assigners work in the following sections.

Global windows

Global windows are never-ending windows unless specified by a trigger. Generally, in this case, each element is assigned to one single per-key global window. If you do not specify any triggers, no computation is triggered.

Tumbling windows

Tumbling windows are fixed-length windows and are non-overlapping. Use tumbling windows to do computation of elements at a specific time. For example, a tumbling window of 10 minutes can be used to compute a group of events occurring in 10 minutes, time.

Sliding windows

Sliding windows are similar to tumbling windows, except that they are overlapping. They are fixed-length windows, overlapping the previous ones by a user-given window slide parameter.

Use this windowing to compute something out of a group of events occurring in a certain time frame.

Session windows

Session windows are useful when window boundaries must be decided based on the input data. Session windows allow flexibility in window start time and window size.

Provide the session gap configuration parameter, which indicates the duration to wait before considering a session as closed.

windowAll

The `windowAll` function allows grouping of regular data streams. This is normally a non-parallel data transformation as it runs on non-partitioned streams of data:

In Java:

```
inputStream.windowAll(TumblingEventTimeWindows.of(Time.seconds(10)));
```

In Scala:

```
inputStream.windowAll(TumblingEventTimeWindows.of(Time.seconds(10)))
```

Similar to regular data stream functions, we have window data stream functions as well. The only difference is they work on windowed data streams. So, window reduce works like the `reduce` function, window fold works like the `fold` function, and there are aggregations as well.

union

The `union` function performs the union of two or more data streams. It combines data streams in parallel. If you combine a stream with itself, it outputs each record twice:

In Java:

```
inputStream. union(inputStream1, inputStream2, ...);
```

In Scala:

```
inputStream. union(inputStream1, inputStream2, ...)
```

Window join

Join two data streams by some keys in a common window. The following example shows the joining of two streams in a window of 5 seconds where the joining condition of the first attribute of the first stream is equal to the second attribute of the other stream:

In Java:

```
inputStream. join(inputStream1)
.where(0).equalTo(1)
.window(TumblingEventTimeWindows.of(Time.seconds(5)))
.apply (new JoinFunction () {...});
```

In Scala:

```
inputStream. join(inputStream1)
.where(0).equalTo(1)
.window(TumblingEventTimeWindows.of(Time.seconds(5)))
.apply { ... }
```

split

Use this function to `split` the stream into two or more streams based on criteria. This is particularly helpful when you get a mixed stream and you may want to process data separately:

In Java:

```
SplitStream<Integer> split = inputStream.split(new
OutputSelector<Integer>() {
@Override
public Iterable<String> select(Integer value) {
List<String> output = new ArrayList<String>();
if (value % 2 == 0) {
output.add("even");
}
else {
output.add("odd");
}
return output;
}
});
```

In Scala:

```
val split = inputStream.split( (num: Int) =>(num % 2) match {
    case 0 => List("even")
    case 1 => List("odd")
})
```

Select

Use this function to select a specific stream from the split stream:

In Java:

```
SplitStream<Integer> split;
DataStream<Integer> even = split.select("even");
DataStream<Integer> odd = split.select("odd");
DataStream<Integer> all = split.select("even","odd");
```

In Scala:

```
val even = split select "even"
val odd = split select "odd"
val all = split.select("even","odd")
```

Project

Use the `project` function to select a subset of attributes from the event stream and send only selected elements to the next processing stream:

In Java:

```
DataStream<Tuple4<Integer, Double, String, String>> in = // [...]
DataStream<Tuple2<String, String>> out = in.project(3,2);
```

In Scala:

```
val in : DataStream[(Int,Double,String)] = // [...]
val out = in.project(3,2)
```

The preceding function selects the attribute numbers `2` and `3` from the given records. The following are the sample input and output records:

```
(1,10.0, A, B )=> (B,A)
(2,20.0, C, D )=> (D,C)
```

Physical partitioning

Using Flink, you can do physical partitioning of the stream data. You can also have the option to provide custom partitioning. Let's examine different types of partitioning in the following sections.

Custom partitioning

As mentioned earlier, you can provide a custom implementation of a partitioner:

In Java:

```
inputStream.partitionCustom(partitioner, "someKey");
inputStream.partitionCustom(partitioner, 0);
```

In Scala:

```
inputStream.partitionCustom(partitioner, "someKey")
inputStream.partitionCustom(partitioner, 0)
```

While writing a custom partitioner, make sure that you implement an efficient `hash` function.

Random partitioning

Random partitioning randomly partitions data streams in an even manner:

In Java:

```
inputStream.shuffle();
```

In Scala:

```
inputStream.shuffle()
```

Rebalancing partitioning

This type of partitioning helps distribute the data evenly. It uses a round-robin method for distribution. This type of partitioning is good when data is skewed:

In Java:

```
inputStream.rebalance();
```

In Scala:

```
inputStream.rebalance()
```

Rescaling

Rescaling is used to distribute the data across operations, perform transformations on subsets of data, and combine them together. This rebalancing happens over a single node only, so it does not require any data transfer across networks:

In Java:

```
inputStream.rescale();
```

In Scala:

```
inputStream.rescale()
```

Broadcasting

Broadcasting distributes all records to each partition. This helps to distribute each and every element to all partitions:

In Java:

```
inputStream.broadcast();
```

In Scala:

```
inputStream.broadcast()Data Sinks
```

Once data transformations are complete, you must save the results. The following are some Flink options to save results:

- `writeAsText()`: Writes records one line at a time as strings.
- `writeAsCsV()`: Writes tuples as comma-separated value files. Row and field delimiters can also be configured.
- `print()`/`printErr()`: Writes records to the standard output. You can also choose to write to the standard error.
- `writeUsingOutputFormat()`: You can also provide a custom output format. While defining the custom format, extend `OutputFormat`, which takes care of serialization and deserialization.

- `writeToSocket()`: Flink supports writing data to a specific socket as well. Define `SerializationSchema` for proper serialization and formatting.

Event time and watermarks

The Flink Streaming API draws its inspiration from the Google Dataflow model. This API supports different concepts of time. The following are the three common places where you can capture time in a streaming environment:

- **Event time**: Event time is the time when the event occurred on its producing device. For example, in an IoT project, it can be the time at which the sensor captures a reading. Generally, these event times need to embed in the record before they enter Flink. During time processing, these timestamps are extracted and considered for windowing. Event time processing can be used for out-of-order events.
- **Processing time**: Processing time is the machine time for executing the stream of data processing. Processing time windowing considers only the timestamps where an event gets processed. Processing time is the simplest way of stream processing, as it does not require any synchronization between processing machines and producing machines. In distributed asynchronous environment processing, time does not provide determinism as it is dependent on the speed at which records flow in the system.
- **Ingestion time**: Ingestion time is the time at which a particular event enters Flink. All time-based operations refer to this timestamp. Ingestion time is a more expensive operation than processing, but gives predictable results. Ingestion time programs cannot handle any out-of-order events as it assigns a timestamp only after the event has entered the Flink system.

The following example shows how to set event time and watermarks. In the cases of ingestion time and processing time, just assign the time characteristics and watermark generation is taken care of automatically. The following is a code snippet for this:

In Java:

```
final StreamExecutionEnvironment env =
StreamExecutionEnvironment.getExecutionEnvironment();
env.setStreamTimeCharacteristic(TimeCharacteristic.ProcessingTime);
//or
env.setStreamTimeCharacteristic(TimeCharacteristic.IngestionTime);
```

In Scala:

```
val env = StreamExecutionEnvironment.getExecutionEnvironment
env.setStreamTimeCharacteristic(TimeCharacteristic.ProcessingTime)
//or
env.setStreamTimeCharacteristic(TimeCharacteristic.IngestionTime)
```

In the case of event time stream programs, specify the way to assign watermarks and timestamps. There are two ways of assigning watermarks and timestamps:

- Directly from a data source attribute
- Using a timestamp assigner

To work with event time streams, assign the time characteristic as follows:

In Java:

```
final StreamExecutionEnvironment env =
StreamExecutionEnvironment.getExecutionEnvironment();
env.setStreamTimeCharacteristic(TimeCharacteristic.EventTime;
```

In Scala:

```
val env = StreamExecutionEnvironment.getExecutionEnvironment
env.setStreamTimeCharacteristic(TimeCharacteristic.EventTime)
```

It is always best to store event time while storing the record in source. Flink also supports some predefined timestamp extractors and watermark generators.

Connectors

Apache Flink supports various connectors that allow data reads/writes across various technologies.

Kafka connector

Kafka is a publish—subscribe distributed message queuing system that allows users to publish messages to a certain topic. These are then distributed to the subscribers of the topic. Flink provides options to define a Kafka consumer as a data source in Flink streaming. To use the Flink Kafka connector, you must use a specific JAR file.

Use the following Maven dependency to use the connector. For example, for Kafka version 0.9, add the following dependency in `pom.xml`:

```
<dependency>
    <groupId>org.apache.flink</groupId>
    <artifactId>flink-connector-kafka-0.9_2.11/artifactId>
    <version>1.1.4</version>
</dependency>
```

Now, let's see how to use the Kafka consumer as the Kafka source:

In Java:

```
Properties properties = new Properties();
properties.setProperty("bootstrap.servers", "localhost:9092");
properties.setProperty("group.id", "test");
DataStream<String> input = env.addSource(new
FlinkKafkaConsumer09<String>("mytopic", new SimpleStringSchema(),
properties));
```

In Scala:

```
val properties = new Properties();
properties.setProperty("bootstrap.servers", "localhost:9092");
// only required for Kafka 0.8
properties.setProperty("zookeeper.connect", "localhost:2181");
properties.setProperty("group.id", "test");
stream = env
.addSource(new FlinkKafkaConsumer09[String]("mytopic", new
SimpleStringSchema(), properties))
.print
```

In the preceding code, we first set the properties of the Kafka host and the zookeeper host and port. Then, we specified the topic name, in this case `mytopic`. So if any messages get published to the `mytopic` topic, they will be processed by the Flink streams.

If you get data in a different format, you can also specify custom schema for deserialization. By default, Flink supports string and JSON deserializers. To enable fault tolerance, enable checkpointing in Flink. Flink takes snapshots of the state in a periodic manner. If there is a failure, it restores to the last checkpoint and restarts the processing. You can also define the Kafka producer as a sink. This writes data to a Kafka topic. To write data to a Kafka topic:

In Java:

```
stream.addSink(new FlinkKafkaProducer09[String]("localhost:9092",
"mytopic", new SimpleStringSchema()))
```

In Scala:

```
stream.addSink(new FlinkKafkaProducer09<String>("localhost:9092",
"mytopic", new SimpleStringSchema()));
```

Twitter connector

With social media and networking sites becoming more powerful everyday, it becomes crucial to be able to fetch data from Twitter and process it. Twitter data can be used to do sentiment analysis for various products, services, applications, and so on.

Flink provides the Twitter connector as one data source. To use the connector, use your Twitter account to create a Twitter application and generate authentication keys to be used by the connector.

The Twitter connector can be used using Java or Scala API. Once tokens are generated, you can write a program to fetch data from Twitter as follows:

1. First, add a Maven dependency:

    ```
    <dependency>
    <groupId>org.apache.flink</groupId>
    <artifactId>flink-connector-twitter_2.11/artifactId>
    <version>1.1.4</version>
    </dependency>
    ```

2. Next, add Twitter as a data source:

    In Java:

    ```
    Properties props = new Properties();
    props.setProperty(TwitterSource.CONSUMER_KEY, "");
    props.setProperty(TwitterSource.CONSUMER_SECRET, "");
    props.setProperty(TwitterSource.TOKEN, "");
    props.setProperty(TwitterSource.TOKEN_SECRET, "");
    ```

```
DataStream<String> streamSource = env.addSource(new
TwitterSource(props));
```

In Scala:

```
val props = new Properties();
props.setProperty(TwitterSource.CONSUMER_KEY, "");
props.setProperty(TwitterSource.CONSUMER_SECRET, "");
props.setProperty(TwitterSource.TOKEN, "");
props.setProperty(TwitterSource.TOKEN_SECRET, "");
DataStream<String> streamSource = env.addSource(new
TwitterSource(props));
```

In the preceding code, we first set properties for the token we got, and then we added `TwitterSource`. If the given information is correct, start fetching the data from Twitter. `TwitterSource` emits the data in a JSON string format. A sample Twitter JSON looks like the following:


```
{
...
"text": ""Loyalty 3.0: How to Revolutionize Customer &amp; Employee
Engagement with Big Data &amp; #Gamification" can be ordered here:
http://t.co/1XhqyaNjuR",
"geo": null,
"retweeted": false,
"in_reply_to_screen_name": null,
"possibly_sensitive": false,
"truncated": false,
"lang": "en",
"hashtags": [{
"text": "Gamification",
"indices": [90,
103]
}],
},
"in_reply_to_status_id_str": null,
"id": 330094515484508160
...
}
```


`TwitterSource` provides various `StatusesSampleEndpoint`, which returns a set of random tweets. If you need to add some filters and do not want to use the default endpoint, you can implement the `TwitterSource.EndpointInitializer` interface.

Once you fetch data from Twitter, you can either process, store, or analyze the data.

RabbitMQ connector

RabbitMQ is a widely used, distributed, high-performance message queuing system. It is used as a message delivery system for high-throughput operations. It allows you to create a distributed message queue and include publishers and subscribers in the queue. For more information about RabbitMQ, visit `https://www.rabbitmq.com/`.

Flink supports fetching and publishing data to and from RabbitMQ. It provides a connector that can act as a data source for data streams.

For the RabbitMQ connector to work, you must provide the following information:

- **RabbitMQ**: Configurations such as host, port, user credentials, and so on.
- **Queue**: The RabbitMQ queue name that you wish to subscribe to.
- **Correlation IDs**: This is a RabbitMQ feature used for correlating the request and response by a unique ID in a distributed world. The Flink RabbitMQ connector provides an interface to set this to `true` or `false` depending on whether you are using it or not.
- **Deserialization schema**: RabbitMQ stores and transports the data in a serialized manner to avoid network traffic. So when the message is received, the subscriber knows how to deserialize the message. The Flink connector provides us with some default deserializers, such as the string deserializer.

The RabbitMQ source provides us with the following options on stream deliveries:

- **Exactly once**: Using RabbitMQ correlation IDs and the Flink checkpointing mechanism with RabbitMQ transactions
- **Atleast once**: When Flink checkpointing is enabled but RabbitMQ correlation IDs are not set

There are no strong delivery guarantees with the RabbitMQ auto-commit mode.

Now let's write a code to get this connector working. Like other connectors, add a Maven dependency to the code:

```
<dependency>
<groupId>org.apache.flink</groupId>
<artifactId>flink-connector-rabbitmq_2.11/artifactId>
<version>1.1.4</version>
</dependency>
```

The following snippet shows how to use the RabbitMQ connector in Java:

```
//Configurations
RMQConnectionConfig connectionConfig = new RMQConnectionConfig.Builder()
.setHost(<host>).setPort(<port>).setUserName(..)
.setPassword(..).setVirtualHost("/").build();

//Get Data Stream without correlation ids
DataStream<String> streamWO = env.addSource(new
RMQSource<String>(connectionConfig, "my-queue", new SimpleStringSchema()))
.print

//Get Data Stream with correlation ids
DataStream<String> streamW = env.addSource(new
RMQSource<String>(connectionConfig, "my-queue", true, new
SimpleStringSchema()))
.print
```

Similarly, in Scala the code can be written as follows:

```
val connectionConfig = new RMQConnectionConfig.Builder()
.setHost(<host>).setPort(<port>).setUserName(..)
.setPassword(..).setVirtualHost("/").build()
streamsWOIds = env.addSource(new RMQSource[String](connectionConfig, " my-
queue", new SimpleStringSchema))
.print
streamsWIds = env.addSource(new RMQSource[String](connectionConfig, "my-
queue", true, new SimpleStringSchema))
.print
```

You may also use the RabbitMQ connector as a Flink sink.

To send processes back to some different RabbitMQ queue, provide three important configurations:

- RabbitMQ configurations
- Queue name – where to send back the processed data
- Serialization schema – schema for RabbitMQ to convert the data into bytes

The following is sample code in Java to show how to use this connector as a Flink sink:

```
RMQConnectionConfig connectionConfig = new RMQConnectionConfig.Builder()
.setHost(<host>).setPort(<port>).setUserName(..)
.setPassword(..).setVirtualHost("/").build();
stream.addSink(new RMQSink<String>(connectionConfig, "target-queue", new
StringToByteSerializer()));
```

The same can be done in Scala:

```
val connectionConfig = new RMQConnectionConfig.Builder()
.setHost(<host>).setPort(<port>).setUserName(..)
.setPassword(..).setVirtualHost("/").build()
stream.addSink(new RMQSink[String](connectionConfig, "target-queue", new
StringToByteSerializer
```

Elasticsearch connector

Elasticsearch is a distributed, low-latency, full text search engine system that allows you to index documents of your choice and then allows you to do a full text search over the set of documents. To know more about Elasticsearch, see `https://www.elastic.co`.

In many scenarios, you may want to process data using Flink and then store it in Elasticsearch. To enable this, Flink supports the Elasticsearch connector. So far, Elasticsearch has had two major releases. Flink supports them both. For Elasticsearch 1.x, the following Maven dependency needs to be added:

```
<dependency>
\<groupId>org.apache.flink</groupId>
<artifactId>flink-connector-elasticsearch_2.11</artifactId>
<version>1.1.4</version>
</dependency>
```

The Flink connector provides a sink to write data to Elasticsearch. It uses two methods to connect to Elasticsearch:

- **Embedded node mode**: In embedded node mode, the sink uses BulkProcessor to send the documents to ElasticSearch. You can configure how many requests to buffer before sending documents to Elasticsearch. The following is the code snippet:

```
DataStream<String> input = ...;
Map<String, String> config = Maps.newHashMap();
config.put("bulk.flush.max.actions", "1");
config.put("cluster.name", "cluster-name");
input.addSink(new ElasticsearchSink<>(config, new
IndexRequestBuilder<String>() {
@Override
public IndexRequest createIndexRequest(String element,
RuntimeContext ctx) {
    Map<String, Object> json = new HashMap<>();
    json.put("data", element);
    return Requests.indexRequest()
    .index("my-index")
```

```
        .type("my-type")
        .source(json);
    }
    }));
```

In the preceding code snippet, we create a hash map with configurations such as the cluster name and how many documents to buffer before sending the request. Then we add the sink to the stream, specifying the index, type, and the document to store. Similarly, the code in Scala is as follows:

```
val input: DataStream[String] = ...
val config = new util.HashMap[String, String]
config.put("bulk.flush.max.actions", "1")
config.put("cluster.name", "cluster-name")
text.addSink(new ElasticsearchSink(config, new
IndexRequestBuilder[String]
{
    override def createIndexRequest(element: String, ctx:
RuntimeContext):
    IndexRequest = {
        val json = new util.HashMap[String, AnyRef]
        json.put("data", element)
        Requests.indexRequest.index("my-index").`type`("my-
type").source(json)
    }
}))
```

- **Transport client mode**: Elasticsearch allows connections through the transport client on port `9300`. Flink supports connecting using those through its connector. Specify all the Elasticsearch nodes present in the cluster in configurations. The following is the snippet in Java:

```
DataStream<String> input = ...;
Map<String, String> config = Maps.newHashMap();
config.put("bulk.flush.max.actions", "1");
config.put("cluster.name", "cluster-name");
List<TransportAddress> transports = new ArrayList<String>();
transports.add(new InetSocketTransportAddress("es-node-1", 9300));
transports.add(new InetSocketTransportAddress("es-node-2", 9300));
transports.add(new InetSocketTransportAddress("es-node-3", 9300));
input.addSink(new ElasticsearchSink<>(config, transports, new
IndexRequestBuilder<String>() {
@Override
public IndexRequest createIndexRequest(String element,
RuntimeContext ctx) {
Map<String, Object> json = new HashMap<>();
json.put("data", element);
```

```
return Requests.indexRequest()
.index("my-index")
.type("my-type")
.source(json);
}
}));
```

Here as well, we provide the details about the cluster name, nodes, ports, maximum requests to send in bulk, and so on. Similar code in Scala can be written as follows:

```
val input: DataStream[String] = ...
val config = new util.HashMap[String, String]
config.put("bulk.flush.max.actions", "1")
config.put("cluster.name", "cluster-name")
val transports = new ArrayList[String]
transports.add(new InetSocketTransportAddress("es-node-1", 9300))
transports.add(new InetSocketTransportAddress("es-node-2", 9300))
transports.add(new InetSocketTransportAddress("es-node-3", 9300))
text.addSink(new ElasticsearchSink(config, transports, new
IndexRequestBuilder[String] {
override def createIndexRequest(element: String, ctx:
RuntimeContext):
IndexRequest = {
val json = new util.HashMap[String, AnyRef]
json.put("data", element)
Requests.indexRequest.index("my-index").`type`("my-
type").source(json)
}
}))
```

Cassandra connector

Cassandra is a distributed, low-latency NoSQL database. It is a key value-based database. Many high-throughput applications use Cassandra as their primary database. Cassandra works with distributed cluster mode, where there is no master-slave architecture. Reads and writes can be felicitated by any node. For more information about Cassandra, visit `http://cassandra.apache.org`.

Apache Flink provides a connector that can write data to Cassandra. In many applications, people may want to store streaming data from Flink in Cassandra.

Like other connectors, to get this we need to add it as a Maven dependency:

```
<dependency>
<groupId>org.apache.flink</groupId>
<artifactId>flink-connector-cassandra_2.11</artifactId>
<version>1.1.4</version>
</dependency>
```

Once the dependency is added, add the Cassandra sink with its configurations, as follows:

In Java:

```
CassandraSink.addSink(input)
.setQuery("INSERT INTO cep.events (id, message) values (?, ?);")
.setClusterBuilder(new ClusterBuilder() {
@Override
public Cluster buildCluster(Cluster.Builder builder) {
return builder.addContactPoint("127.0.0.1").build();
}
})
.build()
```

In Scala:

The preceding code writes stream of data into a table called **events**. The table expects an event ID and a message:

```
CassandraSink.addSink(input)
.setQuery("INSERT INTO cep.events (id, message) values (?, ?);")
.setClusterBuilder(new ClusterBuilder() {
@Override
public Cluster buildCluster(Cluster.Builder builder) {
return builder.addContactPoint("127.0.0.1").build();
}
)
.build();
```

Summary

In this chapter, we learned about Flink's most powerful API, the DataStream API; how data sources, transformations, and sinks work together; and about various technology connectors, such as Elasticsearch, Cassandra, Kafka, RabbitMQ, and so on. In this chapter, we also discussed stream processing using Apache Flink.

In the next chapter, we will switch gears and look at one of the most exciting fields of visualizing data.

10
Visualizing Big Data

This chapter explores one of the most important activities in big data processing and analysis, which is creating a powerful visualization of data and insights. We tend to understand anything graphical better than anything textual or numerical. During the analytical process, you will need to constantly make sense of data and manipulate its usage and interpretation; this will be much easier if you can visualize the data instead of reading it from tables, columns, or text files. When you have used one of the many ways of analyzing data and generated insights that we have seen so far (such as through Python, R, Spark, Flink, Hive, MapReduce, and so on), anyone trying to make sense of the insights will want to understand those in the context of the data. For this purpose, you need some pictorial representation for that as well.

In a nutshell, the following topics will be covered throughout this chapter:

- Introduction
- Tableau
- Chart types
- Using Python
- Using R
- Data visualization tools

Introduction

One of the most valuable means through which we can make sense of big data, and thus make it more useful to most people, is data visualization. Visualization of data depends a lot on the use cases. Graphs and charts are visual representations of data. They provide a powerful means of summarizing and presenting data in a way that most people find easier to comprehend. Charts and graphs enable us to see the main features or characteristics of some data. They not only enable us to present the numerical findings of a study but also provide the shape and pattern of the data, which is critical in data analysis and decision making. There are many key considerations you need to keep in mind when developing data visualizations:

- What type of graphical representation to use for which type of data
- How to design a visualization approach that allows interactive features
- How to search and modify datasets graphically
- How to differentiate between data and the resultant insights
- How to develop a visualization methodology scalable with the growth of your data on a big data scale
- How to address latency issues such that there is no significant lag in visualizing data
- How to optimize design for high velocity or streaming data to show real-time visualizations
- How to visualize data from databases
- How to visualize in memory data

There are many different ways of visualizing data. The following image shows some examples to depict how the choice of a chart type can change the use and effectiveness of visualization:

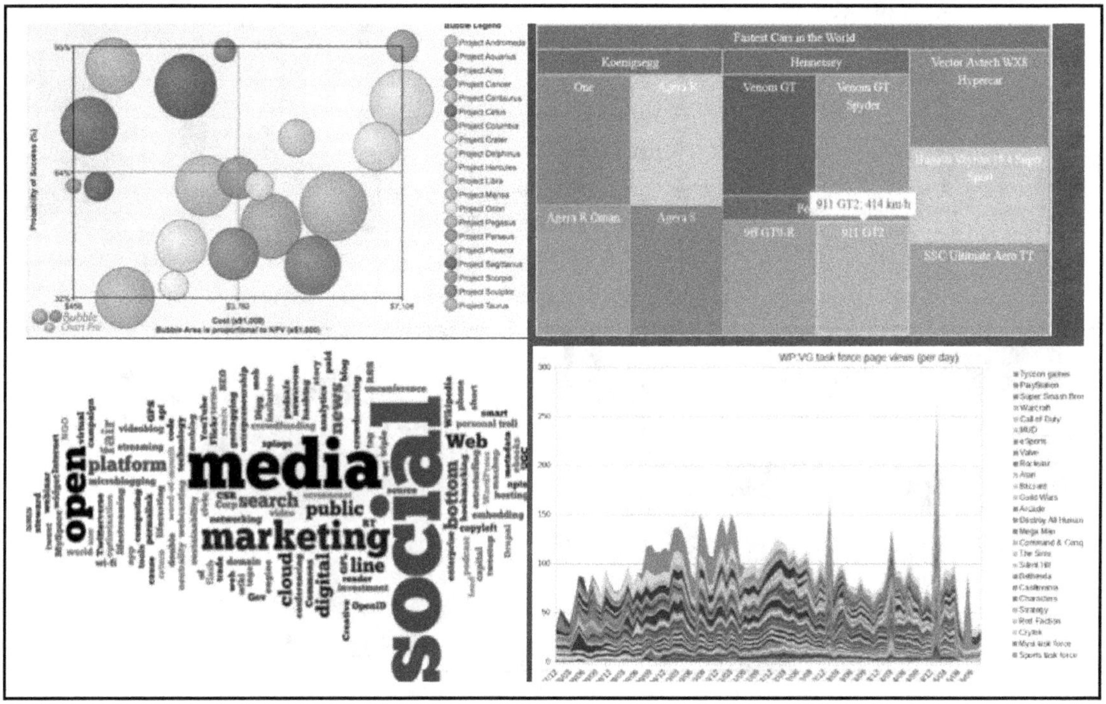

The following are some more examples of visualization:

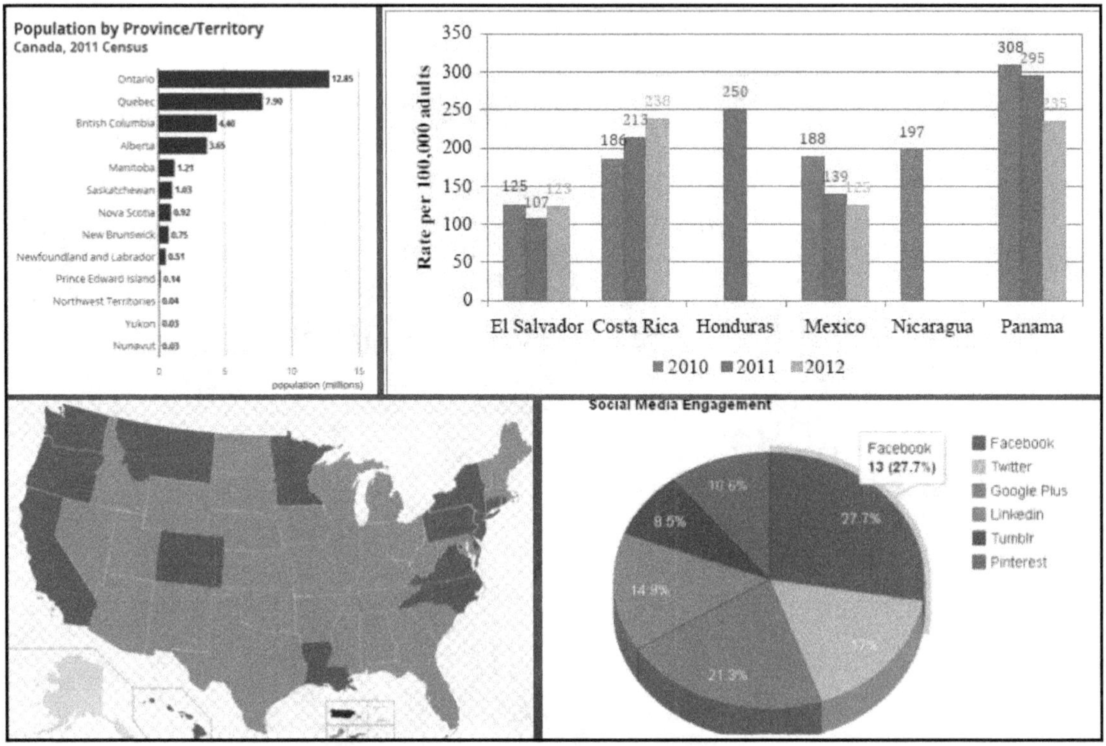

Figure: Screenshot showing some more examples of visualization

Tableau

In this section, we will set up Tableau, which is a very popular visualization tool. For this, we can simply download a trial version of Tableau and install it on our local machine. You can find Tableau at `https://www.tableau.com/`.

The following screenshot shows the download link for Tableau:

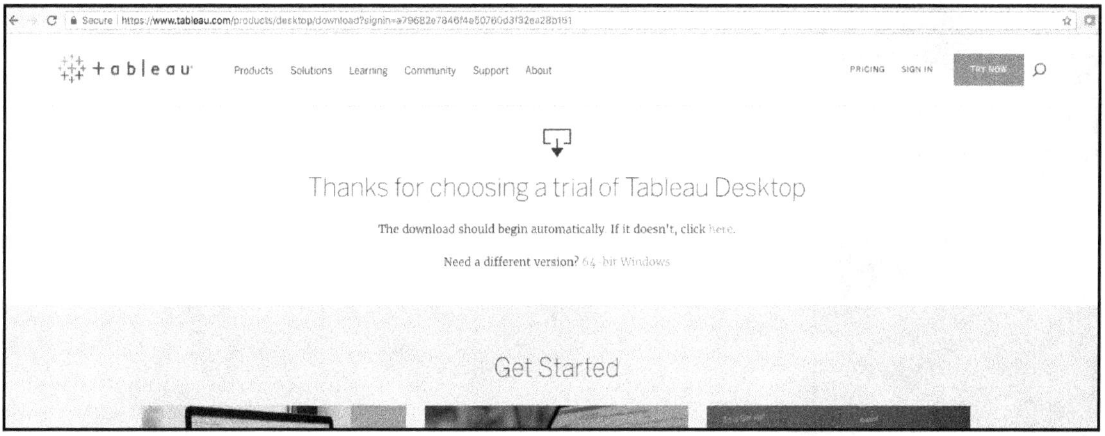

Once you've installed the trial version (or if you already have a licensed copy available), you are ready to go through some basic visualization exercises.

The following is a screenshot of the launch of Tableau, where you will see the various sources of data you can start with:

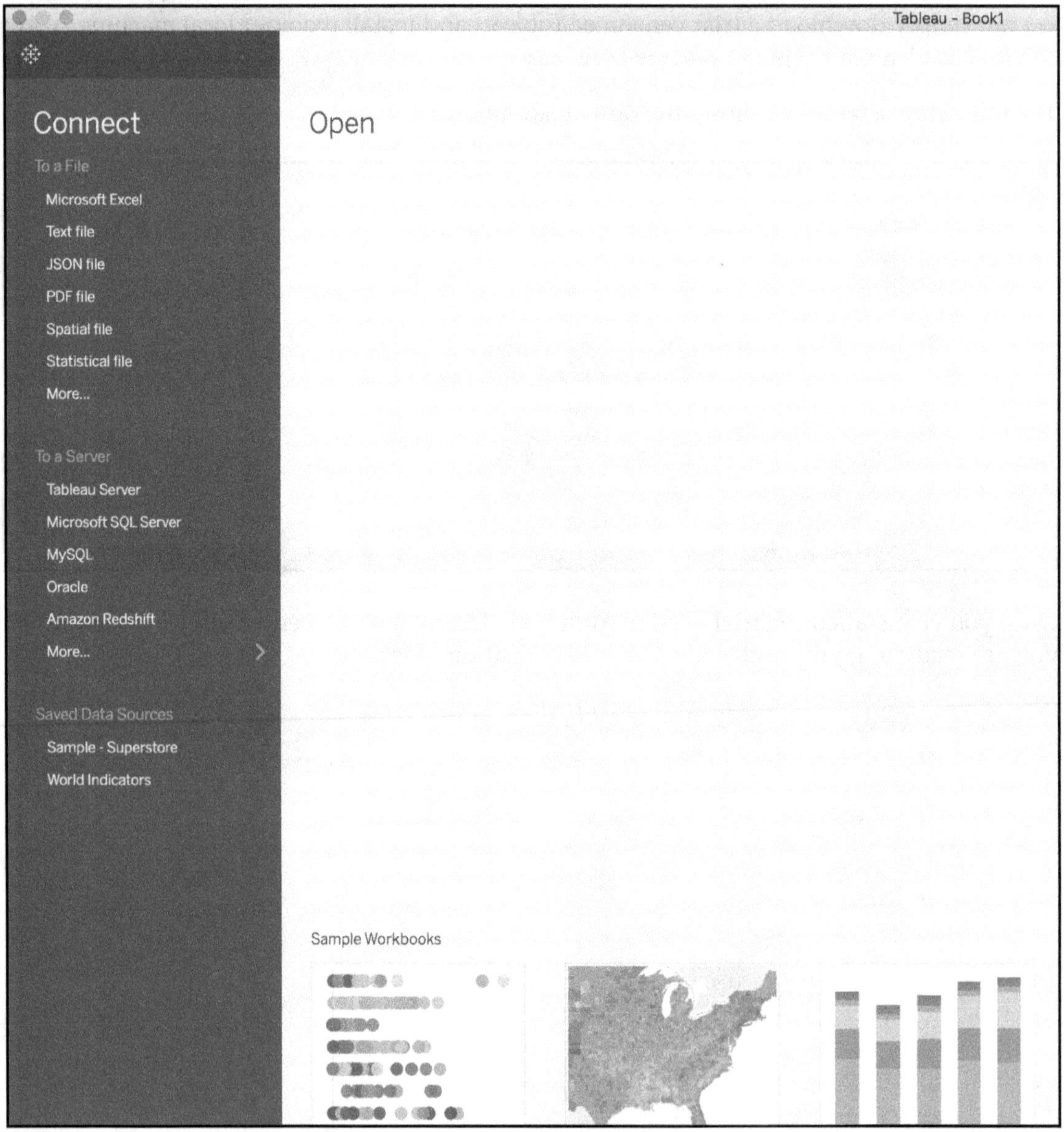

Let's start by opening the file `OnlineRetail.csv`. The following is a screenshot of the blank worksheet:

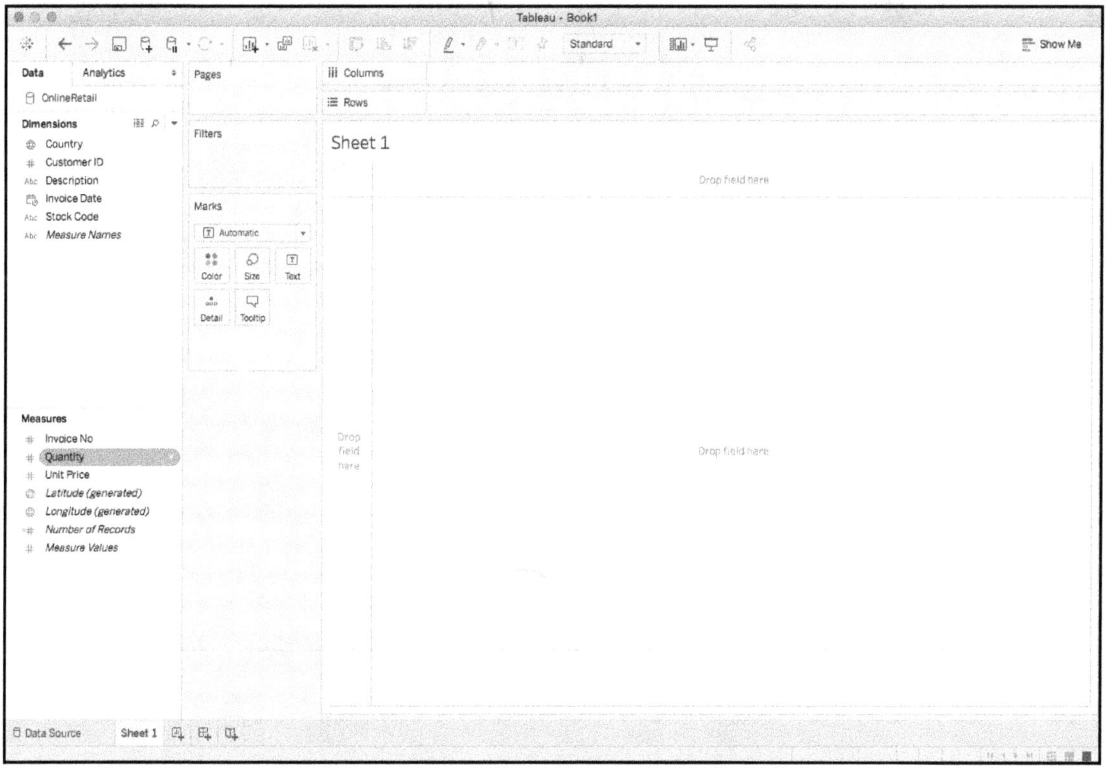

Select the `Quantity` as a column to see a bar chart with one bar, as shown in the following screenshot:

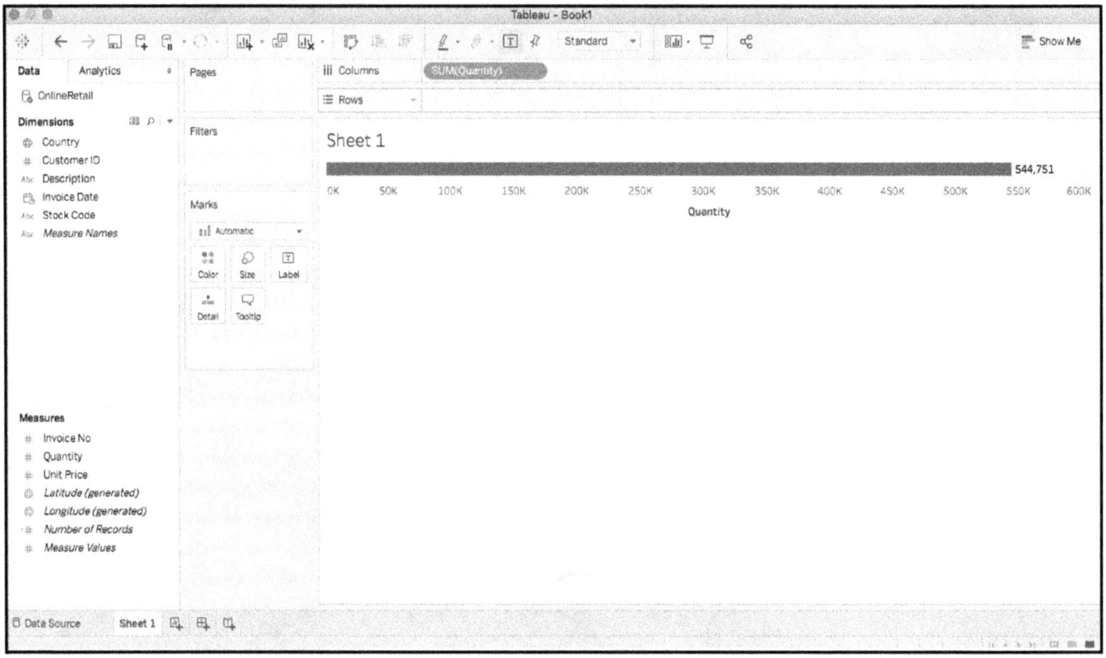

Select the `Description` as a row to see the bar chart showing the quantity for each item, as follows:

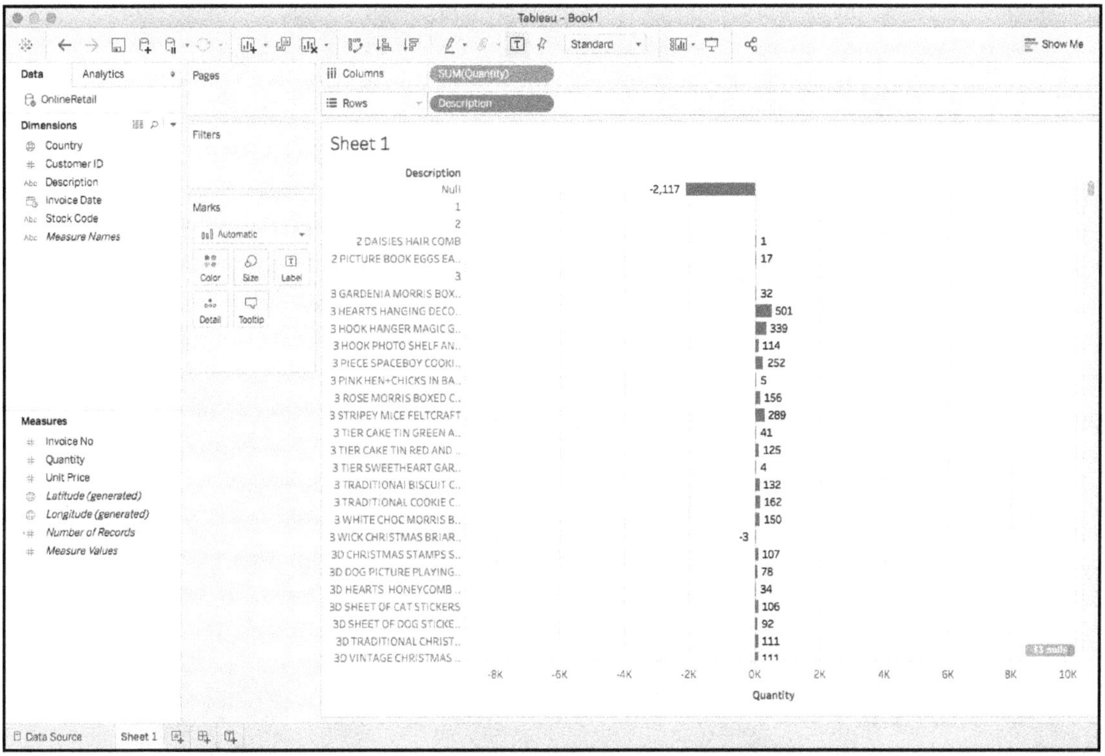

You can apply filters to eliminate the negative quantity values, as shown in this screenshot:

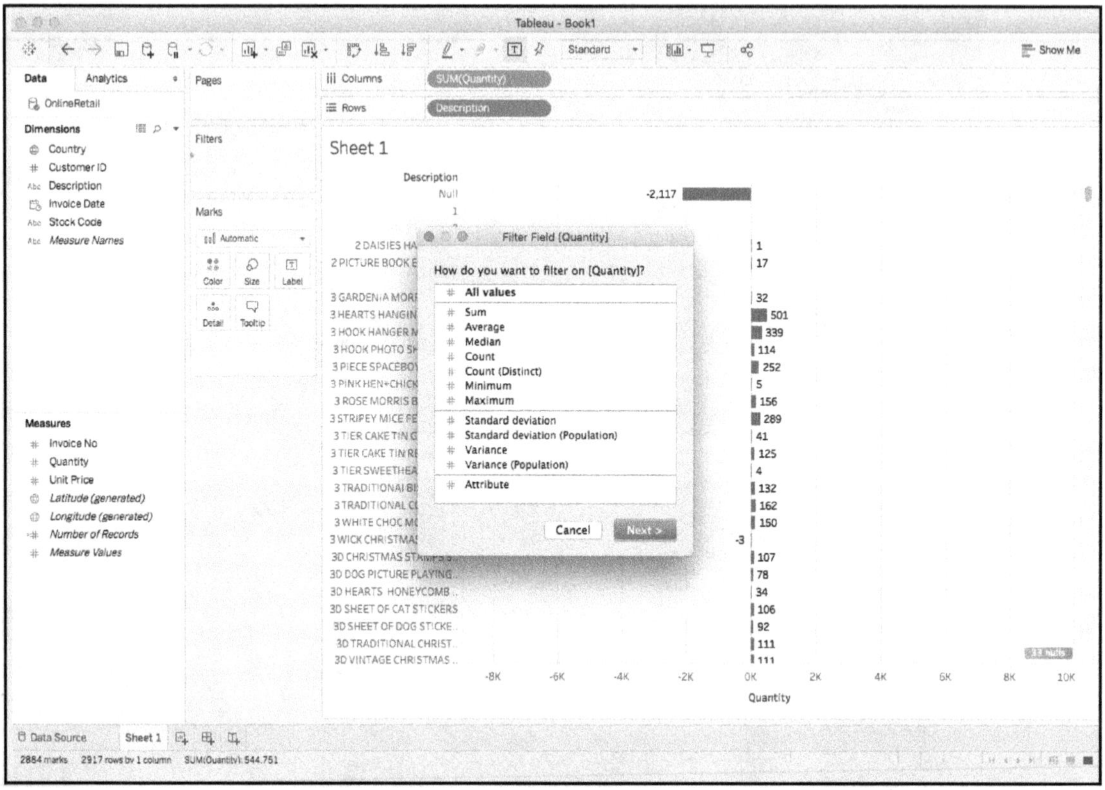

You will see the range of values of any numerical column, such as `Quantity`:

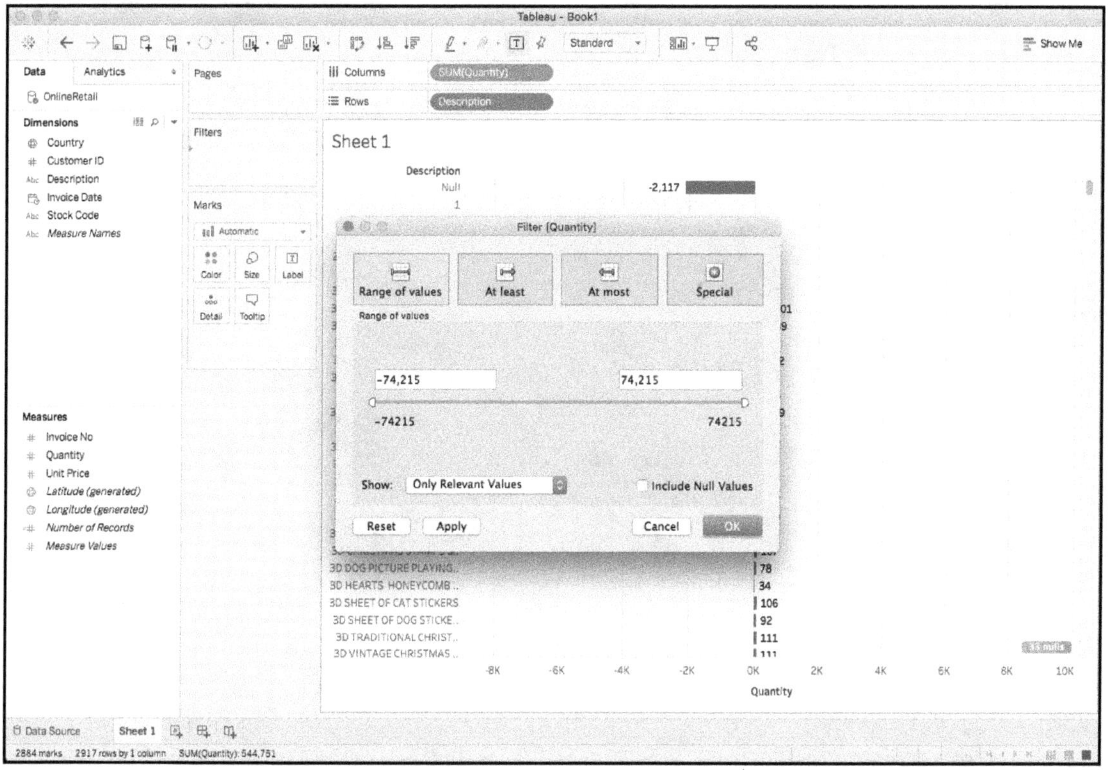

Now, you can select the valid ranges of values for `Quantity`, as follows:

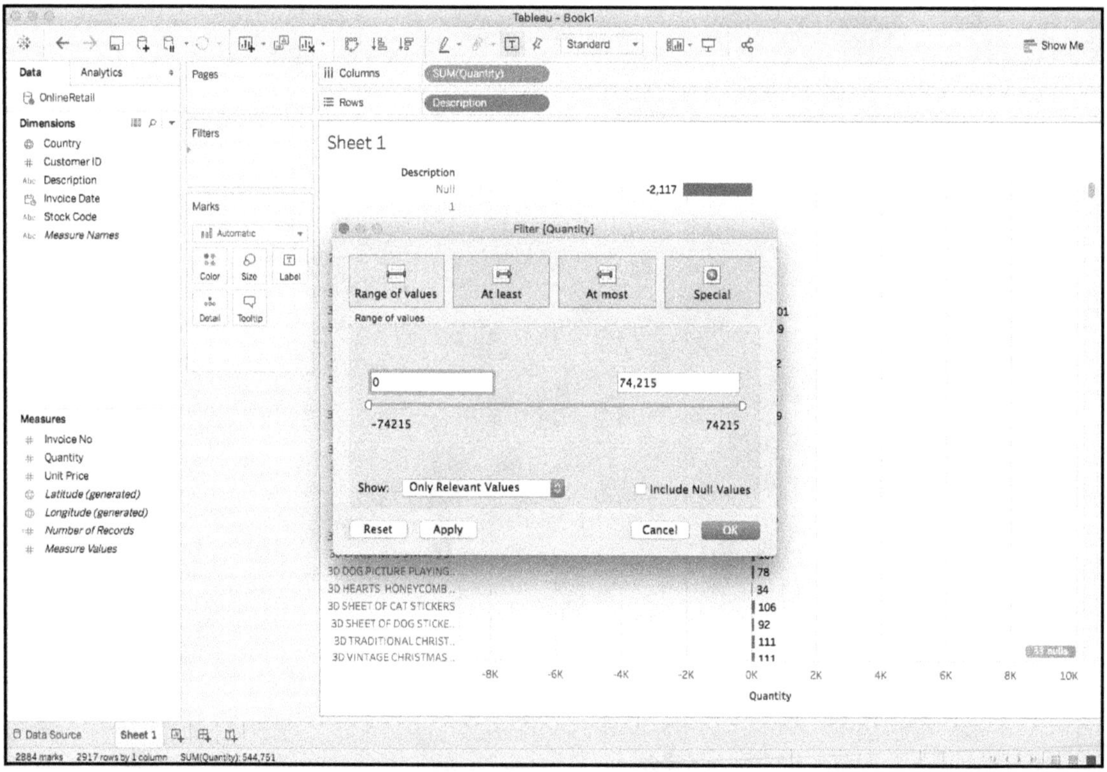

As seen in the following screenshot, only positive values are shown now:

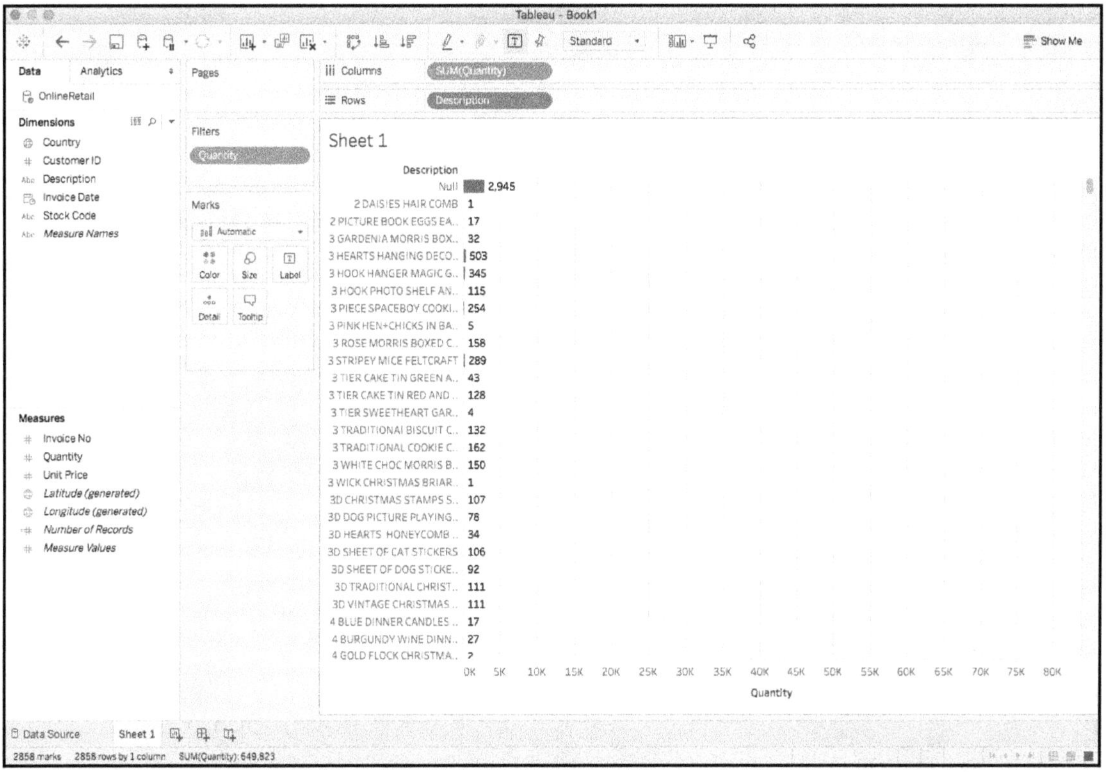

You can sort the chart by `Quantity` so that you see the item `Descriptions` with the largest `Quantity` at the top, as shown in the following screenshot:

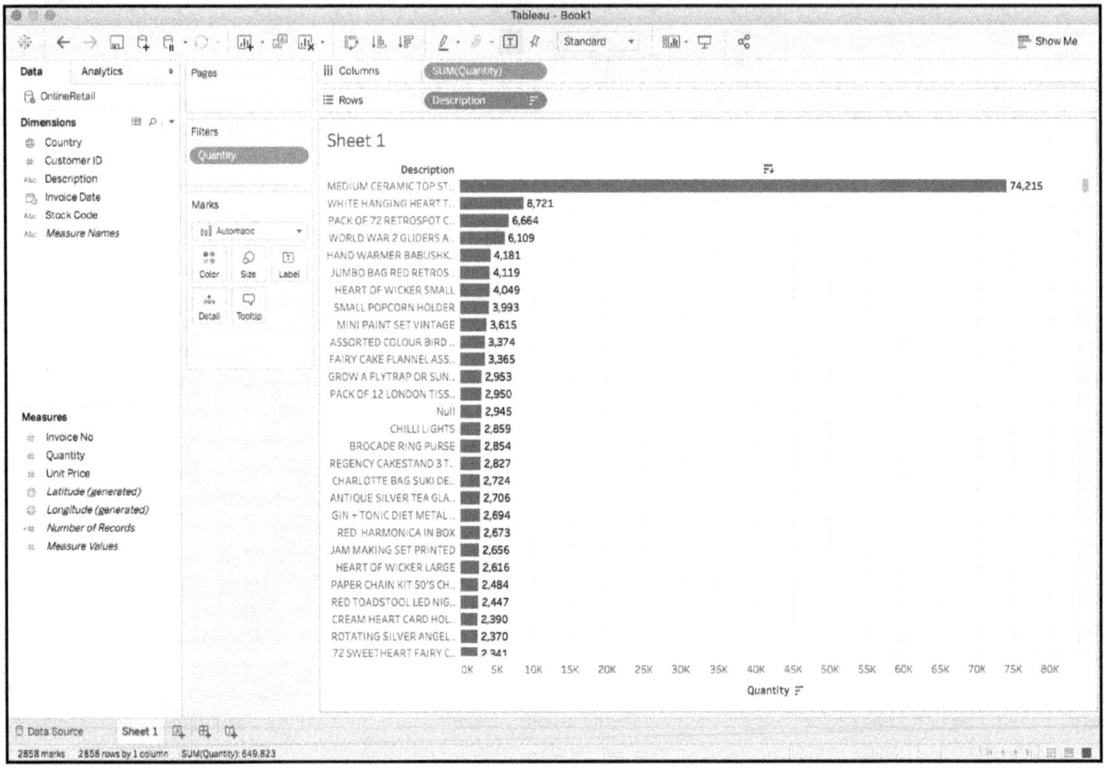

Create a new worksheet, as follows:

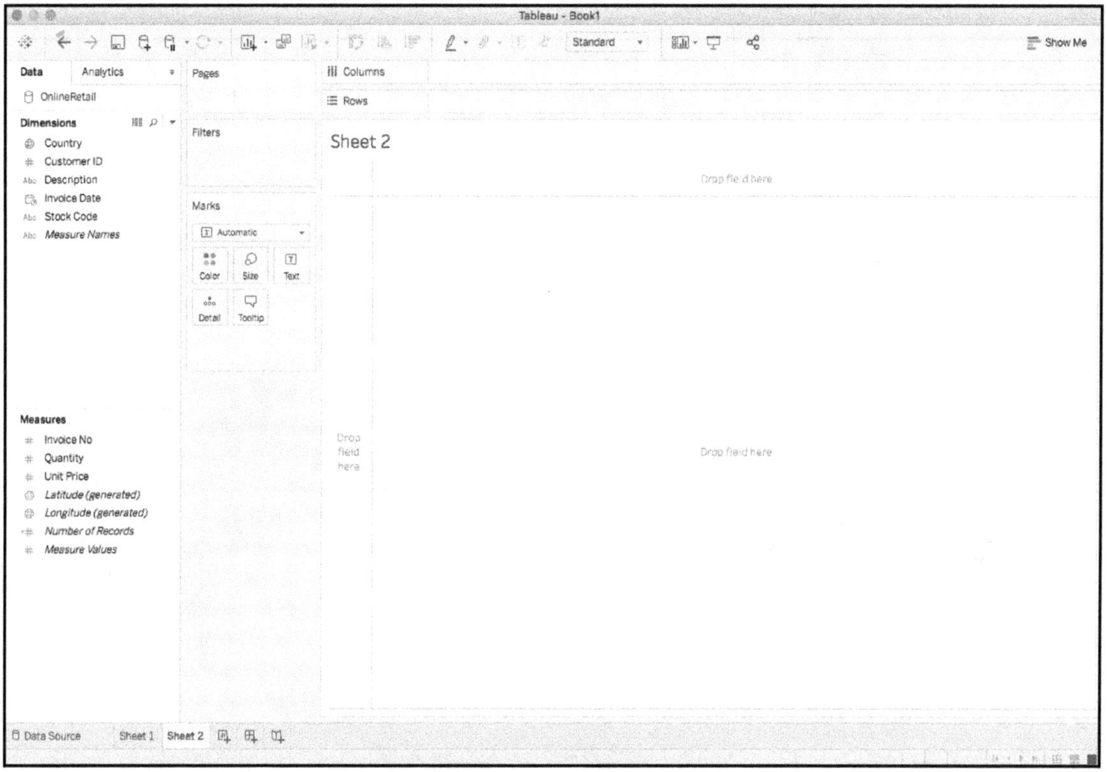

Similar to the previous worksheet, choose `Description` and `Quantity` as shown in the following screenshot:

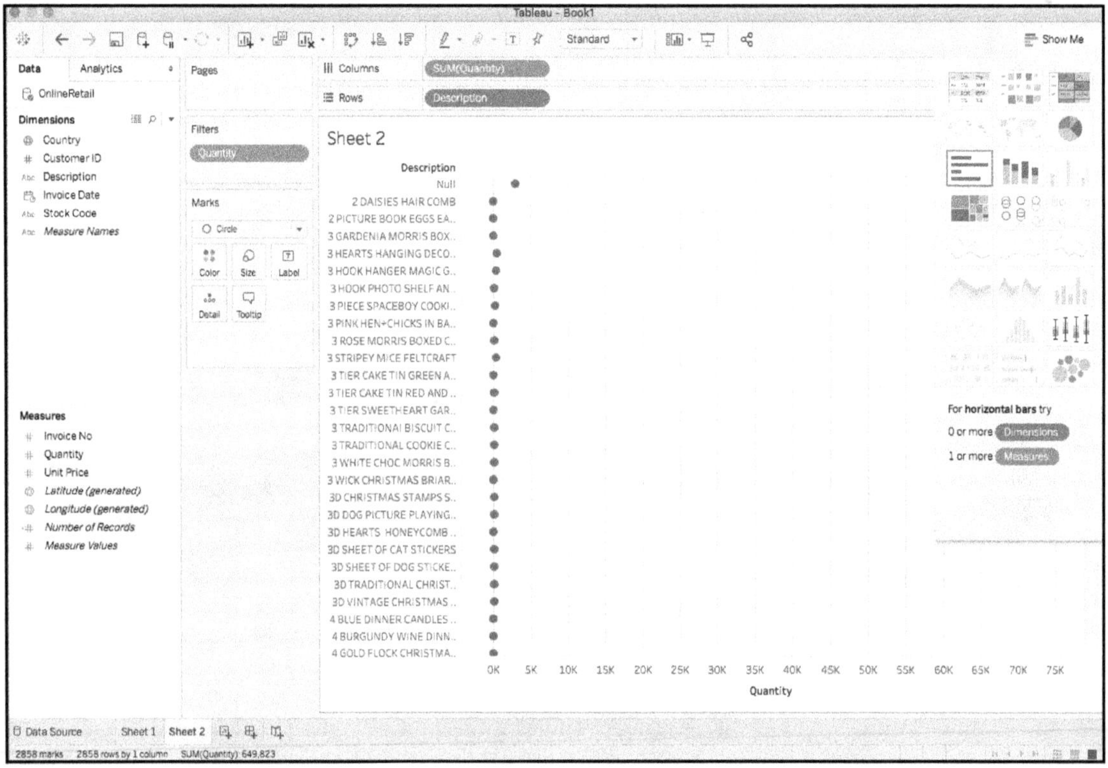

You can choose different chart types from the right-hand side pane; select packed bubbles:

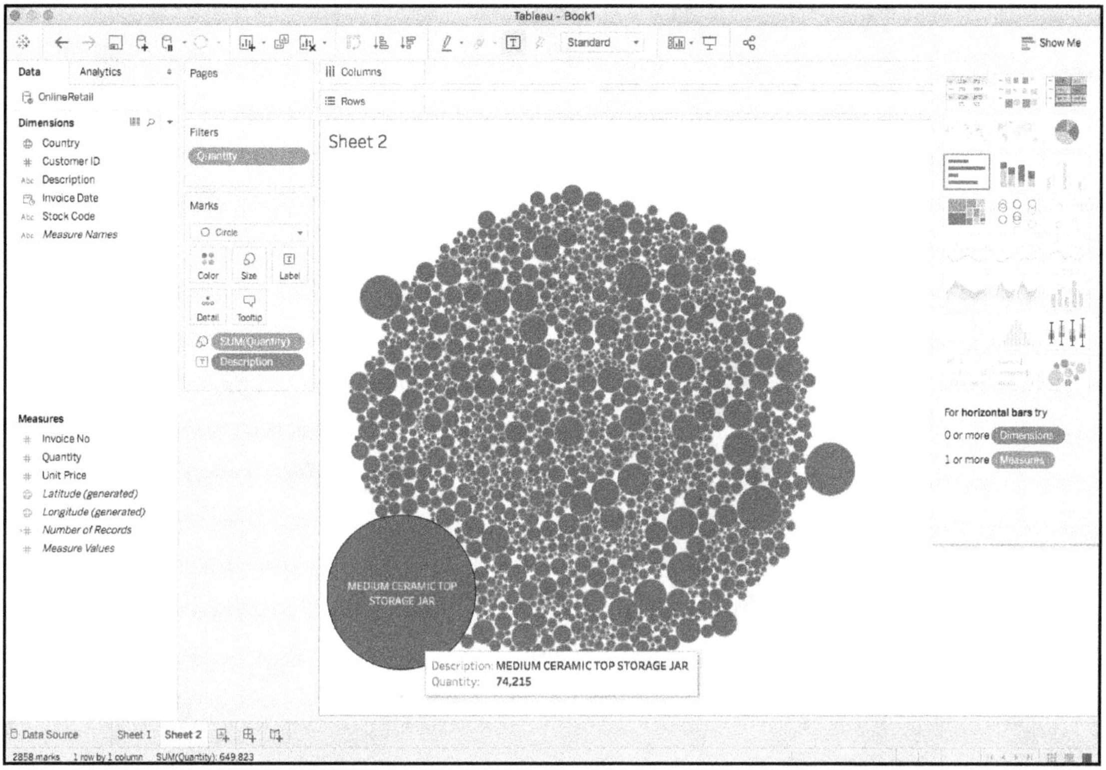

Try choosing treemap as the chart type, as follows:

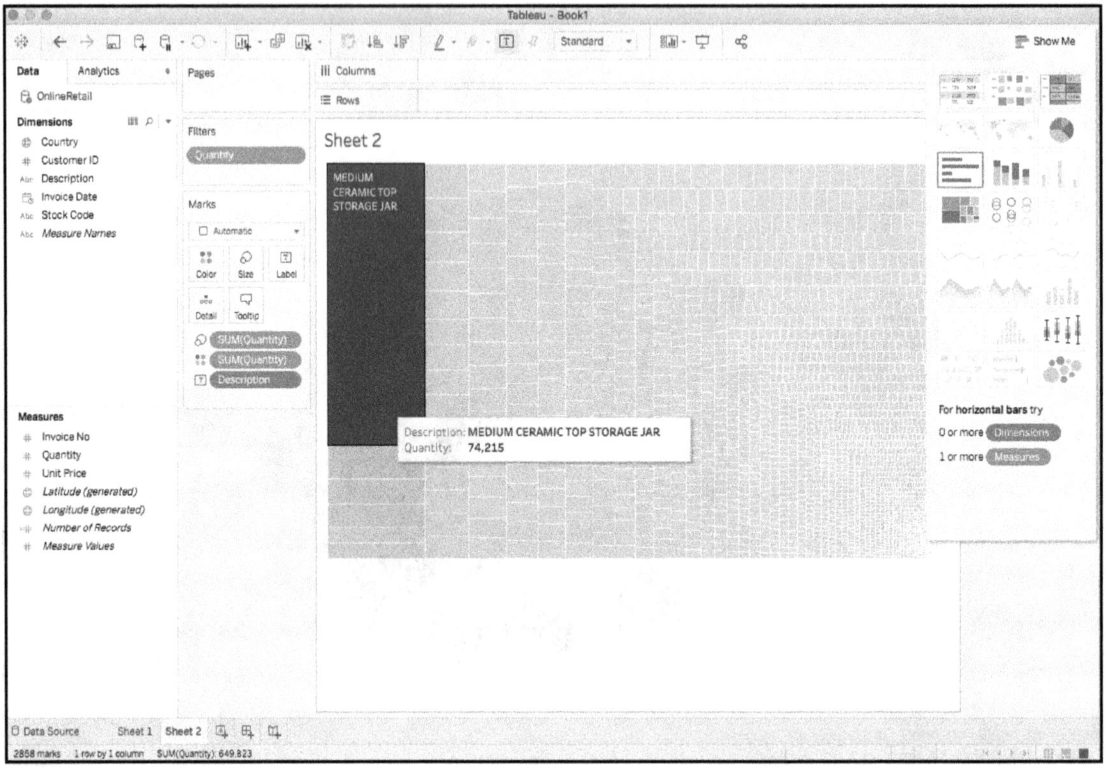

You can change the colors and other properties of a chart, as shown in the following screenshot:

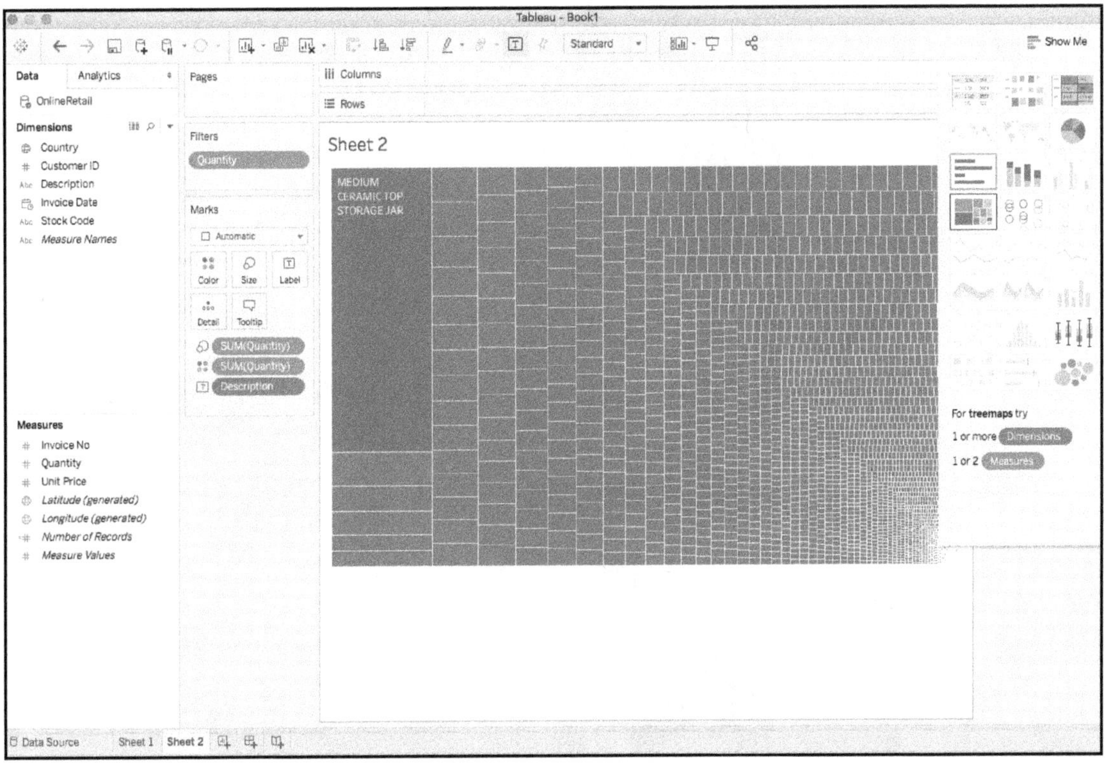

It's easy to exclude any row/column or a value/data point:

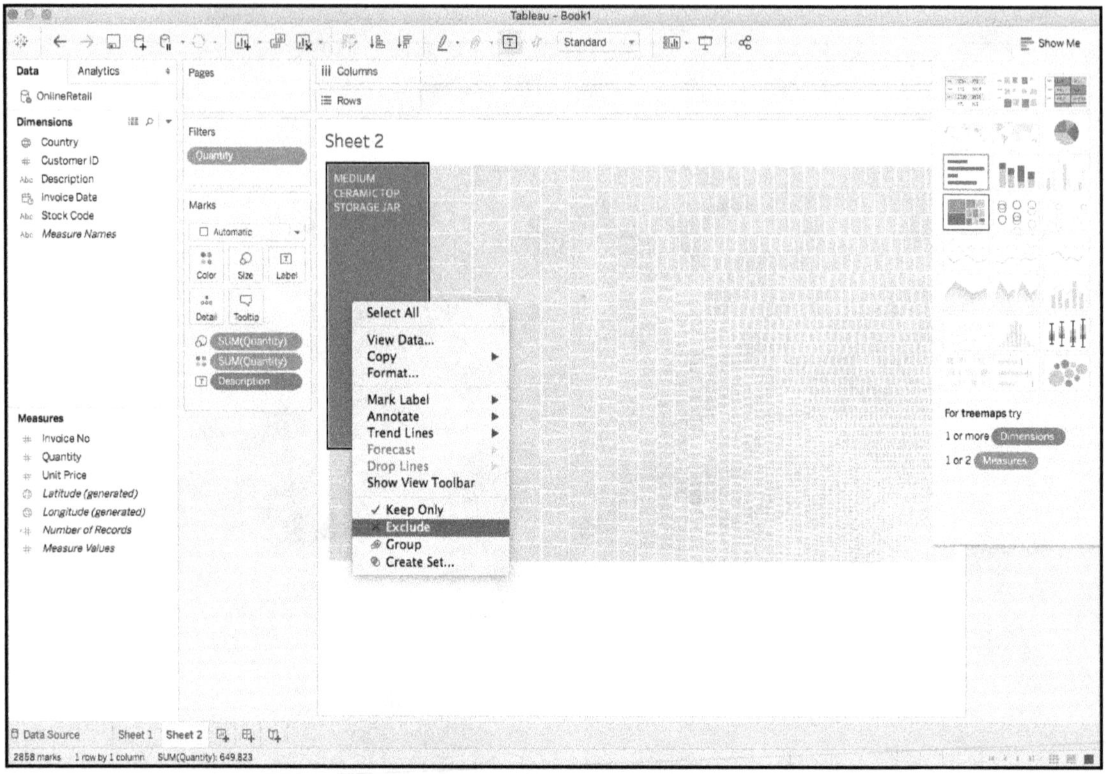

You can also create a **Dashboard** comprising multiple worksheets, as follows:

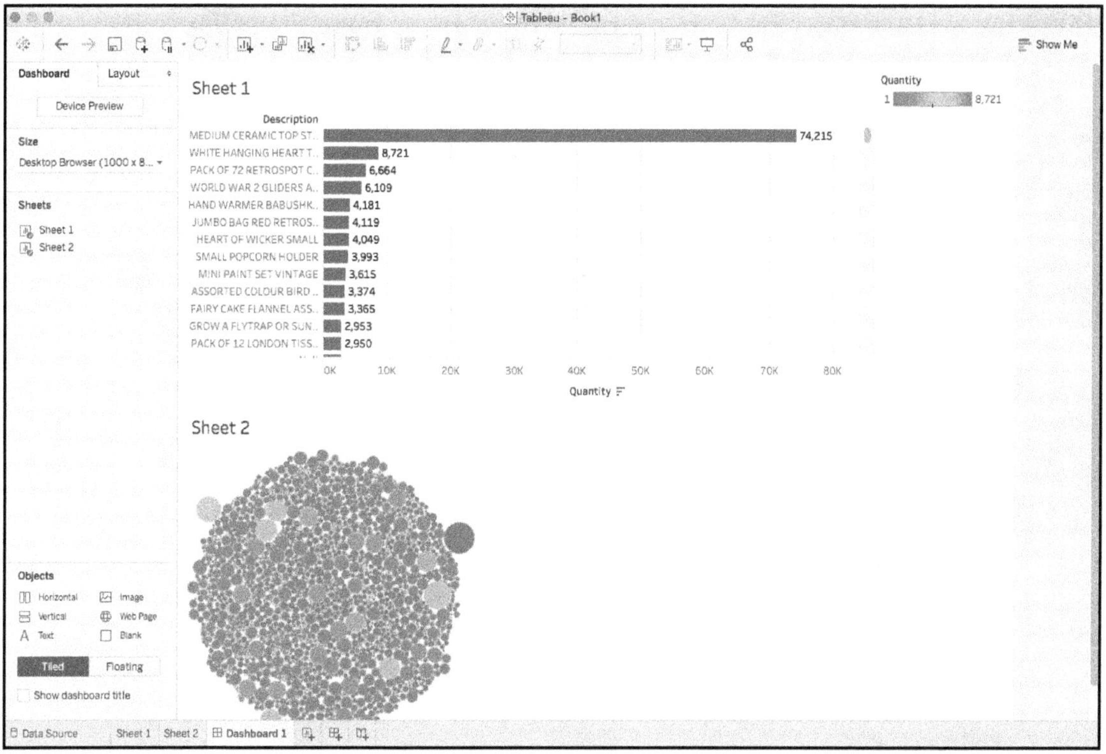

Create some other chart type (say a line chart), as shown in the following screenshot:

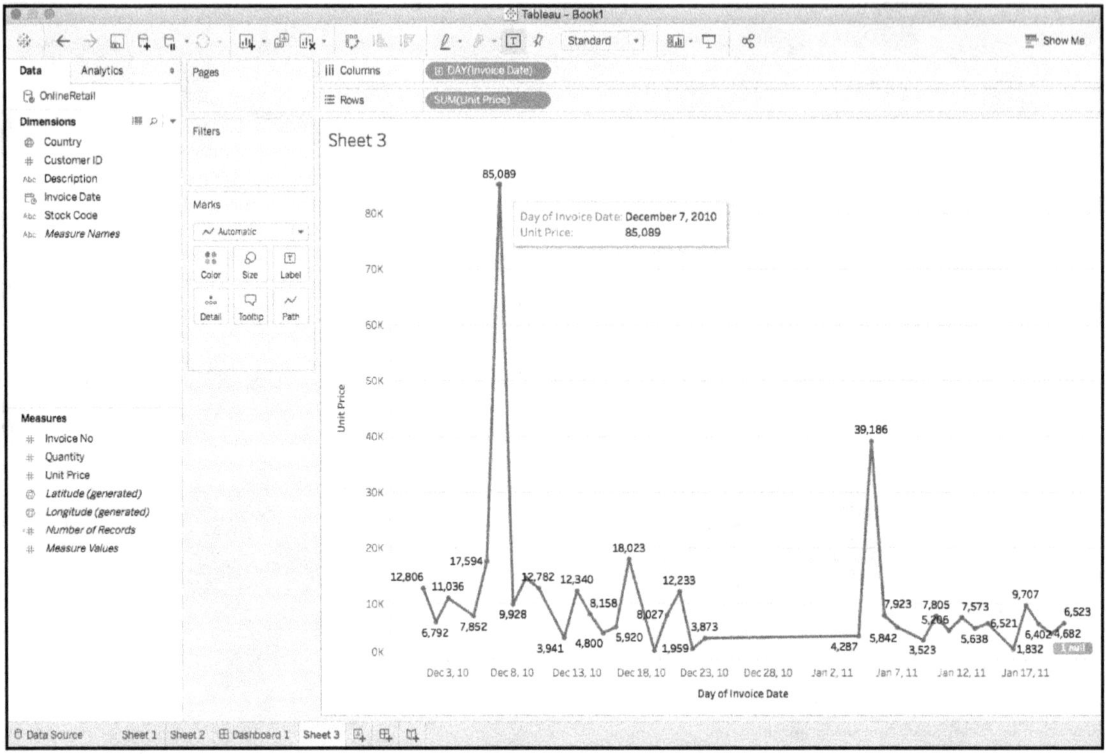

Add the new worksheet to the **Dashboard**, as shown in this screenshot:

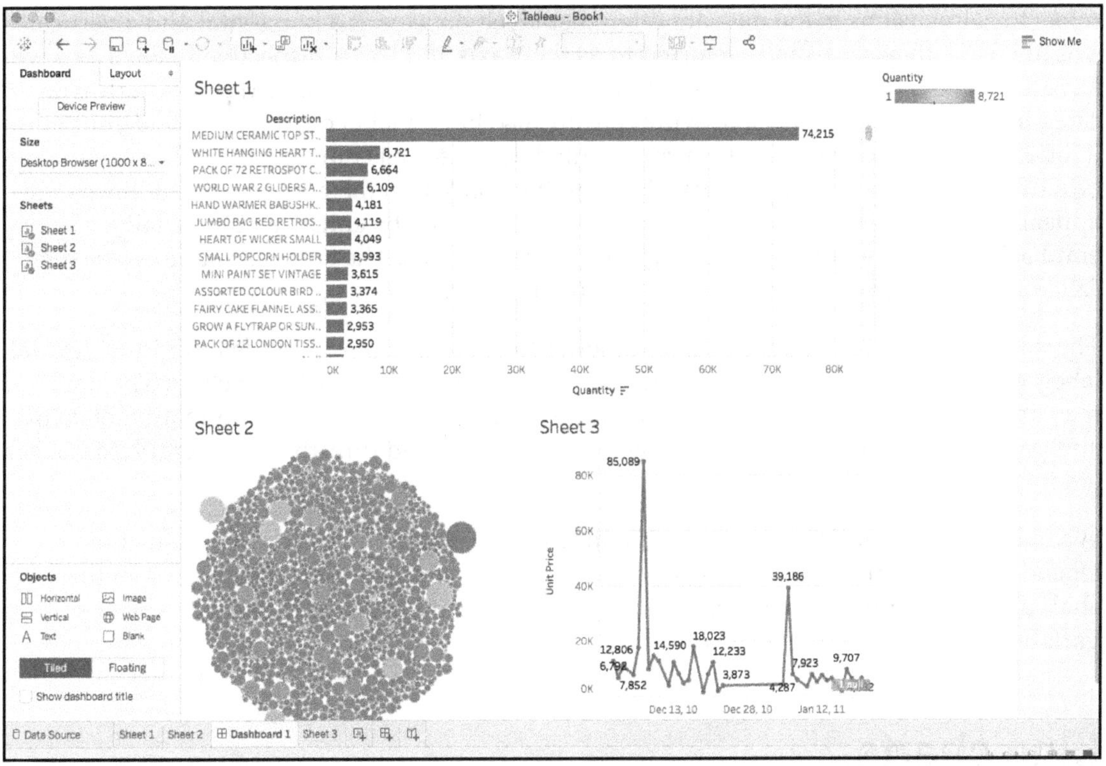

Chart types

A chart can take a large variety of forms; however, there are common features that provide the chart with its ability to extract meaning from data. Typically, the data in a chart is represented graphically, since humans are generally able to infer meanings from pictures quicker than from text. Text is generally used only to annotate the data.

One of the most important uses of text in a graph is the title. A graph's title usually appears above the main graphic and provides a succinct description of what the data in the graph refers to. Dimensions in the data are often displayed on axes. If a horizontal and a vertical axis are used, they are usually referred to as the x axis and y axis respectively. Each axis will have a scale, denoted by periodic graduations and usually accompanied by numerical or categorical indications. Each axis will typically also have a label displayed outside or beside it, briefly describing the dimension represented. If the scale is numerical, the label will often be suffixed with the unit of that scale in parentheses. Within the graph, a grid of lines may appear to aid in the visual alignment of data. The grid can be enhanced by visually emphasizing the lines at regular or significant graduations. The emphasized lines are then called major grid lines and the remainder are minor grid lines.

The data of a chart can appear in all manner of formats, and may include individual textual labels describing the datum associated with the indicated position in the chart. The data may appear as dots or shapes, connected or unconnected, and in any combination of colors and patterns. Inferences or points of interest can be overlaid directly on the graph to further aid information extraction.

When the data appearing in a chart contains multiple variables, the chart may include a legend (also known as a **key**). A legend contains a list of the variables appearing in the chart and an example of their appearance. This information allows the data from each variable to be identified in the chart.

Line charts

Line charts allow looking at the behavior of one or several variables over time and identifying the trends. In traditional BI, line charts can show sales, profit, and revenue development for the last 12 months. When working with big data, companies can use this visualization technique to track total product purchases by weeks, the average number of orders to the sales office by months, and so on.

The following screenshot is an example of a line chart:

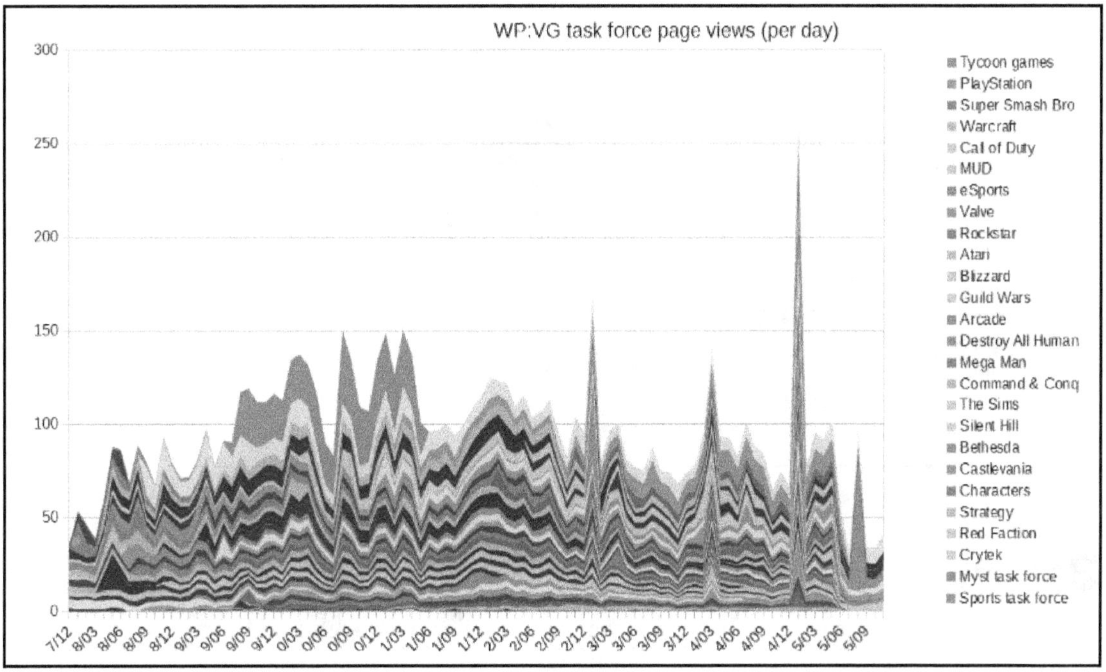

Pie chart

Pie charts show the components of the whole. Companies that work with both traditional and big data may use this technique to look at customer segments or market shares. The difference lies in the sources from which these companies take raw data for the analysis.

The following is an example of a pie chart:

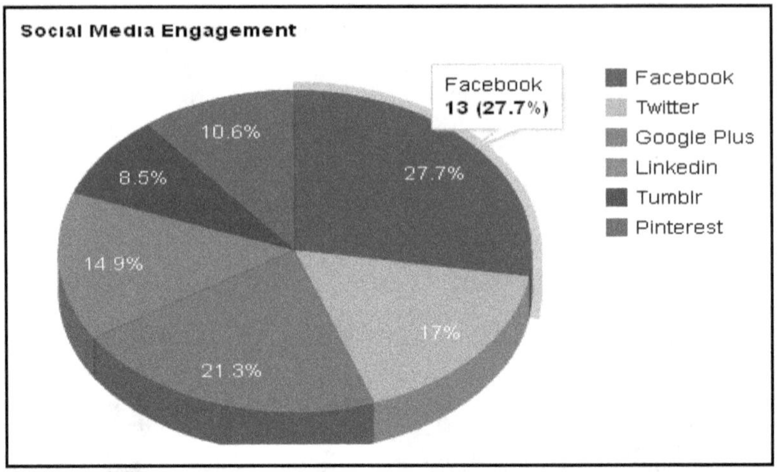

Bar chart

Bar charts allow comparing values of different variables. In traditional BI, companies can analyze their sales by category, the costs of marketing promotion by channel, and so on. When analyzing big data, companies can look at the customer engagement, sales figures by hour, and so on.

An example of a vertical bar chart is as follows:

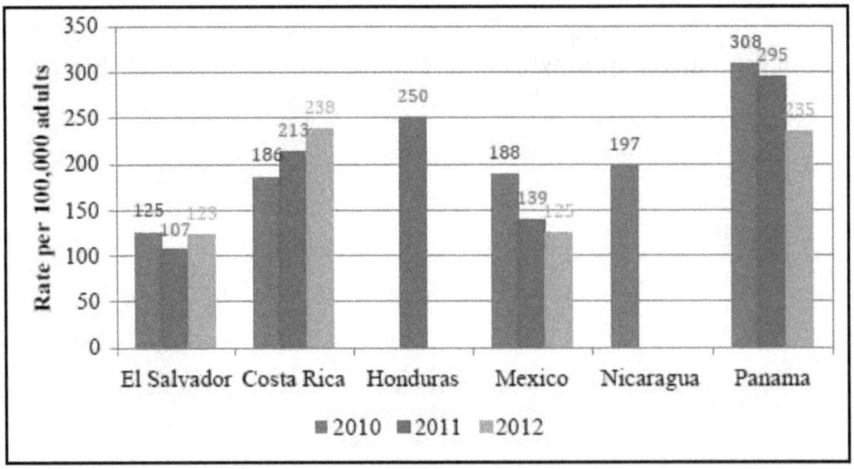

The following screenshot is an example of a horizontal bar chart:

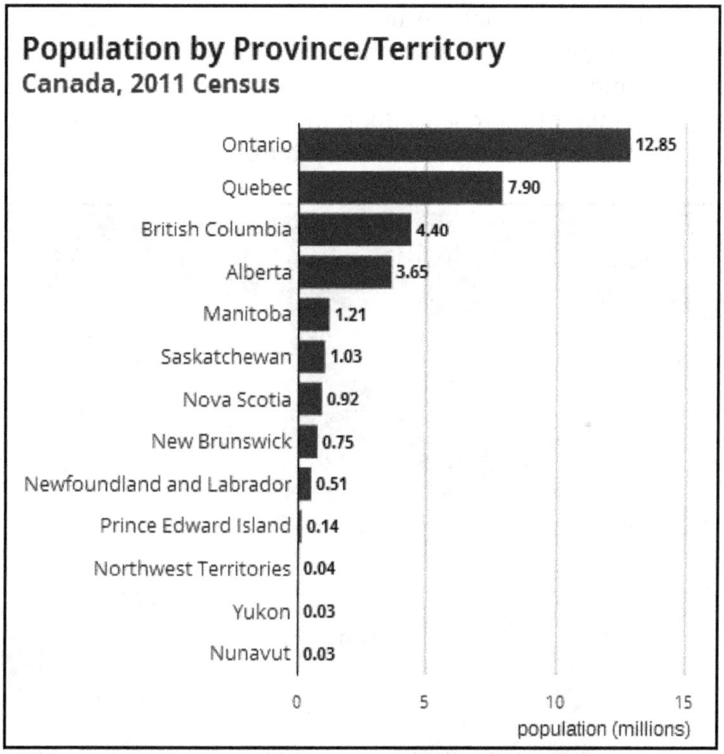

Heat map

Heat maps use colors to represent data. A user may encounter a heat map in Excel that highlights sales in the best performing branch office with green and the worst performing with red. If a retailer is interested in knowing the most frequently visited aisles in the store, they will also use a heat map of their sales floor. In this case, the retailer will analyze big data, such as the data from a video surveillance system:

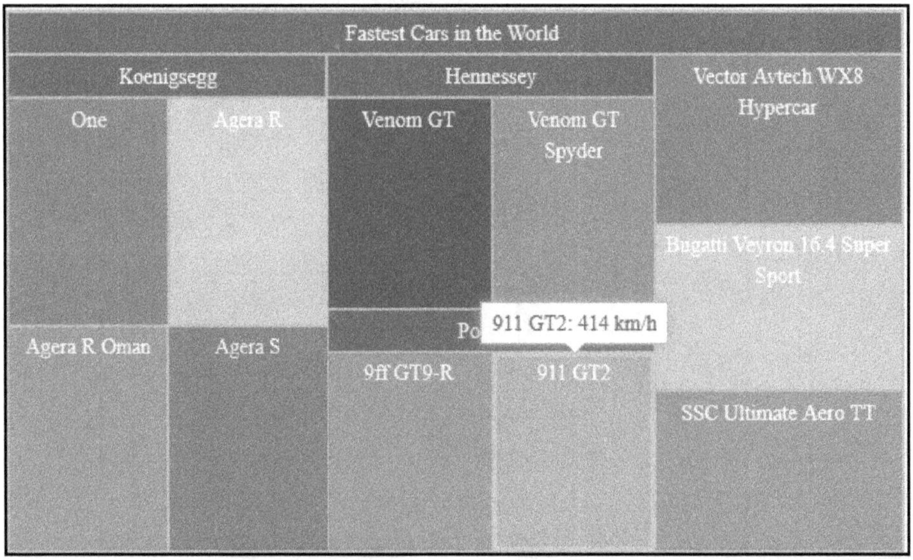

Some really cool visualizations can be seen at `https://blog.hubspot.com/marketing/great-data-visualization-examples` and also at `http://www.mastersindatascience.org/blog/10-cool-big-data-visualizations/`.

Visualization is an art in itself and every use case requires attention to what is being visualized, starting from the chart type, number of data points, colors of the elements, and so on.

Using Python to visualize data

Python provides many extensive capabilities of analysis of big data as well as the plotting and visualization of data.

> *Analyzing and Visualizing Big Data using Python* is covered in `Chapter 4`, *Scientific Computing and Big Data Analysis with Python and Hadoop*.

Here is one such example of using Python, involving a single column:

```
d8 = pd.DataFrame(df, columns=['Quantity'])[0:100]
d8.plot()
```

Here, only the first 100 elements are selected to make the graph less crowded and illustrate the example better.

Now, you'll have:

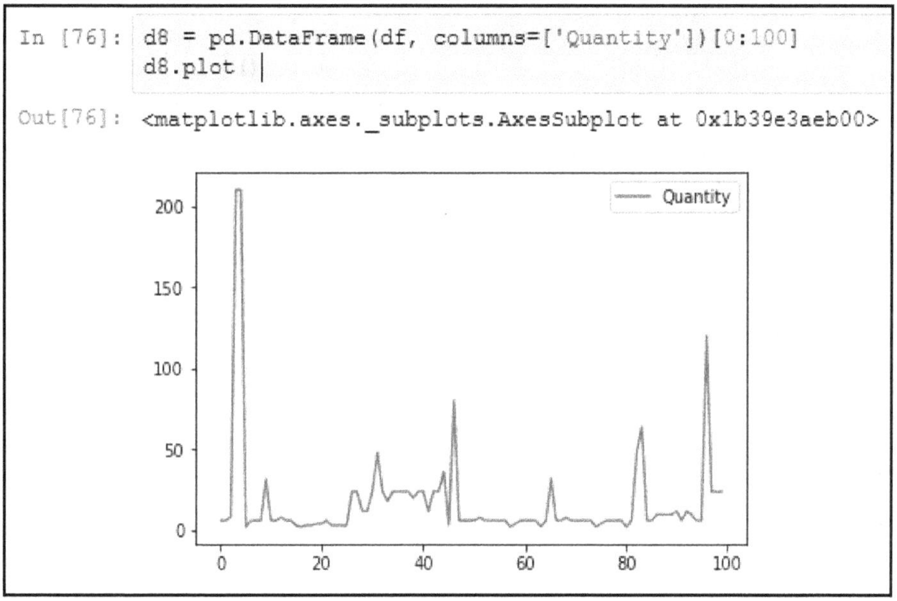

Suppose that you want multiple columns to show up. Look at the following code:

```
d8 = pd.DataFrame(df, columns=['Quantity', 'UnitPrice'])[0:100]
d8.plot()
```

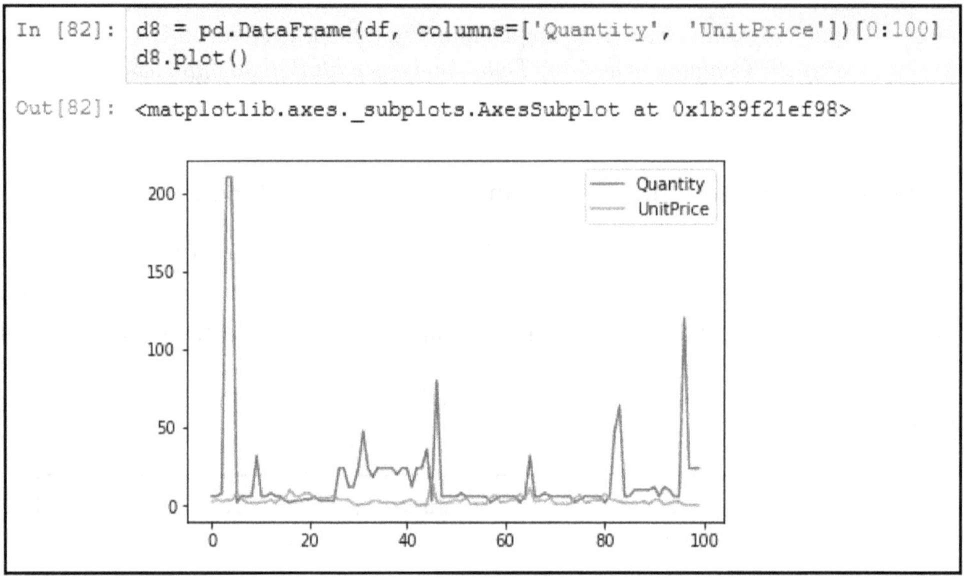

Just remember that it will not plot qualitative data columns such as `Description` but only things that can be graphed, such as `Quantity` and `UnitPrice`.

Using R to visualize data

R provides many extensive capabilities for the analysis of big data as well as the plotting and visualization of data.

TIP

Analyzing and Visualizing Big Data using R is covered in `Chapter 5`, *Statistical Big Data Computing with R and Hadoop.*

Using R, we can also plot a column of choice. Look at this:

```
plot(df$UnitPrice)
```

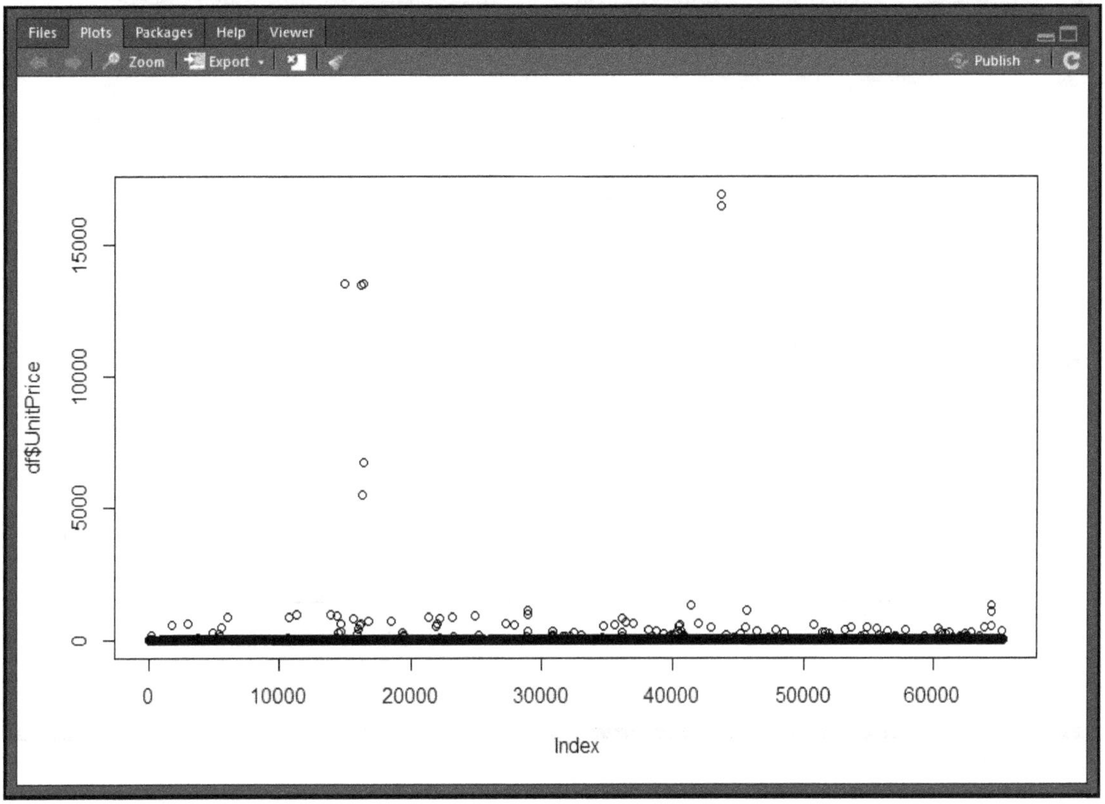

```
plot(d1, type="b")
```

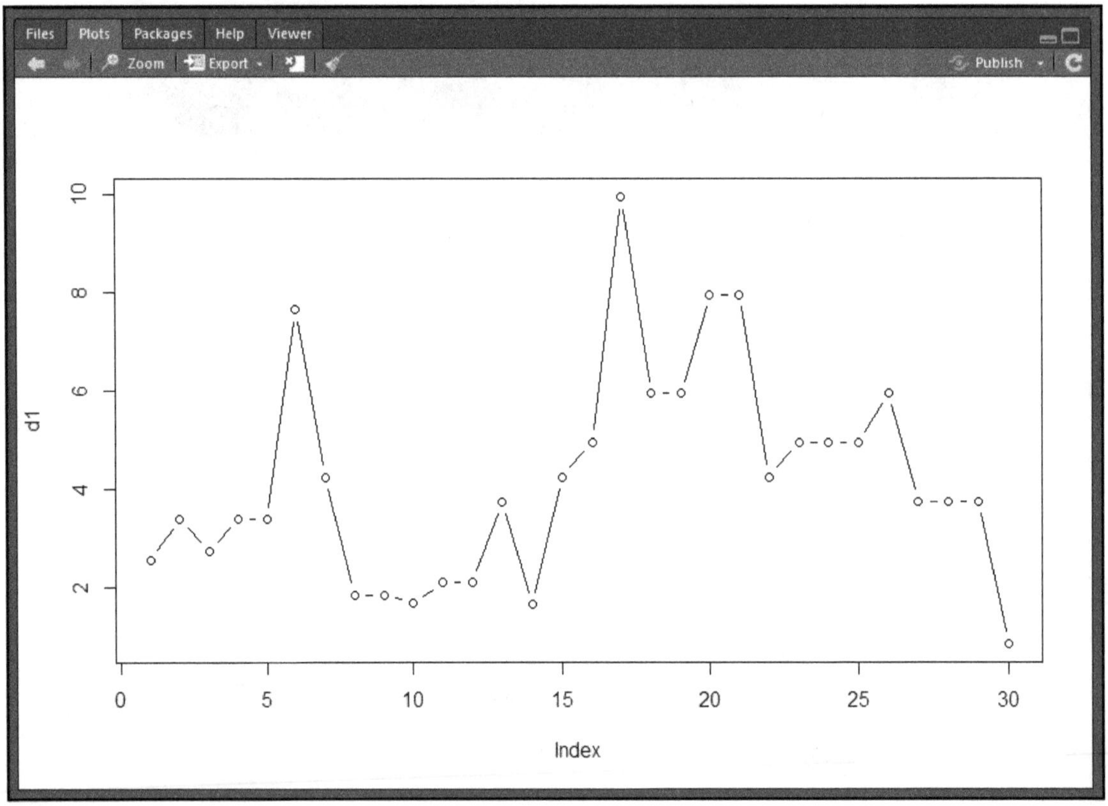

Big data visualization tools

A quick survey of the big data tools marketplace reveals the presence of big names, including Microsoft, SAP, IBM, and SAS. But there are plenty of specialist software vendors offering leading big data visualization tools, and these include Tableau, Qlik, and TIBCO. Leading data visualization products include those offered by the following:

- **IBM Cognos Analytics**: Driven by their commitment to big data, IBM's analytics package offers a variety of self-service options to more easily identify insights. Visit `https://www.ibm.com/analytics/us/en/technology/products/cognos-analytics/`.

- **QlikSense and QlikView**: The Qlik solution touts its ability to perform more complex analysis that finds hidden insights (http://www.qlik.com/us/products/qlik-sense).
- **Microsoft PowerBI**: The Power BI tools enables you to connect with hundreds of data sources, and then publish reports on the Web and across mobile devices. Visit https://powerbi.microsoft.com/en-us/.
- **Oracle Visual Analyzer**: A web-based tool, visual analyzer allows the creation of curated dashboards to help discover correlations and patterns in data. Refer to https://docs.oracle.com/cloud/latest/reportingcs_use/BILUG/GUID-7DC34CA8-3F7C-45CF-8350-441D8D9898EA.htm#BILUG-GUID-7DC34CA8-3F7C-45CF-8350-441D8D9898EA.
- **SAP Lumira**: Calling it self service data visualization for everyone, Lumira allows you to combine your visualizations into storyboards (https://www.sap.com/product/analytics/lumira.html).
- **SAS Visual Analytics**: The SAS solution promotes its *scalability and governance,* along with dynamic visuals and flexible deployment options. Visit https://www.sas.com/en_us/software/business-intelligence/visual-analytics.html.
- **Tableau Desktop**: Tableau's interactive dashboards allow you to *uncover hidden insights on the fly*, and power users can manage metadata to make the most of disparate data sources (https://www.tableau.com/products/desktop).
- **TIBCO Spotfire**: This offers analytics software as a service, and touts itself as a solution that *scales from a small team to the entire organization.* Refer to http://spotfire.tibco.com/.

Summary

In this chapter, we discussed the power of visualization and various concepts behind a good visualization practice. In the next chapter, we will look at the power of Cloud computing and how it is changing the landscape of big data and big data analytics.

SUMMARY

11
Introduction to Cloud Computing

This chapter introduces the concepts of Cloud computing, **Infrastructure as a Service** (**IaaS**), **Platform as a Service** (**PaaS**), and **Software as a Service** (**SaaS**). The top Cloud providers are also discussed briefly.

In a nutshell, the following topics will be covered throughout this chapter:

- Cloud computing basics
- Concepts and terminology
- Goals and benefits
- Risks and challenges
- Roles and boundaries
- Cloud characteristics
- Cloud delivery models
- Cloud deployment models

Whether you are running applications that share photos across millions of mobile users or whether you are supporting the critical operations of your business, a Cloud services platform offers rapid access to flexible and low-cost IT resources. With Cloud computing, you don't need to invest heavily on managing hardware. Instead, you can provision the suitable computing resources that you need to power your ideas or manage your IT department's operations. You can instantaneously access the required resources and pay only as per the usage.

Cloud computing provides a simple way to access servers, storage, databases, and a broad set of application services over the internet. A Cloud services platform such as **Amazon Web Services** (**AWS**) owns and maintains the network-connected hardware required for these application services while you use what you need using a web application.

Concepts and terminology

This section introduces the fundamental concepts of a Cloud and its artifacts.

Cloud

A Cloud refers to a distinct IT environment that is designed for remote provisioning of scalable and measured IT resources. The term originated as a metaphor for the internet to describe a network of networks providing remote access to a set of decentralized IT resources. Before Cloud computing was a formal IT segment, a Cloud symbol was commonly used to represent the Internet in a variety of specifications and mainstream documentation of web-based architectures.

IT resource

An IT resource is a physical or a virtual IT-related artifact that can be either software-based, such as a virtual server or a custom software program, or hardware-based, such as a physical server or a network device.

On-premise

As a distinct and remotely accessible environment, a Cloud represents an option for the deployment of IT resources. An IT resource hosted in a conventional IT enterprise within an organizational boundary (that does not specifically represent a Cloud) is considered to be located on the premises of the IT enterprise, or on-premise (on-premise implies on the premises of a controlled IT environment that is not Cloud-based). This term is used to qualify an IT resource as an alternative to Cloud-based. An IT resource that is on-premise cannot be Cloud-based and vice-versa.

Cloud consumers and Cloud providers

The entity that provides Cloud-based IT resources is the **Cloud provider**. The entity that uses Cloud-based IT resources is the **Cloud consumer**.

Scaling

Scaling represents the ability of an IT resource to handle usage demands.

The following sections describe the types of scaling.

Types of scaling

- **Horizontal scaling**: Scaling out and scaling in
- **Vertical scaling**: Scaling up and scaling down

Horizontal scaling

Allocating or releasing the same type of IT resources is called **horizontal scaling**. Horizontal allocation of resources is referred to as **scaling out** and horizontal releasing of resources is referred to as **scaling in**. Horizontal scaling is a common form of scaling within Cloud environments.

Vertical scaling

Vertical scaling occurs when an existing IT resource is replaced by another of a higher or lower capacity. Replacing an IT resource with another one that has a higher capacity is referred to as **scaling up** and replacing an IT resource with a lower capacity resource is referred to as **scaling down**. Vertical scaling is less common in Cloud environments due to the replacement downtime caused.

Cloud service

Although a Cloud is a remotely accessible environment, not all IT resources within a Cloud can be made remotely accessible. For example, a database or a physical server deployed within a Cloud can be accessible only by other IT resources that are within the same Cloud. A software program with a published API can be deployed specifically to enable access for remote clients.

A Cloud service is any IT resource that is made remotely accessible using a Cloud. Unlike other IT fields that comprise of service technology, such as **service-oriented architecture** (**SOA**), the term **service** within the context of Cloud computing is broad. A Cloud service can exist as a simple web-based software program with a technical interface invoked using a messaging protocol, or as a remote access point for administrative tools or larger environments.

Cloud service consumer

The Cloud service consumer is a temporary role assumed at runtime by a software program while it accesses a Cloud service.

The common types of Cloud service consumers can include software programs and services capable of remotely accessing Cloud services with published service contracts, as well as workstations, laptops, and mobile devices running software capable of remotely accessing other IT resources available as Cloud services.

Goals and benefits

Similar to wholesalers, public Cloud providers base their business model on mass acquisition of IT resources, which are made available to Cloud consumers for attractive prices. This helps organizations to access powerful infrastructure without any infrastructure costs.

The most common economic rationale for investing in Cloud-based IT resources is to reduce initial IT investments, such as hardware, software purchases, and ownership costs. A cloud's measured usage characteristic represents a feature set that allows measured operational expenditures (directly related to business performance) to replace anticipated capital expenditures. This is also referred to as **proportional cost**.

The reduction of costs allow enterprises to start small, to increase IT resource allocation as needed. Moreover, lower initial expenses allow for capital to be redirected to core business investments. Opportunities to decrease costs are derived from the deployment and operation of large-scale data centers by major Cloud providers. Such data centers are commonly located at areas where real estate, IT professionals, and network bandwidth can be obtained at lower costs, allowing higher operational savings.

The same rationale applies to operating systems, middleware or platform software, and application software. Pooled IT resources can be shared by multiple Cloud consumers, resulting in increased or optimal utilization. Operational costs and inefficiencies can be further reduced by using proven practices for optimizing Cloud architecture, management, and governance.

Benefits to Cloud consumers:

- On-demand access to pay-as-you-go computing resources on a short-term basis (such as processors by the hour), and releasing these computing resources when not required
- Access to unlimited computing resources, which are available on demand without the need to prepare for provisioning
- The ability to add or remove IT resources at a rudimentary level, such as modifying available storage disk space by single gigabyte increments
- Infrastructure abstraction of the infrastructure so that applications are not locked into devices or locations and can be easily moved if needed

For example, a company with sizable batch-centric tasks can complete them as quickly as their application software can scale. Using 100 servers for 1 hour costs the same as using 1 server for 100 hours. This elasticity of IT resources achieved without requiring steep initial investments to create a large-scale computing infrastructure can be extremely compelling.

Although the benefits of Cloud computing are obvious, the actual economics can be complex to calculate and assess. The decision to proceed with a Cloud computing adoption strategy will involve much more than a simple comparison between the cost of leasing and the cost of purchasing.

Increased scalability

By providing pools of IT resources, along with tools and technologies designed to leverage them collectively, Clouds can instantly and dynamically allocate IT resources to Cloud consumers, on-demand or using the Cloud consumer's direct configuration. This empowers Cloud consumers to scale their Cloud-based IT resources to accommodate processing fluctuations and peaks automatically or manually. Similarly, Cloud-based IT resources can be released (automatically or manually) as processing demands decrease.

The inherent, built-in feature of clouds to provide flexible levels of scalability to IT resources is directly related to the proportional costs benefits mentioned earlier. Besides the evident financial gain to the automated reduction of scaling, the ability of IT resources to always meet and fulfill unpredictable usage demands avoids potential loss of business that can occur when usage thresholds are met.

Increased availability and reliability

The availability and reliability of IT resources are directly associated with tangible business benefits. Outages limit the time an IT resource can be open for business for its customers, thereby limiting its usage and revenue generating potential. Runtime failures that are not immediately corrected can have a more significant impact during high-volume usage periods. Not only is the IT resource unable to respond to customer requests, but also its unexpected failure can decrease overall customer confidence.

A hallmark of the typical Cloud environment is its intrinsic ability to provide extensive support for increasing the availability of a Cloud-based IT resource to minimize or even eliminate outages, and for increasing its reliability so as to minimize the impact of runtime failure conditions.

Specifically:

- An IT resource with increased availability is accessible for longer periods of time (for example, 22 hours out of a 24 hour day). Cloud providers generally offer resilient IT resources for which they are able to guarantee high levels of availability.
- An IT resource with increased reliability is able to better avoid and recover from exception conditions. The modular architecture of Cloud environments provides extensive failover support that increases reliability.

It is important that organizations carefully examine the SLAs offered by Cloud providers when considering the leasing of Cloud-based services and IT resources. Although many Cloud environments are capable of offering remarkably high levels of availability and reliability, it comes down to the guarantees made in the SLA that typically represent their actual contractual obligations.

Risks and challenges

Several of the most critical Cloud computing challenges, pertaining mostly to Cloud consumers that use IT resources located in public Clouds, are presented and examined.

Increased security vulnerabilities

Migration of business data to the Cloud means that the responsibility of data security becomes shared with the Cloud provider. Remote usage of IT resources requires an expansion of trust boundaries by the Cloud consumer to include the external Cloud. It can be difficult to properly address multi-regional compliance and legal issues due to the fact that third-party Cloud providers will frequently establish data centers in affordable or convenient geographical locations. Cloud consumers will often not be aware of the physical location of their IT resources and data when hosted by public Clouds. For some organizations, this can pose serious legal concerns pertaining to industry or government regulations that specify data privacy and storage policies.

The presence of the multiple boundaries makes it difficult to establish a viable security architecture that spans such trust boundaries without introducing vulnerabilities, unless Cloud consumers and Cloud providers happen to support the same or a compatible security framework. Achieving such compatibility is not easy with public Clouds.

Another consequence of overlapping trust boundaries relates to the Cloud provider's privileged access to Cloud consumer data. The extent to which the data is secure is now limited to the security controls and policies applied by both the Cloud consumer and Cloud provider. Furthermore, there can be overlapping trust boundaries from different Cloud consumers due to the fact that Cloud-based IT resources are commonly shared.

The overlapping of trust boundaries and the increased exposure of data can provide malicious Cloud consumers (human and automated) with greater opportunities to attack IT resources and steal or damage business data. Imagine a scenario whereby two organizations accessing the same Cloud service are required to extend their respective trust boundaries to the Cloud, resulting in overlapping trust boundaries. It can be challenging for the Cloud provider to offer security mechanisms that accommodate the security requirements of both Cloud service consumers.

Reduced operational governance control

Cloud consumers are usually allotted a level of governance control that is lower than that over on-premise IT resources. This can introduce risks associated with how the Cloud provider operates its Cloud, as well as the external connections that are required for communication between the Cloud and the Cloud consumer.

Limited portability between Cloud providers

Due to a lack of established industry standards within the Cloud computing industry, public Clouds are commonly proprietary to various extents. For Cloud consumers that have custom-built solutions with dependencies on these proprietary environments, it can be challenging to move from one Cloud provider to another.

Roles and boundaries

Organizations and humans can assume different types of predefined roles depending on how they relate to and/or interact with a Cloud and its hosted IT resources. Each of the upcoming roles participates in and carries out responsibilities in relation to Cloud-based activity. The following sections define these roles and identify their main interactions.

Cloud provider

The organization that provides Cloud-based IT resources is the Cloud provider. When assuming the role of Cloud provider, an organization is responsible for making Cloud services available to Cloud consumers as per the agreed SLA terms. The Cloud provider is further tasked with any required management and administrative duties to ensure smooth ongoing operation of the overall Cloud infrastructure.

Cloud providers normally own IT resources that are made available for lease by Cloud consumers; however, some Cloud providers also resell IT resources leased from other Cloud providers.

Cloud consumer

A **Cloud consumer** is an organization (or a human) that has a formal contract or arrangement with a Cloud provider to use the IT resources that are made available by the Cloud provider. Specifically, the Cloud consumer uses a Cloud service consumer to access a Cloud service.

Cloud service owner

The person or organization that legally owns a Cloud service is called a **Cloud service owner**. The Cloud service owner can be the Cloud consumer or the Cloud provider that owns the Cloud within which the Cloud service resides.

Cloud resource administrator

A Cloud resource administrator is the person or organization responsible for administering a Cloud-based IT resource (including Cloud services). The Cloud resource administrator can be (or belong to) the Cloud consumer or Cloud provider of the Cloud within which the Cloud service resides. Alternatively, it can be (or belong to) a third-party organization contracted to administer the Cloud-based IT resource.

Additional roles

The NIST Cloud computing reference architecture defines the following supplementary roles:

- **Cloud auditor**: A third party (often accredited) that conducts independent assessments of Cloud environments assumes the role of the Cloud auditor. The typical responsibilities associated with this role include the evaluation of security controls, privacy impacts, and performance. The main purpose of the Cloud auditor role is to provide an unbiased assessment (and possible endorsement) of a Cloud environment to help strengthen the trust relationship between Cloud consumers and Cloud providers.
- **Cloud broker**: This role is assumed by a party that assumes the responsibility of managing and negotiating the usage of Cloud services between Cloud consumers and Cloud providers. Mediation services provided by Cloud brokers include service intermediation, aggregation, and arbitrage.
- **Cloud carrier**: The party responsible for providing the wire-level connectivity between Cloud consumers and Cloud providers assumes the role of the Cloud carrier. This role is often assumed by network and telecommunication providers.

Organizational boundary

An organizational boundary represents the physical perimeter that surrounds a set of IT resources that are owned and governed by an organization.

Trust boundary

When an organization assumes the role of Cloud consumer to access Cloud-based IT resources, it needs to extend its trust beyond the physical boundary of the organization to include parts of the Cloud environment.

Cloud characteristics

An IT environment requires a specific set of characteristics to enable the remote provisioning of scalable and measured IT resources in an effective manner. These characteristics need to exist to a meaningful extent for the IT environment to be considered an effective Cloud.

The following six specific characteristics are common to the majority of Cloud environments:

- On-demand usage
- Ubiquitous access
- Multitenancy (and resource pooling)
- Elasticity
- Measured usage
- Resiliency

On-demand usage

A Cloud consumer can unilaterally access Cloud-based IT resources, giving the Cloud consumer the freedom to self-provision these IT resources. Once configured, usage of the self-provisioned IT resources can be automated, reducing human involvement with the Cloud consumer or Cloud provider. This results in an on-demand usage environment. Also known as **on-demand self-service usage**, this characteristic enables the service-based and usage-driven features found in mainstream Clouds.

Ubiquitous access

Ubiquitous access represents the ability for a Cloud service to be widely accessible. Establishing ubiquitous access for a Cloud service can require support for a range of devices, transport protocols, interfaces, and security technologies. Enabling this level of access generally requires that the Cloud service architecture be tailored to the particular needs of different Cloud service consumers.

Multi-tenancy (and resource pooling)

The characteristic of a software program that enables an instance of the program to serve different consumers (tenants), whereby each is isolated from the other, is referred to as multi-tenancy. A Cloud provider pools its IT resources to serve multiple Cloud service consumers by using multi-tenancy models that frequently rely on the use of virtualization technologies. Through the use of multi-tenancy technology, IT resources can be dynamically assigned and reassigned according to Cloud service consumer demands.

Elasticity

Elasticity is the automated ability of a Cloud to transparently scale IT resources as required in response to runtime conditions or as pre-determined by the Cloud consumer or Cloud provider. Elasticity is often considered a core justification for the adoption of Cloud computing, primarily due to the fact that it is closely associated with the reduced investment and proportional costs benefit. Cloud providers with vast IT resources can offer the greatest range of elasticity.

Measured usage

The measured usage characteristic represents the ability of a Cloud platform to keep track of the usage of its IT resources, primarily by Cloud consumers. Based on what is measured, the Cloud provider can charge a Cloud consumer only for the IT resources actually used and/or for the time frame during which access to the IT resources was granted. In this context, measured usage is closely related to the on-demand characteristics.

Resiliency

Resilient computing is a form of failover that distributes redundant implementations of IT resources across physical locations. IT resources can be preconfigured so that if one becomes deficient, processing is automatically handed over to another redundant implementation. Within Cloud computing, the characteristic of resiliency can refer to redundant IT resources within the same Cloud (but in different physical locations) or across multiple Clouds.

Cloud delivery models

A Cloud delivery model represents a specific, pre-packaged combination of IT resources offered by a Cloud provider. Three common Cloud delivery models have become widely established and formalized:

- IaaS
- PaaS
- SaaS

Infrastructure as a Service

The IaaS delivery model represents a self-contained IT environment that comprises infrastructure-centric IT resources that can be accessed and managed using Cloud service-based interfaces and tools. This environment can include hardware, network, connectivity, operating systems, and other raw IT resources. In contrast to traditional hosting or outsourcing environments, with IaaS, IT resources are usually virtualized and packaged into bundles that simplify runtime scaling and customization of the infrastructure.

The general purpose of an IaaS environment is to provide Cloud consumers with a high level of control and responsibility over its configuration and utilization. The IT resources provided by IaaS are generally not preconfigured, placing the administrative responsibility directly upon the Cloud consumer. This model is used by Cloud consumers who require a high amount of control over the Cloud-based environment they intend to create.

Sometimes Cloud providers contract IaaS offerings from other Cloud providers in order to scale their own Cloud environments. The types and brands of IT resources provided by IaaS products that are offered by different Cloud providers can vary. IT resources available through IaaS environments are generally offered as freshly initialized virtual instances. A central and primary IT resource within a typical IaaS environment is the virtual server.

Platform as a Service

The PaaS delivery model represents a predefined, ready-to-use environment typically comprised of already deployed and configured IT resources. Specifically, PaaS relies on (and is primarily defined by) the usage of a ready-made environment that establishes a set of pre-packaged products and tools used to support the entire delivery life cycle of custom applications.

Common reasons a Cloud consumer would use and invest in a PaaS environment:

- The Cloud consumer wants to extend on-premise environments into the Cloud for scalability and economic purposes
- The Cloud consumer uses the ready-made environment to entirely substitute an on-premise environment
- The Cloud consumer wants to become a Cloud provider and deploys its own Cloud services to be made available to other external Cloud consumers

By working within a ready-made platform, the Cloud consumer is spared the administrative burden of setting up and maintaining the bare infrastructure IT resources provided using the IaaS model.

Software as a Service

A software program positioned as a shared Cloud service and made available as a product or generic utility represents the typical profile of a SaaS offering. The SaaS delivery model is typically used to make a reusable Cloud service widely available (often commercially) to a range of Cloud consumers. An entire marketplace exists around SaaS products that can be leased and used for different purposes and using different terms.

A Cloud consumer is generally granted very limited administrative control over a SaaS implementation. It is most often provisioned by the Cloud provider, but it can be legally owned by whichever entity assumes the Cloud service owner role. For example, an organization acting as a Cloud consumer while using and working with a PaaS environment can build a Cloud service that it decides to deploy in that same environment as a SaaS offering. The same organization then effectively assumes the Cloud provider role, as the SaaS-based Cloud service is made available to other organizations that act as Cloud consumers when using that Cloud service.

Combining Cloud delivery models

The three base Cloud delivery models comprise a natural provisioning hierarchy, allowing opportunities for combined application of the models to be explored. The upcoming sections briefly highlight considerations pertaining to two common combinations.

IaaS + PaaS

A PaaS environment will be built upon an underlying infrastructure comparable to the physical and virtual servers and other IT resources provided in an IaaS environment.

IaaS + PaaS + SaaS

All three Cloud delivery models can be combined to establish layers of IT resources that build upon each other. For example, by adding on to the preceding layered architecture, the ready-made environment provided by the PaaS environment can be used by the Cloud consumer organization to develop and deploy its own SaaS Cloud services, which it can then make available as commercial products.

The following are all the layers in IaaS, PaaS, and SaaS:

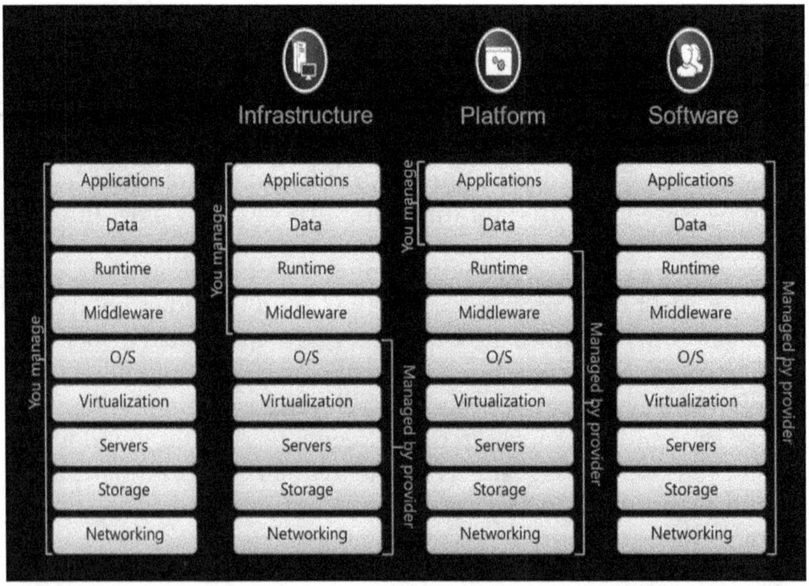

Cloud deployment models

A Cloud deployment model represents a specific type of Cloud environment, primarily distinguished by ownership, size, and access.

The following sections describe the four common Cloud deployment models:

- Public Cloud
- Community Cloud
- Private Cloud
- Hybrid Cloud

Public Clouds

A public Cloud is a publicly accessible Cloud environment owned by a third-party Cloud provider. The IT resources on public Clouds are usually provisioned using the previously described Cloud delivery models and are generally offered to Cloud consumers at a cost or are commercialized using other avenues (such as advertisements).

The Cloud provider is responsible for the creation and ongoing maintenance of the public Cloud and its IT resources. Many of the scenarios and architectures explored in upcoming chapters involve public Clouds and the relationship between the providers and consumers of IT resources using public Clouds.

Community Clouds

A community Cloud is similar to a public Cloud except that its access is limited to a specific community of Cloud consumers. The community Cloud may be jointly owned by the community members or by a third-party Cloud provider that provisions a public Cloud with limited access. The member Cloud consumers of the community typically share the responsibility for defining and evolving the community Cloud.

Membership in the community does not necessarily guarantee access to or control of all of the Cloud's IT resources. Parties outside the community are generally not granted access unless allowed by the community.

Private Clouds

A private Cloud is owned by a single organization. Private Clouds enable an organization to use Cloud computing technology as a means of centralizing access to IT resources by different parts, locations, or departments of the organization. When a private Cloud exists as a controlled environment, the problems described in the *Risks and Challenges* section from `Chapter 3`, *Big Data Processing with MapReduce*, do not tend to apply.

The use of a private Cloud can change how organizational and trust boundaries are defined and applied. The actual administration of a private Cloud environment may be carried out by internal or outsourced staff.

With a private Cloud, the same organization is technically both the Cloud consumer and Cloud provider. In order to differentiate these roles:

- A separate organizational department typically assumes the responsibility for provisioning the Cloud (and therefore assumes the Cloud provider role)
- Departments requiring access to the private Cloud assume the Cloud consumer role

A Cloud service consumer in the organization's on-premise environment accesses a Cloud service hosted on the same organization's private Cloud using a virtual private network.

It is important to use the terms on-premise and cloud-based correctly within the context of a private Cloud. Even though the private Cloud may physically reside on the organization's premises, the IT resources it hosts are still considered Cloud-based as long as they are made remotely accessible to Cloud consumers. The IT resources hosted outside of the private Cloud by the departments acting as Cloud consumers are therefore considered on-premise in relation to the private-cloud-based IT resources.

Hybrid Clouds

A hybrid Cloud is a Cloud environment comprised of two or more different Cloud deployment models. For example, a Cloud consumer may choose to deploy Cloud services processing sensitive data to a private Cloud and other, less sensitive Cloud services to a public Cloud. The result of this combination is a hybrid deployment model.

Shown here is an organization using a hybrid Cloud architecture that utilizes both a private and public Cloud:

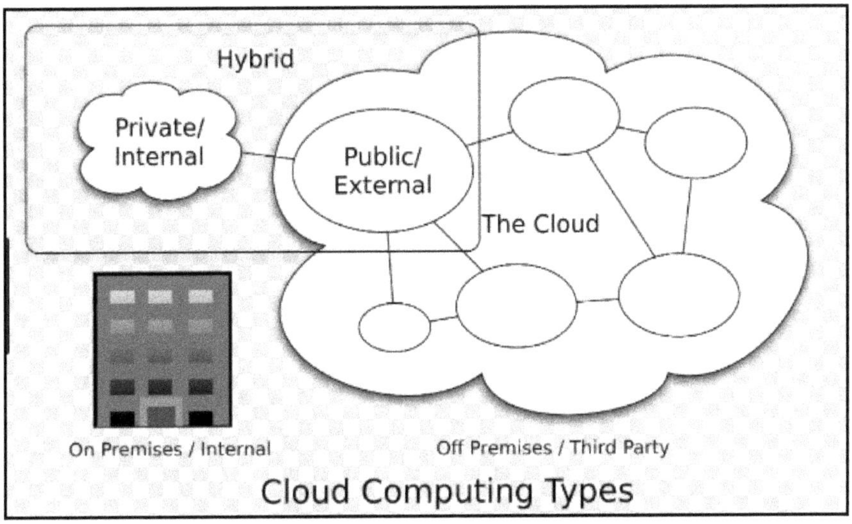

Hybrid deployment architectures can be complex and challenging to create and maintain due to the potential disparities in Cloud environments and the fact that management responsibilities are typically split between private Cloud providers and public Cloud providers.

Summary

In this chapter, we discussed Cloud computing and the key terminology used to understand and implement Cloud computing.

In the next chapter, we will explore one of the most popular Cloud providers from Amazon: AWS.

12

Using Amazon Web Services

This chapter introduces you to the concept of AWS and its services, which are useful for performing big data analytics using **Elastic MapReduce** (**EMR**) while you set up a Hadoop cluster in AWS Cloud. We will look at the key components and services offered by AWS and get an idea of what we can do with the various functionalities offered by the components and services of AWS.

In a nutshell, the following topics will be covered in this chapter:

- Amazon Elastic Compute Cloud
- Launching multiple instances from an AMI
- What is AWS Lambda?
- Introduction to Amazon S3
- Amazon DynamoDB
- Amazon Kinesis Data Streams
- AWS Glue
- Amazon EMR

Amazon Elastic Compute Cloud

Amazon Elastic Compute Cloud (**Amazon EC2**) is a web service that provides secure, resizable computing capacity on a Cloud. It is designed to make web-scale Cloud computing easier for developers.

Amazon EC2's simple web service interface allows you to obtain and configure capacity with ease. It provides you with complete control of your computing resources and let's you use Amazon's computing environment. Amazon EC2 reduces the time required to obtain and boot new server instances to minutes, allowing you to quickly scale capacity (both up and down), as your computing requirements change. Amazon EC2 allows you to save computing costs as you pay only for capacity that you actually use. Amazon EC2 provides developers with the tools to build failure-resilient applications and to isolate them from common failure scenarios.

Elastic web-scale computing

Amazon EC2 enables you to increase or decrease capacity within a span of minutes. You can commission one or several server instances simultaneously. You can also use **Amazon EC2 Auto Scaling** to maintain the availability of your EC2 fleet and automatically scale your fleet up and down depending on your needs, in order to maximize performance and minimize cost. To scale multiple services, you can use **AWS Auto Scaling**.

Complete control of operations

You have complete control of your instances, including root access, and have the ability to interact with them as you would with any machine. You can stop any instance while retaining the data on the boot partition, and then subsequently restart the same instance using web service APIs. Instances can be rebooted remotely using web service APIs, and you also have access to their console output.

Flexible Cloud hosting services

You have the choice of multiple instance types, operating systems, and software packages. Amazon EC2 allows you to select a configuration of memory, CPU, instance storage, and the boot partition size that is optimal for your choice of operating system and application. For example, the choice of operating systems includes numerous Linux distributions and Microsoft Windows Server.

Integration

Amazon EC2 is integrated with most AWS services, such as **Amazon Simple Storage Service** (**Amazon S3**), **Amazon Relational Database Service** (**Amazon RDS**), and **Amazon Virtual Private Cloud** (**Amazon VPC**), to provide complete, secure solutions for computing, query processing, and Cloud storage across a wide range of applications.

High reliability

Amazon EC2 offers a highly reliable environment where replacement instances can be rapidly and predictably commissioned. The service runs within Amazon's proven network infrastructure and data centers. The Amazon EC2 **service-level agreement** (**SLA**) provides 99.99% availability for each Amazon EC2 region.

Security

Cloud security at AWS is the highest priority. As an AWS customer, you will benefit from a data center and network architecture built to meet the requirements of the most security-sensitive organizations. Amazon EC2 works in conjunction with Amazon VPC to provide security and robust networking functionalities for your compute resources.

Inexpensive

Amazon EC2 passes on to you the financial benefits of Amazon's scale. You pay a very low rate for the compute capacity you actually consume. See Amazon EC2's instance purchasing options for more details: `https://aws.amazon.com/ec2/pricing/`.

Easy to start

There are several ways to get started with Amazon EC2. You can use the AWS Management Console, the AWS **command-line tools** which are accessible via the **CLI(Command Line Interface)**, or using the AWS SDKs(Software Development Kit). AWS is easy to start and operate. To learn more, please visit our tutorials at `https://aws.amazon.com/getting-started/tutorials/`.

Instances and Amazon Machine Images

An **Amazon Machine Image** (**AMI**) is a template that contains a software configuration (for example, an operating system, an application server, and applications). From an AMI, you launch an instance, which is a copy of the AMI running as a virtual server in the Cloud. You can launch multiple instances of an AMI, as shown in the following screenshot:

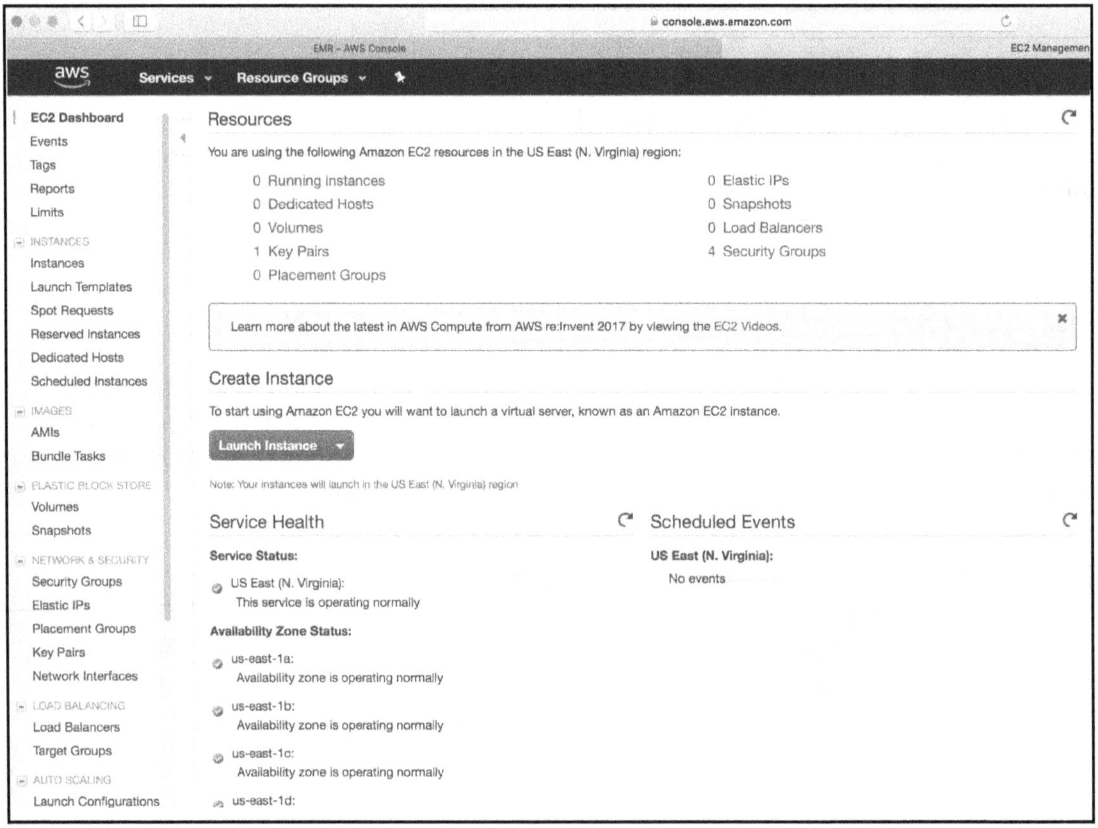

Launching multiple instances of an AMI

Your instances keep running until you stop or terminate them, or until they fail. If an instance fails, you can launch a new one from the AMI.

Instances

You can launch different types of instance from a single AMI. An instance type essentially determines the hardware of the host computer used for your instance. Each instance type offers different compute and memory capabilities. Select an instance type based on the amount of memory and computing power that you need for the application or software that you plan to run on the instance. For more information about the hardware specifications for each Amazon EC2 instance type, see *Amazon EC2* instances at this link `https://aws.amazon.com/ec2/instance-types/`.

After you launch an instance, it looks like a traditional host, and you can interact with it as you would any computer. You have complete control of your instances; you can use `sudo` to run commands that require root privileges.

AMIs

Amazon Web Services (**AWS**) publishes many AMIs that contain common software configurations for public use. In addition, members of the AWS developer community have published their own custom AMIs. You can also create your own custom AMI or AMIs; doing so enables you to quickly and easily start new instances that have everything you need. For example, if your application is a website or a web service, your AMI could include a web server, the associated static content, and the code for the dynamic pages. As a result, after you launch an instance from this AMI, your web server starts and your application is ready to accept requests.

All AMIs are categorized as either backed by Amazon EBS, which means that the root device for an instance launched from the AMI is an Amazon EBS volume, or backed by an instance store, which means that the root device for an instance launched from the AMI is an instance store volume created from a template stored in Amazon S3.

Regions and availability zones

Amazon EC2 is hosted in multiple locations worldwide. These locations are composed of regions and availability zones. Each region is a separate geographical area. Each region has multiple isolated locations known as availability zones. Amazon EC2 provides you with the ability to place resources such as instances and data in multiple locations. Resources aren't replicated across regions unless you do so specifically.

Amazon operates state-of-the-art, highly available data centers. Although rare, failures can occur that affect the availability of instances that are in the same location. If you host all your instances in a single location that is affected by such a failure, none of your instances will be available.

Region and availability zone concepts

Each region is completely independent. Each availability zone is isolated, but the availability zones in a region are connected through low-latency links. The following diagram illustrates the relationship between regions and availability zones:

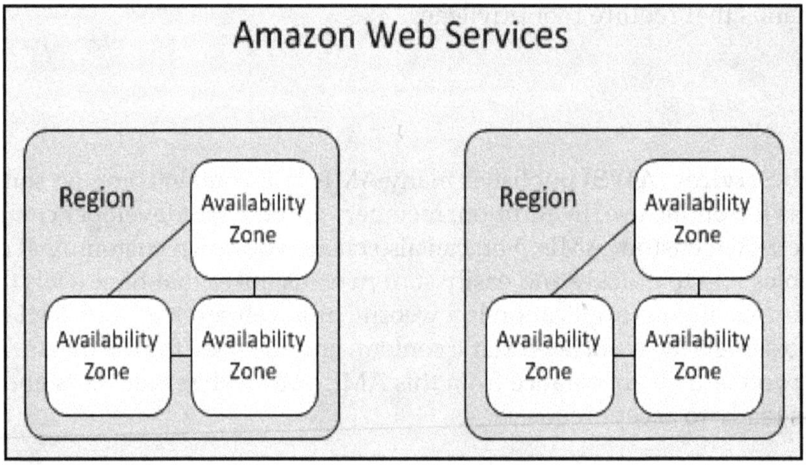

Regions

Each Amazon EC2 region is designed to be completely isolated from the other Amazon EC2 regions. This achieves the greatest possible fault tolerance and stability.

When you view your resources, you'll only see the resources tied to the region you've specified. This is because regions are isolated from each other, and we don't replicate resources across regions automatically.

Availability zones

When you launch an instance, you can select an availability zone or have one assigned for you. If you distribute your instances across multiple availability zones and one instance fails, you can design your application so that an instance in another availability zone can handle requests.

You can also use Elastic IP addresses to mask the failure of an instance in one availability zone by rapidly remapping the address to an instance in another availability zone. For more information, see *Elastic IP Addresses* at this link is `https://docs.aws.amazon.com/AWSEC2/latest/UserGuide/elastic-ip-addresses-eip.html`.

Available regions

Your account determines the regions that are available to you. For example, an AWS account provides multiple regions so that you can launch Amazon EC2 instances in locations that meet your requirements. For example, you might want to launch instances in Europe to be closer to your European customers or to meet legal requirements.

An AWS GovCloud (US) account provides access to the AWS GovCloud (US) region only. For more information, see *AWS GovCloud (US) Region*.

An Amazon AWS (China) account provides access to the China (Beijing) region only.

The following table lists the regions provided by an AWS account:

Region name	Region	Endpoint	Protocol
US East (Ohio)	us-east-2	`rds.us-east-2.amazonaws.com`	HTTPS
US East (N. Virginia)	us-east-1	`rds.us-east-1.amazonaws.com`	HTTPS
US West (N. California)	us-west-1	`rds.us-west-1.amazonaws.com`	HTTPS
US West (Oregon)	us-west-2	`rds.us-west-2.amazonaws.com`	HTTPS
Asia Pacific (Tokyo)	ap-northeast-1	`rds.ap-northeast-1.amazonaws.com`	HTTPS
Asia Pacific (Seoul)	ap-northeast-2	`rds.ap-northeast-2.amazonaws.com`	HTTPS
Asia Pacific (Osaka-Local)	ap-northeast-3	`rds.ap-northeast-3.amazonaws.com`	HTTPS
Asia Pacific (Mumbai)	ap-south-1	`rds.ap-south-1.amazonaws.com`	HTTPS
Asia Pacific (Singapore)	ap-southeast-1	`rds.ap-southeast-1.amazonaws.com`	HTTPS
Asia Pacific (Sydney)	ap-southeast-2	`rds.ap-southeast-2.amazonaws.com`	HTTPS
Canada (Central)	ca-central-1	`rds.ca-central-1.amazonaws.com`	HTTPS

China (Beijing)	cn-north-1	`rds.cn-north-1.amazonaws.com.cn`	HTTPS
China (Ningxia)	cn-northwest-1	`rds.cn-northwest-1.amazonaws.com.cn`	HTTPS
EU (Frankfurt)	eu-central-1	`rds.eu-central-1.amazonaws.com`	HTTPS
EU (Ireland)	eu-west-1	`rds.eu-west-1.amazonaws.com`	HTTPS
EU (London)	eu-west-2	`rds.eu-west-2.amazonaws.com`	HTTPS
EU (Paris)	eu-west-3	`rds.eu-west-3.amazonaws.com`	HTTPS
South America (São Paulo)	sa-east-1	`rds.sa-east-1.amazonaws.com`	HTTPS

Regions and endpoints

When you work with an instance using the command-line interface or API actions, you must specify its regional endpoint. For more information about the regions and endpoints for Amazon EC2, see *Regions and endpoints* at this link: `https://docs.aws.amazon.com/general/latest/gr/rande.html`.

Instance types

When you launch an instance, the instance type that you specify determines the hardware of the host computer used for your instance. Each instance type offers different compute, memory, and storage capabilities and is grouped in an instance family based on these capabilities. Select an instance type based on the requirements of the application or software that you plan to run on your instance.

Tag basics

Tags enable you to categorize your AWS resources in different ways, for example, by purpose, owner, or environment. This is useful when you have many resources of the same type—you can quickly identify a specific resource based on the tags you've assigned to it. Each tag consists of a key and an optional value, both of which you define. For example, you could define a set of tags for your account's Amazon EC2 instances that helps you track each instance's owner and stack level.

Amazon EC2 key pairs

Amazon EC2 uses public key cryptography to encrypt and decrypt login information. Public key cryptography uses a public key to encrypt a piece of data, such as a password, then the recipient uses the private key to decrypt the data. The public and private keys are known as a **key pair**.

Amazon EC2 security groups for Linux instances

A security group acts as a virtual firewall that controls the traffic for one or more instances. When you launch an instance, you associate one or more security groups with the instance. You can add rules to each security group that allow traffic to or from its associated instances. You can modify the rules for a security group at any time; the new rules are automatically applied to all instances that are associated with the security group after a short period. When you decide whether to allow traffic to reach an instance, you can evaluate all the rules from all the security groups that are associated with the instance.

Elastic IP addresses

An Elastic IP address is a static IPv4 address designed for dynamic Cloud computing. An Elastic IP address is associated with your AWS account. With an Elastic IP address, you can mask the failure of an instance or software by rapidly remapping the address to another instance in your account.

Amazon EC2 and Amazon Virtual Private Cloud

Amazon VPC enables you to define a virtual network in your own logically isolated area within the AWS Cloud, known as a VPC. You can launch your AWS resources, such as instances, into your VPC. Your VPC closely resembles a traditional network that you might operate in your own data center, with the benefits of using AWS's scalable infrastructure. You can configure your VPC, or select its IP address range, create subnets, and configure route tables, network gateways, and security settings. You can connect instances in your VPC to the internet. You can connect your VPC to your own corporate data center, making the AWS Cloud an extension of your data center. To protect the resources in each subnet, you can use multiple layers of security, including security groups and network access control lists. For more information, see the *Amazon VPC User Guide* at `https://aws.amazon.com/documentation/vpc/`.

Amazon Elastic Block Store

Amazon Elastic Block Store (**Amazon EBS**) provides block-level storage volumes for use with EC2 instances. EBS volumes are highly available and reliable storage volumes that can be attached to any running instance which are in the same availability zone. EBS volumes attached to an EC2 instance are exposed as storage volumes that persist independently from the life of the instance. With Amazon EBS, you pay only for what you use. For more information about Amazon EBS pricing, see the *Projecting costs* section of the Amazon EBS page `https://aws.amazon.com/ebs/`.

Amazon EBS is recommended when data must be quickly accessible and requires long-term persistence. EBS volumes are particularly well-suited for use as the primary storage for filesystems, databases, or for any applications that require fine granular updates and access to raw, unformatted, block-level storage. Amazon EBS is well suited to both database-style applications that rely on random reads and writes, and to throughput-intensive applications that perform long, continuous reads and writes.

Amazon EC2 instance store

An instance store provides temporary block-level storage for your instance. This storage is located on disks that are physically attached to the host computer. An instance store is ideal for the temporary storage of information that changes frequently, such as buffers, caches, scratch data, and other temporary content, or for data that is replicated across a fleet of instances, such as a load-balanced pool of web servers.

An instance store consists of one or more instance store volumes exposed as block devices. The size of an instance store as well as the number of devices available varies by instance type. While an instance store is dedicated to a particular instance, the disk subsystem is shared among instances on a host computer.

What is AWS Lambda?

AWS Lambda is a compute service that lets you run code without provisioning or managing servers. AWS Lambda executes your code only when needed and scales automatically, from a few requests per day to thousands per second. You pay only for the compute time you consume—there is no charge when your code is not running. With AWS Lambda, you can run code for virtually any type of application or backend service, all with zero administration. AWS Lambda runs your code on a high-availability compute infrastructure and performs all of the administration of the compute resources, including server and operating system maintenance, capacity provisioning and automatic scaling, code monitoring, and logging. All you need to do is supply your code in one of the languages that AWS Lambda supports (currently Node.js, Java, C#, Go, and Python).

You can use AWS Lambda to run your code in response to events, such as changes to data in an Amazon S3 bucket or an Amazon DynamoDB table; to run your code in response to HTTP requests using Amazon API Gateway; or invoke your code using API calls made using AWS SDKs. With these capabilities, you can use Lambda to easily build data processing triggers for AWS services such as Amazon S3 and Amazon DynamoDB to process streaming data stored in Kinesis, or to create your own backend that operates at AWS scale offering superior performance and the necessary security around the system.

You can also build serverless applications composed of functions that are triggered by events and automatically deploy them using **AWS CodePipeline** and **AWS CodeBuild**. For more information, see *Deploying Lambda-based Applications* at `https://docs.aws.amazon.com/lambda/latest/dg/deploying-lambda-apps.html`.

When should I use AWS Lambda?

AWS Lambda is an ideal compute platform for many application scenarios, provided that you can write your application code in languages supported by AWS Lambda (that is, Node.js, Java, Go, C#, and Python) and run within the AWS Lambda standard runtime environment and resources provided by Lambda.

Introduction to Amazon S3

Amazon S3 runs on the world's largest global Cloud infrastructure, and was built from the ground up to deliver a customer promise of 99.999999999% durability. Data is automatically distributed across a minimum of three physical facilities that are geographically separated within an AWS region, and Amazon S3 can also automatically replicate data to any other AWS region.

Learn more about the AWS Global Cloud Infrastructure at `https://aws.amazon.com/`.

Getting started with Amazon S3

Amazon S3 is storage for the internet. You can use Amazon S3 to store and retrieve any amount of data at any time, from anywhere on the web. You can accomplish these tasks using the AWS Management Console, which is a simple and intuitive web interface. This guide introduces you to Amazon S3 and how to use the AWS Management Console to manage the storage space offered by Amazon S3.

Companies today need the ability to easily and securely collect, store, and analyze their data on a massive scale. Amazon S3 is object storage built to store and retrieve any amount of data from anywhere—websites and mobile apps, corporate applications, and data from IoT sensors or devices, and stores data for millions of applications used by market leaders in every industry. S3 provides comprehensive security and compliance capabilities that meet even the most stringent regulatory requirements. It gives customers flexibility in the way they manage data for cost optimization, access control, and compliance. S3 provides query-in-place functionality, allowing you to run powerful analytics directly on your data at rest in S3. And Amazon S3 is the most supported storage platform available, with the largest ecosystem of ISV solutions and systems integrator partners.

Comprehensive security and compliance capabilities

Amazon S3 is the only Cloud storage platform that supports three different forms of encryption. S3 offers sophisticated integration with **AWS CloudTrail** to log, monitor, and retain storage API call activities for auditing. Amazon S3 is the only Cloud storage platform with **Amazon Macie**, which uses machine learning to automatically discover, classify, and protect sensitive data in AWS. S3 supports security standards and compliance certifications including PCI-DSS, HIPAA/HITECH, FedRAMP, the EU Data Protection Directive, and FISMA, helping satisfy compliance requirements for virtually every regulatory agency around the globe.

Learn more about security at `https://aws.amazon.com/security/`.

Learn more about compliance at `https://aws.amazon.com/compliance/`.

Query in place

Amazon S3 allows you to run sophisticated big data analytics on your data without moving the data into a separate analytics system. Amazon Athena provides on-demand query access to vast amounts of unstructured data to anyone who knows SQL. **Amazon Redshift Spectrum** lets you run queries spanning your data warehouse and S3. Only AWS offers Amazon S3 Select (currently in preview for testing purposes), a way to retrieve only the subset of data you need from an S3 object, which can improve the performance of most applications that frequently access data from S3 by up to 400%.

Learn more about querying in place at `https://aws.amazon.com/blogs/aws/amazon-redshift-spectrum-exabyte-scale-in-place-queries-of-s3-data/`.

Flexible management

Amazon S3 offers the most flexible set of storage management and administration capabilities. Storage administrators can classify, report, and visualize data usage trends to reduce costs and improve service levels. Objects can be tagged with unique, customizable metadata so customers can see and control storage consumption, cost, and security separately for each workload. The S3 inventory feature delivers scheduled reports about objects and their metadata for maintenance, compliance, or analytics operations. S3 can also analyze object access patterns to build life cycle policies that automate tiering, deletion, and retention. Since Amazon S3 works with AWS Lambda, customers can log activities, define alerts, and invoke workflows, all without any additional infrastructure.

Learn more about S3 storage management at `https://aws.amazon.com/s3/`.

Most supported platform with the largest ecosystem

In addition to integration with most AWS services, the Amazon S3 ecosystem includes several consulting system integrators and independent software vendor partners, with more joining every month. And the AWS Marketplace offers 35 categories and more than 3,500 software listings from over 1,100 ISVs that are preconfigured to deploy on the AWS Cloud. **AWS Partner Network** (**APN**) partners have adapted their services and software to work with S3 for solutions such as backup and recovery, archiving, and disaster recovery.

Learn more about AWS storage partners at `https://aws.amazon.com/backup-recovery/partner-solutions/`.

Easy and flexible data transfer

You can choose from a wide range of options to transfer your data into (or out of) Amazon S3. S3's simple and reliable APIs make it easy to transfer data over the internet. **Amazon S3 Transfer Acceleration** is ideal for data uploads across large geographical distances. AWS direct connect provides consistently high bandwidth and low latency data transfer for moving large amounts of data to AWS using a dedicated network connection. You can use the AWS Snowball and **AWS Snowball Edge** appliances for petabyte-scale data transfer, or AWS Snowmobile for even larger datasets. **AWS Storage Gateway** provides you with a physical or virtual data transfer appliance to use on-premises to easily move volumes or files into the AWS Cloud.

Learn more about Cloud data migration at `https://aws.amazon.com/cloud-migration/`.

Backup and recovery

Amazon S3 offers a highly durable, scalable, and secure destination for backing up and archiving your critical data. You can use S3's versioning capability to protect your stored data. You can also define life cycle rules to migrate less frequently used data to S3 Standard-Infrequent Access and archive sets of objects to Amazon Glacier.

Learn more about backup and recovery at `https://aws.amazon.com/backup-restore/`.

Data archiving

Amazon S3 and Amazon Glacier provide a range of storage classes to meet the needs of compliance archives for regulated industries or active archives for organizations who need fast, infrequent access to archive data. Amazon Glacier Vault Lock provides **write-once-read-many** (**WORM**) storage to meet compliance requirements for records retention. Lifecycle policies make transitioning data from Amazon S3 to Amazon Glacier simple, helping automate the transition based on customer-defined policies.

Learn more about data archiving at `https://aws.amazon.com/archive/`.

Data lakes and big data analytics

Whether you're storing pharmaceutical or financial data, or multimedia files such as photos and videos, Amazon S3 can be used as your data lake for big data analytics. AWS offers a comprehensive portfolio of services to help you manage big data by reducing costs, scaling to meet demand, and increasing the speed of innovation.

Learn more about data lakes and big data analytics at `https://aws.amazon.com/blogs/big-data/introducing-the-data-lake-solution-on-aws/`.

Hybrid Cloud storage

AWS Storage Gateway helps you build hybrid Cloud storage, augmenting your existing local storage environment with the durability and scale of Amazon S3. Use it to burst a workload from your site into the Cloud for processing and then bring the results back. Tier colder or less valuable data off of your primary storage into the Cloud to lower costs and extend your on-premises investment. Or, simply use it to incrementally move data into S3 as a part of backup or migration projects.

Learn more about hybrid Cloud storage at `https://aws.amazon.com/enterprise/hybrid/`.

Cloud-native application data

Amazon S3 provides high performance, highly available storage that makes it easy to scale and maintain cost-effective mobile and internet-based apps that run fast. With S3, you can add any amount of content and access it from anywhere, so you can deploy applications faster and reach more customers.

Disaster recovery

Amazon S3's secure global infrastructure offers a robust disaster recovery solution designed to provide superior data protection. **Cross-Region Replication** (**CRR**) automatically replicates every S3 object to a destination bucket located in a different AWS region.

Learn more about disaster recovery at `https://aws.amazon.com/disaster-recovery/`.

Amazon DynamoDB

Amazon DynamoDB is a fully managed NoSQL database service that provides fast and predictable performance with seamless scalability. DynamoDB lets you offload the administrative burdens of operating and scaling a distributed database so that you don't have to worry about hardware provisioning, setup and configuration, replication, software patching, or cluster scaling. Also, DynamoDB offers encryption at rest, which eliminates the operational burden and complexity involved in protecting sensitive data. For more information, see *Amazon DynamoDB Encryption at Rest* at `https://docs.aws.amazon.com/amazondynamodb/latest/developerguide/EncryptionAtRest.html`.

With DynamoDB, you can create database tables that can store and retrieve any amount of data, and serve any level of request traffic. You can scale up or scale down your tables throughput capacity without downtime or performance degradation, and use the AWS Management Console to monitor resource utilization and performance metrics.

Amazon DynamoDB provides on-demand backup capabilities. It allows you to create full backups of your tables for long-term retention and archival for regulatory compliance needs. For more information, see *On-Demand Backup and Restore* for DynamoDB.

DynamoDB allows you to delete expired items from tables automatically to help you reduce storage use and the cost of storing data that is no longer relevant. For more information, see *Time To Live*.

DynamoDB automatically spreads the data and traffic for your tables over a sufficient number of servers to handle your throughput and storage requirements, while maintaining consistent and fast performance. All of your data is stored on **solid state disks** (**SSDs**) and automatically replicated across multiple availability zones in an AWS region, providing built-in high availability and data durability. You can use global tables to keep DynamoDB tables in sync across AWS regions. For more information, see *Global Tables*.

Amazon Kinesis Data Streams

You can use Amazon *Kinesis* Data Streams to collect and process large streams of data records in real time. You'll create data-processing applications, known as Amazon Kinesis Data Streams applications. A typical Amazon Kinesis Data Streams application reads data from a Kinesis data stream as data records. These applications can use the Kinesis Client Library, and they can run on Amazon EC2 instances. The processed records can be sent to dashboards, used to generate alerts, dynamically change pricing and advertising strategies, or to send data to a variety of other AWS services. For information about Kinesis Data Streams features and pricing, see Amazon Kinesis Data Streams.

Kinesis Data Streams is part of the Kinesis streaming data platform, along with Amazon Kinesis Data Firehose. For more information, see the Amazon Kinesis Data Firehose Developer Guide. For more information about AWS big data solutions, see *Big Data*. For more information about AWS streaming data solutions, see *What is Streaming Data?*

What can I do with Kinesis Data Streams?

You can use Kinesis Data Streams for rapid and continuous data intake and aggregation. The types of data used includes IT infrastructure log data, application logs, social media, market data feeds, and web clickstream data. Because the response time for the data intake and processing is in real time, the processing is typically lightweight.

The following are typical scenarios for using Kinesis Data Streams.

Accelerated log and data feed intake and processing

You can have producers push data directly into a stream. For example, push system and application logs and they become available for processing in seconds. This prevents the log data from being lost if the frontend or application server fails. Kinesis Data Streams provides accelerated data feed intake because you don't batch the data on the servers before you submit it for intake.

Real-time metrics and reporting

You can use data collected into Kinesis Data Streams for simple data analysis and reporting in real time. For example, your dataprocessing application can work on metrics and reporting for system and application logs as the data is streaming in, rather than waiting to receive batches of data.

Real-time data analytics

This combines the power of parallel processing with the value of real-time data. For example, you can process website clickstreams in real time, and then analyze site usability engagement using multiple different Kinesis Data Streams applications running in parallel.

Complex stream processing

You can create **Directed Acyclic Graphs** (**DAGs**) of Amazon Kinesis Data Streams applications and data streams. This typically involves putting data from multiple Amazon Kinesis Data Streams applications into another stream for downstream processing by a different Amazon Kinesis Data Streams application.

Benefits of using Kinesis Data Streams

While you can use Kinesis Data Streams to solve a variety of streaming data problems, a common use is the real-time aggregation of data, followed by loading that data into a data warehouse or map-reduce cluster.

To ensure durability and elasticity, data is put into Kinesis data streams. The delay between the time a record is put into the stream and the time it can be retrieved (put-to-get delay) is less than 1 second; an Amazon Kinesis Data Streams application can start consuming the data from the stream almost immediately after the data is added. The managed service aspect of Kinesis Data Streams relieves you of the operational burden of creating and running a data intake pipeline. You can create streaming map-reduce type applications, and the elasticity of Kinesis Data Streams enables you to scale the stream up or down, so that you never lose data records prior to their expiration.

Multiple Amazon Kinesis Data Streams applications can consume data from a stream, so that multiple actions, such as archiving and processing, can take place concurrently and independently. For example, two applications can read data from the same stream. The first application calculates running aggregates and updates a DynamoDB table, and the second application compresses and archives data to a data store such as Amazon S3. The DynamoDB table with running aggregates is then read by a dashboard for *up-to-the-minute* reports.

AWS Glue

AWS Glue is a fully managed **extract, transform, and load** (**ETL**) service that makes it simple and cost-effective to categorize your data, clean it, enrich it, and move it reliably between various data stores. AWS Glue consists of a central data repository known as the **AWS Glue Data Catalog**, an ETL engine that automatically generates Python code, and a flexible scheduler that handles dependency resolution, job monitoring, and job retries/reattempts on failure. AWS Glue is serverless, so there's no infrastructure to set up or manage.

Use the AWS Glue console to discover data, transform it, and make it available for searching and querying. The console calls the underlying services to orchestrate the work required to transform your data. You can also use the AWS Glue API operations to interface with AWS Glue services. Edit, debug, and test your Python or Scala Apache Spark ETL code using a familiar development environment.

When should I use AWS Glue?

You can use AWS Glue to build a data warehouse to organize, cleanse, validate, and format data. You can transform and move AWS Cloud data into your data store. You can also load data from disparate sources into your data warehouse for regular reporting and analysis. By storing it in a data warehouse, you integrate information from different parts of your business and provide a common source of data for decision making.

AWS Glue simplifies many tasks when you are building a data warehouse:

- Discovers and catalogs metadata about your data stores into a central catalog.
- You can process semi-structured data, such as clickstream or process logs.

- Populates the AWS Glue Data Catalog with table definitions from scheduled crawler programs.
- Crawlers call classifier logic to infer the schema, format, and data types of your data. This metadata is stored as tables in the AWS Glue Data Catalog and used in the authoring process of your ETL jobs.
- Generates ETL scripts to transform, flatten, and enrich your data from source to target.
- Detects schema changes and adapts based on your preferences.
- Triggers your ETL jobs based on a schedule or event. You can initiate jobs automatically to move your data into your data warehouse. Triggers can be used to create a dependency flow between jobs.
- Gathers runtime metrics to monitor the activities of your data warehouse.
- Handles errors and retries automatically.
- Scales resources, as needed, to run your jobs.

You can use AWS Glue when you run serverless queries against your Amazon S3 data lake. AWS Glue can catalog your Amazon S3 data, making it available for querying with Amazon Athena and Amazon Redshift Spectrum. With crawlers, your metadata stays in sync with the underlying data. Athena and Redshift Spectrum can directly query your Amazon S3 data lake using the AWS Glue Data Catalog. With AWS Glue, you access and analyze data through one unified interface without loading it into multiple data silos.

You can create event-driven ETL pipelines with AWS Glue. You can run your ETL jobs as soon as new data becomes available in Amazon S3 by invoking your AWS Glue ETL jobs from an AWS Lambda function. You can also register this new dataset in the AWS Glue Data Catalog as part of your ETL jobs.

You can use AWS Glue to understand your data assets. You can store your data using various AWS services and still maintain a unified view of your data using the AWS Glue Data Catalog. View the Data Catalog to quickly search and discover the datasets that you own, and maintain the relevant metadata in one central repository. The Data Catalog also serves as a drop-in replacement for your external Apache Hive Metastore.

Amazon EMR

Amazon EMR is a managed cluster platform that simplifies running big data frameworks, such as Apache Hadoop and Apache Spark, on AWS to process and analyze vast amounts of data. By using these frameworks and related open source projects, such as Apache Hive and Apache Pig, you can process data for analytics purposes and business intelligence workloads. You can also use Amazon EMR to transform and move large amounts of data in and out of other AWS data stores and databases, such as Amazon S3 and Amazon DynamoDB.

Amazon EMR provides a managed Hadoop framework that is easy, fast, and cost-effective in order to process vast amounts of data across dynamically scalable Amazon EC2 instances. You can also run other popular distributed frameworks such as Apache Spark, HBase, Presto, and Flink in Amazon EMR, and interact with data in other AWS data stores such as Amazon S3 and Amazon DynamoDB.

Amazon EMR securely and reliably handles a broad set of big data use cases, including log analysis, web indexing, data transformations (ETL), machine learning, financial analysis, scientific simulation, and bioinformatics.

Practical AWS EMR cluster

For this exercise, you will need to create an AWS account using `aws.amazon.com`.

> You will be charged to create and use an EMR cluster so please make sure you are OK with spending money on the cluster (typically $10 a day) and also terminate the cluster as soon as you are done.

Once you log in, you will see the screen shown in the following screenshot:

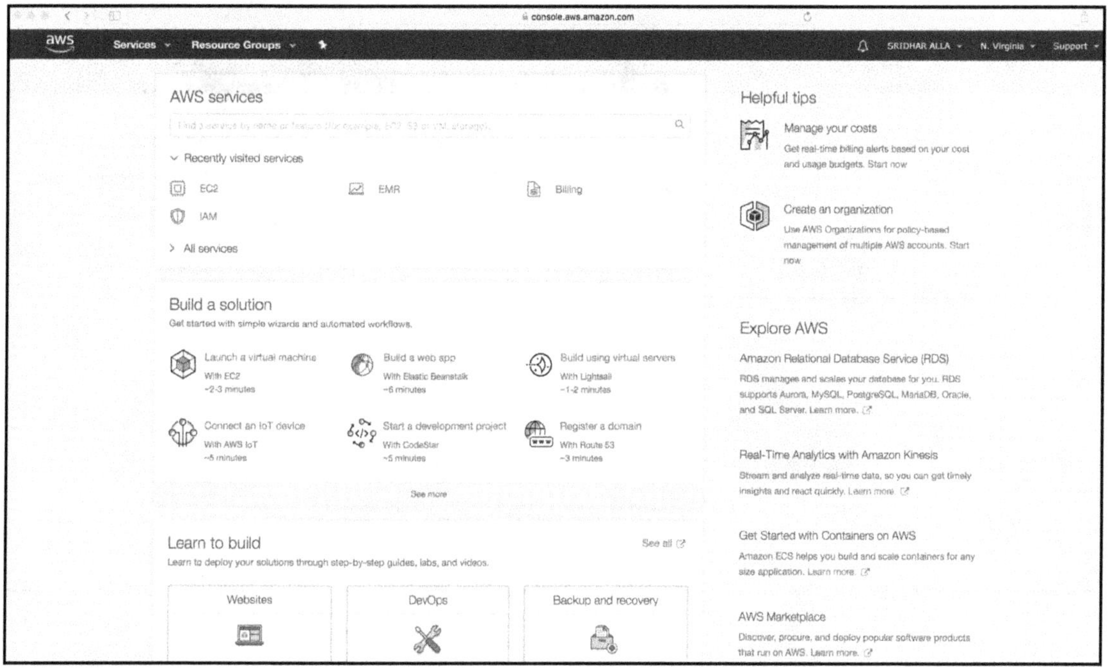

Figure: Screenshot of the screen that will appear after logging into your AWS account

By selecting EMR, as the service, you will be taken to a screen shown in the following screenshot:

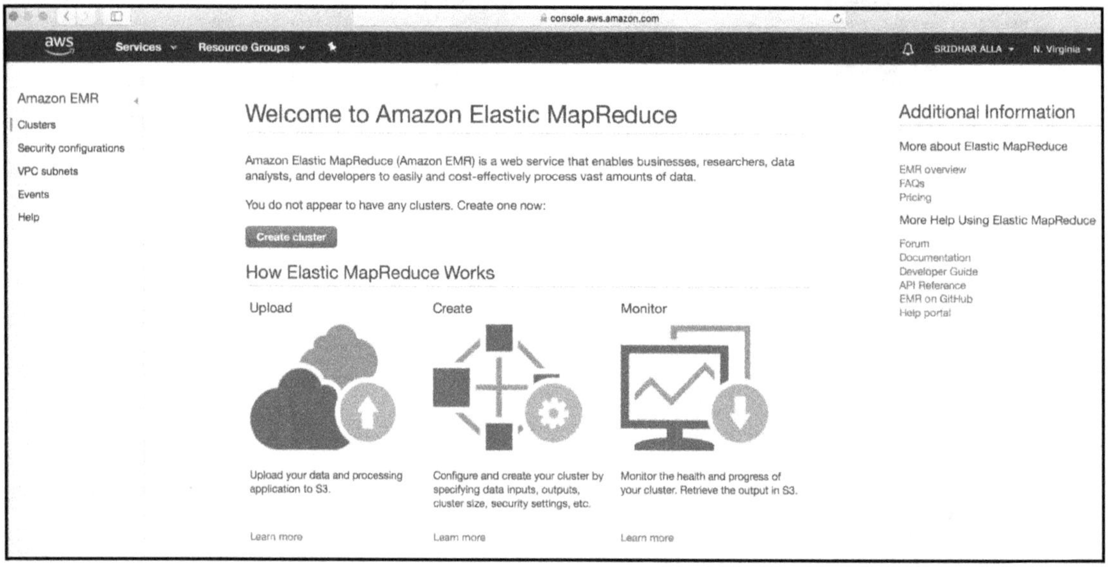

You can create an EMR cluster by selecting the various options as shown in the following screenshot:

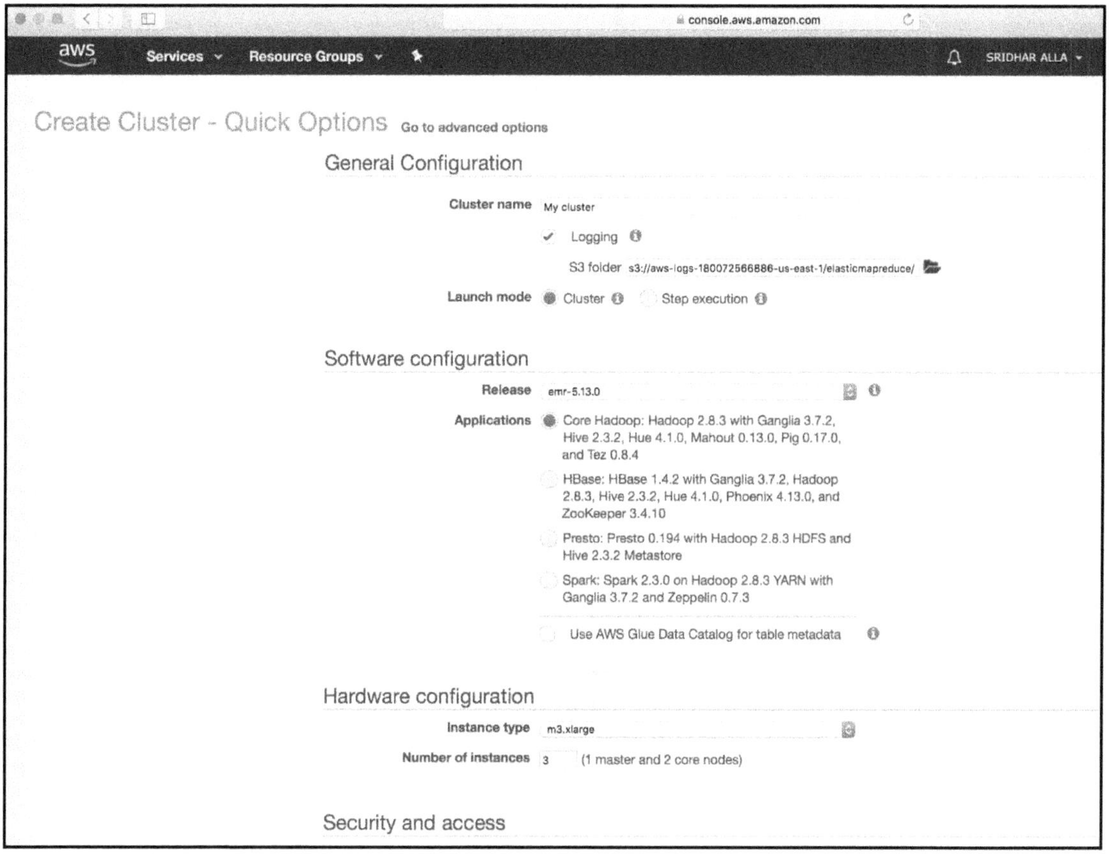

A key pair is a must for EMR so you can open a new tab and go to **EC2 service** in the AWS console:

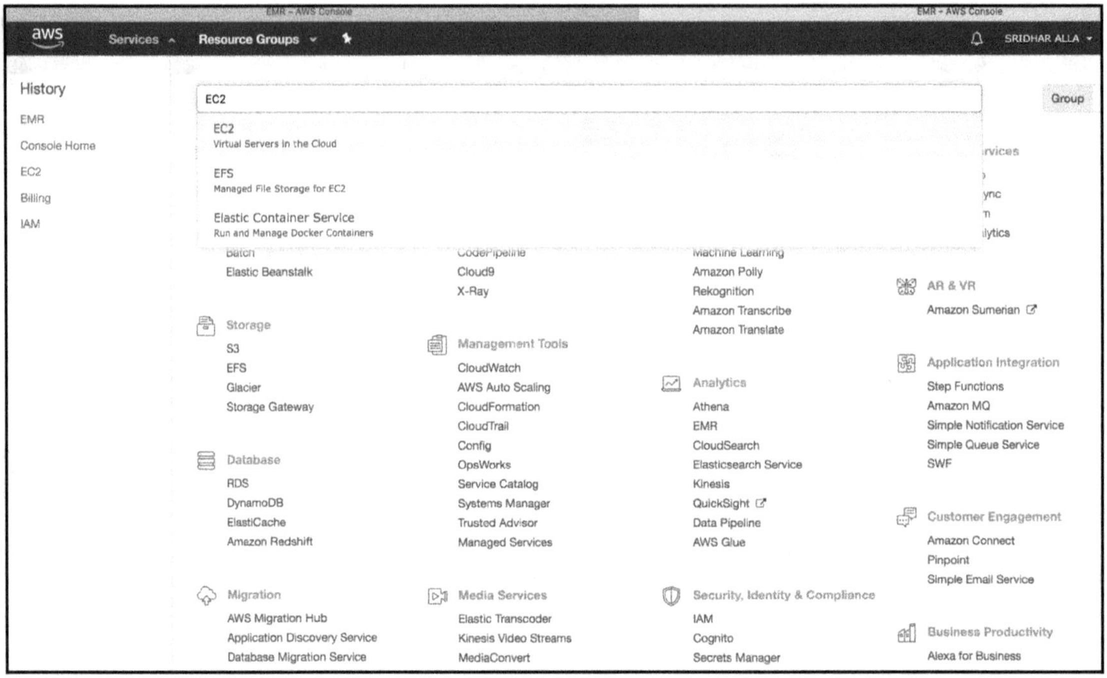

The following is the EC2 dashboard:

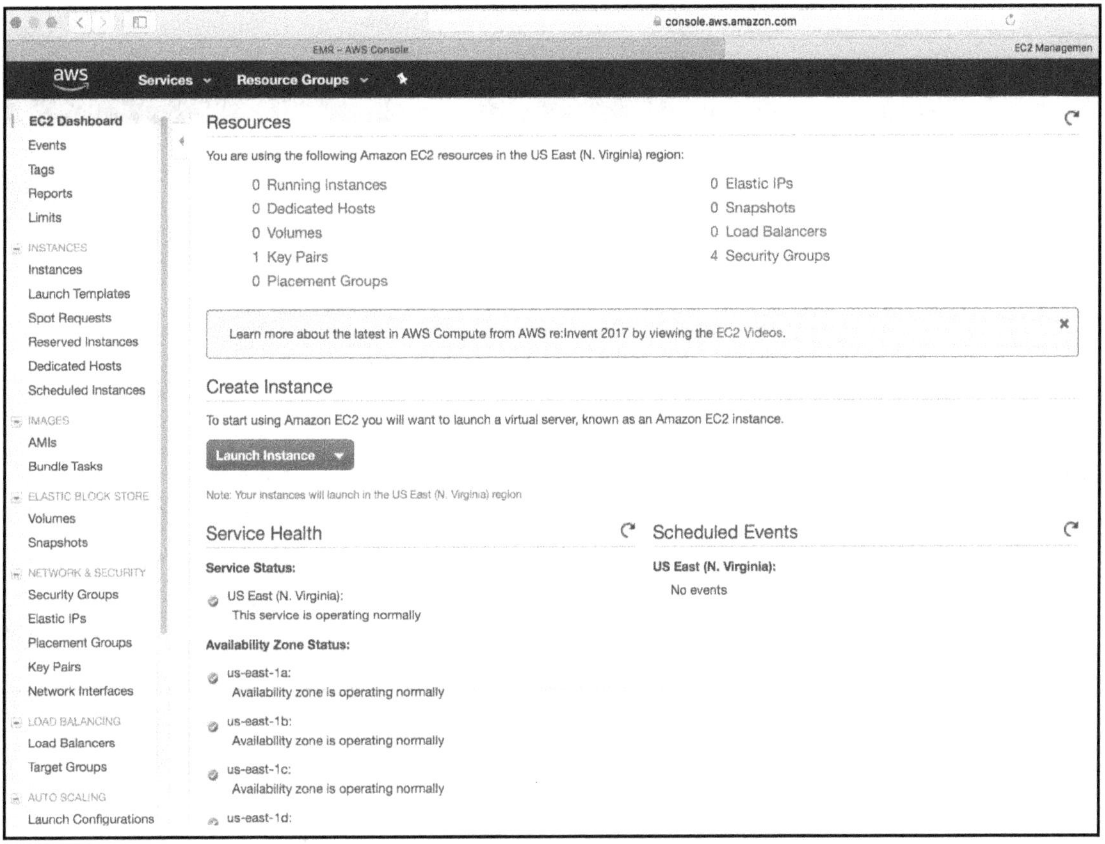

Create a new key pair in the EC2 dashboard by selecting the **Key Pairs** option in the left pane:

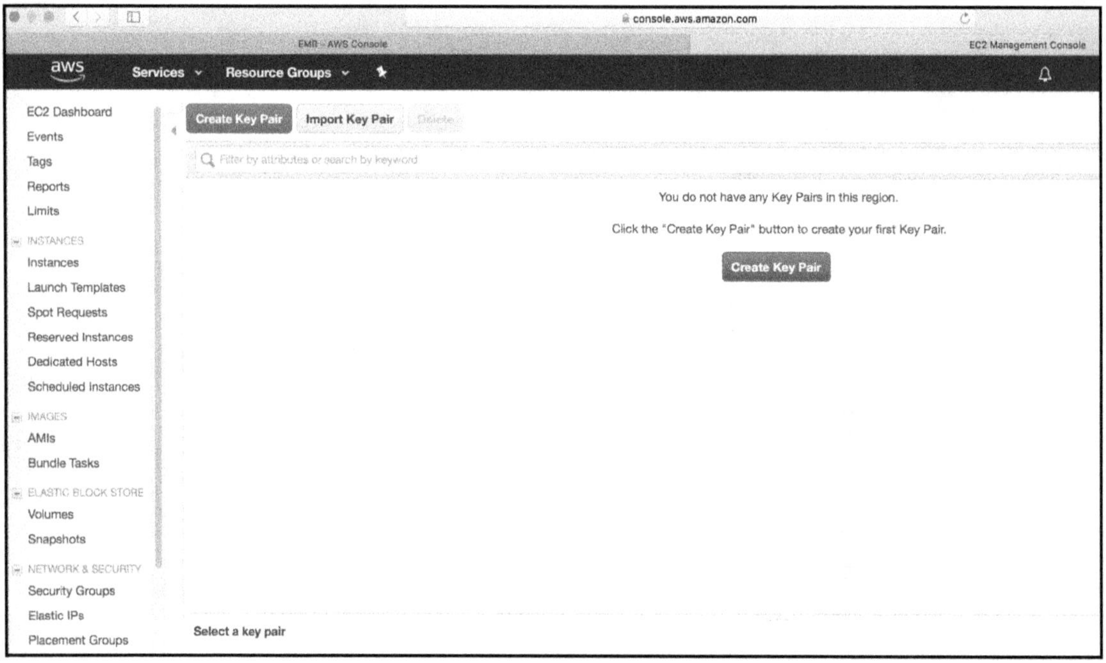

Here is how you can name the key pair:

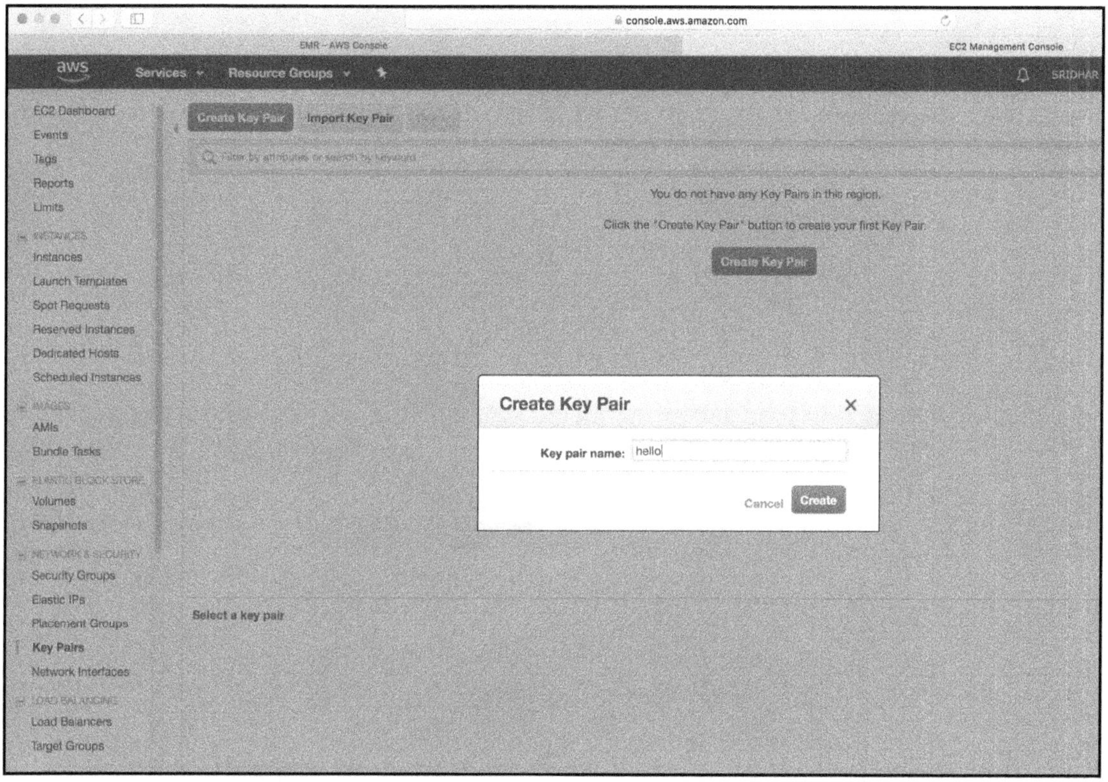

Make sure you copy the key pair, as you will not be able to do so at a later time

Here is the key pair, which you can save for later use:

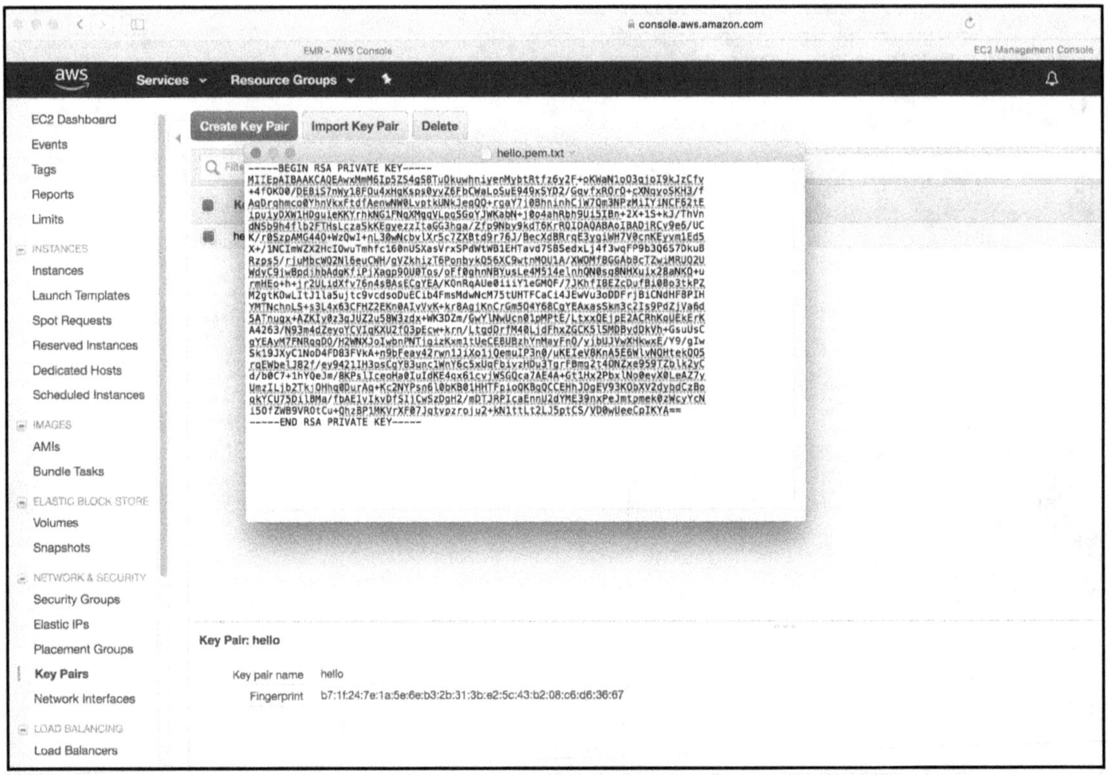

Figure: Screenshot showing the key pair that can be saved for later use

Now, proceed further using the key pair you just generated:

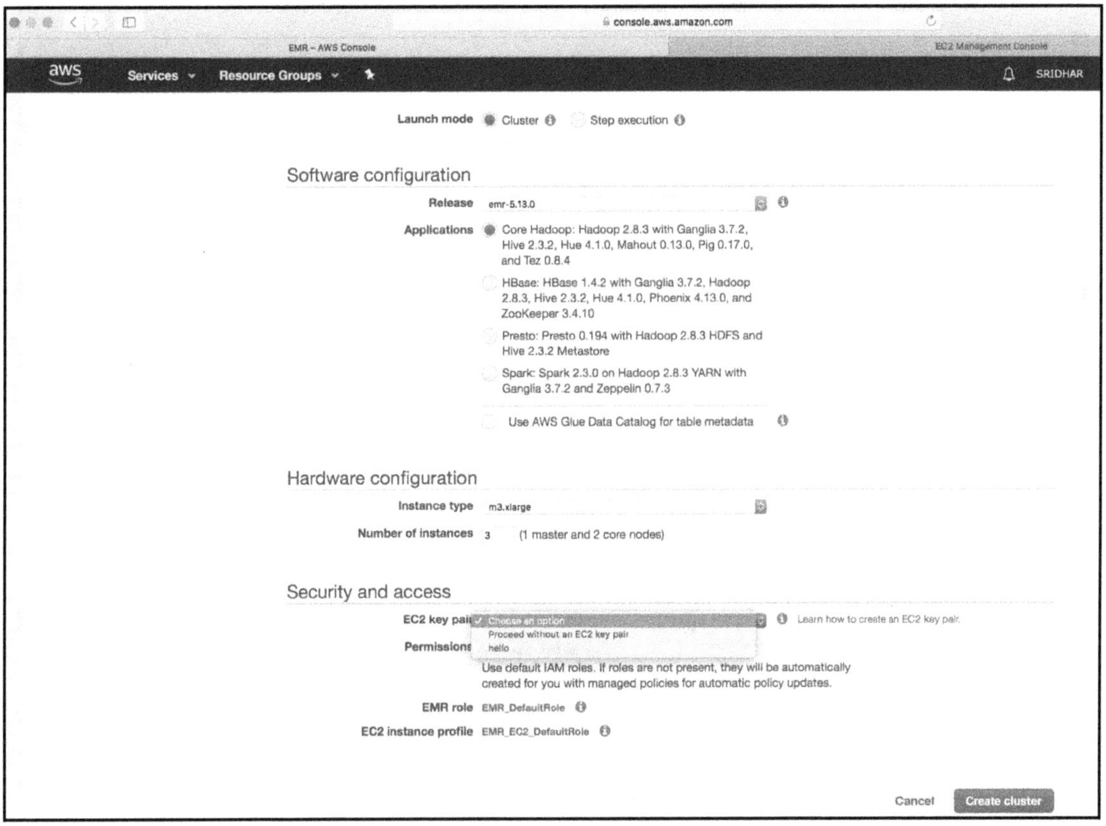

Once you select the key pair, you can now create the cluster:

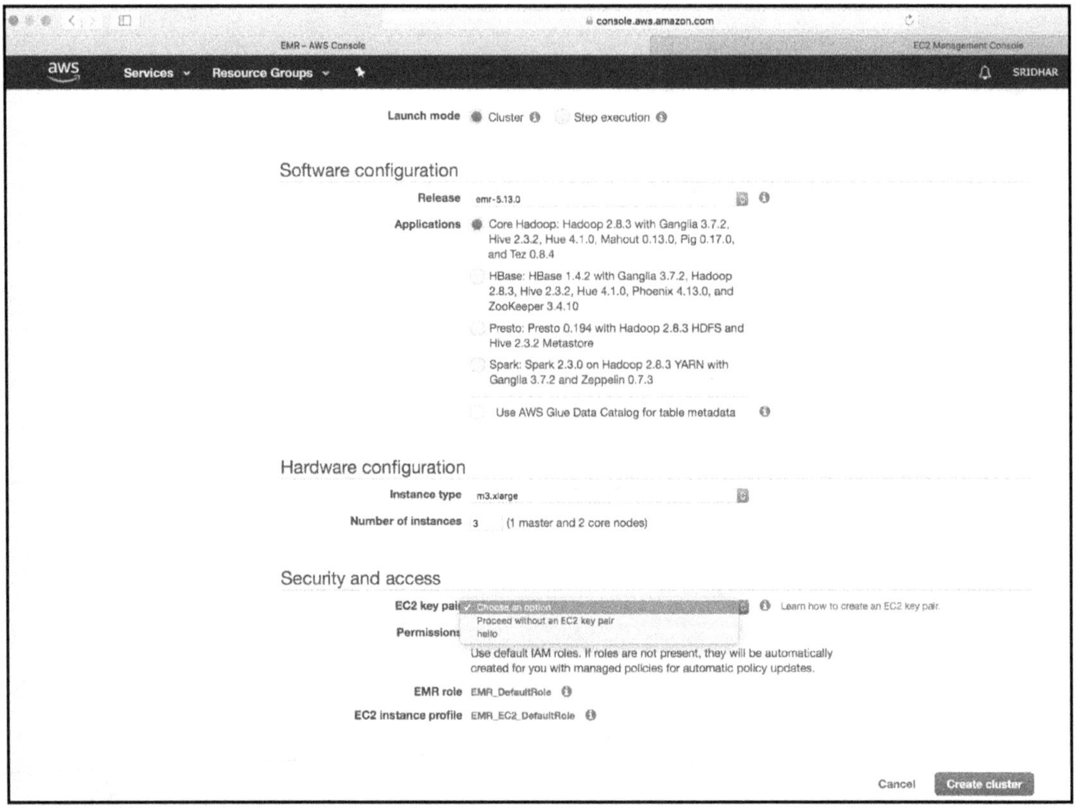

EMR cluster creation takes about 10 minutes.

This is the EMR cluster creation screen:

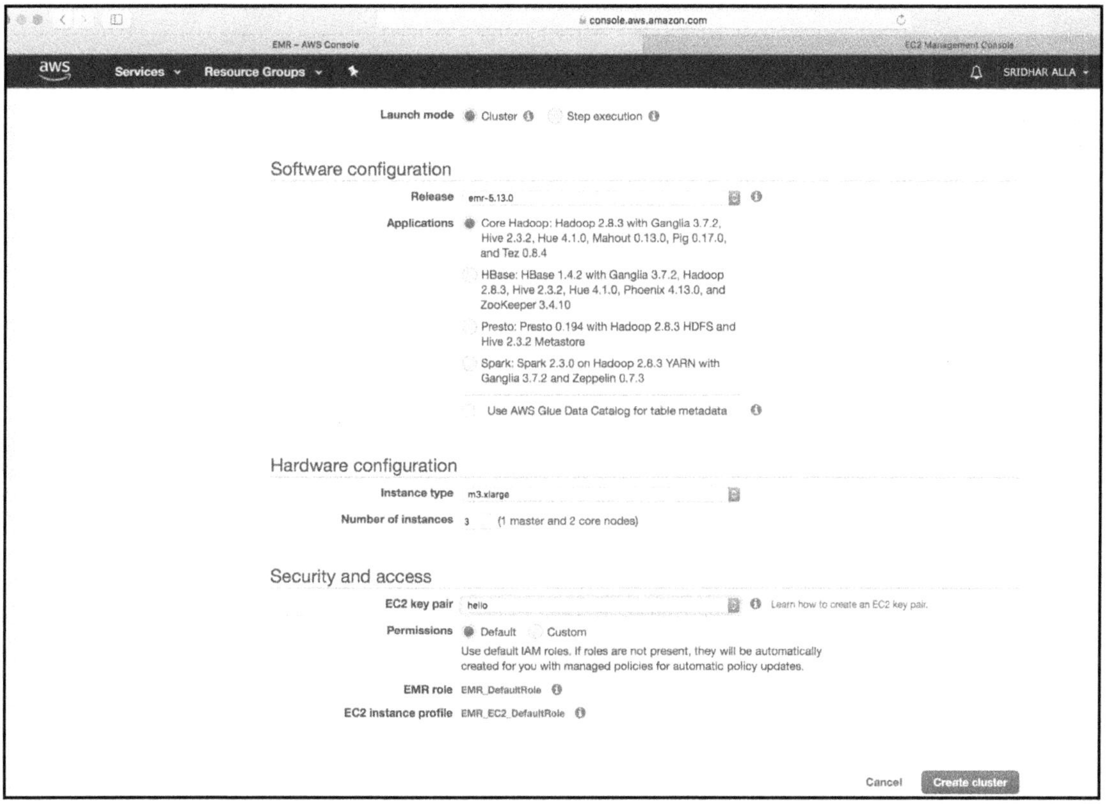

This is the **Summary** tab, which shows the cluster details:

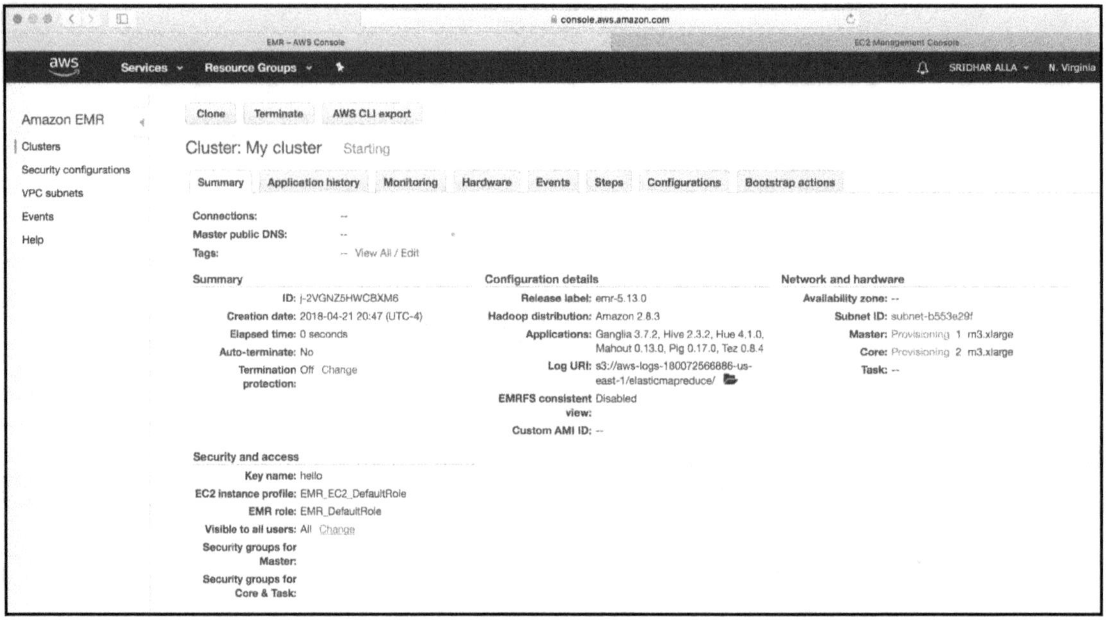

This is the **Hardware** tab, which shows the cluster hardware:

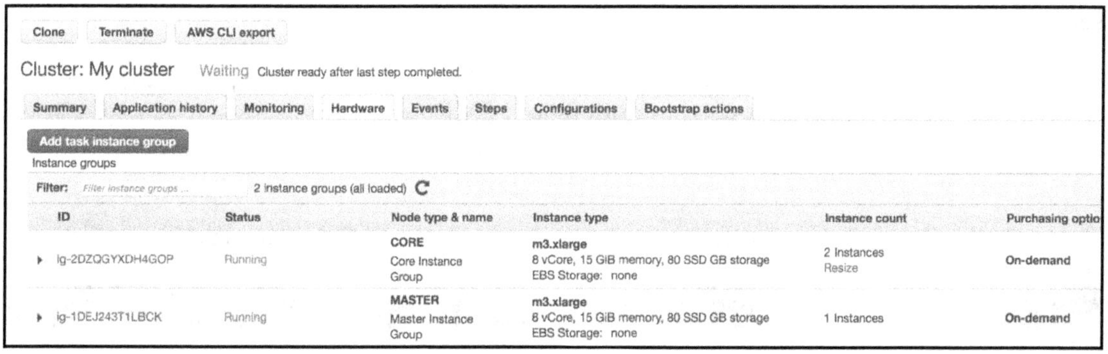

This is the **Events** tab, which shows the cluster events:

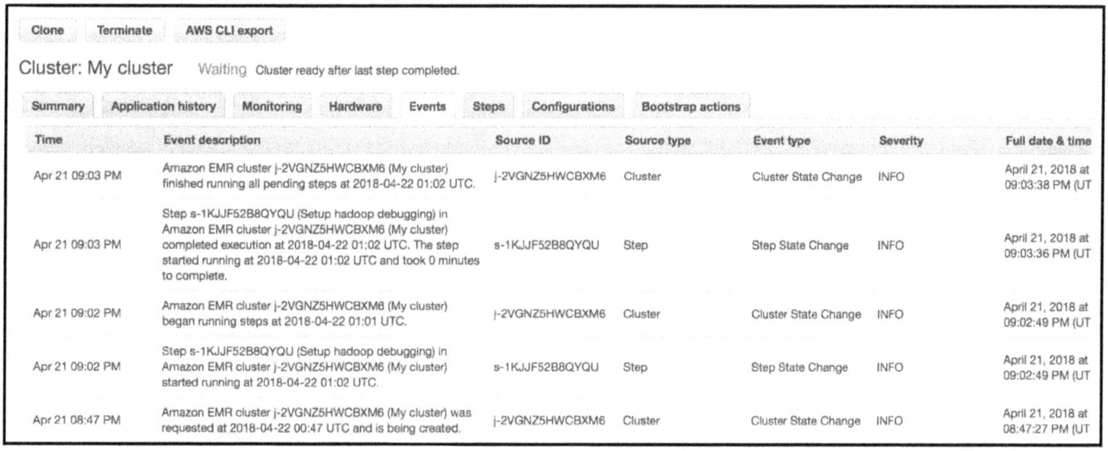

You will not be able to access the EMR cluster due to security settings. So, you have to open the ports to be accessible from outside before you can explore the HDFS and YARN services of the EMR cluster.

Make sure you don't use this insecure EMR cluster for practical purposes. This is just to be used to understand EMR.

These are the **Security Groups** for the cluster, shown in the EC2 dashboard:

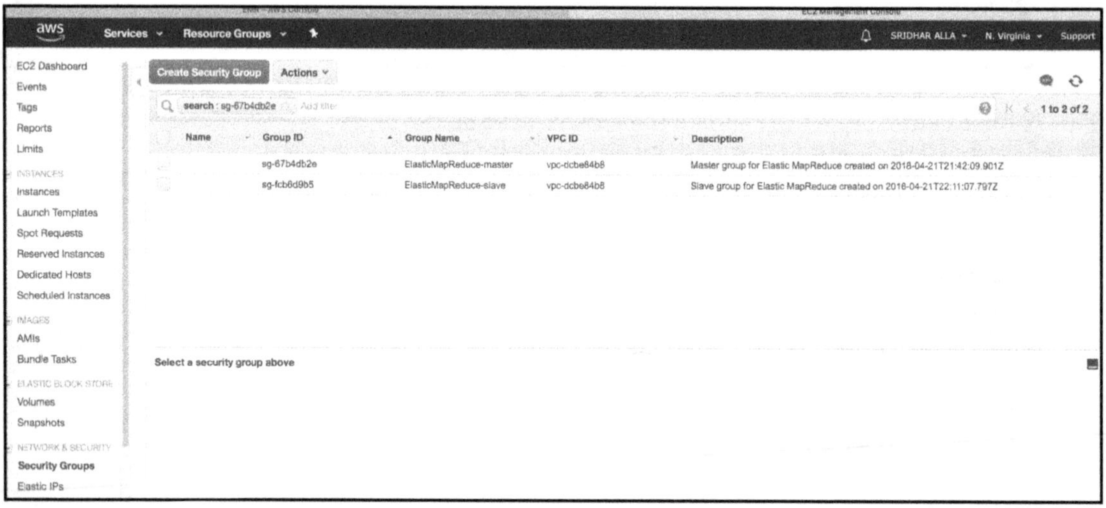

Figure: Screenshot showing security groups for the cluster

Edit the two security groups and allow all TCP traffic from source **0.0.0.0/0**, as shown in the following screenshot:

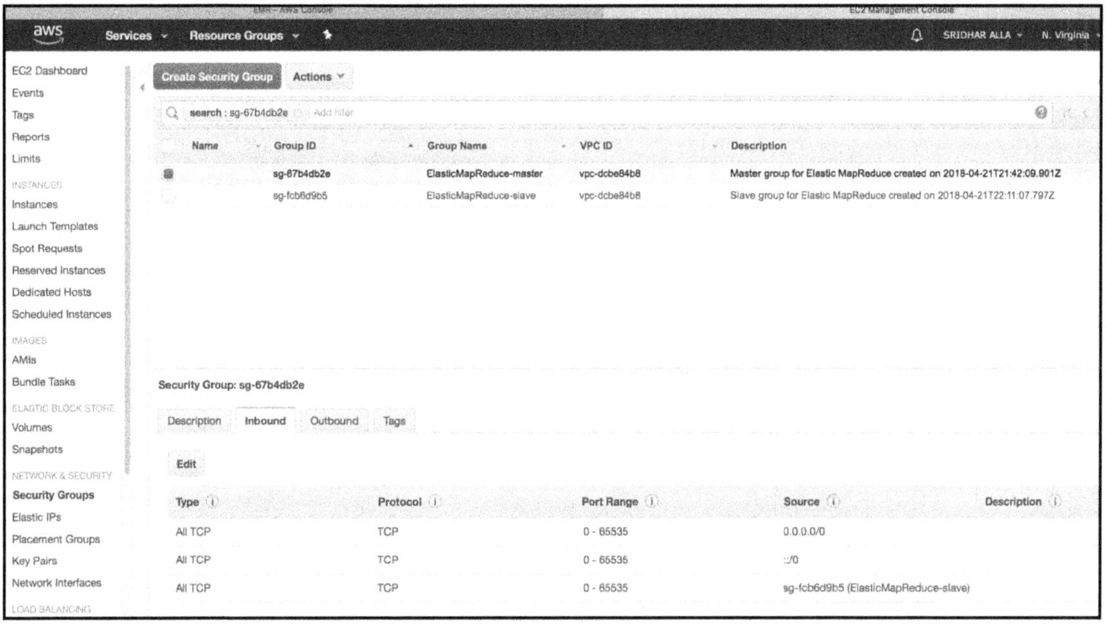

Figure: Screenshot showing how to edit the two security groups

Now, look at the EMR Master IP address (public) and then use that to access the YARN service, `http://EMR_MASTER_IP:8088/cluster`.

This is the resource manager:

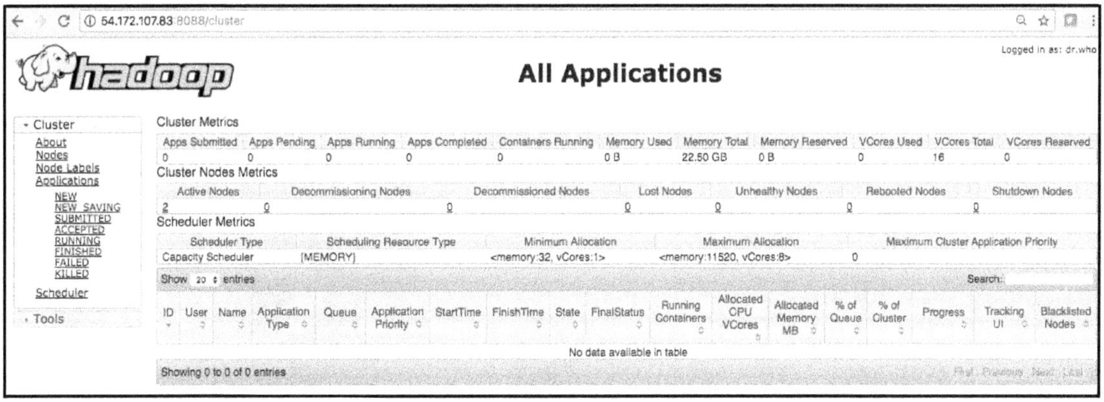

This are the resource manager's queues:

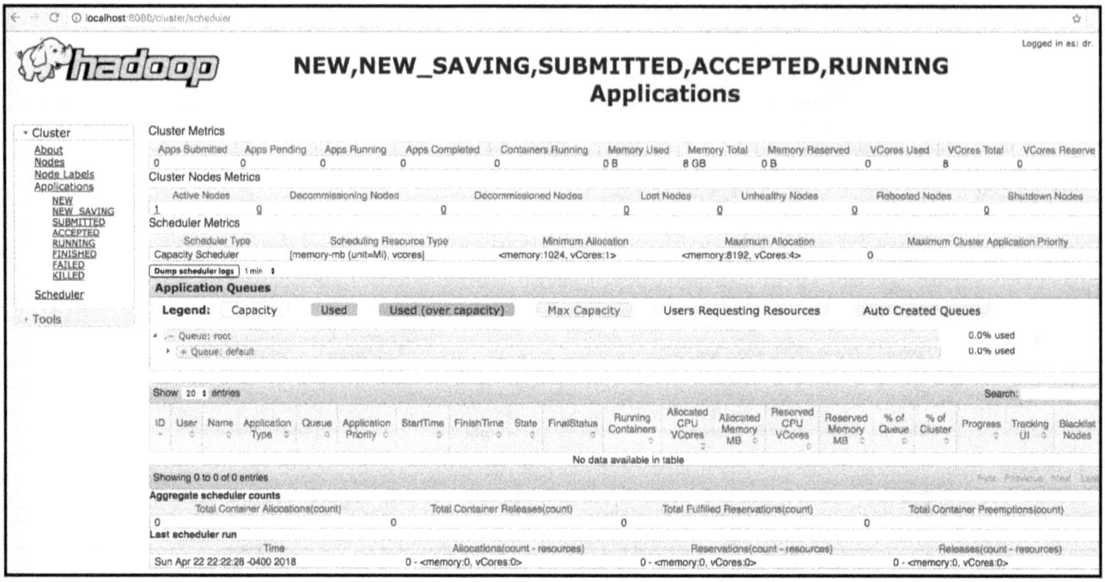

HDFS can also be accessed using the same IP address, `http://<EMR-MASTER-IP>:50070`.

Shown here is the HDFS portal:

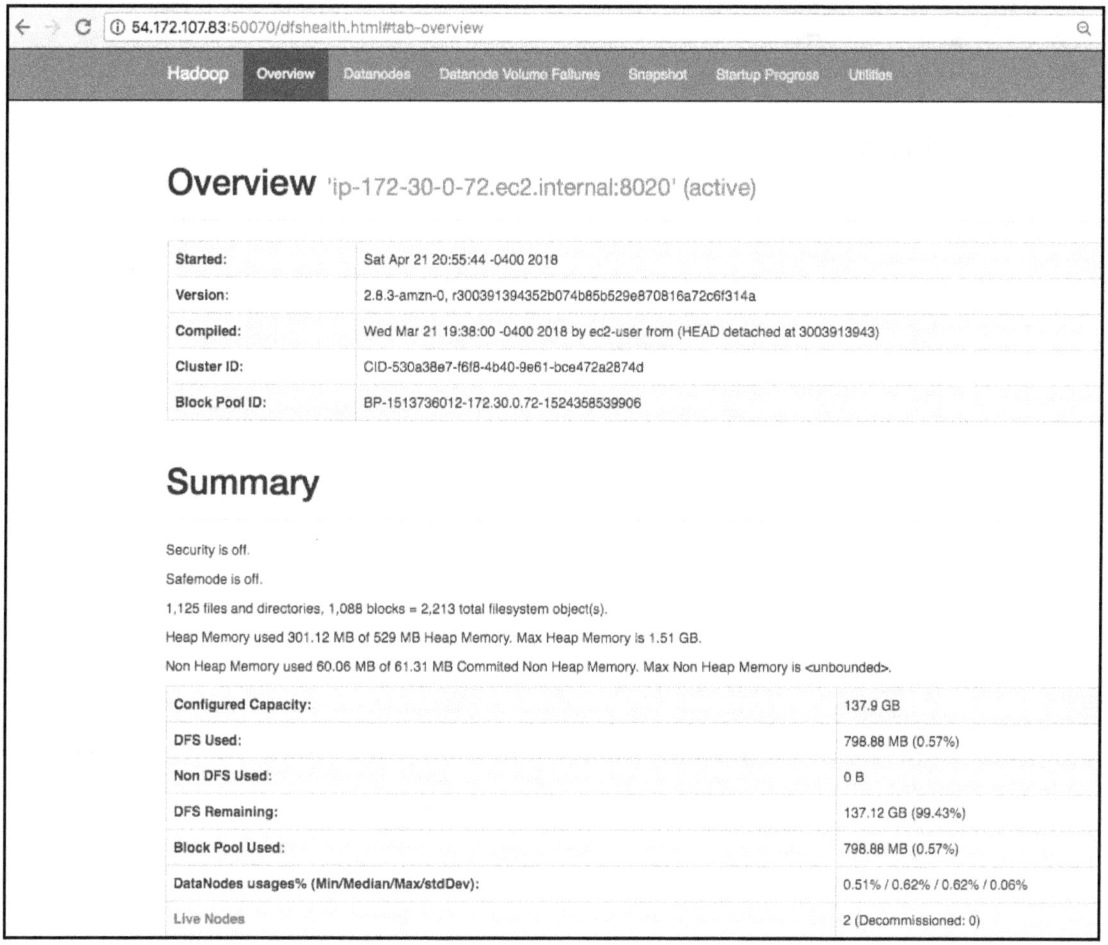

These are the datanodes in the EMR cluster:

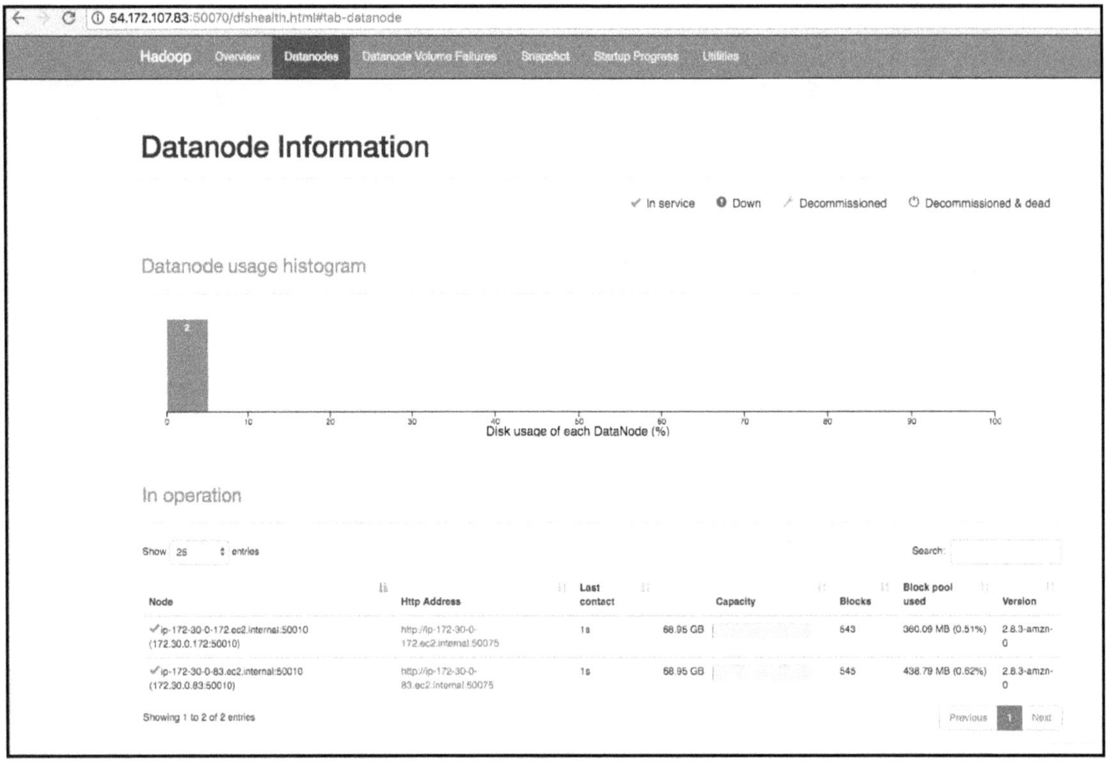

Figure: Screenshot showing datanodes in the EMR cluster

This is the HDFS browser showing the directories and files in your filesystem:

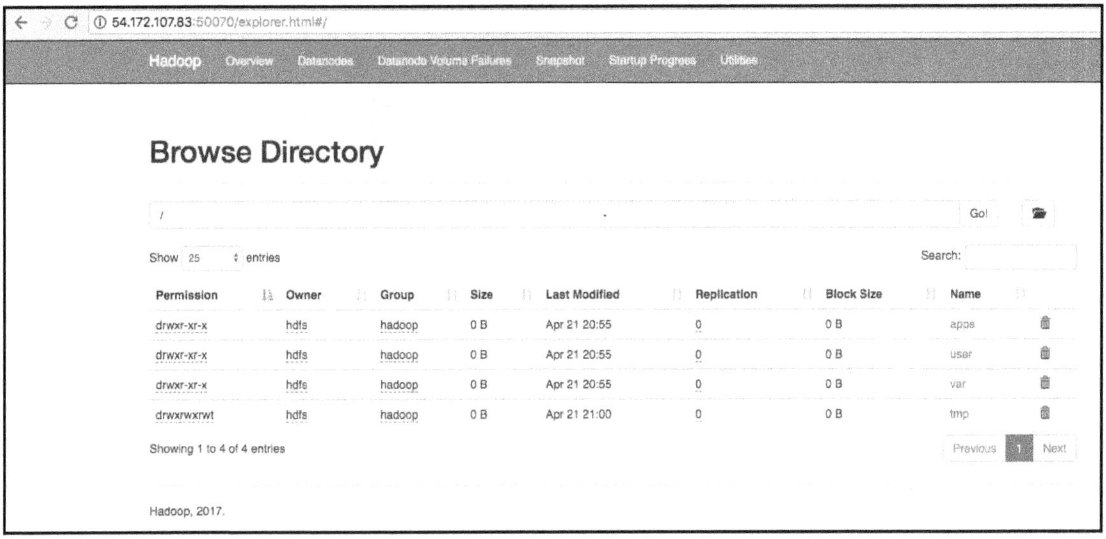

We have demonstrated how easily we can spin up an EMR cluster in AWS.

Please make sure you terminate the EMR cluster at this point.

Summary

In this chapter, we have discussed AWS as a Cloud provider for Cloud computing needs.

In the next chapter, we will bring everything together to understand what it takes to realize the business goals of building a practical big data analytics practice.

Index

A

B

C

D

E

F

G

H

N

O

P

Q

R

S

T

www.ingramcontent.com/pod-product-compliance
Lightning Source LLC
Chambersburg PA
CBHW060643060326
40690CB00020B/4498
9781788628846